THE SPANISH MIDDLE EASTERN & AFRICAN COOKBOOK

THE SPANISH MIDDLE EASTERN & AFRICAN COOKBOOK

Over 330 dishes shown step by step in 1400 colour photographs – classic and regional specialities include tapas and mezzes, spicy meat dishes, tangy fish curries and exotic sweets

PEPITA ARIS   JENNI FLEETWOOD   JOSEPHINE BACON

HERMES HOUSE

This edition is published by Hermes House

Hermes House is an imprint of Anness Publishing Ltd
Hermes House, 88-89 Blackfriars Road, London SE1 8HA
tel. 020 7401 2077; fax 020 7633 9499
info@anness.com

A CIP catalogue record for this book is available from the British Library.

PUBLISHER: Joanna Lorenz
EDITORIAL DIRECTOR: Helen Sudell
EXECUTIVE EDITOR: Joanne Rippin
EDITOR: Susannah Blake
DESIGNERS: Nigel Partridge and Adelle Morris
JACKET DESIGN: Clare Reynolds
PHOTOGRAPHERS: Nicki Downey, Craig Robertson, William Adams-Lingwood, Patrick McLeavey, Martin Brigdale
RECIPIES: Pepita Aris, Ghillie Basan, Rosamund Grant, Rebekah Hassan, Soheila Kimberley
ADDITIONAL TEXT: Josephine Bacon (Africa). Jenni Fleetwood (Middle East)

Thanks to the following agencies for permission to reproduce their images: Ian Aitkin pp19t, 20, 21t&r, 33b; Anthony Blake p 27t; Cephas PIcture Library pp17t, 19b; Corbis pp264b, 267 all, 269, 270b, 290, 291, 292 all, 293, 294b, 295, 296t; Powerstock pp 16, 17b, 21b, 22t&b, 23t&b, 25t&b, 23b, 33t; Travel Ink pp24t&b, 26t&b, 264t, 265, 266, 270t, 271t, 294t, 297bl, 302t; Peter Wilson pp 18t&b, 28t&b, 29, 31t&b, 32t, 33b.

Previously published in two separate volumes, *Spanish Food and Cooking* and *Food and Cooking of Africa and the Middle East.*

10 9 8 7 6 5 4 3 2 1

NOTES

Bracketed terms are intended for American readers.For all recipes, quantities are given in both metric and imperial measures and, where appropriate, in standard cups and spoons. Follow one set, but not a mixture, because they are not interchangeable.
Standard spoon and cup measures are level. 1 tsp = 5ml, 1 tbsp = 15ml, 1 cup = 250ml/8fl oz.
Australian standard tablespoons are 20ml. Australian readers should use 3 tsp in place of 1 tbsp for measuring small quantities of gelatine, flour, salt, etc.
American pints are 16fl oz/2 cups. American readers should use 20fl oz/2.5 cups in place of 1 pint when measuring liquids.
The nutritional analysis given for each recipe is calculated per portion (i.e. serving or item), unless otherwise stated. If the recipe gives a range, such as Serves 4–6, then the nutritional analysis will be for the smaller portion size, i.e. 6 servings. Measurements for sodium do not include salt added to taste.
Medium (US large) eggs are used unless otherwise stated.

CONTENTS

INTRODUCTION

Above: Couscous is a well-known Middle Eastern dish.

Above: Olives are enjoyed throughout Spain.

Standing sentinel over the western entrance to the Mediterranean, with Africa so close that you can sometimes smell its spices, is Spain, a country whose cuisine has been likened to the flamenco, combining passion with restraint and a deep sensuality. This ancient land has played host to Phoenicians, Greeks, Carthaginians, Romans and Visigoths, but no invaders influenced the cuisine of the country more emphatically than did the Moors. These Arab forces originated in the Middle East in the 7th century AD and swept across North Africa before setting their sights on the Iberian Peninsula. By the time they sailed across the straits, their numbers had been swollen by Berber tribesmen who had converted to the Muslim cause, and it was a motley army that finally subjugated Spain. Like all armies, it marched on its stomach, and the food its forces favoured was whatever was most familiar. Middle Eastern and African delicacies were introduced to Spain, enriching the simple, honest cuisine that had evolved over centuries.

THE MOORISH LEGACY

The Moors dominated much of Spain – particularly the south - for the next seven hundred years. Once they had subjugated the country, they largely lived in harmony with their subjects, including the Sephardi Jews, who had settled in Spain after the Diaspora and who had themselves played a role in developing the cuisine that came to be known as Spanish.

The Moors refined the system of irrigation introduced by the Romans and enabled rice to be cultivated for some of Spain's favourite dishes, including *paella*, which some claim is a variation on a Middle Eastern favourite, pilau or pilaff. They were also responsible for bringing pomegranates, figs, citrus fruits, aubergines (eggplants) and almonds to Spain. The latter formed the basis for a popular cold soup that also included ingredients that had been current for centuries: bread, garlic, olive oil and vinegar. Much later, when the explorer Christopher Columbus changed the face of culinary history by importing the first tomatoes and sweet (bell) peppers from the New World, these also found their way into the iced soup, which became known as gazpacho.

Spain introduced tomatoes to the rest of the world, and once it was realised that they were edible as well as ornamental, they became popular throughout the Mediterranean region, filtering back to the Middle East and Africa.

A TWO-WAY TRAFFIC

This traffic in ingredients and recipes is one of the aspects that makes food history so fascinating. Even in Africa, a huge continent with many diverse

Below: Desserts in Africa usually consist of fresh fruit.

Left: Seafood and fresh fish are very popular throughout

Above: Exquisite pastries are enjoyed in the Middle East.

Above: Cinnamon is used in sweet and savoury dishes.

Top: Lamb koftas are instantly identifiable as Middle Eastern. Above: Small fried fish are popular tapas and mezze dishes.

cultures and climates, there are common themes and linkages. Algeria, Morocco and Tunisia, the African countries onthe continent's northern coast – collectively referred to as the Maghreb – have more in common than a shared coastline on the Mediterranean. Their favourite dishes illustrate a deft touch with spices and other flavourings, whether in a robust sauce such as harissa or in a delicate rosewater dessert. Sweet and sour flavours are matched in a masterly fashion, and this delight in creating contrasts is a recurring theme throughout the Middle East and also in Spain.

MEZZES AND OTHER MORSELS

This savouring of contrasting flavours is perfectly illustrated in the *mezze* table of the Middle East, which sets out to offer a vast array of delicious dishes, all served in small portions for the diner's delectation. The theme is explored equally successfully in the Spanish *tapas* tradition. *Tapas*, or *pinchos* as they are called in the Basque Country, are bitesize portions of food traditionally served with drinks in Spanish bars. They range from olives, cubes of Manchego cheese, or salted almonds to more elaborate offerings such as wild boar sausages, *patatas bravas* (potatoes in a chilli sauce), roast quail or eels. A slice of tortilla is a popular choice, or the visitor may be invited to try a feather-light pastry.

Throughout Spain, North Africa and the Middle East, people share a passion for pastries. These may be light multi-layered confections made from a dough resembling filo, as in Moroccan *briouates* or Turkish *boreks*, or the more solid but equally scrumptious *empanadas* from Spain. Typical fillings include honey and nuts, or soft cheese with spinach or a similar vegetable.

Above: The Moors introduced lemons to Spain.

Above: Fried plantain is a popular snack in Africa.

SIMPLE AND SATISFYING

Among the many parallels to be drawn between the food of the countries covered in this book is the appreciation of simple dishes. Fish, for instance, is seldom served in elaborate sauces, but more often grilled (broiled), fried or baked with just a little olive oil and lemon, a few herbs or perhaps some tomatoes and onions. Salads do not always have dressings, and a meal is often rounded off with fresh fruit, rather than a rich dessert. Ingredients are bought daily, and cooks tend to tailor their menus to what is in season, choosing the catch of the day or the butcher's best buy.

Below: In Tangier, where the Spanish influence is still strong, their tagines often include broad beans and chorizo.

HOSPITALITY

Africa, the Middle East and Spain all share a reputation for generous hospitality. The traveller is made welcome, and in the Middle East in particular, guests are inevitably treated to the best their hosts can offer, whether this be fresh sardines, cooked simply over an open fire; a hearty meat stew such as Don Quixote's *olla podrida*, or simply a saucer of olive oil and some cubes of country bread.

Experience that hospitality and offer it to others by sampling the delicious dishes in this book, which brings together the authentic cooking styles and classic foodstuffs of three large and diverse regions. Introductory sections detail the countries covered, their different cooking traditions and ingredients. The following chapters provide recipes that range from appetizers to main courses to refreshing fruit desserts and delectable pastries. Some of the dishes described in the following pages of this book will be old favourites, others may well be unfamiliar. What they have in common is how they will enrich your repertoire of recipes as you take a culinary tour through Spain, Africa and the Middle East.

COOKING IN SPAIN

The wonderful ingredients of Spain – olives, rice, wine, Mediterranean vegetables, cheeses and sausages, and fish and shellfish from the longest coastline in Europe – have shaped the country's individual style of cooking. These ingredients are matched by cooking methods and recipes that best display their virtues.

THE SPANISH CUISINE

The history and religion of Spain are visible on the plate. It is always true, to some extent, that what we eat says who we are. But in no country is it more obvious than in Spain. Ingredients, cooking methods and many recipes all have an easy-to-trace and fascinating past. And Spain's most famous foods – chorizo, cocido, gazpacho, bacalao, paella – have an encoded history.

MOORISH INFLUENCES

"A land which hovers between Europe and Africa, between the hat and the turban" was Richard Ford's description of Spain in 1845. The Moors invaded Spain from North Africa, in AD711, and stayed for nearly 800 years. The Moorish influence is still evident today. To start with, a huge number of food words are derived from the Arabic: *aceite* (oil), *arroz* (rice), *albóndigas* (meatballs), *almendras* (almonds), *almirez* (the mortar) and *almuerzo* itself, the word for lunch.

In the mosques of and palaces of Cordoba, irrigation systems were planned, making possible wonderful gardens such as the Generalife in Granada, as well as Valencia's rice fields. The valleys of the Guadalquiver and Granada bloomed. The grey-green olive and the newly introduced almond transformed the landscape, while orange and lemon trees filled courtyards and surrounded buildings. New crops were planted, including sugar, spinach, aubergines (eggplant) and mint.

From the Moorish cuisine came new culinary methods – cooking in sealed clay pots and wood-burning ovens were introduced. The meat skewer and kebabs arrived, and *churrasco* (pieces of meat cooked on the barbecue) is still a Spanish favourite. Frying with olive oil and preserving in vinegar (*escabeche*) were both Arab practices, the latter eagerly adopted by the locals for preserving surplus fish for a little longer. The mortar and pestle could grind nuts to a smooth cream, used to thicken chilled soups such as the almond *ajo blanco* (white garlic soup) or *salmorejo* (a cream of garlic, bread and vinegar). Both were forerunners of the classic chilled soup, gazpacho.

Above (left and right): Many classic desserts such as fritters drenched in honey and rich fruit syrups show the Moorish origins of much Spanish food.

Many things that are now considered typically Spanish come from this era: almond pastries, fritters in honey, milk puddings, quince paste, peaches in syrup, iced sorbets (sherbets), raisins and pine nuts used together in sauces, and the "caviar", botargo.

The spices brought by the Moors included cinnamon, cumin and nutmeg, served with chicken the way they are now, and the magnificent golden saffron. They enjoyed sour-and-sweet (*agridulce*) mixtures and anise bread. Look around in Spain now and you will find all these things still on the menu.

Left: The Spanish love to cook and eat outdoors and cooking pieces of meat on skewers over a barbecue comes from the Moorish tradition.

Right: The slow-cooked stew of meats and chickpeas, cocido, *was inspired by the Jewish sabbath stew,* adafina.

CATHOLICISM CONQUERS

The *Reyes Católics* – the Catholic kings, Isabella and Ferdinand – conquered Granada, the last Moorish stronghold, in 1492. They threw out the Moors and the Jews, who were the Moorish managerial class, to make one united Catholic kingdom. The Jews, who had been in Spain for many centuries, left several imprints on Spanish cuisine, including *cocido* (meat and chickpea stew). The Christmas *roscón* has common features with the sticky braided *challah*, the Jewish Sabbath loaf.

The new foods enjoyed in this era were spectacularly different, favoured almost entirely for their religious orthodoxy. *Bacalao* (salt cod) was for Church fast days, of which there were some 200, when abstinence from meat – and sex – were required. Pork, which neither displaced peoples would touch, became an integral part of Spanish religion, and therefore everyday life. Eating sausages became a statement of loyalty and proof, if required, of conversion to the Catholic church.

Below: Of all the spices that the Moors brought with them to Spain, rich golden saffron is the one most distinctively associated with Spanish cooking.

Cocido, the national dish

It is ironic that the *cocido*, that pot of long-cooked meats with chickpeas, is the legacy of a people whom the Spanish rejected. Its origins lie in the Jewish *adafina*, the Sabbath casserole, cooked the night before, and also served in three courses. *Pelotas* are still added to *cocido* on big occasions. These are balls of minced (ground) meat or chicken livers, bread and pine nuts that echo the hamine eggs that the Jews added to *adafina*.

Adopted by the Catholic Spaniards, pork and sausages were added to the other meats in the *cocido*, as proof that the eaters were neither Jewish nor Muslim. Made almost entirely with meat, it was at first a thoroughly aristocratic dish. Then, as more chickpeas and potatoes were added, so it slipped down the social scale. Every region adds its own vegetables, and the further from Madrid, the more of a rural *puchero* (bean and sausage or meat stew) it becomes.

Below: Since the days of the Catholic kings, pork sausages such as spicy red chorizo have become the main meat eaten in Spain.

The Sephardim

This was the name given to the Spanish Jews; it is the Hebrew word for Spanish. When the Jews fled from Spain, they took with them many of its vegetables and dishes, including lentils, citron, fried fish, the boiling chicken with the bird's unshed eggs still inside, chicken with olives, and chicken soup with almonds.

HOLY SWEETMEATS

At one time, the church employed one tenth of the population, many of them women. In Old Castile and the south, nuns turned to cookie- and sweetmeat-making for charity. Egg whites were used in sherry-making and the left-over yolks given to the convents. The nuns combined these with cheap sugar from the New World to make little *natillas* (custards) and sweetmeats.

Today, you can still go to closed convents and place your order through the grille or put money on the shelf in a *tornador* (revolving door) and receive back goodies.

The best-known of these are *yemas de San Leandro* (egg yolk balls). Christmas brings red quince jellies, coconut truffles, *mantecados*, *polvorones* and potato cakes called *cubilitos* (little cubes). Other delicacies include the almond and cinnamon cream known as *bien me sabe* (I know it does me good).

Below: Dried salt cod has been enjoyed in Spain for centuries. In times past, the dried fish was carried across the country by muleteers.

FOOD ON THE ROAD

Spain is a country of mountains, and of fierce regionalism. Nevertheless, it has always had its travellers. The muleteers of León were the equivalent of modern-day lorry drivers, criss-crossing Spain with their load of salt cod and news. They had their own recipe, *bacalao ajo arriero* (dry, hard fish rehydrated in a pot with oil and garlic), which is now often transformed into a Christmas *brandade* or into a tomato-based dish.

Tourism is not a new phenomenon in Spain either. Santiago de Compostella has been a major shrine for pilgrims for a millenium. In the 1550s, at the height of its popularity, up to two million people a year, from all over Europe, walked there south of the mountains on the *camino frances*, or along the coast. Scallop shells were their badge, but in their bags they carried bread and smoked sausage. At the pilgrim monasteries, crowds of up to 1,500 were fed on chickpeas and chard.

Another transient people, the gypsies (with a background in Egypt and India) arrived in the 1450s. They settled in Andalusia where they took up the jobs left vacant by the Moors and Jews. They also annexed the folklore of the south and became the smugglers and bandits of the 19th century. Their contribution to the Spanish cuisine was an element of improvisation in food, instead of traditional long-cooked stews.

Above (left and right): The tradition of sweet cookies and custard desserts was once the province of Spanish nuns, who made and sold them for charity.

FOODS FROM NEW LANDS

The introduction of new foods from America after 1492 changed the Mediterranean diet for ever. Spain was transformed from being a bean, grain and meat-eating country, into a place where vegetables were widely enjoyed. An increase in population followed in Spain and Europe.

Chocolate and chilli peppers quickly became firm favourites in the Spanish kitchen: chocolate as a drink, and chillies as a condiment. Tomatoes were adopted and used in sauces, and beans became a firm fixture at the heart of the Spanish cuisine. Potatoes, however, never displaced the great popularity of chickpeas, and corn was adopted only in Spain's fringes. (Could the reason for this be that tobacco was discovered on the same day – and the Spanish preferred the latter?)

From the opposite direction, the Portuguese returning from China in the early 1500s, brought with them sweet oranges. To this day, oranges are still known as *chinas*. The resulting orange trees, which now grow in such abundance all over Spain, have dramatically altered the landscape of the east and south coast.

Right and far right: Spain boasts the longest coastline in Europe and from two oceans come a vast array of fresh seafood, including scampi and sardines.

BETWEEN TWO OCEANS

Spain's longest frontiers are water so it is no wonder the Spanish are seafarers. Spain has always looked outward to the Atlantic as well as inward to the Mediterranean. First came shipping salt, whaling and fishing. Later Cádiz and Sevilla provided the ships and stores for "the Empire on which the sun never sets" – a phrase used to describe Spain before it was borrowed by the British Empire. In Spain, *América* refers to Latin America, which was open territory for the *conquistadores* (adventurers) to make their fortune.

Mediterranean links

Since the Phoenicians first arrived and planted olive trees, Spain has long had links with its Eastern neighbours. In terms of food influences, Spain has given much more than it has received.

The Romans imported Spanish olive oil and adopted Spanish chickpeas to feed their armies. Under the Borgias, Spain introduced beans to Tuscany – and possibly *sofrito* (fried onion-based dishes). When the kings of Aragón ruled Italy, saffron and short-grained rice were planted, which were to become the base of the classic Italian dish, risotto.

France adopted mayonnaise, *aioli*, iced soups, chocolate, haricots and tomatoes, plus the beans and spices that transformed their *cassoulet*. With France's culinary reputation, you might expect to find French dishes in Spain, but there are actually more Spanish dishes to be found in France.

Thanks to the Moorish legacy, a huge range of kitchen skills travelled from Spain to other countries. In return, the best gift to Spain came from France in the form of wine-making skills. These included the technique of maturing wine in oak barrels.

Below: Chillies came from America and became a widely used condiment in Spanish food and cooking.

Below: Lemons were brought to Spain by the Moors, while sweet oranges were brought from China by the Portuguese.

Below: Spanish olives owe their legacy to the Phoenicians who first planted the trees there hundreds of years ago.

THE REGIONS OF SPAIN

The Spanish regions are divided by many mountain ranges. This separates them geographically, but has also led to cultural differences as well. The climate, too, varies enormously, both across the regions and from winter to summer. Both these factors have contributed to the creation of distinctive local food traditions.

THE SOUTH

Typical images of Spain are of the south: blinding sunshine and a cool arch into a Moorish patio where a guitarist is quietly practising; white walls, covered with pots of bright geraniums; horses parading and girls in polka-dot flounced skirts. The great black bull silhouette that advertises Veterano brandy stands proudly on the rims of the brown *sierras* and leaves a lasting impression.

Andalusia

This region encompasses the whole of the south coast, looking east on the Mediterranean from Almeria province, south to Africa from Málaga and out on to the Atlantic beyond Gibraltar. It embraces two sunlit worlds – that of the tourist beaches and another of fishing, farming and flamenco.

Water splashing from fountains, running in rills through gardens, or poured from cans at night on the green plants in every doorway, is the key to the country. For it was these fertile valleys that brought the Moors across the narrow straights from Africa. Now wonderful crops of asparagus and strawberries grow in the Guadalquiver delta and the *vega* of Granada. Valleys of tropical fruit face the sea, ripening in the glorious sunshine. Almería, with the help of irrigation, supplies all of Europe with tomatoes and (bell) peppers. The grey-green olive grows where nothing else will, and orange and lemon trees, loaded with fruit, surround the hamlets.

The province is mountainous with many *sierras*: the Sierra Morena north of Seville and the Sierra Nevada south east of Granada, where the Mulhacén rises 3,482m/11,420ft, its icy diamond piercing the sky beyond Granada. The *pueblos blancos*, white villages, cascade down the brown hillsides. This is the land where tapas were created – a little drink, a little food – as an unwinder at the end of a scorching day.

Andalusia's greatest foods are green olives and the scarlet, dried hams of the *sierras* – hence the name *jamón serrano*. A wide variety of shellfish are found in abundance in the warm Mediterranean, and from the Atlantic come big fish such as sharks and tuna.

In this corner of the province are the sherry *bodegas*, cathedrals where oak barrels, stacked in dark tiers, mature the precious liquid. Sherry flies through the air when the *venecia* (a sampling can fixed on a long rod) dips into the butt and is poured in a graceful arc into a row of glasses held between the fingers of a master.

Splendid church processions and pilgrimages with ox carts, bull fighting and fiestas celebrating horses or sherry, all punctuate the year. They lend formality as well as colour to a region deeply committed to its folklore. Gypsies, especially in Seville and Granada, have created the rhythms of flamenco. They also have a reputation for improvising quick and delicious dishes.

Left: Sun and shade, blinding white walls and pots filled with geraniums are typical of Andalusia's many villages.

Above: Murcia's hot climate and lush plains produce nearly half of Spain's lemons each year.

Andalusia is said to be the "zone of frying"; certainly it is done superbly. But in the villages, old-fashioned stews of beans or chickpeas are just as common. *Gazpacho*, once the only daytime meal of poor labourers (who ate it again hot at night) is these days a chilled tomato and cucumber soup, wonderfully refreshing in the midday heat. There are many different versions of *gazpacho*, but all contain garlic, vinegar and oil.

Sangría, the chilled mixture of wine and citrus juice made in a jug (pitcher), is another summer cooler. It belongs to a world of the *siesta* – afternoons of pure peace, when jobs can be put off until *mañana* (tomorrow).

Murcia

To the east of Andalusia lies Murcia, another Moorish province; indeed, they ruled here, unnoticed, until 1609. This is another market garden area, with the *Huerta de Murcia* growing seas of bright green parsley and broad (fava) beans so tender they are cooked in the pod. It is said you breakfast twice here, once on chocolate and once on (bell) peppers. Stuffed peppers, tomato salad with cumin and an *escabeche* of aubergines (eggplant) with vinegar are popular. But the region is famous for lemons and for Calasparra rice, Spain's best and ideal for paella, as well as for pickled capers.

Moorish dishes include *pastel murciano*, a pigeon pie with elaborate pastry that mimics the *b'stilla* of Morocco, desserts such as *arrope* and *jarabes* (fruit syrups), and *pan de higo* (pressed fig cake). The region also has a connection with Cuba, with dishes such as *arroz cubana* (Cuban rice).

In the salt lagoons of the Mar Menor, grey mullet are reared to eat and for caviar. *Lubina* (sea bass) baked in salt, is an internationally acclaimed dish.

Below: Water was the key to the Moors' success in Andalusia and the fountains of the Genaralife in Granada irrigate one of their greatest gardens.

CENTRAL SPAIN

At 700m/2,300ft, the *Meseta* is the high heart of Spain and comprises nearly half the country. This is *Castilla* (of the castles), a great plain with Madrid in the middle, which divides into two rather different halves.

Northern Castile and León

Tierra de pan y vino (land of bread and wine) is one description of the Duero valley. Bread has mystical significance in the great grain plains of Old Castile. The bread basket of Spain produces round *hogazas*, big close-grained loaves, and houses retain their circular ovens, even when they no longer work.

Legumes are daily fare, well-flavoured with garlic. Chickpeas and lentils grow here, and white *alubias* that are used to make bean stews with oxtail or pigs' ears and sausage. The northern fringe, El Bierzo, is very wild, but known for *empanada de batallón*, a pie that gathers all the good produce of the region together – chicken, rabbit, frogs, chorizos and (bell) peppers. The old kingdom of León is deeply influenced by the French pilgrim route passing through it, which shows in foodstuffs such as sausages. Best known are Burgos's *morcilla*, a black pudding (blood sausage) with rice, and Cantimpalo's *chorizo*, Madrid's choice for their traditional stew-pot, *cocido*.

In the north-east, sheep graze happily in the summer, but winter is icy here and woollen blankets sell well. Soría and Burgos are important centres in this region. Sheep's milk is used to make cheeses – soft, white Burgos and the celebrated *manchego*.

Above: Painted wall tiles in a Madrid restaurant advertise the wood-oven that is used to make notable roast meats.

The region is famous for its wood-fired ovens. In Sepúlvedra they roast *lechazo*, milk-fed lamb, while further west in Arévalo and Segovia, *tostones*, tiny 15–20-day-old suckling pigs are roasted to perfection. The best calves in the country are reared in Ávila.

Fritters, punch cakes and Tordesilla pastries appear in cake shops, while the many convents specialize in *repostería* (confectionery), including *rosquillas fritas* (fried rings), *pastas de té* (tea cakes) and *cocos* (coconut balls).

Madrid

Everyone in Madrid belongs to the country, so they say, and patronizes a regional restaurant. The city's dish is *cocido*, but *callos* (tripe) is so popular that it has moved from the home to become bar fare. Madrid's many restaurants introduced short-order cooking to Spain – *madrileño* used to indicate quicker dishes. The city is spoiled for fish and delicatessens. In May, San Isidro is celebrated with mixed salads and puff pastries.

Left: The fairytale Alcázar *(fortress) of Segovia is one of the many medieval castles scattering central Spain – giving the region its name, Castile.*

New Castile and La Mancha

La Mancha, Don Quixote country, means parched. No wonder Cervantes chose it for his poor knight. The great plains are covered with low vines, with odd corners of saffron planted by the Moors. The intense heat of the summer fuels a preference for strong, robust flavours. *Sopa de ajo* (garlic and bread soup) and dishes with cumin are typical fare. Huge quantities of thyme are mixed with pig's liver, paprika and pine nuts, or go into meatballs and one-pot stews.

The food is simple yet quite delicious – glistening tomato salads, luscious *el asadilla* (baked sweet red peppers) and fabulous marinated vegetables such as aubergines (eggplant) pickled in Almalgro in the Moorish fashion. Genuine *pisto* is simply made using (bell) peppers, tomatoes and courgettes (zucchini). Paprika, for red sausages, is made here and in the neighbouring La Vera valley from *choricero* chillies. *Morteruelo* is a liver pâté with game. Best-known of all, however, is *tortilla* – the thick, solid potato and onion omelette. This classic was originally prepared, it is said, by a peasant for a hungry king. Valdepeñas make the best wines, good enough for a *chateo* (a walk round the bars) in Madrid.

Above: Wild black ibérico pigs forage under the holm oaks of Extremadura, where acorns give their hams special flavour. The region is famous for its pork consumption and its sausages.

Below: In Castile, sheep are valued for their wool and milk, which is turned into cheese. Their meat is eaten while the animals are still young and tender.

Extremadura

The rolling plains are called the *charro* – a land of holm oak and corks, knee-deep in flowers in spring, with more pigs and sheep than people. The explorers Cortes and Pizarro were born here – and left to find something better. Extramadura is poor and there is a good deal of hunting for free food: birds, rabbits, frogs, freshwater fish and summer truffles. Rich tomato sauces are favoured for many of these foods.

Montanchez and Guijelo are famous for *pata negra* (black foot) hams. The black pigs run wild under the oaks, fattening up on acorns. The locals are great consumers of pork. The seasoning of the mince (ground pork) for sausage-making is tested in *prueba* (meatballs). *Pringada* is anything fried in bacon fat. Everything from the pig that can be is made into sausages, and the rest is either pickled, stewed or minced in some manner. The region produces half the pork pâté eaten in Spain.

Migas (fried breadcrumbs) are served with fry-ups, or combined with bacon and chillies. Local hospitality demands that the plates are always piled high. Local paprika colours *el frito* (fried lamb) red; *caldereta extremeña* is lamb stewed with its liver.

THE NORTH COAST

Isolated from the rest of Spain, the wet north has a rugged coast and a Celtic tradition that links it closely to its northern neighbours.

Galicia

Europe's western corner is green and misty, the cabbages rocked by the wind that blows on two coasts. *Hórreos* (stone-roofed storehouses), which are used for storing maize (corn), potatoes and local cheeses, stand guard outside every house.

Below: Vineyards above the Miño River around the village of San Esteban in Galicia produce white wines.

Galicia grows innovative produce for the Madrid markets, including *padrón* peppers, watercress and kiwi fruit. The favourites at home are a special white potato (*cachelo*), which is indispensable for any traditional meal, turnips and, more particularly, *grelos* – the turnip leaves just coming into bud.

The poorer south is covered with chestnut trees, whose nuts were long a basic food but which are now eaten at festivals. Three-quarters of the land provides pasture for dairy cows, whose milk is used to make the famous Galician cheeses such as *tetilla*. Here you will also find the blond breed *rubio gallego*, which supplies much of the country's best meat. Unemployment is rife, however, and the region is called "the goodbye lands" because people leave in the hope of finding a better future in Latin America.

Maize grows on the north coast, and the local breads, heavy in texture, are made with corn meal, barley and rye. Raisins are sometimes added to the corn bread for Christmas.

The Moors never conquered these Celtic lands, which have more in common with Normandy and Wales than they have with provinces further south. Oil and garlic are seldom used in the kitchens of this region and cooking tends to be simple. Fat pigs are prized; the native dish is *lacón*, the salted front leg. Markets sell rolls of back fat for cooking, as well as tripe and numerous types of sausage. Barnyard poultry produce red-yolked eggs, and fat ginger hens are sold with unshed eggs inside.

Cape Finisterre – the world's end and the last stop before America – is known as the Cape of Death, because of the number of ships wrecked there. It provides the best choice and quality of seafood in the world. Half of the mussels eaten in the world grow here.

Windy, westward Santiago de Compostela cathedral, with its cliff-face façade, is a place of world pilgrimage, famous for the grave of St James. The pilgrims' badge is a scallop shell, and even those who do not wear it must surely eat them. Vigo is the biggest fishing port in Europe.

New wineries of gleaming steel make wine from grapes that grow on the south-facing seaside slopes. The white *alberiño* is said to come from a Riesling grape brought by German monks. Its "green" wine is often sparkling – the perfect partner for shellfish.

Galicia has over 200 food festivals a year, celebrated with bagpipes, tambourines and simple dances. An ancient pre-Christian culture lies just beneath the surface, with herbalism and a touch of witchcraft. In the magic ritual of the *queimada*, which is used for divination, a rough brandy (*orujo*) and sugar are flamed. The chief witch, in his straw cape, sets fire to the pot. The lights go down and the flames shoot up.

Above: The stone hórreos *that are used for storing corn cobs and local cheeses can be seen all over Galicia.*

Asturias and Cantabria

The range of mountains that run east to west along the north coast stretch 500km/300 miles, with many peaks at 2,500m/8,000ft. Oak and beechwoods support spectacular wild life – bears, wolves and wild cats, as well as deer, boar and capercaillie. Civilization here dates back to the Bronze Age.

This is "green Spain", with some 250 varieties of apple, and where cider-drinking is a serious sport. Clogs are worn against the frequent drizzle, while cauldrons of stew offer a different form of protection against the cold in this mining country. *Pote asturiana* combines cabbage, beans, salt foreleg, pig fat and ribs. Great melt-in-the-mouth white kidney beans go into *fabada*. In the hinterland of Santander, known as *la montaña*, you will find stews of mutton and beans, as well as the bullet cabbage. There are also bean stews with clams and other shellfish.

All four northern regions are famous for their smoke-cured sausages. The *morcillas* (blood sausages) are dried out, then reydrated in stews. *Botiello* (ribs and tail) are served at carnival.

High up, flower-strewn dairy pastures provide the milk for half of Spain's cheeses. The Picos de Europa have 27 varieties, including the famed *cabrales*. This is a dairy culture, which sends milk and yogurt across Spain; at home the milk and butter are used in rice puddings, apple batter cake and butter sponges for breakfast. The Val de Liébana produces wonderful cheese; it is also an enclave of Mediterranean agriculture, growing tiny, delicious chickpeas as well as fruit.

Oviedo, a centre of coal and iron mining, is a wealthy and fast-living city. It has fabulous seafood such as the *changurro* (spider crab) and many modern creations by talented chefs. This is the largest salmon-producing region in the country. Classically the fish is soaked in milk, salt and lemon, then grilled (broiled) – *a la parrilla*.

Cantabria, the corridor west from the Basque country, is a coast of small bays and little fishing harbours, with the flag-flying casino city of Santander. Sardines are found in abundance and the very popular hake is cooked *a la sidra* (in cider), with mussels and brandy. Squid (*rabas*) are breaded and fried.

Above: Scallop shells are the symbol of St James at Santiago de Compostela. These are painted with his sword.

Below: The Asturias is milk country and the rich pastures that cover the hillsides offer excellent grazing.

ALONG THE PYRENEES

Three very different provinces border France. The successful Basque Country, smaller Navarra and large, poor Aragon.

The Basque country

Snuggled into the Pyrenees by France, el País Vasco has many Michelin-starred restaurants. The lucky Basques have it all; well-hung beef, wild mushrooms, fish and vegetables. Long recognized as Spain's finest cooks, they do things the French way, using butter and cream (unusual for Spain), and take their food very seriously. Basque chefs embraced *la nueva cocina* a quarter of a century ago, seeking a profile that extended beyond Spain.

Eating is thoroughly social, with an eatery per every 1,000 people. The Basques adopted the *pincho* (a *tapa* on a stick) and are sophisticated tapas crawlers. In the *cofradías* (men's clubs), cooking is done by the members, who create dishes with *angulas* (elvers) and *kokotxas* (the tasty part of hake throat).

Basques are nationalists through and through, with their own exotic language. The "TX" of the Basque language can prove tricky. The small glass used for local wine, *txiquito*, is pronounced *chiquito*. The perfumed spider crab is called *txangurro*, pronounced *changurro*. "TX" over a restaurant door anywhere in Spain means that the chef is Basque, which is usually a good sign.

The Basques have a long connection with the sea, with some of the biggest fleets in the world. Cod is mainly fished off the coast of Iceland, to be sold, salted, in *bacalao* shops. Salt fish goes into *zurraputuna*, a soup with bread and chilli, and *porrusaldo*, soup with leeks, which is eaten mid-morning as the workmen's breakfast.

Above: Basque fishermen unload their catch at Getaria. The Basques have the largest fishing fleet in Spain.

Biscay is our name for the waters of Viscaya, whose fish are cooked *a la brasa*, over charcoal. Perfectionists say that fish is only worth eating if it has been line-caught rather than netted.

Basque cuisine boasts four main sauces to serve with fish. White sauce, *pil-pil*, is an emulsion of olive oil and garlic; green *salsa verde* combines wine and parsley and is usually served with hake; *vizcaína* (Biscay) is tomato-based; and the fourth sauce is black, made with the ink of the cuttle fish, and often served with it, *en su tinta*.

Spring brings new peas (*tarvillas*) and beans, eaten with other new shoots in *coussinat*, and fungi stalls at markets. In this maize region, corn meal cakes are made on the griddle. But the locals prefer beans – red, black and all shades between – and sausages.

For dessert there are apples (*reinettas*) and *cañutillas* (cream horns), and this is also Spain's main

Below: The Pyrenees offer grazing for Basque sheep, whose milk is made into the richly flavoured cheese, Idiazábal.

chocolate centre. Firm cheeses revolve around Idiazábal, which are slightly caramelized when smoked.

Rioja is known for its style of wine, which is flavoured from storage in oak casks. It is the best known of Spain's wine and most widely drunk abroad.

Navarra

This tiny region is relatively isolated, with one highway, the great Valley of Roncesvalles, passed through by so many millions of pilgrims. These travellers are remembered with *bacalao al arriero*, now often a cream of salt cod and garlic, and a hank of *chistorra* sausage. The cheese of Roncal is firm and widely enjoyed in France. Mountain dishes include mushrooms with herbs, roast quail in fig leaves in September and brown trout. Lamb is fried in *cochifrito* or stewed with red (bell) peppers as *chilindrón*.

The fashionable, fruity wines are red or rosé. The vineyards face those of Rioja across the Ebro, Spain's greatest river. Peppers, asparagus and lettuces also grow well here. The many almonds grown in the region are ground for cake-making and marzipan, which is extremely popular.

Below: Vineyards in Navarra produce strong but very fruity wines.

Above: Bright yellow sunflowers are grown for their seeds, which are often served as a tapa*, or crushed to make margarine or cooking oil.*

Aragón

Huge Aragón boasts soaring mountains, with many chamois and boar. Game is a speciality, especially the birds that skim over the mountain passes. Pigeons are served in *salmorejo* (garlic and vinegar sauce) and partridges with chocolate, an idea that has caught on across the country. The hams of Teruel, one of the three best in the country, are eaten as *magras con tomate* locally, where slices of ham are served in tomato sauce.

Aragón is sometimes mocked for the simplicity of its cooking – the locals like grills, such as goat on a spit, served with *allioli*. Stews with vegetables, baked dough rounds with sardines and red (bell) peppers, and *migas* (fried breadcrumbs) with chocolate are all popular dishes.

Downwards to the dusty plain, Zaragoza is a large grower of maize (corn), sunflowers and many herbs. Borage is still cultivated and used in the same way as spinach. *Boliches* are white beans of great quality.

Groves of almond trees date from Moorish times, with apple, cherry and peach orchards stretching from Zaragoza to Teruel. Here they make *vi rancios* (fortified dessert wine) and cystallized fruit and candied peels. Delicious almond sweetmeats are a reminder of the long Moorish rule.

THE EAST COAST AND THE ISLANDS

As with the other regions of Spain, the east coast and the islands that lie off the mainland have their own specific culture, flavour and traditions.

Catalonia

The French discovered the excellent fish on the Costa Brava, and named the place the Wild Coast. Ever since then people have crossed Spain's borders to eat *zarzuela* (fish stew studded with shellfish) and *susquet*, with tomato and potatoes. Gerona is famous for its sea bass, and Barcelona for its monkfish in a dark cream of toasted garlic.

Catalunya, the small province next to France, has Spain's business brains and earns one fifth of the national income. The cuisine here leans towards the French tradition of fine cooking mixed with a little Italian spontaneity – and less towards Africa. Sauces are thickened with yolks in the French style and béchamel is used. Ducks are reared, and confit and magrets (breast fillets) are on the menu.

Catalans have long had a tradition of good restaurants – and are now thought of as Spain's best cooks. (French chefs voted *El Bulli* to be the world's top restaurant.) Barcelona is a city of 10,000 eateries, and its market, *la Boquería*, is one of the world's greatest.

Catalan cooking is eclectic. *Allioli* was invented here and first recorded in AD100. Saffron and the tradition of combining meat with fruit go back to the Roman times. Sweet-and-sour is a Moorish taste, while lobster with chocolate came later. Other dishes are inspired by local ingredients – *mar i muntanya* (sea and mountain) refers to dishes that combine seafood and meat such as clams with partridge. Black rice with squid ink is a modern speciality.

Above: A shop window in Catalonia, displays a wonderful selection of foods, including sausages, hams and cheeses.

Almonds, onions, spinach and aubergines (eggplant) remain popular, while the provincial dish is the chickpea *escudella* with pork dumpling, served in two courses. White beans are called *mongetes* here and are cooked with *botifarro*, the local sausage. Vic, a sausage capital, produces a black-and-white speciality, as well as the carmine drumstick, *fuet*.

Quality shows in simple foods such as *pa amb tomàquet* (bread rubbed with garlic, oiled and rubbed with the ripest tomato). There is also the *rovelló* mushroom of autumn (fall), and rich, tangy tomato sauce flavoured with bitter orange peel.

Unlike many homes in Spain, Catalan houses have ovens, and cakes for dessert means puff pastries, sweet *cocas* (like pizzas) and little almond and pine nut cookies. The region is the centre of creative wine-making – and *champán's* biggest house in the world, Cordoníu. There is even a non-drip bottle, in the *porrón*, to drink from.

Left: The Boqueria market in the centre of Barcelona sells the freshest seasonal foods such as rovellones *(bleeding milk cap mushrooms).*

The Levante

The east coast includes Alicante and Valencia and a good many of Spain's sunshine beaches. Paella was invented here by picnicking men, and it is still customary to have a *tío* (uncle) in charge. Lake Albufera has freshwater eels, eaten with pepper (*alli-pebre*). Rice dishes often include special runner (green) beans, or *garrafones* (huge flat dried white beans). These are described as "paving stones across rice" in the dish *arros empedrat*.

Alicante's paella contains chicken and rabbit, rather than seafood. Alternatively, it may be made with pasta instead of rice to make *fideuá*. Fresh sausages, *blancs*, are popular, as is the black *poltrona* sausage.

It was a priest who had the brilliant idea of planting oranges commercially here in the 1780s. Now they are on the trees year-round. There are lemons and dates, too, and muscat grapes that survive the heat until after Christmas. *Horchata*, a cool milky drink made from *chufas* (tiger nuts) is a local speciality. It is also a region of festival cakes and Christmas *turrón* (nougat).

Below: The Forn de Teatre bakery in Mallorca is famous for its ensaimadas *– coils of exquisite pastry.*

Above: Fishing boats bob in the water in the Los Cristianos port in Tenerife.

The Balearic Islands

Mallorca, Menorca and Ibiza are islands with good lobsters and fish, and gulleys full of herbs. The British fleet, which was stationed in Menorca for 150 years, left gin, clover and dairy cows that now provide the milk for the cheese *mahón*. The French discovered *mahonesa* (mayonnaise) here in the 1750s and instantly adopted it.

Food tends to be solid, as in the layered-vegetable *tumbet*, along with rich soups, and snails from the earthenware *greixonera*. Pigs take centre stage, the high point being the exquisite, spreadable, bright orange *sobrasada* sausage, which is widely available outside the Balearics.

An overlay of cultures has left Moorish-influenced *sucrerías* (sweet shops), which sell jams, pastries and an exquisite cheesecake (*flao*).

The Canary Islands

Las Canarias specialize in local fish, which are beautiful in their varying colours, such as the yellow-purple *vieja*, and cooked simply. They are served with unusual wrinkled potatoes (*papas arrugadas*), which are cooked in sea water and served unpeeled. With them comes *mojo*, a green sauce of blended garlic, coriander (cilantro) and vinegar. A climate of eternal spring produces a wealth of vegetables, including corn. The islands are known for small, sweet aromatic bananas, which are a good partner for the rich, amber *malvasía*, a local dessert wine.

THE SOCIAL CONTEXT

The Spanish are a gregarious people and much of their social life revolves around food. Many people breakfast in a bar before going to work; others go out mid-morning.

They can enjoy *café con leche*, *zumo* (juice) and *tostadas* (toast) or, if they are lucky, a sophisticated roll such as *ensaimada* or *sobao*. For anyone in no hurry, there is always hot chocolate served with *churros* – long strips of deep fried batter for dunking in the thick chocolate drink.

Lunch is a big affair, typically starting at around two o'clock but later on feast days. The old pattern, in middle-class households, was to eat meat at lunch, then fish at night, with vegetables as a first course. Now it is one or the other. Children have a *merienda* (drink and snack) at about five o'clock. Women often meet friends for a *merienda* after work. Whole families go for the *paseo* – a seven o'clock promenade. Men might go for an *aperativo*. Supper is late, and is a light meal, often vegetable-based.

Large cities never seem to sleep. Dinner bookings are made for ten o'clock at night, and in Madrid there is a rush hour at three in the morning as everyone goes home to sleep before starting work at eight that morning. And the famous siesta? The lunch hour, for office workers, is two hours long and is mainly spent talking.

MENUS

Salad is universal as a first course in summer. Placed in the centre of the table, everyone uses their own fork to eat from it. A restaurant will offer ham or several cold meats, egg dishes, shellfish and soups. The latter are often heavy, and would be regarded as stews elsewhere. Rice and pasta are listed separately, but are a first course in Spain. Then there is a fish or meat course, perhaps offered *a la brasa* or from the *barbacoa* (cooked over charcoal). Restaurants offer desserts, but at home these are usually reserved for saints' days and fiestas.

COOKING AT HOME

The Spanish tradition is for slow-cooking, which can go on all day. The *puchero*, a pot of mixed pulses and meats or sausage, was made most days and left on the stove, wafting rich aromas around the house. Mothers were kept busy in the kitchen but life is different now, and many women work. The delicatessen round the corner stays open until late and supermarkets, with their ready meals, are open all hours.

Left: Cafés provide drinks thoughout the day, offering a place to pause and relax or to meet friends and family.

Table manners

Good children keep their hands on the table throughout a meal, so nothing can go on "underneath the counter". It is thought very bad manners to leave any food on your plate, and anyone not mopping up with bread is considered *mal educado*.

THE GREAT OUTDOORS

Eating outdoors is part of the Spanish psyche and houses have balconies and patios, and perhaps a little outdoor summerhouse called a *comedor* (eating place) because it is often too hot to sit in the sun. Built-in charcoal barbecues grace many gardens.

The Spanish are great picnickers. On casual occasions, family groups may go for a happy day out in the *campo* (fields), or for a harvest picnic. For more formal gatherings such as pilgrimages and fairs, makeshift booths or houses (*casetas*) are put up for entertainment. They offer dining, dance floors and kitchens with gas tripods over which paella is cooked. As many as 2,000 people may be accommodated for the night at unpublicized local events, in tents that are put up and taken down in a single weekend.

Above: Outdoor cooking is a big part of Spanish life and many homes have a built-in fire or barbecue in the garden.

RESTAURANT CULTURE

Families eat out together at weekends, with all the generations present. This is one of the reasons why restaurants are so numerous and prices remain so affordable. Hospitality is offered in restaurants rather than at home and many eating establishments advertise catering for large numbers. Jokingly called a *palacio de boda* (wedding palaces), big parties celebrate not just weddings but First Communions and golden weddings. Spectacularly tiered cakes may appear at any of the celebrations. These large parties are paid for by the guests, who come with large cash rolls: the bill is paid, then the rest forms the bridal gift.

SPANISH CUISINE

The strength of Spanish cooking lies in careful selection of ingredients, then finding perfect ways of cooking them. What does it matter that a recipe goes back 400 years, or even 800 years? If it tastes good, why change it?

Today freezers and imports may have improved choice somewhat, but essentially Spanish cooking is regional, devoted to *la patria chica* (my home town and the things it does well). The big 1970s influx of tourists coincided with *la nueva cocina* and its message to use locally produced ingredients. The *Denominación de Origen* (D.O.) system, introduced to protect locally distinctive quality food and drink, is broadly extended and covers hams, cheese and peppers as well as wine. The *Paradores* (state-run hotels), also encourage menus that feature local dishes.

The bride's cookbook

The *Manual de Cocina* is the cookbook given to brides. It dates from the 1930s, when Pilar Prima de Rivera, daughter of dictator Miguél, ran the *Sección Feminina*, a politicized women's group. The organization collected simple, classic recipes from across the country. The book has now run to some 30 editions and is as popular as ever.

TAPAS

Tapas are Spain's greatest food invention. "Eat when you drink, drink when you eat" is the philosophy. Spanish men traditionally drink outside the home and rarely alone. Tapas are not meant to be a meal (although a *ración* is a substantial portion). One *tapa* per person and a different one with each drink is the idea, then everyone enjoys tasting and sharing. Tapas food is real food – good local ingredients presented with flair.

The idea comes from Andalusia. It started, so they say, with a piece of bread, soon topped with ham or cheese, balanced over a glass, to keep out the flies – the word *tapa* means a cover. Tapas were once free snacks included in the price of the drink. Now this is a way of life in the south. In dim caverns, where the sherry barrels are stacked high, men revolve the wine in their *copitas*, gently sipping, then select a new wine from a different cask. To compare and contrast is part of the tapas ritual. An old man may sit by the door, with a bucket of *conchas finas*, opening clams slowly and to order. It is a life less hectic than our own.

Below: An old Seville tapas bar sign advertises food to help sell its drinks.

Above: Hams hang behind the bar in a traditional tapas bar in Madrid, while bulls' heads adorn the walls.

CLASSIC TAPAS

Tapas dishes revolve around shellfish. In the southern triangle of sherry towns – between Jerez de la Frontera, El Puerto de Santa Maria and Sanlúcar de Barrameda – you may eat amazing shellfish, including squid eggs, whelks (*cañadillas*) and fritters of minute shrimps. The south is also famous for fried fish, *cazón* (a type of shark) marinated in saffron, and *frita malagueña* (mixed battered seafood).

Charcuterie is an important part of the tradition. Hams hang over every bar, with little upturned paper umbrellas underneath to catch dissolving fat: the incomparable scarlet *jamón serrano.*

SOCIAL AMBIENCE

Tapas bars were once the preserve of men. Now they attract women too but they are still a great place to discuss sport, particularly bullfighting. In this macho atmosphere old foods survive, for example squares of blood (set with vinegar) "to give men strength at night". Tapas also fuel Spain's many fiestas. After all, how could one follow an all-night procession without a little bite to eat? A café terrace is also an ideal place from which to watch the spectacle.

People go to bars for the company, but stay for the temptations. A range of flavours is offered in tiny portions, from the sophisticated and exotic to the bland and soothing. They are laid out on the counter, like jewels in a shop window: yolk-yellow *tortilla*, kidneys in sherry, red-hot potatoes, Russian salad (*ensaladilla*) and stuffed baby squid.

CITY SPECIALITIES

Madrid favours tripe, *boquerones en vinagre* (fresh anchovy fillets cured in vinegar) and, of course, shellfish. The old tradition was to throw prawn and shrimp heads on the floor of the bar to show how popular the place was. In Barcelona, designer bars are all the rage and people go there to see and be seen. Basque bars in cities reflect a much more bourgeois clientele. The phrase *ir de pinchos* means to go for a tapas crawl, which can be a popular way to spend an evening.

Fried tapas in the north evoke an era of nostalgia, with bechamel-based *croquetas* (croquettes), and *gambas en gabardinas* (prawns/shrimp in batter).

Bars are also the place to find local food specialities such as spider crab in San Sebastián, and elvers and hake throats in Bilbao. The morsels can often be very elaborate, high cuisine presented in miniature. Tapas bars are also a wonderful way to sample Spain's best dishes such as *rabo de toro* (bull's tail) and the delicious *escabeche de perdiz* (vinegared partridge).

Above: A bartender in Madrid pulls a caño, *a beer drawn from the pump.*

Right: This smart tapas bar in Bilbao, decorated with ornate gilt, entices a sophisticated and loyal clientele.

Pepitas ...

Think "pippy", for *pepitas* are seeds – little nibbles to pick up in handfuls. Toasted chickpeas, soaked *chufas* (tiger nuts), pistachios and large, soaked yellow lupin seeds, *altramuz*. *Pepitas* themselves are creamy-flavoured pumpkin seeds, but also common are *pipas de girasol* (sunflower seeds).

... and pepitos

A *pepito* is a long soft roll (like a bridge roll), often filled with succulent roast veal. A *montadito* (which literally means mounted) is a piece of bread with a topping such as chorizo or (bell) peppers, perhaps speared with a cocktail stick (wooden toothpick). Though the name *bocadillo* translates as mouthful, it is in fact a substantial sandwich of crusty bread, often with ham and cheese.

Feast Days and Fiestas

In Spain, almost every event involves food. There are special foods for feast days – and feast days solely to celebrate food. Every town, and nearly every village, has its fiesta – over 3,000 occur annually. All are occasions for dressing up, parading the children and drinking with the neighbours.

Holy week is an occasion of high drama but the local saint's day, or an incident in a town's history, will be celebrated with processions and street crowds. The seasons of the year are also greeted with affection.

CHRISTMAS AND NEW YEAR

The Christmas lights go up, and there are *belenes* in shop windows, manger scenes often with a huge cast of characters. On Christmas Eve, *Noche Buena*, it is elvers if you are Basque, or perhaps a salt cod cream (*bacalao al arriero*) after midnight mass in Aragón. The Madrid choice is baked *lubina* (sea bream) and red cabbage; the Catalans eat roast turkey. There are gifts of almond *turrón* and marzipan on the table. Twelfth night is a magical day for children; it is the day they receive gifts. The three kings' arrival in Bethlehem is remembered in the *roscon de reyes*, a crown of rich yeast bread.

On *Noche Vieja* (New Year's Eve), it is grapes at midnight at the Puerta de Sol in Madrid, with costume parties and street festivals in the warmer south. For good luck, people eat one grape for each toll of the midnight bell.

SPRING CARNIVALS

Jueves lardero (Mardi Gras) sees a big carnival in Tenerife, the largest of the Canary Islands. In Andalusia the day is marked with a feast of all good things from the pig, before the start of the 40 meatless days of Lent.

In Valencia, *La Fiesta de Las Fallas* culminates on the saint's day of San José, 19 March. Some 400 huge caricature creations are set alight in one vast bonfire and all-night party. Further south in Alcoy every April, San Jorge is celebrated with a battle reenactment. The saint appears on a white horse to lift the Muslim seige. Black beans with white rice (*moros y cristianos*) are eaten as a reminder.

For Seville's *Feria de Abril*, streets of *casetas* are erected, and days are given over to drinking and dancing. The close is followed by *lunes de la resaca* (hangover Monday).

HOLY WEEK

Semana Santa, the days from Palm Sunday to Easter, is the big festival, particularly in the south. The heavy *pasos* (scenes of Christ's death) and the weeping virgins banked by scented lilies and tall candles are paraded night after night, later and later, before packed crowds and to a constant reverberating noise of drumming.

The Easter foods are few: *torijillos* (fried toast), cheesecake, and perhaps lamb for *Resurreción* day. However, it is *carajillos* (brandy and black coffee) that you will need to cope with the drama and exhaustion of the festival.

Left: The Virgin and Child are paraded around Valencia for the patronal festival. The special relationship of each town to its patron makes her "our" virgin.

Above: The sinister costumes of the penitentes *were adopted in the past to hide the identity of the genuine penitents. Today, they are a traditional part of Holy Week in the south.*

CELEBRATING THE NEW SEASON

Food coming into season is joyfully greeted – the reappearance of freshwater crayfish, the first salmon of the year, a *caracolada* (feast of river snails) in Lerida. Tarragona people wear bibs when they suck the *calçots* (spring onions/scallions) from the barbecued black leaves. In Valls and Cambrils, the celebrations include human towers.

In Murcia, the end of Lent is marked with floats and a parade for the "Burial of the Sardine". The return of sardines to Spanish waters marks the coming of summer. In Malaga, the fish are roasted over beach fires for *la moraga*. Fishermen give thanks on San Pedro and the Virgen de Carmen on 15 July with a flotilla of decorated boats, followed by fish suppers.

For the children
Many festivals start with a carriage procession and a *chupinaza* – pelting children with candy. *Chupa* is a ball of candy on a stick.

SAINTS' DAYS AND PATRONAL FESTIVALS

Spaniards don't have birthdays but instead celebrate their saint's day. For example, if your name is José everyone will remember you on 19 March, with congratulations, flowers and sweets (candy) for the children. It is "your day". Towns, and districts within them, also seek the protection of a saint, whose image is paraded annually. These days are a frenzy of baking.

In Badajoz, people celebrate with little Moorish fritters, and in Logroño they eat yeast buns called *bollas* for San Marco. A topsy-turvy day in Segovia on Santa Agatha, when the men are replaced by "mayoresses", is celebrated by women with moscatel-soaked cake (*ponche segoviana*).

To celebrate San José on 19 March, everyone eats *buñuelos de viento*, little choux puffs that "just blow away". In Madrid these airy pastries are made with lard and *coñac*, and have a special filling of rich, sweet, creamy custard to celebrate San Isidro.

Local cookies come out for fiestas such as the Valencia *Fallas*: baked nut *almendrados*, little *glorias* (pyramids of marzipan and meringue), and sweet pastry *rollets* and *fartons* (fingers of sweet rolled dough, baked and sugared). Santa Clara, patroness of so many nuns, is celebrated in August with *rosquillas* (iced ring doughnuts) and, in the summer, street crowds on the east coast and islands eat *cocas* (flat buns) with candied fruit for St John and St James.

Below: Brightly coloured costumes with a team theme add to the fun at many festivals such as carnaval *in Cádiz.*

SUMMER IN THE SUN

Summer brings the perfect weather for celebrations. Spain's biggest picnic is *El Rocío* when a million people traipse with wagons, drawn by face-fringed oxen, to the shrine of the *Virgen de Rocío* in Andalusia. The Assumption of the Virgin on 15 August is celebrated with days of street fairs, table tennis, dancing, flirting and flamenco, and is a bigger festival than Christmas. Madrid and Barcelona have year-round festivals, including San Isidro each May in Madrid and Festa de la Mercè every September in Barcelona. All of them serve typical local dishes. Pamplona has the most challenging festival of all from 6–14 July to celebrate San Firmín. Called the *encierro* (bull penning), each day, the bulls chase any who are brave enough to participate across the town.

ST JAMES' DAY – SANTIAGO

Spain's National Day on 25 July means fiesta time in Santiago de Compostela. Jostling crowds of people, many of whom have walked the last few kilometres into town, pack the streets around the cathedral. There are balloons, pavement stalls, music, dancing, fireworks and beauty queens. No one is drunk, just happy. *Gigantes y cabezas* amuse the crowds. The giants (men on stilts) represent figures from the past – Queen Isabel or a Moor. They have comic papier-mâché heads and costumes that go down to the shoes.

To feast on, bars serve octopus *a la feria*, gently stewed with paprika. There is also lobster followed by *tarta de Santiago*, a cinnamon almond tart, with a stencil of St James' great two-handed sword outlined in powdered sugar.

Above: Gigantes *feature in many traditional festivals. Valencia is famous for its papier-mâché figures, which are balanced on the shoulders.*

HARVESTS

In the days when grapes were crushed by men dancing in the vats with bare feet, there was close physical contact to the harvest. Today, abundance is celebrated in a different fashion. *La tomatina*, held in Bunyol in Valencia at the end of August, is the messiest of all these festivals. It starts with trying to get a ham off the top of a greasy pole and is followed by 15 minutes of mayhem as thousands of people pelt each other with ripe tomatoes.

Haro, in La Rioja, celebrates San Pedro at the end of June with a "war of the wines". Neighbours dress up in white and bombard each other with wine squirted from a leather bottle. In the Asturian town of Nava, the cider apple harvest is celebrated by a chain of celebrants pouring cider from pitcher to pitcher down the street. There are plenty of free drinks along the way.

Left: Oxen wearing Cleopatra-style headdresses pull the gilded cart that carries the Virgin of El Rocío on Spain's biggest pilgrimage.

MATANZA – PIG KILLING TIME

The *matanza* is the greatest social festival of the year. The proverb goes: "every pig has his St Martin" (pride comes before a fall), and traditionally 10–11 November is the time for pig killing. If you don't have a pig, then you muscle in on someone else's, because it needs a team for sausage-making. The annual event brings families together and lasts for two or more days. The pig's liver, cooked with onions, is served for lunch on the first day, and the kidneys with rice or potatoes is served on the second.

If you can't find a pig, then you can party at a *matanza* feast in a restaurant, accompanied by oboes, drums and dancing of the *paso doble*. Over 30 courses, the skilled chefs demonstrate just what you can do with a pig. Brains and ears, hot and cold, salad and soup make up the delicious first courses. Hot courses follow: roasts, stews of tail, trotters, marinated loin, roast ham, *solomillo* (tenderloin) with occasional garnishes of vegetables, and tiny roast pigs too. All is accompanied by hunting horns, singing and *olé* to everything.

Above: Dancers skip around a maypole at a local festival in Belunchón, Toledo.

Below: Flamenco dancers at the Fiera de Abril in Seville wear the flounced skirts usually associated with Andalusia. Here, they are known as sevillanas.

THE DAY OF THE DEAD

All Saints, on 1 November, is celebrated by families all over Spain, carrying flowers to the graveyards. *Huesos de santos* (saint's bones), made of almond pastry, sweet potato or batter, are eaten. Sometimes they are fried around a piece of bamboo cane, which makes them ghoulishly hollow. Catalans bake little nut *panellets*. In Galicia, there are all-night vigils by candlelight, with chestnuts roasting on braziers and the mists drifting in from the sea.

CELEBRATION EATING

Huge outdoor meals are a typically Spanish event, but crowd cooking from a single pot is a challenge that only the Spanish would accept. In the town square of Valencia, a vast paella pan 4m/4yds across and set over charcoal was used to cook yellow rice for 1,000 people. The ingredients were stirred with wooden oars.

Vast cauldrons, to dance around as well as to eat from, bubble on fires in the middle of public squares in many places. Arévalo, in Castile, celebrates St John of the Cross in December with a *cocido de San Juan* (plates of beans and chorizo). Benifairó de Les Valls, in Valencia, has its *calderete* of everything porcine, with rice and many vegetables.

THE SPANISH KITCHEN

Spanish cooking methods have stayed mainly unchanged over the centuries. Although modern kitchen appliances have taken away some of the labour of food preparation, the pots, pans and techniques remain the same.

COOKING OVER CHARCOAL

This is very much a Spanish tradition. Wood and charcoal fires are still used in homes and many restaurants today. The fire is built on a brick shelf and a metal plate (*la plancha*) sits over the fire at cooking height, with holes for the pots to sit in. It is also used for grilling.

Small terracotta stoves may also be used, heated with charcoal from the main fire in winter, and an outdoor fire in summer. These stoves feature in the 16th-century paintings of Velásquez, and have not changed since that time.

ABOUT THE HOUSE

Spanish winters are chilly, so a *brasero* (two-handled brass tray of hot charcoal) sits under the sitting-room table; a cloth over the table holds in heat, keeping the feet warm. The *brasero* is not actually used for cooking, but is handy for toasting bread.

The cellar (*bodega*) is also of great importance. In the big country *cortijo* (farmhouse complex) the cold cellar stones near the well were often the only cold place. This is where gazpacho was chilled overnight.

Above: Classic earthenware cazuelas *are used for both cooking and serving.*

Below: The shallow paella pan and the deep-frying pan are widely used in the Spanish kitchen.

POTS AND PANS

All over the world the paella pan is identified with Spain. The real Valencian *paellera* has green handles, a dimpled base and is quite thin. They range in size from small to enormous – big enough for a party.

The other traditional frying pan is deep and two-handled, used for stews and for deep-frying fish.

The *puchero* (or *olla*) is the pot that has given its name to many Spanish stews. In central Spain it may be earthenware with a bulbous body, narrow neck and two handles but in other areas it is more frequently an upright, loop-handled, metal or copper pot. The witches' kettle (a round-bellied metal *caldereta* with three legs) is used for fish dishes and the rice dish, *arroz caldoso*. A bigger version of this is *un calderón*, which is used for cooking large stews in public squares at fiestas. It is the classic vessel carried around to Galician fairs by itinerant octopus cookers.

EARTHENWARE DISHES

The earthenware *cazuela* is a splendid invention. Glazed inside, it comes in all sizes from small to very large, and may be rectangular as well as round. In Castile they are used for roasting, and in Catalonia and Levante for oven-baked dishes. Flameproof, when used with a heat diffuser (except over charcoal), the virtue of the *cazuela* is that it retains heat for a long time, but also remains cold, which was crucial in the days before refrigeration.

BOWLS, JARS AND JUGS

There are many traditional bowls and vessels that are still used in kitchens today. *Lebrillos* are earthenware mixing bowls. The *cuenco*, with a small base and straight sides rising to a wide rim, is characteristic, and the large bowl is used in the south. The wooden *artesa* is a trough used for kneading bread and salting hams. Traditional gazpacho bowls are made of olive wood and in the north the saucers used for serving octopus are also wooden.

Storage jars come in many wonderful shapes and sizes and may be lidded or unlidded. Some jars are glazed and painted, while others are simply glazed on the inside. The unglazed *tinaja* is a handleless urn of Moorish origin that is used for storing wine and grain or, in Catalonia, oil. You will see huge ones sitting by the roadside driving south into Valdepeñas.

Below: Small brown casserole dishes cook individual servings.

Above: This earthenware apothecary's jar is a typical type of storage container.

Many modern kitchens have two oil jugs (pitchers) labelled *aceite de pescado* and *aceite de carne* each with its own strainer. The former is used for cooking fish, and the latter for cooking meat. Oil is stored in these jugs after frying for reuse. A popular wedding present is a matching set of oil jugs on a tray, with china vinaigrette bottles and cruets, and a jar for toothpicks.

Below: Traditional gazpacho bowls are made of olive wood.

Traditional drinking jugs

In the Andalusian countryside men go to work carrying a *botijo*, a round pot with a handle and two spouts – one for filling and the other, narrower, one for drinking.

The more elegant Catalan equivalent is the glass *porrón*, which is used for passing hand-to-hand indoors. Its long, thin spout tips into the mouth, but the body of the jug slopes backwards, to prevent spillages.

KITCHEN EQUIPMENT

There are many gadgets in the Spanish kitchen, some for general use and others that are used for a specific dish. Originally, the mortar and pestle were used for the tasks that are now carried out using a food processor or blender. The Spanish *almirez* (mortar), which comes in varying sizes, has four "ears", one of which has a pouring channel. It was introduced to Spain by the Moors and had a huge impact on Spanish cuisine. Dishes such as *salmorejo* (a smooth garlic and tomato soup) became possible, eventually leading to the creation of gazpacho. Purists still press gazpacho through a hair sieve but the mixture can also be pounded or finely chopped. Today, most people chop the vegetables in a *cuenco* (earthenware bowl) using a hand-held blender.

La quemadora is the tool used for caramelizing sugar on *crema catalana* – the metal disc attached to a wooden handle is heated, then held close to the sugared surface to give a caramel finish.

A ridged rolling pin is used to make striped pastry for sweet *empanadillas* (the savoury ones are unstriped) and dariole moulds are used to make *flan* (baked custard). Traditional kitchens also have a box on the wall covered with a cloth, or a drawer in the dresser, for storing stale bread. Bread is bought daily, and eaten with meals. Leftover bread is pounded and used to thicken soups and sauces.

THE OLIVE TREE

One of the oldest cultivated trees, and one of the oldest Mediterranean crops, the olive tree is thought to have been spread throughout Spain by the Phoenicians before 1000BC. Spain is now the largest producer and exporter of olive oil, most of it from the south. These oils are typically rich and fruity, with an olive aroma.

GROWING OLIVES

The Mediterranean basin is defined by where olives will grow. Three-quarters of olive oil comes from the south of Spain, but olives also grow to the west as far north as Madrid and to the Pyrenees at Huesca in the east, with a corridor through La Mancha to Valencia.

Olive trees grow on flat or hilly land, but need winter cold as well as warmth to flourish. They blossom in May in an explosion of white flowers. Half of Spain's olives are the *picual* variety, which turn black on the trees before being picked for oil at the end of November. About 4–5kg/8¾–11lb olives are needed to make a litre of oil.

Left: Unfiltered single-olive oils such as this one are new in Spain.

In Catalonia, oil-making dates back to Roman times, when Spanish oil was a luxury product. The region's favourite tree, the *arbequina*, is small and not particularly vigorous, producing large amounts of small olives that never turn black, even when fully ripe. The oil is smooth and low in astringency with, some say, a slight banana flavour. Catalonia has three *Denominación de Origen* (D.O.) areas (although these represent just 4 per cent of production): Borjas Blancas in Lérida, Siurana west of Tarragona, and Las Garrigues in the southern part of Lérida.

Andalusia has a different oil tradition that dates back to Moorish times. The oil is very fruity, with high astringency. It is made from *picual* with *hojiblanca* (the white-leaf variety of olive). It has a lower oil yield but a fresh taste and strong aroma. The D.O. areas are Córdoba and Jaén: Baena and Priego de Córdoba in the former, and the Sierra de Segura and Sierra Magina in the latter. The Montes de Toledo, Murcia and Aragón also have D.O. areas.

OLIVE OIL

The health benefits of the Mediterranean diet are owed, in part, to olive oil. The oil is rich in oleic acid, which can help to reduce levels of bad cholesterol and raise levels of good cholesterol. It contains vitamin E, a natural oxidant that helps bone formation in the young and old. It also helps reduce blood pressure and may even be an aphrodisiac for women, for it is high in the female hormone oestrogen.

However, it is for its kitchen virtues that the olive has been cultivated. A simple dressing of virgin oil brings out the flavour of food, cold or hot. Olive oil is also the best choice for frying, as the subtle bitterness of Spanish oil counters the rich effect of frying. It can also be used to preserve food – the Moors used it for storing fresh beans. The high acidity of Spanish oil makes it ideal for making sauces and emulsions such as mayonnaise, which was first made in Spain.

*Left: An unfiltered (*opalino*) extra virgin green olive oil*

Once exposed to air, oil deteriorates and should be used within three months, though top-quality oils may keep well for up to a year.

OIL CATEGORIES

Flor de aceite is top of the range – the "flower" of the oil that seeps from the crushed olive paste as it revolves in the barrel. Spain's best oil is clear, golden Nuñez de Prado from Baena. Extra virgin (or cold pressed) is the oil that drips from olives crushed on mats. The difference between extra virgin and virgin is the acidity. Top-quality oils must have less than 0.8 per cent acidity. Spanish oils are always labelled with the acidity and the average is 0.4 to 0.8 per cent (virgin oils may be higher). Unfiltered oils deteriorate more quickly. *Aceite de orujo* is oil extracted chemically from the leftover paste. Branded olive oils (formerly labelled "pure") have about 15 per cent virgin oil added for the flavour. Two well-known Spanish brands are Carbonel and Ybarra.

Denominación de Origen

As with the system for wine, the best olive-producing areas are given D.O. status, and the quality of their products is carefully regulated.

OLIVE OIL SAUCES

Aliñada Virgin oil is often used as a dressing for cooked food. The name literally means embellished.
Ajada This is north coast food. Fish is fried in the oil, then vinegar and paprika are added to make a sauce.
Allioli Garlic and oil are blended to make a thick, white emulsion, which is served with vegetables. The Catalan *allioli amb ous* is allioli with egg yolk, which is served with fish and rice.
Mahonesa Spanish "mayonnaise" takes its name from Mahón in Menorca. It is a rich emulsion of egg yolk and oil and is more subtle than allioli from which it is probably derived. It is the perfect partner for shellfish.
Pil pil Like allioli, this is an emulsified sauce. It combines the gelatine in fish skin with oil. The fish is cooked in the oil, and the oil is then swirled in the hot casserole dish until it thickens.

Making Mahonesa

Put 2 egg yolks in a bowl with a good pinch of salt. Using a hand-held blender, beat well, then add 30ml/2 tbsp vinegar and beat again. Work in up to 250ml/8fl oz/1 cup ordinary (not virgin) olive oil, drizzling very slowly at first, until it becomes thick and creamy. Flavour with lemon juice, extra virgin olive oil and pepper to taste.

Above: Negras perlas are fruity black olives with a mild flavour.

TABLE OLIVES

Lawrence Durrell said that the taste of olives is "older than meat, older than wine, a taste as old as cold water". Spain is the world's chief olive producer, with half the crop being exported. The vast majority of these olives grow on unirrigated land within range of Seville.

Spanish cured olives are mainly picked when they are bright green and unripe. At this point, they are low in oil, being made up of only acid and sugars. In this state, the olives will keep their colour and grassy tang for several months after brining. Left on the tree they turn a mottled purple, and finally black, with a softer, fuller flavour. The *muerta* (dead) just drop from the tree, black and wrinkled.

To remove their bitterness, green olives are washed in several changes of water and then stored for a few days in brine (known as the Seville way) with flavourings, to make *aceitunas aliñadas* (seasoned olives). In Andalusia garlic, oregano and herbs are used; in the Balearics wild fennel and lemon leaves. Pitted olives stuffed with little pieces of cooked pimiento, slivers of almond, anchovy or roasted garlic are also sold, and popularly exported.

Left: Allioli made with egg yolks is a powerful garlic mayonnaise with a history dating back over 2,000 years.

Above: Pimiento-stuffed olives were originally filled by hand.

Above: Manzanillas are the best-known and most popular of Spanish olives.

Types of olive

There are many different varieties of olive, each with their own individual appearance and character.
Arbequina comes from the village of La Arbeca in Lérida. It is very small, greenish-brown and has a high oil content and pleasant bitter-to-aromatic flavour. It is *the* Catalan appetizer.
Cornezuelo is horn-shaped, green and with a white tip. It has a strong flavour with a hint of bitterness.
Cuquillo is round, small, and blue-black. It is often prepared with chopped onion and hot spices, and is good as a partner to beer.
Gordal or **reina** (queen) are trade names for the largest, dark green, fleshy olive, often called *sevilles* in Spain.
Hojiblanco is slightly rectangular in shape. One of the main types of olives, it is more fibrous and less tasty than other varieties.
Manzanilla is apple- or pear-shaped, the best-known and most popular olive. It is suitable for stuffing.
Pelotín from Andalusia, is small, round and green.
Negra is black, spiced or dried and pickled, and perfect with red wine. Large negras are called *negras perlas*.

Cheese and Dairy Produce

Spain produces about 200 varieties of cheese (*queso*), most of them in farmhouse dairies and with limited distribution. A considerable number are exported, with the hard cheeses being the most successful.

Cheeses are shaped according to local tradition. Muslin (cheesecloth) is used to shape the Galician *tetilla* and also *Mahón*, producing very different results. *Camerano* is a ball-shaped cheese, moulded in a basket. Sycamore or maple leaves are pressed on to the wet rind of northern blue cheeses. Esparto grass hoops give Manchego cheese a welt, which becomes broader on the rind of the *Ronda*.

Although goat's, cow's and ewe's milk all produce distinct cheeses with their own unique character, some generic cheeses are made with milk blends. The semi-hard *Aragón* is made with ewe's and goat's milk, as is *Gamonedo*. Some cheese is smoked – most notably the versions of *San Simón*, *Gamonedo* and *Idiazábal*. *Quesucos* (part of the Liébana D.O.) is a mild, smoked, mixed-milk cheese from Santander, pale yellow inside, with "eyes".

Hard cheeses are often served as a tapas dish, while soft ones are served with honey and nuts as dessert. There is little in the way of cheese cooking – only fried hard-cheese cubes, and *flamenquines* (ham and cheese rolls that are breadcrumbed and deep-fried).

Below: Menorcan Mahón is made using cow's milk. Its bright orange rind is produced by rubbing the rind with butter, paprika and oil.

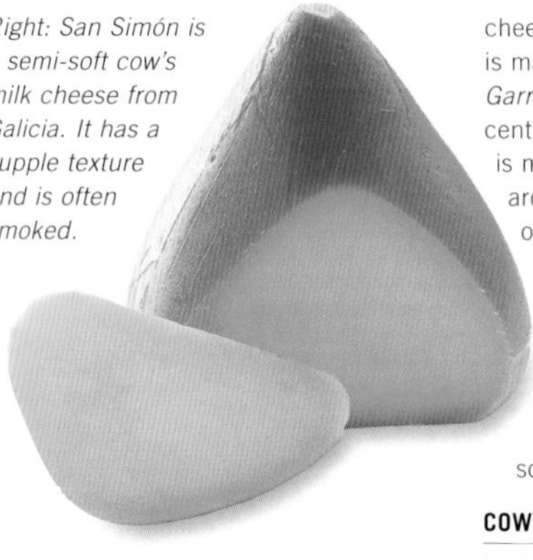

Right: San Simón is a semi-soft cow's milk cheese from Galicia. It has a supple texture and is often smoked.

FRESH AND SOFT CHEESES

Fresh curd cheese (*requesón*) is much liked and made all over Spain. Ewe's milk is normally used to make matured cheese, but there are some soft ones, which include the white *Anso*, from the valley of Huesca; and the mild *Cervera* and *Puzol*, both from Valencia. Two are widely available and typical: *Queso de Burgos* is rindless, often with mould markings, and soft. It is made from scalded curd, which is moulded then salted in brine for 24 hours. *Villalón* or *pata de mulo*, from the Valladolid region, is an elongated cylinder.

GOAT'S MILK CHEESES

In the south, cheeses are predominantly made with goat's milk. Often pressed, their flavour is distinct and clean. They are not pungent like many of the French varieties, and they have a light, crumbly texture. Unaged goat's milk cheeses include *Alicante*, *Camerano* from the Rioja area, and the slightly aromatic *Málaga*, with its buff rind, lightly pressed into an esparto grass mould. Southern goat's cheeses include: *Cádiz*, which is medium-pressed, full of holes, and with a rind marked with esparto; and *Añejo de cabra* from the *Sierra de Huelva*, whose ripened paste is dark orange, with a rough rind. The Canary Islands make only goat's cheese, the best being *Majorero*, which is matured for two months. In the east, *Garroxta* is made all over Catalonia. In central Spain, *Ibores* from Extremadura, is made from *retinto* goat's milk. It is aromatic, slightly sour, with a soft oiled rind coated with paprika. *Soría* has a firm white skin and is lightly salted. *Cabra de Tiétar*, from Ávila, is lightly pressed and briefly matured. *Valdeteja*, from León, has a sharp, goaty smell. It is shaped into a cylinder, has some holes and a crusty rind.

COW'S MILK CHEESES

In the north, the cheeses are made with cow's milk. They are generally eaten quite young and are creamy and soft.

Tetilla, from Pontevedra in Galicia, is white inside, moulded with a cloth and sometimes has a golden rind. Its name literally means teat or nipple, reflecting the shape of the cheese. *Cebrero* (*Piedrafita*), from the mountains of Lugo, looks like a chef's hat; it is tangy and white inside. The mild, yellow *Gallego* (*Ulloa*) is a slightly flattened ball. *León* is a yellow drum, with a close texture and rough yellow rind. The dry, astringent *afuega el pitu*, from Asturias, is shaped in a small cone. *Pasiego prensado*, which is made south-west of Santander, is white and creamy with small holes and a distinctive flavour.

Eggs

Spain is a country of poultry breeders and the use of eggs (*huevos*) in cooking reflects this. Galician free-range (farm-fresh) eggs are famous for the red albumen in their yolks – they are used in Madrid for making tortillas.

Menus still have an egg course and proper attention is given to egg cooking. *Revuelta*, soft scrambled eggs, is the way to display such luxuries as summer truffles and caviars. Eggs make everyday meals with a good deal of spontaneity, such as flamenco eggs and other gypsy recipes.

Above: Idiazábal D.O. has been made for centuries by shepherds in the Urbia and Alara mountains.

San Simón, from the Lugo province in Galicia, is large, shiny, brown and pear-shaped; it is oiled on the outside then smoked, but remains creamy inside.

Extremadura produces two soft-rind, creamy cheeses that are unusual for Spain. *La Serena* D.O., made in Cáceres, and *torta de Casar* are spring cheeses – the latter set with cardoon, which makes it pleasantly bitter. It is very creamy and is usually spooned out of its pink rind.

In the Balearics *Mahón* D.O., from Menorca, owes its existence to the British, who brought Friesian cows to the island, where the salty grazing affects the cheese's taste. It is hand-pressed into rectangles.

BLUE CHEESES

Cabrales D.O. is a real gourmet cheese made from cow's milk (or sometimes a blend) in 25 x 20cm/10 x 8in drums. A worthy competitor to Roquefort, the paste is off-white with blue veins, slightly stonger and more acidic than the French cheese. It is moulded, dry-salted, then matured for about six months in natural limestone caves in the Asturias, then wrapped in plane tree leaves. Related cheeses are *Picón* (part of the *Liébana* D.O.) and *Tresviso*. *Gamonedo*, another Asturian blue made from blended milk, which is unusual both for being smoked for ten to twelve days before maturing, and for its wrapping of fern leaves. The white flesh is blue-veined with oval eyes.

EWE'S MILK CHEESES

In central-north Spain, Castile and León produce most of the ewe's milk. This is the home of hard, pressed cheeses with dark rinds. Made in big drums, they are well-matured, strong, dense and grainy. *Roncal* was Spain's first D.O. cheese. The ivory paste has tiny holes. *Idiazábal* D.O., from the Basque Provinces, is a classic, holey, often smoked cheese. *Zamorano* D.O., from western Castile, is unpasteurized, made from the best milk in Spain.

Other firm cheeses include *Grazalema* from Cadiz, *Orduña* from Navarra, the *Oropesa* from Toledo and Basque *Gorbea*, with a dark shiny rind, flat base and rounded top. *Pedroches* from Córdoba is piquant and salty, which is brought out by storing it in oil.

MILK

Spain's dairy region is the Cantabrian range, along the north coast. Here cows move up to summer pastures in the high mountains. The Spanish drink milk at breakfast time, mixed half and half with coffee. Fresh milk is drunk by children and the elderly or made into *cuajada* (a sort of junket) and yogurt. Milk puddings have always been popular, and whipped cream (*nata*) is often piped over desserts.

BUTTER

Called *mantequilla*, butter is used for frying in the Basque country. This is one important way Basque cooking can be distinguished from the rest of Spain. Their sauces and cakes contain butter, as they now do in Catalonia. Elsewhere, oil and pork fat still dominate.

All about Manchego

Spain's premier cheese is made from the milk of Manchega ewes from the centre of the country. It is made in 3kg/6½lb drums, or occasionally smaller. Sometimes pasteurized, the curds are heated and pressed into esparto grass moulds, which pattern the outside of the cheese. Golden inside, Manchego becomes stronger as it ages and is sold as *semi-curado* (under 13 weeks), *curado* (up to six months), *viejo* (over six months), and also packed in oil. Mature (sharp) cheeses are similar to Parmesan. Exported cheeses, called *ibéricos* are often made using blended milk.

Below: Manchego, from left, aged for 4 months, 6 months and 10 months

VEGETABLES OF THE OLD WORLD

The Spanish really appreciate fresh vegetables. In spring, fresh peas, the first asparagus and shoots of young crops such as garlic are all gathered and served in egg dishes and *menestras* (vegetable stews), where their virtues can shine. New small artichokes (*alcachofas*) are grilled on the first barbecues of summer.

Growing delicate green asparagus (*espárragos*) is a big industry in the south, in the valleys around Granada, while white asparagus, fat like rich men's fingers, are grown in the valley of the Ebro, in Navarre, and canned for sale all over Europe. Other excellent food crops grow there too, including *cogollos* (Little Gem, or Bibb, lettuces). Unusual vegetables such as borage, blue-flowered and hairy stemmed, are still stewed in Aragón. Carrots are another ancient vegetable and flourish in the Spanish sunshine.

Spinach was introduced by the Moors and their *espinacas a la catalana*, with pine nuts and raisins, is still made today. In the south, spinach is replaced by the prolific chard (*acelga*) with similar but coarser leaves. The pearly stalks can be battered and fried.

The true vegetable of the Islamic lands is *berenjena*, the aubergine or eggplant (*albergenies* in Catalan). Many recipes using aubergine go back 800 years. *Almodrote* combines aubergine with garlic, cumin, pine nuts and cheese; *alboronia* is similar to ratatouille, but with no tomatoes.

Above: Large Spanish onions are sweet and mild enough to eat raw.

ONIONS AND GARLIC

The Moors loved onions, especially raw, which is one reason why the Spanish onion is so big and mild. *Sofrito* is the combination of onion and garlic fried together to form the base of numerous sauces. *Cebollones* (*calçots* in Catalan) are oversized spring onions (scallions), with the mild flavour of shallots. Young garlic shoots, plucked when green, are similar and these *ajetes* have a spring cuisine of their own, usually cooked with eggs and seafood. Leeks are popular with the Basques and are used in soups such as *purrusalda*.

Garlic is as old as the Pyramids and in Spain many sauces contain this pungent vegetable. *Ajo-pollo*, which means "the sort of sauce used for chicken", combines crushed garlic with ground almonds and breadcrumbs. Valencian *alli-pebre* is a mixture of garlic and paprika, and *alli oli* is simply a mixture of garlic and oil – the names say it all.

Left: Leafy green spinach has been eaten in Spain for centuries and is used in many Catalan dishes.

All about garlic

Fundamental to Spanish cooking, garlic is often mistakenly thought to dominate it. Its role in the kitchen is reflected in the saying, *estar en el ajo* (to be in the know). Garlic is more than a flavouring – it is good for you too. It lowers cholesterol levels and acts as an antiseptic on cuts. It is said in Spain that garlic gives you guts. After the San Fermín bull running at Pamplona, young men take home strings of garlic to build up their courage for the next year.

Used raw or cooked, garlic has two quite different flavours, the first pungent, the second more suggestive. Any dish *al ajillo* is flavoured with chopped garlic, while *con ajo* means "with whole cloves", which are made sweet and mild with long cooking.

In Spanish cooking, garlic is often the first ingredient into the frying pan. It is used to flavour the oil, but is then discarded before the rest of the ingredients are added. Before adding garlic to an uncooked sauce, make a paste by crushing it with a little salt using the flat side of a knife.

Below: Garlic is widely used in Spanish cooking, adding a distinctive flavour.

Above: Chickpeas, with their lovely, nutty flavour, are the basic carbohydrate of Spanish cuisine.

DRIED BEANS, LENTILS AND PEAS

Dried broad (fava) beans were used widely in Spanish dishes in years past, and are still used in a few dishes today, such as the Valencian *micherones* (stewed with garlic). Dried peas and lentils (*lentejas*) are still weekly fare, partnered with the inevitable chorizo, particularly north of Madrid.

Chickpeas (*garbanzos*) are the potatoes of Spain, growing well through the hot summers. In ancient times, the Romans mocked the chickpea-eating Spanish, suggesting that their enormous consumption of the legume not only indicated stupidity but also induced it. Chickpeas are the least easy of dried beans and peas to spoil, but do not absorb flavour from accompanying ingredients in the way that beans do. Although they need soaking and take up to 2 hours to cook, chickpeas keep their shape well, even when reheated. *Garbanzos con chorizos* (chickpeas with chorizo) is a classic, while chickpeas, chard and salt cod are combined to make a traditional Lenten dish.

Right: Today, fresh broad beans are far more widely used than dried ones, and are celebrated in a national dish, habas con jamón, *with ham.*

CABBAGES, TURNIPS AND CARDOONS

Galician cabbages are huge, but every province likes this vegetable. There are more words for cabbage in Spanish than in English, and more varieties. *Lombardo* (red cabbage) is popular in Madrid and is used to garnish sea bream on Christmas Eve; a *cocido de berza* will contain cabbage. However, it is turnips that Galicians really love, both the root and the green tops (*grelos*) when they just start budding. Cardoon (*cardo*) is the artichoke's bigger cousin and comes into season at the end of the year.

WILD FOOD

Much produce is gathered from the countryside, especially in poorer areas. Lupin seed is a yellow tapas bar nibble, and is sold at fairs as a snack. Wild asparagus is a speciality, picked in April and again before winter. *Targina* is a thistle with short side stems that are eaten in the same way as cardoon or with beans or eggs. Dandelion leaves go into salads, chicory root is dug to make coffee, and fennel is used to season fish. Chestnuts grow in the south of Galicia and were a basic foodstuff until potatoes arrived.

Capers originally grew wild all over the southern coasts. But they are now a huge industry. Both the buds and the plump berries are pickled, the latter eaten in the same way as olives.

Above: Fresh young turnips and their leafy green tops are Galicia's pride.

WILD MUSHROOMS

The Spanish in general are not great mushrooms pickers, and the Galicians are positively against it. However, the Basques and Catalans make up for this. About 50 kinds of mushroom are gathered throughout the year. They are cooked simply, with garlic or eggs, and are used in game casseroles. Ceps (*bolets*) are grilled (broiled) whole.

Setas (wild mushrooms) and *hongos* (fungi) are much in demand, as are *setas de cardo* (oyster mushrooms). In Catalonia, picking the golden yellow *rovolló* is almost an obsession. Called *níscalo* in the rest of Spain, the bleeding milk cap oozes red drops from the stem when it is cut.

The Basque favourite is the tiny yellowish white spring St George's mushroom with its penetrating perfume. Called *zizak* locally, it is *moixernons* elsewhere. Truffles also grow in Spain, and the common *criadillas de tierra* are served in tapas bars in Extremadura during the summer months.

VEGETABLES FROM AMERICA

The colour, sweetness and piquancy of American vegetables, brought home by Christopher Columbus, revolutionized Spanish cooking – and with it, Europe. The Mediterranean climate is ideal for tomatoes, peppers, courgettes (zucchini) and pumpkins. Maize (corn) was adopted in northern Spain, for fattening poultry and as corn meal for bread, and potatoes had their biggest Spanish success fried as *patatas fritas.*

TOMATOES

Today, tomatoes are a great success story in Spain. Three or even four crops a year are produced in the *invernadores* (plastic tunnels) of Almería, and they are loaded into lorries that roar north from southern Spain.

The name *tomate* comes from the Aztec *tomatl*, meaning something plump. The tomato was not an instant success when it was introduced to Spain and was, at first, used simply as the liquid for serving chilli. Tomato sauce was still a novelty as late as the 1820s – and regarded by outsiders as a Spanish curiosity. A *sauce espagnole* in a restaurant in France is a classic meat-stock sauce with tomato in it.

Today tomatoes are combined with sweet (bell) peppers in a huge number of dishes: *gazpacho, pisto, bacalo a la viscaína* (salt cod baked with tomato) and all the dishes called *samfaína*. Tomatoes are sold in two classes: ripest and ripe. The first are for sauces, the second for salads. There are even salads where one tomato is dressed with the juice of another – *ajotomate.*

FRESH PEPPERS

Morrones (bell) peppers, are often two-fist size, fleshy with tough skin, green or the sweeter red. There are other sweet varieties and a long, thin, green one with a thin skin. When soft and baked, red pepper has become an ingredient in its own right, called *pimiento.*

The red *piquillo*, grown in Navarra and Rioja, is the gourmet's pepper. Smaller, stocky and with a point at one end, it is crisper and distinctly piquant. It is often stuffed with cod and baked. It is also wonderful canned, after being roasted over beechwood.

Below: Tomatoes are used subtlely in Spanish cuisine, partnering but never dominating other flavours.

Above: Sweet pimientos *peppers go into many dishes. Little* padróns *are a Galician speciality, popular everywhere.*

The green Galician pepper, *padrón*, is part of a popular joke. As long as a thumb, they are deep-fried and served with a little salt as an appetizer, about twenty to a plate. Though normally sweet, one in that number will be fiery hot, and there is no knowing which.

DRIED CHILLIES

Columbus' mission was to look for the spice, black pepper. He discovered spicy red peppers instead. Towards winter, chilli peppers are hung up all over Spain to dry, particularly in Rioja, in red *ristras* (strings).

The general rule for these chillies is the larger, the milder. Cooking, in particular roasting, makes them sweeter, as the bitterness is in the skin. The flavour of chillies is made more concentrated and robust by drying or toasting. Including vinegar in the recipe gives the same intensified effect.

Choricero This chilli has given its name, colour and piquancy to the red Spanish frying sausage. The chilli is larger than a fist, elongated but rounded, red, and extremely sweet and mild – 1/10 on the Mexican chilli-heat scale. It can be crumbled into dishes or reconstituted in liquid, then the flesh scraped out. One or two per person go into dishes such

Below: Romesco or ñora chillies are usually hung up to dry in long, decorative strings.

as *chilindrón*, (lamb with chilli).

Ñora This is called *romesco* in Catalonia and is a walnut-sized chilli; red and cherry-round. It has a sweet fruit flavour, with a hint of a biting finish – 2/10 on the Mexican chilli-heat scale. It was adopted by the Catalans in the 16th century and is common in Alicante and Murcia. It has very little flesh but the colour and flavour are concentrated, hence its use in salsas, *romescos* of fish, rice and paella. Ancho or jalapeño chillies may be used as substitutes.

Guindilla As long as a finger, this is Spain's hot chilli – 3/10 on the Mexican chilli-heat scale – but it is also medium sweet. It adds zip to dishes such as *gambas pil pil* (prawns with chilli).

BEANS

Large American kidney beans were considered much more elegant and tasty than old, brown beans. *Judias* are green beans (pods) and *alubias* are dried ones. The latter come in all sizes – from the tiniest *arroncini* (rice-sized) to the big *judiones* of El Barco de Ávila and the *garrafones* (carboys) of Valencia – and in all colours: white, to mottled red or green, to purple with green eyes. Spain is the bean capital of the world.

Every province soon adopted and grew their own beans, in fierce regional competition, cooking them with their own sausages. The Basques once specialized in red beans, but now theirs is the "black" bean of Tolosa. The finest beans grown are *fabes de la granja* from Asturias, used to make *fabada*. They are very expensive and sold in numbered cotton bags.

Fresh beans make one national dish, eaten with ham, while *pochas* (kidney beans fresh from the pod) are a little October speciality, stewed with quail. A Spanish type that is just becoming known elsewhere is *ferraura*. Bred from runner beans, they are "flat beans", long, soft-surfaced, stringless green pods – and one of the original ingredients of paella.

Right: Red kidney beans are a Basque favourite stewed with ham bone, red chorizo sausage and black morcilla.

POTATOES AND SQUASH

While potatoes were ignored in northern Europe, they were a success in Seville. They found their true home in Galicia, which now grows *cachelos*, a large white tuber of exceptional quality, near the sea, where it absorbs salt from the soil. They accompany the local *lacón* (cured pork shoulder) or sardines, and are often layered into fish stews.

Sweet potatoes are *batata* (yellow-fleshed; the US yam) and *boniato* (white-fleshed). They are made into little cakes or served in honey.

The *calabaza* (marrow/large zucchini, summer squash or pumpkins) goes into stewpots like *calabazote* (with potatoes and beans). But *calabacín* (courgette/zucchini) was little known until the 1980s, and more of a success in Italy.

Below: In the south, squash are added to gypsy vegetable and bean stews.

SPICES, HERBS AND FLAVOURINGS

The Spanish cuisine has its own range of spices, herbs, condiments and nuts, all of which contribute to the unique and characteristic taste of Spanish food.

SAFFRON

With its aromatic scent and golden colour, *azafrán* is a quintessentially Moorish spice. For paella and fish and shellfish stews, there is no substitute. For chicken, all *pepitorias* (nut sauces), creams, buns and ices, saffron is king.

The purple crocuses from which saffron is obtained flower quite suddenly in mid-October in parched La Mancha, creating purple carpets around the vines. The flowers are plucked by hand, then three orange stamens are pulled from each flower, toasted over charcoal and dried to bring out the flavour. A hard day's work produces only about 50g/2oz saffron.

Mancha selecto is the world's best saffron; it is deep red, with long threads and a high oil content. Spain produces 70 per cent of the world's saffron. Although very expensive, a tiny amount flavours a dish for two to three people.

Spanish saffron is rarely powdered, as this is too easy to adulterate with cheap yellow dyes such as safflower (*cártamo*), colouring (*colorante*), and the chemical tartrazine.

Below: Top quality saffron all comes from Spain, grown in La Mancha.

Above: Warm, spicy, aromatic cumin is a legacy of the Moors and is widely used in southern cooking.

OTHER SPICES

The Moors introduced cumin (*comino*) to Spain and it is widely used with vegetables and tomatoes, and with skewered meats. Coriander seeds (*cilantro*) also came from North Africa, and are often partnered with cumin and used to flavour skewered meat cooked on the barbecue. Coloured yellow with turmeric, pork cubes are sold ready-spiced in many southern butchers. Other popular spice flavourings include turmeric (*cúrcuma*), cloves (*clavos*), cardamom (*cardamoma*) and – to a lesser extent – ginger (*jengibre*).

The Catalans are generous users of black pepper (*pimienta*), whereas the rest of Spain uses paprika (*pimentón*).

There is no clear division between sweet and savoury spices in Spain – another Moorish legacy. Nutmeg (*nuez moscada*) goes into *morcillas* (black pudding) – along with cumin, cinnamon (*canela*) and aniseed (*matalhuva*) – and is also used to flavour custards. Cinnamon is the obligatory flavouring used in rice milk puddings and the ice cream that accompanies fruit. It is also commonly used with poultry and in stews, which also often contain saffron.

Aniseed (*anís*) is a key flavour in Spanish food and drink. It is basic to many liqueurs and its seeds are ground and used in many pastries, doughs and sausages. Another very Spanish flavour is dried orange peel (*cachorreña*), which is pounded and added to shellfish and fish soups.

SALT

Intimately tied to Spain's commercial history, the salt trade is an old one, and grew up around the Mediterranean salt pans. Cadiz supplied salt beef for the ships journeying to the Americas, and the Basques have been shipping home salt cod since the 17th century.

Today salt has changed from being a preservative to being a preference. The Spanish seek out foods that contain salt, especially cured foods such as *mohama*, *cecina*, *anchoas* and *botargo* (tuna, beef, anchovies and grey mullet caviar). Salt adds interest to beans, while eating salt fish on Fridays is a 500-year-old tradition.

Paprika

Pimentón is a basic flavouring in Spanish cooking, used like black pepper, and not just sprinkled for decoration. It is made from a sweet red (bell) pepper with a round body and pointed end. There are three grades of paprika used in Spain: *dulce* (mild), *picante* (which contains a little *guindilla* chilli), and *agridulce* (bittersweet). You can substitute cayenne pepper for *picante*. The main centre of production is the Vera valley, where peppers are smoked before being ground.

Below: Sweet paprika is Spain's most commonly used pepper.

Left: Many varieties of thyme grow in the Spanish sierras.

HERBS

Bay leaves (*hojas de laurel*) Partnered with rosemary and thyme, aromatic bay leaves make up Spain's herbal trinity. The leaves are added to stews and thrown on the barbecue. Fresh leaves are battered, fried and sugared to make sweet *paparejotes*.

Coriander (*cilantro*) Pungent fresh coriander leaves are thought of as the Portuguese herb and only used in Extremadura and the Canary Islands, where the herb is crushed to make the green *mojo verde* sauce for fish. It is also excellent rubbed over pork to flavour the meat before roasting.

Fennel (*hinojo*) This beautiful herb has a slight flavour of aniseed and grows wild everywhere. It is used to flavour the cooking water for shellfish and its tiny aromatic seeds are sometimes added to home-cured olives.

Lemon verbena (*hierba luisa*) Used to make a delicious fragrant tea, this popular herb can be found growing in many Spanish gardens.

Mint (*menta*) Known as *hierba buena*, the good herb, Moroccan mint is a favourite garden plant. It goes into *morcilla* (black pudding) and is used with offal. *Poleo* is Pennyroyal mint (*Mentha pulegium*), which is used for tea – and also in a soup for hangovers.

Oregano (*origano*) This is the sausage herb, and also goes into meat stews and marinades. Its essential oil doesn't deteriorate with long cooking, so it is one of the few herbs that can be added early on in cooking. The related English herb, marjoram (*mejorana*), is thought of as a medicinal herb in Spain.

Parsley (*perejil*, or *julivert* in Catalan) The Spanish grow flat leaf parsley, which is milder than curly parsley. It is a popular herb and is used lavishly in Murcia.

Rosemary (*romero*) Snails eat rosemary, so they are used as "rosemary cubes" to flavour rabbit stews and paella. Big old bushes of the wild herb are also used to fuel bread ovens and wood-burning stoves. Rosemary with thyme and chilli are traditionally used to flavour dried bean dishes.

Thyme (*tomillo*) There are several varieties of thyme with small white flowers, which are used for cooking. *Tomillo salsero* (sauce thyme) is picked in April to give to friends at Christmas. The herb is much used to flavour rabbit and, with summer savory (*ajedrea blanca*), to flavour dried bean dishes.

NUTS

Almonds (*almendras*) These are second only to oranges as a major crop. There are two types. The first is the smaller, bitter almond, which is grown only for almond oil and essence (extract), as it is poisonous if eaten raw. The second type is the sweet *Jordan* almond. Of Spanish origin, its name is a corruption of *jardín* meaning garden. Grown in the south-east, they are long, flat and slender, and the best cocktail almonds in the world. *Marcona* almonds are used to make turrón (*nougat*).

Ground almonds are used in place of flour to thicken sauces in Spain. They are the base of *picada*, which thickens sauces instead of a roux, and any dish called a *pepitoria*. Almonds are also pounded for soups, used in biscuits (cookies) and coated with sugar to make festival *almendras garipinadas* and Catalan *ametlles*.

Hazelnuts (*avellanas*) These nuts grow in mountain regions and were farmed in Tarragona, where they are made into a soup. The Basques use them to thicken stews, and they are added to meringues as far apart as Granada and Asturias.

Sherry vinegar

With its stunning tobacco aromas, sherry vinegar is used in salad dressings and gives a superior finish to sauces. Young sherries, reserved because of their high acidity, are matured in wood and concentrated to intensify their flavour. Aged up to 25 years, a really good sherry vinegar far surpasses a cheap *balsámico*. One of the best is Emilio Lustau 1/24 solera, or look for Xerés.

Pine nuts (*piñones*) These come from the cones of the stone pine, one of the West's ancient fertility symbols. The cones are gathered in winter and are then dried through the next summer. The tiny creamy nuts have a slightly astringent taste and are improved by toasting, which brings out and enhances their flavour. They are good used in salads and sauces, or baked in little cakes, such as festival *paneletts* and nut-covered *piñonates*.

Below: Pine nuts have a distinctive taste and are frequently toasted before being added to dishes.

Below: Hazelnuts are used to flavour sweet dishes such as desserts, cakes and cookies, as well as savoury sauces.

Rice and Pasta

These two staples are at the heart of both everyday family meals and classic celebration dishes in Spain.

RICE

Valencia is forever linked with rice. The Moors planted rice there and it was the only crop that could be grown on the hot Mediterranean littoral in summer.

Rice is eaten on a daily basis in the east and south of Spain. It is eaten plain, added to soupy stews, and combined with beans to make stuffings for vegetables. Many *morcillas* (black puddings) contain rice, especially those made in Burgos, Aragón, Rioja and the Levante. *Arroz con leche* (rice pudding) rivals *flan* (baked custard) as Spain's national dessert.

It is the quality and flavour of rice that matters, so flavourings tend to be simple – a pinch of saffron, perhaps with a little bacon and *morcilla* (black pudding). Alicante *arros amb costra,* a Catalan oven-baked dish, comes with a rice crust concealing the chickpea and sausage stew. *Arros perdiu* (partridge rice) is "trick dish" made for Lent – instead of partridge, it has a whole baked garlic bulb in the centre. Valencian restaurants feature a different rice every day, but the popular choice for Sundays is rice with salt cod.

Below: Bomba is the most readily available variety of paella rice.

Above: Paella, originally from Valencia, is probably Spain's most famous dish. It is eaten for celebrations but is also an incredibly popular dish for tourists.

Short grain rice

The short, fat Spanish grain originates from Japanese round rice, rather than the Indian long grain, and it has a slight bite, like risotto rice. Spain became Europe's largest rice producer because it was the first country to try to find a suitable grain for the Mediterranean climate. A large amount of rice is grown in the Seville area but the best type of rice is *Calasparra,* which grows in Murcia. The grains swell dramatically when cooked in stock, absorbing three or four times their volume of liquid.

Below: The prized Calasparra rice is sold in numbered cotton bags.

Rice pans and dishes

When cooking rice, there are different types of pan for cooking specific dishes. Paella is cooked in the shallow *paellera.* The Valencian model is thin with a dimpled base. The finished dish should be "dry" (but moist), with every grain separate. Strictly speaking, paella is the Valencian name for the dish, and similar dishes elsewhere should simply be called *arroz* (*arros* in Catalan).

"Wet" rice dishes are soupy and eaten with a spoon. They are often fish dishes, cooked in a round-based cooking pot known as a *caldereta.* The pot gives its name to some of the classic wet rice dishes, including *el caldero* (rice with fish). *Arroz a banda* is rice cooked in fish stock, but separately from the fish (which makes another course). It is the perfect dish to reveal just how good plain rice can be, done the Spanish way. These soupy dishes used to be considered far too provincial to appear on restaurant menus, but one exception is the winter *arros amb fesol i naps* (rice with yellow swede/rutabaga and turnip). Another substantial dish is *el perrol,* a cauldron of rice stewed with meat and a large quantity of vegetables.

Paella

The birthplace of paella is the marshland outside the city of Valencia, round Lake Albufera. The area is still a place of ducks and eels. Bamboo groves standing in water separate lake from lake and little bridges carry small roads from village to village. El Palmar, one of the best-known villages, is surrounded by water.

Paella was invented here some 200 years ago. It is a summer dish, intended for picnics, and generally cooked by men in a flat pan set over a charcoal fire. Originally, paella used ingredients from the surrounding area – rice, garlic and parsley, either eels or snails, plus good beans, either flat green beans that look like runner beans or big flat kidney beans called *garrafones*. The seasoning was Spain's best – saffron – while the snails added a hint of rosemary. The rice is cooked very slowly, then covered with newspaper for the last 10 minutes, until all liquid has been absorbed. The paella is allowed to crisp slightly underneath before serving.

Saffron-yellow *paella valenciana*, decorated with mussels and strips of red (bell) pepper, prawns (shrimp) and chicken pieces like buried treasure, is eaten in Spain on every festive occasion. In Valencia, however, it is more of a tourist dish. Locals are more likely to opt for just shellfish or chicken; on the south coast, the usual choice is rabbit.

PASTA

Pasta has been eaten in Spain for longer than it has in north Italy. (There is even a recipe for a noodle soup in Catalonia's first printed cook book, by Rupert de Nolan, in 1477.) Pasta became everyday food in Spain and Italy at the same time, in the late 18th century. Durum wheat, used to make pasta, was planted in Catalonia in the 1950s. Today pasta is made in Andalusia and Extremadura.

The Catalan favourite is *fideos*, a thin, short spaghetti used in soups or served with sauces and sausage. South of paella country is Gandía (home of the Borgias, the family of Pope Alexander VI) where they have a *fideuá* (noodle) festival every year. The big pasta dish these days is shellfish with *fideos* instead of rice, which is a great deal easier to make than paella. It was invented in the 1970s and now features along the entire coast from Málaga to the Costa Brava, including one version where the pasta is dry-fried first.

Canelones (cannelloni) were introduced to Spain by the many Italian chefs who came to work in Barcelona in the 19th century. Flat dry squares, *obleas* (thin wafers), are now sold for making lasagne or for rolling into *canelones*. Home-made pasta was originally made by poor shepherds. They added simple flour-and-water paste squares (Manchego wafers) to stews such as *andrajos*.

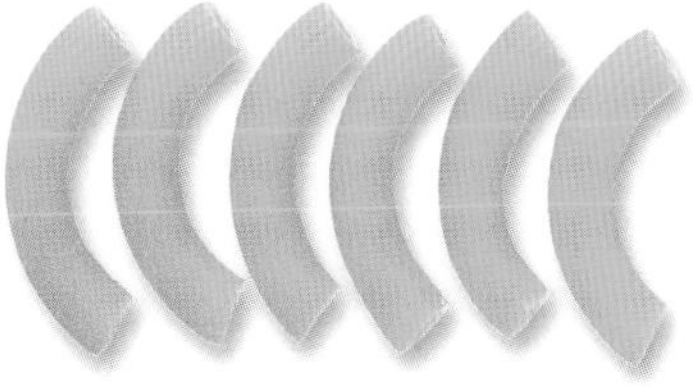

Above: Macaroni is a popular pasta, usually served with grated cheese.

Below: Fideos is a thin and short Spanish pasta – about 5cm/2in long.

Ten tips to good paella

Good paella is not difficult to make, but there are a few simple steps to ensure perfect results.

- Use a wide pan – 20cm/8in is right for two people. A deep pizza pan can be substituted for a paella pan.
- Use paella (or risotto) rice. Use 50–75g/2–3oz/generous ¼–scant ½ cup per person. (Don't stint on the rice.)
- Don't overdo the extras; they are there to flavour the rice. Choose a theme such as rabbit or shellfish.
- Don't be mean with the saffron, and use threads not powder. 0.1g is sufficient for two to three people and for six you will need 0.3g.
- Start with double the amount of stock to the volume of rice – some rices take more. Taste and warm the stock before adding it to the pan, making sure it is deeply flavoured. If the stock is insipid, so will be the paella.
- Don't overfill the pan; a depth of 2cm/¾in is about right.
- Use a wide heat source. Ideally the heat source should equal the diameter of the pan. The Spanish have special wide gas rings for making paella. Cooking over charcoal works well and solid fuel cookers are also suitable.
- If the heat source is smaller than the base of the pan, move the pan every 2–3 minutes, to prevent the middle cooking while the outside remains uncooked.
- The shape and size of the pan and the heat source are the main problems outside Spain. If in doubt, cover the pan with foil and bake in the oven for the second half of the cooking time.
- Let the paella stand, covered, off the heat for 10 minutes at the end of the cooking time, to absorb the last of the liquid. Paella should be a "dry" rice dish.

Atlantic and Mediterranean Fish

Above (from front): Gilthead bream, red bream and blackhead bream

Spain is second only to Japan in fish consumption, with over 500g/1lb eaten per head per week. Madrid has been called "the biggest port in Europe".

The two coasts of Spain are very different. The roaring, scourging Atlantic breaks on Cape Finisterre, where the finest fish in the world are caught. The Mediterranean, lazy and warm, is better for shellfish than fish, the best being caught outside Gibraltar.

Farming fish for salting goes back to Roman times, and today fish from salt flats such as Murcia's *Mar Menor* are prized for their extra flavour. The *salinas* off Cadiz raise gilthead bream, and sea bass and turbot are bred in El Grove on the Galician coast.

Cadiz is probably home to the original take-away (take-out) fried fish shop. Frying is something the Spanish do superbly well, although battered fried fish, called *a la romana*, is credited to the Italians. Málaga is famed for its mixed *pescaito frito*.

Below: Delicately flavoured hake is one of Spain's best-loved fish.

Spain shares the general Mediterranean love of fish stews and some say that the Spanish *bulla baissa* was the origin of French *bouillabaisse*. *Romesco de peix* (mixed fish with Catalan chilli), *zarzuela*, and the similar *suquet*, are incontestably Spanish. On the north coast, and in Galicia, the great *caldieras* layer mixed fish with potatoes. The east coast has *calderos* with rice, which include *cabracho* (the rascasse or large-scaled scorpion fish), the indispensable fish for soups and for making the broth of rice dishes.

EVERYDAY FISH

The most popular everyday fish is salt cod (*bacalao*), then *pescadilla* – a small hake which is fried in a ring, with its tail in its mouth – and many small flat fish such as *gallo* (a type of plaice).

Sardines have an honoured place in Spanish cuisine, with festivals in Bilbao and elsewhere dedicated to the fish. They are enjoyed as an outdoor food and the *moraga*, on the Málaga coast, marks the beginning of summer: fish are skewered on to bamboo sticks, like sails on a tall mast, and are cooked beside the fires on the beaches. Mackerel, *caballo* and *melva* (from warm water) are other popular fish.

LUXURY FISH

Sea bass (*lubina*), turbot (*rodaballo*) and monkfish (*rape*, or *pixin* as it is known in Asturias) are cooked in wine and shellfish sauces, or with cider and potatoes.

Really good fish needs no disguise and *ajada* (a simple mixture of oil, garlic and paprika) frequently partners fish in the north, in the same way that lemons do in the south. A typical dish is *besugo a la espalda*, in which red bream is spatchcocked on the grill and finished with garlic, hot chilli and a few drops of vinegar.

Dorada, the gilthead bream is the finest Mediterranean bream. Like the related *urta*, the sea bream lives on a diet of shellfish, which scents the flesh. Sea bream is most famously cooked with brandy and tomatoes.

Hake (*merluza*), with its delicate flavour and flaky texture, is extremely popular in Spain. It is often partnered with green sauces of asparagus or parsley. The back of the neck may be roasted, and *kokotas* (triangles cut from the lower throat) are a true speciality, often served in *pil pil* (a hot emulsion of garlic and oil). The *lenguado* (Dover or Channel sole) has a major fishing ground in the Bay of Biscay, while grey mullet (*mújol* or *lisa*) is popular in the Levante. Red mullet (*salmonetes*) are beloved by everyone in Spain.

Tiny *chanquetes* (whitebait) now have to be protected to retain stocks, but little anchovies (*boquerones*) are popular everywhere, though they are mainly fished in the Bay of Biscay. Anchovies are one of the best fish for frying and may be presented Málaga-style, fried in a fan pattern. More often they are marinated for tapas because they deteriorate so fast.

Above: Swordfish is a delicious, meaty fish that is very pink when raw but turns a greyish colour when cooked.

Elvers

Angulas, tiny baby eels, are a speciality of the *cofradías*, the Basque all-male gastronomic societies. Once considered only good enough to be fed to pigs, elvers are now an expensive delicacy, eaten around Christmas.

European eels spawn in the Sargasso Sea, between the West Indies and the Azores. The spawn set off for home and, amazingly, they head for the rivers from which their parents came, for example the Nervión, near Bilbao. The elvers of Aguinaga (west of San Sebastián) are the most highly prized. After a three-year journey back across the Atlantic, the elvers grow to 10cm/2in. They are washed ten times, then dipped in a cold tobacco solution to kill them. Sold cooked, they are then tossed in a hot earthenware bowl with oil and garlic. Once cooked, they look rather like spaghetti with only their eyes indicating that they are fish.

Elvers are also bred in Northern Ireland and France for sale in the Spanish market. These are softer and whiter than their wild cousins.

Above: Shark loin is good marinated with aromatic saffron and grilled.

TUNA, SWORDFISH AND SHARK

Tuna are landed at Vigo, from ships that trawl the world. They are also fished off Zahara de los Atunes (outside Gibraltar) with nets in the *alamadraba* – a bloody ritual that goes back as far as Roman times, where men fight the fish.

Tuna steaks are meaty and nutritious, and may be fried, grilled (broiled) or cooked on the barbecue. *Bonito del norte*, white tuna, is cooked in stews with (bell) peppers and potatoes. In Tarragona it is eaten *all cremat* (pot-roast with caramelized garlic).

Swordfish (*pez espada*) is ideal for grilling. Dogfish (*cazón*) and sharks such as *cailón* (porbeagle/mackerel shark) are good marinated and grilled.

FRESHWATER FISH

Spain has many fast-flowing rivers in its mountainous regions. Trout catches in some Pyrenees rivers run at 1,500 a day. León has about 3,000km/1,800 miles of trout rivers, as well as lakes. Brown trout abound in the rivers of western Asturias; *truchas del Bierzo* are well known. *Rea* (sea trout or salmon trout) run up the Galician *rías* (coastal inlets). Brown trout with *jamón serrano* is a famous combination, but otherwise cooking is simple, with fish being poached in cider or the Basque wine, *txacoli*.

Salmon teem in the rivers of Galicia and swim up into the Picos de Europa, south of Santander. Arriondas is the salmon capital of Spain. The same story is told here, as in Scotland, of labourers refusing to eat salmon more than three times a week. The classic salmon recipe is to salt them for one hour, then fry in pork fat. *Lamprea* (lamprey) follow the salmon, especially in the river Miño, while other fish, such as tench, carp and barbel are very much in evidence in Extremadura in summer.

Below: Brown and rainbow trout flourish in the rivers and lakes of Spain.

PRESERVED FISH

The Spanish adore preserved fish, and it is still weekly fare across the country. *Bacalao* is salt cod, which has been used in dishes for centuries. Other fish are salted too, including sardines and anchovies. Numerous fish and shellfish are canned – sometimes simply in brine, in rich, fruity olive oil, or in a spicy marinade such as *escabeche*. Fish caviars are a speciality.

BACALAO

It is ironic that the most commonly eaten fish in Spain – cod – is one that swims on neither of her shores. The Basques fished cod more than a millennium ago off the Gulf of St Lawrence, in the North Atlantic, and brought it back to Spain in salt. With the discovery of the Americas, the Basques were driven away by other fleets and a new fishing ground was established around Iceland and Norway.

Bacalao was called the inland fish, and was sold as stiff kite-shaped boards. With Catholic Spain imposing a Friday fast and a fast for the 40 days of Lent, it became a fixture in the Spanish diet. In these less religious days, where refrigeration is commonplace, *bacalao* has remained popular – probably due to the exquisite balance of salt and fish. In warmer climes, the flavour appears to deepen and salt tastes better in the south than it does in the colder north.

In Madrid, Bilbao and Barcelona, whole shops (*bacalao* boutiques) are devoted to the one product. The fish is sold like meat, ready cut and labelled with the place of origin and the dishes for which the cut is suitable. You can buy loin, strips and cheaper, thinner tail ends. The fatter, whiter Norwegian cuts are preferred for fillet dishes such as the Catalan *a la llauna*. Scottish *bacalao* is yellower and stronger tasting, and should be cooked with rice or potatoes. There are modern cures such as *bacalao inglés* that require less soaking.

There are over 100 classic *bacalao* dishes and many books devoted to *bacalao*. There is even a competition held at Guernika for the best new dish. *Bacalao* dishes are classed as red or white, according to whether they are made with, or without, tomatoes. *Bacalao al ajo arriero* contains tomato and red (bell) peppers. Best of the white dishes is *bacalao pil-pil*. In this dish, the fish is cooked with garlic in oil in an earthenware dish (which retains heat) and is then swung for 15 or so minutes, until the gelatine in the fish skin combines with the oil to make a light, mayonnaise-like sauce.

Salt cod can be eaten at any time of the day. The fishermen in the north eat it for breakfast as *zurruputuna* (salt cod prepared with garlic, chillies and soaked bread). *Purrusaldo* is a robust soup made with salt cod, leek and potato. *Potaje de cuaresma*, made with salt cod, chickpeas and chard, is thought to have come from the monastery of Yuste and is eaten during Holy Week. The Cuenca area has a brandade-style dish, a purée of fish, potato and pine nuts. One of the best-known tapas dishes is *soldaditos de Pavia*, named after the Hussars in their yellow coats – sticks of salt cod are battered, then deep-fried until crisp and golden.

Raw salt cod salads are also very popular. *Rinrán* is a dish of salt cod with potato, olives and (bell) peppers. The Andalusian version of *remojón* pairs salt cod with sliced orange, and in Catalan *esqueixada* it is accompanied by red (bell) peppers and tomatoes.

Below: Salt cod, known as bacalao, *is immensely popular and has remained weekly fare in Spain for centuries.*

Buying and soaking bacalao

The thinner cuts of salt cod are fin and tail pieces and are used to make puréed dishes such as salt cod fritters and soup. The fish doubles in weight during soaking, but half of this will be lost when the skin and bone are removed and discarded. The thickest pieces come from the loin and are used to make dishes such as *pil pil*.

Salt cod requires a minimum of 24 hours soaking, with 2–3 changes of water (more often in summer, because the soaking fish can smell pretty bad). The fish needs to retain some salt to maintain the interest of flavour and texture, but how long to soak the fish is a matter of personal judgement and depends on the dish being prepared.

In Andalusia the custom is to toast the fish first, break it up and then soak it. This has produced a range of dishes called *tiznao* that taste faintly of the fire.

CURED AND PRESERVED FISH

Above: White albacore is the finest type of canned tuna.

Mahogany-coloured *mojama* is the salted, wind-dried back flesh of the bluefin tuna (*atún*) and is a speciality of Seville and Cadiz. *Mojama* used to be street food, but it is becoming less common. It is similar to dried beef and, at its best, the thin ruby-coloured slices are almost transparent.

Canned tuna is Spain's second fish and is eaten weekly by most Spanish families. White albacore *atún blanco* (or *bonito del norte*), the long-finned tuna, is the world's best canned fish – and widely believed to be better canned than fresh. The most common of the tunas, *atún claro*, the yellow fin, is caught off the Cantabrian coast. It has darker and less dense meat – *ventresca* (belly) being the best.

Left: Canned sardines are widely eaten in Spain and are served in many ways.

Larger sardines are salted, both in the north and in Huelva in the south, where they are packed in large barrels. Sardine canning is also a major industry throughout Galicia.

Anchovies are also salted, and are called *anchoas* when canned in oil. In the north, some anchovies are brine-pickled before being packed in oil, and may also be smoked. Catalan La Escala, in the bay of Las Rosas, has a D.O. rating and here anchovies are salt-cured for a year – a process known as tanning – before being packed in oil in glass jars.

Some 140 varieties of fish and shellfish are canned in Galicia. The range of canned shellfish is enormous – from plump clams to scallops and mussels in spicy sauces such as *escabeche*. Tiny squid are canned in their ink, octopus in a variety of sauces, and there are also less familiar delights such as "crab thumbs" (the thickest part of the claw).

Below: Fine Spanish anchoas *are canned in olive oil.*

FISH CAVIARS

Luxurious caviars are a speciality of the Mediterranean. *Huevas de marucca*, from ling, are among the most common; the tiny salty eggs are sold in blocks cut from the pressed roe. The best caviar comes from the Murcian salt lagoons, from the grey mullet and is called *huevas de mújol de Mar Menor*.

Before sturgeon caviar reached Europe, this was used to make the great *botargo* (dark shavings cut from the pressed salted roe). Mixed and single moist roes packed into small jars are also sold and exported. These fish roes are particularly good served with eggs. Golden-brown *huevas de atún* come from the bluefin tuna, and have a sharp, faintly metallic taste. Other roes include the poorest cod (*capelán*), black herring roe and huge red salmon eggs, while restaurants offer caviars from sea bream, hake and anchovy.

Above: Black herring roe (back left) and grey mullet mújol, *or* shikrán, *(front left and right) are both good moist caviars.*

Below: Pressed huevas de marucca *(salted ling roe) is a delicacy but is widely available throughout the country.*

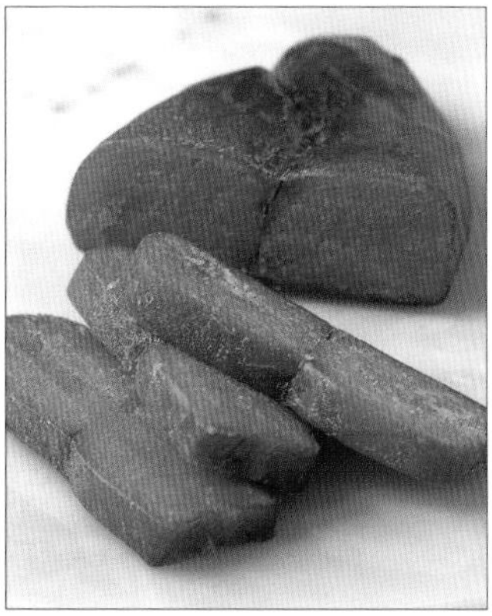

SHELLFISH

Atlantic currents, sweeping on to Cape Finisterre, bring food to an incredible range of shellfish on Europe's most westerly corner, to the Galician *rías* (coastal inlets) and the Spanish north coast. In these waters shellfish grow at great speed. In the Mediterranean the continental shelf is perfect for shellfish. The Spanish are really spoilt for choice.

Spanish shellfish are cooked to demonstrate their superb quality, usually either simply boiled or cooked *a la parrilla* (on the barbecue). Sea salt, and perhaps lemon wedges, are the common accompaniments.

SCALLOPS AND MUSSELS

Santiago de Compostela in Galicia is famous for scallops, and the pilgrims have chosen their shell for their badge. Today scallops are farmed in the quiet bays to the west. Large ones, *vieras*, and little *zamburiñas* (queens or bay scallops) are cooked with their orange roe curled round them. Scallops may be breadcrumbed and fried, cooked with wine and chilli, or with tomato sauce (in St James' style). They feature in the flat Galician pie that is prepared for special occasions.

The mussel beds of Galicia are famous, and Tarragona in the east is also an important mussel area. The bivalves are grown on ropes secured to platforms, out in the western bays. In Galicia, 2.5 million mussels are canned per day, and there are plenty of fresh ones for the whole of Spain, too. It is their sheer size and tenderness that astounds. They are large enough to be breadcrumbed and fried, although wine and parsley mixtures, sometimes with bacon, are more usual. They are also added to many fish dishes and stews. A favourite tapas dish in Madrid is *tigres* – mussels in béchamel sauce with a little chopped (bell) pepper, breadcrumbed then grilled.

Percebes

One of the world's most expensive shellfish, *percebes* are known in English as goose barnacles. You understand why if you see them crowded on the storm-washed rocks. Fixed at the foot, reaching perhaps 5cm/2in high, blackish or mottled, they look like a gaggle of geese with outstretched necks, particularly so because the tips are pointed and white, like a beak.

Percebes are either left raw or briefly boiled. Their orange flesh is squeezed from its casing and served with vinaigrette. Their taste is "essence of seawater".

Left: Carpetshell clams are very popular and are most often served in sauces.

CLAMS AND COCKLES

In Spain clams are common fare. They are boiled for tapas, added to soups and pasta, and used to garnish grander dishes. They are fished on both coasts, but the northern ones are plumper, and a regional speciality. There are many varieties; one of the best is the *almeja fina* (the carpetshell). Most magnificent is the *concha fina* (Venus), which measures about 8cm/3in across, with orange flesh inside. It is opened to order in the sherry bars of the south.

Other bivalves include common cockles, the dog cockle, *almendra de mar*, razor shells and *ostíon*, the Portuguese oyster, found on the Cantabrian coast.

PRAWNS AND SHRIMPS

Saltwater varieties are fished on both coasts. In size order:

Camarones These are the tiniest Spanish shrimps and are caught around Cadiz. They turn white, rather than pink, when cooked, and are made into delicious little fritters.

Quisquilla This term covers all the smaller varieties of prawn (shrimp) that are caught in their thousands off the Spanish coasts. They are added to scrambled eggs and stuffings, or used to add interest to *ensaladilla* (diced vegetable salad) and various sauces.

Gamba These have a good colour and are fished reasonably deep, giving them a good flavour. They are used in some of Spain's most famous dishes. *Gambas en gabardinas* (in overcoats) are battered then fried, while the southern dish *gambas pil pil* (which is quite different from northern *pil pil*) is based on chilli, and is very hot.

Langostino These are the longest Mediterranean prawn, fished from deep water. Sometimes they are called tiger prawns, as some varieties are striped. They are served simply to show off their true flavour – for example in salads.

Below: Cigalas *(scampi) have a fabulous flavour and are fished on every coast.*

Carabinero These prawns grow to 20cm/8in long and are a deep scarlet colour with a violet head. (They are named after the red coats worn by the military.) They lack the flavour of *langostinos* but are excellent in northern matured bean dishes, where the prawn heads add flavour, and in display salads, because the bodies retain their delightful red markings after shelling.

LOBSTERS

Bogavante, the true lobster, is party fare, while *langosta* (in Castilian), the spiny lobster (saltwater crayfish) is eaten to celebrate Spain's national day. Squat (or slipper) lobsters, called *cigarra* in Spain, make cricket-like noises under water. They have insignificant claws, but stocky little tails. St James even has his own lobster, the *santiaguiño*, with a cross on its head.

Scampi (*cigala* or *escarmarlan grande* in Catalan) are "false lobsters". They are a luxury, and four or five make a good portion. Their splendid heads have beady eyes, their long straight claws are pink and scarlet even when raw. They go very well with mayonnaise.

Right: Gambas *are probably the best of all prawns and have a wonderful flavour and lovely texture.*

Freshwater crustaceans

Crayfish (*cangrejos*) are found in the Duero and Tago rivers. There are festivals to celebrate them in Herrera del Pisuergo and at Palencia where the locals eat them in great numbers.

Tiny crayfish also flourish in freshwater reservoirs all over Spain. These crustaceans are sold as *embalsadores* (behind the dam) and are used to make a range of good sauces and soups.

Right: The spider crab is known as centollo *or* txangurro *in Spain*

CRABS

Small shore crabs, such as *necoras*, which have red knees, are served simply boiled, and picked to pieces at the table. They make ideal beach food. *Buey de mar* (ox of the sea) is the large-clawed crab, but the favourite, particularly on the north coast, is the spider crab (*centollo* in Castilian), great beasts on akimbo legs, with stronger and sweeter meat. The classic Basque dish is *txangurro* (dressed meat in the shell); there is one crab per person.

SQUID, CUTTLEFISH AND OCTOPUS

Common to both oceans, squid are universal and a popular food. Few travellers have visited a Spanish beach and not eaten *calamares* (fried squid rings in batter). There are many varieties of squid, and they can vary considerably in size.

Their pink skin turns grey after a time on shore, so choose fresh pink ones when buying. They are also commonly sold cut into rings for stews and should be cooked fast or very slowly, otherwise they will become rubbery. On the north coast breaded squid, known as *raba*, are popular.

Cuttlefish, called *jibia* or *sepia*, and *chocos* and *chiperones* if tiny, are very similar to squid but rounder in shape. They are often sold without the skin when their colour is milky white. When cleaning, be very careful to remove the ink sacs intact because the ink stains. Slit the body open to remove the broad white cuttle bone.

The flesh of the cuttlefish is thick and sweeter than squid. It is ideal for slow simmering or cooking stuffed. The black ink is also used in cooking and classic dishes include *sepia en su tinto* (cuttlefish in their ink) and *arroz negro* (black rice). Ink also features in many signature dishes in top restaurants from Arzak to El Bullí.

Octopus are particularly popular in the north. All the bars in Santiago de Compostela have one sitting like a great wig on a hat-stand. They are mainly cooked with paprika, as in *pulpo de feria*, or they are stewed. Octopus are tough, so traditionally wine corks are added to stews, which are thought to help tenderize the flesh.

Below: Squid are popularly fried in rings, grilled or stuffed and braised.

Beef, Veal, Lamb and Kid

The varieties of meat (*carne*) available in Spain are far wider than elsewhere. The middle classes eat a great deal of meat, while the working classes eat comparatively little; there is virtually no vegetarian cooking. Pulse and vegetable dishes are invariably flavoured with sausages and pork fat.

BEEF AND VEAL

The Spanish have never been great beef eaters. Richard Ford, a century ago, remarked that "bulls are bred for baiting and oxen for the plough, not the spit".

High temperatures elsewhere mean the best beef comes from the north, and Galicia produces about two-thirds of Spanish beef. However, new breeding programmes, and the modern practice of moving cattle indoors, means more beef is now being produced in Catalonia, Aragón and the cereal plains of Castile. Only the Basques will eat "bloody" meat, and red meat is exported in return for veal cattle. The native breed is mahogany-red *retinto*. *Morucho* and *avilana* are work animals.

Spain has at least three sorts of beef. Hung beef is a northern taste, and vast *chuletones* (chops) are enjoyed in this region. Cattle are slaughtered at between two and five years old to produce *carne de buey* (ox) or *vaca* (cow). This lesser quality beef is stewed, famously with chocolate, or with vegetables as in the Catalan *estofat*. Meatballs are sold in every bar and are loved by children, too. Cuts such as salt brisket go into stews.

Younger beef is the popular choice; *añojo* means yearling although, in fact, the cattle are slaughtered at between 10 and 18 months. Joints of meat are frequently labelled with their age and diet. For example, *lomo cebón* is loin fattened on barley.

Above: Ox tail, or bull's tail, benefits from long, slow cooking and is a very popular choice when stewed.

Ternera translates as veal, but it is pink or grey veal, not white. Veal calves are never intensively reared in Spain, and they are often four times the age of Dutch or Italian calves when they are slaughtered. Only in Ávila are calves killed very young. One veal of note is the northern *ternera gallega*, D.O., which comes from the honey-blond *rubio* cattle.

Veal escalopes may be braised with vegetables or fried. *Filetitos* are small escalopes fried with lemon juice, and six or seven make up a single portion. Veal is wonderful with artichokes and sherry, and can be made into excellent stews with young vegetables.

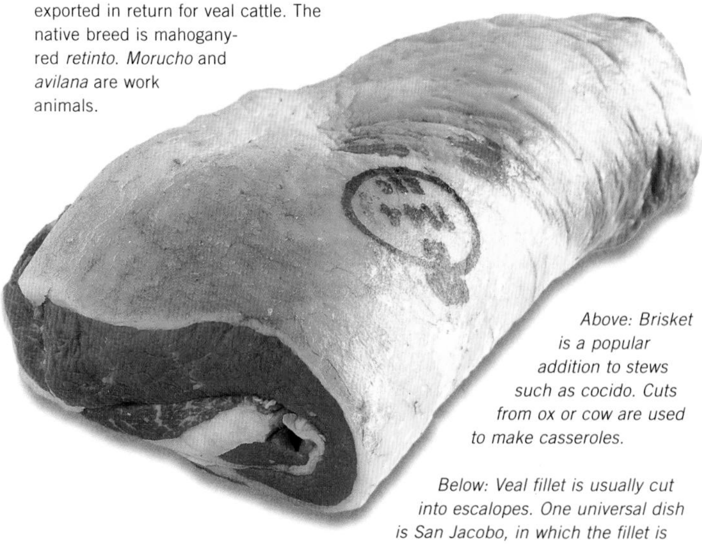

Above: Brisket is a popular addition to stews such as cocido. Cuts from ox or cow are used to make casseroles.

Below: Veal fillet is usually cut into escalopes. One universal dish is San Jacobo, in which the fillet is topped with serano ham, then cheese.

The Moorish oven

Domed ovens built of *adobe* (roofing bricks), which hold the heat, rather than firebricks, are prized for roasting tiny lambs and piglets particularly in Castile, in places such as Aranda de Duero and Haro. These ovens are part of the restaurant structure, and are about 2m/6ft in diameter inside. They are wood-fired, and cooking only takes place when the glowing charcoal subsides. The burned-out coals are pushed to the side, the dishes are put into the oven using long paddles, then the door is sealed. In the hot south, similar ovens are built outside houses for domestic use.

THE FIGHTING BULL

The fighting bull is either slaughtered at the age of one, and the meat is minced (ground), or it lives a life of luxury until it comes to the ring at the age of three or four. The meat from these bulls (*toro de lidia*) is sold in specialist shops. Ex-matadors frequently buy restaurants, and a number of these source beef from the local bullring. The meat is deep black-red (though not tough) and is eaten as steaks in sherry in Jerez, or minced or stewed. The *rabo* (tail) is a popular choice for hotpots, while the testicles – the matadors' titbit – may be breadcrumbed and fried. Valencia produces a special bull ham.

LAMB AND KID

Lamb is very expensive, but it is still the traditional meat in the grazing regions of central and western Spain, and up into the mountains of Aragón and Murcia. Elsewhere, it is an Easter or wedding treat. Spain has 24 million sheep – the same number as when Napoleon marched there during the Peninsular War (1808–14) – which dominate the Meseta, the high heart of Spain. They spend the winter in Extremadura and southern Castile, and once walked north in vast flocks (the *transhumance*) to summer pastures in Cantabria. However, today sheep are transported by train, with Burgos as the commercial sheep centre.

Thyme is used to flavour roast lamb. Lamb chops are popular, and tiny legs of lamb provide an exquisite eating experience. Stews can consist of a whole animal, chopped. *Cochifrito* is flavoured with lemon or vinegar and paprika; *chilindrones*, around Logroño traditionally feature a mild red chilli pepper. *Menestra* are spring stews cooked with young vegetables.

Mutton is used in a few dishes in Aragón and Extremadura, and some of the classic stews such as *chilindrón* and *caldereta* originally used mutton.

Kid (*cabrito* or *choto*) is another luxury meat, either cooked on a spit or in traditional stews such as *tumbet* in Valencia or *caldereta extremeña*, which is thickened with the kid's puréed liver

Spanish stews

Olla puchero Both these words mean cooking pot, the large vessel used to make the daily stew cooked by many families in Spain.

Olla podrida Literally meaning rotten pot, the name of this stew actually means hotchpotch – a mixed stew of beef, bacon, ham and vegetables, simmered so long the ingredients become very soft-textured.

Cocido Meaning boiled or simmered, *cocido* is shorthand for mixed stew.

Cocido madrileño This is the national dish, where several different meats are cooked with chickpeas and fresh vegetables. It makes a three-course feast. Made all over the country, the meat content is reduced the further from the capital you get; every region includes its own sausages and other produce. The Basques like to add red beans, and in Seville both rice and chickpeas are included, with garlic, sweet potatoes and *morcilla* sausage. In the south pears and pumpkins are often used, and in the Canaries, sweet potatoes and fresh corn are added.

Escudella This is the Catalan word for *cocido* or stew. *Escudella i carn d'olla* is a big dish, with the *carn* (pork) as one large dumpling, or it may contain a selection of ham, chicken, veal and *botifarra* sausage, with chickpeas and noodles, plus vegetables. The liquid is served first as soup, the rest follows. *Escudella de pagès* is a country-style stew, with carrots, potatoes and cabbage.

Fabada This is the Asturian stew of dried beans, salt pork and ham, with oak-smoked *morcilla* and *chorizo*.

Caldereta Meaning witch's cauldron, this is the name of the lamb, goat or fish stew that is cooked in it.

Estofado *Estofat* in Catalan, this is meat that is slow-cooked, usually in its fat and juice.

Guiso Also known as *guisado*, this is simply a stew with sauce.

Cochifrito Pieces of lamb or goat are fried, and seasoned with vinegar or lemon and paprika.

Fricandó Small veal pieces are stewed with vegetables such as carrots. The Catalan version contains onions and tomatoes.

Above: In Spain, legs of lamb may be very small – with one leg per person.

Above: Kid is a luxury meat that often replaces lamb in traditional stews.

PORK

The pig represents Spain's history and religion on the plate. To eat pork and sausages became, after the unification of the country at the end of the fifteenth century, a way of demonstrating nationality. (The Muslim Moors and the Jews were forbidden to eat pork.) In a poor, mountainous country, the pig provided the major source of nutrition, and it is still Spain's most widely eaten meat.

Almost every family would once have owned a pig. People in the villages would throw their rubbish into local gullies and streams, and this waste sustained foraging pigs. People who live in apartments in Madrid will still tell you about the family porker in Galicia. The *matanza* (pig killing), when families gather to make sausages and celebrate, is the greatest non-religious festival of the year.

Although cured meat is eaten more often than fresh, pork chops and loin of pork remain Spain's most familiar meat. *Solomillo*, which means fillet of beef in the north, becomes pork in the south; it is delicious *a la trianera* (roasted with sherry). *Magro* is a pork steak, commonly served with a tomato sauce or potatoes. *El frite*, or *cochefrito*, is chopped fried meat flavoured with vinegar and paprika; it is traditionally prepared to test the meat of a newly killed pig. Minced (ground) pork is used in dishes such as *pringa* and *prueba*, which were both devised as a way to test the spicing mix, before stuffing the meat into sausage casings. *Gazpacho manchego* is a delicious coarse pork pâté, and is quite different from the well-known southern gazpacho.

Other cuts of pork are cured, as well as the ubiquitous ham. In the north, the famous cured meat is *lacón*, a front-leg ham. Among the *salazones* (salted meats), there is coarse-salted belly, and also *panceta* (streaky bacon), which is sometimes marinated before being cured and/or smoked. *Torreznos* are pork slices, fried like bacon and served with eggs, a popular dish in the centre of the country and Extremadura. However, their social status is indicated by their name in Cervantes's novel *Don Quixote*: *duelos y quebrantes*, which means sorrow and suffering.

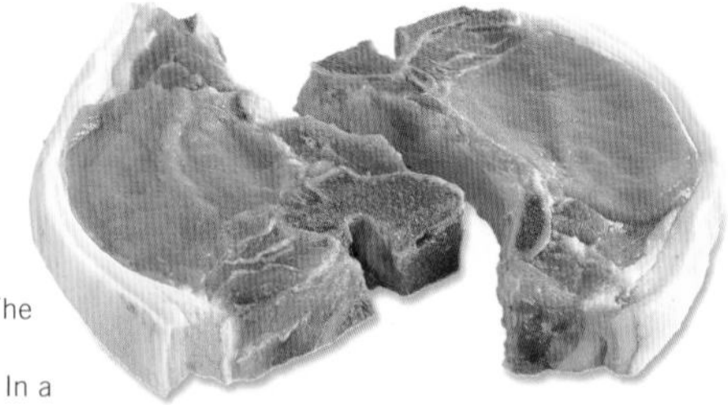

Above: Loin chops are popular in beach bars.

Above: Chump chops are great cooked on la plancha, *the iron grill sheet.*

Below: In Spain, pork loin is trimmed to the meat eye only.

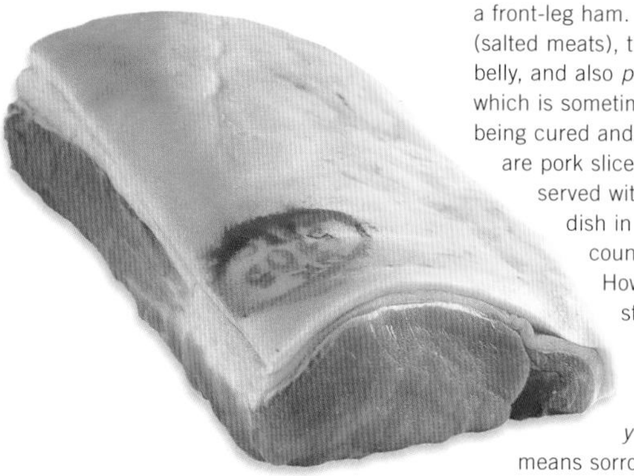

THE BLACK WILD PIG

The native *ibérico* pig is known by its black trotter (*pata negra*). (The phrase *pata negra* is also a slang term used to describe anything good.) There are actually four dark-skinned breeds, the main two having black or red hair. The pigs are trim and graceful, with long legs. They run wild in small groups, in the *sierras* of Andalusia and particularly in Extremadura, in the flower pastures under the holm oaks, called the *dehesa*.

Their numbers are decreasing as their fame rises. Their final food is acorns, which give the meat its full flavour and an old golden tinge. If meat is labelled *bellota*, it means the pig fed entirely on acorns and will therefore have excellent flavour.

Wild pigs are slaughtered at 18 months, weighing about 160kg/352lb – the domestic hog reaches that weight at nine months. Highly prized for ham, they now make up only five per cent of Spanish *serrano* (compared with 25 per cent in the 1950s) 90 per cent of which is taken up by restaurants. Another restaurant speciality is fresh steaks of *cerdo ibérico*; it is dark like beef and tastes like game.

Below: Spanish panceta *is fresh or cured belly. If it is unavailable, Italian pancetta makes an excellent substitute.*

Cooking with pork fat

Pork fat (*manteca*) adds a very characteristic flavour to many Spanish dishes. *Manteca colorada* is fat coloured with paprika. It is delicious spread on bread for breakfast in the south. The fat is also made into *rillettes* (fat packed around cooked, shredded pork).

Tocino is solid fat, fresh or salted, back or belly, for cubing and frying. Like *panceta* (fresh or cured pork belly), it adds flavour and goodness to pulse dishes. Dry or poor-quality *serrano* ham is chopped and used for cooking.

SUCKLING PIG

Truly a wonder, so small and so tender, the suckling pig is known as *cochinillo* in Castilian, *tostón* in central Spain and *porcella* in the Balearics.

Old Castile is famous for its ovens, which are used to roast either milk-fed piglets or lamb. The west, Arévolo and Segovia, is piglet country. There they are roasted in a huge domed brick or refractory oven, heated by holm oak – just imagine thirty piglets sizzling on a revolving turntable.

With the pig being killed at 15 to 20 days old, the shoulder blade is only the size of a car key. To roast the pigs, they are split through the belly and opened out flat with their legs and tail out. Each splayed pig is displayed in an earthenware dish, which catches the fat and juices as the pig roasts. The roasted meat is carved using the side of a plate.

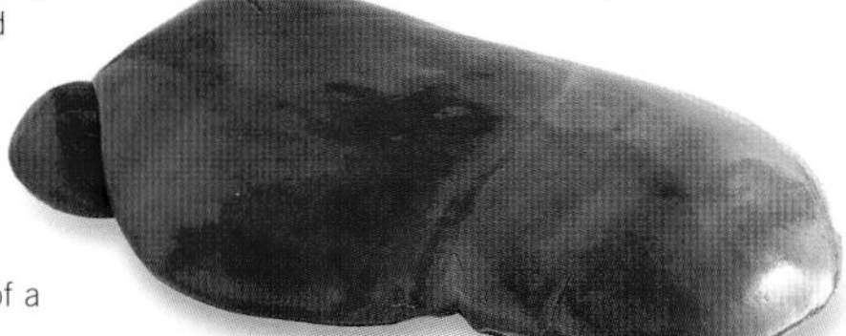

Above right: Calf's liver is good cooked with sweet Malaga wine sauce.

Right: Strongly flavoured pig's liver is stewed and served with sweet, pungent sauces.

OFFAL

It is said that everything from the pig can be eaten except its squeak. The pig is the principal source of offal (variety meats) in Spain, although other animals are also used.

Pigs' heads and tails can be salted. Pickled ears are breaded and fried, as well as being used to make some wonderful delicatessen salads. Trotters and tails may be found in stews and rice dishes. Ham bones are used to flavour beans; as they grow older they become highly prized, with neighbours lending each other bones for stews. Pig's caul is used to baste faggots, and ham fat (*unto*) sold in great rolls, is used for frying – aged fat is prized in Galicia for its extra flavour.

Lamb and veal kidneys are to be found cooked in wine sauces in tapas bars. Sweetbreads (*mollejas*) are usually fried. Brains are used in two good gypsy dishes: they are minced (ground) to stuff *tortilla Sacromonte*; and are served fried, with lemon, as *sesos a la flamenca*. *Criadillas* (testicles) are called white kidneys; a delicacy for matadors, they are breadcrumbed and fried. Another "man's dish" is blood, solidified in squares with vinegar, which is offered in tapas bars.

The first dish to be eaten at the *matanza* (pig killing) is *asadura*, the liver and guts made into a great stew with almonds, garlic and oregano. The similar *chanfaina*, with lungs (lights) and liver, is cooked, often in vast vats for festivals. A more elegant calf's liver dish from the south contains sweet Málaga wine and aromatic herbs.

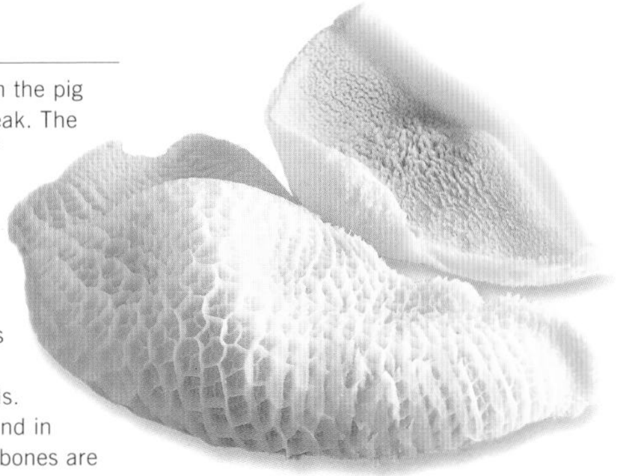

Above: Tripe (callos) *is the essential ingredient used in some distinguished, classic chickpea stews.*

Tripe, called *menudo* in Andalusia, is one of the surprises of Spanish cuisine. Resembling a woollen blanket when raw, it has a repertoire of dishes. *Callos a la madrilena* (from veal or pig) is tavern fare in the capital city. It is seasoned with onion, thyme and tomato, and includes *morcilla*, chorizo and ham too. Depending on the region, tripe is usually cooked with chickpeas or beans, along with a ham bone for extra flavour. One Catalan dish combines tripe with potatoes, pine nuts and a glass of old *rancio* wine.

Pork tongues (*lengua*) are commoner than lambs' tongues. The former are cooked in a Majorcan dish, with pomegranate seeds. But larger veal tongues are also served cold, and as a *fiambre* (pressed delicatessen meat).

White *manitas*, lambs' feet, come 16 to a portion and leave pearl-like bones on the plate. *Zarajos* are the lamb's intestines; they are wrapped around two twigs, then grilled (broiled). Lambs' tails are eaten in Aragón, where they are called mountain asparagus, with (bell) peppers and tomatoes. In the markets you will find beef muzzles, too, and cow's heel with the horn off.

SAUSAGES

The pig is virtually a "larder on trotters" and is valued more for what can be made out of it than for fresh meat. It is turned into sausages, frequently home-made, which will last the whole year. The raw pork is minced (ground), or hand-chopped, mixed with back fat and spices, then stuffed into casings. The bigger the pieces of meat, and the lower the fat content, the sweeter the meat is.

Some sausages (chiefly *morcillas*) include extra ingredients such as onion or rice, and additions such as nuts are included in regions where there was once a strong Moorish presence. Garlic is used in the south and west, but too much would turn the sausage rancid. There are also sausages made using pork blends – with beef, vegetables other than onion, and even the occasional cereal sausage such as the *farinata* of Salamanca. There are game sausages too, made from venison.

The mixture is stuffed into casings made from pigs' guts. These natural casings vary in size so some sausages are fatter than others. The sausages are then hung on strings in the cold dry air and will lose as much as 35 per cent of their weight if left for a full year. Smoked sausages are found across Spain, usually coinciding with the old pilgrim routes, as in Bierzo in León. The dry sausages used in the Asturian *fabada* (pork and bean stew) are smoked and swell with cooking.

Sausages tend to be classed by colour, and this provides some guidance as to how they should be cooked and served. Many dried sausages may be eaten raw, although this is not always the rule.

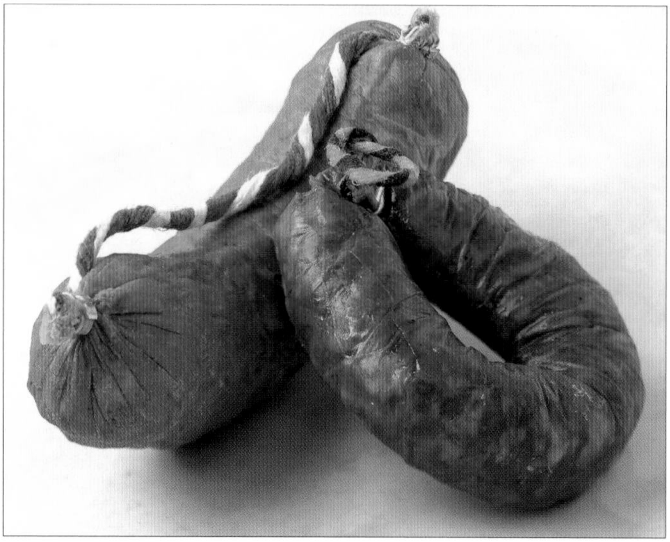

Above: The fat chorizo from Cantimpalo, and the ring-shaped one from Jabugo are two famous versions of this classic spicy paprika sausage.

BLACK SAUSAGES

Morcillas are blood puddings, and are the first to be made from the newly killed pig, straight after slaughter. They are made as links, or as rings in Seville and Ronda in the south. Once made, they are boiled in cauldrons, then dried for storage. Occasionally they may also be smoked, and they are almost always cooked again before being eaten.

These wonderful sausages are a speciality of the north, the most famous being those of Extremadura and Asturias, which are flavoured with aniseed and cloves, and plumped with either rice or onions. Rice is typically used in some parts of Aragón, and the Burgos *morcilla* also contains pine nuts. *Morcilla dulce* is eaten raw, and can be found in tapas bars. The spicing, sweetness and rich tongue-clinging fat make it irresistible.

Botifarra is the black sausage from the east of the country. It is made in links, or occasionally in rings. The *bisbe* (meaning bishop) is an outsize sausage, while the *bull* contains tongue and cheek. There are Valencian *morcillas* too, which are sometimes very spicy, and a Majorcan version, *camiot*, which is flavoured with cumin and cinnamon.

Left: Ring-shaped black and white botifarras *are made in Catalonia.*

RED SAUSAGES

Paprika is used in sausages right across Spain, apart from in Catalonia, the Levante and the Balearics (except for the *sobrasada* from Majorca). Chorizos are named after the *choricero* chilli that gives them both spiciness and colour. There are at least 50 varieties of chorizo, but two main types.

Red chorizos, made in links, contain minced (ground) meat, which is mottled with fat. They may be fried or boiled. The longer varieties are usually sweeter, while small round ones are *picante* (hot and spicy). The knobbly, garlicky *chorizos de Cantimpalos*, from Segovia, are typical of central Spain and are the first choice for the Madrid *cocido* (the national stew of salt and fresh meats).

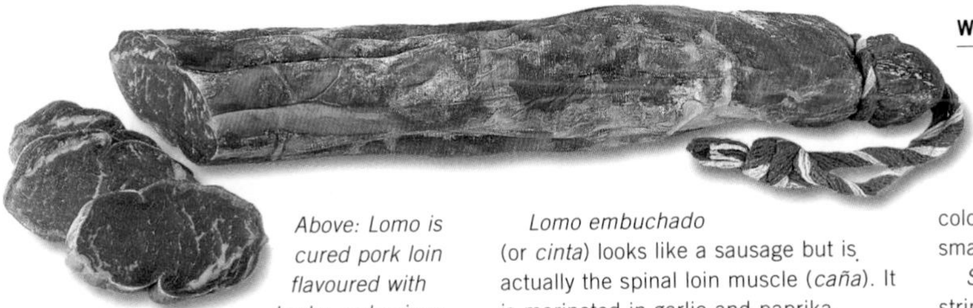

Above: Lomo is cured pork loin flavoured with herbs and spices.

The second type is the tapas or cured chorizo. The meat filling is stuffed into a larger gut casing and so is much longer and fatter. These are sliced thinly and eaten with bread, or they are cut into little batons and added to salads. The meat in these sausages may be marbled or chopped.

There are many varieties of cured chorizo, and each one attracts an enthusiastic and loyal following. *Pamplona* resembles salami, with its thoroughly minced (ground) meat, and the coloured fat that looks like orange rice grains. *Chorizo de Rioja* has big swirls of paprika-red marbled meat around the fat. *Chistorra* is typically Basque and Navarran. This narrow, cigar-shaped sausage includes beef as well as pork. *Morcón* is widely distributed in Andalusia. It is made from marinated loin and shoulder, and seasoned with paprika. It is tied with string to make a round sausage that resembles a hand grenade. There is also a larger Murcian version. However, it is *sobrasada de Mallorca* that probably wears the crown and is the pride of the Balearic islands. The sausage is more or less spherical in shape, although it is sometimes long, and is air-cured for up to a year. It is spreadable and has a smooth pâté-like texture that is achieved by grinding and regrinding the pork several times. The sausage meat is also sold in pots.

Lomo embuchado (or *cinta*) looks like a sausage but is actually the spinal loin muscle (*caña*). It is marinated in garlic and paprika, sometimes with sugar, oregano and nutmeg, then encased and dried for two to six months. A good variety is produced in Teruel. It has a delicate flavour and compact texture, but is expensive so is quite a treat.

Sausages that are named after a place famed for ham also attract a following. *Jabugocitos* are little frying sausages from Jabugo, *guijuelo* is a fat tapas sausage from Extremadura, and *ibéricos* are made from the meat of the prized black pig.

Below: Long, fat cured salchichones *are sliced and served for tapas.*

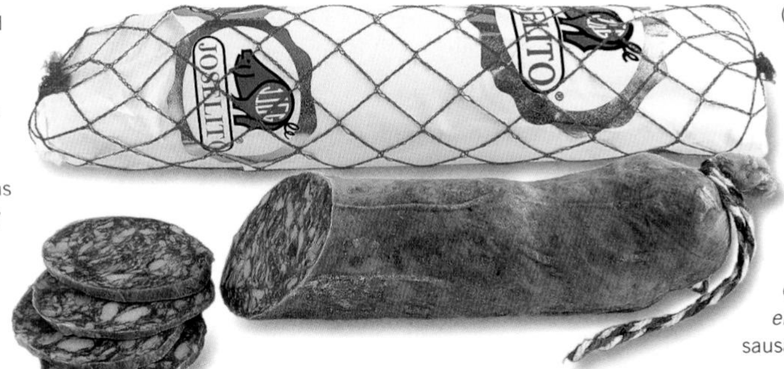

WHITE SAUSAGES

Sausages that are neither black nor red are classified as white sausage, although they are not necessarily white in appearance. The cured varieties are a dark cerise colour inside and are cased in the smaller gut.

Salchichón comes in rings and strings, and is usually powdered on the outside with ambient bacteria. The meat and fat are easily distinguishable. Some famous examples are made in Vic in Catalonia. These sausages are dry, like salami, and laced with peppercorns. *Fuet* is a Catalonian sausage containing white pepper and sugar. It is long and thin so dries fast, and is consequently very chewy.

Longaniza covers a variety of sausages. A few are dry, while others are fresh and coiled in a bowl, and still more hang in a wonderful hank. Short lengths are used for cooking. If the sausages are thin, they tend to be hard, bland and can be rather fatty.

White *botifarras* (known as *blancas*) are the brothers of the black ones. These fresh sausages are usually grilled (broiled), and are often eaten with beans all along the east coast. And of course there are *embutidos* (fresh sausages) that are made everywhere.

Above: Fuet *is a chewy, dry Catalonian sausage.*

HAMS

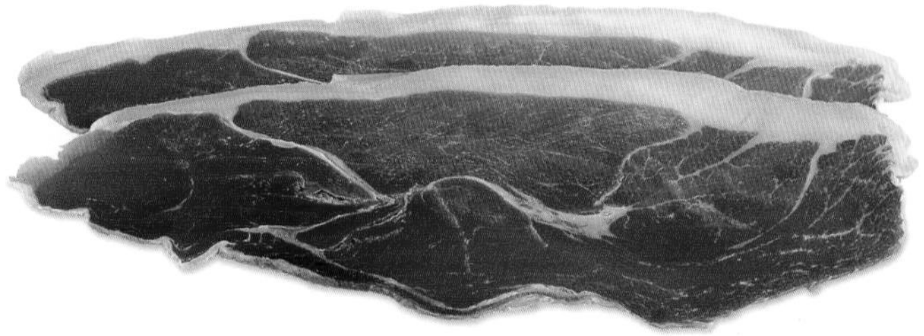

Above: Raw serrano *ham is cured in the cool air of the sierras.*

Spain produces some of Europe's finest hams, one-third of which are exported. About one-fifth of Spanish pigs are used for hams, so it is not surprising more ham is eaten in Spain than elsewhere in Europe – the Basques alone eat nearly one whole ham each per year.

The mountain-cured *jamón serrano* rules supreme, but lesser hams – *jamón cocido* – are cured for boiling. The front leg of the pig (*paleta*, or *lacón* in Galicia) is also cured. It is a coarser cut but with a very even flavour). In the north-west it is used for *caldo gallego*, while *lacón con grelos* (with turnip tops) is definitely their national dish.

JAMON SERRANO

Serrano is the adjective from *sierra* (mountain). It means mountain ham, and indicates that it is raw and dried in cold air. Typically, these hams are long and thin, and almost triangular at the meaty end. Better ones are marketed with the trotter (foot) still attached.

Big names in ham production in Andalusia are Jabugo in the Aracena (near Huelva) and Trévelez, in the high mountains south of Granada. *Jabugo* is probably the Spanish choice for the best ham, but *Trévelez* is better known abroad. Being so far south, these hams need heavier salting, and so are less sweet and melt-in-the-mouth than hams from cooler climes such as those from Extremadura and Lérida.

Teruel in Aragón and *Guijuelo* in Salamanca have D.O. status for local hams. The former is famous for its white hams; the latter for lighter salting and sweet-flavoured hams. The whole of Extramadura is pig country and *Montanchez* in Cáceres and *Cumbre Mayores* are both popular hams.

As well as the big names, who don't need to advertise, as they sell all the ham that they can produce, there are also many small producers. Many hams are sold packed off the bone, or sliced. Other parts of the pig (including the loin and front shoulder) are also cured.

Thinly sliced *serrano* is eaten for tapas or sandwiched with cheese, but it is also used to wrap fish. Little batons are added to salads and bean dishes.

Breeds and grades

White hams come from crosses of Landrace, Duroc and the Large White pigs. Just 5 per cent of hams now come from the incomparable black native pig called *ibérico*. This ham is sold under this name *ibérico* abroad but, in Spain, it is known as *pata negra*. *Ibérico* meat is leaner and tougher than other pigs', while the surface fat attracts a little blue penicillin mould, which adds flavour.

These expensive "black" hams are graded by the animals' food. *Bellota* (acorn) indicates a pig fed in the wild, and this is terribly expensive. *Recebo* refers to a pig fed on a diet of grain and acorns for its last month. *Pienso* means the pig was entirely grain fed.

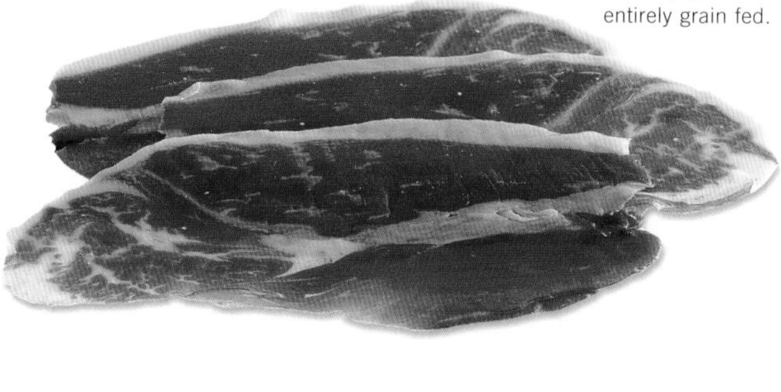

Below: Serrano *ham from the black* ibérico *pig is highly prized.*

Curing

It takes 12 months to cure a *serrano* ham. All hams take at least 9 months to cure, and *pata negra* is cured for 18 months. The ham is salted once, for 40 to 60 days, then matured hanging in the dry winter air. When summer temperatures return, it is cellar-rested.

Fat

The fat is distributed between the muscles in fine layers, increasing the flavour of the meat. When black pigs forage on grass and acorns, this fat has a very high oleic oil content, and so liquifies at a lower temperature than other meat fats. It also has a lower cholesterol content than farmed or other free-range (farm-fresh) meat.

Carving

Serrano hams need their own stands to support them, as they are very long. They are carved into paper-thin slices, lengthways with the grain of the meat. The meat is faintly chewy, varying in colour from deep red to scarlet. The fat appears as tiny lengthways threads in the meat. The best cuts come from close to the bone on the *manza* (the rounder side).

Other salazones

Parts of lamb, kid and beef can also be salted, and smoked for more flavour. *Cecina* (*ceniza* in Catalan) is cured beef that is thinly sliced. There are also bull hams and duck breast hams.

THE BARNYARD

Poultry cluck around the many farms of Spain. However, the chickens are mainly kept for their eggs; the birds are not the main family meat.

CHICKEN

More popular now than it used to be, there was a time when chicken was more expensive than beef. The well-known Catalan dish, chicken with lobster, recalls its luxury status.

There are numerous Spanish chicken dishes, reflecting regional tastes and using local produce. Chicken is cooked with sherry in the south; with (bell) peppers in Rioja; *alli-pebre* (with garlic and paprika) in Valencia, and with tomatoes and cumin in Extremadura.

Below: The boiling hen is tastier than a young chicken and features in many dishes in Spain.

Below: Huge capons are a favourite at Christmas time.

The smell of chickens roasting, basted with pork fat, in chicken shops at the weekend is quite mouthwatering.

Gallina is a boiling hen. In *gallina en pepitoria*, it is simmered slowly, then the sauce is thickened with ground nuts. Capons are sold in the Christmas market in Villalba in Galicia. These large birds weigh about 5kg/11lb. Some are fattened on maize (like foie gras ducks) and they are sold in Madrid dressed and stuffed with Roquefort or chestnuts.

Chicken offal (variety meats) is widely used. The gizzards are added to lentil dishes, and accompany the chicken meats in *arroces* (rice dishes). Chicken livers cooked in sherry is a popular tapas dish.

Above: Guinea fowl are regarded as a substitute for true game birds.

OTHER POULTRY

Goose and duck are cooked in Catalonia, but are not popular in the rest of Spain. Goose with pears (*oca amb peras*) is the famous dish of the region. The Catalans are known for combining birds and fruit, and the reason is not hard to discover – the birds feed on fruit. Duck is combined with figs in another Catalan classic.

Ducks (*pato*) are also reared in Valencia near lake Albufera but they are not widespread elsewhere. Catalonia and Navarra now breed the mallard (a cross between the white duck and the grey barbary), called *anèc* in Catalan. Because of the French influence in these regions, duck hams, foie gras and even duck confit are produced. In Galicia, a popular dish combines duck with turnips. However, Spain's most famous duck recipe comes from Seville. The juice of the Seville orange was added to duck to cut through the fat. Olives do the same job, and there are several dishes that combine duck and olives.

The turkey was introduced to Europe via Spain in the 16th century from America. Called *pavo*, after the peacock (*pavo real*), it was at first cooked like a peacock, stuffed and inserted into a pig's caul. The dark bronze or black turkey are the birds of choice, weighing in at around 3kg/6½–7lb. The best birds come from Aspe, in the Pyrenees.

The guinea fowl (*pintada*) came from Queen Dido's Africa – either directly, or with the Romans. They are now reared in Spain, as are quails (*codornices*).

GAME

Spain is great for wildlife, and out in the country the sign *coto de caza* (shooting reserved) is a constant reminder that hunting is a passion in Spain. *Caza mayor* (game hunting) has always been part of the social/political scene. *Caza menor* (shooting birds) can be pursued by anyone with a gun and a knapsack.

FEATHERED GAME

There are massive migrations of birds across Spain twice a year, on their way to and from Africa. The 27,000 Spanish shooting clubs try to ensure that two-thirds of the birds pass through their land, for breeding. Small birds have always contributed to the poor family's diet: fieldfare, starling, even sparrow, can be added to rice dishes.

Duck

In Spain, duck shooting (*aquatica*) is a specialized sport, with many adherents. There are mallards on all the lakes and salt flats in Spain, and many teal.

Below: The abundant pigeon is meaty and benefits from long, slow cooking.

Above: Tiny quail are one of the most prevalent wild birds found in Spain.

Pigeon

Present all year, pigeons (*palomas*) are netted as they fly over the mountains. They are pot-roasted with vinegar, or with raisins in the Val d'Arran, and stewed with peas or mushrooms in Castile. Murcia has a famous pigeon pie, which mimics the highly spiced Moroccan *b'stilla* (a pie made with filo pastry and a filling of shredded pigeon, ground almonds and spices), revealing its distinct Moorish influences. The pie is then baked until golden and sprinkled with icing (confectioners') sugar and ground cinnamon.

Partridge

The partridge in Spain is the red-legged (French) *perdiz* (which is larger than the grey-legged variety). It is far and away the most popular of game birds. It gorges on the sherry grapes in the south, and from October a million of the birds are eaten each year. La Mancha is the partridge capital of Europe. Once captured, the birds may be kept in cages until needed. Celebrated recipes include partridges in chocolate, Pyrenean mushroom stews, and *perdices en escabeche* (a salad of jellied, vinegared birds). They are also stewed with cabbage, in a dish that dates back to the 1400s, and with beans.

Left: Teal is one of the smallest wild ducks and is highly prized for its fabulous taste and texture.

Quail

In Spain, it is said to rain quails, rather than cats and dogs because there are so many of these tiny birds (about 10 million), which are trapped in their thousands as they fly south each April. The birds are roasted, barded with bacon and stuffed with their own innards, or casseroled with wine and garlic, or with grapes. A speciality is *codornices con pochas*, quail with freshly shelled haricot (navy) beans, as their seasons coincide.

Woodcock

Chocha (woodcock) are found in Galicia in the winter. The small birds are shot for the pot, and you really need to allow two birds per person.

Pheasant

Because it was recorded by the great French chef, Escoffier, *faisan al modo de Alcántara*, pheasant stuffed with duck liver and truffles, became the most famous bird dish in Europe.

FURRED GAME

Ninety per cent of Spain is mountainous and full of game. The mountain goats are the long-horned ibex (*cabra monte*) and the short-horned chamois (*rebeco* in Catalan). Boars (*jabalí*) are hunted by moonlight. They are numerous in the rugged north and in the southern mountains. Because the wild boar does so much damage to young woodland, it is now culled. Boar is stewed with thyme or wine and nuts.

Venison

The red *ciervo común* is Europe's largest deer, pre-eminent in the Sierra Morena and the mountains of the south, in the coastal Coto Doñana, and reintroduced into the northern

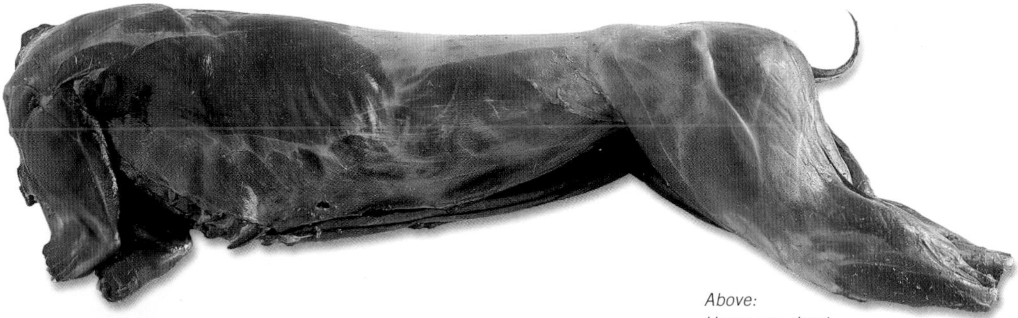

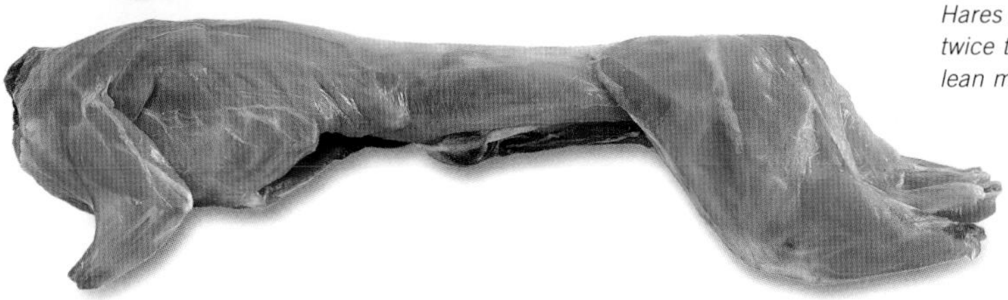

Above: Hares are about twice the size of rabbits and the dark, lean meat has a strong flavour.

Left: Rabbit is so common in Spain that the Romans named the country "rabbit land" – Hispania *– from which the modern name is derived.*

Cantabrian *cordillera*. Here, you can find all three types of deer: the *ciervo común*, the small *corzo* (roe deer), and the *gamo* (fallow deer). Venison (*venado*) is cooked in wine, roasted or grilled (broiled) and served with a creamy *Cabrales* sauce.

Hare

In Extremadura, hare (*liebre*) is served at engagement parties, the sauce finished with blood, sherry and brandy. It is also often cooked with chocolate. Sometimes it is cooked in the field, in a pot with charcoal on the lid, and accompanied by beans. *Morteruelo*, a pâté of mixed game meats pounded together, is a speciality of Cuenca on the edge of La Mancha.

Rabbit

There are rabbits (*conejos*) all across Spain – so many that the Spanish bred spaniels to chase them. Rabbits are often cooked with snails, which impart the flavour of rosemary, or wild thyme. A Navarran speciality is a pie whose pastry is aromatized by thyme and rosemary. In the south, saffron rice with rabbit is eaten in preference to paella. Rabbit is also cooked with vinegar and garlic (*salmorego*), giving rise to the proverb for a good match – *el salmorejo para el conejo.*

Gathering wild food

Hunters out with a gun and a dog often also collect wild mushrooms, herbs, grubs and snails in their knapsacks – for they are free food. Lizards are caught in Extremadura; the hunters tighten a small noose around the tail of the creature. The lizard's white flesh, which tastes like a cross between a young rabbit and a frog, is eaten in little pots with a tomato sauce. Frogs are a popular food, too, and the hind legs may be battered or fried.

There are many different snails that can be eaten, and they come in all sizes and many flavours. The great black *negros* and *moros* are best grilled (broiled) and eaten with vinegar. The most expensive are the prized Valencia *vaquetas de oliva*; grey and black with a flavour of wild rosemary, upon which they feed. They are commonly added to rice dishes such as paella. In Lérida there is the *caracol de viña* (the same as Burgundy's *petit gris* snail), while in Seville there is the small *caracol* (the generic word for a snail) and the larger *cabrilla*, which means chanterelle, with its pretty whorls of black and white.

Preparing snails

To make an appetizer for four people, you will need about 60 snails. They must be purged before cooking.

1 To purge the snails, put them in a bucket with a weighted lid. After 3 days sprinkle in flour, then leave for another 4 days.

2 The day before cooking, splash the snails with a little fresh water. Discard any that aren't moving. Clean the shells with salt and vinegar, then leave them for 30 minutes before rinsing under cold running water.

3 To cook, put the snails in a pan and cover with warm water, then bring slowly to the boil. Drain, then return to the pan and cover in fresh salted water and bring to the boil again, with a handful of herbs such as wild fennel or bruised parsley stalks. Cook for at least 30 minutes.

4 Drain the snails and add them to a spicy tomato sauce. Simmer for 30 minutes, then serve in individual earthenware dishes. To eat, put a pin into the end, and twist the shell anticlockwise (counterclockwise).

FRUIT AND DESSERTS

More often than not, dessert in Spain is simply a beautifully fragrant piece of fruit. There are only a few true desserts, but they are deeply traditional – and usually incredibly sweet.

FRUIT

Spain is blessed with a huge wealth of fruit. The apricot trees are the first to flower every spring. But it is apples (*manzanas*) that are grown across the country, especially Asturias, with *reinetas* (a Cox type) being a speciality. The orchards of Lérida and Navarra are red with *melocotones* (peaches).

Any Spaniard will boast of the date groves of Elche, of the plums (*ciruelas*) and pears (*peras*), and of the Valle de Jerte that is filled with cherries (*cerezas*). Dark *picota* cherries have no stalks. Quinces are made into a delicious orange paste, *membrillo*, which is often served with cheese.

Golden grapes (*uvas*) drape across houses in the south, and the coast from Alicante to Valencia is famous for fat, juicy muscats. They are dried in Málaga as huge black *pasas*. Red-fleshed figs grow wild in the southern scrub, while Granada gained its name from the pomegranate (*granada*). The orange "tomatoes", growing high on bare trees in December, are persimmons (*cakis*).

Below: Pasas de Málaga *are the huge, fat raisins made from muscat grapes.*

Above: Spain is renowned for its honeydew melons.

Left: Strawberries are an important Spanish crop.

Melons (*melones*) have been grown in Spain since the Roman times. The dark-skinned, white-fleshed honeydew melons (*piel de sapo*) are the most highly prized. Strawberries (*fresas*) are another success story. In times past, a train used to run from Madrid to Aranjuez in the summer, carrying picnickers out to the strawberry farms. Now, in Huelva, the strawberries are ripe by Christmas.

Below: Pomegranates are used to make drinks, sorbets and a sauce for chicken.

Citrus fruit

It was the Moors who first planted citrus trees in Spain. The bitter orange came from India in the 11th century, and the juice was squeezed over fish – and still is – in the way we now use lemons. Sweet oranges (*naranjas*) came from China and were planted across the country in the 1550s.

Valencia is the orange capital of Spain and oranges are picked from September to late spring. The small Valencia orange has now been replaced by the seedless Washington navel, and small clementines now represent a quarter of citrus exports. More lemons (*limones*) are grown in Murcia than in Valencia. The summer lemon is the *verna*, with thick peel and juicy flesh, and in winter it is the thin-skinned *fino*.

Tropical fruit

Microclimates allow passion fruit (*pasionara*), loquat (*níspero*) and the custard apple (*cherimoya*) to grow in the south, while in Galicia kiwi and feijoas are cultivated. The Canary Islands are known for a small, sweet banana and the pineapple (*piña*).

Above: Small Valencia oranges have a sweet, tangy, juicy flesh.

FRUIT DESSERTS

Peaches in syrup (*almibar*) are a favourite dessert in Spain, although peaches (or pears) baked whole in red wine are also very popular. Traditional desserts often feature preserved fruit and nuts and are made in winter. Dried figs go into *pan de alá*. The Galicians make superb *marrons glacées* as well as an excellent chestnut and chocolate mousse. They also like freshly roasted chestnuts in a glass of brandy. The Basque Christmas Eve *intxausalsa* is a creamy purée of walnuts.

In Aragón, the crystallized fruit are coated in chocolate. In Cáceres, they make tiny chocolate-coated figs that are out of this world.

MILK PUDDINGS

Custards reign supreme in Spain, and there is a great trio of desserts: *flan* (baked custard), *crema catalana* (crème brulée) and *tocino de cielo,* which is a baked caramel custard turned out and dark-topped. It looks like an uncut slab of pork, hence its name, which means blissful bacon. Custards (*natilla*) are traditionally made in convents, to sell outside. They may be piled high with *suspiros de mona* (poached meringue); the name means nun's sighs and it is said that the nuns making them sigh regretfully, "Would that I could eat them."

Rice found a sweet niche in the north. The Asturian milk pudding, *arroz con leche,* is flavoured with cinnamon or caramel. Fried custard squares (*leche frita*) are a Basque speciality, and further west pancakes (*filloas*) are popular, served with cream and liqueur. Sugared *flores manchegos* are cooked on special irons and are shaped like flowers. Junket (*cuajada*) and whipped cream (*nata*) are topped with nuts, and *mel y mato* is Catalan cream cheese with honey. Two good cheesecakes are the Santander *quesada,* made with fresh *pasiega,* and the Ibizan *flaó,* which is flavoured with mint.

ICES

The Moors in Granada used to send runners up the mountains to cut ice, even in summer, starting a tradition of *granizados* (grainy iced desserts), made with lemon and sweet fruit syrups (*jarabes*), and later with coffee. The popular frozen dessert today is *tarta helada quemada,* which has a crispy caramel topping.

ALMOND SWEETMEATS

The tradition of serving almond sweetmeats such as *alfajores* (almonds crushed to a paste with honey and wrapped in paper) started in the Moorish harems. *Mazapán* (marzipan) was invented in Toledo when the Moors, besieged by Alfonso VI, ran out of bread and turned to almonds instead. The city now sells little baked half moons of marzipan. *Figuritas de mazapán* are sold at Christmas and you will find them in many different shapes, including little fish, animals, bread shapes, and even miniature musical instruments.

Turrón (nougat) used to be seasonal too, but is now available all year round. In Jijona you can buy a soft almond and honey paste, and in Alicante one with whole marcona almonds embedded in it, while *torta imperiale,* sandwiched between layers of rice paper, is the best in Spain. *Almendras garapiñadas* (crunchy nuts tossed in sweet caramel) are sold at street fairs.

Left: Traditional Spanish sweetmeats date back to the Moorish traditions.

Honey

Spain specializes in single-flower honey – and there are a great many varieties due to the many mountains, herbs and flowering trees. Valencia is famous for rosemary, *azahar* (citrus blossom) and thyme honeys. Lavender and thyme honeys are produced in the hills behind Cordoba. *Miel de bosque,* from the blossom of Extrameduran oaks, is very dark. Alcarría D.O. is a famous honey centre in Guadalajarra.

Honey is traditionally served with fruit juice, or with almonds or figs, but it is also served with unusual savoury foods such as *bacalao* and *sobrasada* sausage.

BREAD AND CAKES

Bread is a very important part of the Spanish diet, while cakes and sweet buns are eaten less often than in other countries. Bread shops (*panaderias*) sell bread alone. Cakes and other sweet things are bought from a *pastelería*.

BREAD

As in many European countries, *pan* is Spain's basic food and taken very seriously. Not so long ago consumption was 1kg/2¼lb a head per day. In Galicia, if a piece of bread is dropped, it will be picked up and kissed. It plays a ritual part in weddings, anniversaries and death ceremonies.

Bread accompanies all meals in Spain. It is bought twice a day and eaten very fresh. The *barra* (long loaf) is better, some claim, than French bread. But there are a host of rolls with local names such as *bollas* (balls) and *chicas* (little girls).

Traditional breads

The wheat granary of Spain is the Tierra de Campos in León and south towards Zamora. Here they make the *hogaza* (large loaf) of Castile and the round, white *candeal* bread, which is a classic. In Catalonia, where everything tends to be done slightly differently, the bread is shaped like a three-corned hat, with slashes across the corners. (Salvador Dalí used them to decorate his house.) *Pan cateto* is sourdough bread with a close crumb and chewy crust (*cateto* means country bumpkin); it is dry but long lasting. Bread is also made with pork crackling in it.

Corn meal is used to make corn bread (*pan de maíz*) in Galicia; it is wrapped in leaves and baked overnight in the dying embers of the fire. *Borona* is made with both rye flour and corn meal. Galicians also use bread dough to make their flat two-crust pies, while *bollas preñadas* (pregnant buns) consist of dough folded round sausage meat.

Above: Pan de cebada *is a coarse-textured country bread from Galicia, which is exceptional for its barley flour.*

Cocas

Hot from the bread oven, *cocas* are a speciality of the Balearics and Levante. They resemble an Italian pizza but date back much further than that. Once they were just bread dough topped with sardines or salted meat, but today they are spread with tomato sauce, too, and scattered with onions, black olives and herbs. At festival time, there are sweet ones for sale, topped with glistening candied fruit. *Cocarois* are little pastries, folded over with a filling of meat or vegetables.

Using bread

Bread is used in a variety of ways, both in the kitchen and at the table.

Mojado The bread used to scoop up sauced vegetables and seafood tapas.

Rebanada A slice of bread, which is used as a "polite" plate mop at the end of a course.

Pa amb tomàquet Very lightly toasted bread, topped with olive oil and squashed fresh tomato. It is eaten at the start of every meal in Catalonia.

Torrijas These are bread dipped in milk or wine, then fried and sugared.

Migas Breadcrumbs fried in olive oil and a food for all occasions, for every meal and with almost everything. They can be eaten for breakfast after a night on the town, with bacon and eggs; or with fresh fruit as dessert; even with chocolate and sardines – together.

Sobras Yesterday's stale bread is ideal for frying, before being pounded and used to thicken sauces and soups.

Sopa Stale pieces of bread were once common breakfast fare, dunked in coffee, milk and sugar, and eaten with a spoon.

Jam

The best jam is *cabello de angél* (angel's hair) made from the citron melon (*cidra*) which is large and blotched dark green. Jam is used to fill sweet *empanadillas* and cakes, or spread on bread.

FRITTERS

Dulces de sartén (frying-pan sweets) are the Spanish doughnut, sold on the streets at fairs and in tapas bars. Delicately flavoured with crushed aniseed, and steeped in honey or anis syrup, they betray their Moorish past. *Borrachuelos* are "drunk" on their syrup. Many of them are made in the same way as choux pastry, by beating flour and egg (with wine) in a pan. They may be baked or fried, both of which causes the pastry to puff up.

Plain *empanadillas* (pies) are rolled out with a special rolling pin to stripe the pastry, then sugared; others are filled with angel's hair jam. *Pestiños* (honey-coated fritters) are often hollow – a square folded with opposite corners meeting – to soak up more syrup. *Huesos de santos* (saints' bones) are hollow too, sometimes made of potato dough or almond pastry. *Buñuelos de viento* (*bunyols* in Catalan) are choux puffs, which are eaten on All Saints' Day and at Christmas.

BISCUITS AND COOKIES

Small dry cakes are served with sweet liqueurs, and are often dunked into them. Rings (*rosquillos*) are very common. Many little cookies are made from cinnamon pastry. Others have delightfully descriptive names. S-shaped *mostachones* look like a moustache when two of the cookies are held together; *polverones* (crumble cakes) have a powdery texture. *Mantecados*, which are famous in Old Castile, are lardy cookies containing ground almonds. *Macarrones* (macaroons) are made with whisked egg whites and ground almonds, while *almendrados*, made with almonds, and *almori* (honey cakes) reflect the Moorish influence. Moors' sighs (*suspiros de Moros*) are ground almond meringues.

Nuns are traditionally bakers in Old Castile and the south. The nuns of San Leandro in Seville make *yemas* (yolks), whose name describes their colour, shape and content.

Below: Small, dry rosquillos, *made from a wine pastry, are found all over Spain.*

Above: Sobaos pasiegas, from the dairy valley of Pas, are made with butter.

LITTLE CAKES AND BUNS

Breakfast is the occasion for some real treats. The melting pastry of Majorcan *ensaimada*, curled like a turban, is also a favourite in Madrid. *Sobaos pasiegas* are rich butter sponges baked in little individual rectangles in papers.

Pan quemado is an all-day Valencian snack. The name means burnt bread, because it is brushed with meringue and sugar before baking, to give it a dark golden crust. For tea time in Madrid, custard-filled puff pastry *bartillos* are eaten. *Medias noches* (midnight buns) are worth sneaking down for at night.

Above: Small, soft bread rolls are good at any time of day.

CAKES

Sponge cakes, made with egg whites only, are light and airy and perfect for soaking up syrups and brandies – as is the tradition in Spain. *Brazo de gitano* (gypsy's arm) is the best-known cake – long and brown and rolled up round *cremadina* (custard). The big traditional cake is *Roscón de Reyes*, an enriched bread-dough ring made for Twelfth Night. It is generously topped with almonds and candied fruit, of which there seems to be more every year.

Below: Simple little magdalenas *(butter cakes) make a delightful treat.*

WINE

There are two great wine styles that are particular to Spain – Rioja and sherry. In Rioja, red wine (but also some white wine) is aged in oak casks, which gives it a light aroma of vanilla. Sherry is a highly sophisticated fortified white wine, and classed with the world's great wines. In Spain, it is drunk as a wine, not just as an aperitif as it is elsewhere.

Spain's viticulture is the largest in the world, and is undergoing a rapid modernization programme. Once behind other countries in technology, Spain's expenditure on modern equipment is resulting in better wines all the time.

Spanish wine drinking is not a very complicated matter. There are no rules about matching food and drink and the Spanish enjoy young wines as well as those that have been aged in oak casks in the traditional way.

RED WINE

Much of Spain's wine is red, with top quality wine produced on the northern rivers and hefty reds with a high alcohol content further south.

Wines on the Ebro river

These are the Riojas; they are soft but not delicate, with a fruity taste. They are blended wines, and some wine firms grow no grapes themselves. Good wines are matured partly in casks, partly in the bottle, which gives an opportunity for a "house taste". Popular brands are San Ascensio made by Campo Viejo, the biggest *bodega* (wine firm) in Rioja, CUNE and Banda Azul (Blue Stripe) from top exporter Frederick Paternina.

At the expensive end, two traditional houses, Marqués de Murrieta and Marqués de Riscal make big-bodied, oaky reds. With them a newer house in the same style, Marqués de Muga, makes up "the three mighty Ms" of Rioja. However, many modern *bodegas* favour time maturing in the bottle (not the cask), for example Marqués de Cáceres, Lagunilla and the big exporter Faustino Martínez.

Vintages are important here, as grapes may not always ripen to full potential. There are three regions of Rioja, each with its own distinct style, which will also give clues as to what you are buying. Rioja Baja is low-lying, producing everyday fruity wines. The high Rioja Alta produces wines with more tannin, making them hard and acidic if young, but maturing to a more complex taste. The Rioja Alavesa makes softer, aromatic wines. Part of this region is in Navarra, on the other side of the river, which has a good line in young reds, not unlike Beaujolais.

Right: Campo Viejo is one of the biggest Rioja-producing wine firms in Spain.

Wines on the Duero river

Ribera del Duero produces Vega Sicilia, Spain's masterpiece, which is, unfortunately, almost unobtainable. Based on Cabernet Sauvignon, it is aged in casks for ten years or so, and is often 16 years old when sold. Pesquera del Duero is the affordable alternative.

Central Spain

Valdepeñas produces better-quality reds than La Mancha which surrounds it. Huge *tinajas* (unglazed urns) stand at the roadsides and are used for wine. Here they make *aloques*, strong but light red wines, and *claretes*, not claret but a wine of mixed red and white grapes.

The red grapes

Tempranillo is Spain's principal red grape (*Ull de Llebre* in Catalonia). Used on its own, it makes good, berry-scented young wines, but about 70 per cent of the crop goes into the great Riojas, chiefly supported by the garnacha grape.

Spain's quest for better grapes has been hampered by old D.O. (*Denominación de Origen*) restrictions. However, new grapes and irrigation, which have been introduced increasingly since the 1960s, have helped to improve quality. Landmarks are the Raimat estate in Costers del Segre, while Jean León introduced Cabernet Sauvignon to Penedès. The palm of honour, however, goes to

The language of wine

Drinking wine is part of Spanish culture and has its own terms.

Vino de la mesa This is the house wine, usually in *una jarra* (a jug or pitcher). *Una media* is a 500ml/17fl oz/2¼ cup measure.

Vino corriente This is table wine in its first or second year.

Crianza These wines must be stored for two years after harvest (*cosecha*). For the first six months the wine is stored in casks, whose oak gives the wine its distinctive flavour. Better quality wines may be held back before they are sold. However, you should beware of five- to six-year-old wines because they may have developed a very oxidized, stale taste.

Reserva This means that the wine has been matured for three years. For whites and *rosados* (rosé) wines, this means they are in the cask for six months; for reds, this means at least a year, often much more, plus a year in the bottle. Both modest regional wines and good brands carry this label.

Gran reserva This includes much of the best wine, which is only made in fine vintage years or from the best grapes. Cellar-aged for six years, they have at least two years in the cask and three in the bottle – and are splendid value for the quality of wine offered.

Viña This means vineyard, but is a brand not a place. There are few estate-bottled wines.

two generations of the Torres family in Penedès, who produce splendid new wines (white, pink and red) with fabulous wines such as Gran Coronas' Black Label, Mas la Plana.

Vast acres of Spain are under vines. La Mancha, with half the vineyards in Spain, produces red wine mainly from the *monastrell* grape. Poor Aragón makes purplish reds, often 15 per cent by volume, because the sun raises alcohol content at the same time as it diminishes quality. Cariñena and Borja in the south-east, and Alicante, Jumilla and Yecla nearer the coast all make hefty reds. Priorato may be Spain's answer to Burgundy. Lighter reds come from Utiel-Requeña and Somontana in the north-east.

PINK WINE

The *rosados* (rosé wines) of Navarra such as Gran Feudo are justly famous, and good ones are made in Aragón, Ribera del Duero, Tarragona and Utiel-Requeña. The cherry-coloured wines, a speciality of Ampurdán, are very good.

WHITE WINE

Good whites are produced on Spain's fringes – north and east – with the masterpiece, sherry, in the south.

Green wine

The *Alberiño* grape produces German-style wines on the slopes of Rías Bajas and Ribera del Duero. Delicately fruity, they give a slight prickle in the mouth and are perfect with shellfish.

Chacoli

The Basques are proud of this wine which they call *txacoli*. It is thin, rather acidic, appley and slightly sparkling.

Rioja whites

White wine is made with the traditional *viura* grape, usually without being aged in the cask. Marqués de Cáceres is a good example of the type. CUNE's Monopole *blanco* is balanced between the two styles, while good oaked examples come from Marqués de Murrieta, Monte Real from Bodegas Riojanas and López de Heredía.

French-style whites

Lighter, fruitier and less alcoholic wines are in demand today, so styles are changing accordingly. New technology is also helping to improve white wines. Typical ones are Antonio Barbadillo in Huelva and Palacio de Bornos, made from the *verdejo* grape, in Rueda.

Whites are a tradition on the north-east coast, with French grapes making French-style wines in the cooler hills. Delicate young whites come from Marqués de Alella just outside Barcelona. Torres makes Viña Sol, which is fresh and slightly lemony (from the Spanish *parellada* grape), Gran Viña Sol (half Chardonnay), or the estate-bottled version, green label, which is matured in oak. Torres' Milmanda is the top Chardonnay in Spain.

South-west Spain

The white wines in the south-west have a strong resemblance to sherry and include *cañamero* and *chiclana*. Most famous, however, is Montilla-Moriles, which has the same nutty scent as sherry, though it is made by conventional methods. Alvear is well-known, especially C.B. (the proprietor's initials), which is the white for cooking.

Sparkling wines

Cavas are wines made by the champagne method in Penedès (although the grapes may come from elsewhere), mainly in San Sadurní de Nova. Codorníu is the largest champagne-style wine producer in the world. Their lovely top-of-the-range wine is the Chardonnay *cava*. Raimat is a good alternative, or Freixenet *cordon negro*, in the black bottle. The Spanish favour sweet *champáns* so do look for "brut" on the label.

Right: Freixenet Cordon Negro is a good quality cava *with a lovely flavour.*

Sherry styles

Fino This is the lightest and driest sherry. It is a pale straw colour.

Manzanilla Meaning camomile, this is similar to *fino*, but has a tang aquired as a result of being stored by the sea.

Amontillado This is matured until it is a soft, dark tawny colour.

Palo cortado This is sweeter still.

Oloroso With more body and a nutty flavour, *olorosos*, as a class, are on the sweet side, sometimes reminiscent of port, but they are also made in dry styles.

Cream sherry This has sweet Pedro Ximénes juice added, which gives it a voluptuous flavour.

Sherry

The name sherry is actually a mispronounciation of the place Jerez de la Frontera. Jerez de la Frontera produces exceptional fortified wines, mainly from the *Palomino* grape, and is one of the few places in Spain with a long tradition of fine wines. Because of its high alcohol content (17 per cent by volume) and the way it is made, it is regarded as an aperitif by the outside world. But in Spain it is a white wine, the natural choice for fish, or a flamenco evening, drunk chilled from the tulip-shaped *copita*, which is never more than two-thirds full. Sherry is made in a *solera* system, a tier of barrels, where the bottom barrels are tapped and the upper barrels are made up with younger wine. The sherry is fortified with brandy, then exposed to air in the cask, where a yeast *flor* grows on the surface to protect it. Darker sherries have oxidized more. Among the great names are Tio Pepe, Barbadillo and Domecq's La Ina.

ALCOHOLIC AND OTHER DRINKS

The Spanish are immensely social, and can match any occasion throughout the day with the perfect drink.

SWEET AND FORTIFIED WINES

The scented muscat grape gives its name to many sweet wines including the *moscatels* of Alicante and Valencia and Málaga *Virgen*. The *Malvasía* grape is used to make a honeyed wine of the same name. Pedro Ximénes is made into luscious dessert wines. *Vino de lágrima* is made from very ripe grapes.

Dry or sweet fortified wine (*generoso*) can be enjoyed before or after dinner, as can the mellowed *rancio*. Tarragona is known for the 20-year-old copper-coloured Fondillón.

BRANDY

Coñac is very popular. (Some people even enjoy it with coffee for breakfast.) The Spanish prefer brandies that are caramelized with added syrup and perfume such as Soberano. Magno and Veterano are big medium-priced sellers, while Carlos III (*te-thero*) is more elegant. Catalonia has always produced brandies that are closer to cognac such as Mascaró and Torres' Black label.

Below: The top quality brandy Lepanto is sold in a decanter-shaped bottle.

Above: The light Valencia moscatel *is widely available abroad.*

SPIRITS AND LIQUEURS

Aguardiente is any distilled liquor, often colourless. In the north, the dark *orujo* is a rough, strong brandy, made from grape skins. *Anís* is the true taste of Spain, and there are both dry and *dulce* (sweet) varieties. Aniseed-flavoured and colourless, the famous brands are Anís de Mono and Chinchón. *Dulce* is served neat in liqueur glasses or combined in mixtures such as *sol y sombra* (anís with brandy). *Pacharán* (sloe brandy), such as Zoco, is the top generic liqueur and is drunk on the rocks.

Both gin and rum are popular. Gin is made by the huge firm Larios in the south, while a grape gin is made in Menorca by Xoviguer. Bacardi is made under licence, but there is also brown *ron*. They are drunk short over ice, with mixers, or soda and lemon. *Cubalibre* is rum and coke, poured 50:50.

Above: Anís de Mono comes in a very distinctive cut glass bottle.

Herb liqueurs

Hierbas are popular throughout Spain. Those made in Ibiza are really strong – like the dangerous green absinthe – and should be mixed with ice and water. *Izarra*, meaning star, is the Basque green liqueur, made with 48 herb flowers and plants. It is served chilled in short glasses. *Ponche*, meaning punch, is a sweet, herbalized old brandy that comes in a silver bottle; Cabellero and De Soto are well-known varieties. *Ratafias* are liqueurs flavoured with almonds and are particularly popular in Navarra and Aragón.

In this land of liqueurs there are many more to choose from. Chartreuse is made in Tarragona, for it became the home of monks when they were expelled from France. The golden Calisay is quinine-based, while vanilla is included in Liquor 43 (*Cuarenta y tres*).

Right: Liquor 43 is a brandy-based liqueur with an infusion of forty-three different herbs.

CIDER AND BEER

In the north of Spain, cider (*sidra)* replaces wine as the drink of choice. Strongly alcoholic, it is drunk in *sidrerías* with its own rituals. Guests are not permitted to pour their own *sidra*. The bottle is held high in one hand, the tumbler low in the other, and the cider is poured in a great arc, to aerate it.

Spanish-style beer, *cerveza*, is light and refreshing – well suited to the climate. *Un caño* is beer from the pump. Well-known brands include San Miguel, Aguila and Victoria, which are all pilsner types. Cruz Campo is Seville's best beer, and Majou is the best bitter.

Below: San Miguel is one of the most popular summer beers in Spain.

SUMMER DRINKS

Refrescos are cool, non-alcoholic drinks. The big names in bottled water, *con gas* or *sin gas* (sparkling or still) are Solares, Font Vella and Lanjarón. Vichy Catalan is the leading sparkling water. Spanish lemonades (*gaseoso*) are fizzy and very sweet. Freshly squeezed juice (*zumo*) is available in bars, while the brand Rives produces colourful fruit syrups for diluting, including bright red *granadina* (pomegranate).

Tinto de verano is the beach drink, made with half red wine and half lemonade. More elegant, chilled *horchata* is made from tiger nuts (*chufas*), which grow in the Moorish-owned fine black sand round Alboraya in Valencia. The nuts are ground, diluted with water and sweetened with honey. Good shops such as Santa Catalina in Valencia, make it fresh every day.

Finally, *leche merenguada* is made with half milk and half cream. It is flavoured with cinnamon and lemon, and made light with whisked egg whites – rather like an ice cream.

TEA, CHOCOLATE AND COFFEE

Teas are known as *infusiones*, but hot *te con limón* is less popular than the many herb teas that are available. Camomile (*manzanilla*) is the firm favourite. Other popular flavourings are mint (*poleomenta*), lime (linden) flowers (*tila*) and lemon verbena *(hierba luisa)*.

Chocolate came from America, but acquired its connection with cinnamon in Spain. Louis XIV's Spanish bride took to it with her to France as a breakfast drink. Today, there are still traditional bars dedicated to serving chocolate in Seville. It is sold as a powder or in tablet form with thickener added.

The national passion is for coffee, which is always made the same way – dark and strong. In former days breakfast coffee was poured over bread in a bowl, then hot milk and sugar were added before it was eaten.

Sangría

There are many variations of this classic, refreshing mixture of iced wine and citrus juice.

MAKES ABOUT 2 LITRES/ 4 PINTS

INGREDIENTS

- 2 pared lemon rind strips
- juice of 2 lemons
- juice of 4 oranges
- 30ml/2 tbsp caster (superfine) sugar
- 1 litre/1¾ pints/4 cups red wine, chilled
- 750ml/1¼ pints/3 cups soda water, chilled
- ice cubes

1 Put the lemon rind, fruit juice and sugar in a large jug and chill.

2 To serve, pour the wine, soda water and ice cubes into the jug. Stir, then pour into tall glasses.

A nice cup of coffee

Coffee in Spain is always freshly made and there are many ways to drink it.

Café con leche A mellow coffee drunk at breakfast. It is made with its own volume of hot milk.

Café solo Black coffee.

Un cortado A *demi-tasse*, with room for a little bit of milk.

Café helado This iced coffee is made by pouring hot coffee into a tumbler of ice cubes.

Un blanco y negro A glass of milky iced coffee, heavily scented with cinnamon, and drunk through a straw.

Batido de café A cold coffee milkshake.

Mazagrán Iced coffee with rum.

El carajillo Coffee with brandy.

Un cremàt Brandy or rum flamed with coffee. (*Cremàt* is the Catalan word for burnt.)

TAPAS

In Spain, the motto is "eat when you drink, drink when you eat" – and tapas would seem to have been invented for just this. Tapas are finger food, a choice of delicious morsels to tempt the drinker to have another glass and with it another tapas dish. They range from simple dishes of olives and nuts to richly flavoured shellfish, marinated fish and titbits on skewers.

Olive and Anchovy Bites

These little melt-in-the-mouth morsels are made from two ingredients that are forever associated with tapas – olives and anchovies. The reason for this is that both contain salt, which helps to stimulate thirst and therefore drinking.

MAKES FORTY TO FORTY-FIVE

INGREDIENTS

- 115g/4oz/1 cup plain (all-purpose) flour
- 115g/4oz/½ cup chilled butter, diced
- 115g/4oz/1 cup finely grated Manchego, mature (sharp) Cheddar or Gruyère cheese
- 50g/2oz can anchovy fillets in oil, drained and roughly chopped
- 50g/2oz/½ cup pitted black olives, roughly chopped
- 2.5ml/½ tsp cayenne pepper
- sea salt, to serve

1 Place the flour, butter, cheese, anchovies, olives and cayenne pepper in a food processor and pulse until the mixture forms a firm dough.

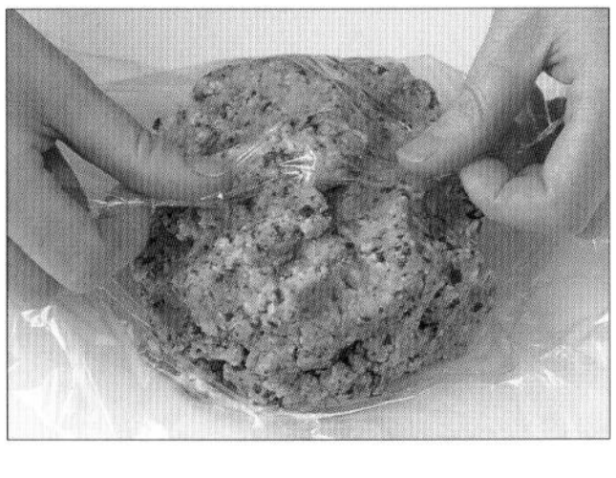

2 Wrap the dough loosely in clear film (plastic wrap). Chill for 20 minutes.

3 Preheat the oven to 200°C/400°F/Gas 6. Roll out the dough thinly on a lightly floured surface.

4 Cut the dough into 5cm/2in wide strips, then cut across each strip in alternate directions, to make triangles. Transfer to baking sheets and bake for 8–10 minutes until golden. Cool on a wire rack. Sprinkle with sea salt.

VARIATIONS

- To add a little extra spice, dust the olive and anchovy bites lightly with cayenne pepper before baking.
- Crisp little nibbles set off most drinks. Serve these bites alongside little bowls of seeds and nuts such as sunflower seeds and pistachios. These come in the shell, the opening of which provides a diversion while gossiping. Toasted chickpeas are another popular tapas snack.

Energy 41Kcal/171kJ; Protein 1.2g; Carbohydrate 1.9g, of which sugars 0.1g; Fat 3.2g, of which saturates 1.9g; Cholesterol 9mg; Calcium 27mg; Fibre 0.1g; Sodium 103mg.

SWEET AND SALTY VEGETABLE CRISPS

THE SPANISH LOVE NEW AND COLOURFUL SNACKS. TRY THESE BRIGHTLY COLOURED CRISPS, WHICH MAKE AN APPEALING ALTERNATIVE TO POTATO CRISPS. SERVE THEM WITH A BOWL OF CREAMY, GARLICKY ALLIOLI, AND USE THE CRISPS TO SCOOP IT UP.

SERVES FOUR

INGREDIENTS
- 1 small fresh beetroot (beet)
- caster (superfine) sugar and fine salt, for sprinkling
- olive oil, for frying
- coarse sea salt, to serve

COOK'S TIP

Beetroot crisps are particularly flavoursome, but other naturally sweet root vegetables, such as carrots and sweet potato, also taste delicious when cooked in this way. You might like to make several different varieties and serve them heaped in separate small bowls.

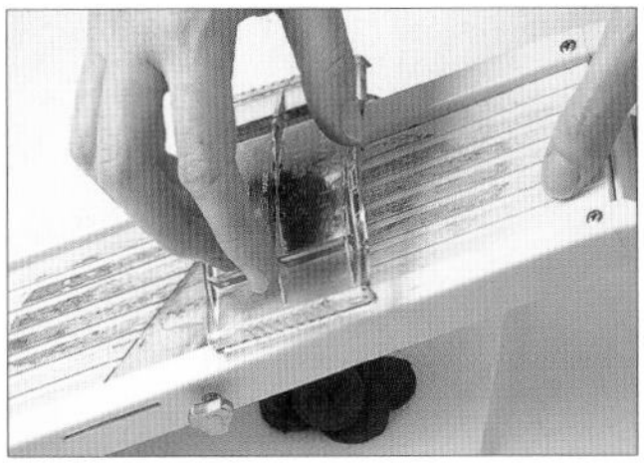

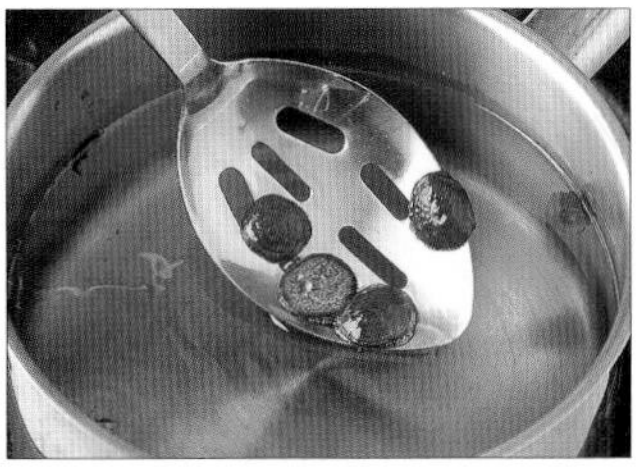

1 Peel the beetroot and, using a mandolin or a vegetable peeler, cut it into very thin slices.

2 Lay the slices on kitchen paper and sprinkle them with sugar and fine salt.

3 Heat 5cm/2in oil in a deep pan until a bread cube turns golden in 1 minute. Cook the slices in batches, until they float to the surface and turn golden at the edge. Drain on kitchen paper and sprinkle with sea salt when cool.

Energy 113Kcal/466kJ; Protein 0.4g; Carbohydrate 3.2g, of which sugars 3.1g; Fat 11g, of which saturates 1.6g; Cholesterol 0mg; Calcium 6mg; Fibre 0.5g; Sodium 508mg.

TAPAS OF ALMONDS, OLIVES AND CHEESE

ALMONDS AND OLIVES USED TO BE SERVED FREE IN ALL TAPAS BARS, AND STILL ARE IN SOME. THEY ARE THE PERFECT NIBBLE OR CASUAL STARTER FOR PRE-DINNER DRINKS. MANCHEGO CHEESE IN OIL IS NOW A DELICIOUS SPANISH EXPORT, ALTHOUGH YOU CAN EASILY MARINATE THE CHEESE YOURSELF.

SERVES SIX TO EIGHT

INGREDIENTS

For the marinated olives

- 2.5ml/½ tsp coriander seeds
- 2.5ml/½ tsp fennel seeds
- 2 garlic cloves, crushed
- 5ml/1 tsp chopped fresh rosemary
- 10ml/2 tsp chopped fresh parsley
- 15ml/1 tbsp sherry vinegar
- 30ml/2 tbsp olive oil
- 115g/4oz/⅔ cup black olives
- 115g/4oz/⅔ cup green olives

For the marinated cheese

- 150g/5oz Manchego or other firm cheese
- 90ml/6 tbsp olive oil
- 15ml/1 tbsp white wine vinegar
- 5ml/1 tsp black peppercorns
- 1 garlic clove, sliced
- fresh thyme or tarragon sprigs
- fresh flat leaf parsley or tarragon sprigs, to garnish (optional)

For the salted almonds

- 1.5ml/¼ tsp cayenne pepper
- 30ml/2 tbsp sea salt
- 25g/1oz/2 tbsp butter
- 60ml/4 tbsp olive oil
- 200g/7oz/1¾ cups blanched almonds
- extra salt for sprinkling (optional)

1 To make the marinated olives, crush the coriander and fennel seeds in a mortar with a pestle. Work in the garlic, then add the rosemary, parsley, vinegar and olive oil. Put the olives in a small bowl and pour over the marinade. Cover with clear film (plastic wrap) and chill for up to 1 week.

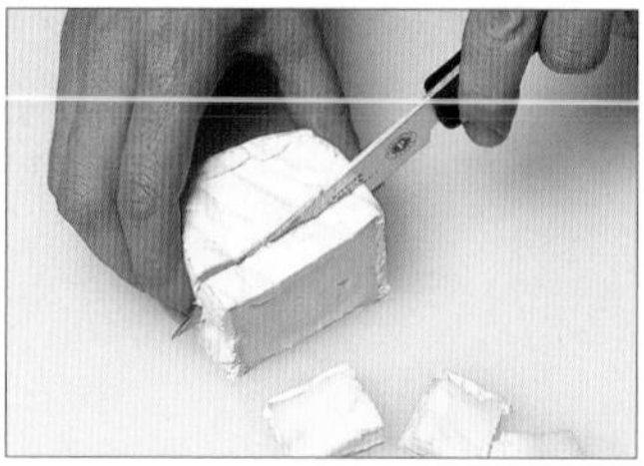

2 To make the marinated cheese, cut the cheese into bitesize pieces, removing any hard rind, and put in a small bowl. Combine the oil, vinegar, peppercorns, garlic, thyme or tarragon and pour over the cheese. Cover with clear film and chill for up to 3 days.

3 To make the salted almonds, combine the cayenne pepper and salt in a bowl. Melt the butter with the oil in a frying pan. Add the almonds and fry them, stirring for 5 minutes, or until golden.

4 Tip the almonds into the salt mixture and toss until the almonds are coated. Leave to cool, then store in an airtight container for up to 1 week.

5 To serve, arrange the almonds, olives and cheese in three separate small, shallow dishes. Garnish the cheese with fresh herbs if you like and scatter the almonds with a little more salt, to taste. Provide cocktail sticks (toothpicks) for guests to pick up the cheese and olives with.

COOK'S TIPS

- Whole olives, sold with the stone, invariably taste better than pitted ones. Don't serve them directly from the brine, but drain and rinse them, then pat dry with kitchen paper. Put the olives in a jar and pour over extra virgin olive oil to cover. Seal and store in the refrigerator for 1–2 months; the flavour of the olives will become enriched. Serve the olives as a tapas dish, or add to salads. When the olives have been eaten, the fruity oil can be used as a dressing for hot food, or made into flavoursome salad dressings.
- A number of exotic stuffed olives are exported from Spain and are widely available in most large supermarkets. Popular varieties include pimiento-stuffed olives, which have been in existence for more than half a century, olives stuffed with salted anchovies, and olives filled with roast garlic.

Energy 436Kcal/1798kJ; Protein 10.3g; Carbohydrate 1.8g, of which sugars 1.1g; Fat 42.7g, of which saturates 9.7g; Cholesterol 25mg; Calcium 217mg; Fibre 2.7g; Sodium 1051mg.

Buñuelos

The name of these cheese puffs literally means puffball. In Spain, they are usually deep-fried but baking is easier and gives wonderful results. The dough is made in the same way as French choux pastry, and the buñuelos should be eaten within a few hours of baking.

SERVES FOUR

INGREDIENTS

- 50g/2oz/¼ cup butter, diced
- 1.5ml/¼ tsp salt
- 250ml/8fl oz/1 cup water
- 115g/4oz/1 cup plain (all-purpose) flour
- 2 whole eggs, plus 1 yolk
- 2.5ml/½ tsp Dijon mustard
- 2.5ml/½ tsp cayenne pepper
- 50g/2oz/½ cup finely grated Manchego or Cheddar cheese

1 Preheat the oven to 220°C/425°F/Gas 7. Place butter and the salt in a pan, then add the water. Bring the liquid to the boil. Meanwhile, sift the flour on to a sheet of baking parchment or greaseproof (waxed) paper.

2 Working quickly, tip the flour into the pan of boiling liquid in one go and stir it in immediately.

3 Beat the mixture vigorously with a wooden spoon until it forms a thick paste that binds together and leaves the sides of the pan clean. Remove the pan from the heat.

4 Gradually beat the eggs and yolk into the mixture, then add the mustard, cayenne pepper and cheese. Place teaspoonfuls of mixture on a non-stick baking sheet and bake for 10 minutes.

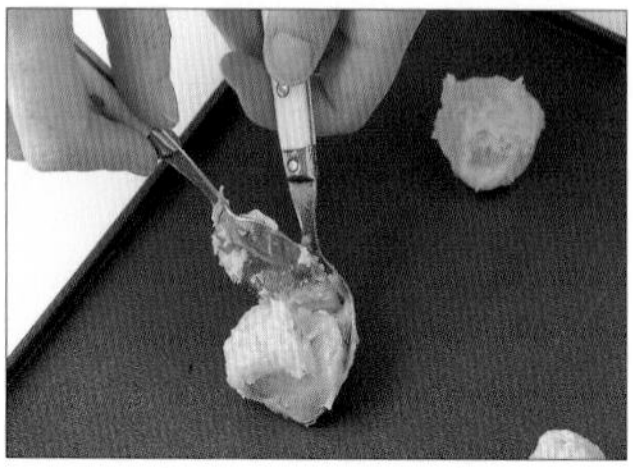

5 Reduce the temperature to 180°C/350°F/Gas 4 and cook for a further 15 minutes until well browned. Serve hot or cool on a wire rack.

Chicharrones

The Spanish eat everything that comes from the pig, and even the humble rind goes to make this delicious little salted, piquant snack. This crispy, crunchy pork crackling is the perfect accompaniment for a glass of wine or chilled bottle of San Miguel.

SERVES FOUR

INGREDIENTS

- 115g/4oz pork rind
- vegetable oil, for frying
- paprika and coarse sea salt, for sprinkling

COOK'S TIPS

- Make these cracklings spicier, if you wish. Paprika is the pepper of Spain, and any kitchen may well have one sweet variety (our common paprika), as well as one smoked and one hot – hot chilli powder, cayenne and Tabasco sauce can all be substituted.
- Strips of streaky (fatty) belly can be used instead of pork rind. Cut the strips into the same lengths, removing any bones. Cook them until all the fat has run out, and they look like crisp honeycombs. These tasty morsels are known as *torreznos*.

1 Using a sharp knife, cut the pork rind into strips. There is no need to be too precise, but try to make the strips roughly 1cm/½in wide and 2.5cm/1in long.

2 Pour the vegetable oil to a depth of 2.5cm/1in in a deep heavy frying pan. Heat the oil and check that it has reached the correct temperature by immersing a cube of bread, which should brown in 1 minute.

3 Cook the strips of rind in the oil for 1–2 minutes, until they are puffed up and golden brown. Remove with a slotted spoon and drain on kitchen paper.

4 Sprinkle the chicharrones with paprika and salt to taste. Serve them hot or cold. Although they are at their best 1–2 days after cooking, they will keep reasonably well for up to 2 weeks in an airtight container.

TOP Energy 295Kcal/1231kJ; Protein 9.8g; Carbohydrate 22.4g, of which sugars 0.5g; Fat 18.9g, of which saturates 10.5g; Cholesterol 184mg; Calcium 155mg; Fibre 0.9g; Sodium 204mg.
BOTTOM Energy 178Kcal/735kJ; Protein 4.6g; Carbohydrate 0g, of which sugars 0g; Fat 17.8g, of which saturates 3.7g; Cholesterol 19mg; Calcium 2mg; Fibre 0g; Sodium 362mg.

PIMIENTO TARTLETS

Known as TARTALITAS DE PIMIENTO *in Spain, these pretty little tartlets are filled with strips of roasted sweet peppers and a deliciously creamy, cheesy custard. They make the perfect snack to serve with drinks.*

SERVES FOUR

INGREDIENTS

- 1 red (bell) pepper
- 1 yellow (bell) pepper
- 175g/6oz/1½ cups plain (all-purpose) flour
- 75g/3oz/6 tbsp chilled butter, diced
- 30–45ml/2–3 tbsp cold water
- 60ml/4 tbsp double (heavy) cream
- 1 egg
- 15ml/1 tbsp grated fresh Parmesan cheese
- salt and ground black pepper

VARIATION

Use strips of grilled aubergine (eggplant) mixed with sun-dried tomatoes in place of the roasted peppers.

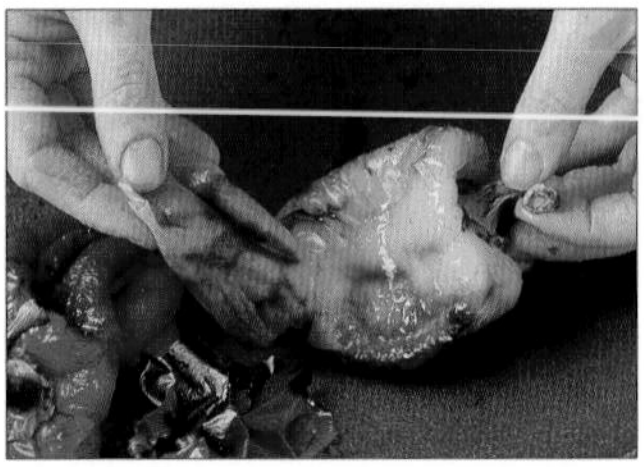

1 Preheat the oven to 200°C/400°F/ Gas 6, and heat the grill (broiler). Place the peppers on a baking sheet and grill for 10 minutes, turning occasionally, until blackened. Cover with a dishtowel and leave for 5 minutes. Peel away the skin, then discard the seeds and cut the flesh into very thin strips.

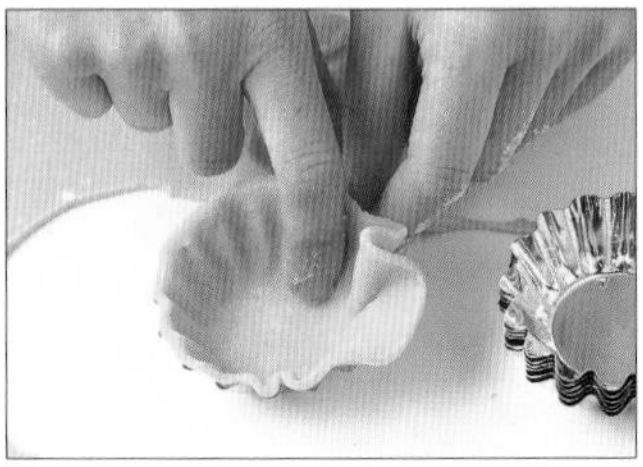

2 Sift the flour and a pinch of salt into a bowl. Add the butter and rub it in until the mixture resembles fine breadcrumbs. Stir in enough of the water to make a firm, not sticky, dough.

3 Roll the dough out thinly on a lightly floured surface and line 12 individual moulds or a 12-hole tartlet tin (muffin pan). Prick the bases with a fork and fill the pastry cases with crumpled foil. Bake for 10 minutes.

4 Remove the foil from the pastry cases and divide the pepper strips among the pastry cases.

5 Whisk the cream and egg in a bowl. Season well and pour over the peppers. Sprinkle each tartlet with Parmesan cheese and bake for 15–20 minutes until firm. Cool for 2 minutes, then remove from the moulds and transfer to a wire rack. Serve warm or cold.

Energy 427Kcal/1778kJ; Protein 8.4g; Carbohydrate 40g, of which sugars 6.4g; Fat 27g, of which saturates 16.1g; Cholesterol 112mg; Calcium 131mg; Fibre 2.8g; Sodium 180mg.

SPINACH EMPANADILLAS

LITTLE PIES ARE PART OF THE MOORISH TRADITION IN SPAIN. THE ARABS FIRST BROUGHT SPINACH TO EUROPE AND PINE NUTS AND RAISINS ARE TYPICAL ARAB FLAVOURINGS. IN SPAIN THE DOUGH FOR THESE PASTRIES IS SOLD READY-CUT INTO ROUNDS, AND THEY ARE DEEP-FRIED.

MAKES TWENTY

INGREDIENTS

- 25g/1oz/¼ cup raisins
- 25ml/1½ tbsp olive oil
- 450g/1lb fresh spinach leaves, washed, drained and chopped
- 6 canned anchovies, drained and chopped
- 2 garlic cloves, finely chopped
- 25g/1oz/¼ cup pine nuts, roughly chopped
- 1 egg, beaten
- 350g/12oz puff pastry
- salt and ground black pepper

1 To make the filling, soak the raisins in a little warm water for 10 minutes. Drain well, then chop roughly.

2 Heat the olive oil in a large pan, add the spinach, stir, then cover and cook over a low heat for about 2 minutes until the spinach starts to wilt. Remove the lid, turn up the heat and cook until any liquid has evaporated.

3 Add the chopped anchovies, garlic and seasoning to the spinach and cook, stirring, for about 1 minute.

4 Remove the pan from the heat, then stir in the soaked raisins and pine nuts, and set aside to cool.

5 Meanwhile, preheat the oven to 180°C/350°F/Gas 4. Roll out the pastry on a lightly floured surface to a 3mm/⅛in thickness.

6 Using a 7.5cm/3in pastry cutter, cut the pastry into 20 rounds, re-rolling any scraps if necessary. Place about 10ml/2 tsp filling in the middle of each round, then brush the edges with a little water.

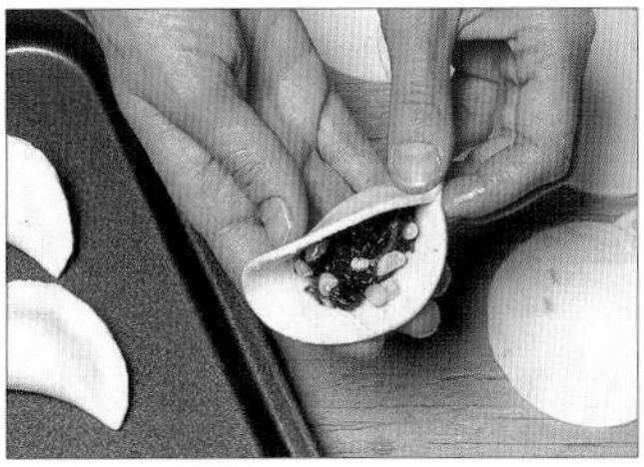

7 Bring up the sides of the pastry and seal well. Press the edges together with the back of a fork. Brush with egg.

8 Place the pies, slightly apart, on a lightly greased baking sheet and bake for about 15 minutes, until puffed up and golden brown.

9 Transfer the pies to a wire rack to cool. They are best served while still slightly warm, but not hot.

VARIATIONS

- Little stuffed pies such as these are typical of Catalonia and the Balearic Islands. Elsewhere in Spain these pies are usually plain, deep-fried and then sugared – the one sweet tapas.
- In the Barcelona food markets, pies filled with a canned tuna and vegetable stuffing are a popular hot snack.

Energy 95Kcal/396kJ; Protein 2.4g; Carbohydrate 7.8g, of which sugars 1.5g; Fat 6.4g, of which saturates 0.3g; Cholesterol 10mg; Calcium 53mg; Fibre 0.5g; Sodium 125mg.

COCA WITH ONION AND ANCHOVY TOPPING

Not unlike Italian pizza, cocas have a very long tradition in Spain. They are essentially fresh bread dough, baked with a variety of savoury toppings, and often include salt fish. The flavourings of this snack go back at least 1000 years.

SERVES SIX TO EIGHT

INGREDIENTS
- 400g/14oz/3½ cups strong white bread flour
- 2.5ml/½ tsp salt
- 15g/½oz easy-blend (rapid-rise) dried yeast
- 120ml/4fl oz/½ cup olive oil
- 150ml/¼ pint/⅔ cup milk and water, in equal quantities, mixed together
- 3 large onions, thinly sliced
- 50g/2oz can anchovies, drained and roughly chopped
- 30ml/2 tbsp pine nuts
- 30ml/2 tbsp Muscatel raisins or sultanas (golden raisins), soaked
- 5ml/1 tsp dried chilli flakes or powder
- salt and ground black pepper

VARIATION
You can eat cocas with a wide range of different toppings. Try spinach sautéed with garlic or sweet red (bell) peppers.

1 Put the flour and salt into a food processor with the yeast. Process, gradually working in 60ml/4 tbsp oil and a little of the milk and water. Gradually add the remaining milk and water, processing until well combined. Turn the dough into a bowl, cover with a dishtowel, then leave in a warm place for about 1 hour to rise.

2 Preheat the oven to 240°C/475°F/Gas 9. Heat the remaining oil in a large frying pan, add the sliced onions, and cook gently until soft.

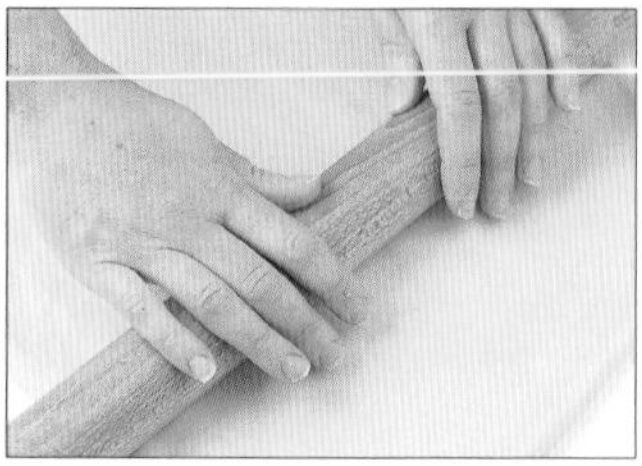

3 Return the dough to the food processor and use the pulse button to work the dough. On a lightly floured surface roll out the dough to a rectangle about 30 × 38cm/12 × 15in. Place on an oiled baking sheet.

4 Cover the dough with the onions. Scatter with the anchovies, pine nuts, raisins or sultanas and chilli flakes or powder and season. Bake for about 10 minutes, until puffed up and the edges are beginning to brown. Serve hot, cut into wedges.

BANDERILLAS

These miniature skewers are very popular in the north of Spain, where they are called pinchos, *which literally means stuck on a thorn. Taste, colour and shape guide the choice of ingredients, which may include cold or cured meat, pickled tuna, salted fish or even hard-boiled eggs. In the South, pickled vegetables are preferred. There, the resemblance to the bullfighter's dart was noticed and so the skewers were renamed.*

SERVES FOUR

INGREDIENTS
- 12 small capers
- 12 canned anchovy fillets in oil, drained
- 12 pitted black olives
- 12 cornichons or small gherkins
- 12 silverskin pickled onions

VARIATION
You can vary the ingredients if you like, using cold meats, cheeses and vegetables. Choose ingredients with different textures, tastes and colours.

1 Using your fingers, place a caper at the thicker end of each anchovy fillet and carefully roll it up, so that the caper is completely enclosed.

2 Thread one caper-filled anchovy, one olive, one cornichon or gherkin and one pickled onion on to each of 12 cocktail sticks (toothpicks). Chill and serve.

TOP Energy 335Kcal/1407kJ; Protein 7.8g; Carbohydrate 47.5g, of which sugars 7.7g; Fat 14g, of which saturates 1.8g; Cholesterol 4mg; Calcium 110mg; Fibre 2.8g; Sodium 252mg.
BOTTOM Energy 34Kcal/140kJ; Protein 2.7g; Carbohydrate 0.4g, of which sugars 0.3g; Fat 2.4g, of which saturates 0.4g; Cholesterol 6mg; Calcium 41mg; Fibre 0.5g; Sodium 702mg.

MARINATED ANCHOVIES

THIS IS ONE OF THE SIMPLEST WAYS TO PREPARE THESE TINY FISH BECAUSE IT REQUIRES NO COOKING. MARINATING IS PARTICULARLY ASSOCIATED WITH ANCHOVIES, WHICH TEND TO LOSE THEIR FRESHNESS VERY QUICKLY. THE SPANISH TERM FOR MARINATED ANCHOVIES IS BOQUERONES, *WHILE* ANCHOAS *IS THEIR WORD FOR THE CANNED, SALTED VARIETY.*

SERVES FOUR

INGREDIENTS
- 225g/8oz fresh anchovies, heads and tails removed, and split open along the belly
- juice of 3 lemons
- 30ml/2 tbsp extra virgin olive oil
- 2 garlic cloves, finely chopped
- 15ml/1 tbsp chopped fresh parsley
- flaked sea salt

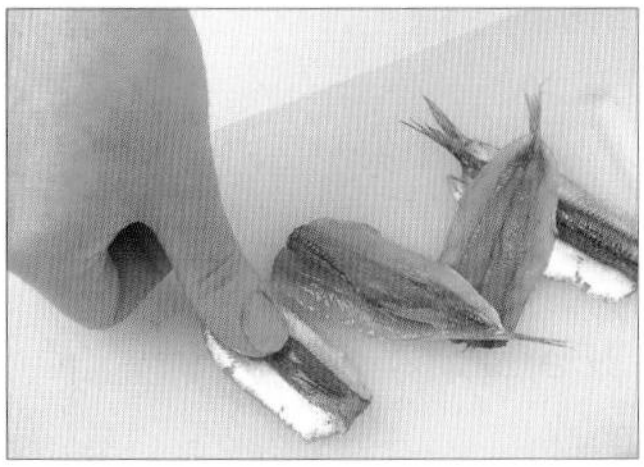

1 Turn the anchovies on to their bellies, and press down with your thumb.

2 Using the tip of a small, sharp knife, carefully remove the backbones from the flattened fish, and arrange the anchovies skin side down in a single layer on a large plate.

3 Squeeze two-thirds of the lemon juice over the fish and sprinkle them with the salt. Cover and leave to stand for 1–24 hours, basting occasionally with the juices, until the flesh is white and no longer translucent.

4 Transfer the anchovies to a serving plate and drizzle with the olive oil and the remaining lemon juice. Scatter the fish with the chopped garlic and parsley, then cover with clear film (plastic wrap) and chill until ready to serve.

Energy 108Kcal/449kJ; Protein 14.2g; Carbohydrate 0g, of which sugars 0g; Fat 5.6g, of which saturates 0.9g; Cholesterol 35mg; Calcium 169mg; Fibre 0g; Sodium 2211mg.

FLASH-FRIED SQUID WITH PAPRIKA AND GARLIC

SQUID ARE PART OF EVERY TAPAS BAR SELECTION, AND ARE USUALLY DEEP-FRIED. HERE IS A MODERN RECIPE, WHICH IS UNUSUAL IN THAT IT USES FRESH CHILLIES. SERVE THE DISH WITH A FINO OR MANZANILLA SHERRY AS A TAPAS DISH. ALTERNATIVELY, SERVE THE CALAMARES ON A BED OF SALAD LEAVES, ACCOMPANIED BY BREAD, FOR A SUBSTANTIAL FIRST COURSE TO SERVE FOUR.

SERVES SIX TO EIGHT

INGREDIENTS

- 500g/1¼lb very small squid, cleaned
- 90ml/6 tbsp olive oil, plus extra
- 1 fresh red chilli, seeded and finely chopped
- 10ml/2 tsp Spanish mild smoked paprika
- 30ml/2 tbsp plain (all-purpose) flour
- 2 garlic cloves, finely chopped
- 15ml/1 tbsp sherry vinegar
- 5ml/1 tsp grated lemon rind
- 30–45ml/2–3 tbsp finely chopped fresh parsley
- salt and ground black pepper

1 Using a sharp knife, cut the squid body sacs into rings and cut the tentacles into bitesize pieces.

2 Place the squid in a bowl and pour over 30ml/2 tbsp of the olive oil, half the chilli and the paprika. Season with a little salt and some pepper, cover with clear film (plastic wrap), place in the refrigerator and leave to marinate for 2–4 hours.

COOK'S TIPS

- Make sure the oil in the pan is very hot before adding the squid. The squid should cook for only 1–2 minutes; any longer and it will begin to toughen.
- Smoked paprika, chiefly from the Valle de Jerte, has a wonderful, subtle flavour. If you cannot find it, you can use mild paprika instead.

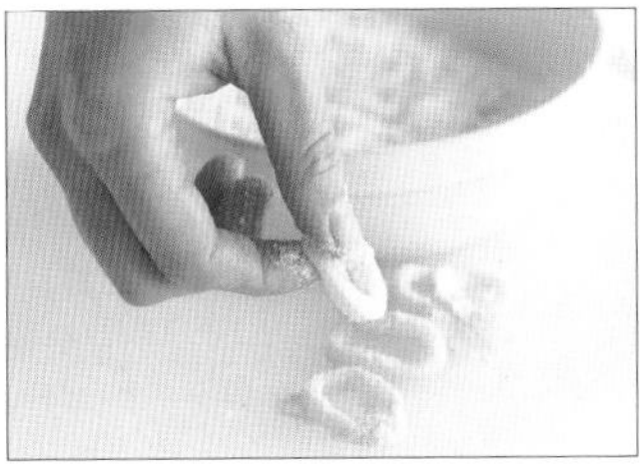

3 Toss the squid in the flour and divide it into two batches. Heat the remaining oil in a wok or deep frying pan over a high heat until very hot. Add the first batch of squid and quickly stir-fry for 1–2 minutes, or until it becomes opaque and the tentacles curl.

4 Add half the garlic. Stir, then turn out into a bowl. Repeat with the second batch, adding more oil if needed.

5 Sprinkle with the sherry vinegar, lemon rind, remaining chilli and parsley. Season and serve hot or cool.

Energy 140Kcal/583kJ; Protein 10.2g; Carbohydrate 3.8g, of which sugars 0.2g; Fat 9.4g, of which saturates 1.4g; Cholesterol 141mg; Calcium 26mg; Fibre 0.4g; Sodium 71mg.

KING PRAWNS IN CRISPY BATTER

A HUGE RANGE OF PRAWNS IS ENJOYED IN SPAIN, EACH WITH ITS APPROPRIATE COOKING METHOD. LANGOSTINOS ARE DEEP-WATER PRAWNS, OFTEN WITH TIGER STRIPES, AND CAN BE AMONG THE BIGGEST. THE BEST WAY TO ENJOY THEM IS DIPPED IN A SIMPLE BATTER AND DEEP-FRIED.

SERVES FOUR

INGREDIENTS

- 120ml/4fl oz/½ cup water
- 1 large egg (US extra large)
- 115g/4oz/1 cup plain (all-purpose) flour
- 5ml/1 tsp cayenne pepper
- 12 raw king prawns (jumbo shrimp), in the shell
- vegetable oil, for deep frying
- flat leaf parsley, to garnish
- lemon wedges, to serve (optional)

COOK'S TIP

Leaving the tails on the prawns makes them easier to pick up and eat, and also look very pretty once cooked.

1 In a large bowl, whisk together the water and the egg. Whisk in the flour and cayenne pepper until smooth.

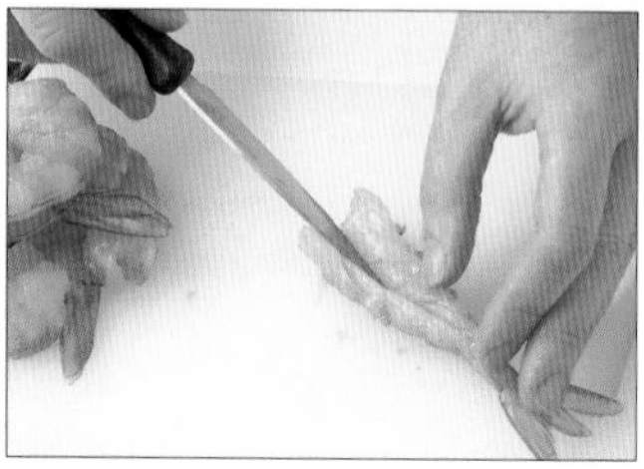

2 Peel the prawns, leaving just the tails intact. Make a shallow cut down the back of each prawn.

3 Using the tip of the knife, pull out and discard the dark intestinal tract.

4 Heat the oil in a large pan or deep-fat fryer, until a cube of bread dropped into the oil browns in 1 minute.

5 Holding the prawns by their tails, dip them into the batter, one at a time, shaking off any excess. Carefully drop each prawn into the oil and fry for 2–3 minutes until crisp and golden. Drain on kitchen paper, garnish with parsley and serve with lemon wedges, if you like.

VARIATION

If you have any batter left over, use it to coat thin strips of vegetables such as sweet potato, beetroot (beet), carrot or (bell) pepper, or use small broccoli florets or whole baby spinach leaves. Deep-fry the vegetables until golden.

Energy 257Kcal/1076kJ; Protein 13.4g; Carbohydrate 22.4g, of which sugars 0.4g; Fat 13.3g, of which saturates 1.9g; Cholesterol 155mg; Calcium 88mg; Fibre 0.9g; Sodium 117mg.

BUTTERFLIED PRAWNS IN CHOCOLATE SAUCE

There is a long tradition in Spain, which originates in Mexico, of cooking savoury food – even shellfish – with chocolate. Known as LANGOSTINOS EN CHOCOLATE *in Spanish, this is just the kind of culinary adventure that Basque chefs love.*

SERVES FOUR

INGREDIENTS
- 8 large raw prawns (shrimp), in the shell
- 15ml/1 tbsp seasoned plain (all-purpose) flour
- 15ml/1 tbsp pale dry sherry
- juice of 1 large orange
- 15g/½oz dark (bittersweet) chocolate, chopped
- 30ml/2 tbsp olive oil
- 2 garlic cloves, finely chopped
- 2.5cm/1in piece fresh root ginger, finely chopped
- 1 small dried chilli, seeded and chopped
- salt and ground black pepper

1 Peel the prawns, leaving just the tail sections intact. Make a shallow cut down the back of each one and carefully pull out and discard the dark intestinal tract.

2 Turn the prawns over so that the undersides are uppermost, and then carefully slit them open from tail to top, using a small sharp knife, cutting them almost, but not quite, through to the central back line.

3 Press the prawns down firmly to flatten them out. Coat with the seasoned flour and set aside.

4 Gently heat the sherry and orange juice in a small pan. When warm, remove from the heat and stir in the chopped chocolate until melted.

5 Heat the oil in a frying pan. Add the garlic, ginger and chilli and cook for 2 minutes until golden. Remove with a slotted spoon and reserve. Add the prawns, cut side down and cook for 2–3 minutes until golden brown with pink edges. Turn the prawns and cook for a further 2 minutes.

6 Return the garlic mixture to the pan and pour the chocolate sauce over. Cook for 1 minute, turning the prawns to coat them in the glossy sauce. Season to taste and serve hot.

Energy 119Kcal/495kJ; Protein 7.2g; Carbohydrate 6.5g, of which sugars 3.6g; Fat 6.8g, of which saturates 1.5g; Cholesterol 73mg; Calcium 38mg; Fibre 0.2g; Sodium 73mg.

Sizzling Prawns

Garlic prawns are hugely popular in Spain, both with and without the addition of chilli. They are normally cooked in small, individual earthenware casseroles, which stand on an iron baking sheet – la plancha. *A frying pan will produce the same result.*

SERVES FOUR

INGREDIENTS

- 1–2 dried chillies (to taste)
- 60ml/4 tbsp olive oil
- 3 garlic cloves, finely chopped
- 16 large raw prawns (shrimp), in the shell
- salt and ground black pepper
- French bread, to serve

VARIATION

To make classic *gambas al ajillo* – garlic prawns (shrimp) – simply omit the chilli. The word *ajillo* tells you how the garlic is prepared. The diminutive means finely chopped, like the garlic in the final dish. The alternative is *gambas con ajo*, which means with garlic. For this dish, slices of garlic are fried until brown, to flavour the oil, then discarded.

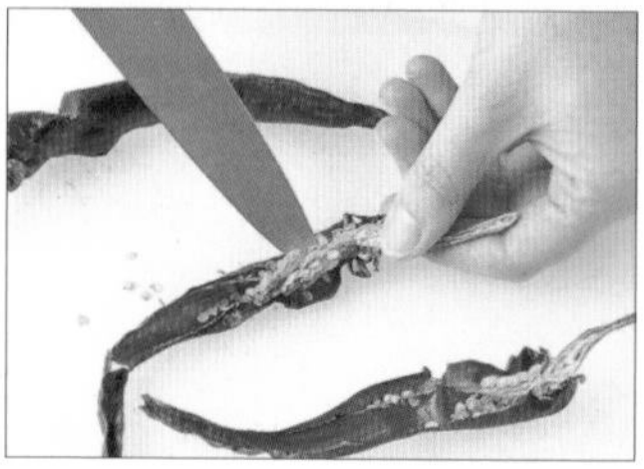

1 Split the chillies lengthways and discard the seeds. It is best to do this with a knife and fork, because the seeds, in particular, contain hot capsicum, which can be very irritating to the eyes, nose and mouth.

2 Heat the oil in a large frying pan and stir-fry the garlic and chilli for 1 minute, until the garlic begins to turn brown.

3 Add the whole prawns and stir-fry for 3–4 minutes, coating them well with the flavoured oil.

4 Remove from the heat and divide the prawns among four dishes. Spoon over the flavoured oil and serve immediately. (Remember to provide a plate for the heads and shells, plus plenty of napkins for messy fingers.)

Energy 161Kcal/668kJ; Protein 13.6g; Carbohydrate 0.8g, of which sugars 0.1g; Fat 11.5g, of which saturates 1.7g; Cholesterol 146mg; Calcium 60mg; Fibre 0.2g; Sodium 143mg.

SPICED CLAMS

SPANISH CLAMS, ESPECIALLY IN THE NORTH, ARE MUCH LARGER THAN CLAMS FOUND ELSEWHERE, AND HAVE MORE SUCCULENT BODIES. THIS MODERN RECIPE USES ARAB SPICING TO MAKE A HOT DIP OR SAUCE. SERVE WITH PLENTY OF FRESH BREAD TO MOP UP THE DELICIOUS JUICES.

SERVES THREE TO FOUR

INGREDIENTS

- 1 small onion, finely chopped
- 1 celery stick, sliced
- 2 garlic cloves, finely chopped
- 2.5cm/1in piece fresh root ginger, grated
- 30ml/2 tbsp olive oil
- 1.5ml/¼ tsp chilli powder
- 5ml/1 tsp ground turmeric
- 30ml/2 tbsp chopped fresh parsley
- 500g/1¼lb small clams, in the shell
- 30ml/2 tbsp dry white wine
- salt and ground black pepper
- celery leaves, to garnish
- fresh bread, to serve

COOK'S TIPS

- There are many different varieties of clam fished off the coast of Spain. One of the best is the *almeja fina* (the carpet shell clam), which is perfect used in this dish. They have grooved brown shells with a yellow lattice pattern.
- Before cooking the clams, check that all the shells are closed. Any clams that do not open after cooking should be discarded.

1 Place the onion, celery, garlic and ginger in a large pan, add the olive oil, spices and chopped parsley and stir-fry for about 5 minutes. Add the clams to the pan and cook for 2 minutes.

2 Add the wine, then cover and cook gently for 2–3 minutes, shaking the pan occasionally. Season. Discard any clams whose shells remain closed, then serve, garnished with the celery leaves.

Energy 126Kcal/526kJ; Protein 12.5g; Carbohydrate 4.5g, of which sugars 2.2g; Fat 6g, of which saturates 0.9g; Cholesterol 50mg; Calcium 69mg; Fibre 0.6g; Sodium 906mg.

MUSSELS WITH A PARSLEY CRUST

The stormy Atlantic coast of Spain produces the best mussels in the world. Known as mejillones in Spain, they grow to enormous size in a very short time, without becoming tough. Here they are grilled with a deliciously fragrant topping of Parmesan cheese, garlic and parsley, which helps to prevent the mussels from becoming overcooked.

SERVES FOUR

INGREDIENTS
- 450g/1lb fresh mussels
- 45ml/3 tbsp water
- 15ml/1 tbsp melted butter
- 15ml/1 tbsp olive oil
- 45ml/3 tbsp freshly grated Parmesan cheese
- 30ml/2 tbsp chopped fresh parsley
- 2 garlic cloves, finely chopped
- 2.5ml/½ tsp coarsely ground black pepper
- crusty bread, to serve

COOK'S TIP

Steaming the mussels produces about 250ml/8fl oz/1 cup wonderful shellfish stock that can be used in other fish and shellfish recipes. Once the mussels have been steamed, remove them from the pan and leave the broth liquor to cool, then store it in a sealed container in the refrigerator or freezer.

Combining fish and shellfish stock is the backbone of many Spanish fish dishes such as *merluza con salsa verde* (hake with green sauce). It is said that the stock from one shellfish makes the best sauce for another.

1 Scrub the mussels thoroughly, scraping off any barnacles with a round-bladed knife and pulling out the gritty beards. Sharply tap any open mussels and discard any that fail to close or whose shells are broken.

2 Place the mussels in a large pan and add the water. Cover the pan with a lid and steam for about 5 minutes, or until the mussel shells have opened.

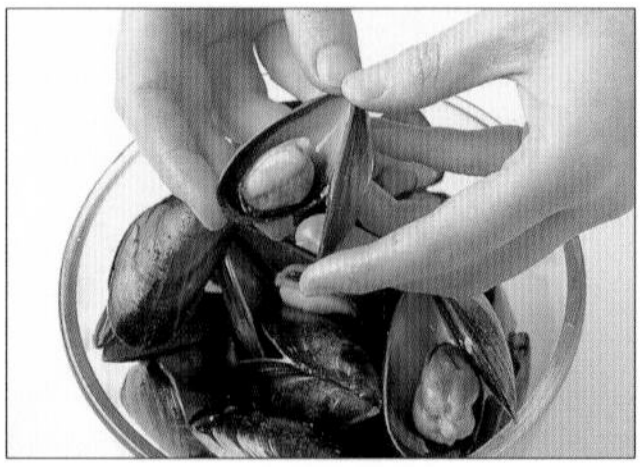

3 Drain the mussels well and discard any that remain closed. Carefully snap off the top shell from each mussel, leaving the actual flesh still attached to the bottom shell.

4 Balance the shells in a flameproof dish, packing them closely together to make sure that they stay level.

5 Preheat the grill (broiler) to high. Put the melted butter, olive oil, grated Parmesan cheese, parsley, garlic and black pepper in a small bowl and mix well to combine.

6 Spoon a small amount of the cheese and garlic mixture on top of each mussel and gently press down with the back of the spoon.

7 Grill (broil) the mussels for about 2 minutes, or until they are sizzling and golden. Serve the mussels in their shells, with plenty of bread to mop up the delicious juices.

COOK'S TIP

Give each guest one of the discarded top shells of the mussels. They can be used as a little spoon to free the body from the shell of the next. Scoop up the mussel in the empty shell and tip the shellfish and topping into your mouth.

Energy 136Kcal/567kJ; Protein 10.6g; Carbohydrate 0.3g, of which sugars 0.3g; Fat 10.3g, of which saturates 4.8g; Cholesterol 33mg; Calcium 222mg; Fibre 0.5g; Sodium 220mg.

CHICKEN CROQUETTES

CROQUETAS *ARE VERY POPULAR TAPAS FARE AND THERE ARE MANY DIFFERENT VARIATIONS.* THIS *ONE IS BASED ON BECHAMEL SAUCE, WHICH IS PERFECT FOR TAKING ON DIFFERENT FLAVOURS SUCH AS HAM OR CHOPPED PEPPERS.* THE *CROQUETTES ARE BEST FRIED JUST BEFORE SERVING.*

SERVES FOUR

INGREDIENTS

- 25g/1oz/2 tbsp butter
- 25g/1oz/¼ cup plain (all-purpose) flour
- 150ml/¼ pint/⅔ cup milk
- 15ml/1 tbsp olive oil, plus extra for deep-frying
- 1 boneless chicken breast with skin, diced
- 1 garlic clove, finely chopped
- 1 small egg, beaten
- 50g/2oz/1 cup stale white breadcrumbs
- salt and ground black pepper
- fresh flat leaf parsley, to garnish
- lemon wedges, to serve

1 Melt the butter in a pan. Add the flour and cook gently, stirring, for 1 minute. Gradually stir in the milk and cook until smooth and thick. Cover and set aside.

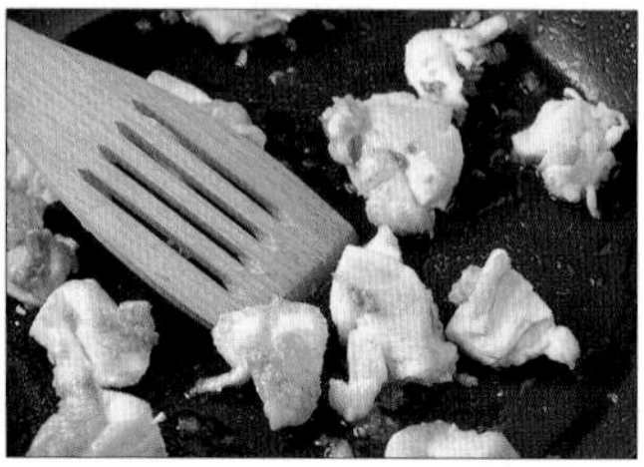

2 Heat the oil in a frying pan and fry the chicken and garlic for 5 minutes.

3 When the chicken is lightly browned and cooked through, tip the contents of the frying pan into a food processor and process until finely chopped. Tip the mixture into the sauce and stir to combine. Season with plenty of salt and pepper to taste, then set aside to cool completely.

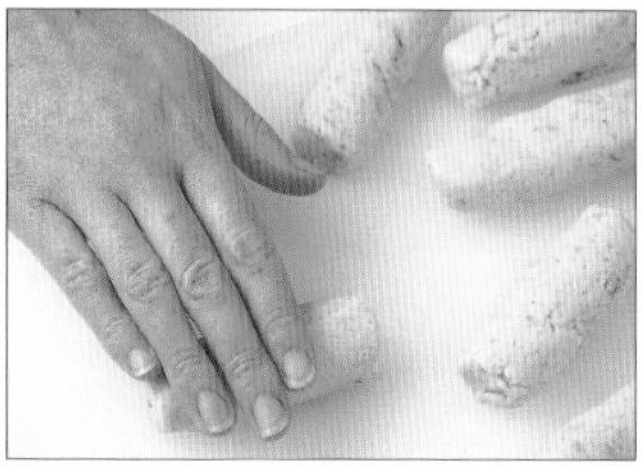

4 Once cooled and firm, shape the mixture into eight small sausage shapes. Dip each one in beaten egg, then roll in breadcrumbs to coat.

5 Heat the oil in a large pan, until a cube of bread dropped in the oil browns in 1 minute. Lower the croquettes into the oil and cook for 4 minutes until crisp and golden. Lift out using a slotted spoon and drain on kitchen paper. Serve with lemon wedges and garnish with fresh flat leaf parsley.

Energy 286Kcal/1195kJ; Protein 13.9g; Carbohydrate 16.4g, of which sugars 2.2g; Fat 18.9g, of which saturates 5.8g; Cholesterol 89mg; Calcium 80mg; Fibre 0.5g; Sodium 189mg.

PINCHITOS MORUÑOS

The Moors introduced both skewers and marinated meat to Spain. These little yellow kebabs are a favourite in Andalusia, where many butchers sell the meat ready marinated. The Arab versions used lamb, but pork is used now, because the spicing fits so perfectly.

SERVES FOUR

INGREDIENTS

- 2.5ml/½ tsp cumin seeds
- 2.5ml/½ tsp coriander seeds
- 2 garlic cloves, finely chopped
- 5ml/1 tsp paprika
- 2.5ml/½ tsp dried oregano
- 15ml/1 tbsp lemon juice
- 45ml/3 tbsp olive oil
- 500g/1¼lb lean cubed pork
- salt and ground black pepper

1 Starting a couple of hours in advance, grind the cumin and coriander seeds in a mortar and work in the garlic with a pinch of salt. Add the paprika and oregano and mix in the lemon juice. Stir in the oil.

2 Cut the pork into small cubes, then skewer them, three or four at a time, on to cocktail sticks (toothpicks). Put the skewered meat in a shallow dish, and pour over the marinade. Spoon the marinade back over the meat to ensure it is well coated. Leave to marinate in a cool place for 2 hours.

3 Preheat the grill (broiler) to high, and line the grill pan with foil. Spread the kebabs out in a row and place under the grill, close to the heat. Cook for about 3 minutes on each side, spooning the juices over when you turn them, until cooked through. Sprinkle with salt and pepper, and serve at once.

Energy 229Kcal/955kJ; Protein 27g; Carbohydrate 0.4g, of which sugars 0.1g; Fat 13.3g, of which saturates 2.9g; Cholesterol 79mg; Calcium 9mg; Fibre 0.1g; Sodium 88mg.

Fried Black Pudding

Spanish morcilla – black pudding – is the first sausage to be made from the freshly killed pig and is very popular throughout Spain. It is flavoured with spices and herbs, usually including garlic and oregano, and has a wonderfully rich, spicy taste.

SERVES FOUR

INGREDIENTS

- 15ml/1 tbsp olive oil
- 1 onion, thinly sliced
- 2 garlic cloves, thinly sliced
- 5ml/1 tsp dried oregano
- 5ml/1 tsp paprika
- 225g/8oz black pudding (blood sausage), cut into 12 thick slices
- 1 thin French stick, sliced into 12
- 30ml/2 tbsp fino sherry
- sugar, to taste
- salt and ground black pepper
- chopped fresh oregano, to garnish

COOK'S TIP

If you can find real *morcilla*, serve it neat: simply fry the slices in olive oil and use to top little rounds of bread. If you cannot find black pudding, you can use red chorizo instead.

1 Heat the olive oil in a large frying pan and fry the sliced onion, garlic, oregano and paprika for 7–8 minutes until the onion is softened and has turned golden brown.

2 Add the slices of black pudding, then increase the heat and cook them for 3 minutes, without stirring. Turn them over carefully with a spatula and cook for a further 3 minutes until crisp.

3 Arrange the rounds of bread on a large serving plate and top each with a slice of black pudding. Stir the sherry into the onions and add a little sugar to taste. Heat, swirling the mixture around the pan until bubbling, then season with salt and black pepper.

4 Spoon a little of the onion mixture on top of each slice of black pudding. Scatter the oregano over and serve.

Energy 477Kcal/2010kJ; Protein 15.3g; Carbohydrate 68.5g, of which sugars 5.1g; Fat 16.8g, of which saturates 5.5g; Cholesterol 38mg; Calcium 199mg; Fibre 3g; Sodium 1147mg.

BARBECUED MINI RIBS

These tasty ribs are known as costillas *in Spain. They are delicious barbecued and almost as good when cooked under a hot grill. If you prefer a sweeter flavour, use freshly squeezed orange juice instead of the sweet sherry.*

SERVES SIX TO EIGHT

INGREDIENTS

- 1 sheet of pork ribs, about 675g/1½lb
- 90ml/6 tbsp sweet oloroso sherry
- 15ml/1 tbsp tomato purée (paste)
- 5ml/1 tsp soy sauce
- 2.5ml/½ tsp Tabasco sauce
- 15ml/1 tbsp light muscovado (brown) sugar
- 30ml/2 tbsp seasoned plain (all-purpose) flour
- coarse sea salt

COOK'S TIP

Oloroso sherry has a full body and sweet flavour sometimes reminiscent of port.

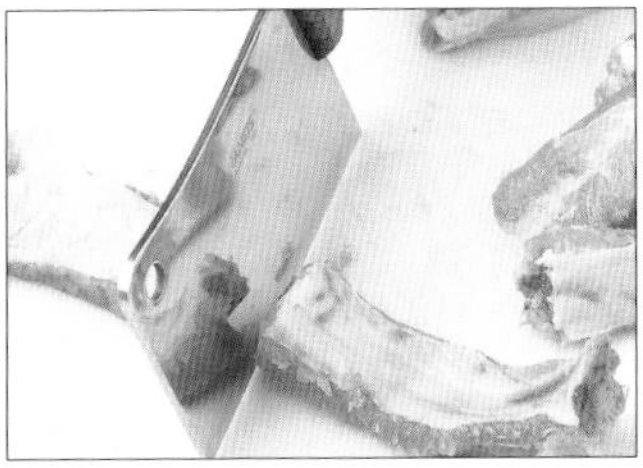

1 Separate the ribs, then, using a meat cleaver or heavy knife, cut each rib in half widthways to make about 30 pieces.

2 Mix the sherry, tomato purée, soy sauce, Tabasco and sugar in a bowl. Stir in 2.5ml/½ tsp salt.

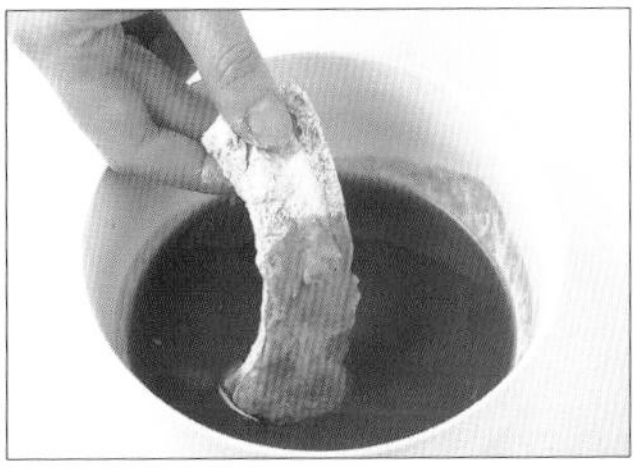

3 Put the seasoned flour in a strong plastic bag, then add the ribs and toss to coat. Dip each rib in the sauce. Cook on a hot barbecue or under a hot grill (broiler) for 30–40 minutes, turning occasionally until cooked and a little charred. Sprinkle with salt and serve.

Energy 197Kcal/825kJ; Protein 16.2g; Carbohydrate 5g, of which sugars 3g; Fat 11.4g, of which saturates 4.4g; Cholesterol 56mg; Calcium 19mg; Fibre 0.1g; Sodium 89mg.

EGGS AND SOUP

Tortilla is the classic dish identified with Spain, and eggs hold a special place in the Spanish heart – for they speak of the barnyard, and the country, where every Spaniard imagines a home. Gazpacho is the world-famous soup but there are many others from shellfish soup to ham-scented broth, and those that might come before a hearty main course.

GAZPACHO

THIS CLASSIC CHILLED SOUP IS DEEPLY ROOTED IN ANDALUSIA. THE SOOTHING BLEND OF TOMATOES, SWEET PEPPERS AND GARLIC IS SHARPENED WITH SHERRY VINEGAR, AND ENRICHED WITH OLIVE OIL. SERVING IT WITH SAUCERFULS OF GARNISHES HAS VIRTUALLY BECOME A TRADITION.

SERVES FOUR

INGREDIENTS
- 1.3–1.6kg/3–3½lb ripe tomatoes
- 1 green (bell) pepper, seeded and roughly chopped
- 2 garlic cloves, finely chopped
- 2 slices stale bread, crusts removed
- 60ml/4 tbsp extra virgin olive oil
- 60ml/4 tbsp sherry vinegar
- 150ml/¼ pint/⅔ cup tomato juice
- 300ml/½ pint/1¼ cups iced water
- salt and ground black pepper
- ice cubes, to serve (optional)

For the garnishes
- 30ml/2 tbsp olive oil
- 2–3 slices stale bread, diced
- 1 small cucumber, peeled and finely diced
- 1 small onion, finely chopped
- 1 red (bell) and 1 green (bell) pepper, seeded and finely diced
- 2 hard-boiled eggs, chopped

COOK'S TIP
In Spain, ripe tomatoes are used for salads and very ripe ones for sauces and soups. No further flavouring ingredients are needed. If you cannot find really ripe tomatoes, add a pinch of sugar to sweeten the soup slightly.

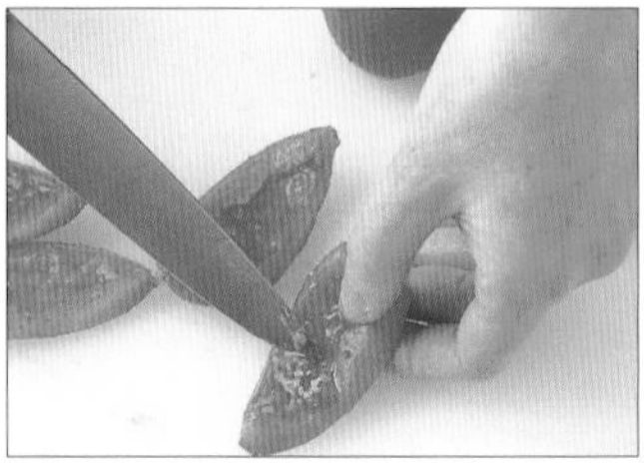

1 Skin the tomatoes, then quarter them and remove the cores and seeds, saving the juices. Put the pepper in a food processor and process for a few seconds. Add the tomatoes, reserved juices, garlic, bread, oil and vinegar and process. Add the tomato juice and blend to combine.

2 Season the soup, then pour into a large bowl, cover with clear film (plastic wrap) and chill for at least 12 hours.

3 Prepare the garnishes. Heat the olive oil in a frying pan and fry the bread cubes for 4–5 minutes until golden brown and crisp. Drain well on kitchen paper, then arrange in a small dish. Place each of the remaining garnishes in separate small dishes.

4 Just before serving, dilute the soup with the ice-cold water. The consistency should be thick but not too stodgy. If you like, stir a few ice cubes into the soup, then spoon into serving bowls and serve with the garnishes.

Energy 356Kcal/1494kJ; Protein 7.6g; Carbohydrate 41.9g, of which sugars 21.5g; Fat 18.8g, of which saturates 2.9g; Cholesterol 0mg; Calcium 90mg; Fibre 6.7g; Sodium 346mg.

CHILLED AVOCADO SOUP WITH CUMIN

ANDALUSIA IS HOME TO BOTH AVOCADOS AND GAZPACHO, SO IT IS NOT SURPRISING THAT THIS CHILLED AVOCADO SOUP, WHICH IS ALSO KNOWN AS GREEN GAZPACHO, WAS INVENTED THERE. IN SPAIN, THIS DELICIOUSLY MILD, CREAMY SOUP IS KNOWN AS SOPA DE AGUACATE.

SERVES FOUR

INGREDIENTS

- 3 ripe avocados
- 1 bunch spring onions (scallions), white parts only, trimmed and roughly chopped
- 2 garlic cloves, chopped
- juice of 1 lemon
- 1.5ml/¼ tsp ground cumin
- 1.5ml/¼ tsp paprika
- 450ml/¾ pint/scant 2 cups fresh chicken stock, cooled, and all fat skimmed off
- 300ml/½ pint/1¼ cups iced water
- salt and ground black pepper
- roughly chopped fresh flat leaf parsley, to serve

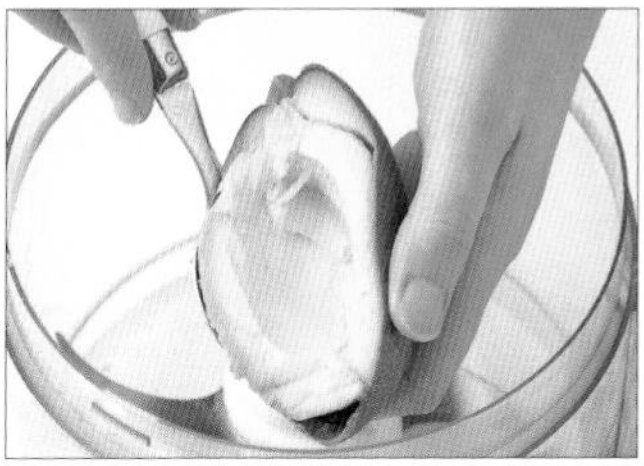

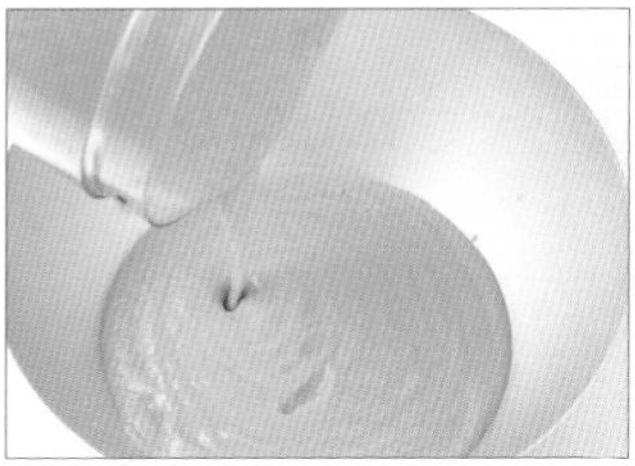

1 Starting half a day ahead, put the flesh of one avocado in a food processor or blender. Add the spring onions, garlic and lemon juice and purée until smooth. Add the second avocado and purée, then the third, with the spices and seasoning. Purée until smooth.

2 Gradually add the chicken stock. Pour the soup into a metal bowl and chill.

3 To serve, stir in the iced water, then season to taste with plenty of salt and black pepper. Garnish with chopped parsley and serve immediately.

Energy 293Kcal/1208kJ; Protein 3.5g; Carbohydrate 3.6g, of which sugars 1.3g; Fat 29.3g, of which saturates 6.2g; Cholesterol 0mg; Calcium 26mg; Fibre 5.4g; Sodium 214mg.

CHILLED ALMOND SOUP WITH GRAPES

Called ajo blanco – white garlic soup – in Spain, this is a chilled Moorish soup of ancient origin. It is a perfect balance of three southern ingredients: crushed almonds, garlic and vinegar, in a smooth purée made luscious with oil.

SERVES SIX

INGREDIENTS
- 115g/4oz stale white bread
- 115g/4oz/1 cup blanched almonds
- 2 garlic cloves, sliced
- 75ml/5 tbsp olive oil
- 25ml/1½ tbsp sherry vinegar
- salt and ground black pepper

For the garnish
- toasted flaked almonds
- green and black grapes, halved and seeded
- chopped fresh chives

1 Break the bread into a bowl and pour in 150ml/¼ pint/⅔ cup cold water. Leave to soak for about 5 minutes, then squeeze dry.

2 Put the almonds and garlic in a food processor or blender and process until very finely ground. Add the soaked white bread and process again until thoroughly combined.

3 Continue to process, gradually adding the oil until the mixture forms a smooth paste. Add the sherry vinegar, followed by 600ml/1 pint/2½ cups cold water and process until the mixture is smooth.

4 Transfer the soup to a bowl and season with plenty of salt and pepper, adding a little more water if the soup is very thick. Cover with clear film (plastic wrap) and chill for at least 2 hours.

5 Ladle the soup into bowls. Scatter the almonds, halved grapes and chopped chives over to garnish.

COOK'S TIP

To accentuate the flavour of the almonds, dry roast them in a frying pan until they are lightly browned before grinding them. This will produce a slightly darker soup.

Energy 245Kcal/1017kJ; Protein 5.7g; Carbohydrate 10.8g, of which sugars 1.3g; Fat 20.2g, of which saturates 2.2g; Cholesterol 0mg; Calcium 67mg; Fibre 1.7g; Sodium 102mg.

SHERRIED ONION SOUP WITH SAFFRON

THE SPANISH COMBINATION OF ONIONS, SHERRY AND SAFFRON GIVES THIS PALE YELLOW SOUP A BEGUILING FLAVOUR THAT IS PERFECT FOR THE OPENING COURSE OF A MEAL. THE ADDITION OF GROUND ALMONDS TO THICKEN THE SOUP GIVES IT A WONDERFUL TEXTURE AND FLAVOUR.

SERVES FOUR

INGREDIENTS

- 40g/1½oz/3 tbsp butter
- 2 large yellow onions, thinly sliced
- 1 small garlic clove, finely chopped
- pinch of saffron threads (0.05g)
- 50g/2oz blanched almonds, toasted and finely ground
- 750ml/1¼ pints/3 cups chicken or vegetable stock
- 45ml/3 tbsp fino sherry
- 2.5ml/½ tsp paprika
- salt and ground black pepper

To garnish

- 30ml/2 tbsp flaked or slivered almonds, toasted
- chopped fresh parsley

1 Melt the butter in a heavy pan over a low heat. Add the onions and garlic, stirring to ensure that they are thoroughly coated in the melted butter, then cover the pan and cook very gently, stirring frequently, for about 20 minutes, or until the onions are soft and golden yellow.

2 Add the saffron threads to the pan and cook, uncovered, for 3–4 minutes, then add the finely ground almonds and cook, stirring the ingredients constantly, for a further 2–3 minutes.

3 Pour in the chicken or vegetable stock and sherry into the pan and stir in 5ml/1 tsp salt and the paprika. Season with plenty of black pepper. Bring to the boil, then lower the heat and simmer gently for about 10 minutes.

4 Pour the soup into a food processor and process until smooth, then return it to the rinsed pan. Reheat slowly, without allowing the soup to boil, stirring occasionally. Taste for seasoning, adding more salt and pepper if required.

5 Ladle the soup into heated bowls, garnish with the toasted flaked or slivered almonds and a little chopped fresh parsley and serve immediately.

VARIATION

This soup is also delicious served chilled. Use olive oil rather than butter, add a little more chicken or vegetable stock to make a slightly thinner soup, then leave to cool and chill for at least 4 hours. Just before serving, taste for seasoning. (Chilled soups need more seasoning than hot ones.) Float one or two ice cubes in each bowl, then garnish with almonds and parsley and serve immediately.

Energy 255Kcal/1054kJ; Protein 5.8g; Carbohydrate 11.5g, of which sugars 8.1g; Fat 19.6g, of which saturates 6.1g; Cholesterol 21mg; Calcium 82mg; Fibre 3.2g; Sodium 68mg.

Catalan Broad Bean and Potato Soup

Habas are fresh broad beans, and are a great deal nicer than the dried variety, known as favas. The word has vanished from the Spanish dictionary and the rather indigestible dried bean has all but disappeared as well. This fresh soup uses a modern herb too – coriander is not a common Spanish ingredient, but it adds a delicious flavour.

SERVES FOUR

INGREDIENTS

- 30ml/2 tbsp olive oil
- 2 onions, chopped
- 3 large floury potatoes, peeled and diced
- 450g/1lb fresh shelled broad (US fava) beans
- 1.75 litres/3 pints/7½ cups vegetable stock
- 1 bunch fresh coriander (cilantro), roughly chopped
- 150ml/¼ pint/⅔ cup single (light) cream, plus a little extra, to garnish
- salt and ground black pepper

1 Heat the oil in a large pan and fry the onions, stirring, for 5 minutes until soft. Add the potatoes, most of the beans (reserving a few for the garnish) and the stock, and bring to the boil. Simmer for 5 minutes, then add the coriander and simmer for a further 10 minutes.

2 Blend the soup in batches in a food processor or blender, then return to the rinsed pan.

3 Stir in the cream, season, and bring to a simmer. Serve garnished with coriander, beans and cream.

Energy 305Kcal/1279kJ; Protein 13g; Carbohydrate 34.3g, of which sugars 9.1g; Fat 13.9g, of which saturates 5.5g; Cholesterol 21mg; Calcium 149mg; Fibre 10g; Sodium 35mg.

SOPA CASTILIANA

THIS RICH, DARK GARLIC SOUP, FROM CENTRAL SPAIN, DIVIDES PEOPLE INTO TWO GROUPS. YOU EITHER LOVE IT OR HATE IT. THE PITILESS SUN BEATS DOWN ON LA MANCHA, ONE OF THE POOREST REGIONS OF SPAIN, AND THE LOCAL SOUP HAS HARSH, STRONG TASTES TO MATCH THE CLIMATE. POACHING A WHOLE EGG IN EACH BOWL JUST BEFORE SERVING TRANSFORMS THE SOUP INTO A MEAL.

SERVES FOUR

INGREDIENTS

- 30ml/2 tbsp olive oil
- 4 large garlic cloves, peeled
- 4 slices stale country bread
- 20ml/4 tbsp paprika
- 1 litre/1¾ pints/4 cups beef stock
- 1.5ml/¼ tsp ground cumin
- 4 free-range (farm-fresh) eggs
- salt and ground black pepper
- chopped fresh parsley, to garnish

VARIATION

If you prefer, you can simply whisk the eggs into the hot soup.

1 Preheat the oven to 230°C/450°F/ Gas 8. Heat the olive oil in a large pan. Add the whole peeled garlic cloves and cook until they are golden, then remove and set aside. Fry the slices of bread in the oil until golden, then set these aside.

2 Add 15ml/1 tbsp of the paprika to the pan, and fry for a few seconds. Stir in the beef stock, cumin and remaining paprika, then add the reserved garlic, crushing the cloves with the back of a wooden spoon. Season to taste, then cook for about 5 minutes.

3 Break up the slices of fried bread into bitesize pieces and stir them into the soup. Ladle the soup into four ovenproof bowls. Carefully break an egg into each bowl of soup and place in the oven for about 3 minutes, until the eggs are set. Sprinkle the soup with chopped fresh parsley and serve immediately.

Energy 200Kcal/836kJ; Protein 9.8g; Carbohydrate 15.6g, of which sugars 0.9g; Fat 11.8g, of which saturates 2.4g; Cholesterol 190mg; Calcium 62mg; Fibre 0.9g; Sodium 396mg.

SOPA DE MARISCOS

THIS HEARTY SEAFOOD SOUP CONTAINS ALL THE COLOURS AND FLAVOURS OF THE MEDITERRANEAN. IT IS SUBSTANTIAL ENOUGH TO SERVE AS A MAIN COURSE, BUT CAN ALSO BE DILUTED WITH A LITTLE WHITE WINE AND WATER, TO MAKE AN ELEGANT APPETIZER FOR SIX.

SERVES FOUR

INGREDIENTS

- 675g/1½lb raw prawns (shrimp), in the shell
- 900ml/1½pints/3¾ cups cold water
- 1 onion, chopped
- 1 celery stick, chopped
- 1 bay leaf
- 45ml/3 tbsp olive oil
- 2 slices stale bread, crusts removed
- 1 small onion, finely chopped
- 1 large garlic clove, chopped
- 2 large tomatoes, halved
- ½ large green (bell) pepper, finely chopped
- 500g/1¼lb cockles (small clams) or mussels, cleaned
- juice of 1 lemon
- 45ml/3 tbsp chopped fresh parsley
- 5ml/1 tsp paprika
- salt and ground black pepper

COOK'S TIP

Good fish and shellfish dishes are normally based on proper fish stock (including the juices saved from opening mussels). This is equivalent to the French *court bouillon*, and takes 30 minutes' simmering. The method used here is one of the quickest, because the prawn heads come off neatly, and the rest of the shells are simply added as they are removed.

1 Pull the heads off the prawns and put them in a pan with the cold water. Add the onion, celery and bay leaf and simmer for 20–25 minutes.

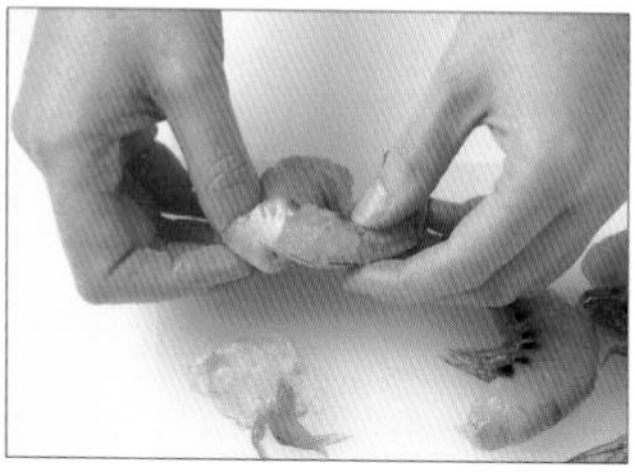

2 Peel the prawns, adding the shells to the stock as you go along.

3 Heat the oil in a wide, deep flameproof casserole and fry the bread slices quickly, then reserve them. Fry the onion until it is soft, adding the garlic towards the end.

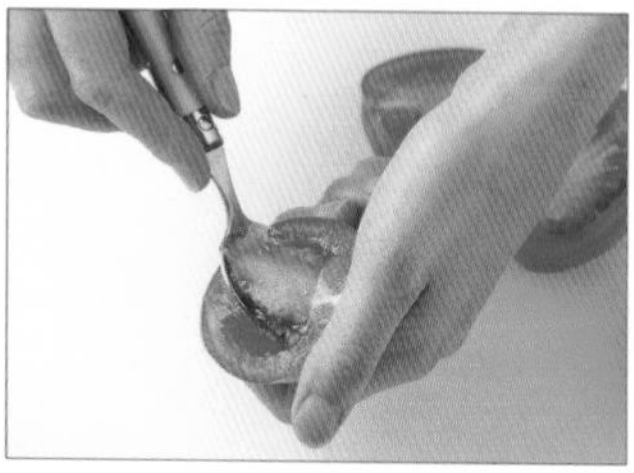

4 Scoop the seeds out of the tomatoes and discard. Chop the flesh and add to the casserole with the green pepper. Fry briefly, stirring occasionally.

5 Strain the stock into the casserole and bring to the boil. Check over the cockles or mussels, discarding any that are open or damaged.

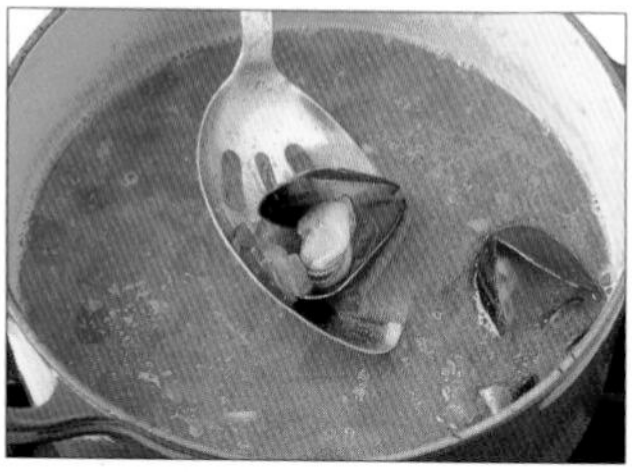

6 Add half the cockles or mussels to the stock. When open, use a slotted spoon to transfer some of them out on to a plate. Remove the mussels or cockles from the shells and discard the shells. (You should end up having discarded about half of the shells.) Meanwhile, repeat the process to cook the remaining cockles or mussels.

7 Return the cockles or mussels to the soup and add the prawns. Add the bread, torn into little pieces, and the lemon juice and chopped parsley.

8 Season to taste with paprika, salt and pepper and stir gently to dissolve the bread. Serve at once in soup bowls, providing a plate for the empty shells.

Energy 241Kcal/1014kJ; Protein 23.6g; Carbohydrate 14.9g, of which sugars 7g; Fat 10.2g, of which saturates 1.6g; Cholesterol 192mg; Calcium 186mg; Fibre 2.1g; Sodium 1173mg.

Fish Soup with Orange

The old name for this soup is Sopa Cachorreña *– Seville orange soup – and it is good served post-Christmas, when bitter Seville oranges are in season. It has a beautiful orange colour. The fish used is normally small hake, but any white fish is suitable.*

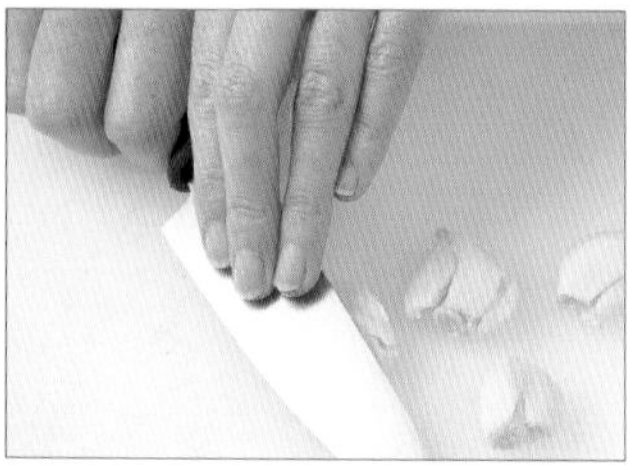

SERVES SIX

INGREDIENTS

- 1kg/2¼lb small hake or whiting, whole but cleaned
- 1.2 litres/2 pints/5 cups water
- 4 bitter oranges or 4 sweet oranges and 2 lemons
- 30ml/2 tbsp olive oil
- 5 garlic cloves, unpeeled
- 1 large onion, finely chopped
- 1 tomato, peeled, seeded and chopped
- 4 small potatoes, cut into rounds
- 5ml/1 tsp paprika
- salt and ground black pepper
- 15–30ml/1–2 tbsp finely chopped fresh parsley, to garnish

1 Fillet the fish and cut each fillet into three, reserving all the trimmings. Put the fillets on a plate, salt lightly and chill. Put the trimmings in a pan, add the water and a spiral of orange rind. Bring to a simmer, skim, then cover and cook gently for 30 minutes.

2 Heat the oil in a large flameproof casserole over a high heat. Smash the garlic cloves with the flat of a knife and fry until they are well-coloured. Discard them and turn down the heat. Fry the onion gently until it is softened, adding the tomato halfway through.

3 Strain in the hot fish stock (adding the orange spiral as well if you wish) and bring back to the boil. Add the potatoes to the pan and cook them for about 5 minutes.

4 Add the fish pieces to the soup, a few at a time, without letting it go off the boil. Cook for about 15 minutes. Add the squeezed orange juice and lemon juice, if using, and the paprika, with salt and pepper to taste. Serve in bowls, garnished with a little parsley.

Energy 245Kcal/1028kJ; Protein 26.7g; Carbohydrate 19.7g, of which sugars 11.1g; Fat 7.1g, of which saturates 1.1g; Cholesterol 30mg; Calcium 89mg; Fibre 3.1g; Sodium 155mg.

CALDO GALLEGO

This classic Galician soup features salt pork and beans with young turnip tops, although purple sprouting broccoli makes a pretty substitute. Make the soup ahead of time, then let the flavours blend. You will need to start making the soup at least a day in advance.

SERVES SIX

INGREDIENTS
- 150g/5oz/⅔ cup haricot beans, soaked overnight in cold water and drained
- 1kg/2¼lb smoked gammon (cured or smoked ham) hock
- 3 potatoes, quartered
- 3 small turnips, sliced in rounds
- 150g/5oz purple sprouting broccoli
- salt and ground black pepper

1 Put the drained beans and gammon into a casserole and cover with 2 litres/3½ pints/8 cups water. Slowly bring to the boil, skim off any scum, then turn down the heat and cook gently, covered, for about 1¼ hours.

2 Drain, reserving the broth. Return the broth to the casserole and add the potatoes, turnips and drained beans.

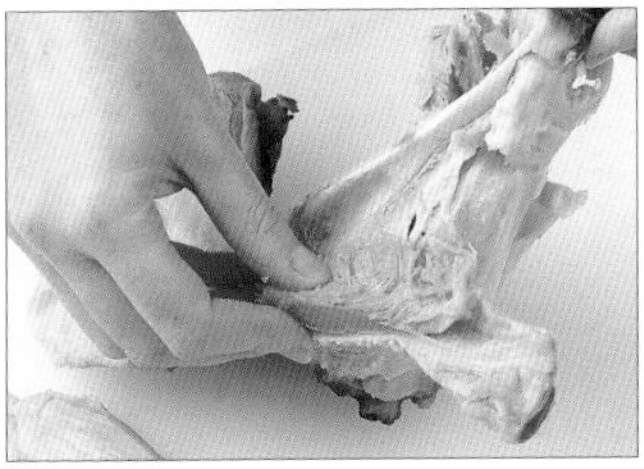

3 Meanwhile, strip all the gammon off the bone and return the bone to the broth. Discard the rind, fat and gristle and chop half the meat coarsely. Reserve the remaining meat for another recipe.

4 Add the chopped meat to the casserole. Discard the hard stalks from the broccoli and add the leaves and florets to the broth. Simmer for 10 minutes. Season generously with pepper, then remove the bone and leave the soup to stand for at least half a day.

5 To serve, reheat the soup, add a little more seasoning if necessary, and ladle into soup bowls.

COOK'S TIP

The leftover gammon can be chopped into bitesize pieces and added to rice or vegetable dishes, or tortillas.

Energy 348Kcal/1458kJ; Protein 36.9g; Carbohydrate 21.1g, of which sugars 3.2g; Fat 13.3g, of which saturates 4.3g; Cholesterol 38mg; Calcium 70mg; Fibre 5.9g; Sodium 1484mg.

Potato Tortilla

The classic tortilla stands on every tapas bar in Spain. The size of a large cake, it is dense and very satisfying. It can be eaten in wedges with a fork – a meal in itself with salad – or cut up into chunks and speared, to be enjoyed as a snack with drinks.

SERVES SIX

INGREDIENTS
- 450g/1lb small waxy potatoes, peeled
- 1 Spanish onion
- 45ml/3 tbsp vegetable oil
- 4 large (US extra large) eggs
- salt and ground black pepper
- fresh flat leaf parsley or tomato wedges, to garnish

1 Using a sharp knife, cut the potatoes into thin slices and slice the onion into thin rings. Heat 30ml/2 tbsp of the oil in a 20cm/8in heavy frying pan.

2 Add the potatoes and the onions to the pan and cook over a low heat for 20 minutes, or until the potato slices are just tender. Remove from the heat.

3 In a large bowl, beat together the eggs with a little salt and pepper. Stir in the cooked potatoes and onion.

4 Clean the frying pan with kitchen paper then heat the remaining oil and pour in the potato mixture. Cook very gently for 5–8 minutes until set underneath. During cooking, lift the edges of the tortilla with a spatula, and allow any uncooked egg to run underneath. Shake the pan from side to side, to prevent sticking.

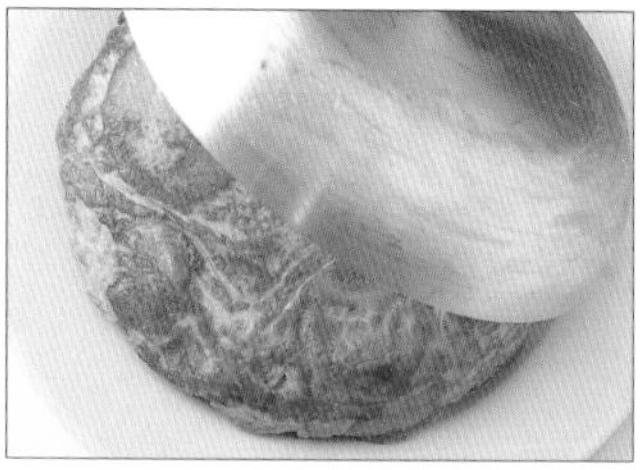

5 Place a large heatproof plate upside-down over the pan, invert the tortilla on to the plate and then slide it back into the pan. Cook for 2–3 minutes more, until the underside of the tortilla is golden brown. Cut into wedges and serve, garnished with fresh flat leaf parsley or tomato wedges.

Energy 163Kcal/681kJ; Protein 5.8g; Carbohydrate 14.7g, of which sugars 2.8g; Fat 9.5g, of which saturates 1.8g; Cholesterol 127mg; Calcium 32mg; Fibre 1.2g; Sodium 56mg.

TORTILLA WITH BEANS

The addition of chopped herbs and a few skinned beans to the classic tortilla makes this a very summery dish. Enjoy it as a light lunch, or cut it into small pieces and serve as a tapas dish. Tortilla is a must in tapas selections.

SERVES TWO

INGREDIENTS

- 45ml/3 tbsp olive oil
- 2 Spanish onions, thinly sliced
- 300g/11oz waxy potatoes, cut into dice
- 250g/9oz/1¾ cups shelled broad (fava) beans
- 5ml/1 tsp chopped fresh thyme or summer savory
- 6 large (US extra large) eggs
- 45ml/3 tbsp mixed chopped fresh chives and fresh flat leaf parsley
- salt and ground black pepper

1 Heat 30ml/2 tbsp of the oil in a 23cm/9in deep non-stick frying pan. Add the onions and potatoes and stir to coat. Cover and cook gently, stirring, for 20–25 minutes until the potatoes are cooked and the onions collapsed.

2 Meanwhile, cook the beans in a pan of boiling salted water for 5 minutes. Drain well and set aside to cool.

3 When the beans are cool enough to handle, peel off and discard the grey outer skins. Add the beans to the frying pan, together with the thyme or summer savory and season with salt and pepper to taste. Stir well to mix and cook for a further 2–3 minutes.

4 Beat the eggs with salt and pepper to taste and add the mixed herbs. Pour the egg mixture over the potatoes and onions and increase the heat slightly. Cook gently for about 5 minutes, or until the egg on the bottom sets and browns. During cooking, gently pull the tortilla away from the sides of the pan and tilt to allow the uncooked egg to run underneath.

5 Cover the frying pan with a large, upside-down plate and invert the tortilla on to it. Add the remaining oil to the pan and heat until hot. Slip the tortilla back into the pan, uncooked side down, and cook for 3–5 minutes until the underneath browns.

6 Slide the tortilla out on to a plate. Cut up into wedges or cubes and serve warm rather than piping hot.

Energy 655Kcal/2737kJ; Protein 34.3g; Carbohydrate 55.2g, of which sugars 15.3g; Fat 35.1g, of which saturates 7.3g; Cholesterol 571mg; Calcium 260mg; Fibre 13.6g; Sodium 250mg.

Spicy Sausage and Cheese Tortilla

This substantial tortilla is delicious hot or cold. Cut it into chunky wedges and serve for supper or a light lunch with a fresh tomato and basil salad. The addition of spicy chorizo and tangy cheese gives it a wonderful, rich flavour.

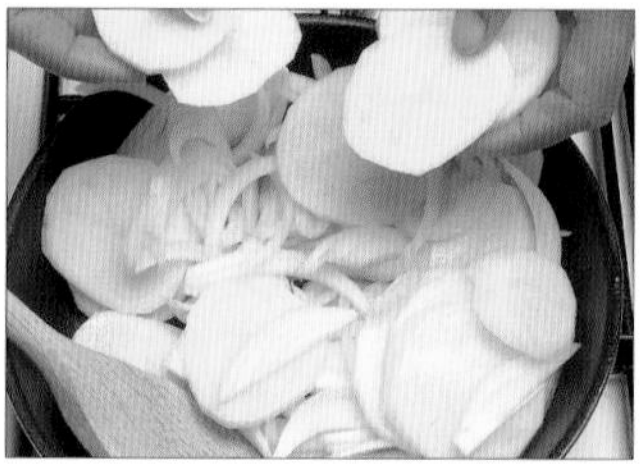

2 Add a further 30ml/2 tbsp oil to the pan and fry the potatoes and onions for 2–3 minutes, turning frequently (the pan will be very full). Cover tightly and cook over a gentle heat for about 30 minutes, turning occasionally, until softened and slightly golden.

3 In a large mixing bowl, beat together the eggs, parsley, cheese, sausage and plenty of seasoning. Gently stir in the potatoes and onions until coated, taking care not to break up the potato too much.

SERVES FOUR TO SIX

INGREDIENTS
- 75ml/5 tbsp olive oil
- 175g/6oz frying chorizo or spicy sausage, thinly sliced
- 675g/1½lb waxy potatoes, thinly sliced
- 2 Spanish onions, halved and thinly sliced
- 4 large (US extra large) eggs
- 30ml/2 tbsp chopped fresh parsley, plus extra to garnish
- 115g/4oz/1 cup grated Cheddar or other hard cheese
- salt and ground black pepper

1 Heat 15ml/1 tbsp of the oil in a 20cm/8in non-stick frying pan and fry the sausage until golden brown and cooked through. Lift out with a slotted spoon and drain on kitchen paper.

4 Wipe out the pan with kitchen paper and heat the remaining 30ml/2 tbsp oil. Add the potato mixture and cook, over a very low heat, until the egg begins to set. Use a metal spatula to prevent the tortilla from sticking and allow the uncooked egg to run underneath.

5 Preheat the grill (broiler) to high. When the base of the tortilla has set, which should take about 5 minutes, protect the pan handle with foil and place the tortilla under the grill until it is set and golden. Cut into wedges and serve garnished with parsley.

Energy 399Kcal/1661kJ; Protein 15.1g; Carbohydrate 25g, of which sugars 5.2g; Fat 26.9g, of which saturates 9.3g; Cholesterol 163mg; Calcium 215mg; Fibre 2.2g; Sodium 451mg.

Piperada Sandwich

The Basque omelette, piperada, *is very different from the cake-like tortilla. It oozes butter and tomato juice, and does not hold its shape at all. That is why it makes such a satisfying filling for a* bocadilla *– the Spanish split-roll sandwich.*

SERVES SIX

INGREDIENTS
- 120–150ml/8–10 tbsp olive oil
- 2 small onions, coarsely chopped
- 4 red, orange or yellow (bell) peppers, seeded and chopped
- 2 large garlic cloves, finely chopped
- pinch of chilli or hot cayenne pepper
- 675g/1½lb ripe tomatoes, peeled, seeded and chopped
- 15ml/1 tbsp chopped fresh oregano or 5ml/1 tsp dried
- 1 long French loaf
- 25g/1oz/2 tbsp butter
- 6 large (US extra large) eggs, beaten
- salt and ground black pepper
- basil leaves, to garnish (optional)

1 Heat 60ml/4 tbsp of the oil in a large heavy frying pan. Add the onions and cook over a gentle heat, stirring occasionally, for about 5 minutes until they are softened but not coloured.

2 Add the peppers, garlic and chilli powder or cayenne pepper to the pan. Cook for a further 5 minutes, stirring, then add the tomatoes, seasoning and fresh or dried oregano. Cook over a moderate heat for 15–20 minutes until the peppers are soft and most of the liquid has evaporated.

VARIATION

If you prefer, serve the piperada as an open sandwich on toasted bread, rather than in a split French stick.

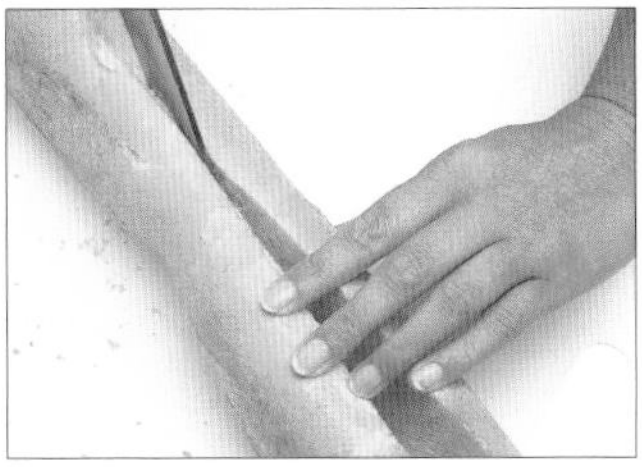

3 Preheat the oven to 200°C/400°F/ Gas 6. Cut the bread in half lengthways, trim off the ends, then cut into six equal pieces and brush with the remaining olive oil. Place the bread on baking trays and bake for 8–10 minutes until crisp and just turning golden.

4 Heat the butter in a pan until it bubbles, add the eggs and cook, stirring, until softly scrambled. Turn off the heat and stir in the pepper mixture. Divide evenly among the pieces of bread and sprinkle with the basil leaves, if using. Serve hot or warm.

Energy 674Kcal/2834kJ; Protein 21.2g; Carbohydrate 92.4g, of which sugars 19g; Fat 27.1g, of which saturates 6.5g; Cholesterol 199mg; Calcium 229mg; Fibre 7.4g; Sodium 934mg.

Scrambled Eggs with Spring Asparagus

Revuelto de espárragos is one of those delicious egg dishes that show off new green spring vegetables to perfection. Delightfully tender fresh asparagus and sweet peas make perfect partners to lightly cooked eggs.

SERVES FOUR

INGREDIENTS

- 1 bunch thin asparagus
- 30–45ml/2–3 tbsp tiny raw mangetout (snow peas)
- 8 large (US extra large) eggs
- 30ml/2 tbsp milk
- 50g/2oz/¼ cup butter
- salt and ground black pepper
- sweet paprika, for dusting

VARIATION

Replace the asparagus with the mangetouts. String 150g/5oz mangetouts, then slice them diagonally into two or three pieces. Cook for 2 minutes.

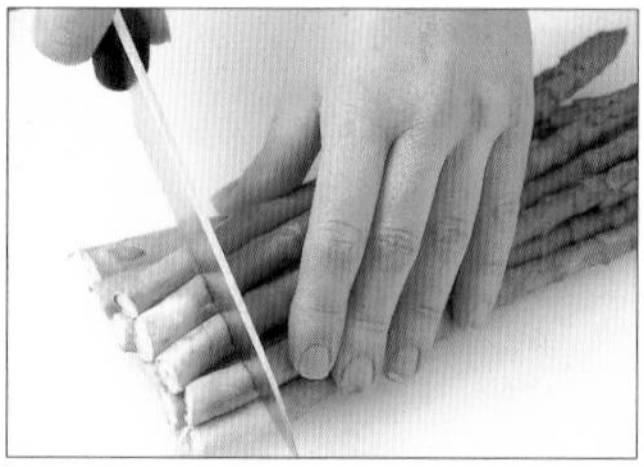

1 Prepare the asparagus. Using a large sharp knife, cut off and discard any hard stems. Cut the stems into short lengths, keeping the tips separate. Shell some of the fatter mangetout pods, to extract the tiny peas.

2 Tip the stems into a pan of boiling water and simmer for 4 minutes. Add the asparagus tips, and cook for another 6 minutes. If including some pea pod strips, cook them for 2 minutes. Break the eggs into a bowl and beat together with the milk, salt and black pepper.

3 Melt the butter in a large frying pan and pour in the eggs, scrambling them by pulling the cooked outsides to the middle with a wooden spoon. When the eggs are almost cooked, drain the asparagus and pea pod strips, if using, and stir into the eggs. Sprinkle the peas over the top, and dust lightly with paprika. Serve immediately.

Energy 252Kcal/1045kJ; Protein 13.8g; Carbohydrate 1.3g, of which sugars 1.2g; Fat 21.7g, of which saturates 9.7g; Cholesterol 408mg; Calcium 78mg; Fibre 0.6g; Sodium 220mg.

SCRAMBLED EGGS WITH PRAWNS

THE SPANISH ARE PARTICULAR ABOUT EGGS, DISTINGUISHING BETWEEN A REVUELTO, *WHICH USES SOFTLY-SET SCRAMBLED EGGS, AND THE MORE SOLID TORTILLA THAT IS COOKED UNTIL SET. THIS* REVUELTO DE GAMBAS *IS AN ECONOMICAL WAY OF USING A FEW SHELLFISH.*

SERVES FOUR

INGREDIENTS

- 1 bunch spring onions (scallions)
- 25g/1oz/2 tbsp butter
- 30ml/2 tbsp oil
- 150g/5oz shelled prawns (shrimp)
- 8 large (US extra large) eggs
- 30ml/2 tbsp milk
- 45ml/3 tbsp chopped fresh parsley
- salt and ground black pepper
- crusty bread, to serve

VARIATION

The green shoots from garlic bulbs are another very popular spring ingredient for this type of dish and can be used in place of the spring onions. Called *ajetes* in Spain, they lend a delicate flavour to eggs.

1 Chop the white of the spring onions and reserve, keeping it separate from 30ml/2 tbsp of the green tops.

2 Heat the butter and oil in a large frying pan. Add the spring onion white and cook briefly. Add the prawns and heat through. (If the prawns are raw, cook them for 2 minutes.)

3 Beat the eggs with the milk and then season. Turn the heat to medium-high and pour the egg mixture over the prawns. Cook for about 2 minutes, stirring with a wooden spoon.

4 Sprinkle with parsley and spring onion greens. Divide among four plates and serve immediately with crusty bread.

Energy 287Kcal/1191kJ; Protein 20.1g; Carbohydrate 1.9g, of which sugars 1.9g; Fat 22.4g, of which saturates 7.4g; Cholesterol 468mg; Calcium 126mg; Fibre 0.9g; Sodium 258mg.

Flamenco Eggs

This dish is a swirl of red, green, yellow and white – as colourful as the moving skirts of flamenco dancers. It is based on whatever ingredients are available. In spring that might mean peas, and late in the year squash or pumpkin. It often contains a few shrimps, too. The Migas (fried breadcrumb) topping is a popular Spanish accompaniment to eggs.

SERVES FOUR

INGREDIENTS
- 30ml/2 tbsp olive oil
- 115g/4oz smoked bacon lardons or diced pancetta
- 2 frying chorizos, cubed
- 1 onion, chopped
- 2 garlic cloves, finely chopped
- 1 red and 1 green (bell) pepper, seeded and chopped
- 500g/1¼lb tomatoes, chopped
- 15–30ml/1–2 tbsp fino sherry
- 45ml/3 tbsp chopped parsley
- 8 large (US extra large) eggs
- salt, paprika and cayenne

For the *migas*
- 4 thick slices stale bread
- oil, for frying
- 2 garlic cloves, bruised

1 Preheat the oven to 180°C/350°F/Gas 4. Warm four individual baking dishes.

2 Heat the oil in a large frying pan and fry the bacon and chorizos, to give off their fat. Add the onion and garlic and cook gently until softened, stirring. Add the peppers and tomatoes and cook and reduce, stirring occasionally. Add some paprika and sherry – the mixture must not be too dry.

3 Divide the vegetable mixture evenly among the baking dishes. Sprinkle with parsley. Swirl the eggs together with a fork (without overmixing) and season well with salt and cayenne. Pour over the vegetable mixture.

4 Bake the eggs and vegetables for 8 minutes, or until the eggs are just set.

5 Meanwhile make the *migas*. Cut the crusts off the bread and reduce to crumbs in a food processor, or use a hand grater.

6 Heat plenty of oil in a large frying pan over a high heat, add the garlic cloves for a few moments to flavour it, then remove and discard them. Throw in the crumbs and brown quickly, scooping them out on to kitchen paper with a slotted spoon. Season with a little salt and paprika, then sprinkle around the edge of the eggs, when ready.

Energy 619Kcal/2580kJ; Protein 26.8g; Carbohydrate 34.7g, of which sugars 14.1g; Fat 42.3g, of which saturates 12.2g; Cholesterol 419mg; Calcium 147mg; Fibre 4.1g; Sodium 1079mg.

PAN-FRIED HAM AND VEGETABLES WITH EGGS

Little vegetable dishes, and ones that contain ham or eggs, or both, are the backbone of the Spanish supper scene. This delicious dish is incredibly simple to make and is hearty enough to serve as a meal in itself. Unlike tortilla, the eggs are not beaten, but are broken into the vegetable mixture and cooked whole.

SERVES FOUR

INGREDIENTS

- 30ml/2 tbsp olive oil
- 1 onion, roughly chopped
- 2 garlic cloves, finely chopped
- 175g/6oz cooked ham
- 225g/8oz courgettes (zucchini)
- 1 red (bell) pepper, seeded and thinly sliced
- 1 yellow (bell) pepper, seeded and thinly sliced
- 10ml/2 tsp paprika
- 400g/14oz can chopped tomatoes
- 15ml/1 tbsp sun-dried tomato purée (paste)
- 4 large (US extra large) eggs
- 115g/4oz/1 cup coarsely grated Cheddar cheese
- salt and ground black pepper
- crusty bread, to serve

1 Heat the olive oil in a deep frying pan. Add the onion and garlic and cook for 4 minutes, stirring frequently.

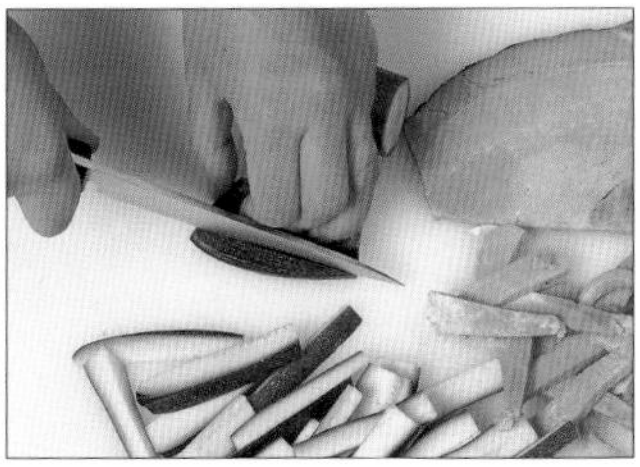

2 Meanwhile, cut the cooked ham and courgettes into 5cm/2in batons.

3 Add the courgettes and peppers to the pan and cook over a medium heat for 3–4 minutes.

4 Stir in the paprika, tomatoes, tomato purée, ham and seasoning. Bring to a simmer and cook gently for 15 minutes.

5 Reduce the heat to low. Make four wells in the tomato mixture, break an egg into each and season. Cook over a gentle heat until the white begins to set. Preheat the grill (broiler). Sprinkle the cheese over and grill for about 5 minutes until the eggs are set.

Energy 365Kcal/1522kJ; Protein 25g; Carbohydrate 14.7g, of which sugars 13.2g; Fat 22.9g, of which saturates 9.3g; Cholesterol 244mg; Calcium 286mg; Fibre 3.7g; Sodium 827mg.

SALADS AND VEGETABLES

Salads start the meal in summer, and are typical of Spain's attitude to cooking, using fresh, local seasonal ingredients. Vegetable dishes are inventive too, eaten as a tapas dish, a course on their own, or perhaps as a supper. Simple ingredients are cleverly paired to show off their qualities to perfection.

Marinated Mushrooms

Champiñones en escabeche is a good way to serve mushrooms in summer, and makes a refreshing alternative to the ever-popular mushrooms fried in garlic. Serve with plenty of crusty bread to mop up the delicious juices.

SERVES FOUR

INGREDIENTS

- 30ml/2 tbsp olive oil
- 1 small onion, very finely chopped
- 1 garlic clove, finely chopped
- 15ml/1 tbsp tomato purée (paste)
- 50ml/2fl oz/¼ cup amontillado sherry
- 50ml/2fl oz/¼ cup water
- 2 cloves
- 225g/8oz/3 cups button (white) mushrooms, trimmed
- salt and ground black pepper
- chopped fresh parsley, to garnish

VARIATION

In Spain, wild mushrooms, known as *setas*, are served in this way.

1 Heat the oil in a pan. Add the onion and garlic and cook until soft. Stir in the tomato purée, sherry, water and the cloves and season with salt and black pepper. Bring to the boil, cover and simmer gently for 45 minutes, adding more water if it becomes too dry.

2 Add the mushrooms to the pan, then cover and allow to simmer for about 5 minutes. Remove from the heat and allow to cool, still covered. Chill in the refrigerator overnight. Serve the mushrooms cold, sprinkled with the chopped fresh parsley.

Energy 80Kcal/329kJ; Protein 1.4g; Carbohydrate 2.1g, of which sugars 1.7g; Fat 5.8g, of which saturates 0.9g; Cholesterol 0mg; Calcium 9mg; Fibre 0.9g; Sodium 14mg.

ENSALADILLA

KNOWN AS RUSSIAN SALAD ELSEWHERE, THIS "SALAD OF LITTLE THINGS" BECAME EXTREMELY POPULAR DURING THE SPANISH CIVIL WAR IN THE 1930S, WHEN MORE EXPENSIVE INGREDIENTS WERE SCARCE. IT MAY EVEN HAVE BEEN INVENTED IN SPAIN – DESPITE ITS NAME.

SERVES FOUR

INGREDIENTS

- 8 new potatoes, scrubbed and quartered
- 1 large carrot, diced
- 115g/4oz fine green beans, cut into 2cm/¾in lengths
- 75g/3oz/¾ cup peas
- ½ Spanish onion, chopped
- 4 cornichons or small gherkins, sliced
- 1 small red (bell) pepper, seeded and diced
- 50g/2oz/½ cup pitted black olives
- 15ml/1 tbsp drained pickled capers
- 15ml/1 tbsp freshly squeezed lemon juice
- 30ml/2 tbsp chopped fresh fennel or parsley
- salt and ground black pepper

For the allioli

- 2 garlic cloves, finely chopped
- 2.5ml/½ tsp salt
- 150ml/¼ pint/⅔ cup mayonnaise

VARIATION

This salad is delicious using any combination of chopped, cooked vegetables. Use whatever is available.

1 Make the allioli. Crush the garlic with the salt in a mortar and whisk or stir into the mayonnaise.

2 Cook the potatoes and diced carrot in a pan of boiling lightly salted water for 5–8 minutes until almost tender. Add the beans and peas to the pan and cook for 2 minutes, or until all the vegetables are tender. Drain well.

3 Tip the vegetables into a large bowl. Add the onion, cornichons or gherkins, red pepper, olives and capers. Stir in the allioli and season to taste with pepper and lemon juice.

4 Toss the vegetables and allioli together until well combined, check the seasoning and chill well. Serve garnished with fennel or parsley.

Energy 385Kcal/1596kJ; Protein 4.6g; Carbohydrate 24.1g, of which sugars 6.9g; Fat 30.7g, of which saturates 4.8g; Cholesterol 28mg; Calcium 39mg; Fibre 4g; Sodium 468mg.

Orange and Red Onion Salad with Cumin

During winter in the south of Spain, when other salad ingredients are in short supply, oranges often form the basis of salads. In this ensalada de naranjas *they are partnered with thinly sliced red onions and black olives, and flavoured with two popular Middle Eastern ingredients – cumin seeds and mint.*

SERVES SIX

INGREDIENTS
- 6 oranges
- 2 red onions
- 15ml/1 tbsp cumin seeds
- 5ml/1 tsp coarsely ground black pepper
- 15ml/1 tbsp chopped fresh mint
- 90ml/6 tbsp olive oil
- salt
- fresh mint sprigs and black olives, to garnish

COOK'S TIP
It is important to let the salad stand before serving. This allows the flavours to develop and the pungent taste of the onion to soften slightly.

1 Using a sharp knife, slice the oranges thinly, working over a bowl to catch any juice. Then, holding each orange slice in turn over the bowl, cut round the middle fleshy section with scissors to remove the peel and pith. Reserve the juice. Slice the two red onions thinly and separate the rings.

2 Arrange the orange and onion slices in layers in a shallow dish, sprinkling each layer with cumin seeds, pepper, mint, olive oil and salt. Pour in the reserved orange juice. Leave to marinate in a cool place for about 2 hours. Just before serving, scatter with the mint sprigs and black olives.

Mixed Salad with Olives and Capers

Colourful salads start many summer meals in Spain, and are a communal affair. The bowl is put in the centre of the table and everyone helps themselves, with a fork.

SERVES FOUR

INGREDIENTS
- 4 large tomatoes
- ½ cucumber
- 1 bunch spring onions (scallions)
- 1 bunch watercress or rocket (arugula), washed
- 8 pimiento-stuffed olives
- 30ml/2 tbsp drained pickled capers

For the dressing
- 1 garlic clove, finely chopped
- 30ml/2 tbsp red wine vinegar
- 5ml/1 tsp paprika
- 2.5ml/½ tsp ground cumin
- 75ml/5 tbsp virgin olive oil
- salt and ground black pepper

COOK'S TIP
In Spain, tomatoes are always used when red and ripe. Firm tomatoes should be used in salads and soft ones in sauces.

1 To peel the tomatoes, place them in a heatproof bowl, pour over boiling water to cover and leave to stand for 1 minute. Lift out with a slotted spoon and plunge into a bowl of cold water. Leave for 1 minute, then drain. Slip off the skins and dice the flesh finely. Put in a salad bowl.

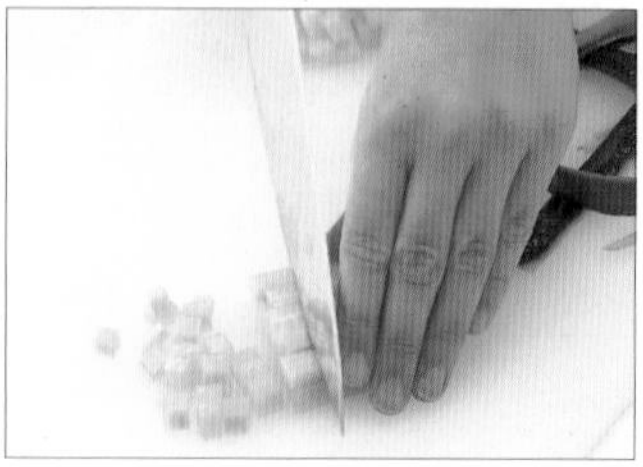

2 Peel the cucumber, dice finely and add to the tomatoes. Trim and chop half the spring onions, and add to the bowl.

3 Toss the vegetables together, then break the watercress or rocket into small sprigs. Add to the tomato mixture, with the olives and capers.

4 Make the dressing. Crush the garlic to a paste with a little salt, using the flat of a knife. Put in a bowl and mix in the vinegar and spices. Whisk in the oil and taste for seasoning. Dress the salad, and serve garnished with the remaining spring onions.

TOP Energy 163Kcal/680kJ; Protein 2.2g; Carbohydrate 14.3g, of which sugars 12.7g; Fat 11.3g, of which saturates 1.6g; Cholesterol 0mg; Calcium 83mg; Fibre 2.7g; Sodium 9mg.
BOTTOM Energy 156Kcal/644kJ; Protein 1.7g; Carbohydrate 4.1g, of which sugars 4.1g; Fat 14.8g, of which saturates 2.2g; Cholesterol 0mg; Calcium 44mg; Fibre 1.8g; Sodium 130mg.

MUSHROOM, BEAN AND CHORIZO SALAD

This really simple salad can be served as an accompaniment to plain fish or chicken dishes, or served with crusty bread as a hearty lunch or supper dish. The combination of spicy sausage, tender, sweet beans and delicate mushrooms is quite delicious.

SERVES FOUR

INGREDIENTS
- 225g/8oz shelled broad (fava) beans
- 175g/6oz frying chorizo
- 60ml/4 tbsp extra virgin olive oil
- 225g/8oz/3 cups brown cap (cremini) mushrooms, sliced
- 60ml/4 tbsp chopped fresh chives
- salt and ground black pepper

COOK'S TIP
Although peeling the skins from broad beans can be time consuming, it is well worth it. Beans with tough, bitter skins will spoil the delicate taste and texture of this lovely salad.

1 Cook the broad beans in a pan of salted boiling water for 7–8 minutes. Drain and refresh under cold water.

2 Remove the skin from the sausage. If it doesn't peel off easily, score along the length of the sausage with a sharp knife first. Cut the chorizo into small chunks. Heat the oil in a small pan, add the chorizo and cook for 2–3 minutes.

3 Put the sliced mushrooms in a bowl and tip in the chorizo and oil. Toss to combine then leave to cool.

4 If the beans are large, peel away the tough outer skins. Stir the beans and half the chives into the mushroom mixture, and season to taste. Serve at room temperature, garnished with the remaining chives.

AVOCADO, ORANGE AND ALMOND SALAD

In Andalusia, avocados have become one of the big cash crops, replacing many orange orchards. In this salad, ENSALADA DE AGUACATES, *the smooth, creamy avocados combine perfectly with locally grown oranges and almonds.*

SERVES FOUR

INGREDIENTS
- 2–3 oranges
- 2 ripe tomatoes
- 2 small avocados
- 60ml/4 tbsp extra virgin olive oil
- 30ml/2 tbsp lemon juice
- 15ml/1 tbsp chopped fresh parsley
- small onion rings
- 25g/1oz/¼ cup split, toasted almonds
- 10–12 black olives
- salt and ground black pepper

COOK'S TIP
Spanish onions are sweet and mild, and pleasant to eat raw, but they are very large. Slice them and use just the small central rings for salads, keeping the large outer rings for frying.

1 Peel the oranges and slice them into thick rounds. Plunge the tomatoes into boiling water for 30 seconds, then refresh in cold water. Peel away the skins, cut the tomatoes into quarters, remove the seeds and chop roughly.

2 Cut the avocados in half, remove the stones and carefully peel away the skin. Cut into chunks.

3 Mix together the olive oil, lemon juice and parsley. Season with salt and pepper, then toss the avocados and tomatoes in half of the dressing.

4 Arrange the sliced oranges on a plate and scatter with the onion rings. Drizzle with the remaining dressing. Spoon the avocados, tomatoes, almonds and olives on top and serve immediately.

TOP Energy 283Kcal/1174kJ; Protein 9.7g; Carbohydrate 11.9g, of which sugars 1.6g; Fat 22.2g, of which saturates 6.1g; Cholesterol 18mg; Calcium 56mg; Fibre 4.5g; Sodium 362mg.
BOTTOM Energy 291Kcal/1204kJ; Protein 3.8g; Carbohydrate 11.4g, of which sugars 10.6g; Fat 25.8g, of which saturates 4.2g; Cholesterol 0mg; Calcium 79mg; Fibre 4.7g; Sodium 295mg.

Charred Artichokes with Lemon Oil Dip

Young artichokes, alcachofas, *are cooked over the first barbecues of the summer. However, they are also very good roasted in the oven. A roast head of garlic combined with olive oil makes a classic, mild sauce –* con mojete *– for vegetables.*

SERVES TWO TO FOUR

INGREDIENTS
- 15ml/1 tbsp lemon juice or white wine vinegar
- 2 globe artichokes
- 45ml/3 tbsp olive oil
- sea salt
- sprigs of fresh flat leaf parsley, to garnish

For the lemon oil dip
- 12 garlic cloves, unpeeled
- 1 lemon
- 45ml/3 tbsp extra virgin olive oil

COOK'S TIP
Artichokes are usually boiled, but if you can get young, tender artichokes, they are delicious roasted over a barbecue.

1 Preheat the oven to 200°C/400°F/Gas 6. Stir the lemon juice or vinegar into a bowl of cold water.

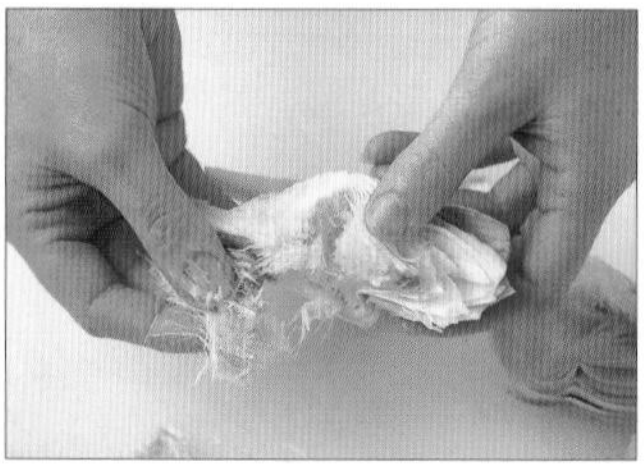

2 Cut each artichoke lengthways into wedges. Pull the hairy choke out from the centre of each wedge and drop the wedges into the acidulated water.

3 Drain the artichokes and place in a roasting pan with the garlic cloves. Toss in the oil. Sprinkle with salt and roast for 40 minutes, stirring once or twice, until the artichokes are tender.

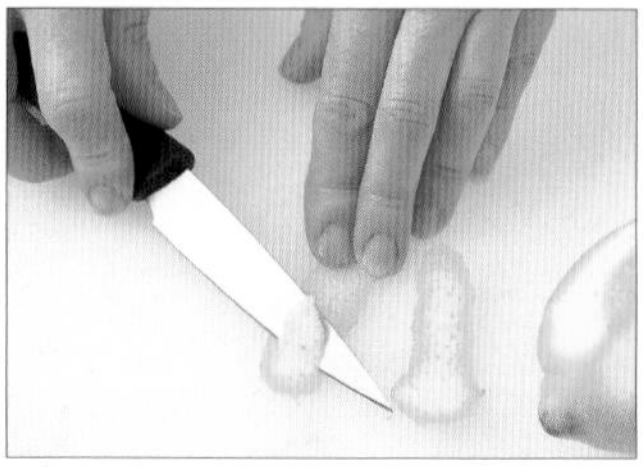

4 Meanwhile, make the dip. Pare away two strips of rind from the lemon and scrape away any pith. Place the rind in a pan with water to cover. Simmer for 5 minutes, then drain, refresh in cold water and chop roughly.

5 Arrange the artichokes on a plate and set aside to cool for 5 minutes. Flatten the garlic cloves so that the flesh pops out of the skins. Transfer the garlic flesh to a bowl, mash to a purée then add the lemon rind. Squeeze the juice from the lemon, then, using a fork, whisk in the olive oil and lemon juice.

6 Serve the artichokes warm. Garnish them with parsley and accompany them with the lemon dip.

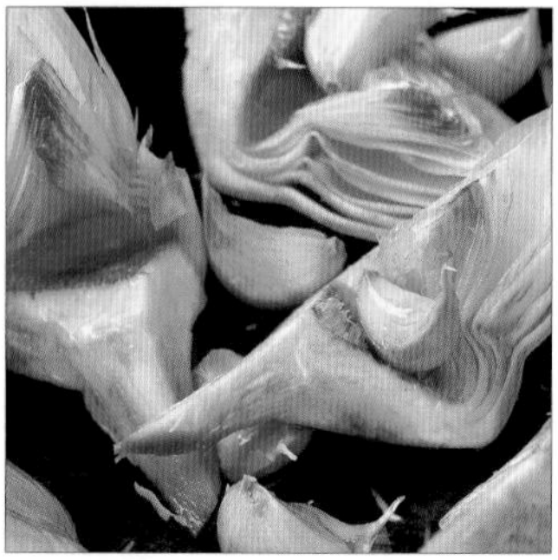

Energy 165Kcal/679kJ; Protein 1.3g; Carbohydrate 2.6g, of which sugars 0.8g; Fat 16.7g, of which saturates 2.4g; Cholesterol 0mg; Calcium 24mg; Fibre 1.1g; Sodium 31mg.

SPINACH WITH RAISINS AND PINE NUTS

RAISINS AND PINE NUTS ARE FREQUENT PARTNERS IN SPANISH RECIPES, AS THE PINE NUTS ARE ASTRINGENT YET RICH, THE RAISINS SWEET. HERE, TOSSED WITH WILTED SPINACH AND CROÛTONS, THEY MAKE A DELICIOUS SNACK OR MAIN MEAL ACCOMPANIMENT.

SERVES FOUR

INGREDIENTS
- 50g/2oz/⅓ cup raisins, preferably Malaga raisins
- 1 thick slice crusty white bread
- 45ml/3 tbsp olive oil
- 25g/1oz/¼ cup pine nuts
- 500g/1¼ lb young spinach, stalks removed
- 2 garlic cloves, finely chopped
- salt and ground black pepper

VARIATION

Swiss chard, also known as spinach beet and leaf beet, may be used instead of the spinach. It has a very similar flavour to spinach, but the leaves require slightly longer cooking.

1 Put the raisins in a small bowl and pour over enough boiling water to cover. Leave the raisins to soak for about 10 minutes, then drain well.

2 Cut off the crusts and cut the bread into cubes. Heat 30ml/2 tbsp of the oil in a frying pan and fry the cubes of bread until golden. Drain.

3 Heat the remaining oil in the pan. Gently fry the pine nuts until just colouring. Add the spinach and garlic and cook quickly, turning the spinach until it has just wilted.

4 Add the raisins and season lightly. Transfer to a warmed dish. Scatter with the croûtons and serve immediately.

Energy 198Kcal/824kJ; Protein 5.2g; Carbohydrate 14.3g, of which sugars 11g; Fat 13.7g, of which saturates 1.6g; Cholesterol 0mg; Calcium 226mg; Fibre 3.1g; Sodium 218mg.

AMANIDA

The word Amanida is Catalan for an arranged salad that includes fish, meat and vegetables in equal proportions. These salads can be a wonder to behold, but are also simple to make, because they combine small quantities of ready-to-eat ingredients.

SERVES SIX

INGREDIENTS
- 1 lolla green lettuce
- 50g/2oz cured, sliced chorizo or in a piece skinned and diced
- 4 thin slices Serrano ham
- 130g/4½oz can sardines in oil, drained
- 130g/4½oz can albacore tuna steak in oil, drained
- 8 canned white asparagus spears, drained
- 2–3 canned palm hearts, drained
- 115g/4oz/⅔ cup tiny arbequina olives
- 115g/4oz/⅔ cup big gordas or queen olives, preferably purplish ones
- 10 medium red tomatoes
- 15ml/1 tbsp chopped fresh parsley, to garnish

For the vinaigrette
- 1 garlic clove, split lengthways
- 30ml/2 tbsp sherry vinegar
- 30ml/2 tbsp red wine vinegar
- 60ml/4 tbsp olive oil
- 60ml/4 tbsp extra virgin olive oil
- salt and ground black pepper

COOK'S TIP
The salad selection is largely about what you can get. Fresh asparagus spears (cut to length) can replace canned ones and celery hearts may replace palm heart.

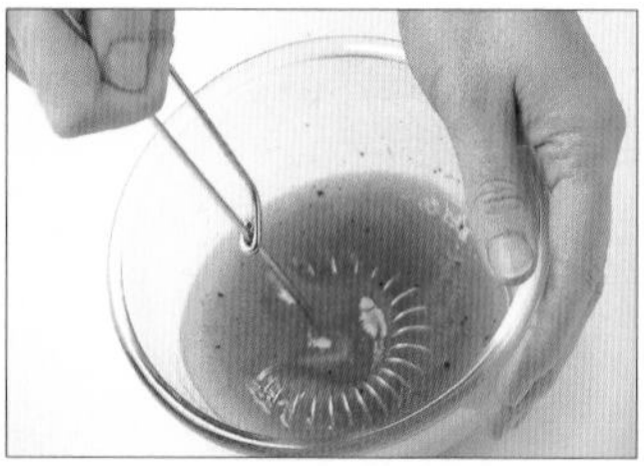

1 Make the vinaigrette. Wipe the cut side of the garlic round a bowl, then discard. Whisk the other ingredients together in the bowl, then tip the vinaigrette into a small jug (pitcher).

2 Choose a large serving plate. Select eight lettuce leaves, to make small bunches round it. Break off the stem ends. Tip the leaves into the vinaigrette bowl and toss to coat in a little dressing. Arrange them around the serving plate.

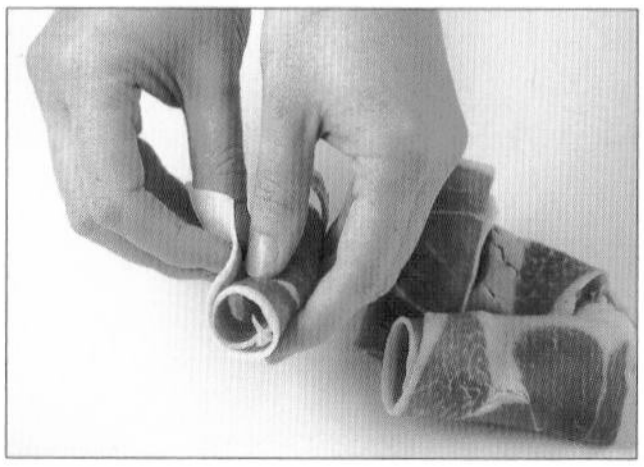

3 Position the chorizo slices on one side of the plate. Roll the ham and arrange opposite. Drain and blot the canned fish and arrange the sardines and tuna across the plate, in a cross.

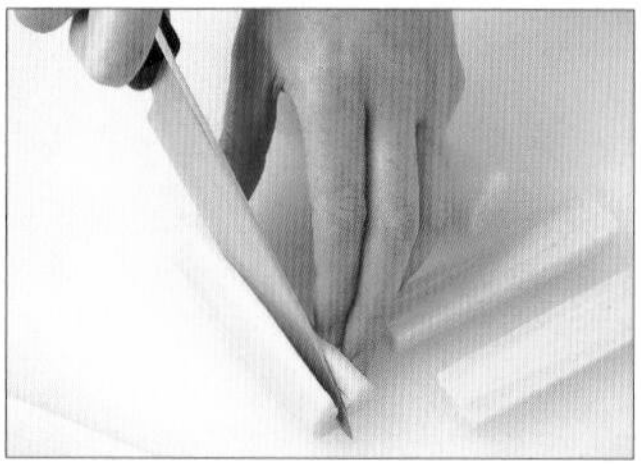

4 Arrange the asparagus, spears outwards, and the palm hearts (split lengthways), on opposite sides of the plate. Pile the two types of olive in the remaining spaces.

5 Put the tomatoes in a bowl and pour over boiling water. Leave to stand for 10 minutes, then drain. Peel and quarter two-thirds of the tomatoes and cut out the centres.

6 Arrange the tomatoes, round side up, in the centre of the plate, just touching all the prepared sections. Prepare more tomatoes as they are needed. Arrange them in a flower shape, each new ring just overlapping the previous one. The final ring, in the centre of the pile, should make a flower shape.

7 Brush vinaigrette dressing over the tomatoes, palm hearts and asparagus spears and season lightly with salt and black pepper. Sprinkle parsley very discreetly on the tomatoes and white vegetables. Serve at room temperature. (Refrigerate if you must, while waiting to serve.)

Energy 304Kcal/1264kJ; Protein 14.7g; Carbohydrate 7.5g, of which sugars 6.8g; Fat 24.2g, of which saturates 4.4g; Cholesterol 37mg; Calcium 169mg; Fibre 3.4g; Sodium 878mg.

BRAISED CABBAGE WITH CHORIZO

CABBAGES – BERZAS – MARK THE LANDSCAPE IN GALICIA, WHERE THE HUGE VEGETABLES GROW MORE THAN HIP HIGH. THEY ARE POPULARLY COOKED IN STEWS IN THE MANY MOUNTAIN REGIONS OF THE SOUTH, AND ARE FREQUENTLY SERVED WITH CHICKPEAS OR SAUSAGES, AS IN THIS RECIPE.

SERVES FOUR

INGREDIENTS

- 50g/2oz/¼ cup butter
- 5ml/1 tsp coriander seeds
- 225g/8oz green cabbage, shredded
- 2 garlic cloves, finely chopped
- 50g/2oz cured chorizo sausage, roughly chopped
- 60ml/4 tbsp dry sherry or white wine
- salt and ground black pepper

VARIATION

Smoked bacon makes a good substitute for chorizo sausage in this recipe, but it should only be cooked briefly.

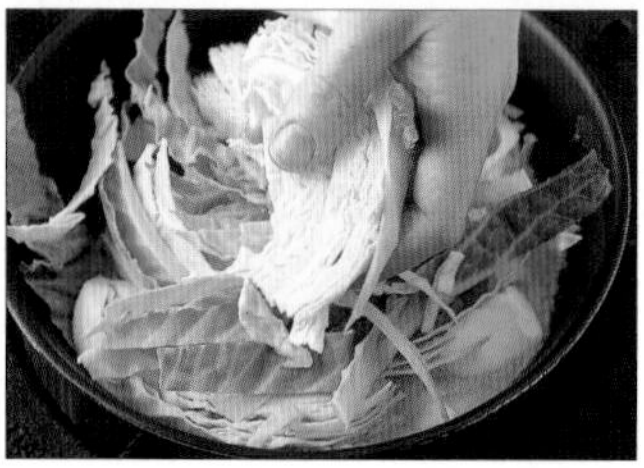

1 Melt the butter in a frying pan, add the coriander seeds and cook for 1 minute. Add the cabbage to the pan with the garlic and chorizo. Stir-fry for 5 minutes until the cabbage is tender.

2 Add the sherry or wine and plenty of salt and pepper to the pan. Cover and cook for 15–20 minutes until the cabbage is tender. Check the seasoning, adding more if necessary, and serve.

Energy 163Kcal/673kJ; Protein 2.1g; Carbohydrate 4.6g, of which sugars 3.3g; Fat 13.4g, of which saturates 7.8g; Cholesterol 32mg; Calcium 37mg; Fibre 1.3g; Sodium 183mg.

La Calçotada

Spring onions (calçot) have their own festival in the province of Tarragona. It is a day to mark the return of better weather, and in the past the onions, which were picked when rather bigger than our standard spring onions, were barbecued in the fields.

SERVES SIX

INGREDIENTS

3 bunches of plump spring onions (scallions), or Chinese green onions, which are about 2.5cm/1in across the bulb
olive oil, for brushing

For the romesco sauce

2–3 *ñoras* or other mild dried red chillies, such as Mexican *anchos* or *guajillos*
1 large red (bell) pepper, halved and seeded
2 large tomatoes, halved and seeded
4–6 large garlic cloves, unpeeled
75–90ml/5–6 tbsp olive oil
25g/1oz/¼ cup hazelnuts, blanched
4 slices French bread, each about 2cm/¾in thick
15ml/1 tbsp sherry vinegar
squeeze of lemon juice (optional)
chopped fresh parsley, to garnish

1 Prepare the sauce. Soak the dried chillies in hot water for about 30 minutes. Preheat the oven to 220°C/425°F/Gas 7.

2 Place the pepper, tomatoes and garlic on a baking sheet and drizzle with 15ml/1 tbsp olive oil. Roast, uncovered, for 30–40 minutes, until the pepper is blistered and blackened and the garlic is soft. Cool slightly, then peel the pepper, tomatoes and garlic.

COOK'S TIP

This piquant romesco sauce is a variation on the classic, roasting the vegetables rather than frying them.

3 Heat the remaining oil in a small frying pan and fry the hazelnuts until lightly browned, then transfer them to a plate. Fry the bread in the same oil until light brown on both sides, then transfer to the plate with the nuts and leave to cool. Reserve the oil from cooking.

4 Drain the chillies, discard as many of their seeds as you can, then place the chillies in a food processor. Add the red pepper halves, tomatoes, garlic, hazelnuts and bread chunks together with the reserved olive oil. Add the vinegar and process to a paste. Check the seasoning and thin the sauce with a little more oil or lemon juice, if necessary. Set aside.

5 Trim the roots from the spring onions or trim the Chinese onion leaves so that they are about 15–18cm/6–7in long. Brush with oil.

6 Heat an oiled ridged grill pan and cook the onions for about 2 minutes on each side, turning once and brushing with oil. (Alternatively, place under a preheated grill (broiler) 10cm/4in away from the heat and cook for 3 minutes on each side, brushing with more oil when turned; roast in a preheated oven at 200°C/400°F/Gas 6 for 5–6 minutes; or barbecue over grey charcoal for 3–4 minutes on each side, brushing with oil as needed.) Serve immediately with the sauce.

Energy 212Kcal/886kJ; Protein 4.9g; Carbohydrate 20.7g, of which sugars 5.1g; Fat 12.8g, of which saturates 1.7g; Cholesterol 0mg; Calcium 58mg; Fibre 2.6g; Sodium 172mg.

PATATAS BRAVAS

THERE ARE SEVERAL VARIATIONS ON THIS CHILLI AND POTATO DISH, BUT THE MOST IMPORTANT THING IS THE SPICING, WHICH IS MADE HOTTER STILL BY ADDING VINEGAR. THE CLASSIC VERSION IS MADE WITH FRESH TOMATO SAUCE FLAVOURED WITH GARLIC AND CHILLI. THE NAME BRAVAS *IMPLIES THAT THE POTATOES ARE SO HOT THAT IT IS MANLY TO EAT THEM.*

SERVES FOUR

INGREDIENTS

- 675g/1½lb small new potatoes
- 75ml/5 tbsp olive oil
- 2 garlic cloves, sliced
- 3 dried chillies, seeded and chopped
- 2.5ml/½ tsp ground cumin
- 10ml/2 tsp paprika
- 30ml/2 tbsp red or white wine vinegar
- 1 red or green (bell) pepper, seeded and sliced
- coarse sea salt, for sprinkling (optional)

1 Scrub the potatoes and put them into a pan of salted water. Bring to the boil and cook for 10 minutes, or until almost tender. Drain and leave to cool slightly. Peel, if you like, then cut into chunks.

2 Heat the oil in a large frying or sauté pan and fry the potatoes, turning them frequently, until golden.

3 Meanwhile, crush together the garlic, chillies and cumin using a mortar and pestle. Mix the paste with the paprika and wine vinegar, then add to the potatoes with the sliced pepper and cook, stirring, for 2 minutes. Scatter with salt, if using, and serve hot as a tapas dish or cold as a side dish.

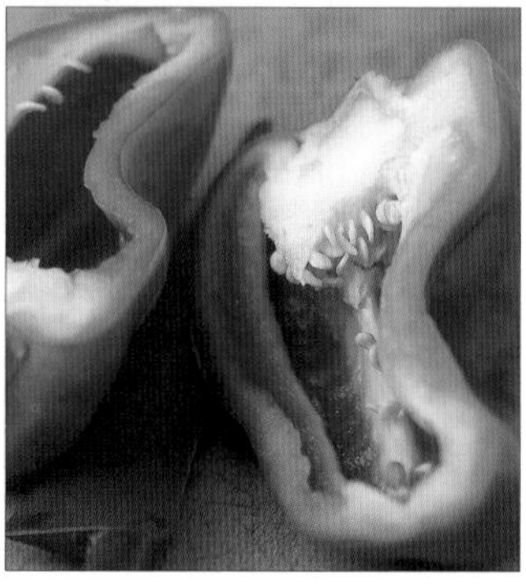

Energy 256Kcal/1070kJ; Protein 3.3g; Carbohydrate 30g, of which sugars 4.9g; Fat 14.4g, of which saturates 2.2g; Cholesterol 0mg; Calcium 14mg; Fibre 2.4g; Sodium 20mg.

MOJETE

THE SPANISH LOVE TO SCOOP UP COOKED VEGETABLES WITH BREAD, AND THE NAME OF THIS DISH, WHICH IS DERIVED FROM THE WORD MEANING TO DIP, REFLECTS THAT. PEPPERS, TOMATOES AND ONIONS ARE BAKED TOGETHER TO MAKE A COLOURFUL, SOFT VEGETABLE DISH THAT IS STUDDED WITH OLIVES. IN THE SUMMER THE VEGETABLES CAN BE COOKED ON THE BARBECUE.

SERVES EIGHT

INGREDIENTS

- 2 red (bell) peppers
- 2 yellow (bell) peppers
- 1 red onion, sliced
- 2 garlic cloves, halved
- 50g/2oz/¼ cup black olives
- 6 large ripe tomatoes, quartered
- 5ml/1 tsp soft light brown sugar
- 45ml/3 tbsp amontillado sherry
- 3–4 fresh rosemary sprigs
- 30ml/2 tbsp olive oil
- salt and ground black pepper
- fresh bread, to serve

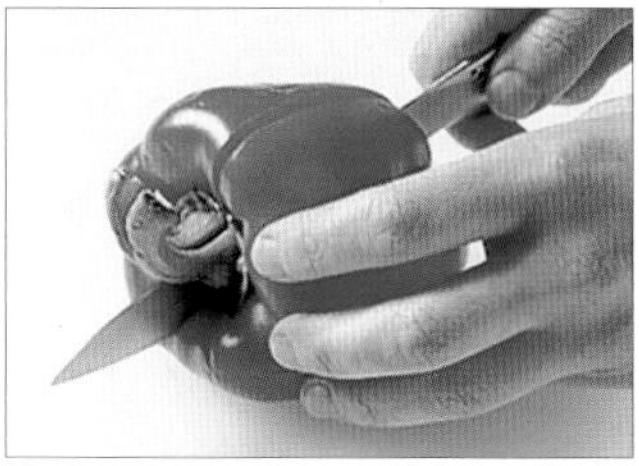

1 Halve the peppers and remove the seeds. Cut each pepper lengthways into 12 strips. Preheat the oven to 200°C/400°F/Gas 6.

2 Place the peppers, onion, garlic, olives and tomatoes in a large roasting pan.

3 Sprinkle the vegetables with the sugar, then pour in the sherry. Season well with salt and pepper, cover with foil and bake for 45 minutes.

4 Remove the foil from the pan and stir the mixture well. Add the rosemary sprigs and drizzle with the olive oil. Return the pan to the oven and cook for a further 30 minutes, uncovered, until the vegetables are very tender. Serve hot or cold with plenty of chunks of fresh crusty bread.

COOK'S TIP

Spain is the world's chief olive producer, with half the crop being exported. Try to use good quality Spanish olives for this recipe. Choose unpitted ones as they have a better flavour.

Energy 84Kcal/349kJ; Protein 1.6g; Carbohydrate 9.3g, of which sugars 8.8g; Fat 4g, of which saturates 0.7g; Cholesterol 0mg; Calcium 19mg; Fibre 2.4g; Sodium 152mg.

STUFFED TOMATOES AND PEPPERS

Colourful peppers and tomatoes make perfect containers for a simple rice, nut and herb stuffing. The vegetables become deliciously sweet and juicy when baked. Serve TOMATES Y PIMIENTAS RELLENOS *as a substantial starter or a supper dish.*

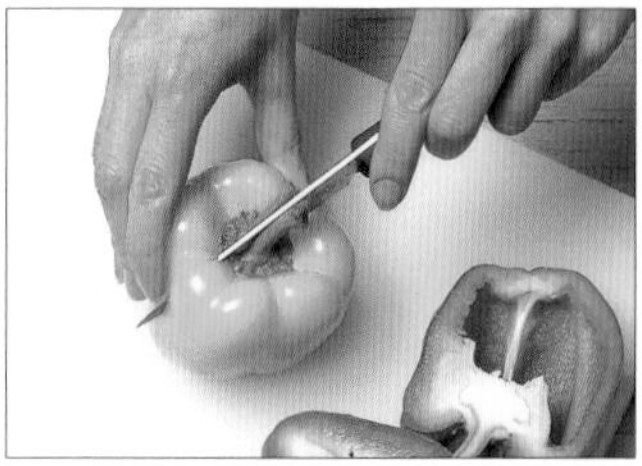

3 Halve the peppers, leaving the cores intact. Scoop out the seeds. Brush the peppers with 15ml/1 tbsp of the oil.

4 Fry the onions and garlic in 30ml/2 tbsp oil. Stir in most of the almonds. Add the rice, tomato pulp, drained raisins, mint and 30ml/2 tbsp parsley. Season well, then spoon the mixture into the vegetable cases.

5 Bake uncovered for 20 minutes. Finely chop the remaining almonds and parsley in a food processor and sprinkle over the top. Drizzle with 15–30ml/1–2 tbsp olive oil. Return to the oven and bake for a further 20 minutes, or until turning golden. Serve, garnished with more chopped parsley if wished.

SERVES FOUR

INGREDIENTS

- 2 large tomatoes
- 1 green (bell) pepper
- 1 yellow or orange (bell) pepper
- 75ml/5 tbsp olive oil
- 2 onions, finely chopped
- 2 garlic cloves, finely chopped
- 75g/3 oz/¾ cup almonds, chopped
- 175g/6oz/1½ cups cooked rice, or 75g/3oz/scant ½ cup long grain rice, cooked and drained
- 30ml/2 tbsp Malaga raisins or muscatels, soaked in hot water
- 30ml/2 tbsp chopped fresh mint
- 45ml/3 tbsp chopped fresh flat leaf parsley
- salt and ground pepper

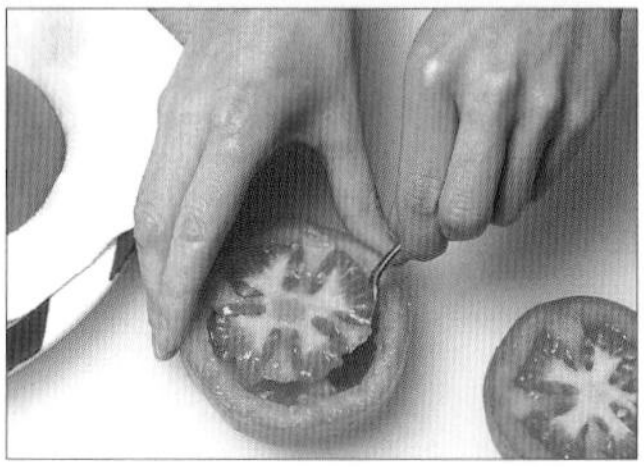

1 Preheat the oven to 190°C/375°F/Gas 5. Cut the tomatoes in half and scoop out the pulp and seeds.

2 Put the tomato halves on kitchen paper with the cut sides down and leave to drain. Roughly chop the centres and seeds and place in a bowl.

VARIATION

Small aubergines (eggplant) or large courgettes (zucchini) are also good stuffed. Scoop out the centres, then oil the vegetable cases and bake for about 15 minutes. Chop the centres, fry to soften and add to the stuffing mixture, then fill and bake as for the peppers and tomatoes.

Energy 387Kcal/1609kJ; Protein 7.7g; Carbohydrate 33.4g, of which sugars 17.3g; Fat 25.6g, of which saturates 3.1g; Cholesterol 0mg; Calcium 108mg; Fibre 5.1g; Sodium 22mg.

STEWED AUBERGINE

THE ARABS INTRODUCED THIS STRANGE VEGETABLE-FRUIT TO ANDALUSIA, WHERE IT WAS COOKED WITH THE ARAB FLAVOURINGS OF CUMIN AND GARLIC. LATER, DISHES SIMILAR TO FRENCH RATATOUILLE BECAME POPULAR. THIS IS A MODERN VERSION OF BERENJENA GUISADA, *WITH RED WINE.*

SERVES FOUR

INGREDIENTS

- 1 large aubergine (eggplant)
- 60–90ml/4–6 tbsp olive oil
- 2 shallots, thinly sliced
- 4 tomatoes, quartered
- 2 garlic cloves, thinly sliced
- 60ml/4 tbsp red wine
- 30ml/2 tbsp chopped fresh parsley, plus extra to garnish
- 30–45ml/2–3 tbsp virgin olive oil (if serving cold)
- salt and ground black pepper

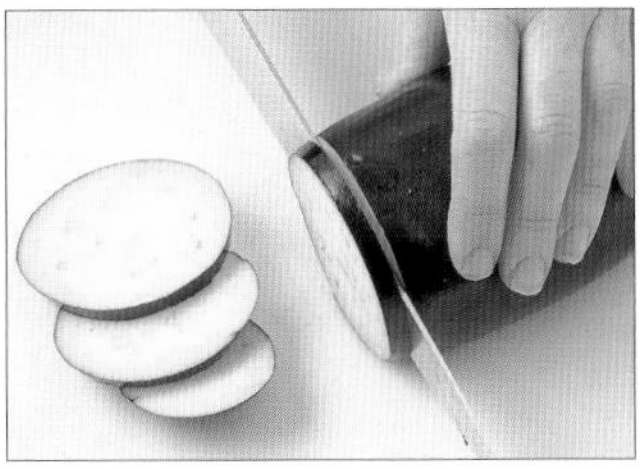

1 Slice the aubergine into 1cm/½in rounds. Place them in a large colander and sprinkle with 5–10ml/1–2 tsp salt. Leave to drain for 30 minutes.

2 Rinse the aubergine slices well, then press between several layers of kitchen paper to remove any excess liquid.

3 Heat 30ml/2 tbsp of the oil in a large frying pan until smoking. Add one layer of aubergine slices and fry, turning once, until golden brown. Remove to a plate covered with kitchen paper. Heat more oil and fry the second batch in the same way.

4 Heat 15ml/1 tbsp of oil in a pan and cook the shallots for 5 minutes until golden. Cut the aubergine into strips. Add, with the tomatoes, garlic and wine. Cover and simmer for 30 minutes.

5 Stir in the parsley, and check the seasonings. Sprinkle with a little more parsley and serve hot. To serve cold, dribble a little virgin olive oil over the dish before it goes on the table.

COOK'S TIP

Be sure to heat the oil before adding the aubergine slices and do not be tempted to add more oil once the aubergines are cooking. They will absorb cold oil, resulting in a greasy dish.

Energy 139Kcal/577kJ; Protein 1.4g; Carbohydrate 5.4g, of which sugars 5g; Fat 11.5g, of which saturates 1.7g; Cholesterol 0mg; Calcium 17mg; Fibre 2.2g; Sodium 12mg.

MENESTRA

THIS VEGETABLE DISH, WHICH CONTAINS AN ASSORTMENT OF YOUNG, NEW VEGETABLES, IS EATEN ALL ALONG THE NORTHERN COAST OF SPAIN TO CELEBRATE THE ARRIVAL OF SPRING. CHOOSE BY EYE, KEEPING THE QUANTITIES IN PROPORTION, AND PAYING CAREFUL ATTENTION TO THE COOKING TIME EACH VEGETABLE REQUIRES TO STAY JUST CRISP.

SERVES SIX

INGREDIENTS

- 15ml/1 tbsp olive oil
- 115g/4oz streaky (fatty) bacon lardons or diced pancetta
- 1 onion, chopped
- 3 garlic cloves, finely chopped
- 90ml/6 tbsp chopped fresh parsley
- 175ml/6fl oz/¾ cup dry white wine
- 150g/5oz green beans
- 200g/7oz bunched young carrots
- 6 small new best potatoes, scrubbed
- 300ml/10fl oz/1¼ cups chicken stock
- 1 corn cob, kernels removed (optional)
- 200g/7oz/2 cups peas
- 50g/2oz mangetout (snow peas)
- salt and ground black pepper
- 2 hard-boiled eggs, chopped, to garnish

VARIATION

Change the vegetables at will – the stalk end of asparagus, for example, is excellent. But don't vary the amount of liquid used in the casserole, or the sauce will become watery.

1 Heat the oil in a small flameproof casserole and fry the bacon or pancetta over a gentle heat for about 5 minutes, or until it crisps. Remove with a slotted spoon and reserve. Add the onion to the casserole and cook in the bacon fat until softened, adding the garlic towards the end.

2 Remove the cooked onion to a food processor, add 30ml/2 tbsp of the chopped parsley and purée with a little of the white wine.

3 Meanwhile prepare all the vegetables. Cut the beans into short lengths, and the carrots to the same size.

4 Bring a pan of salted water to the boil and add the potatoes. Cook for about 10 minutes. Add the carrots to the pan of potatoes, and cook for a further 5 minutes.

5 Meanwhile, return the bacon to the casserole and add the stock. Put in the beans, sweetcorn and peas and lay the mangetout over the top. Half cover the casserole and leave to simmer for 5–10 minutes, until the vegetables are just cooked.

6 Drain the potatoes and carrots and add them to the casserole.

7 Add the rest of the wine and the onion purée to the casserole, warming the liquid and turning the vegetables gently with a wooden spoon. Check the seasoning, adding more if necessary, and serve with the juices. Garnish with chopped egg and the remaining parsley.

VARIATION

This dish can also be made with tender meats such as lamb and veal with various combinations of new vegetables. Good combinations include lamb with artichokes and sherry, and veal with carrots and peas. Chop the meat and fry before adding to the casserole with the vegetables for further cooking.

Energy 193Kcal/804kJ; Protein 9.6g; Carbohydrate 14.3g, of which sugars 5.6g; Fat 9.3g, of which saturates 2.6g; Cholesterol 76mg; Calcium 76mg; Fibre 4.3g; Sodium 284mg.

PISTO MANCHEGO

A rich-flavoured and simple summer vegetable dish, from the poorest and hottest part of Spain, La Mancha. It may be eaten hot, alone or with such things as fried ham and eggs. It also makes a substantial salad, often with canned tuna, or hard-boiled eggs.

SERVES FOUR

INGREDIENTS

- 45–60ml/3–4 tbsp olive oil
- 2 Spanish onions, thinly sliced
- 3 garlic cloves, finely chopped
- 3 large green (bell) peppers, seeded and chopped
- 3 large courgettes (zucchini), thinly sliced
- 5 large ripe tomatoes or 800g/1¾lb canned tomatoes, with juice
- 60ml/4 tbsp chopped fresh parsley
- 2 hard-boiled eggs (optional)
- 30–45ml/2–3 tbsp virgin olive oil (if serving cold)
- salt and ground black pepper

1 Heat the oil in a large heavy pan or flameproof casserole and cook the onions and garlic gently, until soft.

2 Add the peppers, courgettes and tomatoes. Season and cook gently for 20 minutes until the flavours blend.

3 Stir in 30ml/2 tbsp parsley and serve hot, if wished, topped with chopped hard-boiled egg, if using, and more parsley. To serve cold, check the seasoning, adding more if needed, and sprinkle with a little virgin olive oil before adding the garnish.

Energy 198Kcal/824kJ; Protein 6.3g; Carbohydrate 22g, of which sugars 19.2g; Fat 10g, of which saturates 1.6g; Cholesterol 0mg; Calcium 103mg; Fibre 6.4g; Sodium 24mg.

ESCALIVADA

THE CATALAN NAME OF THIS CELEBRATED DISH MEANS "BAKED OVER EMBERS" AND, LIKE MANY OTHER BARBECUE DISHES, IT TRANSFERS VERY SUCCESSFULLY TO THE OVEN. COOKING THE VEGETABLES IN THIS WAY BRINGS OUT THEIR FLAVOUR MAGNIFICENTLY.

SERVES FOUR

INGREDIENTS

- 2–3 courgettes (zucchini)
- 1 large fennel bulb
- 1 Spanish onion
- 2 large red (bell) peppers
- 450g/1lb butternut squash
- 6 whole garlic cloves, unpeeled
- 75ml/5 tbsp olive oil
- juice ½ lemon
- pinch of cumin seeds, crushed
- 4 sprigs fresh thyme
- 4 medium tomatoes
- salt and ground black pepper

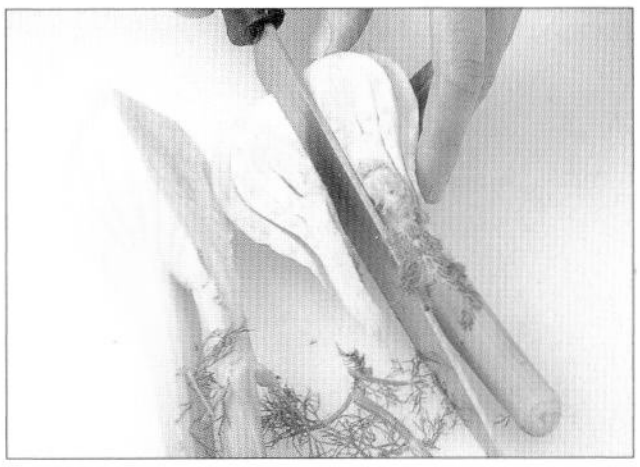

1 Preheat the oven to 220°C/425°F/ Gas 7. Cut the courgettes lengthways into four pieces. Cut the fennel into similar-sized wedges. Slice the onion lengthways into chunks. Halve and seed the peppers, and slice thickly lengthways. Cut the squash into thick chunks. Smash the garlic cloves with the flat of a knife, but leave the skins on.

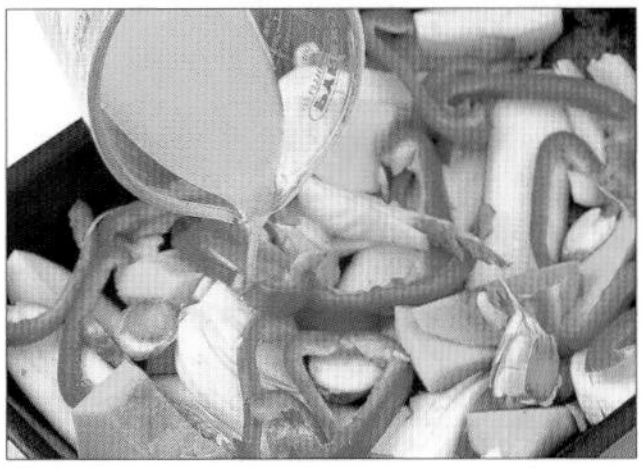

2 Choose a roasting pan into which all the vegetables will fit in one layer. Put in all the vegetables except the tomatoes. Mix together the oil and lemon juice. Pour over the vegetables and toss them. Sprinkle with the cumin seeds, salt and pepper and tuck in the thyme sprigs. Roast for 20 minutes.

3 Gently stir the vegetables in the oil and add the tomatoes. Cook for a further 15 minutes, or until the vegetables are tender and slightly charred around the edges.

VARIATIONS

- This is a very easy, pretty dish and you can vary the choice of vegetables according to what is in the market. Baby vegetables are excellent roasted. Tiny fennel, leeks and squash appear seasonally in supermarkets. Judge the roasting time by their volume.
- Aubergines (eggplant) are frequently included in this mixture, and their flavour is delicious, but they turn a slightly unappetizing grey colour when cooked and served plain.

Energy 224Kcal/928kJ; Protein 5.1g; Carbohydrate 17.6g, of which sugars 15.5g; Fat 15.2g, of which saturates 2.4g; Cholesterol 0mg; Calcium 93mg; Fibre 6g; Sodium 19mg.

BROAD BEANS WITH BACON

This dish is particularly associated with Ronda, in southern Spain, the home of bull fighting, where broad beans are fed to fighting bulls to build them up. It is also found elsewhere in Spain where it is known as HABAS ESPAÑOLAS. *If you have time, remove the dull skins from the broad beans to reveal the bright green beans beneath.*

SERVES FOUR

INGREDIENTS

- 30ml/2 tbsp olive oil
- 1 small onion, finely chopped
- 1 garlic clove, finely chopped
- 50g/2oz rindless smoked streaky (fatty) bacon, roughly chopped
- 225g/8oz broad (fava) beans, thawed if frozen
- 5ml/1 tsp paprika
- 15ml/1 tbsp sweet sherry
- salt and ground black pepper

VARIATION

For a vegetarian version of this dish use sun-dried tomatoes in oil instead of bacon.

1 Heat the olive oil in a large frying pan or sauté pan. Add the chopped onion, garlic and bacon and fry over a high heat for about 5 minutes, stirring frequently, until the onion is softened and the bacon browned.

2 Add the beans and paprika to the pan and stir-fry for 1 minute. Add the sherry, lower the heat, cover and cook for 5–10 minutes until the beans are tender. Season with salt and pepper to taste and serve hot or warm.

Energy 140Kcal/583kJ; Protein 6.6g; Carbohydrate 8g, of which sugars 1.8g; Fat 8.8g, of which saturates 1.9g; Cholesterol 8mg; Calcium 36mg; Fibre 3.9g; Sodium 163mg.

LENTILS WITH MUSHROOMS AND ANIS

The great plains of Castile produce lentils for the whole of Europe. Locally they are weekly fare. In this recipe, LENTEJAS CON CHAMPIÑONES, *they are flavoured with another product of the region, anis spirit, plus a great deal of parsley. Serve this dish on its own, or partnered with grilled pork ribs or slices of pork belly.*

SERVES FOUR

INGREDIENTS
- 30ml/2 tbsp olive oil
- 1 large onion, sliced
- 2 garlic cloves, finely chopped
- 250g/9oz/3 cups brown cap (cremini) mushrooms, sliced
- 150g/5oz/generous ½ cup brown or green lentils, soaked overnight
- 4 tomatoes, cut in eighths
- 1 bay leaf
- 25g/1oz/½ cup chopped fresh parsley
- 30ml/2 tbsp anis spirit or anisette
- salt, paprika and black pepper

COOK'S TIP

If you forget to soak the lentils, add at least 30 minutes to the cooking time.

1 Heat the oil in a flameproof casserole. Add the onion and fry gently, with the garlic, until softened but not browned.

2 Add the sliced mushrooms and stir to combine with the onion and garlic. Continue cooking, stirring gently, for a couple of minutes.

3 Add the lentils, tomatoes and bay leaf with 175ml/6fl oz/¾ cup water. Simmer gently, covered, for 30–40 minutes until the lentils are soft, and the liquid has almost disappeared.

4 Stir in the parsley and anis. Season with salt, paprika and black pepper.

Energy 250Kcal/1053kJ; Protein 12.3g; Carbohydrate 32.7g, of which sugars 10g; Fat 7g, of which saturates 1g; Cholesterol 0mg; Calcium 78mg; Fibre 5.5g; Sodium 32mg.

RICE AND PASTA

Paella – that glorious combination of saffron rice, with shellfish, chicken or rabbit – is probably the dish most commonly associated with Spain. But there are many more classic festival and family dishes that combine rice with vegetables and even bananas. Pasta is a 500-year-old tradition, and comes in the same versatile combinations as the rice.

RICE TORTITAS

LIKE MINIATURE TORTILLAS, THESE LITTLE RICE PANCAKES ARE GOOD SERVED HOT, EITHER PLAIN OR WITH TOMATO SAUCE FOR DIPPING. THEY MAKE AN EXCELLENT SCOOP FOR ANY SOFT VEGETABLE MIXTURE OR DIP – A VERY SPANISH WAY OF EATING.

SERVES FOUR

INGREDIENTS

- 30ml/2 tbsp olive oil
- 115g/4oz/1 cup cooked long grain white rice
- 1 potato, grated
- 4 spring onions (scallions), thinly sliced
- 1 garlic clove, finely chopped
- 15ml/1 tbsp chopped fresh parsley
- 3 large (US extra large) eggs, beaten
- 2.5ml/½ tsp paprika
- salt and ground black pepper

COOK'S TIP

These *tortitas* can be used as a base, for example for cooked chicken livers, instead of the usual sliced bread.

1 Heat half the olive oil in a large frying pan and stir-fry the rice, with the potato, spring onions and garlic, over a high heat for 3 minutes until golden.

2 Tip the rice and vegetable mixture into a bowl and stir in the parsley and eggs, with the paprika and plenty of salt and pepper. Mix well.

3 Heat the remaining oil in the frying pan and drop in large spoonfuls of the rice mixture, leaving room for spreading. Cook the *tortitas* for 1–2 minutes on each side.

4 Drain the *tortitas* on kitchen paper and keep hot while cooking the remaining mixture. Serve hot.

Energy 168Kcal/702kJ; Protein 6.4g; Carbohydrate 13.5g, of which sugars 0.9g; Fat 10.3g, of which saturates 2.1g; Cholesterol 143mg; Calcium 55mg; Fibre 1g; Sodium 60mg.

Artichoke Rice Cakes with Manchego

These unusual little croquetas *contain artichoke in the rice mixture, and they break open to reveal a melting cheese centre. Manchego is made from sheep's milk and has a tart flavour that goes wonderfully with the delicate taste of the rice cakes.*

SERVES SIX

INGREDIENTS

- 1 large globe artichoke
- 50g/2oz/¼ cup butter
- 1 small onion, finely chopped
- 1 garlic clove, finely chopped
- 115g/4oz/⅔ cup paella rice
- 450ml/¾ pint/scant 2 cups hot chicken stock
- 50g/2oz/⅔ cup grated fresh Parmesan cheese
- 150g/5oz Manchego cheese, very finely diced
- 45–60ml/3–4 tbsp fine corn meal
- olive oil, for frying
- salt and ground black pepper
- fresh flat leaf parsley, to garnish

1 Remove the stalks, leaves and choke to leave just the heart of the artichoke; chop the heart finely.

2 Melt the butter in a pan and gently fry the chopped artichoke heart, onion and garlic for 5 minutes until softened. Stir in the rice and cook for about 1 minute.

3 Keeping the heat fairly high, gradually add the stock, stirring occasionally until all the liquid has been absorbed and the rice is cooked – this should take about 20 minutes. Season well, then stir in the Parmesan cheese. Transfer the mixture to a bowl. Leave to cool, then cover and chill for at least 2 hours.

4 Spoon about 15ml/1 tbsp of the mixture into the palm of one hand, flatten slightly, and place a few pieces of diced cheese in the centre. Shape the rice around the cheese to make a small ball. Flatten slightly, then roll in the corn meal, shaking off any excess. Repeat with the remaining mixture to make about 12 cakes.

5 Shallow fry the rice cakes in hot olive oil for 4–5 minutes until they are crisp and golden brown. Drain on kitchen paper and serve hot, garnished with flat leaf parsley.

COOK'S TIP

Manchego is a hard cheese very similar to Italian Parmesan.

Energy 330Kcal/1368kJ; Protein 12g; Carbohydrate 21.8g, of which sugars 0.8g; Fat 20.9g, of which saturates 10.5g; Cholesterol 43mg; Calcium 299mg; Fibre 0.5g; Sodium 312mg.

Simple Rice Salad

In this quick and easy side dish, rice and a selection of chopped salad vegetables are served in a well-flavoured dressing to make a pretty salad.

SERVES SIX

INGREDIENTS
- 275g/10oz/1½ cups long grain rice
- 1 bunch spring onions (scallions), finely sliced
- 1 green (bell) pepper, seeded and finely diced
- 1 yellow (bell) pepper, seeded and finely diced
- 225g/8oz tomatoes, peeled, seeded and chopped
- 30ml/2 tbsp chopped fresh flat leaf parsley or coriander (cilantro)

For the dressing
- 75ml/5 tbsp mixed olive oil and extra virgin olive oil
- 15ml/1 tbsp sherry vinegar
- 5ml/1 tsp strong Dijon mustard
- salt and ground black pepper

1 Cook the rice in a large pan of lightly salted boiling water for 10–12 minutes, until tender but still *al dente*. Be careful not to overcook.

2 Drain the rice well in a sieve (strainer), rinse thoroughly under cold running water and drain again. Leave the rice to cool completely.

3 Place the rice in a large serving bowl. Add the spring onions, peppers, tomatoes and parsley or coriander.

4 Make the dressing. Place all the ingredients in a screw-top jar, put the lid on and shake vigorously until well mixed. Stir the dressing into the rice and check the seasoning.

Energy 279Kcal/1161kJ; Protein 4.8g; Carbohydrate 42.2g, of which sugars 5.3g; Fat 10g, of which saturates 1.4g; Cholesterol 0mg; Calcium 37mg; Fibre 1.9g; Sodium 34mg.

MOORS AND CHRISTIANS

MOROS Y CRISTIANOS IS MADE EVERY YEAR IN VALENCIA AT THE FESTIVAL CELEBRATING AN ANCIENT VICTORY OF THE CHRISTIANS OVER THE MOORS. THE BLACK BEANS REPRESENT THE LATTER, AND THE WHITE RICE THE FORMER. THIS IS AN ELEGANT MODERN VERSION OF A TRADITIONAL DISH.

SERVES SIX

INGREDIENTS

- 400g/14oz/2 cups black beans, soaked overnight
- 1 onion, quartered
- 1 carrot, sliced
- 1 celery stick, sliced
- 1 garlic clove, finely chopped
- 1 bay leaf
- 5ml/1 tsp paprika
- 45ml/3 tbsp olive oil
- juice of 1 orange
- 300g/11oz/1½ cups long grain rice
- salt and cayenne pepper

For the garnish

- chopped fresh parsley
- thin wedges of orange
- sliced red onion

1 Put the beans in a large pan with the onion, carrot, celery, garlic and bay leaf and 1.75 litres/3 pints/7½ cups water. Bring to the boil and cook rapidly for 10 minutes, then reduce the heat and simmer for 1 hour, topping up the water if necessary. When the beans are almost tender, drain, discarding the vegetables. Return the beans to a clean pan.

2 Blend the paprika and oil with cayenne pepper to taste and stir into the beans with the orange juice. Top up with a little water, if necessary. Heat gently until barely simmering, then cover and cook for 10–15 minutes until the beans are completely tender. Remove from the heat and allow to stand in the liquid for 15 minutes. Season with salt to taste.

3 Meanwhile, cook the rice in boiling water until tender. Drain, then pack into a buttered bowl or individual moulds and allow to stand for 10 minutes.

4 Unmould the rice on to a serving plate and arrange the black beans around the edge. Garnish with parsley, orange wedges and red onion slices.

Energy 417Kcal/1756kJ; Protein 18.7g; Carbohydrate 71.8g, of which sugars 3.9g; Fat 6.8g, of which saturates 0.9g; Cholesterol 0mg; Calcium 83mg; Fibre 10.9g; Sodium 16mg.

CUBAN-STYLE RICE

ARROZ A LA CUBANA, GARNISHED WITH FRIED EGGS AND BANANAS, IS POPULAR IN THE CANARY ISLANDS AND CATALONIA. IT MAKES AN EASY AND SUBSTANTIAL SUPPER DISH. BACON IS SOMETIMES ADDED TO THE TOMATO SAUCE, OR IS FRIED AND SERVED WITH THE EGGS.

SERVES FOUR

INGREDIENTS

- 3 garlic cloves
- 120ml/4fl oz/½ cup olive oil
- 300g/11oz/1½ cups long grain rice
- 15g/½oz/1 tbsp butter
- 4 small bananas or 2 large bananas
- 4 large (US extra large) eggs
- salt and paprika

For the tomato sauce

- 30ml/2 tbsp olive oil
- 1 onion, chopped
- 2 garlic cloves, finely chopped
- 800g/1lb 12oz can tomatoes
- 4 thyme or oregano sprigs
- ground black pepper

1 Make the tomato sauce. Heat the oil in a pan, add the onion and garlic and fry gently, stirring, until soft. Stir in the tomatoes and thyme or oregano sprigs and simmer gently for 5 minutes. Add seasoning to taste. Remove the herb sprigs and keep the sauce warm.

2 Put 850ml/1 pint 8fl oz/3½ cups water in a pan with two whole garlic cloves and 15ml/1 tbsp oil. Bring to the boil, add the rice and cook for 18 minutes until it is done, and the liquid has been absorbed.

3 Heat a pan with 30ml/2 tbsp oil and gently fry one chopped garlic clove. Tip in the rice, stir, season well, then turn off the heat and cover the pan.

4 Heat the butter in a frying pan with 15ml/1 tbsp oil. Halve the bananas lengthways and fry briefly on both sides. Keep them warm.

5 Add 60ml/4 tbsp oil to the pan and fry the eggs over a medium-high heat, so that the edges turn golden. Season with salt and paprika. Serve the rice surrounded by tomato sauce and garnish with bananas and fried eggs.

Energy 441Kcal/1834kJ; Protein 8.8g; Carbohydrate 24.8g, of which sugars 22.8g; Fat 35g, of which saturates 7.4g; Cholesterol 198mg; Calcium 52mg; Fibre 3g; Sodium 112mg.

Alicante Crusted Rice

PAELLA CON COSTRA *IS AN UNUSUAL PAELLA WITH AN EGG CRUST THAT IS FINISHED IN THE OVEN. THE CRUST SEALS IN ALL THE AROMAS UNTIL IT IS BROKEN OPEN AT THE TABLE.*

SERVES SIX

INGREDIENTS
- 45ml/3 tbsp olive oil
- 200g/7oz *butifarra*, fresh sausages or frying chorizo, sliced
- 2 tomatoes, peeled, seeded and chopped
- 175g/6oz lean cubed pork
- 175g/6oz skinless, boneless chicken breast or rabbit, cut into chunks
- 350g/12oz/1¾ cups paella rice
- 900ml–1 litre/1½–1¾ pints/3¾–4 cups hot chicken stock
- pinch of saffron threads (0.2g)
- 150g/5oz/⅔ cup cooked chickpeas
- 6 large (US extra large) eggs
- salt and ground black pepper

1 Preheat the oven to 190°C/375°F/Gas 5. Heat the oil in a flameproof casserole and fry the sausage until browned. Add the tomatoes and fry until reduced. Stir in the pork and chicken or rabbit pieces and cook for 2–3 minutes until the meat has browned lightly, stirring.

2 Add the rice to the pan, stir over the heat for about 1 minute, then pour in the hot stock. Add the saffron, season to taste, and stir well.

3 Bring to the boil, then lower the heat and add the chickpeas. Cover the casserole tightly with the lid and cook over a low heat for about 20 minutes or until the rice is tender.

4 Beat the eggs with a little water and a pinch of salt and pour over the rice. Place the casserole, uncovered, in the oven and cook for about 10 minutes, until the eggs have set and browned slightly on top. Serve the paella straight from the casserole.

Energy 535Kcal/2232kJ; Protein 29.3g; Carbohydrate 56g, of which sugars 1.9g; Fat 21.5g, of which saturates 6.3g; Cholesterol 242mg; Calcium 73mg; Fibre 1.6g; Sodium 382mg.

PAELLA VALENCIANA

A world famous mixture of the finest Spanish ingredients, Valencia's paella contains chicken, shellfish and vegetables in succulent saffron rice. It has become a celebration dish throughout Spain, and Spain's best-known dish abroad. To drink, choose a red Valdepeñas, which will go well with the robust flavours of the paella.

SERVES SIX TO EIGHT

INGREDIENTS

- 90ml/6 tbsp white wine
- 450g/1lb fresh mussels, scrubbed
- 115g/4oz/scant 1 cup small shelled broad (fava) beans
- 150g/5oz green beans, cut into short lengths
- 90ml/6 tbsp olive oil
- 6 small skinless, boneless chicken breast portions, cut into large pieces
- 150g/5oz pork fillet, cubed
- 6–8 large raw prawn (shrimp) tails, deveined, or 12 smaller raw prawns
- 2 onions, chopped
- 2–3 garlic cloves, finely chopped
- 1 red (bell) pepper, seeded and sliced
- 2 ripe tomatoes, peeled, seeded and chopped
- 60ml/4 tbsp chopped fresh parsley
- 900ml/1½ pints/3¾ cups chicken stock
- pinch of saffron threads (0.25g), soaked in 30ml/2 tbsp hot water
- 350g/12oz/1¾ cups paella rice, washed and drained
- 225g/8oz frying chorizo, sliced
- 115g/4oz/1 cup peas
- 6–8 stuffed green olives, sliced
- salt, paprika and black pepper

COOK'S TIP

Paella is a very easy dish to make with the right pan and, more importantly, the right heat. Traditionally it is cooked outdoors on a wide bed of hot charcoal. Indoors a big heat source such as a large hot plate is needed.

Without this steady heat, the pan needs to be moved constantly, or the rice cooks in the centre, but not round the outside. Overcome this problem by cooking it in a hot oven.

1 Heat the wine and add the mussels, discarding any that do not close when tapped. Cover and steam until opened. Reserve the liquid and mussels separately, discarding any that do not open.

2 Briefly cook the broad beans and green beans in boiling water, then drain. Pop the broad beans out of their skins.

3 Heat 45ml/3 tbsp oil in a large paella pan or wide flameproof casserole. Season the chicken with salt and paprika, and put in, skin downwards. Fry, turning until browned on all sides. Reserve on a plate. Season the pork with salt and paprika. Add 15ml/1 tbsp oil and fry the seasoned pork until browned evenly. Reserve with the chicken. Fry the prawns briefly in the same pan, but reserve them separately.

4 Heat the remaining oil and fry the onions and garlic for 3–4 minutes until golden brown. Add the red pepper, cook for 2–3 minutes, then stir in the chopped tomatoes and parsley and cook until thick.

5 If cooking in the oven (see Cook's Tip) preheat to 190°C/375°F/Gas 5. Stir the chicken stock, the reserved mussel liquid and the saffron liquid into the vegetables. Season well with salt and pepper and bring the mixture to the boil. When the liquid is bubbling, throw in all the rice. Stir once, then add the chicken pieces, pork, shellfish, beans, chorizo and peas.

6 Transfer the pan to the oven and cook for 15–18 minutes until the rice is done. Alternatively, cook over medium-high heat for about 10 minutes. Then lower the heat and start to move the pan. A big pan needs to shift every 2–3 minutes, moving the edge of the pan round over the heat, then back to the centre. Cook until the rice is done – another 10–12 minutes.

7 Arrange the mussels and olives on top. Cover with a lid (or damp dishtowel) and leave to stand for 10 minutes, until all the liquid is absorbed. Serve straight from the pan.

COOK'S TIP

Spain exports saffron in little boxes labelled with the weight. A 0.3g packet contains 50–60 threads, enough to flavour three small dishes. A dish such as paella needs two-thirds – measured by eye. The amount of rice used in this recipe could take the whole 0.3g – and in Spain it probably would – so enjoy.

Energy 504Kcal/2108kJ; Protein 36.5g; Carbohydrate 47.7g, of which sugars 6.1g; Fat 17.9g, of which saturates 4.7g; Cholesterol 107mg; Calcium 103mg; Fibre 3.4g; Sodium 352mg.

Seafood Paella

This is a great dish to serve to guests on a special occasion. A seafood paella always looks spectacular and a bed of scented rice is the perfect way to display a selection of mariscos (seafood). This particular paella contains a magnificent combination of squid, prawns, mussels and clams as well as spicy chorizo and succulent vegetables.

SERVES FOUR

INGREDIENTS

- 45ml/3 tbsp olive oil
- 1 Spanish onion, chopped
- 2 large garlic cloves, chopped
- 150g/5oz frying chorizo, sliced
- 300g/11oz small squid, cleaned
- 1 red (bell) pepper, cut into strips
- 4 tomatoes, peeled, seeded and diced or 200g/7oz can tomatoes
- 500ml/17fl oz/2¼ cups chicken stock, plus a little extra
- 105ml/7 tbsp dry white wine
- 200g/7oz/1 cup paella rice
- pinch of saffron threads (0.2g), crumbled
- 150g/5oz/1 cup peas
- 12 large cooked prawns (shrimp), in the shell or 8 peeled scampi (extra large shrimp)
- 450g/1lb fresh mussels, scrubbed
- 450g/1lb clams, scrubbed
- 4 cooked king prawns (jumbo shrimp) or scampi, in the shells
- salt and ground black pepper
- chopped fresh parsley and lemon wedges, to garnish

1 Heat the olive oil in a paella pan or large frying pan, add the onion and garlic and fry until translucent. Add the chorizo and fry until lightly golden.

2 If the squid are very small, leave them whole, otherwise cut the bodies into rings and the tentacles into pieces. Add the squid to the pan and sauté over a high heat for 2 minutes.

3 Stir in the pepper and tomatoes and simmer gently for 5 minutes, until the pepper is tender. Pour in the stock and wine, stir well and bring to the boil. Stir in the rice and saffron and season well. Spread the contents evenly over the base of the pan. Bring the liquid back to the boil, then lower the heat and simmer for about 10 minutes.

4 Gently stir the peas, prawns or scampi, mussels and clams into the rice, then cook for a further 15–20 minutes, until the rice is tender and all the mussels and clams have opened. (Discard any that remain closed.) If the paella seems dry, stir in a little more hot stock.

5 Remove the pan from the heat and arrange the king prawns or scampi on top. Cover and leave to stand for 5 minutes. Sprinkle the paella with chopped parsley and serve from the pan, accompanied by lemon wedges.

Energy 607Kcal/2536kJ; Protein 40.8g; Carbohydrate 59.2g, of which sugars 9.4g; Fat 21.4g, of which saturates 5.4g; Cholesterol 279mg; Calcium 204mg; Fibre 4.6g; Sodium 983mg.

VEGETABLE RICE POT

IN THIS ARROZ DE VERDURAS, *FRESH SEASONAL VEGETABLES ARE COOKED IN SLIGHTLY SPICED RICE. ALWAYS TASTE STOCK BEFORE ADDING IT TO RICE: THIS IS YOUR CHANCE TO REDUCE AND CONCENTRATE IT, OR TO ADD WINE, A BIT OF A STOCK CUBE, OR EVEN SOY SAUCE FOR EXTRA FLAVOUR. IF THE STOCK LACKS TASTE, SO WILL THE FINAL DISH.*

SERVES FOUR

INGREDIENTS
- 1 large aubergine (eggplant)
- 45ml/3 tbsp olive oil
- 2 onions, quartered and sliced
- 2 garlic cloves, finely chopped
- 1 red (bell) pepper, halved, seeded and sliced
- 1 yellow (bell) pepper, halved, seeded and sliced
- 200g/7oz fine green beans, halved
- 115g/4oz/1½ cups brown cap (cremini) mushrooms, halved
- 300g/11oz/1½ cups paella rice, washed and drained
- 1 dried chilli, seeded and crumbled
- 1 litre/1¾ pints/4 cups chicken stock
- 115g/4oz/1 cup peas
- 60ml/4 tbsp chopped fresh parsley
- salt and ground black pepper
- fresh parsley or coriander (cilantro) leaves, to garnish

1 Halve the aubergine lengthways, then cut it into slices. Spread them out in a large colander or on a draining board, sprinkle with salt and leave for about 30 minutes to drain, then rinse under cold running water and pat dry with kitchen paper.

2 Heat 30ml/2 tbsp olive oil in a wide flameproof casserole or sauté pan over a high heat. Add the aubergine slices and sauté until slightly golden, stirring occasionally, then transfer to kitchen paper to drain.

3 Add the remaining oil to the pan and cook the onion and garlic until soft. Add the peppers, green beans and mushrooms and cook briefly.

4 Add the drained rice and stir for 1–2 minutes, then add the aubergine and stir. Add the chilli and seasoning. Taste the stock and pour in. Add the peas and parsley and mix together.

5 Bring to boiling point, cover and cook over a low heat, for 20–25 minutes, checking the liquid level towards the end (the rice should absorb the liquid, but not burn). When the rice is tender, turn off the heat, cover the pan and leave to stand for 10 minutes for the remaining liquid to be absorbed. Garnish with parsley or coriander and serve.

VARIATIONS
- Almost any roughly chopped or sliced vegetables can be used in this dish. Broccoli, carrots, cauliflower, courgettes (zucchini) and okra are all suitable – or try using frozen corn in place of all or some of the peas.
- To make a tomato-flavoured rice, use a 400g/14oz can chopped tomatoes in place of 350ml/12fl oz/1½ cups of the chicken stock.

Energy 458Kcal/1911kJ; Protein 11.9g; Carbohydrate 79.7g, of which sugars 14.1g; Fat 10.4g, of which saturates 1.5g; Cholesterol 0mg; Calcium 100mg; Fibre 7.1g; Sodium 13mg.

Calderete of Rice with Allioli

Cooking rice in fish stock gives it such a splendid flavour that it is often eaten on its own – arroz abanda – served in a little cauldron and accompanied by allioli. The fish then follows as a separate course. If you prefer, the fish can be returned to the casserole while the dish is still liquid, and the fish and rice eaten with the sauce.

SERVES SIX

INGREDIENTS

- 1.6kg/3½lb mixed fish on the bone, such as snapper, bream, grey or red mullet, or bass
- 45ml/3 tbsp olive oil
- 6 garlic cloves, smashed
- 1 *ñora* chilli or 1 hot dried chilli, seeded and chopped
- 250g/9oz ripe tomatoes, peeled, seeded and chopped
- pinch of saffron threads (0.25g)
- 30ml/2 tbsp dry Martini or white wine
- 1 tomato, finely diced
- 30ml/2 tbsp chopped fresh parsley
- 400g/14oz/2 cups paella rice, washed
- 115g/4oz tiny unshelled shrimps
- salt and ground black pepper

For the stock

- 1 onion, chopped
- 2 garlic cloves, chopped
- 1 celery stick, chopped
- 1 carrot, chopped
- 1 litre/1¾ pints/4 cups water

For the allioli

- 4 garlic cloves, finely chopped
- 2.5ml/½ tsp salt
- 5ml/1 tsp lemon juice
- 2 egg yolks
- 250ml/8fl oz/1 cup olive oil

1 Remove the heads from the fish. Working from the head end, cut the skin along the top of the back and work the fillets off the bone. Trim as needed, put the fillets on a plate, salt them lightly, cover and place in the refrigerator until required.

2 Make the fish stock. Put the bones, heads, tails and any other remaining bits into a large pan with the onion, garlic, celery, carrot and water. Bring to the boil, then reduce the heat, cover with a lid and simmer gently for about 30 minutes.

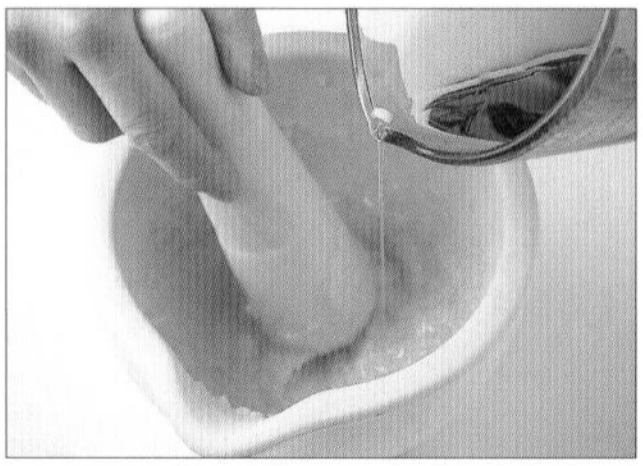

3 Make the allioli. Put the chopped garlic in a large mortar (or small blender) with the salt and lemon juice and reduce to a purée. Add the egg yolks and mix thoroughly. Gradually work in the oil (drop by drop at first if using a mortar) to make a thick, mayonnaise-like sauce.

4 Put 15ml/1 tbsp of the olive oil in a small pan and add the whole smashed garlic cloves and dried chilli pieces. Fry for a few minutes until the garlic looks roasted. Add the chopped tomato halfway through, crumble in the saffron and cook to form a sauce. Pour the sauce into a small blender and purée until smooth.

5 Heat the remaining 30ml/2 tbsp oil in a large pan or a wide flameproof casserole and fry the fish pieces until they begin to stiffen. Strain the fish stock into a jug (pitcher), then add 900ml/1½ pints/3¾ cups stock and the tomato sauce to the fish. Cook the fish gently for a further 3–4 minutes, until slightly underdone.

6 Remove the fish pieces from the pan with a slotted spoon to a serving dish. Season lightly, sprinkle with the Martini or wine, diced tomato and parsley. Cover with foil and keep warm.

7 Add the rice to the stock, stir, season and bring to a simmer. Cook for 18–20 minutes. Before all the liquid is absorbed, stir in the shrimps. When the rice is tender, cover and turn off the heat. Stand until all the liquid is absorbed: about 5 minutes. Serve from the pan, accompanied by the allioli.

8 When the rice course is almost finished, uncover the fish. Stir the fish juices into the remains of the allioli, then pour over the fish. Eat on the same plates as the rice.

Energy 713Kcal/2973kJ; Protein 41.3g; Carbohydrate 55g, of which sugars 1.8g; Fat 35.8g, of which saturates 5.6g; Cholesterol 149mg; Calcium 105mg; Fibre 0.6g; Sodium 281mg.

Fideos con Almejas

Pasta the east coast way, fideos are lengths of spaghetti, shorter than a finger. This sensational dish is rather like paella made with pasta – just as nice, and a great deal easier. It is popular along the Mediterranean coast – the Levante and the South around Malaga. The milky flesh of clams contrasts wonderfully with the firmer pasta and fennel.

SERVES FOUR TO SIX

INGREDIENTS

- 30ml/2 tbsp olive oil
- 1 large Spanish onion, chopped
- 1 garlic clove, finely chopped
- 2 large ripe tomatoes
- 750ml/1¼ pint/3 cups fish stock
- 1kg/2¼ lb clams, cleaned
- 120ml/4fl oz/½ cup anis spirit, such as Ricard or Pernod
- 120ml/4fl oz/½ cup dry white wine, such as Torres Viña Sol
- juice of ¼ lemon
- 300g/11oz spaghetti, broken into 5cm/2in lengths
- 1 fennel bulb, sliced in thin strips
- 30ml/2 tbsp chopped fresh parsley
- salt and ground pepper
- fennel fronds or fresh dill, to garnish

1 Heat the oil in a casserole big enough to contain all the ingredients. Fry the onion gently until soft. Add the garlic.

2 Put the tomatoes in a bowl, pour over boiling water and leave for 10 minutes. Peel the tomatoes on a plate and discard the seeds. Chop the flesh, add to the casserole and strain in the tomato juices into the pan. Cook until reduced to a pulp, then add 250ml/8fl oz/1 cup of the stock.

3 Discard any open or cracked clams. Add the rest to the pan in three batches. As they open, remove most from the shells and transfer to a plate. Discard any clams that remain shut.

4 Add the anis spirit and white wine to the sauce, plus the remaining fish stock and lemon juice, to taste. Add the pasta and sliced fennel. Season and simmer, partially covered, for 10 minutes. Stir every now and then to separate the strands, and to make sure the pasta is not sticking.

5 When the pasta is cooked, stir in the parsley and check the seasoning. Tip the clams across the top and cover tightly. Leave to stand for 10 minutes, so the clams warm through and all the liquid is absorbed. Serve in bowls, sprinkled with the fennel fronds or dill.

Energy 331Kcal/1394kJ; Protein 15.1g; Carbohydrate 43.6g, of which sugars 6.1g; Fat 5.1g, of which saturates 0.8g; Cholesterol 34mg; Calcium 73mg; Fibre 3.2g; Sodium 610mg.

SAN ESTEBAN CANELONES

Catalans are fond of pasta, and canelones *are traditional on* San Esteban, *the day after* Christmas Day, *and are often made in large quantities. Try to keep all the chopped stuffing ingredients the same size – small dice. Spanish stores sell squares of pasta for cooking then rolling, but ready prepared cannelloni tubes have been used here.*

SERVES FOUR TO EIGHT

INGREDIENTS
- 60ml/4 tbsp olive oil
- 1 onion, finely chopped
- 1 carrot, finely chopped
- 2 garlic cloves, finely chopped
- 2 ripe tomatoes, peeled and finely chopped
- 2.5ml/½ tsp dried thyme
- 150g/5oz raw chicken livers or cooked stuffing
- 150g/5oz raw pork or cooked ham, gammon or sausage
- 250g/9oz raw or cooked chicken
- 25g/1oz/2 tbsp butter
- 5ml/1 tsp fresh thyme
- 30ml/2 tbsp brandy
- 90ml/6 tbsp crème fraîche or double (heavy) cream
- 16 no pre-cook cannelloni tubes
- 75g/3oz/1 cup grated fresh Parmesan cheese
- salt and ground black pepper
- green salad, to serve

For the white sauce
- 50g/2oz/¼ cup butter
- 50g/2oz/½ cup plain (all-purpose) flour
- 900ml/1½ pints/3¾ cups milk
- fresh nutmeg, to taste

1 Heat the oil in a large frying pan, add the onion, carrot, garlic and tomatoes and cook over a low heat, stirring, for about 10 minutes or until very soft. Meanwhile, chop all the meats to the same size, keeping the fresh and cooked meat apart.

2 Add the butter, then the raw meat, to the centre of the frying pan and cook until coloured. Then add the remaining meats and sprinkle first with thyme, then with the brandy. Stir, then warm through and reduce the liquid.

3 Pour in the crème fraîche or cream, season to taste and leave to simmer for about 10 minutes. Allow to cool briefly.

4 Preheat the oven to 190°C/375°F/Gas 5. Make the white sauce. Melt the butter in a small pan, add the flour and cook, stirring, for 1–2 minutes. Gradually stir in the milk, a little at a time. Bring to simmering point, stirring until the sauce is smooth. Grate in nutmeg to taste, then season with plenty of salt and black pepper.

5 Spoon a little of the white sauce into a baking dish. Fill the cannelloni tubes with the meat mixture and arrange in a single layer in the dish. Pour the remaining white sauce over them, then sprinkle with the Parmesan cheese. Bake for 35–40 minutes, or until the pasta is tender. Leave for 10 minutes before serving with green salad.

Energy 473Kcal/1981kJ; Protein 26.8g; Carbohydrate 35.9g, of which sugars 8.8g; Fat 24.8g, of which saturates 12.4g; Cholesterol 153mg; Calcium 283mg; Fibre 1.7g; Sodium 474mg.

ANDRAJOS

This is a rich dish of hare, wine and mushrooms, flavoured with herbs and pine nuts. The name means "rags and tatters"; it was a shepherds' dish and the shepherd would have made his own simple flour and water pasta, cut into squares. Dried pasta squares are still sold in Spain to make cannelloni. This recipe uses bought lasagne, which needs to be broken up. The sauce permeates the pasta and transforms the chicken.

SERVES SIX

INGREDIENTS

- 800g/1¾lb hare meat and bone (the front legs and rib end)
- 200ml/7fl oz/scant 1 cup red wine
- 120–150ml/4–5fl oz/½–⅔ cup olive oil
- 150g/5oz smoked bacon lardons, or diced pancetta
- 2 onions, chopped
- 2 fat garlic cloves, finely chopped
- 8 baby onions, peeled
- 4 carrots, diced
- 4 chicken thighs, halved along the bone and seasoned
- seasoned plain (all-purpose) flour, for dusting
- 350g/12oz small open cap mushrooms
- 600ml/1 pint/2½ cups stock
- 5ml/1 tsp dried thyme
- 1 bay leaf
- 250g/9oz dried lasagne sheets
- 90ml/6 tbsp chopped parsley
- 30ml/2 tbsp pine nuts
- salt and ground black pepper

1 Starting at least two days ahead, cut the hare into portions and put in a bowl. Pour over the red wine and 15ml/1 tbsp of the oil and leave to marinate in the refrigerator for at least 24 hours.

COOK'S TIP

This dish uses the front part of the hare, while the back legs and saddle are best kept for a grander dish.

2 Heat 30ml/2 tbsp olive oil in a flameproof casserole, add the bacon or pancetta, chopped onion and garlic and fry until the onion is translucent. Halfway through add the whole baby onions and diced carrots, and continue cooking, stirring occasionally.

3 Heat 45ml/3 tbsp oil in a large frying pan and fry the seasoned chicken pieces on both sides until golden brown. Transfer to the casserole.

4 Remove the hare from the red wine marinade, reserving the liquid. Blot the meat well on kitchen paper and dredge with the seasoned flour until well coated. Add more oil to the frying pan, if necessary, and fry the meat on all sides until browned.

5 Meanwhile, reserve eight of the smallest open cap mushrooms. Quarter the remaining mushrooms and add to the casserole. Continue cooking the hare in the frying pan, stirring every now and then, until browned.

6 When the hare is ready, arrange the pieces in the casserole. Pour the reserved marinade into the frying pan to deglaze it, then pour the juices into the casserole. Add the stock, dried thyme and bay leaf and season with salt and pepper. Cook over a low heat for 1½ hours, until the meat is tender. Leave to cool completely.

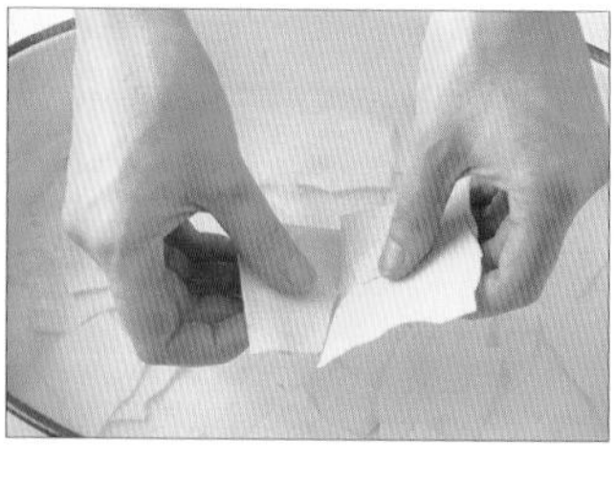

7 When ready to serve, bring plenty of water to the boil in a large roasting pan with 5ml/1 tsp salt and 15ml/1 tbsp oil. Break up the lasagne sheets and spread out the pieces in the pan. Cook for 7–8 minutes until soft, moving the pieces around to prevent them from sticking.

8 Remove all the meat from the bones and return to the casserole with 60ml/4 tbsp of the parsley. Bring to a simmer. Stir the drained pasta into the sauce. Heat 15ml/1 tbsp oil in a small pan and fry the reserved mushrooms, then arrange them on top. Sprinkle with the remaining parsley and the pine nuts, and serve.

Energy 613Kcal/2569kJ; Protein 38.1g; Carbohydrate 52g, of which sugars 8.9g; Fat 27.1g, of which saturates 5.9g; Cholesterol 117mg; Calcium 111mg; Fibre 4.9g; Sodium 406mg.

FISH AND SHELLFISH

Spain is bordered by two different oceans and has the best fishing in the world. Fish and shellfish are one of the glories of Spanish cooking. There is a series of colourful salads and delightful starters, while simple combinations, with lemon or tomato or potatoes, and hearty stews such as Zarzuela make delicious main course.

SEAFOOD SALAD

Ensalada de Mariscos is a very pretty arrangement of fresh mussels, prawns and squid rings served on a colourful bed of salad vegetables. In Spain, canned albacore tuna is also often included in this type of simple salad.

SERVES SIX

INGREDIENTS
- 115g/4oz prepared squid rings
- 12 fresh mussels, scrubbed and beards removed
- 1 large carrot
- 6 crisp lettuce leaves
- 10cm/4in piece cucumber, finely diced
- 115g/4oz cooked, peeled prawns (shrimp)
- 15ml/1 tbsp drained pickled capers

For the dressing
- 30ml/2 tbsp freshly squeezed lemon juice
- 45ml/3 tbsp virgin olive oil
- 15ml/1 tbsp chopped fresh parsley
- salt and ground black pepper

1 Put the squid rings into a metal sieve or vegetable steamer. Place the sieve or steamer over a pan of simmering water, cover with a lid and steam the squid for 2–3 minutes until it just turns white. Cool under cold running water to prevent further cooking and drain thoroughly on kitchen paper.

2 Discard any open mussels that do not close when tapped. Cover the base of a large pan with water, add the mussels, then cover and steam for a few minutes until they open. Discard any that remain shut.

3 Using a swivel-style vegetable peeler, cut the carrot into wafer-thin ribbons. Tear the lettuce into pieces and arrange on a serving plate. Scatter the carrot ribbons on top, then sprinkle over the diced cucumber.

4 Arrange the mussels, prawns and squid rings over the salad and scatter the capers over the top.

5 Make the dressing. Put all the ingredients in a small bowl and whisk well to combine. Drizzle over the salad. Serve at room temperature.

Energy 95Kcal/394kJ; Protein 7.8g; Carbohydrate 1.8g, of which sugars 1.5g; Fat 6.3g, of which saturates 0.9g; Cholesterol 83mg; Calcium 53mg; Fibre 0.9g; Sodium 76mg.

POTATO, MUSSEL AND WATERCRESS SALAD

The mussels found on the Galician coast are the best in the world. The Galicians are also very proud of their potatoes and their watercress. In ENSALADA DE MEJILLONES, PATATAS Y BERROS *a creamy, well-flavoured dressing enhances all these ingredients.*

SERVES FOUR

INGREDIENTS
- 675g/1½lb salad potatoes
- 1kg/2¼lb mussels, scrubbed and beards removed
- 200ml/7fl oz/scant 1 cup dry white wine
- 15g/½oz fresh flat leaf parsley, chopped
- 1 bunch of watercress or rocket (arugula)
- salt and ground black pepper
- chopped fresh chives or spring onion (scallion) tops, to garnish

For the dressing
- 105ml/7 tbsp olive oil
- 15–30ml/1–2 tbsp white wine vinegar
- 5ml/1 tsp strong Dijon mustard
- 1 large shallot, very finely chopped
- 15ml/1 tbsp chopped fresh chives
- 45ml/3 tbsp double (heavy) cream
- pinch of caster (superfine) sugar (optional)

1 Cook the potatoes in salted boiling water for 15–20 minutes, or until tender. Drain, cool, then peel. Slice the potatoes into a bowl and toss with 30ml/2 tbsp of the oil for the dressing.

2 Discard any open mussels. Bring the white wine to the boil in a large, heavy pan. Add the mussels, cover and boil vigorously, shaking the pan occasionally, for 3–4 minutes, until the mussels have opened. Discard any that do not open. Drain and shell the mussels, reserving the cooking liquid.

3 Boil the reserved mussel cooking liquid until reduced to about 45ml/3 tbsp. Strain this through a fine sieve over the potatoes and toss to mix.

4 Make the dressing. Whisk together the remaining oil, 15ml/1 tbsp of the vinegar, the mustard, shallot and chives.

5 Add the cream and whisk again to form a thick dressing. Adjust the seasoning, adding more vinegar and/or a pinch of sugar to taste.

6 Toss the mussels with the potatoes, then gently mix in the dressing and chopped parsley. Arrange the watercress or rocket on a serving platter and top with the salad. Serve sprinkled with extra chives or a little spring onion.

COOK'S TIP

Potato salads such as this one should not be chilled if at all possible because chilling alters the texture of the potatoes. For the best flavour and texture, serve this salad just cool or at room temperature.

Energy 461Kcal/1927kJ; Protein 18.1g; Carbohydrate 28.3g, of which sugars 3.2g; Fat 28g, of which saturates 7.1g; Cholesterol 45mg; Calcium 283mg; Fibre 3.2g; Sodium 210mg.

SKATE WITH BITTER SALAD LEAVES

This dish is popular in Galicia, which is famous for both its skate and its watercress. Skate has a delicious sweet flavour, enhanced here by orange. It contrasts well with any bitter leaves – buy a bag of mixed salad leaves for contrasting textures and flavours.

SERVES FOUR

INGREDIENTS
- 800g/1¾lb skate wings
- 15ml/1 tbsp white wine vinegar
- 4 black peppercorns
- 1 fresh thyme sprig
- 175g/6oz bitter salad leaves, such as frisée, rocket (arugula), radicchio, escarole, lamb's lettuce (mâche) and watercress
- 1 orange
- 2 tomatoes, peeled, seeded and diced

For the dressing
- 15ml/1 tbsp white wine vinegar
- 45ml/3 tbsp extra virgin olive oil
- 1 bunch spring onions (scallions), whites finely chopped
- salt, paprika and black pepper
- crusty bread, to serve

1 Put the skate wings into a large shallow pan, cover with cold water and add the vinegar, peppercorns and thyme. Bring to the boil, then poach gently for 8–10 minutes, until the flesh comes away easily from the bones.

2 Make the dressing. Whisk together the vinegar, oil and spring onions and season with salt, paprika and pepper.

3 Put the salad leaves in a large bowl, pour over the dressing and toss well. Remove the rind from the orange using a zester, then peel it, removing all the pith. Slice into thin rounds.

4 Flake the fish, discarding the bones, and add to the salad. Add a pinch of zest, the orange slices and tomatoes, toss gently and serve with bread.

Energy 226Kcal/950kJ; Protein 30.4g; Carbohydrate 4.9g, of which sugars 4.8g; Fat 9.6g, of which saturates 1.4g; Cholesterol 0mg; Calcium 174mg; Fibre 2g; Sodium 249mg.

SURTIDO DE PESCADO

THE SPANISH ENJOY AND MAKE THE MOST OF PRESERVED FISH. THIS IS A VERY PRETTY DISH, WHICH USES WHATEVER IS EASILY AVAILABLE, AND IT MAKES AN IDEAL LAST-MINUTE PARTY STARTER. IT IS ALSO EASY TO DOUBLE UP FOR A BUFFET. FOR THE BEST RESULTS TRY TO USE SPANISH CANNED FISH.

SERVES FOUR

INGREDIENTS

- 6 eggs
- cos or romaine lettuce leaves
- 75–90ml/5–6 tbsp mayonnaise
- 90g/3½oz jar Avruga herring roe, Eurocaviar grey mullet roe or undyed (or black) lumpfish roe
- 2 × 115g/4oz cans sardines in oil
- 2 × 115g/4oz cans mackerel fillets in oil
- 2 × 150g/5oz jars cockles (small clams) in brine, drained
- 2 × 115g/4oz cans mussels or scallops in tomato sauce
- fresh flat leaf parsley or dill sprigs, to garnish

COOK'S TIP

Smoked salmon, kippers (smoked herrings) and rollmops (pickled herring fillets) can also be included on the platter. Try to maintain a balance between fish or shellfish pickled in brine or vinegar, with those in oil or sauce. Huge Spanish mussels *en escabeche* (spicy sauce) are now available in large supermarkets. Also look out for Spanish fish roes to top the eggs.

1 Put the eggs in a pan with enough water to cover and bring to the boil. Turn down the heat and simmer for 10 minutes. Drain immediately, then cover with cold water and set aside until completely cool. Peel the eggs and slice in half.

2 Arrange the lettuce leaves on a large serving platter, with the tips pointing outwards. (You may need to break off the bottom end of each leaf if the leaves are large).

3 Place a teaspoonful or so of mayonnaise on the flat side of each halved egg and top with a spoonful of fish caviar. Carefully arrange in the centre of the dish.

4 Arrange the sardines and mackerel fillets at four points on the plate. Spoon the pickled cockles into two of the gaps, opposite each other, and the mussels in sauce in the remaining gaps. Garnish with parsley sprigs or dill. Place in the refrigerator until needed.

Energy 596Kcal/2481kJ; Protein 53.7g; Carbohydrate 3.7g, of which sugars 1.9g; Fat 41g, of which saturates 8.9g; Cholesterol 579mg; Calcium 403mg; Fibre 0.5g; Sodium 1323mg.

SARDINES EN ESCABECHE

THE ARABS INVENTED MARINADES AS A MEANS OF PRESERVING POULTRY, MEAT AND GAME, AND ESCABECHE MEANS "ACID" IN ARABIC. IN SPAIN THIS METHOD WAS ENTHUSIASTICALLY ADOPTED AS A MEANS OF KEEPING FISH FRESH. THE FISH ARE ALWAYS FRIED FIRST AND THEN STORED IN VINEGAR.

SERVES TWO TO FOUR

INGREDIENTS

- 12–16 sardines, cleaned
- seasoned plain (all-purpose) flour, for dusting
- 30ml/2 tbsp olive oil
- roasted red onion, green (bell) pepper and tomatoes, to garnish

For the marinade

- 90ml/6 tbsp olive oil
- 1 onion, sliced
- 1 garlic clove, crushed
- 3–4 bay leaves
- 2 cloves
- 1 dried red chilli, seeded and chopped
- 5ml/1 tsp paprika
- 120ml/4fl oz/½ cup wine or sherry vinegar
- 120ml/4fl oz/½ cup white wine
- salt and ground black pepper

1 Using a sharp knife, cut the heads off the sardines and split each of them along the belly. Turn the fish over so that the backbone is uppermost. Press down along the backbone to loosen it, then carefully lift out the backbone and as many of the remaining little bones as possible.

2 Close the sardines up again and dust them with seasoned flour.

3 Heat the olive oil in a frying pan and fry the sardines for 2–3 minutes on each side. With a metal spatula, remove the fish from the pan to a plate and allow to cool, then pack them in a single layer in a large shallow dish.

4 To make the marinade, add the olive oil to the oil remaining in the frying pan. Fry the onion and garlic gently for 5–10 minutes until soft and translucent, stirring occasionally. Add the bay leaves, cloves, chilli and paprika, with pepper to taste. Fry, stirring frequently, for another 1–2 minutes.

5 Stir in the vinegar, wine and a little salt. Allow to bubble up, then pour over the sardines. The marinade should cover the fish completely. When the fish is cool, cover and chill overnight or for up to three days. Serve the sardines and their marinade, garnished with the onion, pepper and tomatoes.

VARIATION

Other oily fish such as herrings or sprats (small whitebait) are very good prepared in this way. White fish can also be used.

Energy 125Kcal/517kJ; Protein 9.6g; Carbohydrate 0g, of which sugars 0g; Fat 9.4g, of which saturates 1.9g; Cholesterol 0mg; Calcium 48mg; Fibre 0g; Sodium 53mg.

FRIED WHITEBAIT WITH SHERRY SALSA

SMALL FRESHLY FRIED FISH ARE OFFERED IN EVERY TAPAS BAR IN SPAIN. BLACK-BACKED ANCHOVIES ARE THE BEST, BUT NEED TO BE COOKED WITHIN A DAY OF CATCHING. TINY CHANQUETES *ARE ALSO GOOD, BUT ANY SMALL FISH, SUCH AS WHITEBAIT, ARE SUITABLE. SERVE THEM WITH LEMON WEDGES.*

SERVES FOUR

INGREDIENTS

- 225g/8oz whitebait
- 30ml/2 tbsp seasoned plain (all-purpose) flour
- 60ml/4 tbsp olive oil
- 60ml/4 tbsp sunflower oil

For the salsa

- 1 shallot, finely chopped
- 2 garlic cloves, finely chopped
- 4 ripe tomatoes, roughly chopped
- 1 small red chilli, seeded and finely chopped
- 30ml/2 tbsp olive oil
- 60ml/4 tbsp sweet oloroso sherry
- 30–45ml/2–3 tbsp chopped mixed fresh herbs, such as parsley or basil
- 25g/1oz/½ cup stale white breadcrumbs
- salt and ground black pepper

1 To make the salsa, place the chopped shallot, garlic, tomatoes, chilli and olive oil in a pan. Cover with a lid and cook gently for about 10 minutes.

2 Pour the sherry into the pan and season with salt and pepper to taste. Stir in the herbs and breadcrumbs, then cover and keep the salsa hot until the whitebait are ready.

3 Preheat the oven to 150°C/300°F/Gas 2. Wash the whitebait thoroughly, drain well and dry on kitchen paper, then dust in the seasoned flour.

4 Heat the oils together in a heavy frying pan and cook the fish in batches until crisp and golden. Drain on kitchen paper and keep warm until all the fish are cooked. Serve at once with the salsa.

Energy 406Kcal/1683kJ; Protein 12.5g; Carbohydrate 12.4g, of which sugars 4.4g; Fat 32.6g, of which saturates 0.9g; Cholesterol 0mg; Calcium 502mg; Fibre 1.2g; Sodium 186mg.

SALT COD FRITTERS WITH ALLIOLI

BACALAO – SALT COD – IS ONE OF THE GREAT SPANISH DELIGHTS, ADDING FLAVOUR TO BLAND INGREDIENTS SUCH AS POTATOES. IF YOU ARE UNFAMILIAR WITH IT, THEN THIS IS A DELIGHTFUL WAY TO TRY IT OUT. BITESIZE FISH CAKES, DIPPED INTO RICH, CREAMY, GARLICKY ALLIOLI, ARE IRRESISTIBLE AS A TAPAS DISH OR APPETIZER.

SERVES SIX

INGREDIENTS

- 450g/1lb salt cod
- 500g/1¼lb floury potatoes
- 300ml/½ pint/1¼ cups milk
- 6 spring onions (scallions), finely chopped
- 30ml/2 tbsp extra virgin olive oil
- 30ml/2 tbsp chopped fresh parsley
- juice of ½ lemon
- 2 eggs, beaten
- plain (all-purpose) flour, for dusting
- 90g/3½oz/1¼ cups dried white breadcrumbs
- olive oil, for shallow frying
- lemon wedges and salad leaves, to serve
- salt and ground black pepper

For the allioli

- 2 large garlic cloves, finely chopped
- 2 egg yolks
- 300ml/½ pint/1¼ cups olive oil
- juice of ½ lemon, to taste

1 Soak the salt cod in cold water for at least 24 hours, changing the water two or three times. The cod should swell as it rehydrates. Sample a tiny piece. It should not taste unpleasantly salty when fully rehydrated. Drain well and pat dry with kitchen paper.

2 Cook the potatoes, unpeeled, in a pan of lightly salted boiling water for about 20 minutes, until tender. Drain. As soon as they are cool enough to handle, peel the potatoes, then mash with a fork or use a potato masher.

3 Pour the milk into a pan, add half the spring onions and bring to a simmer. Add the soaked cod and poach very gently for 10–15 minutes, or until it flakes easily. Remove the cod and flake it with a fork into a bowl, discarding bones and skin.

4 Add 60ml/4 tbsp mashed potato to the cod and beat them together with a wooden spoon. Work in the olive oil, then gradually add the remaining mashed potato. Beat in the remaining spring onions and the parsley.

5 Season with lemon juice and pepper to taste – the mixture may also need a little salt but taste it before adding any. Add one egg to the mixture and beat in until thoroughly combined, then chill until firm.

6 Shape the chilled fish mixture into 12–18 balls, then gently flatten into small round cakes. Coat each one in flour, then dip in the remaining beaten egg and coat with dried breadcrumbs. Chill until ready to fry.

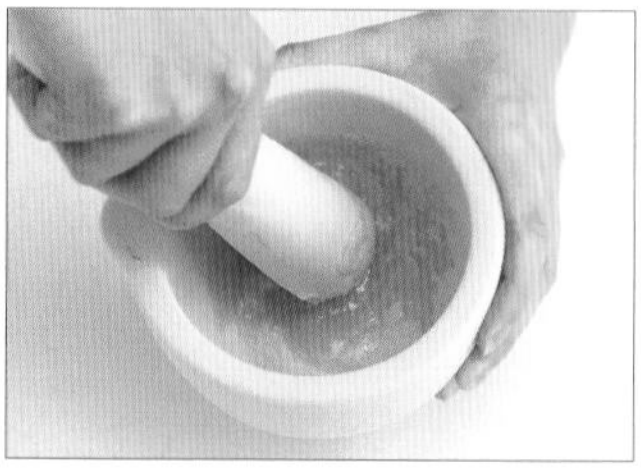

7 Meanwhile, make the allioli. Place the garlic and a good pinch of salt in a mortar and pound to a paste with a pestle. Using a small whisk or a wooden spoon, gradually work in the egg yolks.

8 Beat in about half the olive oil, a drop at a time. When the sauce is as thick as soft butter, beat in 5–10ml/1–2 tsp lemon juice. Continue adding oil until the allioli is very thick. Season to taste, adding more lemon juice if you wish.

9 Heat about 2cm/¾in oil in a large, heavy frying pan. Add the fritters and cook over a medium-high heat for about 4 minutes. Turn them over and cook for a further 4 minutes on the other side, until crisp and golden. Drain on kitchen paper, then serve with the allioli, lemon wedges and salad leaves.

COOK'S TIP

Try to find a thick, creamy white piece of salt cod, preferably cut from the middle of the fish rather than the tail and fin ends. Avoid thin, yellowish salt cod, as it will be too dry and salty.

Energy 645Kcal/2686kJ; Protein 32.3g; Carbohydrate 26.4g, of which sugars 4g; Fat 46.4g, of which saturates 7.6g; Cholesterol 178mg; Calcium 122mg; Fibre 1.2g; Sodium 471mg.

Baked Trout with Rice, Tomatoes and Nuts

Trout is very popular in Spain, particularly in the North, where it is fished in many rivers. Here is a modern recipe for TRUCHA RELLENA, *baked in foil with a rice stuffing in which sun-dried tomatoes have been used in place of the more traditional chillies.*

SERVES FOUR

INGREDIENTS

- 2 fresh trout, about 500g/1¼lb each
- 75g/3oz/¾ cup mixed unsalted almonds, pine nuts or hazelnuts
- 25ml/1½ tbsp olive oil, plus extra for drizzling
- 1 small onion, finely chopped
- 10ml/2 tsp grated fresh root ginger
- 175g/6oz/1½ cups cooked white long grain rice
- 4 tomatoes, peeled and very finely chopped
- 4 sun-dried tomatoes in oil, drained and chopped
- 30ml/2 tbsp chopped fresh tarragon
- 2 fresh tarragon sprigs
- salt and ground black pepper
- dressed green salad leaves, to serve

1 Preheat the oven to 190°C/375°F/Gas 5. If the trout is unfilleted, use a sharp knife to fillet it. Remove any tiny bones remaining in the cavity using a pair of tweezers.

2 Spread out the nuts in a shallow tin (pan) and bake for 3–4 minutes until golden brown, shaking the tin occasionally. Chop the nuts roughly.

3 Heat the olive oil in a small frying pan and fry the onion for 3–4 minutes until soft and translucent. Stir in the grated ginger, cook for a further 1 minute, then spoon into a mixing bowl.

4 Stir the rice, chopped tomatoes, sun-dried tomatoes, toasted nuts and tarragon into the onion mixture. Season the stuffing well.

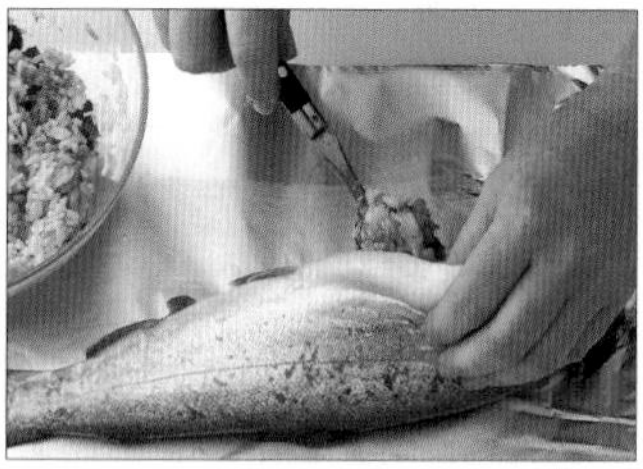

5 Place the trout on individual large pieces of oiled foil and spoon the stuffing into the cavities. Add a sprig of tarragon and a drizzle of olive oil or oil from the sun-dried tomatoes.

6 Fold the foil over to enclose each trout completely, and put the parcels in a large roasting pan. Bake for about 20 minutes or until the fish is just tender. Cut the fish into thick slices. Serve with the salad leaves.

COOK'S TIP

You will need about 75g/3oz/¾ cup of uncooked rice to produce 175g/6oz/1½ cups cooked rice.

Energy 501Kcal/2094kJ; Protein 46g; Carbohydrate 27.8g, of which sugars 5g; Fat 22.8g, of which saturates 3.3g; Cholesterol 160mg; Calcium 144mg; Fibre 3.2g; Sodium 161mg.

TRUCHAS A LA NAVARRA

TRADITIONALLY, THE TROUT WOULD HAVE COME FROM MOUNTAIN STREAMS AND BEEN STUFFED AND WRAPPED IN LOCALLY CURED HAM. ONE OF THE BEAUTIES OF THIS METHOD IS THAT THE SKINS COME OFF IN ONE PIECE, LEAVING THE SUCCULENT, MOIST FLESH TO BE EATEN WITH THE CRISPED, SALT HAM.

SERVES FOUR

INGREDIENTS
- 4 brown or rainbow trout, about 250g/9oz each, cleaned
- 16 thin slices Serrano ham, about 200g/7oz
- 50g/2oz/¼ cup melted butter, plus extra for greasing
- salt and ground black pepper
- buttered potatoes, to serve (optional)

1 Extend the belly cavity of each trout, cutting up one side of the backbone. Slip a knife behind the rib bones to loosen them (sometimes just flexing the fish makes them pop up). Snip these off from both sides with scissors, and season the fish well inside.

2 Preheat the grill (broiler) to high, with a shelf in the top position. Line a baking tray with foil and butter it.

3 Working with the fish on the foil, fold a piece of ham into each belly. Use smaller or broken bits of ham for this, and reserve the eight best slices.

4 Brush each trout with a little butter, seasoning the outside lightly with salt and pepper. Wrap two ham slices round each one, crossways, tucking the ends into the belly. Grill (broil) the trout for 4 minutes, then carefully turn them over with a metal spatula, rolling them across on the belly, so the ham doesn't come loose, and grill for a further 4 minutes.

5 Serve the trout very hot, with any spare butter spooned over the top. Diners should open the trout on their plates, and eat them from the inside, pushing the flesh off the skin.

Energy 369Kcal/1546kJ; Protein 48g; Carbohydrate 0.6g, of which sugars 0.6g; Fat 19.4g, of which saturates 8.8g; Cholesterol 216mg; Calcium 66mg; Fibre 0g; Sodium 821mg.

GRILLED RED MULLET WITH BAY LEAVES

RED MULLET ARE CALLED SALMONETES – LITTLE SALMON – IN SPAIN BECAUSE OF THEIR DELICATE, PALE PINK COLOUR. THEY ARE SIMPLE TO COOK ON A BARBECUE, WITH BAY LEAVES FOR FLAVOUR AND A DRIBBLE OF TANGY DRESSING INSTEAD OF A MARINADE.

SERVES FOUR

INGREDIENTS

- 4 red mullet or snapper, about 225–275g/8–10oz each, cleaned and descaled if cooking under a grill (broiler)
- olive oil, for brushing
- fresh herb sprigs, such as fennel, dill, parsley, or thyme
- 2–3 dozen fresh or dried bay leaves

For the dressing

- 90ml/6 tbsp olive oil
- 6 garlic cloves, finely chopped
- ½ dried chilli, seeded and chopped
- juice of ½ lemon
- 15ml/1 tbsp parsley

COOK'S TIP

If you are cooking on the barbecue, the fish do not need to be scaled.

1 Prepare the barbecue or preheat the grill (broiler) with the shelf 15cm/6in from the heat source.

2 Brush each fish with oil and stuff the cavities with the herb sprigs. Brush the grill pan with oil and lay bay leaves across the cooking rack. Place the fish on top and cook for 15–20 minutes until cooked through, turning once.

3 To make the dressing, heat the olive oil in a small pan and fry the chopped garlic with the dried chilli. Add the lemon juice and strain the dressing into a small jug (pitcher). Add the chopped parsley and stir to combine.

4 Serve the fish on warmed plates, drizzled with the dressing.

COOK'S TIPS

- Nicknamed the woodcock of the sea, red mullet are one of the fish that are classically cooked uncleaned to give them extra flavour. In this recipe however, the fish are cleaned and herbs are used to add extra flavour to the fish.
- If cooking on a barbecue, light the barbecue well in advance. Before cooking, the charcoal or wood should be grey, with no flames.

Energy 294Kcal/1221kJ; Protein 24.2g; Carbohydrate 0.5g, of which sugars 0.1g; Fat 21.8g, of which saturates 2.4g; Cholesterol 0mg; Calcium 91mg; Fibre 0.1g; Sodium 125mg.

PAN-FRIED SOLE WITH LEMON AND CAPERS

Flat fish of different sorts abound in the Mediterranean and are usually fried simply and served with lemon wedges to squeeze over the top. Intensely flavoured capers, which grow extensively in the Balearic Islands, make a pleasant tangy addition.

SERVES TWO

INGREDIENTS
- 30–45ml/2–3 tbsp plain (all-purpose) flour
- 4 sole, plaice or flounder fillets, or 2 whole small flat fish
- 45ml/3 tbsp olive oil
- 25g/1oz/2 tbsp butter
- 60ml/4 tbsp lemon juice
- 30ml/2 tbsp pickled capers, drained
- salt and ground black pepper
- fresh flat leaf parsley, to garnish
- lemon wedges, to serve

COOK'S TIP
This is a flavourful, and quick, way to serve the fillets of any white fish. The delicate flavour is enhanced by the tangy lemon juice and capers.

1 Sift the flour on to a plate and season well with salt and ground black pepper. Dip the fish fillets into the flour, to coat evenly on both sides.

2 Heat the oil and butter in a large shallow pan until foaming. Add the fish fillets and fry over a medium heat for 2–3 minutes on each side.

3 Lift out the fillets carefully with a metal spatula and place them on a warmed serving platter. Season with salt and ground black pepper.

4 Add the lemon juice and capers to the pan, heat through and pour over the fish. Garnish with parsley and serve at once with lemon wedges.

Energy 505Kcal/2113kJ; Protein 51g; Carbohydrate 6.1g, of which sugars 0.4g; Fat 31.1g, of which saturates 9.5g; Cholesterol 153mg; Calcium 150mg; Fibre 0.3g; Sodium 437mg.

SEA BASS IN A SALT CRUST

BAKING FISH IN A CRUST OF SEA SALT ENHANCES THE FLAVOUR AND BRINGS OUT THE TASTE OF THE SEA. IT IS ALSO THE EASIEST WAY THERE IS TO COOK A WHOLE FISH. IN SPAIN THE GILT-HEAD BREAM IS THE FISH MOST OFTEN USED, BUT ANY FIRM FISH, SUCH AS GREY MULLET, STRIPED BASS AND PORGY, CAN BE COOKED THIS WAY. BREAK OPEN THE CRUST AT THE TABLE TO RELEASE THE GLORIOUS AROMA.

SERVES FOUR TO SIX

INGREDIENTS

- 1 sea bass, about 1kg/2¼lb, gutted and scaled
- 1 sprig each of fresh fennel, rosemary and thyme
- mixed peppercorns
- 2kg/4½lb coarse sea salt
- seaweed or samphire, to garnish (optional)
- lemon slices, to serve

COOK'S TIP

In the Mediterranean, fish in salt are often baked whole and ungutted. But supermarkets elsewhere always sell them gutted, so use the opportunity to add flavourings inside.

1 Preheat the oven to 240°C/475°F/ Gas 9. Fill the cavity of the sea bass with the fennel, rosemary and thyme sprigs and grind over some of the mixed peppercorns.

2 Spread half the salt in a shallow baking tray and lay the sea bass on it.

3 Cover the fish all over with a 1cm/½in layer of salt, pressing it down firmly. Bake for 30 minutes, until the salt coagulates and is beginning to colour.

4 To serve, leave the fish on the baking tray and garnish with seaweed or samphire, if using. Bring the fish to the table in its salt crust. Use a sharp knife to break open the crust.

COOK'S TIP

Once baked, the salt sticks to the fish skin, and brings it off. Scrape back the layer of salt and lift out the top fillet in sections. Snip the backbone with scissors and lift out. Discard the herbs and remove the bottom fillet pieces. Add a lemon slice to each plate.

Energy 83Kcal/351kJ; Protein 16.1g; Carbohydrate 0g, of which sugars 0g; Fat 2.1g, of which saturates 0.3g; Cholesterol 67mg; Calcium 109mg; Fibre 0g; Sodium 2023mg.

BACALAO IN SPICY TOMATO WITH POTATOES

Salt cod is a popular ingredient in Spain, not just a Lenten necessity. It is the salt that makes the fish so characterful, so don't oversoak it for this traditional Basque recipe. Look out for a loin piece, which has very little waste; if you can't find one, buy a larger piece to ensure you have enough once any very dry bits have been removed.

SERVES FOUR

INGREDIENTS

- 400g/14oz salt cod loin, soaked in cold water for 24 hours
- 30ml/2 tbsp olive oil
- 1 large onion, chopped
- 2 garlic cloves, finely chopped
- 1½ green (bell) peppers, seeded and chopped
- 500g/1¼ lb ripe tomatoes, peeled and chopped, or a 400g/14oz can tomatoes
- 15ml/1 tbsp tomato purée (paste)
- 15ml/1 tbsp clear honey
- 1.5ml/¼ tsp dried thyme
- 2.5ml/½ tsp cayenne pepper
- juice of ½ lemon (optional)
- 2 potatoes
- 45ml/3 tbsp stale breadcrumbs
- 30ml/2 tbsp finely chopped fresh parsley
- salt and ground black pepper

1 Drain the salt cod and place in a pan. Pour over water to cover generously and bring to the boil. Remove the pan from the heat as soon as the water boils, then set aside until cold.

2 Heat the oil in a medium pan. Fry the onion, and add the garlic after 5 minutes. Add the chopped peppers and tomatoes, and cook gently to form a sauce. Stir in the tomato purée, honey, dried thyme, cayenne, black pepper and a little salt. Taste for seasoning: a little lemon juice will make it tangier.

3 Halve the potatoes lengthways and cut them into slices just thicker than a coin. Drain the fish, reserving the cooking water.

4 Preheat the grill (broiler) to medium with a shelf 15cm/6in below it. Bring the reserved fish cooking water to the boil and cook the potatoes for about 8 minutes. Do not add extra salt.

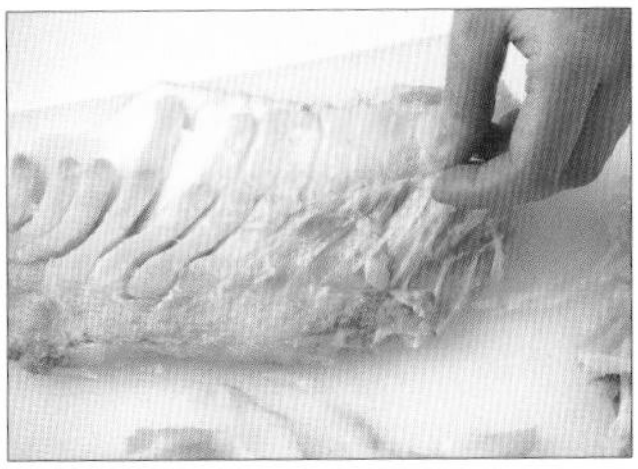

5 Remove the skin and bones from the cod, and pull it into small natural flakes. Spoon one-third of the tomato sauce into a flameproof casserole, top with the potatoes, fish and remaining sauce. Combine the breadcrumbs and parsley and sprinkle over. Heat the dish through under a grill for 10 minutes.

Energy 284Kcal/1193kJ; Protein 23.2g; Carbohydrate 32.9g, of which sugars 15.4g; Fat 7.5g, of which saturates 1.1g; Cholesterol 46mg; Calcium 80mg; Fibre 4.5g; Sodium 180mg.

MACKEREL IN LEMON SAMFAINA

SAMFAINA IS A SAUCE FROM THE EAST COAST OF SPAIN AND THE COSTA BRAVA. IT SHARES THE SAME INGREDIENTS AS RATATOUILLE AND IS RATHER LIKE A CHUNKY VEGETABLE STEW. THIS VERSION IS PARTICULARLY LEMONY, TO OFFSET THE RICHNESS OF THE MACKEREL.

SERVES FOUR

INGREDIENTS

- 2 large mackerel, filleted, or 4 fillets
- plain (all-purpose) flour, for dusting
- 30ml/2 tbsp olive oil
- lemon wedges, if serving cold

For the samfaina sauce

- 1 large aubergine (eggplant)
- 60ml/4 tbsp olive oil
- 1 large onion, chopped
- 2 garlic cloves, finely chopped
- 1 large courgette (zucchini), sliced
- 1 red and 1 green (bell) pepper, seeded and cut into squares
- 800g/1¾lb ripe tomatoes, roughly chopped
- 1 bay leaf
- salt and ground black pepper

1 Make the sauce. Peel the aubergine, then cut the flesh into cubes, sprinkle with salt and leave to stand in a colander for 30 minutes.

2 Heat half the oil in a flameproof casserole large enough to fit the fish. Fry the onion over a medium heat until it colours. Add the garlic, then the courgettes and peppers and stir-fry.

3 Add the tomatoes and bay leaf, partially cover and simmer over the lowest heat, letting the tomatoes just soften without losing their shape.

4 Rinse off the salt from the aubergine. Using three layers of kitchen paper, squeeze the cubes dry.

5 Heat the remaining oil in a frying pan until smoking. Put in one handful of aubergine cubes, then the next, stirring with a wooden spoon and cooking over a high heat until the cubes are brown on all sides. Stir into the tomato sauce.

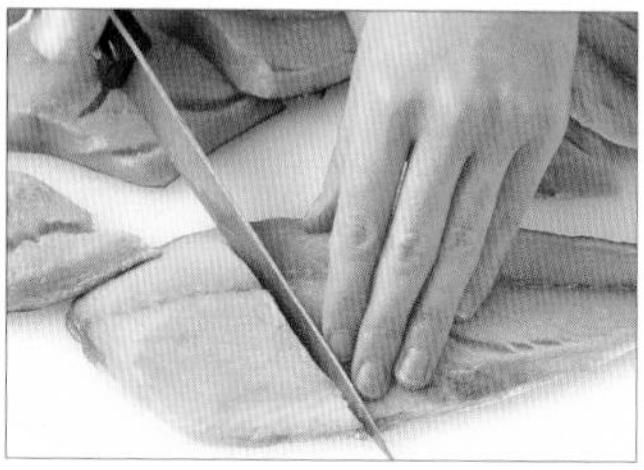

6 Cut each mackerel fillet into three, and dust the filleted side with flour. Heat the oil in a frying pan over a high heat and put the fish in, floured side down. Fry for 3 minutes until golden. Turn and cook for another 1 minute, then slip the fish into the sauce and simmer, covered, for 5 minutes. Adjust the seasonings before serving.

COOK'S TIP

The fish can be served hot or cold. If serving cold, present the mackerel skin-side up, surrounded by vegetables, and garnished with lemon wedges.

Energy 474Kcal/1967kJ; Protein 23.8g; Carbohydrate 19.2g, of which sugars 17.4g; Fat 34g, of which saturates 6.1g; Cholesterol 53mg; Calcium 70mg; Fibre 6.1g; Sodium 83mg.

MONKFISH WITH PIMIENTO AND CREAM SAUCE

THIS RECIPE COMES FROM RIOJA COUNTRY, WHERE A SPECIAL HORNED RED PEPPER GROWS AND IS USED TO MAKE A SPICY SAUCE. HERE, RED PEPPERS ARE USED WITH A LITTLE CHILLI WHILE CREAM MAKES A MELLOW PINK SAUCE. TO DRINK, CHOOSE A MARQUES DE CÁCERES WHITE RIOJA.

SERVES FOUR

INGREDIENTS
- 2 large red (bell) peppers
- 1kg/2¼lb monkfish tail or 900g/2lb halibut
- plain (all-purpose) flour, for dusting
- 30ml/2 tbsp olive oil
- 25g/1oz/2 tbsp butter
- 120ml/4fl oz/½ cup white Rioja or dry vermouth
- ½ dried chilli, seeded and chopped
- 8 raw prawns (shrimp), in the shell
- 150ml/¼ pint/⅔ cup double (heavy) cream
- salt and ground black pepper
- fresh flat leaf parsley, to garnish

1 Preheat the grill (broiler) to high and cook the peppers for 8–12 minutes, turning occasionally, until they are soft, and the skins blackened. Leave, covered, until cool enough to handle. Skin and discard the stalks and seeds. Put the flesh into a blender, strain in the juices and purée.

2 Cut the monkfish or halibut into eight steaks (freeze the bones for stock). Season well and dust with flour.

3 Heat the oil and butter in a large frying pan and fry the fish for 3 minutes on each side. Remove to a warm dish.

4 Add the wine or vermouth and chilli to the pan and stir to deglaze the pan. Add the prawns and cook them briefly, then lift out and reserve.

5 Boil the sauce to reduce by half, then strain into a small jug (pitcher). Add the cream to the pan and boil briefly to reduce. Return the sauce to the pan, stir in the puréed peppers and check the seasonings. Pour the sauce over the fish and serve garnished with the cooked prawns and parsley.

Energy 524Kcal/2185kJ; Protein 47.5g; Carbohydrate 6.5g, of which sugars 6.2g; Fat 32.2g, of which saturates 16.9g; Cholesterol 129mg; Calcium 62mg; Fibre 1.4g; Sodium 125mg.

HAKE AND CLAMS WITH SALSA VERDE

MERLUZA EN SALSA VERDE IS A FAVOURITE BASQUE WAY OF COOKING HAKE, WHICH IS ONE OF THE MOST POPULAR AND PLENTIFUL FISH IN SPAIN. AS THEY BAKE, THE CLAMS OPEN UP AND ADD THEIR DELICIOUS SEA JUICES TO THE GREEN WINE AND PARSLEY SAUCE.

SERVES FOUR

INGREDIENTS

- 4 hake steaks, about 2cm/¾in thick
- 50g/2oz/½ cup plain (all-purpose) flour, for dusting, plus 30ml/2 tbsp
- 60ml/4 tbsp olive oil
- 15ml/1 tbsp lemon juice
- 1 small onion, finely chopped
- 4 garlic cloves, finely chopped
- 150ml/¼ pint/⅔ cup fish stock
- 150ml/¼ pint/⅔ cup white wine
- 90ml/6 tbsp chopped fresh parsley
- 75g/3oz/¾ cup frozen petits pois
- 16 fresh clams, cleaned
- salt and ground black pepper

COOK'S TIP

To make fish stock, put 450g/1lb fish bones, head and skin in a large pan with 1 sliced onion, 1 sliced carrot, ½ sliced celery stalk, 3–4 thick parsley stalks, snapped in places, 1 bay leaf, 10ml/2 tsp lemon juice or wine vinegar and 175ml/6fl oz/¾ cup dry white wine or vermouth. Bring to the boil, then reduce the heat and simmer for 30 minutes. Strain. If you can't buy fish bits, collect fish leftovers in the freezer: prawn (shrimp) heads, the spines from cooked fish, poaching water from a salmon, and mussel or clam stock from opening the shellfish. It is also worth buying a small whole fish to add to the stock.

1 Preheat the oven to 180°C/350°F/Gas 4. Season the fish, then dust with flour. Heat half the oil in a large pan, add the fish and fry for 1 minute on each side. Transfer to an ovenproof dish and sprinkle with the lemon juice.

2 Heat the remaining oil in a clean pan and fry the onion and garlic, stirring, until soft. Stir in the 30ml/2 tbsp flour and cook for about 1 minute.

3 Slowly add the stock and wine to the pan, stirring until thickened. Add 75ml/5 tbsp of the parsley and the petits pois to the sauce and season with plenty of salt and pepper.

4 Pour the sauce over the fish, and bake for 15–20 minutes, adding the clams 3–4 minutes before the end of the cooking time.

5 Discard any clams that do not open once cooked, then sprinkle the fish with with the remaining parsley and serve.

VARIATION

In Rioja country, on the banks of the River Ebro, this dish often includes fresh young asparagus tips as well as peas. Simply replace half the peas with asparagus tips.

Energy 274Kcal/1139kJ; Protein 26.5g; Carbohydrate 4.2g, of which sugars 1.8g; Fat 14.3g, of which saturates 2.1g; Cholesterol 40mg; Calcium 64mg; Fibre 1.7g; Sodium 357mg.

VIEIRAS DE SANTIAGO

SCALLOPS ARE THE SYMBOL OF ST JAMES (SANTIAGO), AND THIS DISH IS ASSOCIATED WITH HIS SHRINE AT SANTIAGO DE COMPOSTELLA IN GALICIA. THE FLAMED SCALLOPS ARE COVERED IN TOMATO SAUCE AND ARE SERVED HOT IN THE CURVED SHELL, WITH CRISP BREADCRUMBS ON TOP.

SERVES FOUR

INGREDIENTS

- 30ml/2 tbsp olive oil
- 1 onion, finely chopped
- 2 garlic cloves, finely chopped
- 200g/7oz can tomatoes
- pinch of cayenne pepper
- 45ml/3 tbsp finely chopped fresh parsley
- 50ml/2fl oz/¼ cup orange juice
- 50g/2oz/4 tbsp butter
- 450g/1lb large shelled scallops, or 8–12 large ones on the shell, detached and cleaned
- 30ml/2 tbsp anis spirit, such as Ricard or Pernod
- 90ml/6 tbsp stale breadcrumbs
- salt and ground black pepper

1 Heat the oil in a pan and fry the onion and garlic over a gentle heat. Add the tomatoes and cook for 10–15 minutes, stirring occasionally. Season with a little salt and cayenne pepper.

2 Transfer the tomato mixture to a small food processor or blender, add 30ml/2 tbsp of the parsley and the orange juice and blend to form a smooth purée.

3 Preheat the grill (broiler) with the shelf at its highest. Arrange four curved scallop shells, or flameproof ramekin dishes, on a baking tray.

4 Heat 25g/1oz/2 tbsp of the butter in a small frying pan and fry the scallops gently, for about 2 minutes, or until sealed but not totally cooked through.

5 Pour the anis spirit into a ladle and set light to it. Pour over the scallops and shake the pan gently until the flames die down. Divide the scallops among the prepared shells (or dishes) and salt them lightly. Add the pan juices to the tomato sauce.

6 Pour the tomato sauce over the scallops. Mix together the breadcrumbs and the remaining parsley, season very lightly and sprinkle over the top.

7 Melt the remaining butter in a small pan and drizzle over the breadcrumbs. Grill (broil) the scallops for about 1 minute to colour the tops and heat through. Serve immediately.

COOK'S TIP

If you can lay your hands on the curved shells of scallops, wash and keep them after use. Fresh scallops are usually sold on the flat shell so the second shell, which can be used as a little dish, is now quite a rarity.

Energy 394Kcal/1652kJ; Protein 29.7g; Carbohydrate 25.5g, of which sugars 4.4g; Fat 18.1g, of which saturates 7.8g; Cholesterol 80mg; Calcium 95mg; Fibre 1.8g; Sodium 459mg.

CHAR-GRILLED SQUID

CALAMARES A LA PLANCHA ARE TRADITIONALLY COOKED ON THE HOT GRIDDLE THAT IS AN ESSENTIAL PART OF EVERY SPANISH KITCHEN. THE METHOD IS FAST AND SIMPLE AND REALLY BRINGS OUT THE FLAVOUR OF THE SQUID. THIS DISH IS AN IDEAL FIRST COURSE FOR FOUR PEOPLE, OR CAN BE SERVED ON A BED OF RICE AS A MAIN DISH FOR TWO.

SERVES TWO TO FOUR

INGREDIENTS

- 2 whole cleaned squid, with tentacles, about 275g/10oz each
- 75ml/5 tbsp olive oil
- 30ml/2 tbsp sherry vinegar
- 2 fresh red chillies, finely chopped
- 60ml/4 tbsp dry white wine
- salt and ground black pepper
- hot cooked rice, to serve (optional)
- 15–30ml/1–2 tbsp chopped parsley, to garnish

1 Make a lengthways cut down the side of the body of each squid, then open it out flat. Score the flesh on both sides of the bodies in a criss-cross pattern with the tip of a sharp knife. Chop the tentacles into short lengths. Place all the squid pieces in a non-metallic dish.

2 Whisk together the oil and vinegar in a small bowl. Add salt and pepper to taste, pour over the squid and toss to mix. Cover and leave to marinate for about 1 hour.

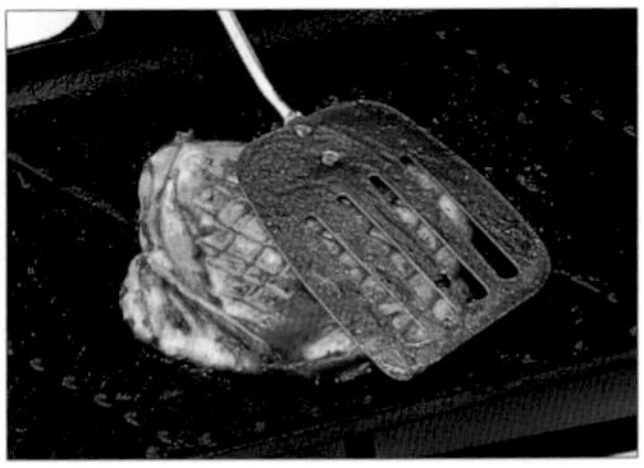

3 Heat a ridged griddle pan until hot. Add the body of one of the squid and cook over a medium heat for 2–3 minutes, pressing the squid with a metal spatula to keep it flat. Repeat on the other side. Cook the other squid body in the same way.

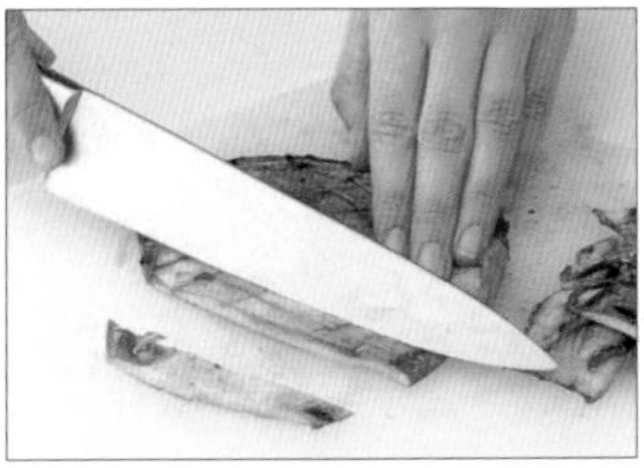

4 Cut the squid bodies into diagonal strips. If serving with rice, arrange the squid strips criss-cross on top. Keep hot.

5 Add the chopped tentacles and chillies to the pan and toss over a medium heat for 2 minutes. Stir in the wine, then drizzle over the squid. Garnish with chopped parsley.

Energy 249Kcal/1038kJ; Protein 21.5g; Carbohydrate 2.1g, of which sugars 0.4g; Fat 16.2g, of which saturates 2.5g; Cholesterol 309mg; Calcium 42mg; Fibre 0.6g; Sodium 156mg.

Calamares Rellenos

Squid are often just stuffed with their own tentacles but, in this recipe, ham and raisins, which contrast wonderfully with the subtle flavour of the squid, are also included. The stuffed squid are cooked in a richly flavoured tomato sauce and make a perfect appetizer. To serve as a main course, simply accompany with plain boiled rice.

SERVES FOUR

INGREDIENTS

- 2 squid, about 275g/10oz each
- 60ml/4 tbsp olive oil
- 1 small onion, finely chopped
- 2 garlic cloves, finely chopped
- 50g/2oz Serrano ham or gammon steak, diced small
- 75g/3oz/scant ½ cup long grain rice
- 30ml/2 tbsp raisins, chopped
- 30ml/2 tbsp finely chopped fresh parsley
- ½ small (US medium) egg, beaten
- plain (all-purpose) flour, for dusting
- 250ml/8fl oz/1 cup white wine
- 1 bay leaf
- 30ml/2 tbsp chopped fresh parsley
- salt, paprika and black pepper

For the tomato sauce

- 30ml/2 tbsp olive oil
- 1 onion, finely chopped
- 2 garlic cloves, finely chopped
- 200g/7oz can tomatoes
- salt and cayenne pepper

1 Make the tomato sauce. Heat the oil in a flameproof casserole large enough to hold the squid. Cook the onion and garlic over a gentle heat. Add the tomatoes and cook for 10–15 minutes. Season with salt and cayenne pepper.

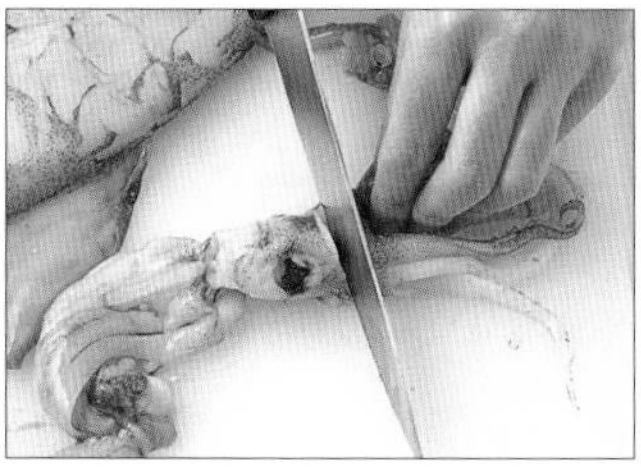

2 To prepare the squid, use the tentacles to pull out the body. Cut off the tentacles, discarding the eyes and everything below. Flex the bodies to pop out the spinal structure. Chop the fin flaps and rinse the bodies well.

3 Heat half the oil in a pan and gently fry the onion and garlic together. Add the ham and squid tentacles and stir-fry. Off the heat stir in the rice, chopped raisins and parsley. Season well and add the egg to bind the ingredients.

4 Spoon the mixture into the squid bodies, then stitch each of them shut using a small poultry skewer. Blot the bodies with kitchen paper, then flour them very lightly. Heat the remaining oil in a frying pan and fry the squid, turning until coloured on all sides.

5 Move the squid with two spoons and arrange them in the tomato sauce. Add the wine and bay leaf. Cover the casserole tightly and simmer for about 30 minutes, turning the squid over halfway through cooking if the sauce does not cover them completely. Serve sliced into rings, surrounded by the sauce and garnished with parsley.

Energy 433Kcal/1810kJ; Protein 26.8g; Carbohydrate 26.4g, of which sugars 9.1g; Fat 20.4g, of which saturates 3.3g; Cholesterol 340mg; Calcium 61mg; Fibre 1.5g; Sodium 325mg.

Octopus Stew

In Galicia, octopus stews are particularly popular and a common tapas dish is a simple stew with paprika, served on little wooden plates. Here the octopus is stewed with tomatoes and potatoes, to make a substantial main course. It is an ideal make-ahead dish, because octopus can be tough, and benefits from long cooking to tenderize it.

SERVES FOUR TO SIX

INGREDIENTS

- 1kg/2¼lb octopus, cleaned
- 45ml/3 tbsp olive oil
- 1 large red onion, chopped
- 3 garlic cloves, finely chopped
- 30ml/2 tbsp brandy
- 300ml/½ pint/1¼ cups dry white wine
- 800g/1¾lb ripe plum tomatoes, peeled and chopped or 2 × 400g/14oz cans chopped tomatoes
- 1 dried red chilli, seeded and chopped
- 1.5ml/¼ tsp paprika
- 450g/1lb small new potatoes
- 15ml/1 tbsp chopped fresh rosemary
- 15ml/1 tbsp fresh thyme leaves
- 1.2 litres/2 pints/5 cups fish stock
- 30ml/2 tbsp chopped fresh flat leaf parsley leaves
- salt and ground black pepper
- rosemary sprigs, to garnish
- salad leaves and French bread, to serve

1 Cut the octopus into large pieces, put in a pan and pour over enough cold water to cover. Season with salt, bring to the boil, then lower the heat and simmer for 30 minutes to tenderize it. Drain and cut into bitesize pieces.

2 Heat the oil in a large shallow pan. Fry the onion until lightly coloured, then add the garlic and fry for 1 minute. Add the octopus and fry for 2–3 minutes, stirring, until coloured.

3 Pour the brandy over the octopus and ignite it. When the flames have died down, add the wine, bring to the boil and bubble gently for about 5 minutes. Stir in the chopped tomatoes, with the chilli and paprika, then add the potatoes, rosemary and thyme. Simmer gently for 5 minutes.

4 Pour in the fish stock and season. Cover and simmer for 20–30 minutes, stirring occasionally, until the octopus and potatoes are tender and the sauce has thickened slightly.

5 To serve, check the seasoning and stir in the parsley. Garnish with rosemary and accompany with salad and bread.

COOK'S TIPS

- Octopus skin can be removed with salted fingers. Large octopus often have scaly rings inside the suckers. Run your fingers down the tentacles to pop out.
- You can make this dish the day before. Simply leave to cool, then chill. To serve, reheat gently, then check the seasoning and stir in the parsley.

Energy 316Kcal/1332kJ; Protein 32.4g; Carbohydrate 18.5g, of which sugars 6.8g; Fat 8.3g, of which saturates 1.5g; Cholesterol 80mg; Calcium 80mg; Fibre 2.4g; Sodium 23mg.

MARMITAKO

This is a traditional fisherman's stew, often made at sea, with meaty tuna steaks. The substantial fish is wonderfully balanced by sweet peppers and cider, all topped by potatoes. It takes its name from the cooking pot, known in France as a "marmite". Traditionally a one-pot dish, it speeds things along to fry the fish separately.

SERVES FOUR

INGREDIENTS

- 60ml/4 tbsp olive oil
- 1 onion, chopped
- 2 garlic cloves, finely chopped
- 3 green (bell) peppers, seeded and chopped
- ½ dried hot chilli, seeded and chopped
- 4 light tuna or bonito steaks, about 150g/5oz each
- 400g/14oz can tomatoes with juice
- 10ml/2 tsp paprika
- 3 potatoes, diced
- 350ml/12fl oz/1½ cups dry (hard) cider
- salt and ground black pepper
- 30ml/2 tbsp chopped fresh parsley, to garnish

1 Heat half the oil in a shallow flameproof casserole big enough to take the fish. Fry the onion gently until softened, then add the garlic. Add the peppers and chilli and stir-fry gently.

2 Season the fish steaks. Heat the remaining oil in a frying pan and fry the fish steaks for 2 minutes on each side over a high heat. Add the tomatoes to the casserole and stir-fry briefly. Add the paprika, then salt and pepper to taste.

VARIATION

Veal steaks or chops can be cooked in the same way. Fry for 5 minutes on each side in step 2, then continue as with fish.

3 Slip the fish steaks into the sauce, moving the peppers into the spaces between them. Cover with the potatoes, pushing them as flat as possible. Add the cider and bring to a simmer. Cover and cook very gently for about 45 minutes, or until the potatoes are done. Check the seasoning, sprinkle with the chopped parsley and serve immediately, straight from the casserole.

Energy 449Kcal/1883kJ; Protein 38.9g; Carbohydrate 26.9g, of which sugars 14.5g; Fat 18.9g, of which saturates 3.6g; Cholesterol 42mg; Calcium 59mg; Fibre 3.8g; Sodium 96mg.

ZARZUELA

THE NAME OF THIS DISH TRANSLATES AS "LIGHT MUSICAL COMEDY", REFLECTING THE COLOUR AND VARIETY OF THE STEW, WHICH IS FULL OF ALL SORTS OF FISH AND SHELLFISH. IT IS DISTINGUISHED FROM OTHER FISH STEWS BY CONTAINING TOMATO AS WELL AS SAFFRON. IT'S A SPLENDID FEAST AND NOT DIFFICULT TO MAKE. IF YOUR PAN IS LARGE ENOUGH, INVITE MORE GUESTS AND SIMPLY ADD A LOBSTER, A GOOD PIECE OF HAKE, ANOTHER BASS AND MORE PRAWNS, COCKLES AND OTHER SHELLFISH. TO DRINK, CHOOSE A BOTTLE OF TORRES GRAN VIÑA SOL.

SERVES SIX

INGREDIENTS

- 250g/9oz monkfish on the bone
- 1 gurnard, snapper or other whole white fish, about 350g/12oz
- 1 sole, plaice or flounder or other whole flat fish, about 500g/1¼lb, cleaned
- 60ml/4 tbsp olive oil
- 8 small squid, with tentacles
- plain (all-purpose) flour, for dusting
- 30ml/2 tbsp anis spirit, such as Ricard or Pernod
- 450g/1lb mussels, cleaned
- 250ml/8fl oz/1 cup white wine
- 4 large scampi (extra large shrimp), with heads, uncooked
- 12 raw king prawns (jumbo shrimp), with heads
- 115g/4oz prawns (shrimp)
- salt and ground black pepper
- 45ml/3 tbsp chopped fresh parsley, to garnish

For the stock

- 1 onion, chopped
- 1 celery stick, chopped
- 1 bay leaf

For the fish broth

- 30ml/2 tbsp oil
- 1 large onion, finely chopped
- 2 garlic cloves, finely chopped
- 500g/1¼lb ripe tomatoes, peeled, seeded and chopped
- 2 bay leaves
- 1 dried chilli, seeded and chopped
- 5ml/1 tsp paprika
- pinch of saffron threads (0.2g)
- salt and ground black pepper

1 Prepare the fish. Remove the flesh from the bones and cut into portions. You should have about 500g/1¼lb white fish, both firm and soft. Salt the fish and reserve on a plate in the refrigerator. (Reserve the bones and heads for making the stock.)

2 Make the stock. Put the onion, celery, bay leaf and the fish bones and heads in a pan, pour in 600ml/1 pint/2½ cups water, and bring to the boil, then simmer for about 30 minutes.

3 Make the broth in a large flameproof casserole. Heat the oil and fry the onion and garlic gently until soft. Add the chopped tomatoes, bay leaves, dried chilli, paprika and crumbled saffron and cook gently to make a sauce.

4 To cook the fish and shellfish, heat the oil in a large frying pan. Put in the squid tentacles, face down, and cook for 45 seconds, to make "flowers". Reserve on a plate.

5 Flour and fry the monkfish and white fish for 3 minutes on each side, then the flat fish for 2 minutes on each side. Cut the squid bodies into rings and fry. Pour the anis spirit into a ladle, flame it and pour over the fish remaining in the pan. Remove the fish and reserve.

6 Strain the fish stock into the casserole and add the wine. Bring to a simmer. Add the mussels in two batches. Cover for a couple of minutes, then remove to a plate, discard any closed mussels, and remove the upper shells.

7 Add the scampi and cook for about 8 minutes, then lift out using a slotted spoon. Cut with scissors along the under side from the head to the tail. Add the raw prawns for 3–4 minutes, then lift out and reserve.

8 About 20 minutes before serving, assemble the casserole. Add the seafood to the hot broth in the following order, bringing the liquid back to simmering each time: firm white fish, soft white fish (with squid rings and pan juices), large shellfish in the shell, cooked shellfish in the shell, then any small shelled prawns. If the liquid level falls below the seafood, make it up with more wine. Check the seasonings.

9 Rearrange the soup with the best-looking shellfish and squid flowers on top. Scatter over the mussels, cover and leave to steam for 2 minutes. Garnish with parsley. Take the casserole to the table with a plate for shells.

COOK'S TIP

Don't leave anything stewing in the broth. Keep the broth warm on a low heat, with the fish at room temperature.

Energy 442Kcal/1858kJ; Protein 58.5g; Carbohydrate 6.9g, of which sugars 4.7g; Fat 16.1g, of which saturates 2.6g; Cholesterol 420mg; Calcium 169mg; Fibre 1.3g; Sodium 415mg.

Poultry and Game Birds

Chicken was once considered a luxury in Spain and there are many traditional recipes. Try serving chicken with spicy red pepper sauce, in saffron rice, with spiced figs, or with ham and peppers. Other poultry, such as duck and turkey, are also on many menus, while game birds are immensely popular. They may be stuffed with grapes, marinaded in wine, cooked with mushrooms or served in delicious sauces.

CHICKEN LIVERS IN SHERRY

HIGADILLAS CON JEREZ IS VERY POPULAR, MADE WITH TRADITIONAL SPANISH INGREDIENTS. IT MAKES A DELICIOUS LITTLE TAPAS DISH AND IS PARTICULARLY GOOD EATEN WITH BREAD OR ON TOAST. FOR A MORE ELEGANT PRESENTATION, SERVE PILED ON TOP OF LITTLE RICE TORTITAS.

SERVES FOUR

INGREDIENTS

- 225g/8oz chicken livers, thawed if frozen, trimmed
- 15ml/1 tbsp olive oil
- 1 small onion, finely chopped
- 2 small garlic cloves, finely chopped
- 5ml/1 tsp fresh thyme leaves
- 30ml/2 tbsp sweet oloroso sherry
- 30ml/2 tbsp crème fraîche or double (heavy) cream
- 2.5ml/½ tsp paprika
- salt and ground black pepper
- fresh thyme, to garnish

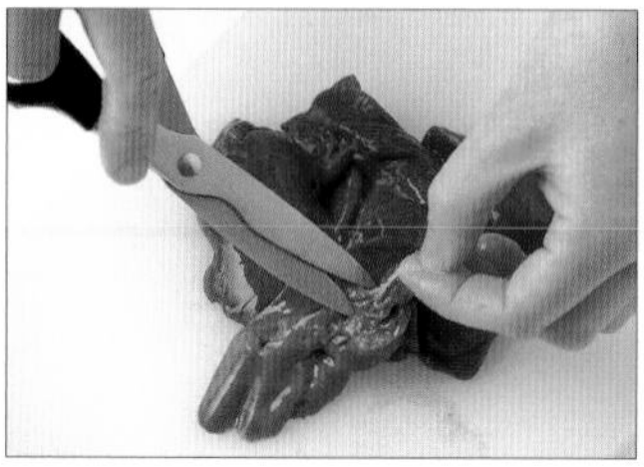

1 Trim any green spots and sinews from the chicken livers. Heat the oil in a frying pan and fry the onion, garlic, chicken livers and thyme for 3 minutes.

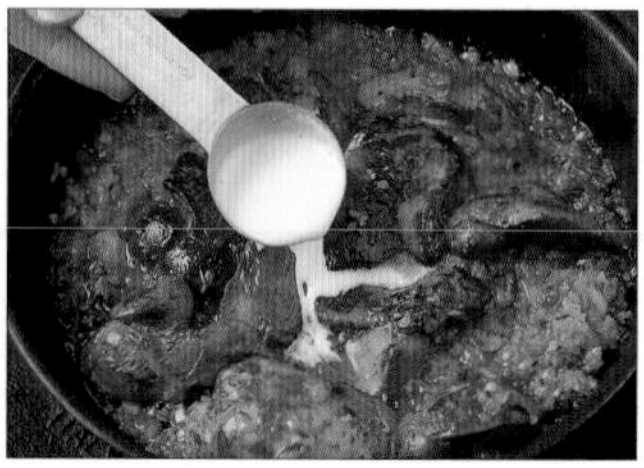

2 Stir the sherry into the livers, then add the cream and cook briefly. Season with salt, pepper and paprika, garnish with thyme and serve immediately.

Energy 129Kcal/537kJ; Protein 10.3g; Carbohydrate 1.8g, of which sugars 1.5g; Fat 8.1g, of which saturates 3.3g; Cholesterol 224mg; Calcium 13mg; Fibre 0.2g; Sodium 46mg.

Orange Chicken Salad

With their tangy flavour, orange segments are the perfect partner for tender chicken in this tasty rice salad. To appreciate all the flavours fully, serve the salad at room temperature. It makes the perfect dish for a hot summer day.

SERVES FOUR

INGREDIENTS

- 3 large seedless oranges
- 175g/6oz/scant 1 cup long grain rice
- 10ml/2 tsp strong Dijon mustard
- 2.5ml/½ tsp caster (superfine) sugar
- 175ml/6fl oz/¾ cup vinaigrette
- 450g/1lb cooked chicken, diced
- 45ml/3 tbsp chopped fresh chives
- 75g/3oz/¾ cup almonds or cashew nuts, toasted
- salt and ground black pepper
- mixed salad leaves, to serve

COOK'S TIP

To make a simple vinaigrette, whisk 45ml/3 tbsp wine vinegar with 90ml/6 tbsp olive oil. Add 60ml/4 tbsp extra virgin olive oil and season well.

1 Pare one of the oranges thinly, removing only the rind, not the white pith. Put the pieces of orange rind in a pan and add the rice. Pour in 475ml/16fl oz/2 cups water, add a pinch of salt and bring to the boil. Cover and cook over a very low heat for about 15 minutes, or until the rice is tender and all the water has been absorbed.

2 Meanwhile, peel the oranges, removing all the white pith. Working over a plate to catch the juices, separate them into segments. Tip in the orange juice from the plate and add to the vinaigrette with the mustard and sugar, whisking to combine. Check the seasoning.

3 When the rice is cooked, remove it from the heat and discard the pieces of orange rind. Spoon the rice into a bowl, let it cool slightly, then add half the dressing. Toss well, then set aside to cool completely.

4 Add the chicken, chives, toasted nuts and orange segments to the cooled rice. Pour over the remaining dressing and toss gently to combine. Serve on a bed of mixed salad leaves.

Energy 655Kcal/2732kJ; Protein 36.1g; Carbohydrate 51.8g, of which sugars 16.4g; Fat 33.9g, of which saturates 4.7g; Cholesterol 79mg; Calcium 132mg; Fibre 4g; Sodium 353mg.

CHICKEN WITH LEMON AND GARLIC

Pollo con limón y ajillo is one of the simplest and most delicious ways to serve chicken. It makes a good tapas dish, served with cocktail sticks to pick up the little strips of richly flavoured chicken, or a supper for two, with fried potatoes.

SERVES TWO TO FOUR

INGREDIENTS

- 2 skinless chicken breast fillets
- 30ml/2 tbsp olive oil
- 1 shallot, finely chopped
- 4 garlic cloves, finely chopped
- 5ml/1 tsp paprika
- juice of 1 lemon
- 30ml/2 tbsp chopped fresh parsley
- salt and ground black pepper
- fresh flat leaf parsley, to garnish
- lemon wedges, to serve

VARIATION

For a variation on this dish, try using strips of turkey breast or pork fillet. They need slightly longer cooking. The whites of spring onions (scallions) can replace shallots, and the chopped green tops replace the parsley.

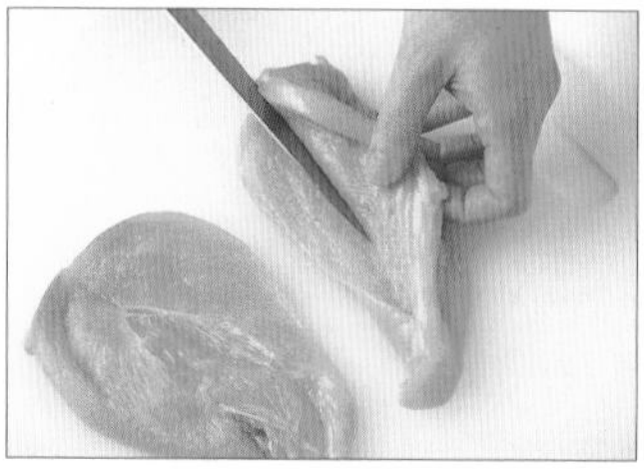

1 Remove the little fillet from the back of each breast. If the breast still looks fatter than a finger, bat it with a rolling pin to make it thinner. Slice all the chicken meat into strips.

2 Heat the oil in a large frying pan. Stir-fry the chicken strips with the shallot, garlic and paprika over a high heat for about 3 minutes until cooked through.

3 Add the lemon juice and parsley and season with salt and pepper to taste. Serve hot with lemon wedges, garnished with flat leaf parsley.

COOK'S TIP

Chicken breasts have a little fillet strip that easily becomes detached. Collect these, in a bag or container in the freezer, for this dish.

Energy 138Kcal/579kJ; Protein 18.5g; Carbohydrate 1.5g, of which sugars 1.1g; Fat 6.5g, of which saturates 1g; Cholesterol 53mg; Calcium 30mg; Fibre 0.8g; Sodium 49mg.

CRUMBED CHICKEN WITH GREEN MAYONNAISE

PECHUGAS DE POLLO REBOZADAS ARE SOLD READY-PREPARED IN EVERY BUTCHER'S IN THE SOUTH. IDENTICAL TO SCHNITZEL, THESE CRISPY, GOLDEN CHICKEN BREAST PORTIONS SHOW THE JEWISH INFLUENCE ON COOKING IN THE REGION. LEMON WEDGES ARE A POPULAR ACCOMPANIMENT.

SERVES FOUR

INGREDIENTS

- 4 boneless chicken breasts fillets, each weighing about 200g/7oz
- juice of 1 lemon
- 5ml/1 tsp paprika
- plain (all-purpose) flour, for dusting
- 1–2 eggs
- dried breadcrumbs, for coating
- about 60ml/4 tbsp olive oil
- salt and ground black pepper
- lemon wedges (optional), to serve

For the mayonnaise

- 120ml/4fl oz/½ cup mayonnaise
- 30ml/2 tbsp pickled capers, drained and chopped
- 30ml/2 tbsp chopped fresh parsley

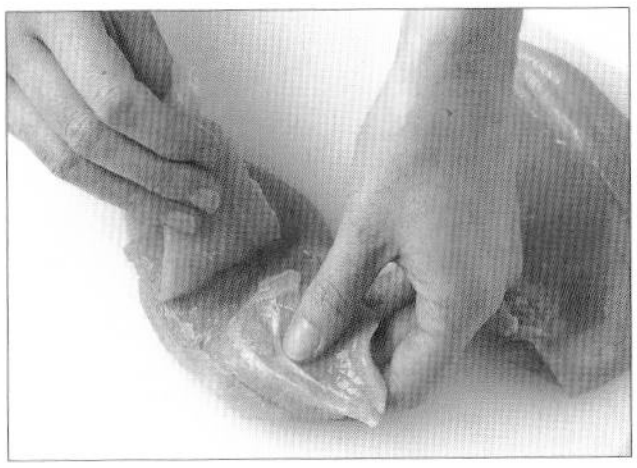

1 Start a couple of hours ahead, if you can. Skin the chicken breasts. Lay them outside down and, with a sharp knife, cut horizontally, almost through, from the rounded side. Open them up like a book. Press gently, to make a roundish shape, the size of a side plate. Sprinkle with lemon juice and paprika.

2 Set out three plates. Sprinkle flour over one, seasoning it well. Beat the egg with a little salt and pour into the second. Sprinkle the third with dried breadcrumbs. Dip the breasts first into the flour on both sides, then into the egg, then into the breadcrumbs. Chill the crumbed chicken, if you have time.

3 Put the mayonnaise ingredients in a bowl and mix well to combine.

4 Heat the oil in a heavy frying pan over a high heat. Fry the breast portions, two at a time, turning after 3 minutes, until golden on both sides. Add more oil for the second batch if needed. Serve at once, with the mayonnaise and lemon wedges, if using.

Energy 612Kcal/2551kJ; Protein 53.5g; Carbohydrate 12.5g, of which sugars 1g; Fat 39.1g, of which saturates 6.4g; Cholesterol 258mg; Calcium 69mg; Fibre 0.9g; Sodium 389mg.

Pollo a la Española

This colourful chicken dish is made throughout Spain in an infinite number of variations. Cubed Serrano ham can replace the bacon, but the fat the latter gives off is a constant theme in the Spanish kitchen, so helps to add to its character.

SERVES FOUR

INGREDIENTS
- 5ml/1 tsp paprika
- 4 free-range or corn-fed chicken portions
- 45ml/3 tbsp olive oil
- 150g/5oz smoked bacon lardons, or diced pancetta
- 1 large onion, chopped
- 2 garlic cloves, finely chopped
- 1 green (bell) pepper
- 1 red (bell) pepper
- 450g/1lb tomatoes or 400g/14oz canned tomatoes
- 30ml/2 tbsp chopped fresh parsley
- salt and ground black pepper
- boiled rice, to serve (optional)

1 Rub paprika and salt into the chicken portions. Heat 30ml/2 tbsp oil in a large frying pan. Put in the chicken portions, skin side down, and fry gently.

2 Heat 15ml/1 tbsp oil in a flameproof casserole and add the bacon or pancetta.

3 When the bacon or pancetta starts to give off fat, add the chopped onion and garlic, frying very gently until soft.

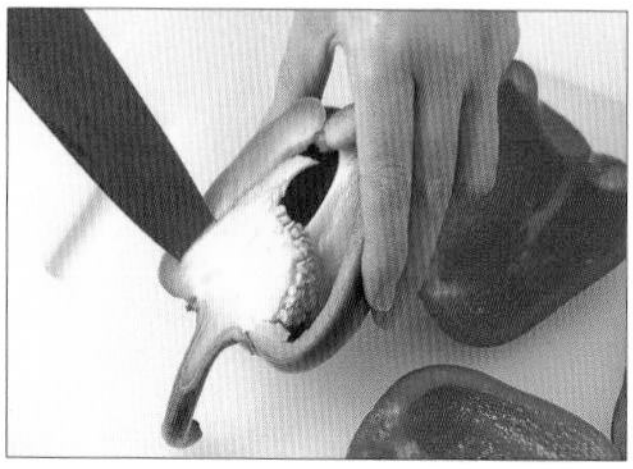

4 Remove and discard the stalks and seeds from the peppers and roughly chop the flesh. Spoon off a little fat from the chicken pan, then add the peppers, fitting them into the spaces between the chicken portions, and cook gently.

5 When the onions are soft, stir in the tomatoes and season. Arrange the chicken pieces in the sauce, and stir in the cooked peppers.

6 Cover the casserole tightly and simmer over a low heat for 15 minutes. Check the seasoning, stir in the chopped parsley and serve with rice, if you like.

Energy 513Kcal/2152kJ; Protein 68.5g; Carbohydrate 13.9g, of which sugars 12.1g; Fat 20.7g, of which saturates 5.2g; Cholesterol 199mg; Calcium 62mg; Fibre 3.7g; Sodium 640mg.

ARROZ CON POLLO

MANY SPANISH FAMILIES EAT RICE ONCE A WEEK, REFERRING TO IT AS ARROZ UNLESS IT IS PAELLA. RICE WITH CHICKEN IS A CASSEROLE, WITH MORE LIQUID THAN A PAELLA. SEASONAL VEGETABLES ARE INCLUDED AND EVEN PEAS AND SWEETCORN CAN BE USED.

SERVES FOUR

INGREDIENTS

- 60ml/4 tbsp olive oil
- 6 chicken thighs, free-range if possible, halved along the bone
- 5ml/1 tsp paprika
- 1 large Spanish onion, roughly chopped
- 2 garlic cloves, finely chopped
- 1 chorizo sausage, sliced
- 115g/4oz Serrano or cooked ham or gammon, diced
- 1 red (bell) pepper, seeded and roughly chopped
- 1 yellow (bell) pepper, seeded and roughly chopped
- 225g/8oz/1 generous cup paella rice, washed and drained
- 2 large tomatoes, chopped or 200g/7oz can chopped tomatoes
- 120ml/4fl oz/½ cup amontillado sherry
- 750ml/1¼ pints/3 cups chicken stock
- 5ml/1 tsp dried oregano or thyme
- 1 bay leaf
- salt and ground black pepper
- 15 green olives and chopped fresh flat leaf parsley, to garnish

1 Heat the oil in a wide flameproof casserole. Season the chicken pieces with salt and paprika. Fry until nicely brown all over, then reserve on a plate.

2 Add the onion and garlic to the pan and fry gently until beginning to soften. Add the chorizo and ham or gammon and stir-fry. Add the chopped peppers. Cook until they begin to soften.

3 Sprinkle in the drained rice and cook, stirring, for 1–2 minutes. Add the tomatoes, sherry, chicken stock and dried herbs and season well. Arrange the chicken pieces deep in the mixture, and tuck in the bay leaf.

4 Cover and cook over a very low heat for 30–40 minutes, until the chicken and rice are done. Stir, then garnish and serve.

Energy 595Kcal/2484kJ; Protein 34.3g; Carbohydrate 60.9g, of which sugars 12.1g; Fat 20.2g, of which saturates 4.7g; Cholesterol 129mg; Calcium 60mg; Fibre 3.1g; Sodium 600mg.

Pollo con Langostinos

Chicken with prawns is another gorgeous Catalan dish. The sauce is thickened with a picada *of ground toasted almonds, which is more convenient than making a roux with butter and flour at the last moment. This special* picada *traditionally includes crumbled butter biscuits, which were considered more sophisticated than the bread that normally goes into* picada*. The sauce is finished with cream and cayenne, as a modern touch – a splendid dinner-party dish. Serve with a glass of Torres Gran Viña Sol.*

SERVES FOUR

INGREDIENTS

- 1.3kg/3lb free-range chicken
- 75–90ml/5–6 tbsp olive oil
- 1 large onion, chopped
- 2 garlic cloves, finely chopped
- 400g/14oz tomatoes, peeled and seeded then chopped or 400g/14oz can tomatoes, drained
- 1 bay leaf
- 150ml/¼ pint/⅔ cup dry white wine
- 450g/1lb large raw prawns (shrimp), or 16 large shelled prawn tails
- 15g/½oz/1 tbsp butter
- 30ml/2 tbsp anis spirit, such as Ricard or Pernod
- 75ml/2½fl oz/⅓ cup double (heavy) cream
- 1.5ml/¼ tsp cayenne pepper
- salt, paprika and ground black pepper
- fresh flat leaf parsley, to garnish
- boiled rice or raw spinach salad, to serve

For the *picada*

- 25g/1oz/¼ cup blanched almonds
- 15g/½oz/1 tbsp butter
- 1 garlic clove, finely chopped
- 3 Marie, Rich Tea or plain all-butter biscuits (cookies), broken
- 90ml/6 tbsp chopped fresh parsley

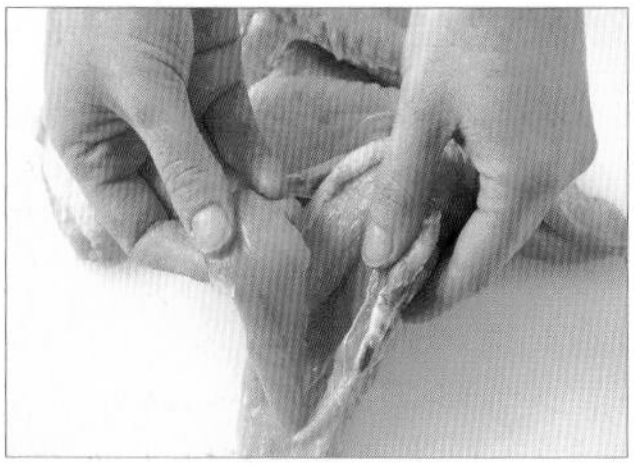

1 Cut the chicken into eight serving portions, then separate the small fillet from the back of each breast portion. Rub salt and paprika into the chicken.

2 Heat 30ml/2 tbsp oil in a wide flameproof casserole and fry the onion and garlic until soft. Put in the chicken pieces, skin downwards, and fry over a medium heat, turning until they are golden on all sides.

3 Meanwhile, make the *picada*. Dry-fry the almonds in a small frying pan, shaking it regularly, until they are just coloured. Transfer them to a blender.

4 Add 15g/½oz/1 tbsp butter to the pan and gently fry the garlic, then add it to the blender, with the broken biscuits. Reduce the biscuits to crumbs then add the chopped parsley and blend to a purée, adding a little of the wine intended for the casserole.

5 Add the tomatoes to the casserole, tuck in the bay leaf and cook down to a sauce, stirring occasionally. Pour in the remaining wine, season to taste with salt and ground black pepper, and leave to simmer gently.

6 Check the shelled prawn tails, if using: if they have a black thread along the back, nick it out with a knife. Heat 15ml/1 tbsp oil and the 15g/½oz/1 tbsp butter in the frying pan and add the prawns. Cook over a medium heat for 2 minutes on each side.

7 Pour the anis spirit into a ladle and set light to it. Off the heat pour this over the prawns and let it burn off. Stir in the juices from the casserole, then add the pan contents to the casserole.

8 Remove the bay leaf from the pan and stir in the *picada*, then the cream. Add cayenne to taste and check the seasonings, adding a little more if necessary. Heat through gently and serve garnished with more parsley.

VARIATIONS

The classic version of this dish is beef fillet with lobster. Also try veal with scampi, or partridge with large prawns, for equally delicious results.

Energy 899Kcal/3732kJ; Protein 55.8g; Carbohydrate 22.2g, of which sugars 13.1g; Fat 61.4g, of which saturates 21.1g; Cholesterol 433mg; Calcium 207mg; Fibre 3.7g; Sodium 463mg.

Chicken Chilindrón

This famous chicken dish from Navarre has a spicy red pepper sauce. In the past, the dried choricero *pepper – the one that gives chorizos their colour and spice – was used alone, but nowadays the dish is often made with fresh red peppers, spiced with chilli. The name* chilindrón *refers to a game of cards. Serve with a Tempranillo wine.*

SERVES FOUR

INGREDIENTS

- 675g/1½lb red (bell) peppers
- 4 free-range chicken portions
- 10ml/2 tsp paprika
- 30ml/2 tbsp olive oil
- 1 large onion, chopped
- 2 garlic cloves, finely chopped
- 200g/7oz Serrano or other ham, in one piece, or a gammon chop
- 200g/7oz can chopped tomatoes
- 1 dried *guindilla* or other hot dried chilli, chopped, or 2.5ml/½ tsp chilli powder, to taste
- salt and ground black pepper
- chopped fresh parsley, to garnish
- small new potatoes, to serve

1 Preheat the grill (broiler) to high. Put the peppers on a baking sheet and grill (broil) for 8–12 minutes, turning occasionally, until the skins have blistered and blackened. Place the blackened peppers in a bowl, cover with clear film (plastic wrap) and leave to cool.

2 Rub salt and paprika into the chicken portions. Heat the oil in a large frying pan and add the chicken portions, skin-side down. Fry over a medium-low heat, turning until golden on all sides.

3 Meanwhile, select a casserole into which the chicken will fit comfortably. Spoon in 45ml/3 tbsp fat from the other pan. Fry the onion and garlic until soft. Dice the ham or gammon and add, stirring occasionally, for a few minutes.

4 Add the chopped tomatoes to the casserole, with the chopped dried chilli or chilli powder. Cook for 4–5 minutes, letting the sauce reduce.

5 Peel the skins off the peppers and discard these and the stalks. Put the peppers into a blender and strain in the juices, discarding the seeds. Process, then add the purée to the casserole and stir in. Heat through.

6 Add the chicken pieces to the casserole, bedding them down in the sauce. Cook, covered, for 15 minutes and check the seasonings, adding more if necessary. Garnish with a little parsley and serve with small new potatoes.

Energy 405Kcal/1702kJ; Protein 60.2g; Carbohydrate 18.8g, of which sugars 16.6g; Fat 10.3g, of which saturates 2.2g; Cholesterol 169mg; Calcium 49mg; Fibre 4.3g; Sodium 734mg.

CHICKEN CASSEROLE WITH SPICED FIGS

The Catalans have a reputation for serving fruit with poultry and meat. Figs grow wild around many country farms and the poultry feed on the fallen fruit, so a dish combining chicken and figs seems like a natural combination. Here POLLO CON HIGOS *is cooked with a beautifully spiced sauce, which goes perfectly with a Catalan Cabernet Sauvignon.*

SERVES FOUR

INGREDIENTS

- 50g/2oz bacon lardons or pancetta, diced
- 15ml/1 tbsp olive oil
- 1.3–1.6kg/3–3½lb free-range or corn-fed chicken, jointed into eight pieces
- 120ml/4fl oz/½ cup white wine
- finely pared rind of ½ lemon
- 50ml/2fl oz/¼ cup chicken stock
- salt and ground black pepper
- green salad, to serve

For the figs

- 150g/5oz/¾ cup granulated sugar
- 120ml/4fl oz/½ cup white wine vinegar
- 1 lemon slice
- 1 cinnamon stick
- 120ml/4fl oz/½ cup water
- 450g/1lb fresh figs

1 Prepare the figs. Simmer the sugar, vinegar, lemon and cinnamon with the water for 5 minutes. Add the figs and cook for 10 minutes. Remove from the heat and leave to stand for 3 hours.

2 Fry the bacon or pancetta until golden. Transfer to an ovenproof dish. Add the oil to the pan. Season the chicken, brown on both sides, then transfer to the ovenproof dish.

3 Preheat the oven to 180°C/350°F/Gas 4. Drain the figs. Add the wine and lemon rind to the pan and boil until the wine has reduced and is syrupy. Pour over the chicken.

4 Cook the chicken in the oven, uncovered, for about 20 minutes, then add the figs and chicken stock. Cover and return to the oven for a further 10 minutes. Serve with a green salad.

Energy 596Kcal/2522kJ; Protein 52.7g; Carbohydrate 75.8g, of which sugars 75.8g; Fat 9g, of which saturates 2g; Cholesterol 148mg; Calcium 206mg; Fibre 5.2g; Sodium 324mg.

ROAST TURKEY WITH BLACK FRUIT STUFFING

COLUMBUS INTRODUCED TURKEYS FROM AMERICA TO SPAIN, AND AT FIRST THEY WERE COOKED LIKE PEACOCKS – STUFFED, THEN ROASTED INSIDE A PIG'S CAUL. THE SAUSAGEMEAT INSIDE THIS BIRD IS BLACK MORCILLA, *AND PRUNES AND RAISINS MAKE IT EVEN MORE SWEET AND FRUITY. THE SAUCE IS FLAVOURED WITH SWEET GRAPE JUICE AND AN INTRIGUING SPLASH OF ANIS.*

SERVES EIGHT

INGREDIENTS

- 3kg/6½lb bronze or black turkey, weighed without the giblets
- 60ml/4 tbsp oil
- 200g/7oz rashers (strips) streaky (fatty) bacon

For the stuffing

- 45ml/3 tbsp olive oil
- 1 onion, chopped
- 2 garlic cloves, finely chopped
- 115g/4oz fatty bacon lardons
- 150g/5oz *morcilla* or black pudding (blood sausage), diced
- 1 turkey liver, diced
- 50g/2oz/½ cup Muscatel raisins, soaked in 45ml/3 tbsp anis spirit, such as Ricard, and chopped
- 115g/4oz ready-to-eat pitted prunes, chopped
- 50g/2oz/½ cup almonds, chopped
- 1.5ml/¼ tsp dried thyme
- finely grated rind of 1 lemon
- freshly grated nutmeg
- 60ml/4 tbsp chopped fresh parsley
- 1 large (US extra large) egg, beaten
- 60ml/4 tbsp cooked rice or stale breadcrumbs
- salt and ground black pepper

For the sauce

- 45ml/3 tbsp plain (all-purpose) flour
- 350ml/12fl oz/1½ cups turkey giblet stock, warmed
- 350ml/12fl oz/1½ cups red grape juice
- 30ml/2 tbsp anis spirit, such as Ricard
- salt and ground black pepper

1 Make the stuffing. Heat 30ml/2 tbsp oil in a pan and fry the onion, garlic and bacon. Remove to a large bowl. Fry the *morcilla* or black pudding for 3–4 minutes and the liver for 2–3 minutes.

COOK'S TIP

Allow 30 minutes to prepare and stuff the bird, and put the turkey in the oven 2¾ hours before carving.

2 Add the soaked raisins, prunes, almonds, thyme, lemon rind, nutmeg, seasoning and parsley. Stir in the egg and rice or breadcrumbs.

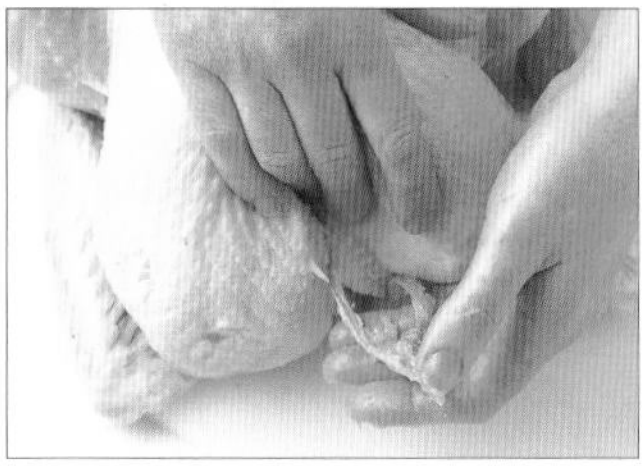

3 About 3 hours before carving, preheat the oven, with a low shelf, to 200°C/400°F/Gas 6. Remove the turkey's wishbone, running fingernails up the two sides of the neck to find it. Just nick it out. Season the turkey inside, stuff and retruss it. Season outside. Keep at room temperature.

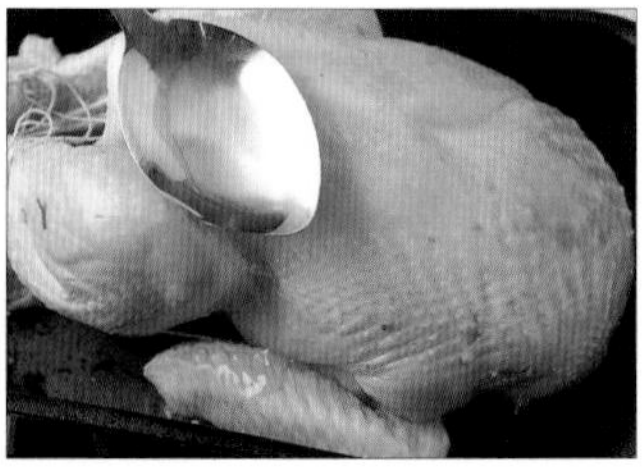

4 Heat a roasting pan in the oven with 60ml/4 tbsp oil. Put in the turkey and baste the outside. Lay the bacon over the breast and legs. Reduce the oven temperature to 180°C/350°F/Gas 4 and roast for 2¼–2½ hours, basting once. To test, insert a skewer into the thickest part of the inside leg. The juices should run clear. Remove the trussing thread and transfer the turkey to a heated serving plate. Keep warm.

5 Make the sauce. Skim as much fat as possible from the roasting pan. Sprinkle in the flour and cook gently for a few minutes, stirring. Stir in the warm turkey stock and bring to simmering point. Add the grape juice and anis, and bring back to simmering. Taste for seasoning. Pour into a jug (pitcher). Carve the turkey and serve with the sauce.

VARIATION

To make a red stuffing, use frying chorizo instead of *morcilla* or black pudding. Flavour the stuffing with half a chopped dried chilli, and replace the prunes with chopped green or black olives.

Energy 531Kcal/2227kJ; Protein 60.3g; Carbohydrate 24g, of which sugars 7.4g; Fat 21.2g, of which saturates 5.7g; Cholesterol 233mg; Calcium 67mg; Fibre 0.9g; Sodium 439mg.

SPICED DUCK WITH PEARS

This Catalan speciality, known as ÀNEC AMB PERES *in the local language, is a fabulous combination of poultry and fruit. Ducks are not common in other regions of Spain. Try to buy a Barbary duck if you can. This dish features the* PICADA*, a great Catalan invention made of pounded nuts, which both flavours and thickens the final sauce. Serve with a bottle of Gran Sangre de Toro, which will stand up well to this robustly flavoured dish.*

SERVES SIX

INGREDIENTS

- 6 duck portions, preferably Barbary, either breast or leg pieces
- 15ml/1 tbsp olive oil
- 1 large onion, thinly sliced
- 1 cinnamon stick, halved
- 4 thyme sprigs
- 475ml/16fl oz/2 cups duck or chicken stock
- 3 firm, ripe pears
- 30ml/2 tbsp olive oil
- 25g/1oz/¼ cup raisins
- salt and ground black pepper
- young thyme sprigs or fresh parsley, to garnish
- mashed potatoes and green vegetables, to serve (optional)

For the *picada*

- 30ml/2 tbsp olive oil
- ½ slice stale bread, without crusts
- 2 garlic cloves, sliced
- 15g/½oz/12 almonds, toasted
- 15g/½oz/12 hazelnuts, toasted
- 15ml/1 tbsp chopped fresh parsley
- salt and ground black pepper

1 Preheat the oven to 180°C/350°F/Gas 4. Season the duck portions, pricking the skins with a fork. Fry them, skin side down, for about 5 minutes, until they give off fat. Turn them over and fry on the other side more briefly.

2 Transfer the duck to an ovenproof dish and drain off all but 15ml/1 tbsp of the fat left in the pan.

3 Add the onion to the pan and fry for 5 minutes. Add the cinnamon, thyme and stock and bring to the boil. Pour over the duck, reserving a little of the stock, and bake for 1¼ hours.

4 Make the *picada*. Heat the olive oil in a frying pan and fry the bread over a high heat. Drain on kitchen paper and reserve. Briefly fry the garlic and reserve with the bread.

5 Put all the nuts in a mortar and pound, or reduce to a paste in a food processor or blender. Add the bread, torn into pieces, and the garlic, and reduce to a thick, smooth paste with a little pan stock. Add the parsley and seasoning.

COOK'S TIP

A good stock is essential for this dish. Buy a large duck (plus two extra duck breasts if you want the portions to be generous) and joint it yourself, using the giblets and carcass for stock. Alternatively, buy duck portions and a carton of chicken stock.

6 Peel, core and halve the pears. Fry quickly in the oil in the frying pan until beginning to colour on the cut sides.

7 Add the *picada* to the ovenproof dish with the raisins and pears. Bake for a further 15 minutes until the pears are tender. Season to taste and garnish with thyme or parsley. Serve with mashed potatoes and vegetables, if you wish.

Energy 439Kcal/1833kJ; Protein 41g; Carbohydrate 12.6g, of which sugars 11.3g; Fat 25.3g, of which saturates 5.5g; Cholesterol 220mg; Calcium 52mg; Fibre 2.3g; Sodium 237mg.

BRAISED QUAIL WITH WINTER VEGETABLES

QUAIL ARE BOTH PLENTIFUL AND VERY POPULAR IN SPAIN, ESPECIALLY DURING THE HUNTING SEASON, WHEN EVERY MAN TURNS OUT WITH A GUN, A DOG AND A KNAPSACK. ROASTING AND BRAISING ARE THE TWO CLASSIC TECHNIQUES FOR COOKING QUAIL. HERE, IN CORDONICES ESTOFADAS, *THEY ARE COOKED AND SERVED IN A RED WINE SAUCE, THEN ELEGANTLY DISPLAYED ON CRISP CROÛTES.*

SERVES FOUR

INGREDIENTS
- 4 quail, cleaned
- 175g/6oz small carrots, scrubbed
- 175g/6oz baby turnips
- 60ml/4 tbsp olive oil
- 4 shallots, halved
- 450ml/¾ pint/scant 2 cups red wine
- 30ml/2 tbsp Spanish brandy
- salt and ground black pepper
- fresh flat leaf parsley, to garnish

For the croûtes
- 4 slices stale bread, crusts removed
- 60ml/4 tbsp olive oil

1 Preheat the oven to 220°C/425°F/Gas 7. Season the quail with salt and freshly ground black pepper.

2 Using a sharp knife, cut the carrots and baby turnips into chunks. (If the carrots are very small, you can leave them whole if you prefer.)

3 Heat half the olive oil in a flameproof casserole and add the quail. Fry until browned all over, using two wooden spoons or a pair of tongs to turn the birds. Remove from the casserole and set aside.

4 Add more olive oil to the casserole with all the vegetables and shallots. Cook until just colouring. Return the quail to the casserole, breast-sides down, and pour in the red wine. Cover the casserole and transfer to the oven. Cook for about 30 minutes, or until the quail are tender.

5 Meanwhile, make the croûtes. Using a 10cm/4in plain cutter stamp out rounds from the bread. Heat the oil in a frying pan and cook the bread over a high heat until golden on both sides. Drain on kitchen paper and keep warm.

6 Place the croûtes on heated plates and set a quail on top of each one. Arrange the vegetables around the quail, cover and keep hot.

7 Boil the cooking juices hard until reduced to a syrupy consistency. Add the brandy and warm through, then season the sauce with salt and black pepper to taste. Drizzle the sauce over the quail and garnish with parsley, then serve immediately.

Energy 845Kcal/3524kJ; Protein 75.2g; Carbohydrate 23.3g, of which sugars 9g; Fat 42.3g, of which saturates 7.6g; Cholesterol 0mg; Calcium 174mg; Fibre 3.2g; Sodium 365mg.

Marinated Pigeon in Red Wine

Great clouds of migrating pigeons fly over the mountains of Spain twice a year, and shooting them is a big sport. Here they are marinated in spiced vinegar and red wine, then cooked in the marinade. Reared squab can also be used. Cabbage is a familiar partner to pigeon, but puréed celeriac also goes very well.

SERVES FOUR

INGREDIENTS

- 4 pigeons (squabs), each weighing about 225g/8oz, cleaned
- 30ml/2 tbsp olive oil
- 1 onion, roughly chopped
- 225g/8oz/3 cups brown cap (cremini) mushrooms, sliced
- plain (all-purpose) flour, for dusting
- 300ml/½ pint/1¼ cups beef or game stock
- 30ml/2 tbsp chopped fresh parsley
- salt and ground black pepper
- fresh flat leaf parsley, to garnish

For the marinade

- 15ml/1 tbsp olive oil
- 1 onion, chopped
- 1 carrot, chopped
- 1 celery stick, chopped
- 3 garlic cloves, sliced
- 6 allspice berries, bruised
- 2 bay leaves
- 8 black peppercorns, bruised
- 120ml/4fl oz/½ cup red wine vinegar
- 150ml/¼ pint/⅔ cup red wine

1 Starting a day ahead, combine all the ingredients for the marinade in a large dish. Add the pigeons and turn them in the marinade, then cover and chill for 12 hours, turning occasionally.

VARIATION

If you are unable to buy pigeon, this recipe works equally well with rabbit or hare. Buy portions and make deep slashes in the flesh so that the marinade soaks in and flavours right to the centre.

2 Preheat the oven to 150°C/300°F/Gas 2. Heat the oil in a large, flameproof casserole and cook the onion and mushrooms for about 5 minutes, until the onion has softened.

3 Meanwhile, remove the pigeons to a plate with a slotted spoon and strain the marinade into a bowl, then set both aside separately.

4 Sprinkle the flour on the pigeons and add them to the casserole, breast-sides down. Pour in the marinade and stock, and add the chopped parsley and seasoning. Cover and cook for 1½ hours or until tender.

5 Check the seasoning, then serve the pigeons on warmed plates with the sauce. Garnish with parsley.

Energy 314Kcal/1307kJ; Protein 31.4g; Carbohydrate 1.7g, of which sugars 1.2g; Fat 20.2g, of which saturates 0.9g; Cholesterol 0mg; Calcium 47mg; Fibre 1.4g; Sodium 120mg.

Pechugas de Pichones con Setas

Pigeons are caught in nets as they come skimming through the mountain passes. The sport combines well with mushroom picking – another Spanish diversion. Use the strongest-flavoured mushrooms you can find. The pigeon breasts are cooked in their own rich sauce, then elegantly displayed on the serving dish.

SERVES SIX

INGREDIENTS

- 6 pigeons (or squabs), cleaned
- 90ml/6 tbsp olive oil
- 1 large onion, chopped
- 2 garlic cloves, finely chopped
- 450g/1lb/6 cups brown cap (cremini) or small open cap field (portabello) mushrooms (use wild mushrooms, if possible)
- 150g/5oz Serrano or other ham, diced
- 150ml/¼ pint/⅔ cup red wine
- salt and ground black pepper
- 60ml/4 tbsp chopped fresh parsley, to garnish
- fried potatoes, to serve

For the stock

- 1 large onion, unpeeled, roughly chopped
- 2 carrots, roughly chopped
- 1 celery stick, roughly chopped
- 6 tough parsley stalks, snapped or bruised
- 1 bay leaf
- 1 garlic clove, unpeeled but smashed
- 4 sprigs of fresh thyme
- 12 black peppercorns, crushed

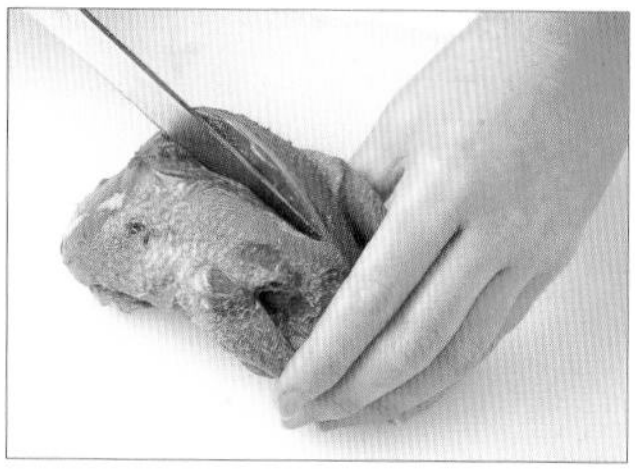

1 First prepare the pigeons. Find the wishbone by pushing your forefinger and thumb in the neck end. It runs up each side; snap it out. Once this is gone, it is easy to take off the breast portions. Cut down on one side of the breastbone with a large knife, then scrape along the rib cage, to get the breast meat off whole. Repeat this, and season the meat.

2 Cut the pigeon carcasses across the ribs and flatten them in a large pan. Add all the stock ingredients and just cover with water. Simmer gently for about 1½ hours to make a rich dark stock. Allow to cool slightly, then strain into a large bowl.

3 Heat 30ml/2 tbsp of the olive oil in a large shallow flameproof casserole and fry the onion and garlic gently for a few minutes, until soft. Meanwhile, pull the mushroom stalks out of the caps, then chop the stalks finely and add to the casserole, with the ham cubes. Fry briefly, stirring. Pour in the wine and 250ml/8fl oz/1 cup of the stock. Simmer gently to reduce a little.

COOK'S TIP

The Spanish definitely prefer wild birds – and they are available in abundance while they are in season. Squabs are the same family as pigeons, but are dovecote birds. They are plumper and slightly blander and benefit from this richly flavoured sauce.

4 Heat 30ml/2 tbsp oil in a large frying pan. Put the pigeon breasts in the pan, skin downward and fry for 2 minutes on each side. Remove to the casserole and simmer for 2–3 minutes.

5 Fry the mushroom caps, in 30ml/2 tbsp oil, in the same pan. Arrange the breasts in a ring on an oval platter. Pile the mushrooms in the centre. Spoon the ham and sauce over the pigeon, and sprinkle with parsley.

Energy 395Kcal/1644kJ; Protein 35.3g; Carbohydrate 0.6g, of which sugars 0.5g; Fat 26.1g, of which saturates 1.9g; Cholesterol 15mg; Calcium 25mg; Fibre 0.8g; Sodium 416mg.

GUINEA FOWL WITH SAFFRON AND NUT SAUCE

THE ARABS INTRODUCED SAFFRON TO SPAIN AND THIS IS A MOORISH SAUCE, OF SAFFRON, TOASTED ALMONDS GROUND WITH PARSLEY AND SEVERAL SPICES. PEPITA IS THE SPANISH WORD FOR A SEED OR NUT, HENCE THE NAME PINTADA EN PEPITORIA. *SERVE WITH A RIOJA RESERVA, TO DRINK.*

SERVES FOUR

INGREDIENTS

- 25g/1oz/¼ cup blanched almonds
- pinch of saffron threads (0.1g)
- 120ml/8 tbsp chicken stock
- 1.2–1.3kg/2½–3lb guinea fowl
- 60ml/4fl oz/½ cup olive oil
- 1 thick slice of bread, without crusts
- 2 garlic cloves, finely chopped
- 120ml/4fl oz/½ cup fino sherry
- 1 bay leaf, crumbled
- 4 thyme sprigs
- 15ml/1 tbsp finely chopped fresh parsley
- pinch of freshly grated nutmeg
- pinch of ground cloves
- juice of ½ lemon
- 5ml/1 tsp paprika
- salt and ground black pepper

1 Preheat the oven to 150°C/300°F/ Gas 2. Spread the almonds on a baking sheet and toast in the oven for about 20 minutes until golden brown.

2 Crumble the saffron with your fingers into a jug (pitcher) or small bowl, pour over 30ml/2 tbsp hot chicken stock and leave to soak.

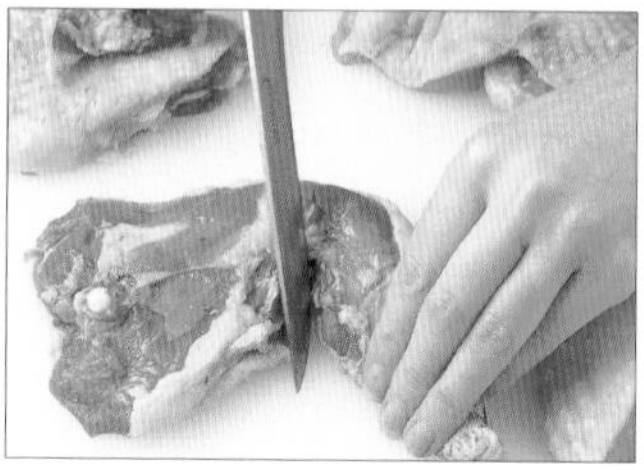

3 Cut the bird into eight serving pieces, discarding the wing tips, backbone, breastbones and leg tips. This will give you two legs (split them at the joint), two wings with one-third of the breast attached, and two short breast pieces.

4 Heat the olive oil in a wide shallow flameproof casserole and fry the bread slice on both sides. Fry the garlic quickly, then remove both to a blender.

5 Season the poultry well and fry them, turning until golden on all sides. Add the remaining stock and the sherry to the pan, stirring to deglaze the pan. Add the bay leaf and thyme and cover. Cook gently for 10 minutes.

6 Grind together the bread, garlic and almonds. Add the parsley, saffron liquid, nutmeg and cloves, and purée. Stir into the poultry juices, add the lemon juice and paprika, season and serve.

Energy 532Kcal/2223kJ; Protein 67.7g; Carbohydrate 1.2g, of which sugars 1g; Fat 24.8g, of which saturates 4.8g; Cholesterol 0mg; Calcium 124mg; Fibre 1g; Sodium 188mg.

Perdices con Uvas

Partridges are Spain's commonest game birds. They have a natural affinity with grapes, as wild birds often attack the harvest. Game hens or any plump small bird can be used for this pot roast, where grapes are used for the garnish and the sauce.

SERVES FOUR

INGREDIENTS
- 4 partridges, cleaned
- 500g/1¼lb red grapes, split and seeded, plus extra to garnish
- 45–60ml/3–4 tbsp olive oil
- 4 rashers (slices) smoked streaky (fatty) bacon, halved across
- 1 onion, chopped
- 2 garlic cloves, finely chopped
- 1 bay leaf
- 120ml/4fl oz/½ cup dry white wine
- 250ml/8fl oz/1 cup game or chicken stock
- freshly grated nutmeg
- salt and ground black pepper
- 30ml/2 tbsp chopped fresh parsley, to garnish

1 Season the birds inside and out, then stuff with 250g/9oz grapes. Put 45ml/3 tbsp oil in a flameproof casserole into which the birds will fit snugly.

2 Fry the bacon until crisp, then reserve on a plate. Put the birds into the casserole breast sides down and fry until coloured. Turn them with two spoons, frying and turning until brown all over. Remove.

3 Fry the onion and garlic, adding a little more oil if needed, until softened.

4 Return the birds to the casserole and arrange two pieces of bacon on top of each. Push 125g/5oz grapes in round them, and add the bay leaf. Pour in the white wine and stock. Add plenty of black pepper. Simmer, covered, for 30 minutes.

5 Remove the birds and bacon to a plate. Spoon the casserole contents into a food processor, discarding the bay leaf, and purée. Add plenty of nutmeg and check the seasoning.

6 Return the birds to the pan, pour the sauce around them, and add 125g/5oz grapes. Heat through. Serve, garnished with extra grapes, crumbled bacon and a little parsley.

Energy 868Kcal/3639kJ; Protein 114.1g; Carbohydrate 20.6g, of which sugars 20.3g; Fat 34.9g, of which saturates 8.4g; Cholesterol 14mg; Calcium 164mg; Fibre 1.1g; Sodium 572mg.

MEAT AND FURRED GAME

From beef with chocolate sauce to kidneys in sherry and the ever-popular meatballs in tomato sauce, there are dishes for every occasion. Try beef steaks with blue cheese sauce, a spring stew of veal with young vegetables, a lamb dish with lemon, a Pyrennean stew with fresh and dried peppers, or classic pulse dishes such as fabada and cocido. Oxtail stewed is reminiscent of the Spanish bulls, while rabbit in garlic sauce is a recipe dating back to before Roman times.

CHORIZO WITH CHESTNUTS

Chestnuts are native to Galicia and are a popular addition to a variety of dishes. Chorizos y castanas makes a good side dish for roast turkey and a popular supper dish served on its own. Add a little chilli if you like things hot and spicy.

SERVES THREE TO SIX

INGREDIENTS
- 15ml/1 tbsp olive oil
- 4 red chorizo sausages, sliced
- 200g/7oz/1¼ cups peeled cooked chestnuts
- 15ml/1 tbsp paprika
- salt and ground black pepper
- crusty bread, to serve

COOK'S TIP
In Spain, chorizo for frying is sold as red links. Both mild and spicy types are available. Similar kinds of red sausage are made in Italy and Mexico.

1 Heat the oil in a wide frying pan and put in the chorizo slices in a single layer. Cook the chorizo for 3–4 minutes, turning frequently, until it starts to give off its oil.

2 Tip in the peeled chestnuts and toss until warm and covered with the chorizo oil. Add the paprika and season with salt and ground black pepper. Serve hot with crusty bread.

ALBÓNDIGAS CON SALSA DE TOMATE

Spanish men like to find traditional dishes in their favourite tapas bar. These tasty meatballs in tomato sauce are usually served in little brown, individual casserole dishes, accompanied by crusty bread. They make a good supper, too, with a green salad or pasta.

SERVES FOUR

INGREDIENTS
- 225g/8oz minced (ground) beef
- 4 spring onions (scallions), thinly sliced
- 2 garlic cloves, finely chopped
- 30ml/2 tbsp grated fresh Parmesan cheese
- 10ml/2 tsp fresh thyme leaves
- 15ml/1 tbsp olive oil
- 3 tomatoes, chopped
- 30ml/2 tbsp red or dry white wine
- 10ml/2 tsp chopped fresh rosemary
- pinch of sugar
- salt and ground black pepper
- fresh thyme, to garnish

VARIATION
Albóndigas are equally good made of half beef and half pork, or a mixture of meats, including ham. In the sausage-making areas, particularly Extremadura, they may be made completely of pork. Meatballs, called *la prueba* ("the try-out"), are made to test the seasoning.

1 Put the minced beef in a bowl. Add the spring onions, garlic, Parmesan and thyme and plenty of salt and pepper.

2 Stir well to combine, then shape the mixture into 12 small firm balls.

VARIATION
To make *biftek andaluz* (the nearest thing Spain has to a beefburger), shape the meat mixture into four wide patties and fry. Serve the patties on a slice of grilled (broiled) beefsteak tomato, or surrounded by tomato sauce. Top with a fried egg for decoration, if you like.

3 Heat the olive oil in a large, heavy frying pan and cook the meatballs for about 5 minutes, turning frequently, until evenly browned all over.

4 Add the chopped tomatoes, wine, rosemary and sugar to the pan, with salt and ground black pepper to taste.

5 Cover the pan and cook gently for about 15 minutes until the tomatoes are pulpy and the meatballs are cooked through. Check the sauce for seasoning and serve the meatballs hot, garnished with the thyme.

TOP Energy 202Kcal/842kJ; Protein 5.6g; Carbohydrate 16.2g, of which sugars 3.5g; Fat 13.2g, of which saturates 4.2g; Cholesterol 25mg; Calcium 58mg; Fibre 1.8g; Sodium 362mg.
BOTTOM Energy 206Kcal/857kJ; Protein 14.7g; Carbohydrate 2.5g, of which sugars 2.5g; Fat 14.6g, of which saturates 5.9g; Cholesterol 41mg; Calcium 105mg; Fibre 0.9g; Sodium 135mg.

Riñones al Jerez

Kidneys cooked in sherry are extremely popular in tapas bars, and make an excellent family supper. As a first course, partner the dish with fried toast triangles or crusty bread. A fino Montilla wine, less well known than sherry but with the same dry qualities, could replace the sherry. C.B. Montilla is often the choice in Andalusia for this dish.

SERVES FOUR

INGREDIENTS
- 12 plump lamb's kidneys
- 60ml/4 tbsp olive oil
- 115g/4oz smoked bacon lardons, or diced pancetta
- 1 large onion, chopped
- 2 garlic cloves, finely chopped
- 30ml/2 tbsp plain (all-purpose) flour
- 150ml/¼ pint/⅔ cup fino sherry or C.B. Montilla wine
- 15ml/1 tbsp tomato purée (paste)
- 30ml/2 tbsp chopped fresh parsley
- salt and ground black pepper
- new potatoes, boiled and buttered, to serve (optional)

1 Halve and skin the kidneys, then remove the cores. Cut the kidneys into cubes. Heat half the oil in a large frying pan and fry the bacon or pancetta until the fat starts to run. Add the onion and garlic and fry until softened. Remove to a plate.

2 Add the remaining oil to the pan and divide the kidneys into four batches. Put in one handful, and stir-fry over a high heat until sealed. Push them to the pan rim and stir-fry the next batch. They should be sealed, and not be allowed to give off juice. Remove to a plate and repeat until they are all cooked.

3 Return the onion and bacon mixture to the pan. Sprinkle with flour and cook, stirring gently. Add the sherry or Montilla wine and stir until thickened. Add the tomato purée and parsley. Return the kidneys to the pan, and heat through. Season well and serve hot with buttered new potatoes, if you like.

Energy 496Kcal/2074kJ; Protein 48.6g; Carbohydrate 10.8g, of which sugars 4g; Fat 24.5g, of which saturates 6.2g; Cholesterol 806mg; Calcium 49mg; Fibre 1.1g; Sodium 752mg.

LIVER AND BACON CASSEROLE

In Spain, liver means pig's liver, and is cooked here in a well-seasoned sauce. Lambs are killed when they are very small and the liver is not much of a meal. The pig's liver is the first thing to be eaten from the new pig, and so is associated with one of the big feasts of the year, Matanza. You can substitute lamb's liver if you prefer.

SERVES THREE TO FOUR

INGREDIENTS

- 450g/1lb pig's or lamb's liver, trimmed and sliced
- 60ml/4 tbsp milk (for pig's liver)
- 30ml/2 tbsp olive oil
- 225g/8oz rindless smoked lean bacon rashers (strips), cut into pieces
- 2 onions, halved and sliced
- 175g/6oz/2¼ cups brown cap (cremini) mushrooms, halved
- 25g/1oz/2 tbsp butter
- 30ml/2 tbsp plain (all-purpose) flour
- 150ml/¼ pint/⅔ cup hot chicken stock
- 15ml/1 tbsp soy sauce
- 5ml/1 tsp paprika
- salt and ground black pepper

1 If using pig's liver, soak it in the milk for 1 hour for a milder flavour, then blot dry with kitchen paper.

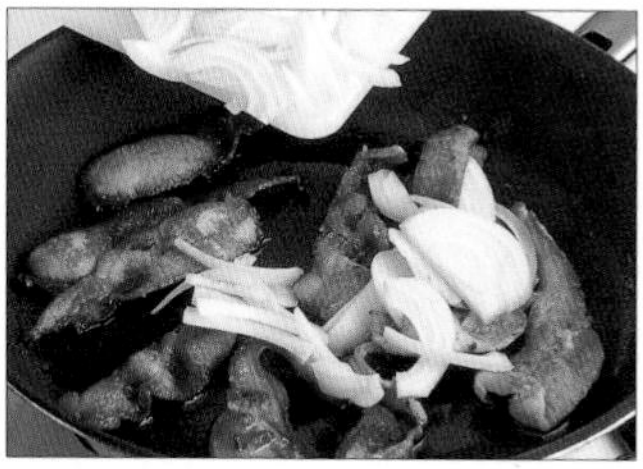

2 Heat the oil in a frying pan and stir-fry the bacon until crisp. Add the onion and cook, stirring, until softened. Add the mushrooms and fry for 1 minute.

3 Using a slotted spoon, remove the bacon and vegetables from the pan and keep warm. Add the liver to the fat remaining in the pan and cook over a high heat for 3–4 minutes, turning once to seal the slices on both sides. Remove from the pan and keep warm.

4 Melt the butter in the pan, sprinkle the flour over and cook briefly. Stir in the stock, soy sauce and paprika and bring to a simmer. Return the liver and vegetables. Simmer gently for 3–4 minutes. Check the seasoning.

VARIATION

Bread is the classic accompaniment to this dish, but macaroni or a choice of vegetables make equally good partners.

Energy 459Kcal/1913kJ; Protein 36.1g; Carbohydrate 16.6g, of which sugars 6.1g; Fat 23.9g, of which saturates 10g; Cholesterol 336mg; Calcium 50mg; Fibre 2.1g; Sodium 1275mg.

FABADA

THIS BEAN AND SAUSAGE HOTPOT FROM THE WILD MOUNTAINS OF ASTURIAS ON THE NORTHERN COAST OF SPAIN, HAS ACHIEVED WORLD FAME. IT USED TO CONTAIN DRIED BROAD (FAVA) BEANS, WHICH GAVE IT THE NAME, BUT WHEN THESE OLD-FASHIONED BEANS WERE ABANDONED AND MODERN FABES *– WHITE KIDNEY BEANS – WERE ADOPTED, IT BECAME A TRULY GREAT DISH. CURED SAUSAGES, A PORK KNUCKLE AND BELLY PORK LEND THE BEANS AN INCREDIBLE RICHNESS, WHICH IS ENHANCED BY SAFFRON AND PAPRIKA. IT IS A GOOD DISH FOR WINTER EVENINGS, SERVED WITH GLASSES OF CIDER.*

SERVES EIGHT

INGREDIENTS

- 500–800g/1¼–1¾lb belly pork, in thick slices
- 1 smoked gammon (smoked or cured ham) knuckle, about 675g/1½lb, skin slashed
- 800g/1¾lb dried cannellini beans, soaked overnight (see Cook's Tip)
- 5ml/1 tsp black peppercorns, crushed
- 15ml/1 tbsp paprika
- pinch of saffron threads (0.2g)
- 1 bay leaf
- 30ml/2 tbsp oil (optional)
- 4 garlic cloves, chopped
- 3 red chorizo sausages, thickly sliced
- 175g/6oz *morcilla* or black pudding (blood sausage), thickly sliced
- ground black pepper (optional)

1 Using a very large stockpot (with a capacity of at least 6 litres/10 pints/25 cups), put the pork belly and knuckle into the pot with water to cover. Bring to the boil, then drain the meat and return it to the stockpot.

COOK'S TIP

The quality of the bean is a feature of the dish so try to use luxury Spanish beans, now widely exported. *Fabes* are like very large, white cannellini beans. If luxury Spanish beans are unavailable use *lingots* (the French *cassoulet* bean) or large white kidney bean.

2 Add the drained beans to the pot and pour over 2.3 litres/4 pints/10 cups water. Bring to the boil very slowly, then boil for 10 minutes. Reduce the heat and add the peppercorns, paprika, crumbled saffron and the bay leaf.

3 Simmer very gently over a very low heat for 2 hours. (It is best to put the pot over a small burner, turned low.) Check occasionally that the beans are still covered with liquid, but do not stir energetically or the beans will break up.

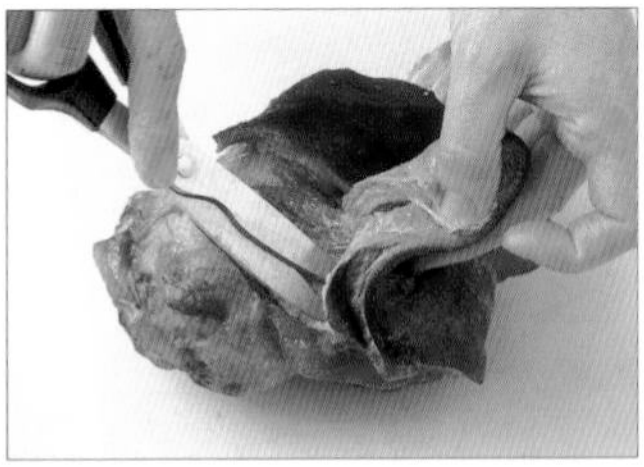

4 Remove the pork belly and knuckle and set them aside to cool. Strip off the skin and fat, and take 30ml/2 tbsp chopped fat for frying (or use oil). Heat this in a frying pan and cook the garlic lightly, then spoon it into the beans.

VARIATION

Most Spanish bean stews are flavoured with meat from the pig and are then enriched with pork fat. However, in the north, beans are cooked with clams.

5 Fry the chorizo and *morcilla* or black pudding lightly in the same pan. Gently stir into the bean pot.

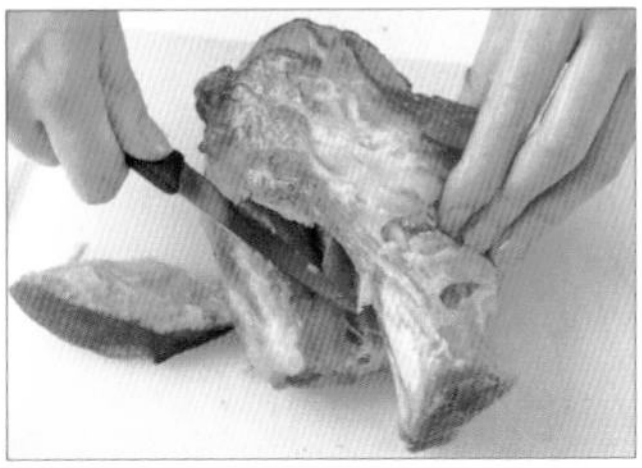

6 Remove all the meat from the ham bone. Chop it with the pork and return to the stockpot. Simmer for a few minutes. Check the seasonings (there should be enough salt from the meat already) and serve.

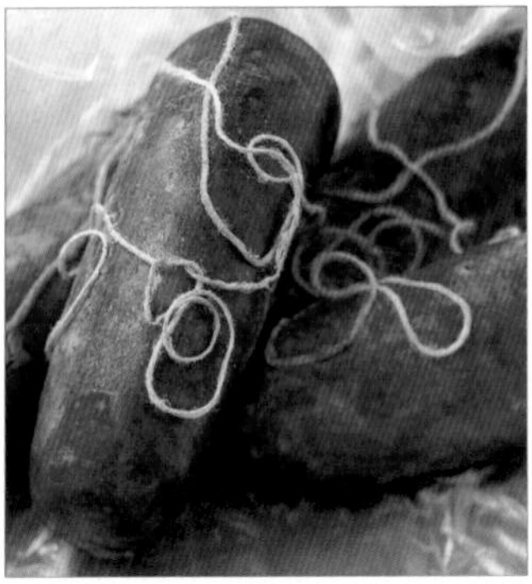

Energy 808Kcal/3379kJ; Protein 46.5g; Carbohydrate 55.1g, of which sugars 3.7g; Fat 46.2g, of which saturates 17.4g; Cholesterol 94mg; Calcium 164mg; Fibre 16.1g; Sodium 1106mg.

Black Bean Stew

Tolosa in the Basque country is famous for its black bean stew – potaje de alubias negras – made spicy with various sausages and pickled pork. Here is a simplified version, with extra fresh vegetables that add wonderfully to its flavour.

SERVES FIVE TO SIX

INGREDIENTS

- 275g/10oz/1½ cups black beans, soaked overnight in cold water
- 675g/1½lb boneless belly pork rashers (strips)
- 60ml/4 tbsp olive oil
- 350g/12oz baby (pearl) onions
- 2 celery sticks, thickly sliced
- 150g/5oz chorizo, cut into chunks
- 10ml/2 tsp paprika
- 600ml/1 pint/2½ cups light chicken or vegetable stock
- 2 green (bell) peppers, seeded and cut into large pieces
- salt and ground black pepper

1 Drain the beans into a pan and cover with fresh water. Bring to the boil and boil rapidly for 10 minutes. Drain the beans and put in an ovenproof dish.

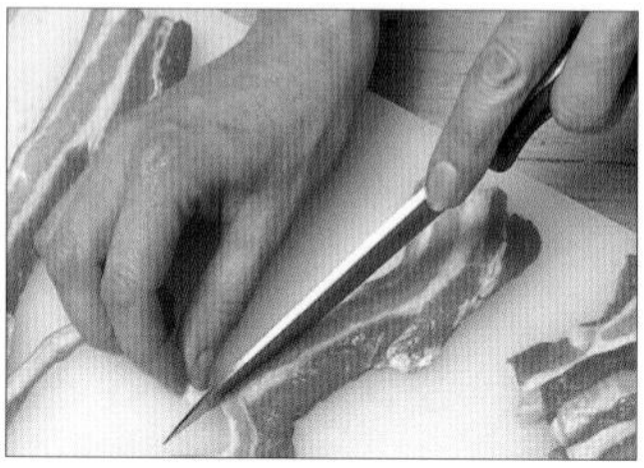

2 Preheat the oven to 160°C/325°F/Gas 3. Cut away any rind from the pork, then cut it into large chunks.

3 Heat the oil in a large frying pan and fry the onions and celery for 3 minutes. Add the pork and fry for 10 minutes, or until the pork is browned.

4 Add the chorizo and fry for 2 minutes, then sprinkle in the paprika. Tip the mixture into the beans and mix well to combine thoroughly.

5 Add the stock to the pan and bring to the boil, then pour over the meat and beans. Cover and bake for 1 hour.

6 Stir the green peppers into the stew and return to the oven for a further 15 minutes. Season and serve hot.

VARIATION

This is the sort of stew to which you can add a variety of winter vegetables, such as chunks of leek, turnip and celeriac.

Energy 616Kcal/2564kJ; Protein 32.2g; Carbohydrate 31.1g, of which sugars 8.8g; Fat 41.1g, of which saturates 12.7g; Cholesterol 88mg; Calcium 102mg; Fibre 9.3g; Sodium 1651mg.

STUFFED ROAST LOIN OF PORK

PORK IS SPAIN'S MOST POPULAR MEAT, THE LOIN PARTICULARLY SO. FOR THIS DISH, LOMO DE CERDO RELLENO, *YOU NEED THE WHOLE CUT WITH THE FLAP ON THE SIDE TO ENCLOSE THE STUFFING, WHICH IS RICHLY FLAVOURED WITH FIGS. MEAT AND FRUIT ARE A POPULAR CATALAN COMBINATION.*

SERVES FOUR

INGREDIENTS

- 60ml/4 tbsp olive oil
- 1 onion, finely chopped
- 2 garlic cloves, chopped
- 75g/3oz/1½ cups stale breadcrumbs
- 4 ready-to-eat dried figs, chopped
- 8 pitted green olives, chopped
- 25g/1oz/¼ cup flaked almonds
- 15ml/1 tbsp lemon juice
- 15ml/1 tbsp chopped fresh parsley
- 1 egg yolk
- 1kg/2¼lb boned loin of pork with the side flap attached
- salt, paprika and black pepper

1 Preheat the oven to 200°C/400°F/ Gas 6. Heat 45ml/3 tbsp of the oil in a pan, add the onion and garlic, and cook gently until softened. Remove the pan from the heat, and stir in the breadcrumbs, figs, olives, almonds, lemon juice, parsley and egg yolk. Season with salt, paprika and pepper.

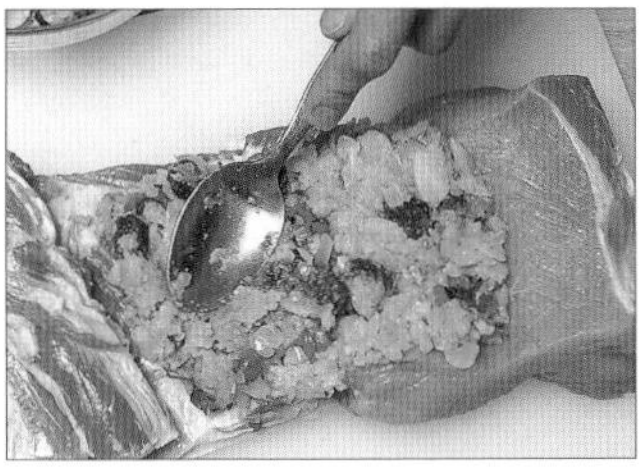

2 Remove any string from the pork and unroll the belly flap, cutting away any excess fat or meat to enable you to do so. Spread half the stuffing over the flat piece and roll it up, starting from the thick side. Tie the joint at intervals with string to hold it together.

3 Pour the remaining oil into a small roasting pan and add the pork. Roast for 1¼ hours. Meanwhile, form the remaining stuffing mixture into balls and add to the pan, 15–20 minutes before the end of cooking time.

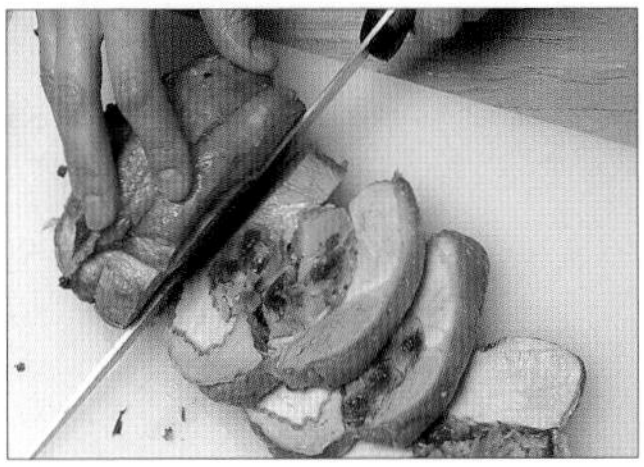

4 Remove the pork from the oven and leave it rest for 10 minutes. Carve into thick slices and serve with the stuffing balls and any juices from the pan. This dish is also good served cold.

Energy 852Kcal/3567kJ; Protein 83.3g; Carbohydrate 46.8g, of which sugars 30.7g; Fat 38g, of which saturates 8.6g; Cholesterol 245mg; Calcium 233mg; Fibre 6.2g; Sodium 556mg.

PORK EMPANADA

This flat, two-crust Galician pie is famous because there is no occasion on which it is not served. It is festival food; it greets the boats of returning fishermen and it is the men's lunchbox staple. Fillings vary enormously, and may include fish such as sardines, or scallops for special occasions. These pies are good hot or cold.

SERVES EIGHT

INGREDIENTS

- 75ml/5 tbsp olive oil
- 2 onions, chopped
- 4 garlic cloves, finely chopped
- 1kg/2¼ lb boned pork loin, diced
- 175g/6oz smoked gammon (smoked or cured ham) or raw ham, diced
- 3 red chorizo or other spicy sausages (about 300g/11oz)
- 3 (bell) peppers (mixed colours), seeded and chopped
- 175ml/6fl oz/¾ cup white wine
- 200g/7oz can tomatoes
- pinch of saffron threads (0.1g)
- 5ml/1 tsp paprika
- 30ml/2 tbsp chopped fresh parsley
- salt and ground black pepper

For the corn meal dough

- 250g/9oz corn meal
- 7g/2 tsp easy-blend (rapid-rise) dried yeast
- 5ml/1 tsp caster (superfine) sugar
- 250g/9oz plain (all-purpose) flour, plus extra for dusting
- 5ml/1 tsp salt
- 200ml/7fl oz/scant 1 cup warm water
- 30ml/2 tbsp oil
- 2 eggs, beaten, plus 1 for the glaze

1 Make the filling. Heat 60ml/4 tbsp oil in a frying pan and fry the onions, adding the garlic when the onions begin to colour. Transfer to a flameproof casserole. Add the pork and gammon or ham to the pan, and fry until coloured, stirring. Transfer to the casserole.

2 Add 15ml/1 tbsp oil, the sausage and the peppers to the pan and fry. Transfer to the casserole. Deglaze the pan with the wine, allowing it to bubble and reduce. Pour into the casserole.

3 Add the tomatoes, saffron, paprika and parsley and season. Cook gently for 20–30 minutes. Leave to cool.

4 Meanwhile make the dough. Put the corn meal into a food processor. Add the dried yeast with the sugar. Gradually add the flour, salt, water, oil and 2 eggs and beat, to make a smooth soft dough.

5 Turn the dough into a clean bowl, cover with a dishtowel and leave in a warm place for 40–50 minutes, to rise.

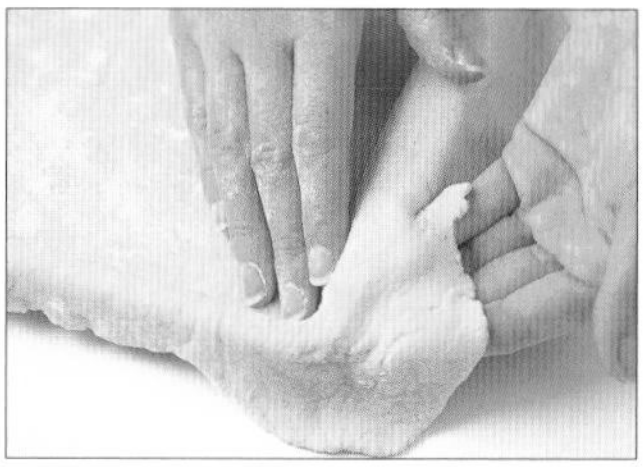

6 Preheat the oven to 200°C/400°F/Gas 6. Grease a shallow roasting pan or dish 30 × 20cm/12 × 8in. Halve the dough. Roll out one half on a floured surface, a little larger than the pan. Lift this in place, leaving the border hanging over the edge.

7 Spoon in the filling. Roll out the lid and lay it in place. Fold the outside edge over the lid (trimming as necessary) and press gently all round with a fork, to seal the pie. Prick the surface and brush with beaten egg.

8 Bake the pie for 30–35 minutes (covering the ends if they brown too much). Cut the pie into squares.

Energy 757Kcal/3166kJ; Protein 54g; Carbohydrate 61.3g, of which sugars 9.6g; Fat 32.1g, of which saturates 9.2g; Cholesterol 165mg; Calcium 108mg; Fibre 3.9g; Sodium 844mg.

SKEWERED LAMB WITH RED ONION SALSA

The Moors first introduced skewered and barbecued meat to Spain, where it has been popular for over 1,500 years. These spiced skewers are accompanied by a simple salsa.

SERVES FOUR

INGREDIENTS

- 500–675g/1¼–1½lb ready-trimmed, cubed lamb
- 5ml/1 tsp ground cumin
- 10ml/2 tsp paprika
- 30ml/2 tbsp olive oil
- salt and ground black pepper

For the red onion salsa

- 1 red onion, very thinly sliced
- 1 large tomato, seeded and chopped
- 15ml/1 tbsp red wine vinegar
- 3–4 fresh basil or mint leaves, roughly torn

VARIATION

Skewer squares of (bell) pepper, and whole bay leaves between the cubes of spicy, marinated meat.

1 Season the lamb with the cumin, paprika, oil and black pepper. Toss well to coat. Leave in a cool place for several hours, or in the refrigerator overnight, so that the lamb absorbs all the spicy flavours.

2 Spear the cubes of lamb on four skewers, leaving one end of each of the skewers free for picking up.

3 To make the salsa, put the sliced onion, tomato, vinegar and basil or mint leaves in a small bowl and stir together. Season to taste with salt and pepper.

4 If cooking on a barbecue, the charcoal should be grey with no flames before you start cooking. Alternatively, preheat the grill (broiler) with the shelf about 15cm/6in from the heat source. Generously brush the grill pan with oil.

5 Season the lamb with salt and cook for 5–10 minutes, turning the skewers occasionally, until the lamb is well browned but still slightly pink in the centre. Serve hot, with the salsa.

COOK'S TIP

If using wooden skewers, soak them in cold water first, to prevent them burning.

COCHIFRITO

Aragon and Navarre in the Pyrenees are known for their fine ingredients – and also for their simple cooking. "If the quality is there, no need to employ tricks in the kitchen" runs the Spanish proverb. The meat is fried simply and flavoured with lemon juice and paprika in this dish. It captures the very essence of lamb.

SERVES FOUR

INGREDIENTS

- 800g/1¾lb very well-trimmed, tender lamb (see Cook's Tip), in cubes or strips
- 30ml/2 tbsp olive oil, plus extra
- 1 onion, chopped
- 2 garlic cloves, finely chopped
- 5ml/1 tsp paprika
- juice of 2 lemons
- 15ml/1 tbsp finely chopped fresh parsley
- salt and ground black pepper

COOK'S TIP

The sweetest lamb is cut from the shoulder. However, it also contains quite a lot of fat, often in layers through the meat, so allow extra weight, and cut it out.

1 Season the lamb with salt and ground black pepper. Heat the 30ml/2 tbsp olive oil in a large frying pan or casserole over a high heat and add the meat in handfuls. Add the onion at the same time, and keep pushing the meat around the pan with a spatula. Add more meat to the pan as each batch is sealed. Add the chopped garlic and a little more oil if necessary.

2 When the meat is golden and the onion soft, sprinkle with paprika and lemon juice. Cover and simmer for 15 minutes. Check the seasonings and add a dusting of parsley, then serve.

VARIATION

This dish may also be made using pork in place of the lamb – the name *cochifrito* means little pig, fried.

TOP Energy 296Kcal/1236kJ; Protein 25.6g; Carbohydrate 4.4g, of which sugars 2.9g; Fat 19.7g, of which saturates 7.3g; Cholesterol 95mg; Calcium 48mg; Fibre 0.8g; Sodium 113mg.
BOTTOM Energy 422Kcal/1761kJ; Protein 39.8g; Carbohydrate 3.1g, of which sugars 2.2g; Fat 28g, of which saturates 11.2g; Cholesterol 152mg; Calcium 33mg; Fibre 0.7g; Sodium 174mg.

LAMB WITH RED PEPPERS AND RIOJA

World-famous for its red wine, Rioja also produces excellent red peppers. It even has a red pepper fair, at Lodoso, every year. Together they give this lamb stew a lovely rich flavour. Boiled potatoes make a very good accompaniment.

SERVES FOUR

INGREDIENTS

- 15ml/1 tbsp plain (all-purpose) flour
- 1kg/2¼lb lean lamb, cubed
- 60ml/4 tbsp olive oil
- 2 red onions, sliced
- 4 garlic cloves, sliced
- 10ml/2 tsp paprika
- 1.5ml/¼ tsp ground cloves
- 400ml/14fl oz/1⅔ cups red Rioja
- 150ml/¼ pint/⅔ cup lamb stock
- 2 bay leaves
- 2 thyme sprigs
- 3 red (bell) peppers, halved and seeded
- salt and ground black pepper
- bay leaves and thyme sprigs, to garnish (optional)

1 Preheat the oven to 160°C/325°F/Gas 3. Season the flour, add the lamb and toss lightly to coat.

2 Heat the oil in a frying pan and fry the lamb until browned. Transfer to an ovenproof dish. Fry the onions and garlic until soft. Add to the meat.

3 Add the paprika, cloves, Rioja, lamb stock, bay leaves and thyme and bring the mixture to a gentle simmer. Add the halved red peppers. Cover the dish with a lid or foil and cook for about 30 minutes, or until the meat is tender. Garnish with more bay leaves and thyme sprigs, if you like.

Energy 708Kcal/2952kJ; Protein 52.1g; Carbohydrate 20g, of which sugars 14.4g; Fat 39.8g, of which saturates 14.7g; Cholesterol 190mg; Calcium 69mg; Fibre 3.8g; Sodium 231mg.

VEAL CASSEROLE WITH BROAD BEANS

This delicate stew, flavoured with sherry and plenty of garlic, is a spring dish made with new vegetables – MENESTRA DE TERNERA. *For a delicious flavour be sure to add plenty of parsley just before serving. Lamb is equally good cooked in this way.*

SERVES SIX

INGREDIENTS

- 45ml/3 tbsp olive oil
- 1.3–1.6kg/3–3½ lb veal, cut into 5cm/2in cubes
- 1 large onion, chopped
- 6 large garlic cloves, unpeeled
- 1 bay leaf
- 5ml/1 tsp paprika
- 240ml/8fl oz/1 cup fino sherry
- 100g/4oz/scant 1 cup shelled broad (fava) beans
- 60ml/4 tbsp chopped fresh flat leaf parsley
- salt and ground black pepper

1 Heat 30ml/2 tbsp oil in a large flameproof casserole. Add half the meat and brown well on all sides. Transfer to a plate. Brown the rest of the meat and remove from the pan.

2 Add the remaining oil to the pan and cook the onion until soft. Return the meat to the casserole and stir well to mix with the onion.

3 Add the garlic cloves, bay leaf, paprika and sherry. Season with salt and black pepper. Bring to simmering point, then cover and cook very gently for 30–40 minutes.

4 Add the broad beans to the casserole about 10 minutes before the end of the cooking time. Check the seasoning and stir in the chopped parsley just before serving.

Energy 366Kcal/1533kJ; Protein 47.9g; Carbohydrate 6.7g, of which sugars 3.8g; Fat 11.7g, of which saturates 2.8g; Cholesterol 182mg; Calcium 57mg; Fibre 2.2g; Sodium 248mg.

Cocido

The Spanish national dish, cocido is also Madrid's most famous stew. The name simply means "boiled dinner" and it used to be made more than once a week. A pot of fresh and salt meat with chicken and sausages is simmered with chickpeas and some fresh vegetables. The broth makes a soup course and then the rest is displayed on two splendid platters. Serve with a bottle of Viña Arana from La Rioja Alta or Bodegas Bilbainas Viña Pomal.

SERVES EIGHT

INGREDIENTS

- 500–800g/1¼–1¾lb cured brisket or silverside (pot roast)
- 250g/9oz smoked streaky (fatty) bacon, in one piece, or 250g/9oz belly pork
- 1 knuckle gammon (smoked or cured ham) bone, with some meat still attached
- 500–750g/1¼–1¾lb beef marrow bone, sawn through
- 1 pig's trotter (foot), sawn through
- 1 whole garlic bulb
- 2 bay leaves
- 5ml/1 tsp black peppercorns, lightly crushed
- 250g/9oz/1¼ cups dried chickpeas, soaked overnight and drained
- 2 quarters corn-fed chicken
- 1 small onion, studded with 2 or 3 cloves
- 2 large carrots, cut into big pieces
- 2 leeks, cut into chunks
- 500g/1¼lb small new potatoes, scrubbed
- 2 red chorizo sausages
- 1 *morcilla* or 250g/9oz black pudding (blood sausage)
- 30ml/2 tbsp long grain rice
- 1 small (bell) pepper, finely diced
- salt

1 Put the salt meat – brisket or silverside, bacon or pork and knuckle – into a large pan and cover with water. Bring slowly to the boil, simmer for 5 minutes to remove excess salt, and drain.

VARIATIONS

The types of meat used in this hearty stew can be varied. Just make sure that you include a salty meat, a meat on the bone, a smoked meat, a piece of pork, a piece of beef and a piece of chicken – plus a paprika sausage.

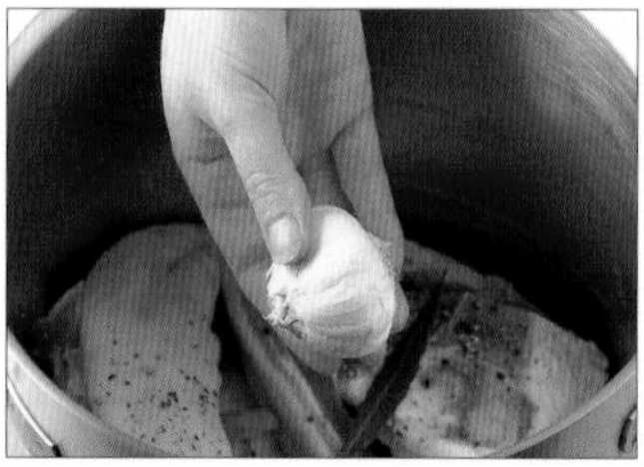

2 Using a very large stockpot (with a capacity of at least 6 litres/10 pints/ 5 quarts), pack in all the meat, skin side down, with the marrowbone and trotter. Add the garlic bulb, bay leaves and peppercorns, with water to cover. Bring to simmering point, skimming off any scum, with a slotted spoon.

3 Add the drained chickpeas, cover and simmer on the lowest possible heat for 1½ hours, checking occasionally that there is enough liquid.

4 Add the chicken and onion to the pot. Cook until the chickpeas are done.

5 Start the vegetables. Put the carrots, leeks and potatoes into a large pan with the chorizo (but not the *morcilla* or black pudding). Cover with water and bring to the boil. Simmer for 25 minutes, until the potatoes are cooked. About 5 minutes before the end, add the *morcilla* or black pudding.

6 Strain off enough broth from the meat pot (about 1.2 litres/2 pints/5 cups) into a pan, for soup. Bring back to the boil, sprinkle in the rice and cook for 15 minutes. Add the diced pepper and cook for 2–3 minutes more. Serve the soup as the first course.

7 Drain the vegetables and sausages and arrange on a platter. Serve as a separate second course or as an accompaniment with the meat.

8 Slice the meats, removing the marrow from the bone and adding it to the chickpeas. Arrange with all the meats on a heated serving platter, moistening with a little broth.

Energy 618Kcal/2588kJ; Protein 47.9g; Carbohydrate 40g, of which sugars 6.6g; Fat 30.7g, of which saturates 11.3g; Cholesterol 128mg; Calcium 136mg; Fibre 6.1g; Sodium 1195mg.

Ropa Vieja

The name of this dish means "old clothes", which sounds a good deal more romantic than leftovers. It is a dish for using up meats from the cocido, and the recipe shows both Jewish and Arab influences. It is normally made with cold roast beef, but it is ideal for finishing up cold turkey and other Christmas meats and even stuffing.

SERVES FOUR

INGREDIENTS
- 2 small aubergines (eggplant)
- 90ml/6 tbsp olive oil
- 1 large onion, chopped
- 3 garlic cloves, finely chopped
- 1 fresh, or baked, red (bell) pepper, seeded and sliced (optional)
- 400g/14oz can tomatoes
- 250ml/8fl oz/1 cup meat stock
- 2.5ml/½ tsp ground cumin
- 2.5ml/½ tsp ground allspice
- pinch of ground cloves
- 2.5ml/½ tsp cayenne pepper
- 400g/14oz cooked beef, cubed (or mixed turkey, ham, etc)
- 400g/14oz can chickpeas, drained
- salt and ground black pepper
- chopped fresh mint, to garnish (optional)

1 Cut the aubergines into cubes and put them into a colander. Sprinkle with 10ml/2 tsp salt, turning the cubes over with your hands. Leave to drain for about 1 hour. Rinse, then squeeze them dry using kitchen paper.

2 Meanwhile put 30ml/2 tbsp oil in a wide flameproof casserole and fry the onion and garlic until soft.

3 If using the fresh pepper, add it to the casserole and stir-fry until softened.

4 Add the tomatoes and the chopped baked pepper, if using, the meat stock, cumin, allspice, ground cloves and cayenne pepper. Season to taste. Add the cubed meat and simmer gently.

5 Heat 45ml/3 tbsp oil over a high heat in a large frying pan. Fry the aubergine cubes, in batches if necessary, until they are brown on all sides. (If you need to add more oil, add it to an empty pan, and reheat to a high heat, before adding more aubergine cubes.)

6 Add the aubergine and chickpeas to the casserole and bring to a simmer, adding a little more stock to cover, if necessary – the dish should be almost solid. Check the seasonings, garnish with mint, if using, and serve.

Energy 458Kcal/1919kJ; Protein 30.1g; Carbohydrate 35.2g, of which sugars 15.4g; Fat 23g, of which saturates 3.9g; Cholesterol 58mg; Calcium 99mg; Fibre 9.4g; Sodium 1221mg.

SOLOMILLO WITH CABRALES SAUCE

WELL-HUNG BEEF IS A FEATURE OF THE BASQUE COUNTRY, SERVED HERE WITH CABRALES, THE BLUE CHEESE FROM SPAIN'S NORTHERN MOUNTAINS. FRENCH ROQUEFORT IS ALSO EXTREMELY POPULAR, BECAUSE IT APPEALS TO THE SPANISH LOVE OF SALTY FLAVOURS. IN THIS RECIPE THE SALT AND BRANDY IN THE SAUCE ARE PERFECTLY BALANCED BY THE CREAM.

SERVES FOUR

INGREDIENTS
- 25g/1oz/2 tbsp butter
- 30ml/2 tbsp olive oil
- 4 fillet steaks, cut 5cm/2in thick, about 150g/5oz each
- salt and coarsely ground black pepper
- fresh flat leaf parsley, to garnish

For the blue cheese sauce
- 30ml/2 tbsp Spanish brandy
- 150ml/5fl oz/⅔ cup double (heavy) cream
- 75g/3oz *Cabrales* or Roquefort cheese, crumbled

COOK'S TIP

Cabrales is also known as *Picón* and *Treviso* and has a slightly more acidic flavour than Roquefort.

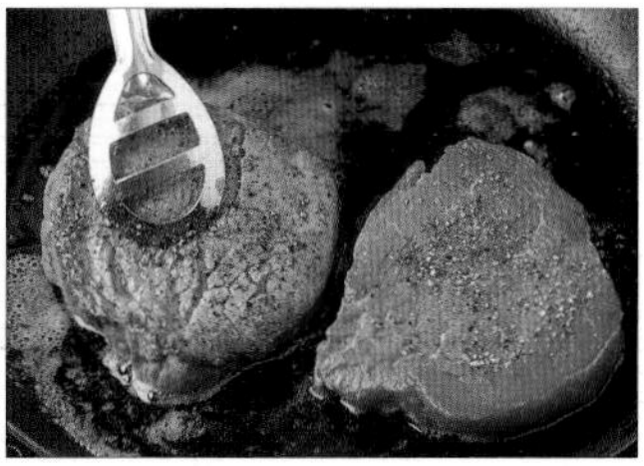

1 Heat the butter and oil together in a heavy frying pan, over a high heat. Season the steaks well. Fry them for 2 minutes on each side, to sear them.

2 Lower the heat slightly and cook for a further 2–3 minutes on each side, or according to your taste. Remove the steaks to a warm plate.

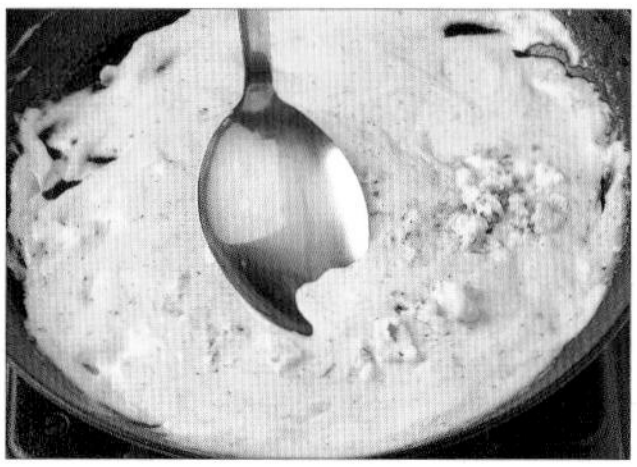

3 Reduce the heat and add the brandy, stirring to pick up the juices. Add the cream and boil to reduce a little.

4 Add the crumbled cheese and mash it into the sauce using a spoon. Taste for seasoning. Serve in a small sauce jug (pitcher), or poured over the steaks. Garnish the beef with parsley.

Energy 573Kcal/2374kJ; Protein 36.3g; Carbohydrate 0.7g, of which sugars 0.7g; Fat 45.4g, of which saturates 24.4g; Cholesterol 170mg; Calcium 117mg; Fibre 0g; Sodium 341mg.

CARNE CON CHOCOLATE

Chocolate came to Europe via Spain. It is not naturally sweet and so chocolate squares are used in Spain in the way that other countries use gravy browning. It gives this stew a rich darkness, which is enhanced by the brandy. Serve with a Rioja Reserva.

SERVES SIX

INGREDIENTS
- 60ml/4 tbsp olive oil
- 1kg/2¼lb trimmed stewing beef
- 5ml/1 tsp paprika
- 150g/5oz smoked bacon lardons, or diced pancetta
- 1 large Spanish onion, chopped
- 4 carrots, sliced thickly
- 1 large leek, white only, sliced
- 6 garlic cloves
- 225g/8oz brown cap (cremini) mushrooms, sliced
- 4 tomatoes, peeled, seeded and chopped
- 45ml/3 tbsp plain (all-purpose) flour
- 12 peppercorns, crushed
- 1 pig's trotter (foot), sawn through
- 250ml/8fl oz/1 cup dry red wine
- 1 bay leaf
- 4 sprigs of thyme
- 120ml/4fl oz/½ cup Spanish brandy
- 300ml/10fl oz/1¼ cups meat stock
- 450g/1lb small potatoes, peeled
- 25g/1oz dark (bittersweet) chocolate, grated
- salt and ground black pepper
- 45ml/3 tbsp chopped fresh parsley, to garnish

1 Preheat the oven to 180°C/350°F/Gas 4. Heat 30ml/2 tbsp oil in a large frying pan. Season the cubed beef with paprika and fry in two batches, over a high heat, turning until browned on all sides. Reserve the first batch on a plate when done. Add a little more oil, if needed, and fry the second batch.

2 Meanwhile heat 15ml/1 tbsp oil in a large flameproof casserole and fry the bacon or pancetta. When the fat starts to run, add the onion, carrots and leek and cook gently until the onion softens.

3 Smash the garlic cloves with the flat of a knife and add them to the pan, with the mushrooms and tomatoes. Stir and cook gently, then sprinkle with the flour and cook briefly.

4 Add the meat, salt and peppercorns to the casserole. Tuck in the trotter. Add a little wine, stir to deglaze, then add all the wine, stirring well. Add the bay leaf and thyme. Pour in the brandy and stock to cover. Return to a simmer, then cover and cook in the oven for 1¼ hours.

5 Cook the potatoes in a pan of boiling water for 15 minutes. Add them to the casserole with the chocolate. Simmer for another 30 minutes. Remove the trotter, check the amount of liquid and taste for seasoning. Sprinkle with chopped parsley and serve.

Energy 368Kcal/1534kJ; Protein 12.2g; Carbohydrate 30.1g, of which sugars 11.7g; Fat 16.4g, of which saturates 4.5g; Cholesterol 27mg; Calcium 67mg; Fibre 4.4g; Sodium 356mg.

Rabo de Toro

In the Spanish kitchen, the most famous part of the bull is his tail – although most people are more likely to cook with oxtail. Either makes a rich, succulent meat stew, which can be prepared several days ahead, and tastes even better reheated.

SERVES SIX

INGREDIENTS

- 60ml/4 tbsp olive oil
- 2 onions, chopped
- 30ml/2 tbsp plain (all-purpose) flour
- 1.6kg/3½lb oxtail, chopped across
- 6 carrots
- 2 large garlic cloves, smashed
- 1 bay leaf
- 2 thyme sprigs
- 2 leeks, sliced thinly
- 1 clove
- pinch of freshly grated nutmeg
- 350ml/12fl oz/1½ cups red wine
- 30ml/2 tbsp vinegar
- 350ml/12fl oz/1½ cups stock
- 30ml/2 tbsp fino sherry
- 60ml/4 tbsp chopped fresh parsley
- salt, paprika and black pepper
- boiled potatoes, to serve

1 Starting a day ahead, preheat the oven to 150°C/300°F/Gas 2. Heat 30ml/2 tbsp oil in a large frying pan, add the onions and fry until softened. Remove to a casserole (in which the oxtail will fit in a single layer).

2 Season the flour with salt, paprika and pepper and dust the oxtail pieces all over. Add the remaining oil to the pan and put in the oxtail pieces, on their sides at first. Fry, turning them to brown all over, then fit them into the casserole, standing upright.

3 Cut the carrots into short lengths and push into the spaces between the pieces of oxtail in the casserole. Tuck in the garlic cloves, bay leaf and thyme sprigs and add the sliced leeks.

4 Add the clove, grated nutmeg and more black pepper. Pour in the wine, vinegar and just enough stock to cover. Bring to simmering point, then cover the casserole with a lid and put in the oven. Cook for about 3 hours, or until the meat is falling off the bones.

5 Skim the fat off the top of the stew. Spoon the larger meat pieces on to a plate and remove the bones and fat.

6 Push all the remaining oxtail and the carrots to one end of the pan and discard the bay leaf and thyme. Spoon the garlic and some of the soft vegetables into a food processor and purée with the sherry. Return the meat and purée to the casserole and heat through. Stir in the parsley, check the seasonings and serve with boiled potatoes.

Energy 409Kcal/1709kJ; Protein 32.6g; Carbohydrate 11.5g, of which sugars 7.2g; Fat 21.3g, of which saturates 1.1g; Cholesterol 0mg; Calcium 65mg; Fibre 2.4g; Sodium 212mg.

VENISON CHOPS WITH ROMESCO SAUCE

ROMESCO IS THE CATALAN WORD FOR THE ÑORA CHILLI. IT LENDS A SPICY ROUNDNESS TO ONE OF SPAIN'S GREATEST SAUCES, FROM TARRAGONA. THE SAUCE ALSO CONTAINS GROUND TOASTED NUTS AND OFTEN ANOTHER FIERCER CHILLI. IT CAN BE SERVED COLD, AS A DIP FOR VEGETABLES, BUT THIS SPICY VERSION IS THE IDEAL PARTNER FOR GAME CHOPS – VENADO CON ROMESCO. *BOAR CHOPS CAN ALSO BE USED BUT NEED LONGER COOKING. CHOOSE GRAN SANGRE DE TORO TO DRINK.*

SERVES FOUR

INGREDIENTS

- 4 venison chops, cut 2cm/¾in thick and about 175–200g/6–7oz each
- 30ml/2 tbsp olive oil
- 50g/2oz/4 tbsp butter
- braised Savoy cabbage, to serve

For the sauce

- 3 *ñora* chillies
- 1 hot dried chilli
- 25g/1oz/¼ cup almonds
- 150ml/¼ pint/⅔ cup olive oil
- 1 slice stale bread, crusts removed
- 3 garlic cloves, chopped
- 3 tomatoes, peeled, seeded and roughly chopped
- 60ml/4 tbsp sherry vinegar
- 60ml/4 tbsp red wine vinegar
- salt and ground black pepper

1 To make the romesco sauce, slit the chillies and remove the seeds, then leave the chillies to soak in warm water for about 30 minutes until soft. Drain the chillies, dry them on kitchen paper and chop finely.

2 Dry-fry the almonds in a frying pan over a medium heat, shaking the pan occasionally, until the nuts are toasted evenly. Transfer the nuts to a food processor or blender.

3 Add 45ml/3 tbsp oil to the frying pan and fry the bread slice until golden on both sides. Lift it out with a slotted spoon and drain on kitchen paper. Tear the bread and add to the food processor or blender. Fry the chopped garlic in the oil remaining in the pan.

4 Add the soaked chillies and tomatoes to the processor or blender. Tip in the garlic, with the oil from the pan and blend the mixture to form a smooth paste.

5 With the motor running, gradually add the remaining olive oil and then the sherry and wine vinegars. When the sauce is smooth and well blended, scrape it into a bowl and season with salt and ground black pepper to taste. Cover with clear film (plastic wrap) and chill for 2 hours.

6 Season the chops with pepper. Heat the olive oil and butter in a heavy frying pan and fry the chops for about 5 minutes each side until golden brown and cooked through.

7 When the chops are almost cooked, transfer the romesco sauce to a pan and heat it gently. If it is too thick, stir in a little boiling water.

8 Serve the sauce with the chops, accompanied by braised cabbage.

Energy 614Kcal/2555kJ; Protein 41.3g; Carbohydrate 6.2g, of which sugars 2.9g; Fat 48.4g, of which saturates 12.6g; Cholesterol 114mg; Calcium 39mg; Fibre 1.3g; Sodium 215mg.

Rabbit Salmorejo

The Carthaginians named Spain "Rabbit Land" and the Romans kept the name, referring to the country as Hispania. The modern name, España, is clearly derived from this old name and serves to remind us how common rabbits are throughout Spain. This is an updated version of one of the classic Mediterranean rabbit stews. Salmorejo indicates pounded garlic, bread and vinegar, while wine is a modern touch.

SERVES FOUR

INGREDIENTS

- 675g/1½lb rabbit, jointed
- 300ml/½ pint/1¼ cups dry white wine
- 15ml/1 tbsp sherry vinegar
- several oregano sprigs
- 2 bay leaves
- 30ml/2 tbsp plain (all-purpose) flour
- 90ml/6 tbsp olive oil
- 175g/6oz baby (pearl) onions, peeled and left whole
- 4 garlic cloves, sliced
- 150ml/¼ pint/⅔ cup chicken stock
- 1 dried chilli, seeded and finely chopped
- 10ml/2 tsp paprika
- salt and ground black pepper
- fresh flat leaf parsley sprigs, to garnish (optional)

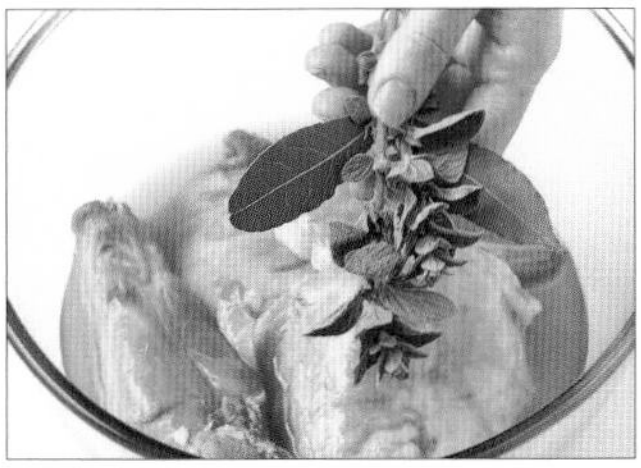

1 Put the rabbit in a bowl. Add the wine, vinegar, oregano and bay leaves and toss together. Marinate for several hours or overnight in the refrigerator.

2 Drain the rabbit, reserving the marinade, and pat it dry with kitchen paper. Season the flour and use to dust the marinated rabbit.

3 Heat the oil in a large, wide flameproof casserole or frying pan. Fry the rabbit pieces until golden on all sides, then remove them and set aside. Fry the onions until they are beginning to colour, then reserve on a separate plate.

4 Add the garlic to the pan and fry, then add the strained marinade, with the chicken stock, chilli and paprika.

5 Return the rabbit to the pan with the onions. Bring to a simmer, then cover and simmer gently for about 45 minutes until the rabbit is tender. Check the seasoning, adding more vinegar and paprika if necessary. Serve the dish garnished with a few sprigs of flat leaf parsley, if you like.

COOK'S TIP

If wished, rather than cooking on the stove, transfer the stew to an ovenproof dish and bake in the oven at 180°C/350°F/Gas 4 for about 50 minutes.

Energy 878Kcal/3656kJ; Protein 31.5g; Carbohydrate 13.8g, of which sugars 7.1g; Fat 25g, of which saturates 5.8g; Cholesterol 147mg; Calcium 102mg; Fibre 0.9g; Sodium 66mg.

Desserts and Baking

Iced desserts were introduced to Spain by the Moors, who also created luxurious dishes of fruit in syrups. Caramel is a much-loved flavour and is used in a winter fruit salad of oranges and a drunken cake soaked in brandy. Custards are also popular and come with a crisp caramel topping or baked with a caramel syrup. As well as desserts there are delicious pastries and cookies, light breakfast rolls and solid, satisfying loaves baked with barley and brown flour.

Rum and Raisin Ice Cream

Helado con ron y pasas is an ice cream with a long tradition in Spain. Dark rum comes from the former Spanish island of Cuba, while the Malaga region produces some of the best Muscatel raisins in the world, huge and black – though from a white grape.

SERVES FOUR TO SIX

INGREDIENTS
- 150g/5oz/1 cup large Muscatel raisins, Malagan if possible
- 60ml/4 tbsp dark rum
- 4 egg yolks
- 75g/3oz/6 tbsp light brown sugar
- 5ml/1 tsp cornflour (cornstarch)
- 300ml/½ pint/1¼ cups full-fat (whole) milk
- 300ml/½ pint/1¼ cups whipping cream
- wafers or biscuits (cookies), to serve

1 Put the raisins in a bowl, add the rum and mix well. Cover and leave to soak for 3–4 hours or overnight.

2 Whisk together the egg yolks, sugar and cornflour in a large bowl until the mixture is thick and foamy. Heat the milk in a large heavy pan to just below boiling point.

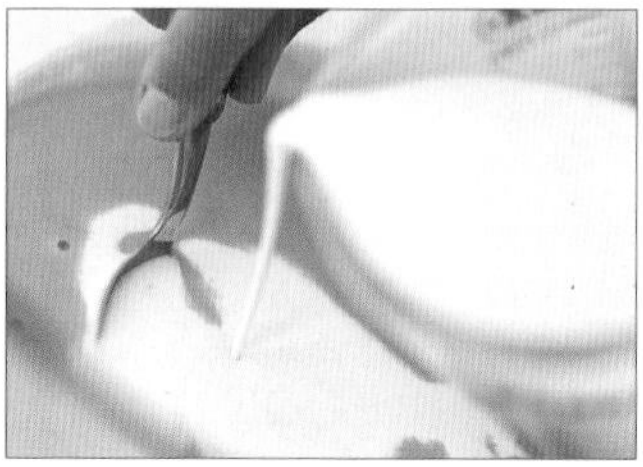

3 Whisk the milk into the eggs, then pour back into the pan. Cook over a gentle heat, stirring with a wooden spoon, until the custard thickens and is smooth. Leave to cool.

4 Whip the cream until it is just thick but still falls from a spoon, then fold it into the cold custard. If you have an ice cream maker, pour the mixture into the machine tub, then churn until thick. Transfer to a freezerproof container. Working by hand, pour the mixture into a plastic tub or similar freezerproof container. Freeze for 4 hours, beating once in a food processor after 2 hours, then beat again after 4 hours.

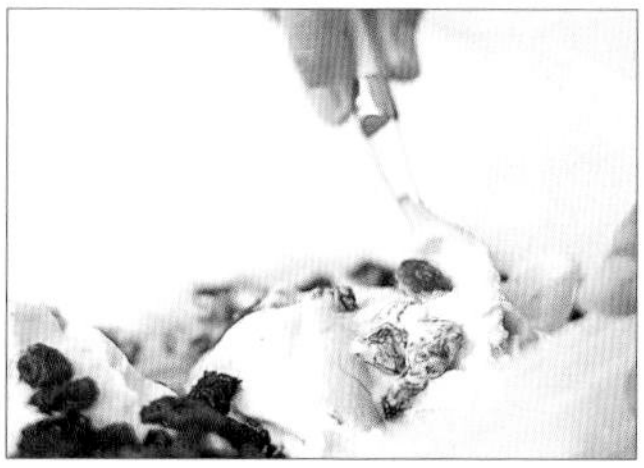

5 Fold the soaked raisins into the soft ice cream, then cover and freeze for 2–3 hours, or until it is firm enough to scoop. Serve in bowls or tall glasses, with wafers or dessert biscuits.

Energy 397Kcal/1654kJ; Protein 5.2g; Carbohydrate 34.9g, of which sugars 34.1g; Fat 24.8g, of which saturates 14.2g; Cholesterol 190mg; Calcium 123mg; Fibre 0.5g; Sodium 56mg.

SORBETE DE LIMÓN

THE MOORS INTRODUCED ICES TO ANDALUCIA A THOUSAND YEARS AGO. EATING THIS SMOOTH, TANGY SORBET, YOU CAN IMAGINE YOURSELF IN A PALACE LIKE THE ONE AT GRANADA, LOUNGING ON SILKEN CUSHIONS, WITH THE STARS ABOVE, NIGHTINGALES SINGING AND THE FOUNTAINS TINKLING.

SERVES SIX

INGREDIENTS
- 200g/7oz/1 cup caster (superfine) sugar
- 300ml/¼l pint/1¼ cups water
- 4 lemons, washed
- 1 large (US extra large) egg white
- a little granulated sugar, for sprinkling

1 Put the sugar and water into a heavy pan and bring slowly to the boil, stirring occasionally, until the sugar has just dissolved.

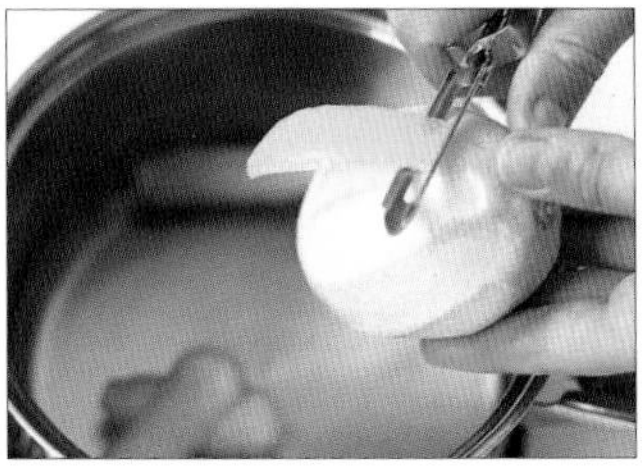

2 Using a swivel vegetable peeler, pare the rind thinly from two of the lemons directly into the pan. Simmer for about 2 minutes without stirring, then remove the pan from the heat. Leave the syrup to cool, then chill.

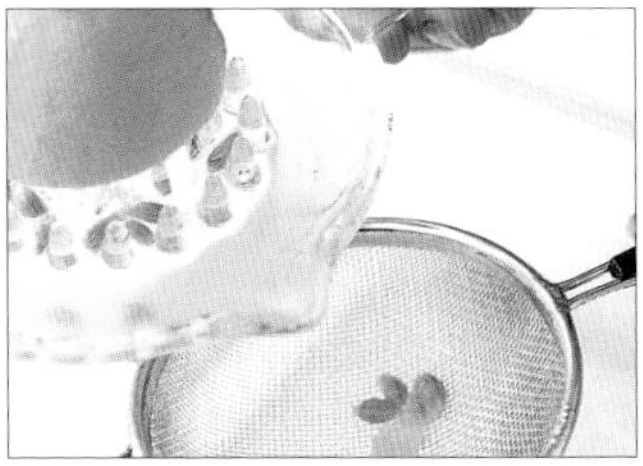

3 Squeeze the juice from all the lemons and carefully strain it into the syrup, making sure all the pips are removed. Take the lemon rind out of the syrup and set it aside until you make the garnish.

4 If you have an ice cream maker, strain the syrup into the machine tub and churn for 10 minutes until thickening.

5 Lightly whisk the egg white with a fork and pour it into the machine. Continue to churn for 10–15 minutes, until firm enough to scoop.

6 Working by hand, strain the syrup into a plastic tub or a similar shallow freezerproof container and freeze for 4 hours, until the mixture is mushy.

7 Scoop the mushy mixture into a food processor and beat until smooth. Lightly whisk the egg white with a fork until it is just frothy. Spoon the sorbet back into its container and beat in the egg white. Return to the freezer for 1 hour.

8 To make the sugared rind garnish, use the blanched rind from step 2. Cut into very thin strips and sprinkle with granulated sugar on a plate. Scoop the sorbet into bowls or glasses and decorate with sugared lemon rind.

VARIATION
Sorbet (sherbet) can be made from any citrus fruit. As a guide, you will need 300ml/½ pint/1¼ cups of fresh fruit juice and the pared rind of half the squeezed fruits. For example, use four oranges or two oranges and two lemons, or, to make a grapefruit sorbet, use the rind of one ruby grapefruit and the juice of two.

Energy 138Kcal/588kJ; Protein 0.9g; Carbohydrate 35.6g, of which sugars 35.6g; Fat 0.1g, of which saturates 0g; Cholesterol 0mg; Calcium 39mg; Fibre 0g; Sodium 13mg.

HONEY-BAKED FIGS WITH HAZELNUT ICE CREAM

TWO WILD INGREDIENTS – FIGS AND HAZELNUTS – ARE USED TO MAKE THIS DELECTABLE DESSERT, HIGOS CON HELADO DE AVELLANA. *FRESH FIGS ARE BAKED IN A LIGHTLY SPICED LEMON AND HONEY SYRUP AND ARE SERVED WITH HOME-MADE ROASTED HAZELNUT ICE CREAM.*

SERVES FOUR

INGREDIENTS

- finely pared rind of 1 lemon
- 1 cinnamon stick, roughly broken
- 60ml/4 tbsp clear honey
- 8 large figs

For the hazelnut ice cream

- 450ml/¾ pint/scant 2 cups double (heavy) cream
- 50g/2oz/¼ cup caster (superfine) sugar
- 3 large (US extra large) egg yolks
- 1.5ml/¼ tsp vanilla essence (extract)
- 75g/3oz/¾ cup hazelnuts

1 Make the ice cream. Gently heat the cream in a pan until almost boiling. Meanwhile, beat the sugar and egg yolks in a bowl until creamy.

2 Pour a little hot cream into the egg yolk mixture and stir with a wooden spoon. Pour back into the pan and mix well. Cook over a low heat, stirring constantly, until the mixture thickens slightly and lightly coats the back of the spoon – do not allow it to boil.

3 Pour the custard into a bowl, stir in the vanilla essence and leave to cool.

4 Preheat the oven to 180°C/350°F/Gas 4. Place the hazelnuts on a baking sheet and roast for 10–12 minutes, or until golden. Leave the nuts to cool, then grind them in a food processor.

5 If you have an ice cream machine, pour in the cold custard and churn until half set. Add the ground hazelnuts and continue to churn until the ice cream is thick. Freeze until firm.

6 Working by hand, pour the custard into a freezerproof container and freeze for 2 hours, or until the custard feels firm around the edges. Turn into a bowl and beat with an electric whisk or turn into a food processor and beat until smooth. Stir in the hazelnuts and freeze until half set. Beat once more, then freeze until firm.

7 Preheat the oven to 200°C/400°F/Gas 6. Remove the ice cream from the freezer and allow to soften slightly.

8 To make the syrup, put the lemon rind, cinnamon stick, honey and 200ml/7fl oz/scant 1 cup water in a small pan and heat slowly until boiling. Simmer the mixture for 5 minutes, then leave to stand for 15 minutes.

9 Using a sharp knife, cut the figs almost into quarters but leaving the figs still attached at the base. Pack them into a casserole, in a single layer, and pour the honey syrup round and over them. Cover the dish tightly with foil and bake for 10 minutes.

10 Arrange the figs on small serving plates, with the cooking syrup poured round them. Serve accompanied by a scoop or two of the ice cream.

COOK'S TIPS

- When toasting the hazelnuts, keep a close eye on them because they can scorch very quickly, spoiling the flavour of the ice cream.
- In southern Spain, red-fleshed figs with a wonderfully sweet flavour grow wild in the scrub.

Energy 1027Kcal/4272kJ; Protein 10.1g; Carbohydrate 76.2g, of which sugars 75.8g; Fat 77.9g, of which saturates 39.6g; Cholesterol 305mg; Calcium 336mg; Fibre 8.1g; Sodium 92mg.

BITTER CHOCOLATE MOUSSES

THE SPANISH INTRODUCED CHOCOLATE TO EUROPE, AND CHOCOLATE MOUSSE REMAINS A FAVOURITE DESSERT IN A COUNTRY THAT USUALLY FAVOURS CUSTARDS AND FRESH FRUIT. THESE DELICIOUS CREMAS DE CHOCOLATE *ARE RICH WITH CHOCOLATE, WITH A HINT OF ORANGE LENT BY THE LIQUEUR.*

SERVES EIGHT

INGREDIENTS

- 225g/8oz dark (bittersweet) chocolate, chopped
- 30ml/2 tbsp orange liqueur or a good Spanish brandy such as Torres
- 50g/2oz/¼ cup unsalted (sweet) butter, cut into small pieces
- 4 large (US extra large) eggs, separated
- 90ml/6 tbsp whipping cream
- 45ml/3 tbsp caster (superfine) sugar

COOK'S TIP

The addition of 1.5ml/¼ tsp cream of tartar to the egg whites helps them to stabilize and hold the volume.

1 Place the chocolate and 60ml/4 tbsp water in a heavy pan. Melt over a low heat, stirring. Off the heat whisk in the orange liqueur or brandy and butter. Beat the egg yolks until thick and creamy, then slowly beat into the melted chocolate until well blended.

2 Whip the cream until soft peaks form, then stir a spoonful into the chocolate mixture to lighten it. Gently fold in the remaining whipped cream.

3 In a clean, grease-free bowl, use an electric mixer to slowly whisk the egg whites until frothy. Increase the speed and continue until the egg whites form soft peaks. Gradually sprinkle the sugar over the egg whites and continue beating until the whites are stiff and glossy. (Be careful not to over-whisk the eggs.)

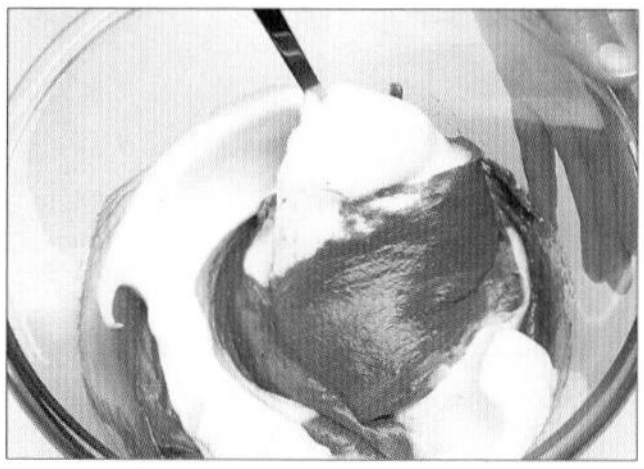

4 Using a rubber spatula or large metal spoon, stir a quarter of the egg whites into the chocolate mixture to lighten it, then gently fold in the remaining whites, cutting down to the bottom of the bowl, along the sides and up to the top in a semicircular motion until they are just combined. Don't worry about a few white streaks.

5 Gently spoon the mixture into eight individual dishes or a 2 litre/3½ pint/8 cup bowl. Chill for at least 2 hours until set before serving.

Energy 300Kcal/1251kJ; Protein 4.8g; Carbohydrate 24.1g, of which sugars 23.8g; Fat 20.3g, of which saturates 11.6g; Cholesterol 122mg; Calcium 34mg; Fibre 0.7g; Sodium 78mg.
Energy 300Kcal/1251kJ; Protein 4.8g; Carbohydrate 24.1g, of which sugars 23.8g; Fat 20.3g, of which saturates 11.6g; Cholesterol 122mg; Calcium 34mg; Fibre 0.7g; Sodium 78mg.

FLAN

THESE LITTLE BAKED CARAMEL CUSTARDS, MADE IN BUCKET-SHAPED MOULDS, ARE THE BEST-KNOWN AND MOST POPULAR OF ALL SPANISH DESSERTS. IF YOU DON'T OWN SMALL MOULDS, YOU CAN MAKE ONE LARGE FLAN INSTEAD BUT IT WILL NEED TO BE COOKED FOR A LITTLE LONGER.

SERVES EIGHT

INGREDIENTS
- 250g/9oz/1¼ cups granulated sugar
- 1 vanilla pod (bean) or 10ml/2 tsp vanilla essence (extract)
- 400ml/14fl oz/1⅔ cups milk
- 250ml/8fl oz/1 cup whipping cream
- 5 large (US extra large) eggs
- 2 egg yolks

1 Select your moulds – eight metal dariole moulds, about 120ml/4fl oz/½ cup each, or a soufflé dish 1 litre/1¾ pints/4 cups in capacity. Arrange in a roasting pan.

2 Put 175g/6oz/⅞ cup of the sugar in a small heavy pan with 60ml/4 tbsp water. Bring to the boil over a high heat, swirling the pan to dissolve the sugar. Boil, without stirring, for about 5 minutes until the syrup turns a dark caramel colour.

3 If using individual moulds, pour a little caramel into each one. If using a single mould, lift it with oven gloves and quickly swirl the dish to coat the base with the caramel. (The caramel will harden quickly as it cools.)

4 Preheat the oven to 160°C/325°F/Gas 3. If using, split the vanilla pod lengthways and scrape out the seeds. Pour the milk and cream into a pan, add the vanilla seeds or essence and bring the mixture close to the boil, stirring. Remove from the heat and allow to stand for 15–20 minutes.

5 In a bowl, whisk the eggs and extra yolks with the remaining sugar for 2–3 minutes until creamy. Whisk in the warm milk and cream mixture, and then strain it into the caramel-lined mould(s). Cover with foil.

6 Pour boiling water into the pan, to come halfway up the sides of the mould(s). Bake until the custard is just set (20–25 minutes for small moulds; about 40 minutes for a large one. A knife inserted to test should come out clean.) Remove from the water, leave to cool, then chill overnight.

7 To turn out, run a palette knife around the custard(s). Cover a large mould with a serving dish and, holding tightly, invert the dish and plate together. Lift one edge of the mould, waiting for the caramel to run down, then remove the mould. Cover the small moulds with saucers and invert them to serve.

Energy 326Kcal/1367kJ; Protein 7.1g; Carbohydrate 35.9g, of which sugars 35.9g; Fat 18.3g, of which saturates 9.8g; Cholesterol 205mg; Calcium 118mg; Fibre 0g; Sodium 77mg.

Crema Catalana

This fabulous Spanish dessert of creamy custard topped with a net of brittle sugar, may well be the original of all crème brûlées. Cremat *is the Catalan word for "burnt", and this was probably part of its original name.*

SERVES FOUR

INGREDIENTS
- 475ml/16fl oz/2 cups milk
- pared rind of ½ lemon
- 1 cinnamon stick
- 4 large egg yolks
- 105ml/7 tbsp caster (superfine) sugar
- 25ml/1½ tbsp cornflour (cornstarch)
- ground nutmeg, for sprinkling

COOK'S TIP

A special tool known as a *quemadora* is sold to caramelize the top of this dessert. A metal disc on a wooden handle is heated like a hot poker, then held over the sugar crust.

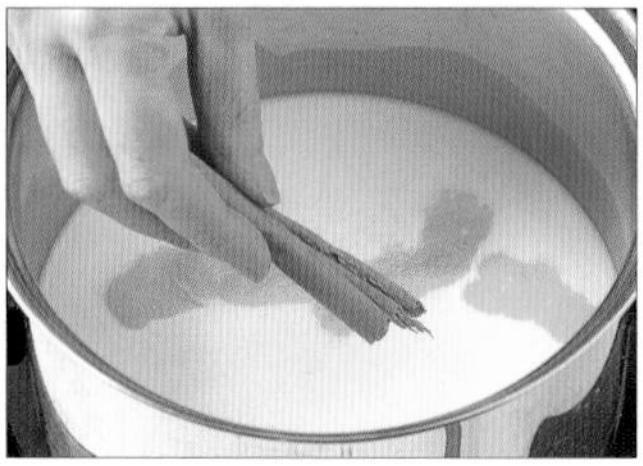

1 Put the milk in a pan with the lemon rind and cinnamon stick. Bring to the boil, then simmer for 10 minutes. Remove the lemon rind and cinnamon. Put the egg yolks and 45ml/3 tbsp sugar in a bowl, and whisk until pale yellow. Add the cornflour and mix well.

2 Stir a few tablespoons of the hot milk into the egg yolk mixture, then tip back into the remaining milk. Return to the heat and cook gently, stirring, for about 5 minutes, until thickened and smooth. Do not boil.

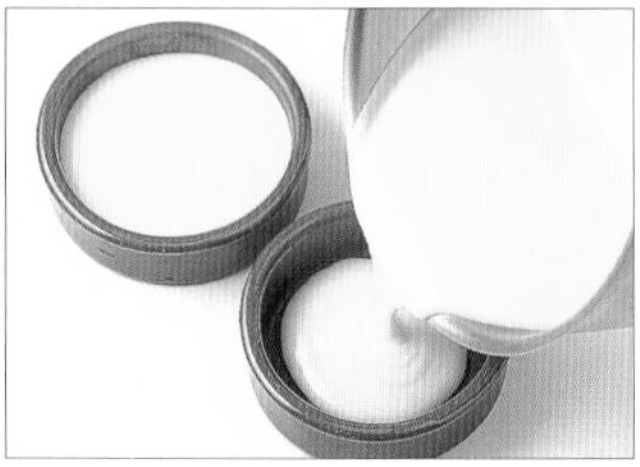

3 Pour the custard into four shallow ovenproof dishes, about 13cm/5in in diameter. Leave to cool, then chill for a few hours, or overnight, until firm.

4 No more than 30 minutes before serving, sprinkle each dessert with 15ml/1 tbsp of the sugar and a little nutmeg. Preheat the grill (broiler) to high. Place the dishes under the grill, on the highest shelf, and cook until the sugar caramelizes. This will only take a few seconds and it will caramelize unevenly. Leave the custards to cool for a few minutes before serving.

Energy 241Kcal/1020kJ; Protein 7.1g; Carbohydrate 38.8g, of which sugars 33g; Fat 7.6g, of which saturates 2.9g; Cholesterol 209mg; Calcium 181mg; Fibre 0g; Sodium 65mg.

ARROPE

THIS IS AN OLD ARAB RECIPE WHOSE NAME MEANS "SYRUP"; THIS VERSION COMES FROM THE PYRENEES REGION. IN SOUTHERN SPAIN, GRAPES, QUINCE AND MELON MIGHT BE USED. ARROPE *STARTS AS A LOVELY FRUIT COMPOTE AND ENDS UP AS A SYRUPY JAM, TO BE SCOOPED UP WITH BREAD.*

SERVES TEN

INGREDIENTS

- 3 firm peaches, unpeeled
- 1kg/2¼lb/5 cups granulated sugar
- 3 large eating apples
- finely grated rind of 1 lemon
- 3 firm pears
- finely grated rind of 1 orange
- 1 small sweet potato, 150g/5oz prepared weight
- 200g/7oz butternut squash, peeled and prepared weight
- 250ml/8fl oz/1 cup dark rum
- 30ml/2 tbsp clear honey

1 Cut the peaches into eighths, without peeling them, and place in the bottom of a large flameproof casserole. Sprinkle with 15ml/1 tbsp of the sugar.

2 Peel and core the apples and cut them into 16 segments, then arrange on top of the peaches. Sprinkle the lemon rind over the top, along with 15ml/1 tbsp of the sugar. Prepare the pears in the same way as the apples, place in the casserole, then sprinkle over the orange rind, followed by 15ml/1 tbsp of the sugar.

3 Slice the sweet potato into pieces half the size of the pears and spread them over the top. Prepare the squash in the same way, layering it on top. Sprinkle with 15ml/1 tbsp of the sugar. Cover with a plate that fits inside the rim, and weigh down with a couple of cans. Stand for a minimum of 2 hours (maximum 12) for juice to form.

4 Remove the cans and plate, put the casserole over a fairly low heat and bring to a simmer. Cook and soften the fruit for 20 minutes, stirring once or twice to prevent sticking.

5 Add the remaining sugar, in three or four batches, stirring to dissolve each batch before adding the next. Bring the mixture up to a rolling boil, over a medium high heat, and boil very steadily for 45 minutes. Stir and lift off any scum.

6 The syrup should be considerably reduced. Test by pouring a spoonful on a plate. It should wrinkle when a spoon is pulled across (like jam in the early stages, before a full set is achieved).

7 Off the heat, add the rum and honey and stir well to combine. Return the casserole to a moderate heat and cook for a further 10 minutes, stirring frequently to prevent the fruit sticking to the base of the pan. The colour will deepen to russet brown. Remove the pan from the heat and set aside to cool.

8 If the resulting compote is a little too stiff, then stir in some more rum before serving.

COOK'S TIP

Arrope is immensely rich, so portions should be small. By the time you reach the bottom of the pot it becomes very thick and sticky, and is best scooped up on bits of bread.

Energy 517Kcal/2200kJ; Protein 1.5g; Carbohydrate 121g, of which sugars 118.6g; Fat 0.2g, of which saturates 0g; Cholesterol 0mg; Calcium 72mg; Fibre 2.7g; Sodium 15mg.

ORANGES WITH CARAMEL WIGS

NARANJAS CON PELUCAS IS A PRETTY VARIATION ON THE NORMAL ORANGE SALAD. THE SLIGHTLY BITTER, CARAMELIZED ORANGE RIND AND SYRUP HAS A WONDERFUL FLAVOUR AND TEXTURE THAT SITS IN PERFECT CONTRAST TO THE SWEET, JUICY ORANGES.

SERVES SIX

INGREDIENTS
- 6 oranges
- 120g/4oz/generous ½ cup caster (superfine) sugar
- 120ml/4fl oz/½ cup boiling water
- cocktail sticks (toothpicks)

1 Using a vegetable peeler, thinly pare the rind off a few of the oranges to make 12 long strips.

2 Using a sharp knife, peel all the oranges, reserving the rind and discarding the pith. Reserve the juice and freeze the oranges separately for 30 minutes.

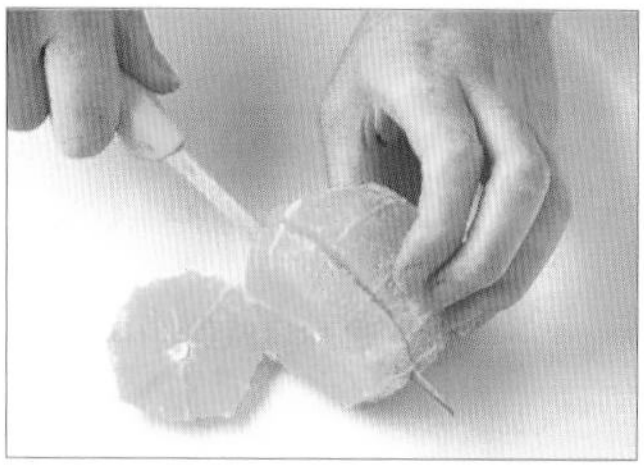

3 Slice the oranges, reform and secure with a cocktail stick (toothpick). Chill.

4 To make the wigs, simmer the rind for about 5 minutes, drain, rinse, and then repeat. Trim with scissors.

5 Put half the sugar into a small pan and add 15ml/1 tbsp water. Heat gently until the mixture caramelizes, shaking the pan a little if one side starts to brown too fast. As soon as the mixture colours, dip the bottom of the pan into cold water. Add 30ml/2 tbsp hot water and the orange rind to the caramel, then stir until the caramel dissolves. Turn the rind on to a plate, to cool.

6 Make a caramel syrup for serving. Put the remaining sugar in a small pan with 15ml/1 tbsp water, and make caramel as before. When it has coloured nicely, stand well back, pour in the boiling water and stir with a wooden spoon to dissolve. Add the reserved juices and pour into a serving jug (pitcher).

7 To serve, arrange the orange strips in a criss-cross pattern on top of each orange. Remove the cocktail sticks and pour a little caramel syrup round the base of each orange.

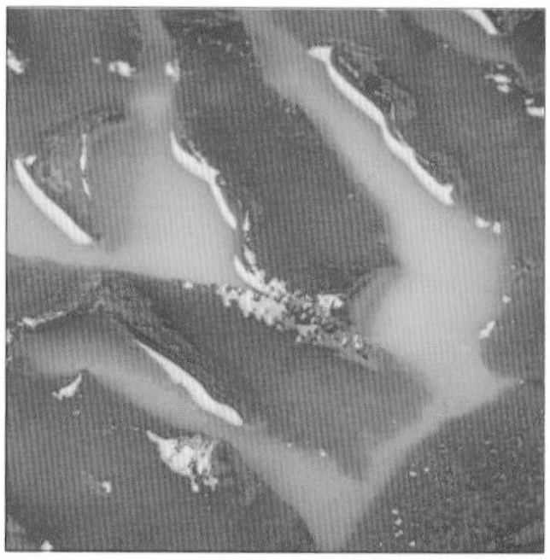

Energy 154Kcal/657kJ; Protein 1.8g; Carbohydrate 38.9g, of which sugars 38.9g; Fat 0.2g, of which saturates 0g; Cholesterol 0mg; Calcium 84mg; Fibre 2.6g; Sodium 9mg.

HAZELNUT MERINGUES WITH NECTARINES

MERINGUES GO BACK TO MOORISH TIMES, AND HAZELNUTS, FROM THE WOODED PYRENEES, ARE A POPULAR FLAVOURING. SERVE THEM AS AN ACCOMPANIMENT TO PEACHES IN SYRUP, OR TRY THEM WITH CREAM WHIPPED WITH MALAGA'S DESSERT WINE, AND STUFFED WITH FRESH NECTARINES.

SERVES FIVE

INGREDIENTS

- 3 large (US extra large) egg whites
- 175g/6oz/generous ¾ cup caster (superfine) sugar
- 50g/2oz/½ cup chopped hazelnuts, toasted
- 300ml/½ pint/1¼ cups double (heavy) cream
- 60ml/4 tbsp sweet Malaga dessert wine
- 2 nectarines, stoned (pitted) and sliced
- fresh mint sprigs, to decorate

COOK'S TIP

Peaches can be used in place of the nectarines, but are better peeled. To remove the skins, place the peaches in a bowl and pour over boiling water to cover. Leave to stand for a few minutes, then drain. The skins should peel off very easily.

1 Preheat the oven to 140°C/275°F/Gas 1. Line two large baking sheets with baking parchment.

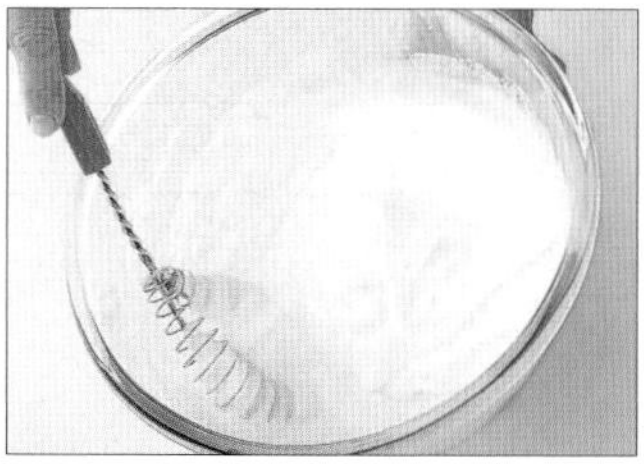

2 Whisk the egg whites in a grease-free bowl until they form stiff peaks when the whisks are lifted. Gradually whisk in the caster sugar a spoonful at a time, until a stiff, glossy meringue forms.

3 Using a large metal spoon, gently fold two-thirds of the chopped toasted hazelnuts into the whisked egg whites.

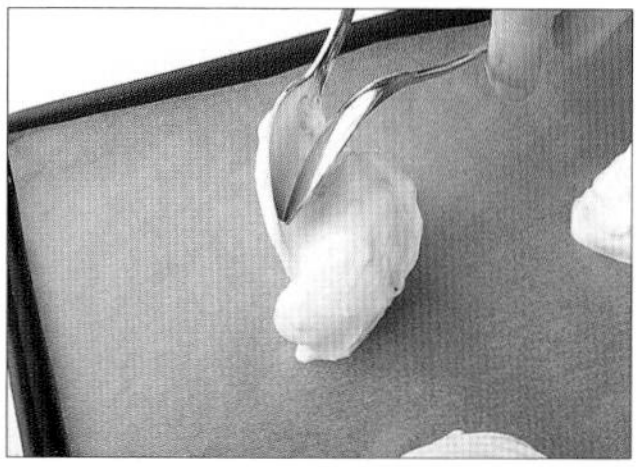

4 Divide the meringue mixture between the baking sheets, spooning five ovals on to each one. Scatter the remaining toasted hazelnuts over the meringues on one baking sheet, then flatten the tops of the others using the back of a spoon.

5 Bake the meringues for 1–1¼ hours until crisp and dry, then lift them off the baking parchment and leave to cool.

6 Put the cream and dessert wine in a bowl and whisk to form soft peaks. Spoon some of the cream on to each of the plain meringues. Arrange a few nectarine slices on each.

7 Put one cream-topped meringue and one nut-topped meringue on each dessert plate. Garnish with fresh mint and serve immediately.

Energy 542Kcal/2259kJ; Protein 5g; Carbohydrate 44.3g, of which sugars 44.1g; Fat 38.6g, of which saturates 20.5g; Cholesterol 82mg; Calcium 69mg; Fibre 1.4g; Sodium 52mg.

Citrus Fruit Flambé with Pistachio Praline

A fruit flambé makes a dramatic finale for a dinner party. Topping this refreshing citrus fruit dessert with crunchy pistachio praline makes it extra special.

SERVES FOUR

INGREDIENTS
- 4 oranges
- 2 ruby grapefruit
- 2 limes
- 50g/2oz/¼ cup butter
- 50g/2oz/⅓ cup light muscovado (brown) sugar
- 45ml/3 tbsp Cointreau
- fresh mint sprigs, to decorate

For the praline
- oil, for greasing
- 115g/4oz/½ cup caster (superfine) sugar
- 50g/2oz/½ cup pistachio nuts

1 First, make the pistachio praline. Brush a baking sheet lightly with oil. Place the caster sugar and nuts in a small heavy pan and cook gently, swirling the pan occasionally until the sugar has melted.

2 Continue to cook over a fairly low heat until the nuts start to pop and the sugar has turned a dark golden colour. Pour on to the oiled baking sheet and set aside to cool. Using a sharp knife, chop the praline into rough chunks.

3 Cut off all the rind and pith from the citrus fruit. Holding each fruit in turn over a large bowl, cut between the membranes so that the segments fall into the bowl, with any juice.

4 Heat the butter and muscovado sugar together in a heavyd frying pan until the sugar has melted and the mixture is golden. Strain the citrus juices into the pan and continue to cook, stirring occasionally, until the juice has reduced and is syrupy.

5 Add the fruit segments and warm through without stirring. Pour over the Cointreau and set it alight. As soon as the flames die down, spoon the fruit flambé into serving dishes. Scatter some praline over each portion and decorate with mint. Serve at once.

Energy 446Kcal/1872kJ; Protein 4.8g; Carbohydrate 65.2g, of which sugars 64.8g; Fat 17.4g, of which saturates 7.4g; Cholesterol 27mg; Calcium 127mg; Fibre 4.4g; Sodium 155mg.

Cold Lemon Soufflé with Caramelized Almond Topping

This terrific-to-look-at, refreshing dessert soufflé is light and luscious.

SERVES SIX

INGREDIENTS
- oil, for greasing
- grated rind and juice of 3 large lemons
- 5 large (US extra large) eggs, separated
- 115g/4oz/½ cup caster (superfine) sugar
- 25ml/1½ tbsp powdered gelatine
- 450ml/¾ pint/scant 2 cups double (heavy) cream

For the decoration
- 75g/3oz/¾ cup flaked almonds
- 75g/3oz/¾ cup icing (confectioners') sugar
- 3 physalis

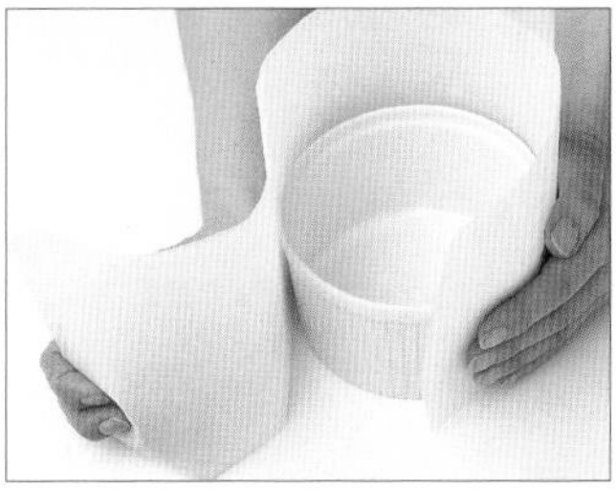

1 Make the soufflé collar. Cut a strip of baking parchment long enough to fit around a 900ml/1½ pint/3¾ cup soufflé dish and wide enough to extend 7.5cm/3in above the rim. Fit the strip around the dish, tape, then tie it around the top of the dish with string. Brush the inside of the paper lightly with oil.

2 Put the lemon rind and egg yolks in a bowl. Add 75g/3oz/6 tbsp of the caster sugar and whisk until light and creamy.

3 Place the lemon juice in a small heatproof bowl and sprinkle over the gelatine. Set aside for 5 minutes, then place the bowl in a pan of simmering water. Heat, stirring occasionally, until the gelatine has dissolved. Cool slightly, then stir the gelatine mixture into the egg yolk mixture.

4 In a separate bowl, lightly whip the cream to soft peaks. Fold into the egg yolk mixture and set aside.

5 Whisk the egg whites in a grease-free bowl until stiff peaks form. Gradually whisk in the remaining caster sugar until the mixture is stiff and glossy. Quickly and lightly fold the whites into the yolk mixture. Pour into the prepared dish, smooth the surface and chill for 4–5 hours or until set.

6 Make the decoration. Brush a baking sheet lightly with oil. Preheat the grill (broiler). Scatter the almonds over the sheet and sift the icing sugar over. Grill (broil) until the nuts are golden and the sugar has caramelized. Allow to cool, then remove the mixture from the tray with a palette knife and break it into pieces.

7 When the soufflé has set, carefully peel off the paper. Pile the caramelized almonds on top of the soufflé and decorate with the physalis.

Energy 647Kcal/2686kJ; Protein 10.3g; Carbohydrate 35.2g, of which sugars 34.9g; Fat 52.8g, of which saturates 27.2g; Cholesterol 293mg; Calcium 112mg; Fibre 0.9g; Sodium 90mg.

Apple-Stuffed Crêpes

Spain's dairy country lies along the cooler northern coast and crêpes are extremely popular there. The Asturias, which run east to west along the coast, are apple and cider country, too, and crêpes, which are known as FRISUELOS, *are made with a variety of sweet fillings, such as this succulent apple one.*

SERVES FOUR

INGREDIENTS

- 115g/4oz/1 cup plain (all-purpose) flour
- pinch of salt
- 2 large (US extra large) eggs
- 175ml/6fl oz/¾ cup milk
- 120ml/4fl oz/½ cup sweet cider
- butter, for frying
- 4 eating apples
- 60ml/4 tbsp caster (superfine) sugar
- 120ml/8 tbsp clear honey, and 150ml/¼ pint/⅔ cup double (heavy) cream, to serve

COOK'S TIP

For the best results, use full-fat (whole) milk in the batter.

1 Make the batter. Sift the flour and salt into a large bowl. Add the eggs and milk and beat until smooth. Stir in the cider. Leave to stand for 30 minutes.

2 Heat a small heavy non-stick frying pan. Add a little butter and ladle in enough batter to coat the pan thinly.

3 Cook the crêpe for about 1 minute until it is golden underneath, then flip it over and cook the other side until golden. Slide the crêpe on to a plate, then repeat with the remaining batter to make seven more. Set the crêpes aside and keep warm.

4 Make the apple filling. Core the apples and cut them into thick slices. Heat 15g/½oz butter in a large frying pan. Add the apples to the pan and cook until golden on both sides. Transfer the slices to a bowl with a slotted spoon and sprinkle with sugar.

5 Fold each pancake in half, then fold in half again to form a cone. Fill each with some of the fried apples. Place two filled pancakes on each dessert plate. Drizzle with a little honey and serve at once, accompanied by cream.

Energy 344Kcal/1461kJ; Protein 7.8g; Carbohydrate 72.1g, of which sugars 50.2g; Fat 4g, of which saturates 1.3g; Cholesterol 98mg; Calcium 122mg; Fibre 2.3g; Sodium 63mg.

TORRIJAS

Translated as "poor knights", these sugared toasts are perfect for almost every occasion. They make a good tea-time snack for children, or to accompany a cup of hot chocolate. As a party dessert they are the equivalent of France's toasted brioche – an accompaniment to ice cream, or to any baked fruit. They are also very popular by themselves.

SERVES FOUR

INGREDIENTS
- 120ml/4fl oz/½ cup white wine
- 2 large eggs
- 12 thick rounds of stale French bread
- 60–90ml/4–6 tbsp sunflower oil
- ground cinnamon, and caster (superfine) sugar, for dusting

COOK'S TIP
These toasts are often enjoyed at festivals and are a typical dish from Madrid (although variations can be found all over Europe). Milk can be used in place of white wine, if liked, making them suitable for children.

1 Pour the wine into a shallow dish and dip the bread rounds into it.

2 Beat the eggs together in another shallow dish. Dip half the bread rounds into the beaten egg on each side so that they are completely covered.

3 Heat 60ml/4 tbsp oil in a pan until very hot and fry the bread rounds for about 1 minute on each side until crisp and golden. Reserve on kitchen paper, then dip and fry the rest, adding more oil if necessary. Serve hot, sprinkled with cinnamon and sugar.

Energy 419Kcal/1763kJ; Protein 12.2g; Carbohydrate 56.3g, of which sugars 3g; Fat 15.7g, of which saturates 2.4g; Cholesterol 95mg; Calcium 138mg; Fibre 2.4g; Sodium 652mg.

Leche Frita with Black Fruit Sauce

The name of this dessert means "fried milk", but it is really custard squares. It is very popular in the Basque country, and has a melting, creamy centre and crunchy, golden coating. Here, it is served hot with a dark fruit sauce, but it is also good cold.

SERVES SIX TO EIGHT

INGREDIENTS

- 550ml/18fl oz/2½ cups full-fat (whole) milk
- 3 finely pared strips of lemon rind
- ½ cinnamon stick
- 90g/3½oz/½ cup caster (superfine) sugar, plus extra for sprinkling
- 60ml/4 tbsp cornflour (cornstarch)
- 30ml/2 tbsp plain (all-purpose) flour
- 3 large (US extra large) egg yolks
- 2 large (US extra large) eggs
- 90–120ml/6–8 tbsp stale breadcrumbs or dried crumbs
- sunflower oil, for frying
- ground cinnamon, for dusting

For the sauce

- 450g/1lb blackcurrants or blackberries
- 90g/3½oz/½ cup granulated sugar, plus extra for dusting

1 Put the milk, lemon rind, cinnamon stick and sugar in a pan and bring to the boil, stirring gently. Cover and leave to infuse for 20 minutes.

2 Put the cornflour and flour in a bowl and beat in the egg yolks with a wooden spoon. Add a little of the milk and beat to make a smooth batter.

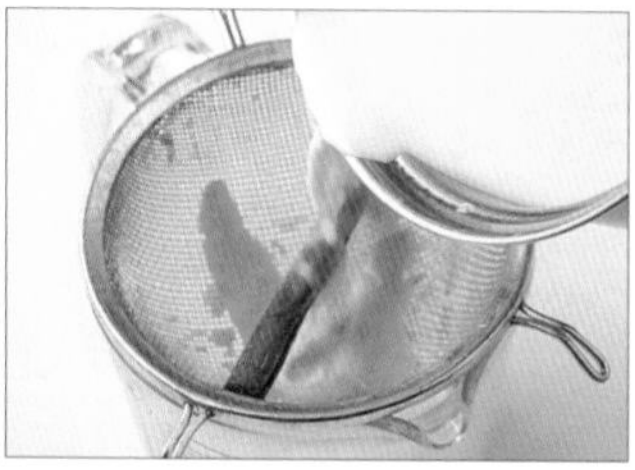

3 Strain the remaining hot milk into the batter, then pour back into the pan. Cook over a low heat, stirring constantly. (The mixture won't curdle, but it will thicken unevenly if you let it.) Cook for a couple of minutes, until it thickens and separates from the side of the pan.

4 Beat the mixture hard with the spoon to ensure a really smooth consistency. Pour into an 18–20cm/7–8in, 1cm/½in-deep rectangular dish, and smooth the top. Cool, then chill until firm.

5 Make the fruit sauce. Cook the blackcurrants or blackberries with the sugar and a little water for about 10 minutes until soft.

6 Reserve 30–45ml/2–3 tbsp whole currants or berries, then put the rest in a food processor and blend to make a smooth purée. Return the purée and berries to the pan.

7 Cut the chilled custard into eight or twelve squares. Beat the eggs in a shallow dish and spread out the breadcrumbs on a plate. Lift half of the squares with a metal spatula into the egg. Coat on both sides, then lift into the crumbs and cover all over. Repeat with the second batch of squares.

8 Pour about 1cm/½in oil into a deep frying pan and heat until very hot.

9 Lift two or three coated squares with a palette knife (metal spatula) into the oil and fry for a couple of minutes, shaking or spooning the oil over the top, until golden. Reserve on kitchen paper, while frying the other batches.

10 To serve, arrange the custard squares on plates and sprinkle with sugar and cinnamon. Pour a circle of warm sauce round the squares, distributing the whole berries evenly.

COOK'S TIP

In Spain, milk is usually drunk at breakfast or used for cheese. In northern Spain, the milk has a wonderful quality and has been given special status as a dessert ingredient. Most popular of all the milk desserts are *leche frita, flan* and *filloas* (thin pancakes).

Energy 257Kcal/1089kJ; Protein 6.9g; Carbohydrate 45.9g, of which sugars 30.6g; Fat 6.4g, of which saturates 2.7g; Cholesterol 133mg; Calcium 159mg; Fibre 2.3g; Sodium 143mg.

GUIRLACHE

This is an Arab sweetmeat from the Pyrenees, combining toasted nuts and caramel to produce a crisp nut brittle – a forerunner of some familiar chocolate bar fillings. It is less well known than turrón, the Spanish Christmas nougat, which is made with similar ingredients and is widely available commercially.

MAKES ABOUT 24 PIECES

INGREDIENTS
- 115g/4oz/1 cup almonds, half blanched, half unblanched
- 115g/4oz/1 cup hazelnuts, half blanched, half unblanched
- 5ml/1 tsp almond oil or a flavourless oil
- 200g/7oz/1 cup granulated sugar
- 15ml/1 tbsp lemon juice

COOK'S TIP
Guirlache may be served as an after-dinner treat. It is also very good pulverized and used as a topping for mousses and whipped cream. It also makes wonderful ice cream.

1 Preheat the oven to 150°C/300°F/ Gas 2. Scatter the nuts on a baking sheet and toast for about 30 minutes, shaking the sheet occasionally. The nuts should smell pleasant and have turned brown and be very dry.

2 Coarsely chop the toasted nuts or crush them roughly with a rolling pin. Cover another baking tray with foil and grease it generously with the oil.

3 Put the sugar in a pile in a small pan and pour the lemon juice round it. Cook over a high heat, shaking the pan, until the sugar turns a coffee colour. (As it cooks, the pile of sugar will melt and collapse into caramel.)

4 Immediately tip in the nuts and stir once, then pour the mixture on to the foil and spread out into a thin, even layer. Leave the mixture to harden.

5 Once set, break up the caramel into pieces and store in an airtight tin.

Energy 94Kcal/395kJ; Protein 1.7g; Carbohydrate 9.3g, of which sugars 9.1g; Fat 5.8g, of which saturates 0.5g; Cholesterol 0mg; Calcium 23mg; Fibre 0.7g; Sodium 1mg.

PANELLETS

THE CATALAN NAME FOR THESE NUTTY FESTIVAL CAKES MEANS "LITTLE BREAD", BUT THEY ARE, IN FACT, MUCH CLOSER TO MARZIPAN, WITH A SLIGHTLY SOFT CENTRE THAT IS PRODUCED BY THEIR SECRET INGREDIENT – SWEET POTATO. PATISSERIES MAKE HUNDREDS OF THESE LITTLE CAKES FOR ALL SAINTS' DAY, ON 1ST NOVEMBER, WHEN FAMILIES TAKE FLOWERS TO THE GRAVEYARDS.

MAKES ABOUT 24

INGREDIENTS

- 115g/4oz sweet potato
- butter, for greasing
- 1 large (US extra large) egg, separated
- 225g/8oz/2 cups ground almonds
- 200g/7oz/1 cup caster (superfine) sugar, plus extra for sprinkling
- finely grated rind of 1 small lemon
- 7.5ml/1½ tsp vanilla essence (extract)
- 60ml/4 tbsp pine nuts
- 60ml/4 tbsp pistachio nuts, chopped

1 Dice the sweet potato, and cook it in a pan of boiling water for 15 minutes, or until soft. Drain and leave to cool.

2 Preheat the oven to 200°C/400°F/Gas 6. Line one or two baking sheets with foil and grease well with butter.

3 Put the cooled sweet potato in a food processor and process to make a smooth purée, then work in the egg yolk, ground almonds, sugar, lemon rind and vanilla essence to make a soft dough. Transfer the dough to a bowl and chill for 30 minutes.

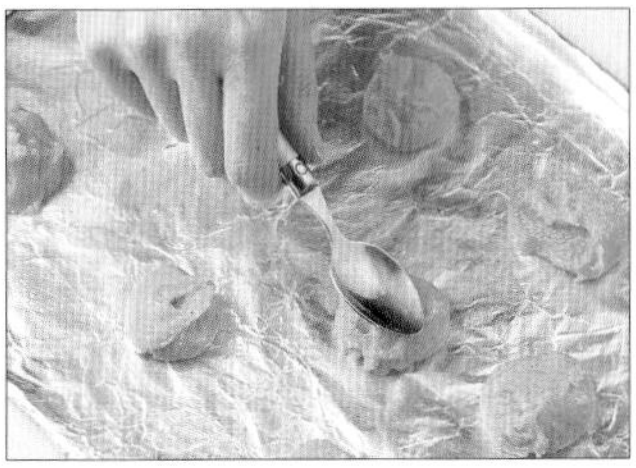

4 Spoon walnut-sized balls of dough on to the foil, spacing them about 2.5cm/1in apart, then flatten them out slightly.

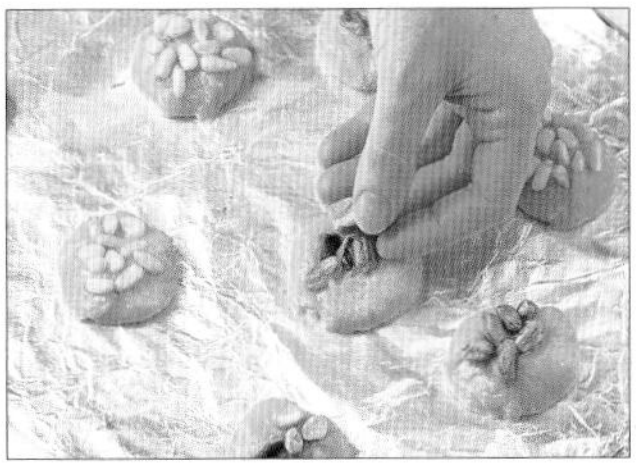

5 Lightly beat the egg white and brush over the cakes. Sprinkle half the cakes with pine nuts, slightly less than 5ml/1 tsp each, and half with pistachio nuts. Sprinkle lightly with sugar and bake for 10 minutes, or until lightly browned.

6 Leave to cool on the foil, then lift off with a metal spatula.

Energy 123Kcal/515kJ; Protein 2.9g; Carbohydrate 10.6g, of which sugars 9.6g; Fat 8g, of which saturates 0.7g; Cholesterol 8mg; Calcium 30mg; Fibre 0.9g; Sodium 20mg.

PESTIÑOS

THE ARABS INVENTED ALL SORTS OF SWEET BITES, TO EAT AFTER THE MAIN COURSE OR WITH DRINKS. BATHED IN SCENTED HONEY SYRUP, PESTIÑOS *WERE OFTEN DEEP-FRIED AND KNOWN AS* DULCES DE SÁRTEN, *WHICH MEANS "SWEETS FROM THE FRYING PAN". HOWEVER, AT HOME IT IS A GOOD DEAL EASIER TO BAKE THEM AND THEY PUFF BEAUTIFULLY IN THE OVEN.*

MAKES ABOUT THIRTY

INGREDIENTS

- 225g/8oz/2 cups plain (all-purpose) flour, plus extra for dusting
- 60ml/4 tbsp sunflower oil
- 15ml/1 tbsp aniseed, lightly crushed
- 45ml/3 tbsp caster (superfine) sugar
- 250ml/8fl oz/1 cup water
- 60ml/4 tbsp anisette
- 3 small (US medium) eggs

For the anis syrup

- 60ml/4 tbsp clear honey
- 60ml/4 tbsp anisette

1 Preheat the oven to 190°C/375°F/Gas 5. Sift the flour on to a sheet of baking parchment. Heat the oil in a small pan with the crushed aniseed, until the aniseed releases its aroma. Strain the oil into a larger pan and add the sugar, water and anisette. Heat to a rolling boil.

2 Remove the pan from the heat and add the sifted flour, all in one go. Beat vigorously with a wooden spoon until the mixture leaves the sides of the pan clean. Leave to cool.

3 Meanwhile lightly beat the eggs. Gradually incorporate the egg into the dough mixture, beating hard. You may not need to use all the egg – the paste should be soft but not sloppy. Reserve any remaining beaten egg.

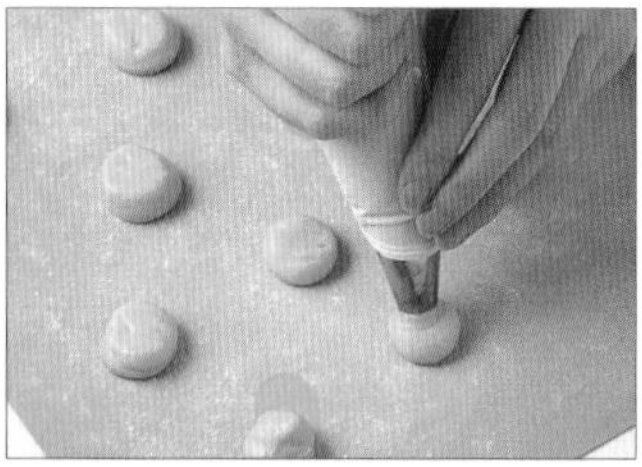

4 Grease and flour two baking sheets. Fit a plain nozzle to a piping (pastry) bag and pipe small rounds of dough about 2.5cm/1in across on the sheets, spacing them about 2.5cm/1in apart. Brush with the remaining beaten egg.

5 Bake for about 30 minutes, or until lightly brown and an even texture right through. (Lift one off the sheet to test.)

6 Melt the honey in a small pan and stir in the anisette. Just before serving, use a slotted spoon to dunk the *pestiños* into the syrup.

COOK'S TIP

Anisette is a sweet aniseed liqueur that gives the syrup a wonderful flavour. If you cannot find anisette, use another anis spirit such as Ricard instead.

Energy 67Kcal/280kJ; Protein 1.3g; Carbohydrate 8.9g, of which sugars 3.2g; Fat 2.1g, of which saturates 0.3g; Cholesterol 19mg; Calcium 14mg; Fibre 0.2g; Sodium 8mg.

CHURROS

This Spanish breakfast doughnut is sold in all tapas bars, which so conveniently transform into cafés in the morning. Freshly fried, churros accompany a cup of hot chocolate or coffee. They are also served as festival fare, piped into great vats of oil, cut into loops, then tied with grass string and sold to eat while walking along.

MAKES TWELVE TO FIFTEEN

INGREDIENTS
- 200g/7oz/1¾ cups plain (all-purpose) flour
- 1.5ml/¼ tsp salt
- 30ml/2 tbsp caster (superfine) sugar
- 250ml/8fl oz/1 cup water
- 60ml/4 tbsp olive or sunflower oil
- 1 egg, beaten
- caster (superfine) sugar and ground cinnamon, for dusting
- oil, for deep-frying

1 Sift the flour, salt and sugar on to a plate or piece of baking parchment. Put the water and oil in a pan and bring to the boil.

2 Tip the flour mixture into the pan and beat with a wooden spoon until the mixture forms a stiff paste. Leave to cool for 2 minutes, then gradually beat in the egg to make a smooth dough.

3 Oil a large baking sheet. Sprinkle plenty of sugar on to a plate and stir in a little cinnamon.

4 Spoon the dough into a large piping (pastry) bag fitted with a 1cm/½in plain piping nozzle. Pipe little coils or "S" shapes on to the baking sheet.

5 Heat 5cm/2in of oil in a large pan to 168°C/336°F, or until a little piece of dough dropped into the oil sizzles on the surface.

6 Using an oiled metal spatula, lower several of the piped shapes into the oil and fry for about 2 minutes until light golden.

7 Drain the churros on kitchen paper, then dip them into the sugar and cinnamon mixture, to coat. Cook the remaining churros in the same way and serve immediately.

Energy 111Kcal/464kJ; Protein 1.7g; Carbohydrate 12.5g, of which sugars 2.3g; Fat 6.4g, of which saturates 0.9g; Cholesterol 13mg; Calcium 22mg; Fibre 0.4g; Sodium 5mg.

Basque Apple Tart

Tarta de Manzana or pastel vasco, as it is also known, is made with a heavy sweet pastry, which has the texture and taste of cake. It often has a custard centre. This one has an apple filling, but other fresh fruit, such as apricots or plums, work just as well.

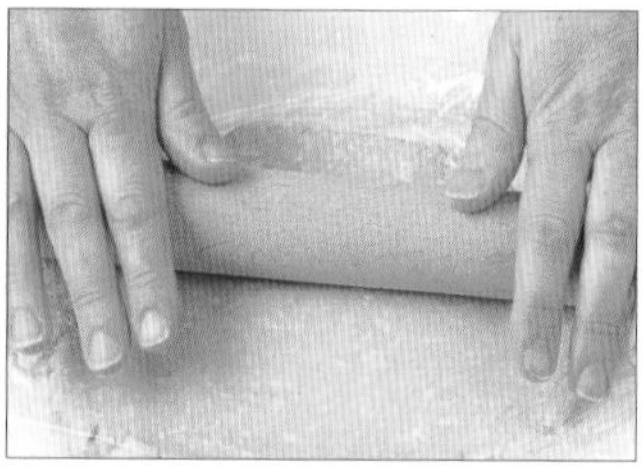

4 Place the larger piece of dough on a lightly floured piece of clear film (plastic wrap) and cover with another piece of film. Roll out to a 25cm/10in round. Remove the top layer of film and lift up the dough on the second film. Place the dough face down in the tin and peel off the film. Press into the tin so that it stands just clear of the top.

SERVES SIX

INGREDIENTS

- 215g/7½oz/scant 2 cups plain (all-purpose) flour, plus extra for rolling
- 5ml/1 tsp baking powder
- pinch of salt
- 115g/4oz/½ cup cold unsalted (sweet) butter, cubed
- finely grated rind of ½ lemon
- 75g/3oz/scant ½ cup caster (superfine) sugar, plus extra for sprinkling
- 2 small (US medium) eggs
- 3 eating apples, peeled, cored and cubed
- ground cinnamon, for sprinkling
- whipped cream, to serve

1 Sift the flour, baking powder and salt into a food processor. Add the butter and grated lemon rind and process briefly to combine, then add the sugar, 1 whole egg and the yolk of the second egg to the flour mixture and process to make a soft dough.

2 Divide the dough into two pieces, one portion nearly double the size of the other. Pat the dough into two flat cakes. Wrap tightly in clear film (plastic wrap) and chill for at least 2 hours until firm.

3 Preheat the oven to 180°C/350°F/Gas 4. Place a baking sheet in the oven and grease a 20cm/8in loose-based flan tin (tart pan).

5 Pack the tin with the apples and sprinkle with cinnamon. Roll out the second piece of dough in the same way, to exactly the same size as the tin. Lay the dough on top of the apples and fold the overlapping edges of the bottom piece of dough inward. Gently press the edges together with a fork, to seal.

6 Prick the dough a few times, brush with egg white and sprinkle with sugar. Place on the hot baking sheet and bake for 20 minutes, then reduce the temperature to 160°C/325°F/Gas 3 for a further 25–30 minutes until golden.

7 Leave the tart to cool in the tin for 30 minutes, then unmould and cool on a wire rack. Serve with whipped cream.

Energy 368Kcal/1545kJ; Protein 6.8g; Carbohydrate 45.5g, of which sugars 18.2g; Fat 19.1g, of which saturates 10.8g; Cholesterol 136mg; Calcium 77mg; Fibre 1.9g; Sodium 154mg.

BISCOCHO BORRACHO

THE NAME OF THIS MOIST, NUTTY DESSERT TRANSLATES AS "DRUNKEN CAKE", INDICATING THAT IT IS SOAKED IN BRANDY-FLAVOURED SYRUP. THE CAKE CAN BE LAYERED WITH CREAM, BUT THIS VERSION IS MADE IN A MOULD, THEN TURNED OUT. PIPE WITH WHIPPED CREAM IF YOU LIKE.

SERVES SIX TO EIGHT

INGREDIENTS

- butter, for greasing
- 90g/3½oz/¾ cup plain (all-purpose) flour
- 6 large (US extra large) eggs
- 90g/3½oz/½ cup caster (superfine) sugar
- finely grated rind of 1 lemon
- 90ml/6 tbsp toasted flaked almonds
- 250ml/8fl oz/1 cup whipping cream, to serve

For the syrup

- 115g/4oz/generous ½ cup caster (superfine) sugar
- 120ml/4fl oz/½ cup boiling water
- 105ml/7 tbsp Spanish brandy

1 Starting 1–2 days ahead, preheat the oven to 200°C/400°F/Gas 6. Butter a shallow tin (pan), about 28 × 18cm/ 11 × 7in. Line the tin with baking parchment and butter well.

2 Sift the flour a couple of times into a bowl. Separate the eggs, putting the whites into a large bowl. Put the yolks in a food processor with the sugar and lemon rind and beat until light. Whisk the whites to soft peaks, then work a little white into the yolk mixture.

3 Dribble two spoonfuls of the yolk mixture across the whites, sift some flour over the top and cut in gently with a large spoon. Continue folding together in this way until all the egg yolk mixture and flour have been incorporated.

4 Turn the mixture into the prepared tin and smooth over. Bake for 12 minutes. Leave the cake to set for 5 minutes, then turn out on to a wire rack. Peel off the paper and leave to cool completely.

5 Make the syrup. Place 50g/2oz/¼ cup sugar into a small pan and add 15ml/ 1 tbsp water. Heat until it caramelizes, shaking the pan a little if one side starts to brown too fast. As soon as it colours, dip the base of the pan into a bowl of cold water. Add the remaining sugar and pour in the boiling water. Bring back to a simmer, stirring until the sugar has dissolved. Pour into a jug (pitcher) and add the brandy.

6 Put the cake back into the tin and drizzle half the syrup over it. Choose a 700ml/1½ pint/3 cup capacity mould or tin; cut the cake into scallops with a spoon and layer half into the bottom of it. Scatter 30ml/2 tbsp almonds over the top, and push them down the cracks. Top with the remaining cake and nuts.

7 Pour the remaining syrup over the cake, cover with foil and weight down the top. Chill until ready to serve.

8 To serve, whip the cream. Run a knife round the mould and turn the cake out on to a long dish. Scatter with almonds and serve with the cream.

Energy 414Kcal/1728kJ; Protein 8.9g; Carbohydrate 37.7g, of which sugars 28.8g; Fat 23.2g, of which saturates 9.6g; Cholesterol 176mg; Calcium 96mg; Fibre 1.2g; Sodium 64mg.

BREAKFAST ENSAIMADAS

Originally from Majorca these snail-shaped buns, made of the lightest possible dough, are a delicious traditional treat. They are now eaten in Madrid and throughout southern and eastern Spain for breakfast. Traditionally lard or saim, as it is known in Spain, was used to brush over the tops, but nowadays butter is used and adds a delicious richness.

MAKES SIXTEEN ROLLS

INGREDIENTS

- 225g/8oz/2 cups unbleached strong white bread flour
- 2.5ml/½ tsp salt
- 50g/2oz/¼ cup caster (superfine) sugar
- 15g/½ oz fresh yeast
- 75ml/5 tbsp lukewarm milk
- 1 egg
- 30ml/2 tbsp sunflower oil
- 50g/2oz/¼ cup butter, melted
- icing (confectioners') sugar, for dusting

COOK'S TIP

Coating the dough with butter helps to separate the coils as they expand.

1 Lightly grease two baking sheets. Sift the flour and salt together in a large mixing bowl and add the sugar.

2 In a small bowl, cream the yeast and lukewarm milk together. Pour the mixture into the centre of the flour, then sprinkle a little of the flour evenly over the top of the liquid. Leave in a warm place for about 15 minutes until frothy.

3 Turn the mixture into a food processor and process briefly to combine. In a small bowl, beat together the egg and sunflower oil, then pour the mixture into the food processor and work to a smooth dough. Process the dough for several minutes, until it becomes smooth and elastic.

4 Put the dough in a lightly oiled bowl, cover with clear film (plastic wrap) and leave to rise, in a warm place, for 1 hour, or until doubled in size.

5 Put the dough in the food processor and use the pulse button to work until smooth. Turn out on to a lightly floured surface and divide into 16 equal pieces.

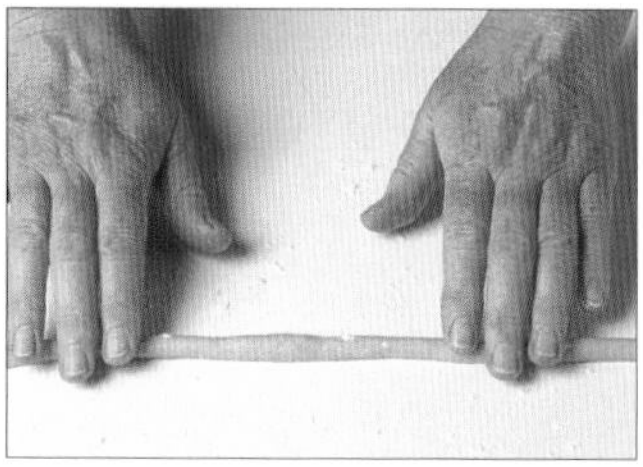

6 Shape each piece of dough into a thin rope about 38cm/15in long. Pour the melted butter on to a plate and dip each piece of dough into it to coat.

7 On the baking sheets, curl each rope into a loose spiral, spacing them well apart. Tuck the ends under to seal. Cover with clear film and leave to rise, in a warm place, for about 45 minutes, or until doubled in size.

8 Preheat the oven to 190°C/375°F/Gas 5. Brush the rolls with water and dust with icing sugar. Bake for about 10 minutes, or until light golden brown. Cool on a wire rack. Dust again with icing sugar and serve warm.

Energy 103Kcal/431kJ; Protein 1.9g; Carbohydrate 14.4g, of which sugars 3.7g; Fat 4.6g, of which saturates 2g; Cholesterol 19mg; Calcium 29mg; Fibre 0.4g; Sodium 26mg.

TWELFTH NIGHT BREAD

JANUARY 6TH, EPIPHANY, CELEBRATES THE ARRIVAL OF THE THREE KINGS AT CHRIST'S MANGER AND IN SPAIN, IT IS THE DAY FOR EXCHANGING CHRISTMAS GIFTS. THIS ROSCON DE REYES *– THE KINGS' RING – IS SPECIALLY BAKED FOR THE OCCASION. TRADITIONALLY IT CONTAINS A BEAN, A TINY CHINA BABY OR A SILVER COIN, AND THE LUCKY PERSON TO FIND IT IS DECLARED KING OF THE PARTY.*

SERVES TWELVE

INGREDIENTS
- 450g/1lb/4 cups unbleached strong white bread flour
- 2.5ml/½ tsp salt
- 25g/1oz fresh yeast
- 140ml/scant ¼ pint/scant ⅔ cup mixed lukewarm milk and water
- 75g/3oz/6 tbsp butter
- 75g/3oz/6 tbsp caster (superfine) sugar
- 10ml/2 tsp finely grated lemon rind
- 10ml/2 tsp finely grated orange rind
- 2 eggs
- 15ml/1 tbsp brandy
- 15ml/1 tbsp orange flower water
- silver coin or dried bean (optional)
- 1 egg white, lightly beaten, for glazing

For the decoration
- a mixture of glacé (candied) fruit slices
- flaked almonds

1 Lightly grease a large baking sheet. Sift together the flour and salt into a large bowl. Make a well in the centre.

2 In a bowl, mix the yeast with the milk and water until the yeast has dissolved. Pour into the centre of the flour and stir in enough of the flour from around the sides of the bowl to make a thick batter.

3 Sprinkle a little of the remaining flour over the top of the batter and leave to turn spongy, in a warm place, for about 15 minutes or until frothy.

4 Using an electric whisk or a wooden spoon, beat together the butter and sugar in a bowl until soft and creamy.

5 Add the citrus rinds, eggs, brandy and orange flower water to the flour mixture and mix to a sticky dough.

6 Beat the mixture until it forms a fairly smooth dough. Gradually beat in the butter mixture and beat for a few minutes until the dough is smooth and elastic. Cover with lightly oiled clear film (plastic wrap) and leave to rise, in a warm place, for about 1½ hours, or until doubled in size.

7 Punch the dough down and turn out on to a lightly floured surface. Gently knead for 2 or 3 minutes, incorporating the lucky coin or bean, if using.

8 Using a rolling pin, roll out the dough into a long strip measuring about 65 x 13cm/26 x 5in.

9 Roll up the dough from one long side like a Swiss roll (jelly roll) to make a long sausage shape. Place seam side down on the prepared baking sheet and seal the ends together. Cover with lightly oiled clear film and leave to rise, in a warm place, for 1–1½ hours, or until doubled in size.

10 Preheat the oven to 180°C/350°F/Gas 4. Brush the dough ring with lightly beaten egg white and decorate with glacé fruit slices, pushing them slightly into the dough. Sprinkle with flaked almonds and bake for 30–35 minutes, or until risen and golden. Turn out on to a wire rack to cool.

Energy 214Kcal/903kJ; Protein 4.6g; Carbohydrate 35.7g, of which sugars 7.1g; Fat 6.6g, of which saturates 3.6g; Cholesterol 45mg; Calcium 62mg; Fibre 1.2g; Sodium 51mg.

Pan de Cebada

Galicia is known for its country breads, which often include flours other than wheat. Maize grows in northern Spain and is used to make coarse corn meal; cebada means barley. Together barley and maize flours give this bread a close, heavy texture and a rich taste.

MAKES ONE LARGE LOAF

INGREDIENTS

- corn meal, for dusting

For the sourdough starter

- 175g/6oz/1½ cups corn meal
- 225g/8oz/2 cups strong wholemeal (whole-wheat) bread flour
- 75g/3oz/⅔ cup barley flour

For the dough

- 20g/¾oz fresh yeast
- 45ml/3 tbsp lukewarm water
- 225g/8oz/2 cups strong wholemeal bread flour
- 15ml/1 tbsp salt

COOK'S TIP

Allow 2 days to make the bread. It keeps very well and, once baked, will last for a week or more – if you haven't eaten it long before then.

1 Make the starter. In a pan, mix the corn meal with 300ml/½ pint/1¼ cups water, then blend in another 300ml/½ pint/1¼ cups of water. Cook over a gentle heat, stirring, until thickened. Transfer to a large bowl and cool.

2 Put the mixture into a food processor. Work in the wholemeal and barley flours and process thoroughly.

3 Return the starter to the bowl, cover with clear film (plastic wrap) and leave in a warm place for 36 hours.

4 To make the dough, put the yeast and water in a small bowl and cream together. Return the sourdough starter to the food processor, pour in the yeast mixture and process to combine well. Gradually add the wholemeal flour, with the salt, and work the whole dough until it becomes smooth and elastic.

5 Transfer the dough to a lightly oiled bowl, cover with clear film and leave, in a warm place, for 1½–2 hours until nearly doubled in size.

6 Return the dough to the food processor and use the pulse button to work it to a smooth dough. Dust a baking sheet with corn meal, and shape the dough on it to a plump round. Sprinkle with a little corn meal. Cover with a large upturned bowl. Leave to rise, in a warm place, for about 1 hour, or until nearly doubled in size.

7 Preheat the oven to 220°C/425°F/Gas 7 and place an empty roasting pan in the bottom of the oven.

8 Pour 300ml/½ pint/1¼ cups cold water into the roasting pan. Lift the bowl off the risen loaf and put the baking sheet in the oven. Bake the bread for 10 minutes. Remove the pan of water, reduce the oven temperature to 190°C/375°F/Gas 5 and bake for about 20 minutes. Cool on a wire rack.

Energy 2360Kcal/9994kJ; Protein 72.3g; Carbohydrate 503.4g, of which sugars 8.1g; Fat 15.1g, of which saturates 1.4g; Cholesterol 0mg; Calcium 431mg; Fibre 39.9g; Sodium 5909mg.

PAN GALLEGO

THIS GALICIAN BREAD IS DISTINGUISHED BY ITS PRETTY TWISTED TOP. THE OLIVE OIL GIVES IT A SOFT CRUMB AND THE MILLET, PUMPKIN AND SUNFLOWER SEEDS SCATTERED THROUGH THE LOAF PROVIDE AN INTERESTING COMBINATION OF TEXTURES.

MAKES ONE LARGE LOAF

INGREDIENTS

- corn meal, for dusting
- 350g/12oz/3 cups unbleached strong white bread flour
- 115g/4oz/1 cup strong wholemeal (whole-wheat) bread flour
- 10ml/2 tsp salt
- 20g/¾oz fresh yeast
- 275ml/9fl oz/generous 1 cup lukewarm water
- 30ml/2 tbsp olive oil or melted lard
- 30ml/2 tbsp pumpkin seeds
- 30ml/2 tbsp sunflower seeds
- 15ml/1 tbsp millet

1 Sprinkle a baking sheet with corn meal. Put the flours and salt together in a food processor and process to mix.

2 In a small bowl, mix the yeast with the water. Add to the flours with the olive oil or melted lard and process to make a firm dough. Continue until the dough is smooth and elastic.

3 Place the dough in a lightly oiled bowl, then cover it with clear film (plastic wrap) and leave to rise, in a warm place, for about 1½–2 hours, or until doubled in size.

4 Return the dough to the processor and use the pulse button to work the dough smooth. Turn out on a lightly floured surface and gently knead in the pumpkin seeds, sunflower seeds and millet. Cover the dough again and leave to rest for 5 minutes.

5 Shape the dough into a round ball and twist the centre to make a cap. Transfer to the prepared baking sheet and dust with corn meal. Cover with a large upturned bowl and leave to rise, in a warm place, for 45 minutes, or until doubled in size.

6 Meanwhile, place an empty roasting pan in the bottom of the oven. Preheat the oven to 220°C/425°F/Gas 7.

7 Pour about 300ml/½ pint/1¼ cups cold water into the roasting pan. Remove the bowl from on top of the loaf and place the loaf (still on the baking sheet) in the oven, on the shelf above the roasting pan. Bake for 10 minutes.

8 Remove the pan of water from the oven and bake the bread for a further 25–30 minutes, or until it is well browned and sounds hollow when tapped on the base. Transfer the bread to a wire rack to cool.

Energy 2274Kcal/9586kJ; Protein 65g; Carbohydrate 363.6g, of which sugars 9.1g; Fat 71.7g, of which saturates 8.2g; Cholesterol 0mg; Calcium 644mg; Fibre 26g; Sodium 3947mg.

Pineapple and Lime Agua Fresca

The vivid colours of this fresh fruit drink give some indication of its wonderful flavour. It makes a delicious midday refresher, mid-afternoon break, or chilled pick-me-up at the end of a hard day.

SERVES FOUR

INGREDIENTS
- 2 pineapples
- juice of 2 limes
- 475ml/16fl oz/2 cups still mineral water
- 50g/2oz/¼ cup caster (superfine) sugar

COOK'S TIP
When peeling a pineapple cut off the top and bottom and remove the skin with a spiral action, cutting deeply enough to remove most of the "eyes". Any remaining "eyes" can be cut out using a small knife.

1 Peel the pineapples and chop the flesh, removing the core and "eyes". You should have about 450g/1lb flesh. Put this in a food processor or blender and add the lime juice and half the mineral water. Purée to a smooth pulp. Stop the machine and scrape the mixture from the side of the goblet once or twice during processing.

2 Place a sieve (strainer) over a large bowl. Tip the pineapple pulp into the sieve and press it through with a wooden spoon. Pour the sieved mixture into a large jug, cover and chill in the fridge for about 1 hour.

3 Stir in the remaining mineral water and sugar to taste. Serve with ice.

Energy 111Kcal/476kJ; Protein 0.5g; Carbohydrate 28.8g, of which sugars 28.8g; Fat 0.2g, of which saturates 0g; Cholesterol 0mg; Calcium 19mg; Fibre 0g; Sodium 13mg.

Lime Agua Fresca

This is the lime version of real English lemonade. Traditionally, lime peel would have been ground in a MOLCAJETE *to extract the oil. Mexican limes –* LIMONES *– are harder and more tart than the smooth-skinned varieties most often sold in Western supermarkets.*

SERVES SIX

INGREDIENTS

- 1.75 litres/3 pints/7½ cups water
- 75g/3oz/6 tbsp caster (superfine) sugar
- 10 limes, plus slices, to decorate

1 Pour the water into a jug (pitcher), add the sugar and stir until all the sugar has dissolved. Chill for at least 1 hour.

2 Using a zester or grater, remove the rind from the limes, taking care to take only the coloured zest, not the pith. Squeeze the juice from the limes and add this to the chilled sugar water, with the lime rind. Stir well and chill again until required. Serve with ice in tall glasses, decorated with lime slices.

COOK'S TIP

To extract the maximum amount of juice from the limes, roll firmly between your palms for a few moments, or pierce with a skewer, put in a bowl, and microwave on maximum power for 10–15 seconds before juicing. This works with all citrus fruits.

Energy 51Kcal/215kJ; Protein 0.1g; Carbohydrate 13.3g, of which sugars 13.3g; Fat 0g, of which saturates 0g; Cholesterol 0mg; Calcium 8mg; Fibre 0g; Sodium 1mg.

Cafe con Leche

Many Mexicans start the day with this spiced milky coffee, and those who have enjoyed a hearty midday meal will often opt for a cup of it with a sweet pastry as the afternoon merienda. *It is also popular throughout the Caribbean and Central and South America, where it is sometimes flavoured with cocoa or chocolate either with or instead of the traditional cinnamon sticks.*

SERVES FOUR

INGREDIENTS
- 50g/2oz/⅔ cup ground coffee
- 475ml/16fl oz/2 cups boiling water
- 475ml/16fl oz/2 cups milk
- 4 cinnamon sticks, each about 10cm/4in long
- sugar, to taste

1 Put the coffee in a cafetière (press pot) or jug (pitcher), pour on the boiling water and leave for a few minutes until the coffee grounds settle at the bottom.

2 Push down the plunger of the cafetière or strain the jug of coffee to separate the liquid from the grounds. Pour the strained coffee into a clean jug.

3 Pour the milk into a heavy-based pan, add the cinnamon sticks and bring to the boil, stirring occasionally.

4 Using a slotted spoon, lift out the cinnamon sticks and use a smaller spoon to press down on them to release any liquid they have absorbed. Set the cinnamon sticks aside for serving.

5 Add the coffee to the hot milk, then pour into cups. Add a cinnamon stick to each cup. Drinkers should add sugar to taste.

Horchata

This delicious, aromatic rice drink tastes wonderfully creamy, yet does not contain a drop of milk. Mexicans swear by it as a means of settling stomach upsets or curing hangovers, and it is often served at breakfast.

SERVES FOUR

INGREDIENTS
- 450g/1lb/2¼ cups long grain rice
- 750ml/1¼ pints/3 cups water
- 150g/5oz/1¼ cups blanched whole almonds
- 10ml/2 tsp ground cinnamon
- finely grated rind of 1 lime, plus strips of rind, to decorate
- 50g/2oz/¼ cup sugar

1 Tip the rice into a sieve and rinse thoroughly under cold running water. Drain, tip into a large bowl and pour over the water. Cover and soak for at least 2 hours, preferably overnight.

2 Drain the rice, reserving 600ml/1 pint/2½ cups of the soaking liquid. Spoon the rice into a food processor or blender and grind as finely as possible.

3 Add the almonds to the processor or blender and continue to grind in the same way until finely ground.

4 Add the cinnamon, grated lime rind and sugar to the ground rice and ground almonds. Add the reserved soaking water from the rice and mix until all the sugar has dissolved.

5 Serve in tall glasses with ice cubes. Decorate with strips of lime rind.

TOP Energy 55Kcal/233kJ; Protein 4.1g; Carbohydrate 5.6g, of which sugars 5.6g; Fat 2g, of which saturates 1.3g; Cholesterol 7mg; Calcium 143mg; Fibre 0g; Sodium 51mg.
BOTTOM Energy 109Kcal/458kJ; Protein 5.5g; Carbohydrate 14.6g, of which sugars 14.6g; Fat 3g, of which saturates 0.6g; Cholesterol 0mg; Calcium 31mg; Fibre 0g; Sodium 61mg.

COOKING IN AFRICA

This vast region has a rich diversity of flavours and cooking styles, an amalgam of influences from within and outside the continent. Africa has three distinct areas, North African, sub-Saharan and southern African, each of which have their own characteristics. Within these regions are further diversities dictated by cultural traditions, geography and accessibility to influences and ingredients from the rest of the world.

THE AFRICAN CONTINENT

Africa can be divided into three principal areas, both geographically and from a culinary point of view: North Africa, sub-Saharan Africa and the expanse of southern Africa.

Above: Men in a rowing-boat, and in a dhow in the background, use traditional methods to catch fish in the River Nile.

NORTH AFRICA

This area is itself divided into the narrow, fertile coastal strip along the Mediterranean and on either side of the Nile, which was the hub of the ancient world, and the desert. Typically Mediterranean produce – olives, grapes, figs, dates, pomegranates and almonds – are enjoyed in the fertile areas of the north, and rich creamy milk and dairy products are provided by water buffalo in the well-watered areas. Flocks of sheep and goats that feed on the sparse vegetation of the Saharan hinterland provide most of the meat in the diet.

Egypt

The cuisine in Egypt is very similar to that of its Middle Eastern neighbours. Many dishes are made with legumes – lentils, beans and chickpeas – including two of the national dishes, ful medames and falafel. Rice and cracked wheat are both staples. Okra, that most pan-African of vegetables, is used to thicken soups and stews, as is *meloukhia*, a bright green, spinach-like leaf. *Meloukhia* soup is a universally popular dish that may be made with the fresh leaf when in season, or with dried, powdered *meloukhia*. Because most of the population is crowded between large stretches of water – the Mediterranean and the Nile – fish are of prime importance. Tilapia flourish in the brackish waters of the Great Bitter Lake, now part of the Suez Canal, where they are also farmed. Sardines, red and grey mullet and tuna are among the fish caught in the Mediterranean. Nile perch are the favourite freshwater fish.

The Maghreb

The cuisine of the three countries of the Maghreb – Algeria, Morocco and Tunisia – is distinctive, ranging from highly sophisticated in the towns to basic in the countryside, the Atlas Mountains and the desert. Magical spice mixtures are typical of the Maghreb, including ras al hanout, in which ground cumin and hot red pepper from the Sudan, known as *filfil soudani*, predominate.

The staple of these countries is couscous, made from durum (hard) wheat or semolina. The grains are soaked in hot water and separated individually by hand, while being evenly coated with smen – clarified butter – by continuous rubbing. This is a long and monotonous task that can take up to eight hours. It is a common sight in a North African village to see women sitting outside their front doors, a large metal bowl of couscous on their knees, as they chat to their neighbours while

Left: A herd of the distinctive cattle of the Dinka people graze on the fertile lands of the Massai Mara in Kenya.

endlessly performing the lifting and rubbing movement to separate and soften the grains. In the towns, the packets of ready-made couscous – couscous *tout prêt* – show that fast food has penetrated even here, and making couscous is now a matter of minutes, rather than hours. Morocco is also famous for its *warka*, a thin dough similar to filo that is made into pies and pastries, in particular Bistilla, the famous pigeon pie. In Tunisia, the same dough is called *brik*.

THE SAHARA

The vast white expanse on the map below the countries of North Africa, and encroaching into their boundaries, is the Sahara: the world's largest desert, which can easily be seen from outer space. Here, existence has always been at subsistence level; food is hoarded and diets are meagre.

SUB-SAHARAN AFRICA

The countries of Senegal, Mali, Niger and Chad are all former French colonies, so traces of French culture remain, especially in the more fertile Senegal. The Sahara gives way here to the Sahel, a semi-arid plain where rainfall is still too low to produce crops. Protein here has added importance, but the inhabitants subsist on imported food and fermented milk, smen and dried fish from the coasts. Meat is a luxury food, eaten during festivals in the form of *mechoui*: spit-roasted lamb or goat, stuffed with rice and vegetables. Dried tomatoes and aubergines (eggplants) enliven the diets in these countries, and they are also available in Libya and, in the north the Sudan.

Despite the dryness, the countries of the Horn of Africa – eastern Sudan, Ethiopia, Somalia and the tiny state of Djibouti – have their own treasure: coffee, which is drunk at high strength. Ethiopians roast the dried, greenish beans only when they are about to drink them. The freshly roasted beans are then ground down as finely as possible and boiled in water to form the thick, syrupy drink that is familiar throughout North Africa and the Middle East.

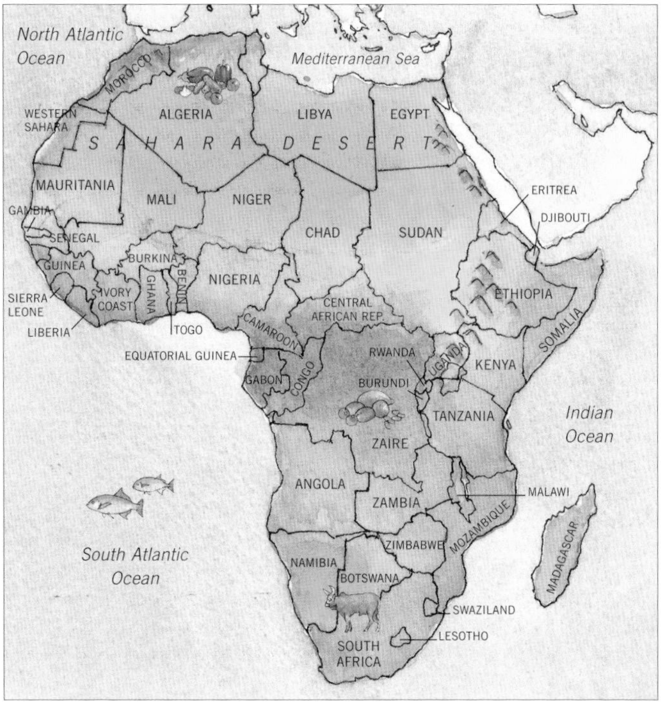

Although Ethiopians eat rice, they also have their own distinctive bread, which is made not from wheat but from a millet-like grain called teff. Unlike the tough flat breads of the Touareg and other nomads, Ethiopian bread, known as *injera*, is soft and pliable, made with a very liquid yeasty dough. It looks rather like terry towelling and has a very sour flavour because it has been leavened with wild yeasts. It is used to mop up the fiery sauces that accompany Ethiopian meat and vegetable stews.

West and Central Africa

Below the Sahara lie the thick rainforest areas of West and Central Africa, with their steamy heat, and where it is said that if you plant a stick in the ground it will take root and bear leaves like the biblical Aaron's rod. The staples here are mealies, corn cobs and cassava root, and similar large fleshy roots such as eddoes and cocoyams (colocasia). There is a profusion of vegetables, dominated by okra, squashes and beans. Most of the animal protein is in the form of fish from inland and coastal waters, as meat is in short supply.

Southern Africa

The terrain that makes up the south of Africa is a patchwork of deserts and fertile land, on which the European settlers established a strong farming tradition, allowing more intensive and productive agriculture, with pasture for cattle to graze on.

In South Africa there are strong differences between the diet of native peoples in the bush and the town-dwellers, black and white. The South Africans have developed their own distinctive foods, including dried meats – biltong – and sausages – *boerewors* – and *boboties*, a mixture of ground meat and spices.

THE AFRICAN KITCHEN

Food is scarce and precious in some areas of Africa, particularly the arid regions, and meat is rarely eaten. Dried and preserved foods are important elements in the diet, with fresh fish available only on the coast and from areas with lakes and rivers. Grains – rice, barley, wheat, maize, millet and *acha* – as well as dried beans are the backbone of the diet throughout Africa.

TRADITIONS PASSED DOWN

The North African kitchen is a sophisticated one, whose traditions date back thousands of years and whose recipes have been recorded in Arabic down through the centuries. Only in North Africa are so many cooking techniques used. Throughout the rest of the continent recipes are handed down from mother to daughter, and rarely written down. Measurements are flexible, and are usually made by handfuls, cups, calabashes and old tins, in particular Players cigarette tins, which are used in the tropics.

Throughout Africa cooking is performed almost exclusively by women, and in sub-Sarahan and southern regions the cooking techniques are slow and sometimes laborious. The pounding of mealies and yams, the fluffing of couscous grains, the peeling and shelling of beans and peas, the trimming of vegetables, the preparation of aromatic stews – these are all tasks that the average African girl learns from her mother from an early age.

Cassava, which originates from South America, contains quantities of hydrocyanic acid, making it too poisonous to be simply peeled and boiled, like a potato. In West and East Africa, it is cooked and then pounded to ensure that the acid evaporates. The sight of village women pounding cassava, using a huge pestle in a decorative wooden mortar, has been a familiar one for centuries.

Pounded yams are called *foufou*, which has a consistency similar to that of couscous. *Foufou* is a staple food of Nigeria. Rice is also an important staple, and Jollof Rice can be considered the Nigerian national dish.

Above: Women in Kenya pound cassava with a pestle in a mortar to release the poisonous hydrocyanic acid.

FOREIGN INFLUENCES

Africa has been subject to several foreign influences throughout the centuries, and this is reflected in its regional cuisine. In West Africa, it was traders – and eventually slavers – from western Europe, especially Portugal and England, and later those from the Americas, who traded with the Ashanti Empire, with its huge wealth of gold and diamonds. It is surprising how many of the African staple foods actually derive from elsewhere. Many, such as cassava, coconut, pomegranates and bananas, were brought in trading ships carried on the strong currents that run through the Indian and Atlantic Oceans between India and Africa or South America and Africa. The Arabs were early traders, bringing many spices with them, especially to East Africa.

One example of a staple ingredient introduced from outside the continent is the opuntia cactus, known in French as *figue de barbarie* (Barbary fig) – Barbary being the old name for the North African coast. However, it is not an indigenous plant, since cacti are native only to the deserts of south-western, North and Central America. It was introduced to North Africa soon after the discovery of the Americas and has flourished ever since.

Another example is the ubiquitous mint tea of Morocco. This would appear to be an ancient tradition, yet in reality it dates from as recently as 1854, when British merchants needed an alternative outlet for their wares that could not be sold in eastern Europe and Turkey owing to the Crimean War. They sold the tea cheaply in Tangiers and Essaouira (the modern name for Mogador), and the Moroccans adapted it to their own tastes, substituting milk with fresh mint leaves.

Right: Beans, grains and pulses are sold in bulk in African markets. Note the variety of measuring equipment.

EUROPEAN COLONISTS

Southern Africa, with its variety of terrains, including more temperate climates suitable for wheat cultivation, is the most heavily influenced by the foods of the former colonists. There is strong Portuguese influence in Angola and Mozambique, British influence in Zimbabwe, and British and Dutch influence in South Africa.

French influence

Not surprisingly, with its strong food culture, French food has influenced all the former French possessions, and the baguette is as universal in North and Saharan Africa as is the local flat bread. Pâté from chicken livers is another French introduction, and coffee is ground and drunk the French way. French cooking styles have had a beneficial effect on local dishes, including such delights as yam soufflé (*soufflé d'ignames*), eaten in Madagascar. Vegetables from French seeds such as carrots, French (green) beans and cabbage are added to stews of local foods in Senegal, where French influence is strongest and ties to France are among the closest in Africa.

Below: A woman slices fish in Kayar, Senegal, where fresh fish is plentiful.

Portuguese influence

The Portuguese influence on African cooking has been extremely important, with the contribution of two basic Portuguese foods: capsicums (chilli and bell peppers) and dried cod. The peppers, originally brought from South America, have permeated the whole of Africa, with Tunisia, Saharan and West Africa being particularly fond of peppery stews spiced with large amounts of small chilli peppers. Dried fish, usually dried cod or hake, is imported into Africa in large amounts. This is an important protein element in countries in which protein is scarce and expensive. The cod is soaked in several changes of water for 24 hours, then steamed or boiled with *foufou* and vegetables, including the ubiquitous chilli sauce (piri-piri) or chilli peppers.

Asian influence

The foods of the Republic of South Africa are also heavily influenced by the large population who came from the Indian subcontinent and very much by the "Cape Malays". These were settlers from south-east Asia, the former Malaya, Singapore and Indonesia, who arrived in the 19th century at the same time as the Indians, and who had an important influence on the national diet.

Merchants from the Indian subcontinent, whose highly spiced curries are very much in tune with the African palate, have also influenced the local cuisine. The fragrant curries of Kenya, Tanzania and South Africa, especially in cities with a large population from the subcontinent, such as Mombasa and Durban, are typical of Indian and Pakistani influence.

AFRICAN FEASTS AND FESTIVALS

Each African country enjoys its own regional dishes, sometimes influenced by their religious beliefs but more often by the ingredients that are available to them. In many parts of Africa meat is an important part of celebratory eating as it is not eaten on a daily basis.

NORTH AFRICA

Islamic traditions dictate social customs and entertaining in the countries of North Africa. For example, during the month of Ramadan, when eating and drinking are forbidden during daylight hours, each country has its own traditional food on which to break the fast in the evening. In most of North Africa, Harira, a soup made with chickpeas or lentils, will be served; however, in Egypt it will be a dish made from lentils and rice known as Mejedra.

In the Horn of Africa, Muslims celebrate both Eids (the two Muslim festivals of ul-Fitr and ul-Adha) with *sheer korma*, made with vermicelli and various nuts, including pistachio nuts, almonds and charoli nuts. The charoli nut is similar to a hazelnut and is found all over Asia and in Muslim Africa.

Whole sheep and goats are roasted for religious festivals, such as Eid, and in parts of the Maghreb, camels are also eaten. Stuffed camel stomach is a delicacy that may be served at a Moroccan feast for celebrating a special occasion such as a wedding. Naturally, there will be a dish of couscous, often a couscous royale, a massive dish where the grain is piled high in a huge metal dish, garnished with vegetables and sprinkled with rosebuds. This will be accompanied by a spicy sauce made from the stock in which the vegetables were stewed, laced with spices – ground cumin, saffron, ginger, chilli pepper and cardamom.

Choua, a dish of stewed lamb, may also be served, and the elegant pigeon pie known as Bastilla as well as other pies made with phyllo (or filo) dough. The meal will be rounded off by apricots, almonds, dates, figs and sweetmeats, such as baklava or halva. No alcohol is consumed as it is forbidden to Muslims.

Above: The feast of Eid ul-Fitr marks the end of Ramadan. Here in the market of Habta in Sharqiya, Egypt, men are buying food for the celebration.

SUB-SAHARAN AFRICA

In the countries of sub-Saharan Africa, which are predominantly non-Muslim, the feasts that are reserved for religious festivals and weddings may last for days. In Kenya, no wedding feast is complete without *ugali*, a kind of maize porridge, which can also be made from millet or cassava flour. *Ugali* is often accompanied by green bananas, wrapped in banana leaves and cooked on open fires. Another accompaniment to *ugali* and green bananas is *chiswa*, white ants or termites boiled and then fried. Perhaps more to European taste are the *simsim balls*: made from toasted, ground sesame seeds, which are also served with the maize porridge.

In Nigeria, a festive meal will include Chicken Suya, grilled chicken with a fragrantly spicy coating. The classic Nigerian dish, Jollof Rice, is always on offer, as well as fried plantains and bean porridge, a spicy stew of field beans. Beans also feature in the snack food called Ackroes: fried bean cakes served to visitors, which are also available from street stalls all over Nigeria. Puff-puff – little puffs of fried dough – and meat pies are also served as appetizers at parties, although they can also be bought in the street. In the Cameroon, a wedding feast will certainly feature a dish called Folon, a stew of chicken and prawns (shrimp) flavoured with coconut water and folon leaf, a bitter leaf native to the Cameroon.

In sub-Saharan tropical Africa, palm wine and beer are the favourite drinks for celebrations: Star Beer in Ghana, Tusker Beer in Kenya. Local breweries can be found throughout the region, but many still prefer to drink Guinness.

SOUTHERN AFRICA

Celebrations in South Africa usually centre on the barbecue, known as a *braai* (pronounced "bry"). These barbecues originated as spit roasts in the late 17th century at celebrations held by the Dutch governor of what is now Cape Province. Later, the voortrekkers, the Dutch settlers, had to cook their meat in this way due to lack of other facilities. Cooks in different regions use different ingredients for the braai. In the Karoo, the central desert, mutton, lamb and eland are popular. In Natal, on the east coast, barracuda and yellowtail fish are wrapped in banana leaves and served with typical Zulu accompaniments such as mealies (corn on the cob), cornmeal breads and fritters. The South African lager, Castle, is popular as well as their wide range of sherries and wines.

On the island of Madagascar the wedding feast will be of fresh seafood and rice, as well as manioc flour (gari or tapioca) to accompany the Romazava: a meat and vegetable stew spiced with ginger. *Ranovola*, a watery rice drink, is enjoyed at celebrations, and in the north of the island there is *trembo* (fermented coconut juice).

Sweetmeats of various kinds are always served at weddings. Particular favourites include coconut and honey sticks in Mali, and *kashata na nazi* (coconut candy) in Uganda. These are the same sweets that are served for any other kind of entertaining. Pastries are always popular: the Arab *sambusak* metamorphosed into the Indian samosa, and both are served throughout Africa. These small triangular pastries may be filled with either sweet or savoury mixtures before being fried.

Above: In rural Africa weddings involve the entire community. Here Sudanese men participate in a wedding dance.

Below: Men of the Masai tribe roast a white bull for the festival of Olingsher, when boys of the village come of age.

African Ingredients

In the arid regions of Africa all foods are scarce and precious, and are carefully prepared. The favourite grains, rice and millet, maize and acha, are pounded and dried then made into a liquid porridge or couscous-like cooked grain. Dried beans, dried *meloukhia* and dried okra are sometimes the only vegetables available, supplemented during the rainy season with squashes, fresh beans and green leafy vegetables. Fermented foods – pickles, rancid clarified butter and yogurt – are important items of the diet, as are dried fish, sardines and prawns (shrimp), in areas away from lakes and the sea. Fish is an important item of diet where it is available, mainly Nile perch and tilapia.

Above: Fishermen work in the water and on traditional boats for tuna and pomfret in the Indian Ocean, off the coast of Mombasa, Kenya.

GRAINS

A wide range of grains is eaten: various types of millet, including finger millet (*eleusine*), sorghum and teff (in the Horn of Africa). The main staples are rice in Egypt and couscous, cracked grain, usually durum wheat, in the Maghreb (Algeria, Morocco and Tunisia). Couscous is sometimes made from barley, especially among the Kabyles of Algeria. Sesame (*simsim* or *benné*) is an African plant that is rich in oil and, like peanuts, the oil can be extracted and used for cooking.

Left: Grains play a central part in the African diet, and are still farmed using traditional methods.

PROTEIN

Because meat is expensive and scarce in most parts of the African continent, certainly among the poor and the tribal peoples, vegetable protein is extremely important. This is provided by the native peanut and other varieties of nuts, and various types of beans and peas throughout the continent. Almonds grow in North Africa and are often added to savoury dishes, such as couscous. Kola nuts are popular because they act as a stimulant. They grow in the tropical rainforests of West Africa and are chewed fresh, or dried and ground to a powder for making into a drink. One type can be found as far south as Angola. The seeds may be white or pink, but purple is preferred. The nut is often eaten as a digestive before a meal, as it is claimed that its slightly bitter flavour makes food subsequently eaten taste sweet. It is customary for a bride and groom to exchange kola nuts at a Nigerian wedding. Similar to the kola nut is the misnamed Java olive, which grows throughout Africa.

Black-eyed beans (peas) and cowpeas are typical ingredients in Africa's classic stews, which mainly consist of vegetables and dried beans, occasionally supplemented with a little fish, and even more occasionally with meat or poultry.

Fish are valuable adjuncts to the diet and both saltwater and freshwater fish are eaten all over the continent, as are prawns, shrimps and mussels.

Meat comes in the form of lamb and goat, camel (mainly for festive occasions), and game such as gazelle and cane-rat (also known as *agouti*). All over Central Africa wild game, known as "bush meat" is eaten: including kudu and eland, and, in parts of West Africa, even monkey.

In areas where dairy cattle are bred, such as among the Dinka peoples, whose territory extends across southern Sudan, Uganda and northern Kenya, the animals are a sign of wealth. As such they are far too valuable to be slaughtered. The dairy herds are, however, regularly bled from the neck and the nutrition-rich blood is mixed with *chisaka* – African spinach or amaranth – and stewed. This mixture is eaten with *ugali* (maize meal).

Above: Cloves are spread out to dry in the sun on the island of Zanzibar.

FRUIT AND VEGETABLES

A wide variety of fruits are grown in the region, many of them unknown and unavailable outside Africa. Vegetables are an important ingredient in Africa, especially leaves and greens, but also staples such as yams and plantains.

DAIRY PRODUCTS

Fermented milks of all kinds are widespread. Many peoples simply milk their flocks and pour the liquid into a gourd that is left in a tree for four or five days until the milk has fermented. Fermented milk, yogurt and butter are often given to children.

SPICES

Spices are a favourite and essential ingredient in African cuisine. Some are produced and sold locally, but most of them are grown in East Africa on the island of Zanzibar.

Below: Spices are used extensively in Africa, and are often made into mixes.

Below: Many varieties of nuts are cultivated in Africa, but also grow wild.

Below: Giant snails and prawns, popular in Ghana, are used to flavour stews.

PRESERVED FOOD AND OILS

Refrigeration is still rare in much of Africa, but advancements in modern food preservation techniques, especially canning, have been a boon to tropical Africa. Pickled, dried and preserved food is an African tradition that continues to be as important today as it was in the past. Alongside the mounds of colourful fruits and vegetables, the open-air markets feature huge cans of condensed milk and butter or ghee (clarified butter or vegetable fat), as well as corned beef and lamb to supplement the meagre diet in the arid lands. Oils extracted from nuts and seeds are also used in different parts of the continent.

PRESERVES

Dried and puréed tomatoes are popular ingredients. It is not unusual to see women sieving and drying tomatoes on large mats in villages. Garden eggs – aubergines (eggplants) – are also dried for use when they are out of season.

Below: Various types of vegetables are pickled throughout Africa, peppers and turnips are particular favourites.

DRIED FISH

In areas of Africa away from lakes or the sea, dried fish is an important part of the diet. Many kinds are dried, including sardines, prawns and shrimps, which are used mainly in stews. However, salt cod, eaten widely in sub-Saharan Africa, is imported.

CANNED AND BOTTLED FOODS

As well as canned tomatoes and tomato purée (paste), which are imported, there are many locally produced canned and bottled foods that are used in African cooking.

Pickles

Vegetables pickled in brine are eaten throughout the continent. In North Africa, pickles (*torshi*) are made from aubergines, turnips, (bell) peppers, onions, and cucumbers, usually coloured pink with beetroot juice.

Smen

Used throughout Africa, smen is clarified butter used for cooking. It is also preserved and laid down in the same way that Europeans lay down vintage wines. Sometimes it is preserved for many years, stored in jars and kept in cellars.

Above: Dried shrimps and anchovies are both used in African stews.

Spiced ghee and shea butter

In Ethiopia, *niter kebbeh*, or spiced ghee, is used for cooking. This is made by adding onion, garlic, ginger, turmeric, cardamom, cinnamon, clove and nutmeg to unsalted (sweet) butter.

Shea butter is a solid fat prepared from the seeds of a tree found in Ghana and Nigeria. The oval fruits contain a thin pulp and a large, oval, shiny brown seed. The pulp is allowed to rot away through exposure to the sun and the kernels are then roasted and pounded to make butter. The Hausa people of northern Nigeria prefer not to roast the nut before its butter is extracted. The fat then extracted is less odorous and more to European taste. Shea butter is also boiled in water and exported to Europe where it is added to margarine. It is also used in cosmetics.

Dairy fats

Fermented milk and butter are very important in the African diet. Buttermilks and mixtures that are a kind of intermediate stage between yogurt and clarified butter are used in cooking and added to all types of foods to enrich them. Buttermilks are often given to babies that are being weaned and to young children. In Senegal, a thick buttermilk mixture known as *nebam sirne* is highly prized as a cooking medium. It is mostly home-made but small factories have begun producing it commercially. *Nebam sirne* may also be used fresh or, like smen, be kept for years to mature.

Coconut

Coconut milk is available in cans and can be stored indefinitely. A favourite cooking medium, creamed coconut is used for many types of fried snacks sold as street food in tropical Africa.

OILS

As well as smen, there are several varieties of oils that are used for cooking throughout Africa.

Palm oil

Also known as palm kernel oil, palm oil is reddish in colour, due to its high vitamin A content. It is made from the kernel of a palm tree native to West and Central Africa, from Benin to the Congo Valley, and is a valuable export. The nut produced by this palm is the dendé nut. This is a rare example of an African food travelling to South America. It was probably taken to Brazil by Portuguese slave traders; at any event it is now popular there, especially in the province of Salvador, whose inhabitants are largely of African origin. The fibrous pulp of the dendé nut is very oily, and the stone (pit), which is the size of a walnut, has a white, oily kernel. In the 19th century, Europeans realized the potential of palm oil for making margarine, as it solidifies much more quickly than other vegetable oils. Palm oil is exported from tropical Africa.

Above: A selection of oils used in African cooking: in front is coconut oil, palm oil on the left and olive oil on the right. The oils at the back are corn oil on the right and the lighter groundnut oil on the left.

Below: Shea butter, bottom, and coconut cream, top, are highly nutritious fats used African cooking.

Nut oils

Other oils used in African cooking include peanut, sesame seed and corn, which are all crushed and their oil extracted. Sesame oil has a strong flavour and fragrance and is used in dishes that can withstand it.

Bush butter is derived from a tropical tree that is known as the African pear, native pear, *safu* or *eben*. The purplish plum-sized fruit grows in tropical Africa and is added to stews and curries. It has a high protein content.

Other oils

Cotton oil is an important oil for cooking in the dry areas of the continent that produce the finest cotton. The biggest African producers, and also exporters, of cotton oil are Egypt and the Sudan.

Sunflower oil is a lighter oil, which is used in Kenyan and Nigerian cooking, especially for frying.

Olive oil is also used, especially in North African countries, although less extensively than elsewhere in the Mediterranean region.

GRAINS, BEANS AND SEEDS

Africa has a variety of staple foods, filling starches for a continent where famine is not uncommon. To complement the grains are many different beans and lentils, another important form of protein.

GRAINS

In the more temperate climates of North Africa – Egypt, Algeria, Morocco and Tunisia – where the climate allows for as many as three wheat or barley harvests a year, the staple grains are coarsely ground to make couscous. Millet and sorghum are grains that are used for animal feed outside Africa, but here they are important ingredients in the human diet.

Wheat

The wheat used to make couscous is a hard wheat: durum wheat. Wheat is also made into bread: the flat breads of North Africa or the thick, porous *injera* of Ethiopia, which is used as much as an eating implement as a food, for mopping up the rich, thick sauces of Ethiopian stews known as *wat*.

Rice

Another staple eaten in all parts of the continent is rice, which is grown in Egypt, along the Nile, and other river valleys in Africa. The so-called Carolina rice was introduced into the United States from Africa by the slave ships, which carried it to feed their human cargo. This rice variety is still cultivated and eaten throughout tropical Africa and in Egypt.

Left: Two African varieties of grain, Carolina rice (top) and millet or acha *(bottom), and sesame seeds (middle).*

Cornmeal

The other universal grain is cornmeal or maize, originally imported from the Americas in the 16th century. Maize is dried and served as cornmeal for use as a thickener for stews, such as *kenkey* and *banku*, both eaten in the Congo with spicy vegetable stews.

Millet

Also known as *acha, giro,* hungry rice and *fonio*, millet has been long used in western Europe as birdseed but is gaining popularity as a healthy, wholegrain food. It is another popular staple in Africa. The nutty, slightly bitter flavour combines well with stews. It is native to Africa, looks a little like maize, and grows about 4m/13ft tall, like corn on the cob. It is a fast-growing crop that needs little water, so it flourishes in the dryer parts of the continent. It stores well without deteriorating, which is another reason for its popularity in the Horn of Africa, where drought and famine are not unknown.

Millet is mixed with other food in some countries: in Nigeria, for example, it is mixed with baobab grain or the dry pulp of the baobab fruit.

Right: Green (top) and grey, or Puy lentils (bottom) grow wild around the Mediterranean and are a valuable vegetable protein.

Sorghum

Also known as *dawa* or guinea corn, sorghum is related to millet and is native to the drier uplands, and has been cultivated in Ethiopia for thousands of years. It is also especially popular in West Africa. Two varieties, black African and white pearl, are popular for grinding into a porridge, but because the grain contains no gluten it cannot be made into bread. Certain cultivars have sap in their thick stems that can be turned into syrup. It will not crystallize into grains because it does not have enough sucrose. Sorghum syrup is dark brown and sticky and tastes a little like molasses, but it has a milder flavour.

Teff

The teff seed is an important grain in Ethiopia. It is the smallest grain seed: 150 grains being equal in size to one grain of wheat. It is low in gluten and high in protein and carbohydrates, a good source of calcium and iron, and high in fibre, and consequently has become the latest fashionable wholegrain in the United States and western Europe and is now available from health food stores.

Cassava

Known by various names, including *gari,* cassava flour may be made in the home, but it is also produced commercially. It is cooked with water and eaten as a filling staple.

Above: Cassava flour (top) and cornmeal are staples of sub-Saharan Africa and come from South America. They are eaten with stews.

DRIED BEANS

All types of bean are valuable additions to the diet in Africa. The field bean, the forerunner of the broad (fava) bean, is a staple in the Egyptian diet, as are lentils – both the puy and the green.

Chickpeas

Native to North Africa, chickpeas feature in stews and all savoury dishes, although they are also coated with icing sugar and eaten as candies in the winter. Chickpeas are almost always found dried, but they are in season in May, and fresh green chickpeas are a delicious snack eaten in Egypt and throughout North Africa. The Indian influence is apparent where chickpeas are split after drying and made into channa dhal. This is then fried as chickpea fritters. These fritters are popular all along the coasts of West and East Africa and in South Africa.

Below: The peanut (groundnut) is native to Africa, and is a legume or pulse, like a pea or bean. The pods develop underground, hence its name.

Above: Field beans are used to make ful medames, which is considered the national dish of Egypt. These beans are also known as horse-beans.

Field beans

In Egypt, the day usually begins with a bowl of ful medames – field beans stewed in water, with olive oil, lemon juice, cumin, onion and garlic, sometimes with the addition of a quartered hard-boiled egg.

Pigeon peas

Like all varieties of peas, pigeon peas are native to Africa. They may be eaten fresh or dried and, if very young, boiled in the pod. When dried, they are added to soups and stews.

Peanuts

Known for their high protein and fat content, peanuts are native to Africa and an important ingredient where animal protein is scarce. Mainly known as groundnuts, peanuts are cooked in stews. They also yield valuable groundnut oil. Groundnut stew is the national dish of Ghana, a stew that includes meat and aubergines as well as roasted peanuts. It is served with rice and small side dishes of raw onion rings, banana slices sprinkled with cayenne pepper, chutney, grated coconut and more toasted peanuts. Peanuts are grown in large plantations and are exported, dried, roasted or as oil, to Europe. Peanut flour is mixed with other flours to enrich the diet.

SEEDS

Benné, or sesame seed, is another highly nutritious native African plant. The seeds may be toasted and ground, and served with honey or sugar as cakes, or sprinkled on savoury rice or other starches to enrich the main meal. The oil from the seed is also used for adding flavour to cooking.

The oil-yielding niger seed is from the same family as the sunflower but is native to East Africa, and is cultivated in Ethiopia. Niger seeds are eaten fried, in pickles or in cakes. The oil the seeds yield has a nutty flavour, and is sometimes used as a substitute for ghee or smen.

Below: Blackeyed peas or beans (top) and pigeon peas (bottom) take the place of the field bean in sub-Saharan Africa as a source of protein.

Spices and Herbs

One feature that is typical of African food throughout the continent is the love of spices and, in particular, hot peppery sauces. Fresh herbs are less widely used, and are mainly lemongrass, mint, basil and rocket.

SPICES

Many of the spices used in African cooking were imported by the Arab traders, but are now grown locally or come from East Africa, the Sudan, Ethiopia and, especially, Zanzibar. The climate and growing conditions in the picturesque island of Zanzibar, with its strongly Arab-influenced culture and lifestyle, are similar to those of the original Spice Islands: the Dutch East Indies. In the early 18th century, the Arabs brought spices to Zanzibar, now also known as Spice Island, for cultivation, and the island still supplies much of Africa with these essential cooking ingredients.

The island is still the prime source of the world's supply of cloves, and, unsurprisingly, cloves are used extensively in the cookery of the region. Other spices grown in Zanzibar are pepper, cardamom, ginger and nutmeg. These spices are important in the local cuisine, which is heavily influenced by the large population from the Indian subcontinent. Curry powder, also known as *mchusi*, has become a much-used ingredient in the African kitchen, thanks to the Asian influence from traders and settlers. As well as these cultivated and exported spices, there are also spices that are native to Africa, and which still grow wild throughout the region. These include dried baobab leaves and fruits, and grains of selim (also known as African nutmeg). Okra, when dried, is also used as a spice. Potash, from the Bitter Lakes, is used as a substitute for salt and as a raising agent. Egusi seeds, the seeds of certain varieties of watermelon, are used to flavour soups, and are beneficial to the diet owing to their oil content.

Left: Ground coriander is used in North Africa in stews, kebabs and meatballs.

Saffron

The classic spice of North Africa is saffron. Once grown even as far north as the United Kingdom (as in Saffron Walden), the saffron crocus is now mainly grown in Morocco, and is exported around the world. In North African cooking it is an important ingredient in a variety of stews and is used to flavour and colour rice with its subtle fragrance and bright yellow hue. Another spice that is used in African cooking for its rich yellow colour, as well as its flavour, is turmeric.

Cloves

Cloves were originally imported from the Spice Islands by the Arabs, who traded extensively along the East Coast of Africa. They are grown throughout northern and eastern Africa and used lavishly in cooking. In Zanzibar, cloves are chewed to sweeten the breath.

Ginger

Ginger, like cloves, is used in many African dishes, and is a particularly favourite spice for flavouring stews.

Nutmeg

The fruit seed is about the size of an apricot. It has a lacy covering known as mace, which tastes similar to the nut and is also used as a spice. Nutmeg is used in sweet and savoury dishes.

Below: Saffron, the most prized and rare of all spices, has a subtle taste and imparts a golden colour to food.

Below: Turmeric, also known as the poor man's saffron, has a stronger flavour and is extensively used in Indian-influenced dishes.

Below: Ginger root can be used fresh, but more often is dried and used in its powdered form.

Above: *Scotch bonnets are colourful African varieties of chilli pepper that are also grown in the West Indies.*

Chillies

The hot peppers used to make the dipping sauces and pastes are almost certainly an import from South America from the days of the early traders in the 17th century, although this applies to many foods in Africa, because the climates of both continents are similar. In fact, there was a local pepper that was used in quantity before chillies became available. It is known as *melegueta* pepper or, more poetically, as grains of paradise. The plant is a tall reed that has elongated red and orange fruits. These fruits contain as many as 100 seeds, which are the "grains of paradise" themselves. Melegueta pepper became popular in Europe soon after West Africa was discovered by explorers, and was shipped in large quantities, but its popularity declined and it is now hard to find outside its native area.

Below: Chilli powder is a preservative, which kills bacteria on fresh food, an added benefit in hot countries where food quickly becomes bad.

SPICE MIXES

These include the ras el hanout of Algeria and Morocco, the harissa of Tunisia, the berbere of Ethiopia and the pilpil of Angola and Mozambique. In North Africa, Tunisian dishes are the most fiery, with Algeria and Morocco tending to favour more subtle flavours. Tunisian harissa, usually the famous Le Phare du Cap Bon variety, can now be found in food stores all over the world in its distinctive yellow "toothpaste" tube.

Berbere

This is an Ethiopian blend of spices added to many local dishes, from baked fish to chicken stews.

8 white cardamoms
10 dried red chillies
5ml/1 tsp cumin seeds
5ml/1 tsp coriander seeds
5ml/1 tsp fenugreek seeds
8 cloves
5ml/1 tsp allspice berries
10ml/2 tsp black peppercorns
5ml/1 tsp ajowan seeds
5ml/1 tsp ground ginger
2.5ml/½ tsp ground nutmeg
15ml/1 tbsp salt

Heat a heavy frying pan. Bruise the cardamom pods and add to the pan with the chillies, cumin, coriander, fenugreek, cloves, allspice, peppercorns and ajowan seeds. Toast the spices until they give off a rich aroma. Remove the seeds from the cardamoms and discard the husks. Grind all the spices to a fine powder. Mix in the ginger, nutmeg and salt. You can use the mix at once or store it in a jar.

All three countries of the Maghreb make extensive use of a mixture called ras el hanout (meaning "head of the shop") consisting of as many as twenty spices dominated by cumin and hot red pepper, although the mixture varies depending on where it is made. In Ethiopia, bitter spices and herbs, such as fenugreek and ajwan, are included in spice mixtures and added to stews.

In Egypt, the classic spice mixture is a dried one known as duqqa (which derives from an Arabic word meaning "pounded"). The ingredients in duqqa, and their proportions, vary from one family to another but generally include sesame and coriander seeds, dried crushed mint, salt and pepper. It may also include chickpea flour and crushed millet. It is usually sprinkled on bread dipped in olive oil.

HERBS

Fresh herbs are used less than spices in African cooking. Lemongrass is used in Kenya, strongly influenced as it is by its Asian population. Lemongrass can be dried, whole or shaved, powdered or distilled into a fragrant oil. It has a fragrant citrus flavour and aroma.

Basil was known in ancient Egypt and is still used in many Egyptian dishes. Mint is an essential ingredient for mint tea in the Maghreb, and flat leaf parsley is used lavishly in many soup and salad recipes as an ingredient in its own right.

Below: Lemon grass is used extensively in the cooking of Kenya. It can be shaved and dried, as here.

Fresh Vegetables

African cooking has always placed great reliance on locally grown fresh vegetables, and in spite of imported or canned foods, this is still the case.

Green leafy vegetables

A winter luxury in the arid lands, green leafy vegetables are available only when the summer sun does not shrivel the leaves. *Meloukhia* is a green, spinach-like vegetable with a slightly slimy consistency that is used to make soup and added to stews in Egypt and Saharan Africa. Spinach is used in stews and fritters. Bitterleaf is another variety of green vegetable available in East and West Africa. The leaves of bean plants and pumpkins are eaten as green vegetables. Cassava leaves are also eaten.

Amaranth, also known as African spinach, is another popular green vegetable. Marrow greens and cowpea leaves are enjoyed, as are sweet potato tops, which, unlike the tops of ordinary potato, are not poisonous.

Above: Turnips and their tops are an essential ingredient in the stew that accompanies couscous in North Africa.

The leaves of other root vegetables are also added to soups and stews in Africa. No part of the plant is wasted; turnip tops and mustard greens (still eaten in the southern states of the USA by people of African origin) and the green leaves of okra (a type of hibiscus) are all added to soups and stews. The tough, fibrous leaves of the banana and plantain are used as disposable plates and to package foods, such as gari (cassava or tapioca flour) for steaming and boiling. In West Africa, a favourite way to use green vegetables is in palaver sauce. Whatever green leaves are available are used to make this sauce, although it should always contain bitterleaf. A little meat, including offal (variety meats), and shellfish are added, as well as watermelon, or egusi, seeds. The mixture is then sprinkled with palm oil. The dish is known as *plassas* in Sierra Leone and *ban flo* in Ghana.

The green leaves of the manioc plant are the main ingredients in *kpwem*, a soup from southern Cameroon. The leaves should be as young and tender as possible. They are stewed with ground peanuts and a little palm oil.

Above: Pumpkin is an important food all over Africa, mainly as an ingredient for stew. In Libya, it is pickled and mashed and eaten with couscous.

Squashes

Pumpkins, squashes and gourds all flourish in the heat, and many varieties of these are eaten, even the liffa, the gourd from which loofahs are made. Squashes and pumpkins are particularly popular, finding their way into most stews. Gourds are not only eaten but are also used as containers (calabashes), utensils (cut in half and used as ladles) and as drinking vessels.

Aubergines

In Kenya, aubergine is known as eggplant or *brinjal*, the latter being the

Below: From top to bottom, cocoyam, cassava yam, guinea yam (left) and soft yam (right).

Above: Okra is valued for the gelatinous texture it gives to stews and soups. It is also known as gumbo.

Above: Plantains are members of the banana family. They are eaten green or ripe, baked or boiled or fried.

Above: Garlic, the pungent Mediterranean plant, is used extensively as a flavouring all over Africa.

Right: Ackee is usually sold in cans.

Indian name. Garden eggs are a white or greenish-yellow variety of aubergine, which are eaten mainly in West Africa. A favourite Nigerian dish is chicken gumbo, for which chicken is stewed with garden eggs.

Okra

Gumbo is also another name for okra, the vegetable that is perhaps most closely associated with Africa. In North Africa, okra is deep-fried in oil, which eliminates any trace of sliminess. However, the slimy texture is valued elsewhere in Africa, for the bulk it gives to stews.

Peppers

Chilli peppers and sweet (bell) peppers, known as bell chillies, are eaten all over the continent. They vary in size and shape from tiny red birdseye chillies and so-called cherry peppers to larger, elongated, milder green (bell) peppers.

Yams

The cocoyam and Guinea soff yam are varieties of yam that are probably indigenous to West Africa. The Guinea soff yam is known locally as *allato*; it may be white or yellow. Yellow yams should not be confused with the sweet potato, which is often known as yellow yam in the United States.

Ackee

Now associated principally with Jamaica, the ackee was originally introduced there from West Africa in the 18th century. The fruit is fluffy and yellow like scrambled egg, but the centre is poisonous, so ackee is always sold canned outside its native habitat.

Plantains

A member of the banana family, plantains are inedible raw, and are cooked extensively in Africa in many different ways.

OTHER VEGETABLES

Colocassia is a root eaten since antiquity, when it was Europe's equivalent of the potato. Colocassia is still eaten widely in Africa, as are eddoes, a taproot related to colocassia. Tomatoes, potatoes and carrots were introduced by the Europeans. The onion, garlic, and other members of the allium family are grown throughout northern Africa.

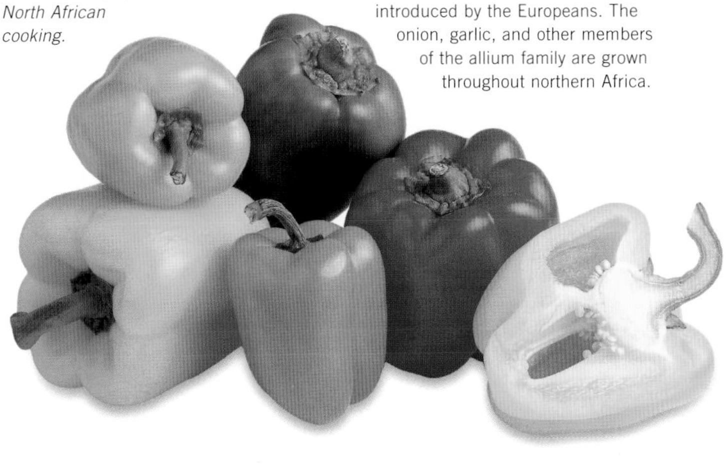

Below: Bell peppers or capsicums, originally from central and South America, are popular in North African cooking.

Fresh Fruit

Africa is famous for its fruits, although many of the native fruits are rarely seen outside the continent, baobab fruits being one example. The baobab is a huge tree that grows all over tropical Africa, from Senegal to Zimbabwe, and can live to be 3,000 years old. It is very strange looking in that the branches look more like roots, as if it were growing upside down. The fruit, which grows up to 30cm/1ft long, contains tartaric acid and vitamin C, and can either be sucked or soaked in water to make a refreshing drink. The fruits are also dried and roasted then ground up to make a coffee-like drink or used as a flavouring and spice.

Other wild fruits, which grow in Kenya, are *muratina*, *burarakambi*, *chufutu* and *busemwa*. Many fruits that are considered to be indigenous are, in fact, not native to the continent, such as orange, tangerine, coconut, banana, mango and papaya.

Surinam cherry

The acerola, or Surinam cherry, originally from the Caribbean, has become very popular in the Horn of Africa. It cannot be eaten fresh as it is too acidic, but makes wonderful jams, jellies and preserves.

Citrus fruit

Imported via India, most citrus fruits probably originally came from China. They have taken to the African climate and are available throughout the year, which makes them widely used. They have largely been spread not by human plantations but by birds, especially parrots, and grow wild in the forests of Kenya and Zimbabwe. Of course, they are carefully cultivated in North Africa, and Algeria has produced its own varieties, such as the clementine and the tangerine, which are an important Christmas export.

Right: Tangerines are cultivated in Algeria, and are harvested between the months of November and April.

Banana

It is surprising to think that bananas, which are an African staple, are not native to the continent, but originally came from India. In addition to the fruit itself, which is eaten ripe, as a fruit, or unripe, as a vegetable, the leaves make wrappers for food, and disposable plates. Green bananas are certain unripe varieties that are used as a vegetable. They are boiled, with or without their skins.

Right: Prickly pears come from the opuntia cactus. The flesh inside is sweet, though full of seeds.

African horned melon

Also known by the name of kiwano, this extraordinary fruit is bright orange and covered with small bumps or protrusions. The flesh is green and it has small crunchy pips similar to passion fruit.

Dates and figs

Luscious dates and figs are native to coastal regions of North Africa. They are dried and exported southwards to Saharan and sub-Saharan Africa. Dates are important in the practice of Islam, as the prophet Mohammed

Below: Jackfruit or jakfruit are large fruits with nutritious seeds that must be boiled before being eaten.

Below: Dates are ideal food for hot regions as in their dried form they keep for months.

Below: The kiwano, or African horned melon, is spectacular with its bright orange skin, thick spines, green flesh and black seeds.

advocated breaking the Ramadan fast by eating dates and drinking water. Figs are mainly found in North Africa, and are used in desserts, as well as eaten fresh and dried.

Locust bean

Also known as carob, this bean grows in the drier parts of North Africa on a large, handsome tree. The long brown beans have a sweet pulp, which is enjoyed by children and also fed to domestic animals. The beans are also fermented and then cooked with the *meloukhia* leaf, especially in Saharan Africa, where the resulting dish is known as *crain crain*.

Below right: Physalis is grown in, and exported widely from, Cape Province, hence its other name of Cape gooseberry.

Physalis

Also known as a Cape gooseberry, the physalis looks like an orange cherry, encased in a papery calyx, and is rich in vitamin C. It is often used for decoration because of its attractive appearance. Despite the profusion in which it grows around the Cape of Good Hope in South Africa, it is really a native fruit of Peru.

Jackfruit

Another fruit originally from the Indian continent is the jackfruit, the largest of the tree-born fruits. It can weigh as much as 41kg/90lb. The fruit growing on the tree is a strange sight because it grows directly out of the trunk on a short stem. Inside the fruit, the thick, warty flesh is yellow, very sweet, and firm rather than fibrous. The large seeds, known as jacknuts, are also edible but are eaten boiled.

The jackfruit has an unpleasant smell, but this does not permeate the flesh. The flesh must be eaten as soon as it is ripe because the fruit will continue to ripen after the flesh is cut.

Below: Pineapples are have become an important import from the Ivory Coast.

Cactus fruit

Also known as prickly pear, this small greenish-orange fruit is from the opuntia cactus, the cactus fruit is native to the Americas, and possibly China, and was introduced into the Middle East and North Africa by merchant traders in the 16th century.

Pineapple

Just as Kenya is famous for its exports of vegetables, most of which were originally from the Americas, so the Ivory Coast and Malawi are exporters of another South American fruit, the pineapple. Miniature pineapples, grown more for their beauty than their usefulness, are also exported.

Right: Watermelon is an African native fruit that has spread all over the world.

Grapes

Vines are indigenous to North Africa and there has always been a flourishing wine trade there. Algeria, Morocco and Tunisia also all produce table grapes, and raisins, for export.

Watermelon

The watermelon has been grown in Africa for centuries and is depicted on Egyptian wall paintings, although earlier varieties were small and probably bitter. They are now universally sweet and very large and are grown throughout Africa. The two main varieties of watermelon are round with a dark-green skin and deep-red flesh, or elongated with a pale green skin or a skin striped with darker green. Watermelons were taken to the Americas via the slave trade.

Fish and Shellfish

Fresh fish and shellfish are found all along the coasts. Fishing methods in Africa (except for South Africa) remain traditional: fish are speared or caught in nets by fishermen in boats working as a team, and lake fish are often netted by a single fisherman. Fish forms a vital part of the African diet, even inland, although the problem of keeping fish fresh is a serious one where refrigeration is still a luxury.

Thébouidienne is a classic fish stew from Senegal, in which any white fish is stewed slowly in a casserole with cabbage, sweet potato, bell chillies, pimentos and chilli peppers. The stew is served on a bed of rice. In the Ivory Coast, the fish is casseroled similarly, but the flavourings are pumpkin, marrow and fresh coconut, strips of which are laid over the fish. To this is added rice, fried onions and seasoning, it is then simmered in coconut water until tender.

FRESH FISH

The following fish are to be found in the rivers or seas of the African continent, but they can all be substituted with similar-sized white fish that may be more easily available.

Below: The brightly coloured parrot fish is popular in West Africa.

Above: Red mullet is an important catch in the Mediterranean and is used for a variety of North African dishes.

Nile perch and tilapia

Both these freshwater fish are eaten in Egypt and the Sudan, with the Nile perch the most frequently consumed. They are usually fried in oil.

Jobfish

A member of the snapper family, the jobfish lives in the waters of the Indian Ocean and is sold along the coast in Kenya, Tanzania and Mozambique. It is an attractive orange or lavender colour.

Red mullet

Among the finest of all sea fish, the flesh of red mullet is lean and firm, and its flavour is robust and distinctive. Because of this, red mullet is a favourite in North African countries, where it is used in a wide variety of dishes. It is caught in the Mediterranean, so does not feature in the more southern areas of Africa.

Parrotfish

The parrotfish is a colourful fish that lives on coral reefs, and is popular in the fish stews of West Africa. In Liberia, it is often cooked with coconut cream and served with *foufou* (mashed cassava or yam). The fish are sautéed in butter or ghee, seasoned with salt and pepper and fried. They are then stewed in coconut milk in a covered pan. The cover is then removed and the sauce reduced until it is creamy.

Other species

In West and South Africa, it is the fish of the southern Atlantic that are caught, including grey mullet and albacore, swordfish and marlin as well as species

Cape Kedgeree

Although originally a curry, Cape kedgeree from South Africa is no longer a spicy dish, owing to the influence of the British and Dutch. Fish that has been precooked – usually red mullet or snoek – is mixed with cooked rice (there should be twice as much fish as rice) and chopped egg whites. It is then seasoned with salt and pepper and simmered in evaporated milk or single cream. The yolks of hardboiled eggs are then pushed through a sieve and used to garnish the dish before it is served.

of shark and snoek. In East Africa, the best ocean catch is considered to be shark, known as *papa*, which is mainly cut into strips, dried and sent inland. The snoek is an oily fish and as such is particularly delicious dried or smoked. Other varieties used are yellowtail, steenbrass and Hottentot fish.

DRIED FISH

A highly prized ingredient in Africa, many different types of small fish are dried and used extensively for flavouring foods. Particular favourites are dried anchovies, which are sold in great piles in all African markets, and used in meat dishes as well as fish-based recipes such as the stews of Senegal and Mali, Uganda, Kenya and Tanzania. In the western Cape province, fatty fish including mullet and herring are strung up in bunches to dry in the sun, to make a dried fish called *hardums*.

Below: Oysters are often eaten as an appetizer in the restaurants of Kenya.

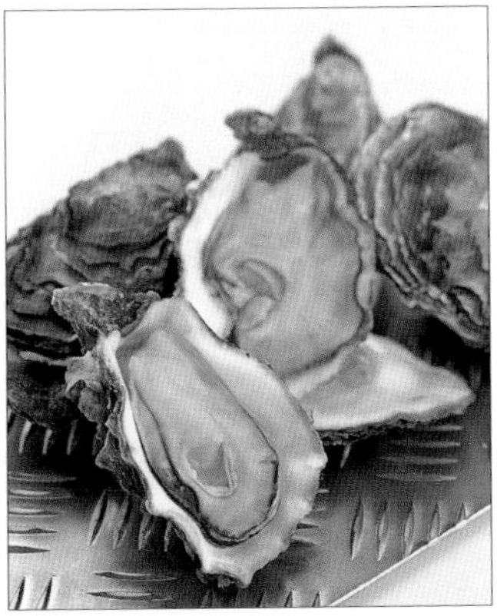

Above: Salt cod before soaking.

Fish calulu is an Angolan fish stew, which is made from a mixture of dried and fresh fish. The dried fish are softened in hot water then stewed with the fresh fish, seasoned with garlic, salt, vinegar and lemon. Alternate layers of the dried and fresh fish are then placed in a large pan with sliced onion, tomatoes, spinach or sweet potato leaves and sliced okra. This is then simmered in palm oil until cooked. The rich stew is usually served with a manioc flour porridge known as *funge*.

Salt fish

Also known as stockfish, salted cod is an important ingredient in cooking throughout sub-Saharan Africa. The fish is imported from countries bordering the North Atlantic, such as Portugal. It is rock hard when purchased, and needs soaking for at least 24 hours in several changes of water before it is ready for cooking.

In Tanzania, the cod is made into a stew called *dagaa*, which is made with tomatoes, onions, chilli and coconut milk.

SHELLFISH

Seafood is a particular favourite of South Africans, where freshly caught lobsters and scallops are widely available. Throughout the rest of Africa shrimps or prawns are dried, and used as flavourings.

Oysters

The oysters of the East African coast are said to be the most delicious in the world. They are regularly served as an appetizer in Kenyan restaurants, European-style with rose-marie sauce and wedges of lemon.

Prawns and shrimps

In Egypt, fresh prawns (shrimp) are a favourite appetizer. In Nigeria they are made into pancakes, using a batter made from ground white haricot beans, tomatoes, onions, cooked prawns and eggs. The pancakes are deep fried, and are often available as street food.

The Indian influence in South Africa is obvious from the fish curries that are often made with prawns. The curries are served with rice and a variety of raitas, such as onion rings, bananas, sliced cucumbers, chutney and shredded coconut. A similar curry is made in East Africa, with small shrimps.

Below: Fresh prawns (shrimp) are a popular ingredient, and when dried they are used extensively throughout Africa.

Meat and Poultry

Red meat is a luxury, especially in central Africa, but poultry, such as the guinea fowl, a bird native to Africa and probably domesticated here as long as five thousand years ago, is an important source of meat. In Africa, meat and fish are often cooked together in the same dish, especially in the former Portuguese colonies of Angola and Mozambique, in a dish known as *futu*, which should have twice as much meat as fish.

Above: Beef is a luxury food throughout Africa, except in South Africa, where cattle are bred for meat.

RED MEAT

The most popular red meats in the Maghreb (Algeria, Morocco and Tunisia) and Saharan Africa, where the animals are raised for milk and meat as well as for their skins or fleece, are that of sheep and goats. The meat is ground, or it might be cut into small pieces or ground with spices and spit-roasted. It may also be added to stews. Only kid is roasted, as older goat is too tough and so it is usually boiled or stewed. Curried goat is a popular dish in Nigeria, and *nyama choma* is very popular in Kenya. This dish consists of goat kebabs served with cooked green banana mash.

Below: Goat is popular in Kenya and Nigeria; it is a tough meat that needs long, slow cooking.

Above: Lamb, in chunks or minced, is the favourite meat of North African cuisine.

In those parts of Kenya and the Sudan where herders count their wealth in cattle, the animals are too valuable to be eaten, so beef is not commonly eaten in East Africa. The Masai, for example, would never eat cattle. However, it is extremely popular in South Africa, where it is used is many different ways, including curries and barbecues. In the Cameroon it is stewed in a fragrant curry with coconut and pineapple. Hump-backed cattle, or zebu, of the type found in India, are also bred in Africa, although more for their milk than meat.

Below: Buffalo is one of the game meats that is hunted and eaten in Africa.

Although pork is forbidden by Islamic law, and not eaten in Muslim countries, it is popular among non-Muslims in West and South Africa in the form of stews and barbecued spare ribs.

GAME

The cane-rat or grasscutter (known as *agouti* in French-speaking Africa) is a rodent that may be as much as 60cm/24in long, not including the tail. It is widely eaten in sub-Saharan Africa. The bush-pig is related to the wart-hog and is eaten in tropical Africa. It has a gamey flavour, tasting more like wild boar. In Central Africa, even monkey and bat are eaten. Gazelle, kudu, eland and other game animals are also eaten in the savannah and in the Sahel, where they roam. Ostrich has lately gained in popularity, as the red meat is lean and flavoursome. The Cape buffalo is hunted and eaten in Africa. The meat from most of these game animals can be airdried and smoked to make biltong.

INSECTS

In Africa, insects are widely eaten, and are a good source of free protein, including grubs, white ants, termites and especially locusts. Plagues of locusts were once common, and eating them was a good way of getting animal protein and helping to protect the crops at the same time, as they were caught before they could damage the crops. Those who have eaten locusts describe them as delicious: crunchy on the outside and creamy within.

Other insects that are eaten include crickets, grasshoppers and flying ants. Even worms and caterpillars are sold as

Right: Biltong is dried meat most commonly made from beef or buffalo.

fried snacks, in towns and cities as well as in more isolated rural areas.

BILTONG

In Southern Africa, and South Africa in particular, beef and other lean meats can be seasoned and dried to make biltong. Game is often preserved this way, including animals such as eland, zebra and ostrich, A long piece of muscle is trimmed into an oval shape and then rubbed with salt, pepper, coriander and fennel. The meat is soaked in vinegar and left to marinate for a few days. It is then hung up in the open air to dry in the wind. When dried out, it is smoked.

If made from game, the biltong is so hard that it can be grated. In South Africa it is often eaten this way as a snack, on top of buttered bread.

CHICKEN

Eggs and chicken are important items in the diet of the those who live in the cities, and those who can afford it put chicken in their stews. Chicken eaten in town or cities in Africa may be the plump, domesticated fowl or even broiler fowl, but in the villages all over Africa chickens roam freely and are consequently lean and tough.

Broiling chicken is known in French West Africa as *poulet bicyclette* (bicycle chicken). No one quite knows why this term is used, perhaps because they are as lean as if they had kept fit by riding a bicycle, but more probably because they are kept for laying and eaten only if they are unfortunate enough to be "road kill". These chickens need long, slow cooking in stews such as Ashanti Chicken from Ghana, where the chicken is slow-cooked with yams, tomatoes and mint leaves, and Yassa Chicken, a traditional recipe from the Camance region of Senegal. Here the chicken is first fried in peanut oil, then slowly stewed in water with spices, including mustard and chilli peppers, lemon juice, vinegar, cabbage and carrots for at least six hours. It is served with *foufou,* cooked and mashed green banana, or rice. Rabbit and guinea fowl can be treated in the same way.

In Angola, chicken is often barbecued (grilled), such as peri-peri chicken, where the bird is first marinated in paprika, hot chilli powder, lemon juice, cloves and ginger.

In North Africa, rich omelettes similar to those eaten in Iran are popular. Chicken irio, a Kikuyu dish from Kenya, is made from eggs, puréed beans, maize and potatoes or cassava, and served with curried chicken.

PIGEON

In the Maghreb and Egypt, pigeon is also an important food item. Pigeons are raised in special towers and their meat is used in roast pigeon with pine nuts and honey or in Bastilla, the famous Moroccan pie.

GUINEA FOWL

There are four species of guinea fowl, all of which are native to Africa, and their ranges extend from the north to south of the Sahara. Guinea fowl were probably domesticated by the ancient Egyptians, but they are expensive and eaten mainly on feast days.

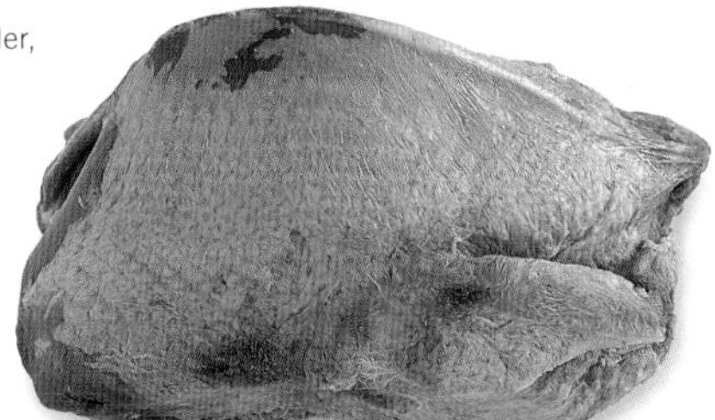

Above: Pigeon is a great delicacy in Egypt and Morocco, where the birds are bred for the table.

Below: Guinea fowl is a domesticated bird that is native to Africa. The flesh is well flavoured and gamey.

Breads and Beverages

Africa is the home of bread, for it is here that the ancient Egyptians first mixed flour with water and left it in the sun. The natural yeasts in the air did the rest. Similarly, most beverages are based on fermentation, including the so-called palm wines of Central Africa.

BREADS AND PASTRIES

In Africa breads are generally flat breads made from wheat. The Ethiopians have two main forms of bread. One is *hambasha*, a firm dough kneaded like a European bread and flavoured with black onion seed or nigella, ground cumin and ground coriander. *Injera* is made with a loose dough, usually made with teff, an indigenous grain grown in the Ethiopian highlands. *Injera* is eaten as a bread, but it is also laid flat on the table and used like the trencher of the Middle Ages – a kind of edible plate on which stew is poured, allowing the bread to soak up the juices as the meal progresses. Diners also use the bread to scoop up meat and vegetable stews. For this purpose, it is cut into long strips.

Phyllo or brik dough is a thin pastry dough, almost identical to filo pastry or strudel dough. One of its uses is to make a pastry from Tunisia that has a filling of egg, vegetables and tuna.

BEVERAGES

Two of the most universally drunk beverages in the world, coffee and beer, were given to the world by Africa.

Above: Phyllo, *the pastry dough that is the trademark of Moroccan cooking.*

Coffee and tea

The coffee shrub grows wild in Ethiopia, and the beans are harvested both from the wild plant and from cultivated varieties. The Ethiopians prefer to dry the beans just until they are still green, then roast and grind them as needed. The coffee drunk all over North and Saharan Africa is prepared in the same way as in the Middle East: ground to a powder, then added to water and boiled over an open fire. Sometimes cardamom or cinnamon is added. In southern Africa coffee is made by percolating rather than boiling, and in South Africa it is drunk with milk.

Tea, both black and green varieties is grown in East and West Africa. In the Maghreb it is taken with a form of spearmint, which is particularly aromatic, rather than milk. Copious amounts of tea are drunk throughout Africa, with meals and on its own. Like coffee, it is the drink of hospitality. Red tea, or Rooibos is a herbal tea that is a favourite drink in South Africa.

Milk

Fresh milk is a luxury in hot climates without refrigeration, but goat's milk and fermented milks (yogurt and kefir-type drinks) are drunk in tropical Africa. Camel milk is also drunk in the Sahara.

Beer

Originally, beer was invented by the ancient Egyptians, who baked cakes of barley then let them ferment in water to produce a rich yeast, beer being an accidental by-product of the process. Thus, beer was developed before people discovered what an improvement yeast made when added to the baked paste of water and flour that came to be eaten as bread. Africans now consume much less beer than people on other continents: about 9 litres/16 pints per capita per year, compared to 21 litres/37 pints as a world average.

Tusker beer is the national drink of Kenya: a light, refreshing beer that

Below: Flat bread, baked on stones or on the floor of the oven, is probably similar to ancient Egyptian bread.

Below: Castle lager, South Africa's most popular beer. All non-Muslim African countries brew their own brands.

Above: Tusker beer, Kenya's own brand, is exported widely, and very much appreciated by Kenyan expatriates.

Above: Coconut water, left, is often drunk in a cocktail. Van der Hum, right, is South Africa's coffee liqueur.

should be drunk ice cold. There are also breweries producing alcohol-free beers, including ABC in Egypt. In South Africa, apart from the popular lagers and ales, such as Castle lager, beer is also brewed illegally and sold at unlicensed bars, known by the Irish name of "shebeens".

Spirits and liqueurs

In Madagascar, rum and fermented coconut water are popular drinks, especially in the north of the island. Africans also brew and distil alcohol from millet. Palm wine is made in tropical Africa. Van der Hum is a liqueur made from brandy and rum steeped in orange peel, orange blossoms, cloves, nutmeg, cinnamon and cardamom. It was originally made by the Dutch settlers, and was named after the Dutch admiral who liked it.

WINES OF AFRICA

Grape-growing began in Algeria in ancient times, and wines were even exported to Rome. Viticulture was revived in 1830, with the arrival of French colonists. In the 1870s, vineyards in France were ravaged by the insect pest phylloxera, and many wine-makers moved to Algeria, where they planted the best French vine stocks. The vineyards are concentrated in three regions: Oran, Constantine and Algiers. The grape varieties grown are mainly Cinsault, Carignan and Grenache, but in some regions Cabernet, Syrah and Merlot are also used. Although the wines of Algeria have suffered from a poor reputation in the past, they are improving. Red wines account for 65 per cent of production, owing to the southern climate, although there are some good whites, especially Coteaux du Zaccar and Médéa. In Oran, Oued-Imbert wines are red, white and rosé. The red wines are generally heavy, coarse and dark, with a high alcohol content and low acidity. They are mainly exported to France, to be blended with wines of the Midi to increase their low alcohol content and add colour and body.

Tunisian vines grow mainly around Cap Bon. Many are dessert wines of the muscat variety, and some of the reds are mixed with rectified spirit to produce a drink called mistelle. The rosé wines are considered among the best in North Africa. Moroccan wines come mainly from the region around Meknès, although vines are grown in Rabat, Casablanca, Fez, Oujda and Marrakech. There are white and red grapes, one variety of which, the Rafsai white grape of the Rif mountain region, is now being vinified. North-eastern Morocco produces rosé wines of comparable quality to Algeria's.

The wines of South Africa have a well established reputation. The first vine cuttings were brought there in 1654, probably from the Rhineland. Wine was made in the Cape by the Dutch colonists for the first time in 1659. The French Huguenots, who first arrived in 1688 and settled in the Franschek Valley, extended the vineyards and improved the quality of the vines. Today, the two vine-growing areas are the Coastal Belt and the Little Karoo. Harvesting is between February and April, before autumn. Many of the vineyards grow in beautiful countryside, presided over by period Dutch plantation houses, some still owned by the original families.

Right: Fairview Pinotage, on the right, is made with a grape created in South Africa. Danie de Wet Chardonnay is a white wine that has won great praise.

Cooking in the Middle East

For centuries the Middle East has had an unrivalled reputation for hospitality, and many of the world's favourite foods originated there. The style of cooking varies from the deceptively simple to the sumptuous and sophisticated recipes that are the legacy of the Ottoman Empire. Herbs and spices – often little known in the West – are used with consummate care, and even the most ordinary meal can be magical.

Historical Background

Exactly what constitutes the Middle East varies, depending upon which authority you consult. Some include the Maghreb – Algeria, Morocco and Tunisia – on the basis that these predominantly Muslim African countries share so much common ground with their eastern neighbours; some exclude Israel but include Afghanistan and some cling doggedly to the older term Near East, which used to comprise the Balkan States and the area of the Ottoman Empire. In this book we include Egypt's Middle Eastern culinary tradition. Therefore, the Middle East, the "belly of the Orient", includes Egypt, Iran, Iraq, Israel and the Palestinian Territories, Jordan, Lebanon, Saudi Arabia, Syria, Turkey, Yemen and the Gulf States of Kuwait, Bahrain, Qatar, the United Arab Emirates and Oman.

All these countries, with the exception of Israel, are strongly Islamic. In Iran, for example, 99 per cent of its population are Muslim; in Jordan the figure is around 96 per cent and in Kuwait around 85 per cent. Lebanon has a 60:40 Muslim:Christian split. Iranians speak Persian (Farsi), Israelis Hebrew and Turks Turkish, but elsewhere the first language is Arabic. English is also widely spoken.

A FERTILE BEGINNING

Two mighty civilizations set the stage for the Middle Eastern story. Both developed in lush valleys and both owed their early stimulus to agriculture. The first of these was in ancient Egypt, in the extraordinarily fertile Nile Valley. The river flooded every year with predictable regularity. This laid down rich deposits of silt, which enabled wheat and other crops to be grown with ease. Beyond the river, irrigation made farming possible even in the surrounding desert, and the co-operation this required was one of the aspects that led to an ordered society.

In what is now Iraq, there was another mighty river valley. This was Mesopotamia, the land between the Tigris and Euphrates rivers. It formed part of a larger area known as the Fertile Crescent, which stretched in an arc from Israel to the Persian Gulf. Here, as in Egypt, irrigation made large-scale agriculture possible. Nomadic hunter-gatherers became farmers, cultivating wheat, barley, figs, dates and pomegranates in the rich alluvial soil. There were marsh fowl and fish in the Delta, and these were incorporated into a diet that was not so very different from modern Iraqi fare.

FOOD FIT FOR PHAROAHS

The daily diet for most inhabitants of ancient Egypt was bread, vegetables and fruit, with perhaps a little fresh or dried fish. *Meloukhia*, a green vegetable that resembles spinach, was used for soup. The wealthier inhabitants might also have meat – duck, goose or maybe gazelle. Dried beans and lentils were widely eaten, just as they are today, and sweetmeats were popular. The earliest recorded Egyptian recipe is for a sweetmeat, a mixture of dates, walnuts and cinnamon, rolled into balls and coated with honey and ground nuts.

Below: Bedouin shepherds in Syria tend to their sheep.

A PATTERN OF CONQUEST

Egypt fell to Rome in 34 BC. Food played a role even in this event, for the conquest was prompted in part by Rome's desire for Egypt's vast grain reserves. In Mesopotamia, the Sumerians had long since been vanquished by the Akkadians, and a succession of new rulers took their place. Eventually, Mesopotamia, too, became a province of Rome. This pattern of events continued throughout the Middle East – with different principal characters – for centuries. Countries were invaded, bitter battles were fought and then there followed a period of relative calm and stability. The invading armies brought with them their favourite dishes and learned to like the local food as well, and when they swept on, as they inevitably did, they took with them the ingredients and cooking methods they had acquired.

This helps to explain why, wherever you go in the Middle East, you will encounter the same recipes. The names will be different and there will be subtle local nuances, but each will be recognizable. Of course, there are individual specialities, too. Iran (formerly Persia), for example, has a rich repertoire of rice dishes and a reputation for subtle spicing. The country was at one time on the famous Silk Route, so Persians had access to exotic ingredients to augment a diet that was already rich and varied.

Recipes of Arab origin, like Tabbouleh, and stuffed lamb with baba ganoush, were disseminated during the Arab Conquest, which began in the 7th century AD, when an army of the Prophet Muhammad's followers conquered all the lands that comprise present-day Syria, Lebanon, Israel, Iraq, Iran, Jordan and Egypt.

THE OTTOMAN EMPIRE

The cuisine of the Middle East may have been shaped by these disparate influences, but it was the Turkish Ottomans who refined it. They came to power at the beginning of the 14th century. Within 150 years they had conquered Constantinople (now

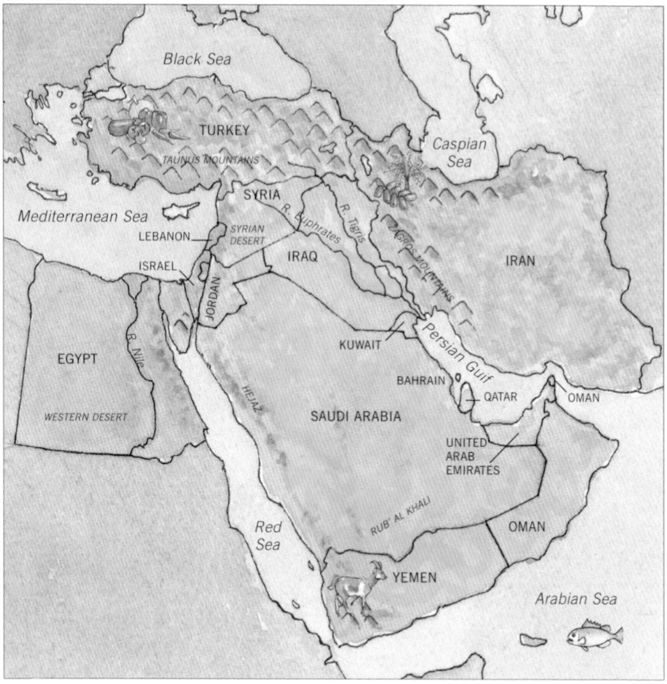

Istanbul), the former Byzantine capital, and built the fabulous Topkapi Palace. Banquets at the palace became legendary. Food was prepared by a team of cooks, including butchers, bakers, pastry cooks, confectioners, yogurt and cheese makers and experts in pickling and preserving vegetables and fruit. Only the finest ingredients were used. The empire that eventually stretched from Cairo to Budapest, and from Tripoli to Baghdad, provided plenty of ingredients and inspiration.

FOREIGN INFLUENCES

After the First World War, which signalled the end of the Ottoman Empire, Britain administered Palestine, Transjordan, Iraq and Egypt, whereas France took control of Lebanon and Syria. France had the greater impact, not so much in the way of introducing typical French dishes, but rather in refining the cooking and presentation of local specialities.

Omani cuisine reveals several foreign influences. Between the 17th and 19th centuries, Oman was a powerful seafaring nation that rivalled Portugal and England in the Gulf, the Indian Ocean and the coasts of India and East Africa. Returning sailors introduced spices from Zanzibar and curries from India. The food in Yemen has an Indian flavour, too, thanks to interaction with Indian merchants. Chillies are used more widely in Yemen than anywhere else in the Middle East.

Israel has a dynamic and very varied cuisine. Since the establishment of the State of Israel in 1948, hundreds of thousands of Jews from many countries have emigrated there, each national group bringing their traditional dishes to add to the Kosher tradition. Chopped liver from Alsace, polenta fritters from Italy, cherry soup from Hungary, *pierogi* from Poland – all these plus a host of typically Middle Eastern dishes are to be found on the menu.

A Cuisine Steeped in Tradition

Social mores and religious observance play a large role in the way food is prepared, cooked and served in the Middle East. Muslims and Jews both abstain from eating pork, and there are strict laws governing the way permitted animals are slaughtered. Custom dictates how food is served and to whom, and there are largely unspoken but firmly entrenched traditions surrounding the role of the host and the offering of hospitality.

MUSLIM RELIGIOUS OBSERVANCE

Islamic doctrine is enshrined in the Koran, or Qur'an. The word literally means "recitation" and is held to be the word of God (Allah) as dictated to the Prophet Mohammad by the Angel Jibril (Gabriel). There are five articles of faith, the first of which is the doctrine that there is only one true God and his name is Allah. The prime observances or duties Muslims must perform include public acknowledgement of Allah and of Muhammad as his prophet; praying five times a day; giving alms; making a pilgrimage to Mecca at least once in a lifetime and fasting from sunrise to sunset every day during Ramadan.

Above: Bedouin women eat after they have served the men, sitting outside their tent in the Sinai Desert.

Food that may be eaten is described as halal (lawful). This includes beef, goat, lamb and poultry slaughtered in the permitted manner. Pork is taboo. Game may be eaten in certain circumstances, provided the hunter is a Muslim or the child of a Muslim. Fish with scales are halal, provided they were alive when taken from the water. This also applies to prawns (shrimp), but lobster, crab, shellfish and fish that lack scales, such as shark, are not allowed. All alcohol and other stimulants are forbidden.

In addition to the Koran, Muslims honour the Hadith, or Tradition, a record of the sayings of Muhammad, together with accounts by others of how the Prophet himself lived. The Hadith offers additional guidance on how adherents should conduct themselves, and has quite a bit to say on the subject of food. Some of the tenets are simply good practice; for example, Muslims are

Below: A stall in the famous night-time marketplace Jema al Fnr, Marrakesh, Morocco, renowned for fabulous food.

The Laws of Kashrut

Observant Jews also adhere to strict dietary laws. Only certain meats and types of fish are permitted, and animals must be dispatched by a *shochet,* or ritual slaughterer. Blood must be removed from the animal immediately after slaughter. Dairy foods and meat must not be cooked together, and if meat has been eaten, a period of time must elapse before any type of dairy food can be consumed. Wine, beer and spirits are permitted, with some limitations. There are special observances for the Sabbath, and for festivals such as Pesach (Passover) and Purim.

advised to wash fruit thoroughly but not to peel it before eating, water should be sipped, not gulped, and no Muslim should drink from a cup with a cracked rim. Food must not be wasted. Any leftovers must be fed to animals or used in another dish. This has led to the development of some intriguing recipes, including Fattoush, a salad composed largely of stale bread and vegetables.

THE HONOURED GUEST

The offering of hospitality is deeply ingrained in the Arab psyche. As an old proverb declares: "Three things are no disgrace to man, to serve his guest, to serve his horse and to serve in his own house." In Bedouin society, this concern for the well-being of a guest is particularly marked. A traveller seeking food and accommodation will not be turned away. Even an enemy must be taken in for 48 hours if need be, and then given safe conduct as he proceeds on his journey.

In Bedouin society, as is the Arab pattern, men and women eat separately. The women prepare the food, but do not eat until after the men have finished their meal. A Western female guest will be accorded the same courtesies as her husband, however. The meal begins with the ceremonial washing of hands. Guests sit cross-legged on the carpeted floor of the tent and the meal is placed in the centre. Traditionally, this is likely to be *mansaf*, Jordan's national dish. The word means "big tray", which is an accurate description. A very large tray is covered with several sheets of flat bread. On top of this is piled rice mixed with roasted pine nuts and almonds, and over that is heaped pieces of succulent cooked lamb. The whole dish is bathed in a yogurt sauce, which is regularly replenished as the meal proceeds. No utensils are used. Instead, everyone eats with the right hand, the left being reserved for personal hygiene.

Before taking the first bite, prayers may be said. During the meal, the guest will be encouraged to eat his fill, and more than his fill. When everyone has eaten, coffee will be served and it is accepted form for a guest to drink several small cups before signifying – with a wave of the empty cup – that he has had enough.

If there are obligations on the host, there are also expectations of the guest. He may be offered a special delicacy, like the eyes or testicles. This titbit must not be refused. It is expected that a guest will eat heartily and show appreciation. Finally, a guest should not overstay his welcome. As Muhammad said: "It is not right for a guest to stay so long as to incommode his host."

MODERN TRENDS

Although the Bedouin model of hospitality may not be encountered very often by the average visitor to the Middle East, kindness and courtesy remain a mark of even the most ordinary encounter. Meals will be prepared with elaborate care, because to take time and trouble honours the guest. Cooking will probably begin early in the day, so that there will be plenty of tasters – the mezzes – for the visitor to sample before moving on to the main course. The meal will be ample and the host will be satisfied only if waistbands are put under strain. Guests will be offered the best chairs and everything will be done to make them feel at home. In contemporary households, men and women may eat together, and serve alcohol, even in Muslim homes.

Above: Ancient farming methods in rural areas of the Middle East reflect the enduring social traditions of the culture.

Daily Eating Patterns

In the Middle East, it is invariably the women who cook, clean and care for children. This is the case even when the woman works full time, as more and more women do. In Israel, the pattern is altering somewhat, particularly among young couples where both are wage earners, but in Arab-Muslim societies in particular, women are the ones who go to market, prepare the food and, in many cases, serve their menfolk first before they and their children have their meal. Convenience foods, like finely ground or minced meat for meatballs and kebabs, ready-to-use shredded pastry and filo pastry, prepared mezzes and salads from shiny supermarkets, make women's lives easier, but many still prefer the old ways, and buy their produce from the *souk* or market.

THE DAILY DIET

In most of the Middle East, the pattern of meals is more or less the same. The day begins early for many people, because it makes sense to get as much work done as possible before it becomes unbearably hot.

For the business person, breakfast might simply consist of a bowl of yogurt with some honey or preserves, or a couple of bite-size pastries bought from the bakery on the way to the office. Many people start the day with bread, olives, soft cheese, tomato and cucumber, but the traditional breakfast, enjoyed from Alexandria to Aqaba, is *foul*. The word can be spelled in many different ways, but the dish is always basically the same: cooked dried broad (fava) beans mashed with oil and lemon juice. The Jordanians add some chopped chilli and the Lebanese like to stir in chopped fresh coriander (cilantro). In Turkey, a favourite breakfast dish is *menemen*, which

Above: Dinner in a Jordanian restaurant, where food is served from a large plate set in the centre of the table.

Below: The markets of the Middle East are full of fresh fruit and vegetables, which are bought on a daily basis.

consists of a thick tomato sauce spiked with chilli. Hollows are made in the sauce and an egg is broken into each. When the eggs are cooked, the dish is topped with crumbled feta cheese and served with flat bread.

Lunch is eaten between 1.00 and 3.00 p.m. Rural dwellers often make this their main meal, but in the cities, people prefer a snack and will often choose two or three mezzes with some bread and perhaps a piece of fruit. Those eating at home might plump for a bowl of beef and herb soup with yogurt, or spinach and lemon soup with meatballs. There'll always be bread, even if all it accompanies is a little cheese and a few olives.

Hummus, which is chickpea purée, is popular, as is the broad bean equivalent, byesar. Office workers may choose some street food, such as Falafel served in pitta bread with onion slices and tomatoes.

The evening meal can be eaten at any time between 8.00 and 11.00 p.m. This is generally the main meal of the day for city people. It will begin in a leisurely fashion, with the serving of mezzes. The main course might be anything from grilled (broiled) fish or poultry to a meat dish. Offal (variety meats) is very popular in the Middle East, or a simple stew may be offered. If you are in Iran, this is likely to be a Khoresh, served over rice. Bread will accompany the meal and there will probably be several salads, all served with a dollop of yogurt on the side. Dessert will be fresh fruit – perhaps a slice of chilled melon – or just a single perfect peach. If it is a special occasion, a sticky pastry such as baklava or kodafa may be served, or a piece of basbousa, the coconut halva beloved of the Egyptians. Creamy rice puddings, scented with rosewater or spiced with cardamom are also popular.

Above: Street food has an important role in the Middle East, and stalls laden with vast arrays of sweetmeats are common.

RAMADAN

During the month of Ramadan, the ninth month in the Islamic calendar, Muslims fast. Most families rise very early, long before daybreak, to share a meal – *sahur*. When it is light enough (when "the white thread can be distinguished from the black thread of dawn") the fast begins and all who are able must refrain from eating or drinking until the sun goes down.

In the evening the fast is broken with another meal – *iftar*. This is very much a family time, although guests are very welcome, and the meal is often shared with others, especially those considered to be less fortunate than their hosts. Ramadan ends with the festival of Eid ul-Fitr, when gifts are exchanged and parties held.

THE MIDDLE EASTERN KITCHEN

The food of the Middle East, like that of the Mediterranean, is fundamentally healthy. There are regions where meat is the mainstay, and the diet is high in animal fats, but most people eat plenty of vegetables and fruit, fresh fish and a relatively small amount of meat, which is generally grilled (broiled) over an open fire. For energy, they rely on slow-release carbohydrates like pulses. The extra-sweet pastries for which the region is famous are eaten as treats with coffee or tea, rather than as daily desserts, so don't have the devastating impact on the diet that might be assumed.

The exciting world of Middle Eastern ingredients is encapsulated in the open-air markets throughout the regions, where the senses are stimulated by the sight of glossy purple aubergines (eggplants), bright red cherries, yellow quinces, baskets of fresh greens and sacks of lentils. The aroma of lemons, warm spices and fresh coffee fills the air. Having filled your basket, you are invited to munch on a handful of nuts or sample a few marinated olives before stepping into a shop for more mysterious items, like pomegranate molasses, *pekmez* and *zahtar*.

Below: Turkish coffee, thick, black and sweet, is served after dinner, or with a sweetmeat in the afternoon.

Above: Fresh vegetables locally grown are an important part of cooking in the Middle East. Here an Egyptian farming family pick their peppers.

FAVOURITE FOODS

Wheat is the favourite grain, and bread is always on the table. There is a wide variety of breads, including leavened and unleavened loaves and flat breads. All the bread must be eaten; leftovers will be incorporated into a tasty dish. Rice, introduced from India, is also widely eaten, especially in Iran. As well as forming a main part of the meal, it is also used to make stuffings for vegetables and vine leaves and there are numerous recipes for rice mixed with vegetables or lentils. Short-grain rice is used for puddings and soups.

The most popular meat is lamb, followed closely by chicken, which is cooked in a variety of ways, perhaps spatchcocked and cooked over a brazier – to be enjoyed as a street food – or simmered in yogurt until tender. Middle Eastern cooks also specialize in the cooking of offal (variety meats). Everything from liver and kidneys to trotters and testicles is eaten, and some of the tastiest spiced dishes are made from these apparently unpromising ingredients. Fish is very popular in coastal regions, especially in Turkey and

Below: These distinctive oval-shaped olives have been grown in the Middle East for centuries.

Oman, and freshwater or sea fish are generally preferred to shellfish. Many recipes for cooking fish include spicy sauces or herb stuffings, and nuts and fruit may also be added to complement the flavours of the fish.

Vegetables and fruits are important in their own right, but are also used in stews and ragoûts. Particularly popular are aubergines, courgettes (zucchini), spinach and green beans. There is a wide range of salads, often served with labna (white cheese) or yogurt. Salads always appear as part of mezze – a selection of small dishes served as a first course or to accompany a main dish. Garlic is popular in Mediterranean lands, but elsewhere in the Middle East it is regarded as being rather brash and is often omitted from recipes.

Luscious Middle Eastern fruits, such as melon and pomegranate, are enjoyed after a meal, and many fruits, both fresh and dried, will also be cooked with savoury foods. Deliciously sweet Middle Eastern pastries, however, are traditionally served with afternoon coffee and not as a dessert. Coffee and tea are widely drunk. Both are served without milk. Fruit drinks and drinks that are based on yogurt are on offer everywhere, but alcohol is less widely available due to the Muslim prohibition on its consumption.

The following pages introduce and explain some of the regions' raw ingredients, used for everyday cooking throughout the Middle East, as well as traditional breads, pastries and drinks.

Above: Dried beans and peas are staple ingredients and are used widely in many traditional dishes.

Nations of nut lovers

Almonds, cashew nuts, pine nuts, peanuts, hazelnuts and pistachio nuts are extremely popular in the Middle East. Nuts serve as snacks, street food and as the basis for sauces like *tarator* – a lemon, garlic and pine nut mixture traditionally served with fish. Ground nuts are used, often with dried fruits, in stuffings for poultry and as fillings for sweet pastries. *Ma'amoul*, for example, can have a walnut and cinnamon filling, a pistachio and rosewater filling, a ground almond and orange flower water filling or any combination of these, with dates or other dried fruit. Nuts are often combined with seeds, as in the Egyptian snack food *dukkah*, which is a mixture of crushed roasted hazelnuts or chickpeas with sesame and coriander seeds.

Many of the ingredients featured are widely available in general stores and supermarkets; for some of the others you might need to find a specialist supplier, or make a substitute.

Below: Dried fruits are used widely in the Middle East, as snacks and desserts, and as an ingredient in both sweet and savoury dishes.

Below: Ras al hanout is a spice mix used throughout the Middle East.

WHEAT, RICE AND BEANS

First cultivated in Mesopotamia some ten thousand years ago, wheat is an extremely important crop in the Middle East, where some kind of bread is eaten at every meal. Rice is also widely eaten, while beans add variety and protein.

Above: Bulgar wheat is used for salads as well as an accompaniment to stews.

WHEAT

An unfussy cereal, wheat will flourish in a range of climates, although it does best in cooler conditions. In most areas of the Middle East wheat is therefore a winter crop. The main areas of cultivation are Turkey, central Iran, coastal Lebanon and Israel, northern Syria and Iraq, Jordan and the Nile Delta.

There are two main varieties: bread wheat and durum wheat, which is used for pasta and semolina. What distinguishes bread wheat is its high gluten content. This elastic protein substance is what makes leavened bread maintain its rise. It does this by strengthening the dough so that it traps the carbon dioxide produced when yeast ferments.

Bulgur wheat

Sometimes described as the world's first processed food, bulgur wheat is durum wheat that has been ground into particles after being cleaned, lightly boiled, dried and hulled. Before use, it needs only brief cooking, or can simply be soaked in boiling water. In the Middle East it is widely used in pilaffs, salads – especially Tabbouleh – and the legendary Lebanese dish, Kibbeh. Bulgur wheat is also the basis of several sweet dishes, and is mixed with fermented yogurt and then dried to make another pelleted product, *kishk*, which is used to thicken stews.

Whole-wheat grains, called *kamh* in Egypt, are boiled in milk and water to make a porridge-like mixture, which is generally eaten with yogurt and honey.

Below: Semolina is used to make porridge, puddings and desserts.

Semolina and wheat

Also known as *smeed*, semolina is coarsely milled durum wheat. The Berbers use it to make a thick gruel, and it is also an ingredient in some desserts and cakes, especially halva. Couscous is made from semolina.

Wheat flour is used for breadmaking, and is also the basis of the thin, crisp pastry that we know as filo or phyllo. The Turkish version, yufka, comes in various thicknesses. Fine yufka is used for pastries, while the thicker type of dough is used for a stuffed bread called *gözleme*.

Below: Fine yufka, made from semolina and used for pastries.

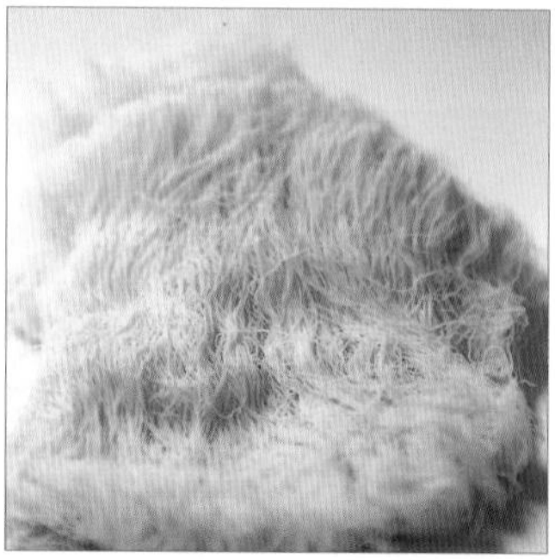

RICE

Long-grain rice arrived in the Middle East from northern India and Afghanistan, which helps to explain why fine varieties like basmati are generally preferred in countries like Iran and Iraq. In Egypt, where rice was traded through Alexandria's "Pepper Gate" towards the end of the first century AD, the grain was originally perceived as a medicinal

Below: Couscous is perhaps the most common ingredient in the Middle East.

Below: Long-grain rice, such as this Iranian rice, is the most popular variety.

food and used to treat stomach ailments. Today, Egyptians eat around 43kg/94lb per person annually, making them among the world's highest consumers. Despite this impressive figure, the richly fertile Nile Delta produces so much rice (three times the average yield) that Egypt is the only Middle Eastern country with a surplus. Most of this goes to its close neighbours: the Middle East is the world's third biggest importer of rice, after Europe and Brazil.

Middle Eastern cooks use rice in a wide variety of ways, but no nation is as adept at cooking it as the Iranians. Rice is grown along the Caspian coast. There are several varieties, including the much-prized *domsiah*. In Persian cooking (still called Persian, despite the name of the country being changed to Iran), light, fluffy rice with each grain separate is a speciality. Rice is so important that the stew served with it, Khoresh, is somewhat dismissively referred to as a sauce. Persians have also perfected the art of cooking rice so that a crisp crust forms on the base of the pan. This is the tahdeeg, which is broken up and served to guests.

BEANS AND LENTILS

Beans, peas and lentils have been cultivated and dried in the Middle East for centuries, and today's pulses (legumes) were developed from wild plants that originally grew in the lands bordering the Eastern Mediterranean. There are numerous mentions of pulses in the Bible, the most famous of which describes the incident when Esau sold his birthright for "a pottage of lentiles". A direct descendant from that famous bowl of lentil soup is *mujaddarah*, a lentil and rice stew that is traditionally eaten by Christian communities in Lebanon during Lent. The name means "smallpox" and it refers to the way in which the lentils stud the white rice and create a spotted appearance.

Dried beans and peas

Of the many varieties of dried bean eaten in the Middle East, broad (fava) beans are probably the most common. A small brown variety called ful or foul is the basis of Egypt's national dish, ful medames. The soaked beans are cooked very simply, with onion skin and whole eggs, and the thick broth that results is eaten throughout the Middle East for breakfast, lunch, dinner and as a street snack.

In Israel, white haricot (navy) beans are widely used, especially in the long-simmered stew known as Cholent. Black-eyed beans (peas) are popular, too. Chickpeas are extensively used throughout the region, particularly for Hummus and Falafel. Small and khaki-coloured, chickpeas look a little like pale hazelnuts. They retain their shape when cooked and are delicious in a spinach salad. Chickpea flour is frequently used as a thickener.

Above: Hummus, made from chickpeas, is a popular mezze dish.

Below: Dried haricot beans from Israel, where they are a particular favourite.

Lentils

Cheap, nutritious and easy to cook, lentils are widely used in the Middle East. The small red split lentil is favoured in Egypt and Syria, whereas Lebanese cooks tend to prefer the green or brown varieties.

Green shoots for Christmas

As Christmas approaches in the Lebanon, Christian children layer chickpeas, lentils and beans between pieces of cotton wool. These are placed on saucers and watered regularly until the shoots are about 15cm/6in long. When the family sets up the nativity scene, the shoots are placed in the manger and on the floor of the stable to represent hay.

Herbs and Spices

Judicious use of herbs and spices is the secret of many Middle Eastern dishes. Although there are some countries where fiery food is enjoyed, such as Yemen, the preference tends to be for mild, warm spices and cool, fresh herbs such as mint and parsley.

The Middle East is also home to some fascinating spice blends. Until recently these were little known outside their countries of origin, but the universal demand for new taste sensations has led to their being packaged and marketed worldwide.

Mint

Mint is an essential fresh herb in Middle Eastern cooking. It is used with lamb dishes, as an ingredient in salads and vegetable dishes, as a flavouring for yogurt sauces and with fruit. A sprig of fresh mint is often added to a glass of the sweet black tea that is such a feature of Middle Eastern life.

Parsley

You are unlikely to find curly parsley in the Middle East, but the flatleaf variety is extremely popular. This is particularly true in Lebanon, where cooks add extravagant handfuls of chopped parsley to dishes like Tabbouleh. In Iran, flat leaf parsley is one of the herbs used in *kuku sabzi*, a baked egg dish, rather like a large omelette, which is served to celebrate the New Year.

Coriander

This herb, also known as cilantro, is a member of the parsley family native to the Middle East and Mediterranean. In Middle Eastern cooking it is the leaves

Above: Mint is used in enormous quantities in Turkey, for tea and salads.

and seeds that are most commonly used. Fresh coriander has a spicy citrus and ginger flavour, quite different from that of flat leaf parsley, which it resembles. The small, round seeds look like pale, creamy peppercorns; they are used whole in pickles, but are more often roasted and ground. Freshly ground coriander has a mild, warm flavour that is discernible in many Middle Eastern dishes, especially meatballs and stews.

Dill

Although most people associate dill with Scandinavia, the herb is actually native to western Asia and is hugely popular in the Middle East. The feathery, fern-like leaves and seeds have a flavour redolent of caraway. Dill goes particularly well with fish, but in the Middle East is also popularly used with vegetables. Fresh dill is often strewn into rice dishes, and is frequently partnered with broad (fava) beans.

Thyme

The aroma of wild thyme is familiar to anyone who has journeyed to the Eastern Mediterranean. In the Middle East, the herb is known by its Arabic name of *zahtar*. Confusingly, the same name is also used to describe a popular spice mix based on thyme.

Cardamom

Ancient Egyptians chewed cardamom pods to whiten their teeth and sweeten their breath. The spice grows mainly in India, and reached the Middle East via Iran. It consists of small fleshy pods, which reveal tiny seeds when split. Green, white (bleached) and black cardamoms are grown, the former being the most popular. The seeds have a warm, slightly citrus flavour. Coffee flavoured with cardamom – *gahwa* – is a favourite drink among Arabs, and is served with considerable ceremony.

Cumin

A native of Upper Egypt and the Mediterranean, cumin has been a favourite spice in the Middle East for centuries. The ancient Egyptians were reputedly very fond of it, and cumin seeds have been found in the tombs of the pharaohs. Today, cumin is widely cultivated throughout the Middle East. Turkey and Iran are particularly important producers of cumin seeds,

Below: Flatleaf parsley is used generously in dishes such as tabbouleh.

Below: Thyme is a woody herb that retains much of its flavour when dried.

Below: Dill is used in fish and vegetable dishes and goes well with broad beans.

Above: Ground cinnamon

Above: White cumin

Above: Black cumin seeds

Above: Ground sumac

with Iran being a source of black cumin as well as the more familiar brownish-yellow variety.

Paprika

Made from a mild red sweet pepper, this sweet, pungent spice is more popular in Turkey than other parts of the Middle East.

Saffron

Used sparingly, this costly spice imparts a delicate flavour and yellow colour to foods, but it can taste musty if overdone. The familiar thin red threads are the stigmas of a crocus that grows well in Iran and Turkey. The threads are usually steeped in a liquid before being used. Ground saffron is also available.

Cinnamon

The rolled bark of an evergreen tree related to the laurel, cinnamon is a sweet, warm spice. It was known to the ancient Egyptians, who used it in religious ritual as well as in the kitchen.

Below: Harissa, a Tunisian spice mix, is also used in the Middle East.

Modern Middle Eastern cooks enjoy its mellow fragrance in both sweet and savoury dishes. In Turkey it is used to flavour tea, while in Azerbaijan it is an important ingredient in beef soup. Cinnamon is also mixed with ground nuts to make a variety of sweet pastries.

Other spices

Sumac is derived from the red berries of a bush that grows throughout the Middle East. The dried berries can be used whole, but are more often ground or cracked, then soaked in water. The liquid that results has a slightly sour, fruity flavour, which gives a pleasing astringency to stews. The berries can be ground and used as a rub for chicken, steaks or kebabs, and is also sprinkled over salads.

Hawaij

This earthy spice blend comes from Yemen. It tastes great in stews, soups and sauces and is also good sprinkled on vegetables before they are roasted. Try it as a rub for lamb chops that are to be grilled (broiled) or barbecued. You can buy ready mixed hawaij in packets, but it is easy to make:

Place 30ml/2 tbsp black peppercorns in a mortar and add 15ml/1 tbsp caraway seeds, 5ml/1 tsp cardamom seeds and several pinches of saffron threads. Use a pestle to grind the mixture.

Add 10ml/2 tsp each of ground cumin and turmeric. Mix together. Use as indicated in recipes. Surplus hawaij should be kept in a sealed jar in a cool, dark place.

Tamarind is another souring agent. It is not as widely used in the Middle East as it is in India, but a drink made from it is popular. Mahlebi is a ground spice, made from the kernel found inside the stone of a small black cherry that grows in Turkey and elsewhere in the Middle East. It has a nutty flavour, suggestive of almonds and cherries, and is used in cakes, breads and pastries.

Spice mixes

The Middle East is a source of some excellent spice mixes, many of which are now available in the West. Harissa, actually a North African mix, is used in couscous, and is widely available. Try baharat, a warm blend of paprika, nutmeg and cardamom that tastes good in meat and vegetable dishes. Kabsa, from Saudi Arabia, is a fiery mixture that typically contains cayenne pepper, cinnamon, cumin, black peppercorns, nutmeg, cardamom, lime rind, cloves and coriander. Zahtar is a blend of sesame seeds, thyme and sumac.

Below: Zahtar is a dry spice mix often used to flavour an olive oil dip.

OLIVES AND OLIVE OILS

There's something miraculous about a tree that can live for hundreds of years on poor soil, baked by the sun and denied regular rainfall, yet still produce fruits that are not only delicious in their own right, but also yield an exquisite oil. Perhaps this explains why olives have always had such cultural and spiritual significance. The olive branch is an ancient symbol of peace and the oil is used to anoint adherents of several religions. Olive oil was used in ancient Egypt as part of the embalming process and is central to the ritual of Christian baptism. Jars of cured olives have been found in the tombs of the Pharaohs, presumably placed there to give them sustenance in the afterlife. Muhammad advised his followers to eat the olive's oil and massage it over their bodies.

The olive tree has been cultivated for more than six thousand years. Whether it originated in Syria or Crete is a matter of constant conjecture (and heated argument) but there is ample evidence of its being traded in both these places by 2500 BC. The Minoans introduced olives and olive oil to mainland Greece. Soon, thanks to Phoenician traders, the fruit and oil were both widely known throughout the Mediterranean region.

Freshly picked olives are extremely bitter and have a metallic taste. When it was discovered that preserving them made them infinitely more palatable, their popularity was assured. The oil, meanwhile, had myriad uses: in lamps, it burned beautifully without smoking; when perfumed, it made a fine medium for massage; it had proven medicinal qualities and could even be used to lubricate chariot axles (and was reputed to have made it easier to manoeuvre the huge stones into position when the pyramids were built). And, of course, it could be used as a marinade, as a cooking medium and as a preservative.

The Roman empire played an important role in disseminating the olive, introducing it to countries it had conquered, and expanding olive cultivation in lands where it was already well known, such as Palestine. It was the Romans who developed the screw press, used for the efficient extraction of olive oil. Meanwhile, in more remote Arab lands, farmers continued to tend their trees as they had done for generations, harvesting the olives in due season, preserving them or pressing them to remove the oil.

Olive oil was not the only cooking medium in ancient times. Arabs also favoured oils derived from nuts of various types and used sesame, sunflower and corn oil. In many areas, especially among nomadic tribes,

Above: Market stalls all over the Middle East sell a wide variety of olives.

Below: Black olives have been left on the tree to ripen the longest.

Below: These distinctive brown olives are very popular in the Middle East.

Below: Fresh olives have to be preserved before they are edible.

Above: *Virgin olive oil is prized for its distinctive flavour.*

animal fats such as sheep tail fat and butter were preferred, since these could be extracted or churned from the milk of their herd animals.

Today, however, olive oil is the main type of oil used for cooking and as a condiment in much of the Middle East, especially in Syria, Turkey, Jordan and Lebanon. Syria and Turkey are both important oil producers – not in the same league as Spain, Italy and Greece, but still in the top ten of producers.

TYPES OF OLIVE

There's always a crowd around the olive stall in a Middle Eastern market. Everyone has a favourite fruit, and there will often be intense discussion as to the virtues of this glossy black olive or that smaller green one, or whether olives in brine taste better than those that have been cured in salt. The colours of the olives are an indication not of the variety, but rather of ripeness. Immature olives are green, and at this stage the flavour is quite acrid. The fruit must be treated with lye before being preserved. As the olives ripen, the colour changes to khaki, brown, red, purple and finally black. The longer the olives stay on the tree, the sweeter they become. Black olives also yield more oil than green ones.

Table olives – as distinct from olives grown specifically for their oil – are generally preserved in brine, although some will be packed in oil, cured in salt or merely packed in water. Graded by size, the smallest weigh around 3.2g/$\frac{1}{16}$ oz whereas the largest, aptly described as "supercolossal", tip the scales at around 15g/$\frac{1}{4}$oz.

OLIVE OIL

Increasingly, olive oils are being appreciated for their individual flavours. Some are mild and buttery; others are fruity or have a distinctly peppery flavour. Colours range from palest yellow to deep, intense green. Some oils come from a single type of fruit, others are blends. Middle Eastern oils are now attracting the attention of discriminating buyers. Highly regarded extra virgin oils are Mishelanu from Galilee in Israel and Rashaya from Lebanon. Sadoun is an interesting oil from Jordan.

Marinated olives

For a tasty snack or mezze, try marinated olives. Tip 450g/1lb black olives into a bowl. Pour over 30ml/2 tbsp red wine vinegar, then add 1 garlic clove, cut into slivers, with 2 whole red chillies and 3–4 slices of lemon. Mix well, then spoon the olives into a large jar or several smaller jars, and pour in enough olive oil to cover them. Cover tightly and leave for 2–3 weeks at room temperature.

Above: *Various types of oil, from very dark green virgin olive oil at the front, is flanked by sesame oil to the left, and a lighter olive oil to the right.*

Grades of oil

Olive oil is graded in terms of its acidity level and how many pressings it has had. In addition to the categories below, there are blended oils and oils flavoured with aromatics and herbs.

- Extra virgin olive oil, which comes from the first pressing of the olives, has low acidity and a superior flavour. It is not recommended for frying, but is the perfect choice for salad dressings.
- Virgin olive oil has a slightly higher level of acidity than extra virgin and is also a first-pressed oil.
- Pure olive oil has been refined and blended and has a lighter, more subtle flavour than virgin olive oil. It is suitable for all types of cooking and can also be used as a dressing.

FISH, MEAT AND POULTRY

The diet of the average man or woman in the Middle East, unless he or she lives in a modern city, is likely to be limited to what is fished, raised or grown in the immediate vicinity. Fish is a valuable addition to the diet and is often more affordable than meat, which is saved for special occasions. Lamb is widely enjoyed in many different forms. Chicken is also popular; it is common to buy live birds from market, which are dispatched and prepared at home.

Below: Grey mullet, a favourite Middle Eastern fish, are often cooked with dill.

FISH

Most of the countries in the Middle East have extensive coastlines. In many parts a fisherman can still make a decent living and those who fish the eastern Mediterranean have better hauls than their counterparts to the west. The Arabian Sea also yields a rich harvest, whereas the Red Sea is the source of colourful reef fish, as well as king prawns (jumbo shrimp) and tasty flat lobsters. Oman has some of the finest fishing territories in the Middle East, and shark, tuna and grouper, are landed in its waters. From the Black Sea come delicious fresh anchovies, while the Caspian is home to the sturgeon, from which comes the expensive delicacy, caviar.

Shellfish are not as widely eaten as sea fish or freshwater fish. This is largely because Jews who observe the dietary laws of Kashrut must abstain from eating any kind of shellfish and crustaceans, as well as squid, octopus and certain types of fish. Muslims may not eat lobster or crab, although prawns are permissible if taken from the water alive. The Koran also forbids the eating of fish that do not have scales, such as shark or catfish. The following are some of the more popular varieties of fish available and eaten in the Middle East.

Caviar and bottarga

The finest caviar is said to be beluga, from the large Caspian sturgeon; oseotre comes from the Danube sturgeon (also found in the Caspian) while sevruga comes from the small Caspian sturgeon. Sadly, all these fish are now endangered species, with beluga on the critical list. Many people now prefer to buy bottarga (shown below), the salted and dried roe of the grey mullet.

Red mullet

Common in Mediterranean waters, red mullet are considered to be among the best tasting sea fish. Perhaps that's one reason why they are given the grand title of Sultan Ibrahim in the Middle East. Red mullet are often cooked whole, either in the pan or – more often – on the barbecue (grill) where they may be wrapped in vine leaves to protect the flesh. Egyptians like to serve red mullet with a sauce made from chopped hazelnuts and pine nuts.

Grey mullet

A favourite way of cooking this fish is to stuff it with dill – a herb that is extremely popular in the Middle East – and grill (broil) it, dousing it with arak or raki (both spirits) from time to time.

Red snapper

Around the Arabian Sea, these handsome fish are often called job or jobfish. Red snapper are generally pan fried or baked. The flesh is robust enough to compete with quite strong flavours, and Egyptians like to bake red snapper in a lightly spiced tomato sauce.

Tilapia

The succulent white flesh of tilapia is quite sweet, and goes well with fruity flavours. In Egypt and Israel the fish is sometimes marketed as St Peter's fish, which can be confusing, as John Dory has the same nickname.

Trout

This is a popular fish, especially in Turkey and Iran, where the rivers and lakes of the Alborz mountains north of Tehran are well stocked with trout, and fishing is a popular pastime.

Below: Brown trout and rainbow trout are both farmed extensively throughout the Middle East.

MEAT

The quality of meat available varies considerably, but Middle Eastern cooks have devised numerous ways of making even the least promising cuts taste good. All parts of the animal are eaten, and some offal (variety meats) is considered to be a delicacy.

Lamb is the meat of choice throughout the Middle East. Very little pork is consumed, since neither observant Jews nor Muslims may eat it, and beef's availability is limited, largely because there is not enough suitable grazing for the best beef animals, nor is the climate ideal. Goat (kid) is eaten, as is – on occasion – young camel. Game is also served, particularly in Iran, which has wild deer, and some of the biggest wild boar in the world.

Above: Lamb is used in a great variety of dishes throughout the region.

Beef

There has been a gradual shift towards more beef consumption, particularly in larger, more cosmopolitan cities, and in Iran and Iraq, where beef and lamb are often used interchangeably. This is particularly true in the case of Koftas (meatballs). Beef is also eaten in stews, such as the Persian Khoresh.

Lamb

Used in a variety of recipes, lamb is roasted, chargrilled, baked, braised, stewed and used as a filling. Ground or minced lamb is baked as a loaf or transformed into meatballs, which are cooked in a rich tomato sauce or threaded on to skewers and cooked on an open fire. Very finely ground or pounded lamb, mixed with bulgur wheat, is the basis for the famous Lebanese and Syrian dish Kibbeh. Lamb kidneys are enjoyed skewered or sautéed, and lambs liver, often cooked with paprika and garlic, is a favourite dish in Turkey.

POULTRY

Spatchcocked chickens are a favourite street food basted with oil and lemon juice, with herbs or a sprinkling of sumac. Roast chicken is popular, too, and is often stuffed with spiced dried fruit and nuts. Chicken is cooked in yogurt for the Persian dish Tah Chin, which makes it beautifully tender. Perhaps the Middle East's most famous chicken dish is Khoresh Fesenjan, from Iran – a colourful mixture of chicken, pomegranates and walnuts. Also popular, especially in Egypt, is pigeon. In the Nile Delta pigeons are plump and of a good size. Egyptians like them roasted or grilled (broiled).

Roast pigeon, Egyptian-style

Pigeon is always popular in Egypt. This dish, Hamam Mashwi, is one of the simplest ways of cooking young birds, the marinade makes the flesh and keeps it moist.

4 plump young pigeons
1 large onion, finely chopped
juice and zest of 2 lemons
30ml/2 tbsp olive oil
salt

Preheat the oven to 180°C/350°F/Gas 4. Clean the pigeons, and rinse them under cold water. Drain and pat dry with kitchen paper. Place side by side in a shallow dish and strew with the chopped onion. Grate the zest of the lemons over the birds, then use your hands to work the onion and lemon rind into the skin. Mix the juice from the lemons with the olive oil and pour over the pigeons. Cover and leave to marinate in a cool place for 4–6 hours.

Place the pigeons, with the marinade, in the roasting pan, sprinkle with salt and roast for 45–55 minutes, or until the birds are fully cooked, basting frequently.

Below: Shin of beef is an ideal cut for slow stewing in a casserole.

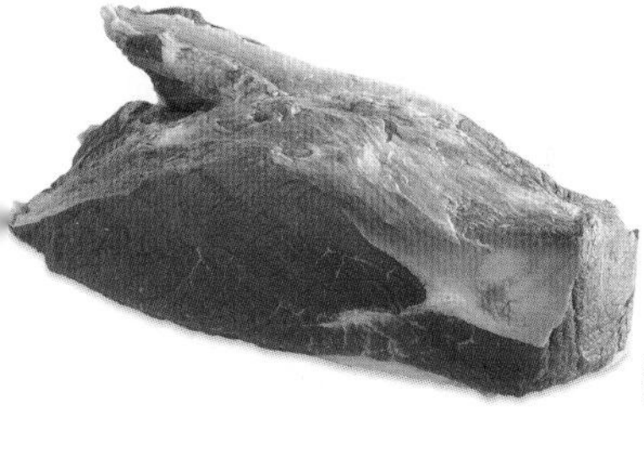

Below: Jointed chicken is used in many different Middle Eastern dishes.

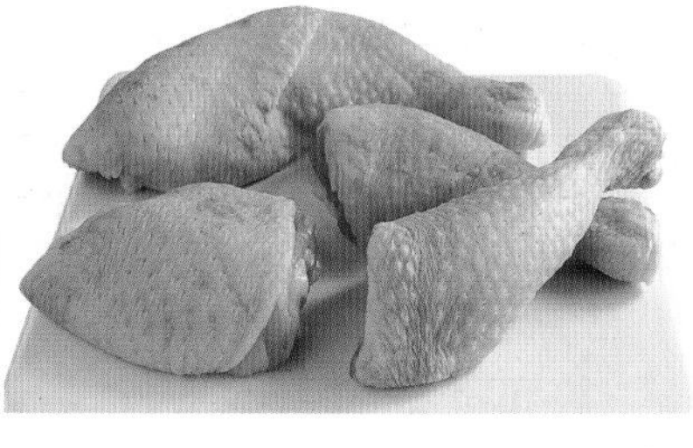

Below: Pigeon is farmed in the Nile Delta and is enjoyed roasted or grillled.

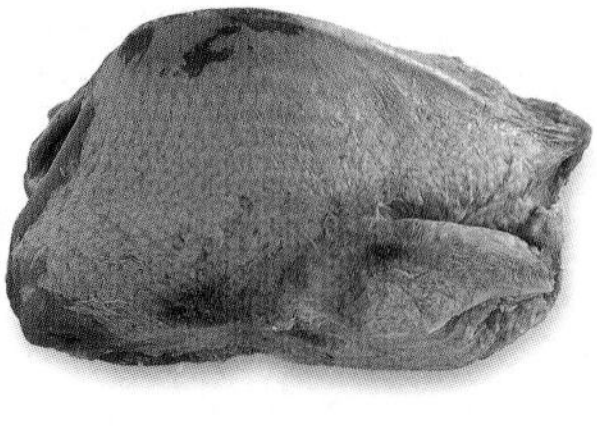

FRESH FRUIT AND VEGETABLES

Middle Eastern markets are a kaleidoscope of colour. Baskets of tomatoes, piles of dusky purple aubergines (eggplants), scented lemons, fat peaches, exotic pomegranates and okra pods are all there for the buying. Shopping for ingredients, especially fruit and vegetables, is a serious business for the Middle Eastern cook. First a circuit must be made of the market to locate the finest produce, and then the niceties must be observed – an inquiry as to the health of the stallholder's sister, perhaps, or a remark about the weather. After this, honour is satisfied and the purchase is completed.

FRUIT

It is traditional throughout the Middle East for a meal to conclude with fresh fruit. A slice of chilled melon, perhaps, a bowl of cherries or just a perfect peach. In winter, such fresh fruit as is available may be added to a dried fruit compote, or a rice pudding topped with berries picked earlier in the year and preserved for just such an occasion. Fresh fruit is used in salads, as when pomegranate arils are mixed with fresh greens, or added to stews. Lemon is the linchpin of Middle Eastern cooking, but other types of citrus are important, too. From Israel, one of the world's most important citrus producers, come Jaffa oranges, white and pink grapefruit and kumquats. Lebanon is famous for soft fruits, Iran for cherries and melons and Turkey for superb figs. Baalbek, the former Phoenician city close to Beirut, is known for its magnificent apricots. It is said that their flesh is so fine that when the fruit is held up to the light, the stone can be seen inside. Apples are grown in the more temperate areas; bananas, pineapples and mangoes grow in coastal regions with good irrigation.

Above: Apricots are a particular favourite in the Middle East.

Below: Figs are eaten fresh, or cooked in a variety of delicious desserts.

Figs

Turkey is one of the world's leading exporters of this delicious fruit. Smyrna figs are sweet and succulent, with golden flesh, while Mission figs are deep purple, with red flesh. Figs are delicious on their own, but can also be split and opened out to hold a nut filling, baked with honey or served with white cheese.

Below: Quinces have a delectable fragrance and mild, sweet flesh.

Quinces

These are fabulous fruit that originated in Turkestan and Persia. In colder climes, they do not achieve their full potential, but when they are placed in the heat they fill the air with their exquisite perfume.

Quinces make delicious jams and jellies, but are also good in meat dishes, and stuffed quince – *dolmeh beh* – is excellent. This Persian dish involves coring the fruit, packing it with a meat and split pea mixture and cooking it in a sweet-and-sour sauce.

Pomegranates

On the tree, pomegranates look like polished cricket balls, but cut them and you find jewelled treasure. Inside the fruit, each seed is encased in a translucent sac of pulp. These arils, as they are called, are deliciously refreshing, but getting at them is no mean feat. It is important to avoid the bitter pith, so the arils must either be picked out individually, using a pin, or pressed into a bowl and then picked over by hand. Middle Eastern cooks use pomegranate seeds in salads, in savoury dishes and in desserts. They are inordinately fond of pomegranate juice, which they sweeten and serve very cold. Juicing a pomegranate is easy – just press it down very gently on a citrus squeezer.

Below: The jewel-like seeds of the pomegranate are sharp and refreshing.

Above: This flavoursome, ridged tomato is grown in the Lebanon.

VEGETABLES

There's something almost decadent about the vegetables of the Middle East. No prissy broccoli or prudish peas here, but instead voluptuous violet aubergines (eggplants), perky (bell) peppers, courgettes (zucchini) – so prolific as to be positively indecent – and shiny round tomatoes, exquisitely sweet, thanks to being grown in bright sunshine in unpolluted desert air. Also on the menu are artichokes, fresh broad (fava) beans, long thin cucumbers, leafy spinach and glossy pumpkin, which is served as a vegetable and also transformed into a candied sweet. Okra, with its mucilaginous texture, isn't to everyone's taste, but the pods are delicious in a chickpea stir-fry or a tomato stew. Peppers are widely used, and are just one of the vegetables that Middle Eastern cooks like to stuff with rice and herbs or a savoury meat mixture. And let's not forget salads: these are universally popular and, thanks to modern farming methods, even the driest desert regions are now capable of producing crisp, fresh greens. A salad will often be delivered to the restaurant table along with the menu, so that diners can take the edge off their appetites while they make their meal choices. Salads form part of every mezze spread, often with yogurt dressings, and are also served as separate courses in their own right. Most of the vegetables that feature in Middle Eastern cooking will be familiar to cooks everywhere, but the following warrant a little more explanation.

Desert truffles

Oil is not the only treasure to lie beneath desert sands. From Egypt to Iraq, a rich harvest of truffles is gathered each year. Called *terfas* by the Bedouin of the Western Desert, and *kamaa* in Syria, they are not so strongly flavoured as European truffles, but are still delicious – and much more affordable.

Artichokes

As soon as globe artichokes are in season they are seized upon by cooks eager to use them for mezze or in main-course dishes. When very young, before the choke has formed, the entire artichoke is edible.

Okra

Also called ladies' fingers, or *baamieh* in Arabic, okra pods are shaped like slim, tapering lanterns. If the pods are cooked whole, as in a stir-fry, they stay crisp, with no trace of slime, but cut them and cook them in a stew, and the rows of seeds release a sticky liquid. This has the effect of thickening the sauce, but in a glutinous way that is not to everyone's taste. Okra goes well with tomatoes, chillies and ginger.

Below: Aubergines come in several shapes and sizes, and can also be white or purple and white in colour.

Above: Artichokes are used extensively in Middle Eastern mezzes and salads.

Aubergines

Known as eggplants in America and *brinjals* in India, these tasty vegetables come in several different shapes and sizes. They are especially appreciated in Turkey, a nation that is said to have more than two hundred recipes for preparing them.

Middle Eastern recipes often recommend salting aubergines to draw out some of their bitter juices, but this is seldom necessary in the West, where the vegetables available are usually young and tender.

DRIED FRUIT AND FLAVOURINGS

Most Arabs have a sweet tooth, which is hardly surprising when you consider that sweet, succulent dates have been part of their diet since childhood. Dried fruits and nuts are favourite snacks, and the penchant for mixing sweet with savoury flavours means that dried fruits are a feature of both meat dishes and desserts. Fruit syrups are highly concentrated and can be overwhelming. For more subtlety, select one of those signature Middle Eastern flavours: rosewater or orange flower water.

POPULAR VARIETIES OF DRIED FRUIT

Middle Eastern cooks often use dried fruit to add a touch of sweetness to a savoury dish. A mixture of nuts and dried cherries, apricots and barberries might be used to stuff a chicken, for example, or meatballs might be studded with the tiny black currants referred to as bird grapes. In

Above: Once dried and packed, dates will last for months.

Azerbaijan, dried fruit is the basis of a beef soup flavoured with mint and cinnamon, whereas in Israel dried apricots and prunes are cooked with vegetables to make *tzimmes*. Raisins, sultanas (golden raisins) and currants

Above: Sun-dried apricots.

are produced in the Mediterranean region, especially in Turkey.

Dates

Plump and succulent, dates are among the most delicious of fruit, whether you enjoy them fresh from the tree or dried. The date palm is extensively cultivated throughout the Middle East. Iraq leads the world in date production, closely followed by Iran and Saudi Arabia. For centuries, dates have been an important food for Arab tribesmen and traders. An excellent energy source, they are easily portable and provide valuable minerals, making them a good match for the fermented milk and occasional meat meals that are standard desert fare.

There are more than three hundred date varieties, classified by how much moisture they contain.

Soft dates are deliciously sweet and juicy. Arabs like to eat them before they are fully ripe, when the flesh is still crunchy and the flavour has a tart undertone. Ripe dates of this type taste like toffee and are almost as sticky. Popular varieties include the Khadrawi, which comes from Iraq, and the Bahri, from Israel and Egypt. Another date that is widely grown in Egypt is the Halawi, which is soft fleshed and slightly chewy. The queen among soft dates is, however, the Medjool, a Moroccan variety that is now cultivated in the Middle East, California and South Africa. Plump and voluptuous, this deep red-coloured date has little fibre and a superb flavour.

Semi-dry dates are firmer than soft varieties and have a lower moisture content. Deglet Noor, Dayri and Zahidi fall into this category. These dates are often sold in boxes, with what look like plastic twigs for winkling them out.

Dry dates are hard and fibrous, almost nutty in texture. These are the dates traditionally eaten

Clockwise from top left: sultanas, currants, and raisins.

by nomadic Arabs, who refer to them as bread dates. The dryness is natural, but they are sometimes dried even more so that they can be ground to a powder.

Below: Two different sizes of dried figs.

Compressed dates are dried fruit that have been tightly packed together in blocks. Very high in sugar, they are largely intended for baking, and are often softened in water before use.

Dried figs

Turkey is the world's major producer of dried figs. Smyrna figs from Izmir are particularly prized, but the purple Mission figs are popular too. Travellers to Turkey will often see the flattened fruit, suspended in loops from reeds or spread on hurdles to dry in the sun. Drying concentrates the natural sugars, which in turn helps to preserve the fruit. Tiny dried figs are eaten like sweets in the Middle East; larger fruits are stuffed and baked, or stewed in water scented with rosewater to make a compote.

Dried apricots

Called *zard-alu* or "yellow plum" by the Persians and *mishmish* in Arabic, apricots have been sun-dried for centuries in the Middle East. In addition to being dried individually, apricots are compressed to make *qamar el-deen*, thin sheets of fruit leather that make a drink when dissolved in boiling water. During Ramadan, serving this drink often signals the end of the daily fast.

Dried barberries and sour cherries

An Iranian speciality, dried barberries are often sprinkled over pilaffs or added to stews. The berries themselves are a small, wild, red fruit, about the size of redcurrants. They are too bitter to eat fresh but become sweeter dried. Dried sour cherries are used to flavour stews in Turkey, Iran and Syria.

Below: Dried sour cherries.

Above: Flower waters: on the left orange flower water, on the right rosewater.

Dried pomegranate seeds

When dried, the arils, or seeds, of pomegranates can be used in place of raisins in desserts and also to flavour vegetables and lentil dishes in Iran and Iraq. The pomegranates from which the arils are extracted are a sour variety, not suitable for eating raw.

FRUIT SYRUPS

Popular throughout the Middle East, fruit syrups are used in marinades, meat dishes and desserts, but their primary function is as a flavouring for long, cold drinks. A small amount of syrup, topped up with iced water or soda (carbonated) water makes a sweet but refreshing beverage.

Also known as *visne*, cherry syrup is the sweetened juice of sour cherries. It is sold by street sellers and makes a pretty drink when diluted over ice.

Made from concentrated grape juice, *pekmez* is remarkably sweet, despite the fact that the only sugar comes from the grapes themselves. Used sparingly, pekmez can add an interesting flavour to chicken and also works well in a dried fruit compote. Also known as *halek*, *dibis* is a concentrated date syrup. Popular in Israel, it is widely sold in jars, but can also be made at home by soaking dried dates in water until plump, then boiling them in water until soft. After being puréed, the date mixture is then cooked again until it reduces to a thick, syrupy paste to be diluted with water. Also called pomegranate molasses, this syrup is a delicious product with the consistency of treacle. It goes well in dressings and has long been an important ingredient in Persian cooking.

FLOWER WATERS

Rosewater has a unique flavour, delicate yet always clearly discernible. Distilled from the petals of the pink damask rose, it is used throughout the Middle East, in cakes, desserts and ice creams. Perhaps best known for its role in *lokum* (Turkish delight), rosewater is the perfect partner for iced melon.

Orange flower water is made from bitter orange blossoms. It is used to flavour pastries and cakes, and is the basis for the well-known Lebanese "café blanc", which is actually a beverage made by boiling the essence with water.

Below: Clockwise from bottom right: date syrup, sour grape juice, pomegranate paste, rosehip syrup and sour cherry juice.

Breads, Pastries and Cakes

The expression "daily bread" is nowhere more accurate than in the Middle East, where peasant workers eat over 1kg/ 2¼lb a day and it is enjoyed at every meal. Cakes and pastries, for which the region is equally famous, are as lavish as the loaves of bread are plain. Many of them are extremely sweet: the perfect accompaniment to a cup of strong, black Turkish coffee.

Above: A selection of the bread sold each day all over the Middle East.

BREADS

Although bread is of enormous value merely as sustenance, it also plays a role in religious observance throughout the Middle East. The baking and buying of bread is a social event, too. Many Middle Eastern housewives work together to bake for themselves and the community, or take their risen dough to the village baker.

Above: Pide.

Below: Simits.

Below: Ekmek.

Muslims are enjoined to treat bread with respect. It should be torn, not cut with a knife, which would show disrespect to what they regard as a gift from Allah. When it is brought to the table it should be eaten immediately, taking precedence over other foods. Any bread remaining at the end of a meal must be used, perhaps in the delicious salad known as Fattoush. Even crumbs must be gathered up and either eaten by those present or fed to animals. This rule – that no food must be wasted – is fundamental to the teachings of Islam.

The royal bakers who prepared food for the pharaohs are known to have made more than 30 different types of bread. Across the whole of the Middle East today, the number is much higher. Flat breads, such as *lavash*, plump loaves such as *hashas*, sheets, crusty bread rings, puffy individual breads that reveal pockets when split – the range of both leavened and unleavened loaves is vast. What they have in common is that they must be eaten fresh. Bread stales rapidly in the Middle East, but this is not a problem since bread is baked at home or in a bakery at least once a day.

Right: A pile of lavash, *the flat bread used to scoop up food at mealtimes.*

Pide

This is the Turkish version of the bread the Greeks call pitta. It can be shaped in rounds or be slipper-shaped. When baked in a very hot oven, the dough puffs up so that the centre remains hollow, making each individual bread the perfect receptacle for a salad, some cheese or a few chunks of grilled (broiled) lamb slid from a skewer. *Pide* is often served with mezzes.

Aiysh

This is similar to *pide*, but smaller and thicker. This Egyptian bread, which has been made in the same way for thousands of years, is found throughout the Middle East. It is generally made with wholemeal (whole-wheat) flour and ranges in shape from 15cm/6in rounds to ovals of up to 38cm/15in. In Yemen the bread is known as *saluf*; in Jordan and Palestine as *shrak*; and in Syria as *aiysh shami*.

Ekmek

The word simply means "bread" in Turkey, but usually refers to a large round or oval leavened bread made simply from a plain white or wholemeal dough. *Sutlu Ekmek*, for example, is made by arranging a circle of round rolls around a central roll in a baking pan so that they rise and stick together to form a single loaf.

Khoubz

Virtually identical to *aiysh*, this flat, slightly leavened bread is popular in the Levant and Arabian peninsula. Originally made with finely ground wholemeal flour similar to chapati flour, it is now more often made using white flour.

Simits

Shaped in golden bread rings, *simits* are traditionally coated with sesame seeds, and are sold in the streets. They look like bagels and are made in the same way, being first poached in water and then baked.

Barbari

These flattish white breads from Iran come in various sizes and shapes, and are dimpled or slashed to give the surface a fretwork effect. They may be brushed with oil before being baked, and spiced versions are often topped with cumin or caraway seeds.

Lavash

This pancake-thin bread originated in Armenia, but is now popular throughout the Middle East. It can be round, oval or square, and is made in various sizes, the largest sheets measuring up to 60cm/24in across. A large *lavash*, placed in the centre of the table, will serve the entire party. Guests tear off as much as they need and use the bread as a wrap or for scooping up sauce.

Challah

Traditionally made for the Jewish Sabbath or for religious festivals, this braided bread has a deep brown crust. The dough is made using eggs and vegetable oil, which gives the baked bread a texture somewhere between that of a brioche and a soft white loaf.

Above: Briouates are one of the many varieties of sweet pastries available.

PASTRIES AND CAKES

Middle Eastern pastries are the stuff of dreams. Whisper-thin pastry, cooked to crisp perfection, is filled with some of the most delicious concoctions imaginable. Ground pistachio nuts and cardamom, dates and almonds, candied apricots, coconut and semolina custard – these are just some of the many possibilities. Further flavouring comes from lemon or lime rind, warm spices or the subtle yet pervasive taste of flower waters. Syrup or honey is often poured over the hot pastries as they emerge from the oven, soaking in to become sensationally sticky. Eat something like this at the end of a large meal and it seems over-sweet, over-indulgent and decidedly over the top. But cut a small portion and enjoy it in the middle of the afternoon with a cup of strong, black Turkish coffee, as people in the Middle East do, and its appeal becomes immediately obvious.

Pastries are popular street foods and it is not unusual to see a vendor performing a seemingly impossible balancing act as he hurries to his pitch with a large tray of pastries on his head. Among the most popular treats is *kodafa*, a rich cheesecake made with an unusual shredded pastry called *kadaif*. The *kodafa* is strewn with pistachio nuts and served with a honey and saffron syrup scented with orange flower water.

It is in Israel and other communities with large Jewish populations that the largest variety of cakes are to be found. Almond cakes, Russian poppy seed cake, Polish apple cake and honey cake are the legacy of those who left the lands of their birth to settle in Israel. Many of them are made without flour; groundnuts and matzo meal are used instead, with beaten egg whites as the raising agent. This allows them to be eaten during Pesach, when leavened foods are forbidden.

Coffee, Tea and Social Drinking

Aside from water, coffee and tea are the most widely drunk beverages in the Middle East. Each has its own rituals regarding preparation and serving. Tea and coffee ease introductions, cement friendships and oil the wheels of commerce. Anyone contemplating making a major purchase is liable to be offered a cup of coffee or glass of tea to ease the pain of parting with money. Muslims may not drink alcohol, so fresh fruit drinks and beverages made from fruit syrups are freely available, as are several milk- or yogurt-based beverages.

COFFEE

There's some disagreement about whether the coffee plant originated in Ethiopia or the Middle East, but Yemen can certainly lay claim to being one of the first countries to cultivate coffee on a large scale. The southern part of the country is suited to coffee production, and the terraced slopes of the mountains are criss-crossed with coffee plants, each row protected from the harsh sun by a row of poplar trees. The arabica coffee from the south-western tip of the Arabian Peninsula is rich and mellow, with underlying acidity and a chocolate aftertaste. It was originally exported through the port of Mocha. This not only gave it its name – Yemen Mocha – but also led to the word "mocha" being used to describe any chocolate-coffee flavour.

The coffee trade in Yemen reached its peak in the 17th and 18th centuries. Today it is in decline, due in part to increased demand for *qat*. This leafy narcotic, a source of a natural amphetamine, is regularly chewed by a large percentage of the population, and coffee bushes are constantly being grubbed up so that more *qat* (*Catha edulis*) trees can be planted.

None of this has diminished the popularity of coffee, however. Arabs, particularly those who live in Yemen and Saudi Arabia, brew the beverage without sugar, in kettles or pots called *dallahs*. The coffee is then poured into tall pots, many of which are exquisitely crafted, before being served in cups.

Turkish coffee

This thick, sweet beverage is not a specific type of coffee, but rather a method of preparation that was developed in the Middle East in the early 16th century. Traders introduced it to the Ottoman court, and the proper preparation of Turkish coffee soon became a vital skill. Women in the harem were instructed in the art, and young girls had to become expert if they hoped to find suitable husbands.

Above: Mint tea is a refreshing drink in the heat of the summer.

A small open pot with a long handle is used for brewing Turkish coffee. Generally made of tin-lined brass, it is called an *ibrik* or *cezve*. Legend has it that the desert sands become so hot during the day that coffee can be brewed directly on them as evening falls, but the more usual method is for the pot to be placed on the stove or in the embers of a fire. Any arabica coffee can be used, but it must be ground very finely, so that it resembles a powder. Ground cardamom or ginger can be added, giving a distinctive flavour.

When making Turkish coffee, the aim is to allow the brew to bubble up several times without boiling over, so that a thick froth forms on top of the liquid. When the coffee is poured out, it should be left to stand briefly so that the ground coffee sinks. It forms a sludge on the bottom of the cup, which should not be drunk.

The amount of sugar in the coffee varies. Technically there are six levels of sweetness, but in practice most people ask for *sekerli* (very sweet), *orta sekerli* (with a little sugar) or *sekersiz* (without sugar). These are Turkish terms; elsewhere in the Middle East different classifications are used. Arabic or Bedouin coffee, on the other hand, is

Below: Turkish coffee will have a froth on the top if it has been made correctly.

Above: Fruit juices (clockwise from front) rosehip, pomegranate and peach.

drunk without sugar. This green or grey liquid, with its slightly bitter taste, is enjoyed in Syria and Jordan.

TEA

Although coffee is widely drunk, especially in Lebanon, tea, or *chai,* is the favourite drink in many parts of the Middle East. Like coffee, it is served with considerable ceremony, and – again like coffee – it is drunk without milk and with sugar. It is the custom in some areas for the recipient to place a cube of sugar between their front teeth, and sip the tea through it. Tea is often flavoured with mint or with spices such as ginger or cinnamon. In Turkey, herb and fruit teas made from sage, rose hips and apples are on sale.

SOFT DRINKS

Fresh fruit juices are widely available from stand-up juice bars, but long, cold drinks made from concentrated fruit syrups topped up with iced water are even more popular. In Egypt, hibiscus juice – often called "red tea" – is a favourite drink, along with apricot juice, tamarind juice and a drink made from dates. Cherry juice is popular in Iran, whereas orange and tamarind juice, either separately or as a mixture, are enjoyed in Israel. Liquorice juice is a more unusual choice, found in Egypt

Above: Sugar cane juice is a very sweet drink served in the Middle East.

and Jordan, and there are several extremely sweet drinks, including honey water and sugar cane juice, both of which are served ice cold.

YOGURT AND MILK DRINKS

Yogurt, diluted with water, is a favourite thirst-quencher for the desert Bedouin. In Syria and Turkey, this drink is called *aryan.* It is often served with mint. *Salep* is a hot milk drink flavoured with cinnamon and thickened with sahlab, ground orchid root. *Boza* is a fermented wheat drink that has a reputation for being especially nourishing and healthy.

Wines of the Middle East

The main wine-producing countries of the Middle East are Israel, Lebanon and Turkey. Historically, Israel has been best known for kosher wine, but now produces Cabernet, Sauvignon Blanc, Grenache and Semillon. Lebanon's wine industry is centred on the Bekkah Valley and produces some fine red wines, largely derived from Cabernet Sauvignon grapes. Turkey produces a considerable amount of wine, and quality reds from Thrace, Anatolia and the Aegean region are highly regarded.

Above: Aryan *is made of yoghurt that has been diluted with water.*

ALCOHOLIC DRINKS

The Koran forbids the drinking of alcohol. In some countries this taboo is strictly enforced. In Saudi Arabia, for example, the sale and/or consumption of any type of alcohol is strictly prohibited, and strict penalties are imposed on anyone caught flouting the law. Elsewhere in the Middle East, the situation is somewhat more relaxed. In Jordan, for example, alcohol is available in many hotels and restaurants, but drinking alcohol in public can cause deep offence. Turkey is more liberal, and has Western-style bars and pubs, though these remain largely male preserves. Beer, brewed under licence, is available, as is wine.

The most popular spirit is raki, a potent aniseed-flavoured drink distilled from grain, which clouds when mixed with water, a phenomenon that has earned it the nickname *aslan sutu* (lion's milk).

Right: The favourite spirit in the Middle East is aniseed-flavoured raki.

Soups, Mezzes and Appetizers

In the Middle East, and some African countries, the first course is seen as a main component of the meal, rather than simply a morsel to tempt the appetite. In Iran, soup is held in such high regard that the kitchen is known as "the house of the soup maker". The art of the appetizer reaches its apogee in Lebanon, where a mezze consists of dozens of different dishes, balanced to offer a feast of colours and flavours. This chapter explores some of the options, from simple marinated olives to stuffed vegetables and exquisite salads.

Chilled Almond and Garlic Soup with Roasted Chilli and Grapes

The cold and chilled soups of North Africa are ancient in origin and were originally introduced to Morocco by the Arabs. This particular milky white soup has travelled further with the Moors into Spain. Heavily laced with garlic, it is unusual but deliciously refreshing in hot weather, and makes a delightful, tangy first course for a summer lunch party.

SERVES FOUR

INGREDIENTS

- 130g/4½oz/¾ cup blanched almonds
- 3–4 slices day-old white bread, crusts removed
- 4 garlic cloves
- 60ml/4 tbsp olive oil
- about 1 litre/1¾ pints/4 cups iced water
- 30ml/2 tbsp white wine vinegar
- salt

To garnish

- 1 dried red chilli, roasted and thinly sliced
- a small bunch of sweet green grapes, halved and seeded
- a handful of slivered almonds

COOK'S TIP

Almonds can be bought ready-blanched, but you can also blanch them yourself in boiling water. To blanch almonds using a microwave oven, place them in a bowl, cover with boiling water and microwave on High for 2 minutes. Drain, and peel off the skins.

1 Place the blanched almonds in a blender or food processor and process to form a smooth paste. Add the bread, garlic, olive oil and half the water and process again until smooth.

2 With the motor running, continue to add the remaining water in a slow, steady stream until the mixture is smooth with the consistency of single (light) cream. Add the vinegar and salt.

3 Transfer the soup to a serving bowl and then chill for at least 1 hour.

4 When the soup is chilled, stir gently before serving into individual bowls. Garnish each bowl with the sliced roasted chilli, halved grapes and a few slivered almonds.

Energy 352Kcal/1459kJ; Protein 8.6g; Carbohydrate 13.8g, of which sugars 3.4g; Fat 29.5g, of which saturates 3.1g; Cholesterol 0mg; Calcium 102mg; Fibre 2.8g; Sodium 110mg.

Cinnamon-Scented Chickpea and Lentil Soup with Fennel and Honey Buns

This thick lentil and vegetable soup, flavoured with ginger and cinnamon, varies from village to village and town to town. It is believed to have originated from a semolina gruel that the Berbers prepared to warm themselves during the cold winters in the Atlas Mountains. Over the centuries, it has been adapted and refined with spices and tomatoes from the New World.

SERVES EIGHT

INGREDIENTS

- 30–45ml/2–3 tbsp smen or olive oil
- 2 onions, halved and sliced
- 2.5ml/½ tsp ground ginger
- 2.5ml/½ tsp ground turmeric
- 5ml/1 tsp ground cinnamon
- pinch of saffron threads
- 2 x 400g/14oz cans chopped tomatoes
- 5–10ml/1–2 tsp caster (superfine) sugar
- 175g/6oz/¾ cup brown or green lentils, picked over and rinsed
- about 1.75 litres/3 pints/7½ cups meat or vegetable stock, or water
- 200g/7oz/1 generous cup dried chickpeas, soaked overnight, drained and boiled until tender
- 200g/7oz/1 generous cup dried broad (fava) beans, soaked overnight, drained and boiled until tender
- small bunch of fresh coriander (cilantro), chopped
- small bunch of flat leaf parsley, chopped
- salt and ground black pepper

For the buns

- 2.5ml/½ tsp dried yeast
- 300g/11oz/2¾ cups unbleached strong white bread flour
- a pinch of salt
- 15–30ml/1–2 tbsp clear honey
- 5ml/1 tsp fennel seeds
- 250ml/8fl oz/1 cup milk
- 1 egg yolk, stirred with a little milk

1 Make the fennel and honey buns. Dissolve the yeast in about 15ml/1 tbsp lukewarm water. Sift the flour and salt into a bowl. Make a well in the centre and add the dissolved yeast, honey and fennel seeds. Gradually pour in the milk, using your hands to work it into the flour along with the honey and yeast, until the mixture forms a dough – if the dough becomes too sticky to handle, add more flour.

2 Turn the dough out on to a floured surface and knead well for about 10 minutes, until it is smooth and elastic. Flour the surface under the dough and cover it with a damp cloth, then leave the dough to rise until it has doubled in size.

3 Preheat the oven to 230°C/450°F/ Gas 8. Grease two baking sheets. Divide the dough into 8 balls. On a floured surface, flatten the balls of dough with the palm of your hand, then place them on a baking sheet. Brush the tops of the buns with egg yolk, then bake for about 15 minutes, until they are risen slightly and sound hollow when tapped underneath. Transfer to a wire rack to cool.

4 To make the soup, heat the smen or olive oil in a stockpot or large pan. Add the onions and stir over a low heat for about 15 minutes, or until they are soft.

5 Add the ginger, turmeric, cinnamon and saffron, then the tomatoes and a little sugar. Stir in the lentils and pour in the stock or water. Bring the liquid to the boil, then reduce the heat, cover and simmer for about 25 minutes, or until the lentils are tender.

6 Stir in the cooked chickpeas and beans, bring back to the boil, then cover and simmer for a further 10–15 minutes. Stir in the fresh herbs and season the soup to taste. Serve piping hot, with the fennel and honey buns.

Energy 376Kcal/1594kJ; Protein 18.7g; Carbohydrate 66.4g, of which sugars 12g; Fat 5.9g, of which saturates 1g; Cholesterol 2mg; Calcium 181mg; Fibre 8.6g; Sodium 70mg.

MOROCCAN PUMPKIN SOUP

MODERN MOROCCAN STREET STALLS AND MARKETS ARE PILED HIGH WITH COLOURFUL SEASONAL PRODUCE. THE PUMPKIN SEASON IS PARTICULARLY DELIGHTFUL, WITH THE HUGE ORANGE VEGETABLES DISPLAYED ON TABLES AND WOODEN CARTS. THE SELLERS PATIENTLY PEEL AND SLICE THE PUMPKINS READY FOR MAKING THIS SIMPLE AND TASTY WINTER SOUP, WITH ITS HINT OF SUGAR AND SPICE.

SERVES FOUR

INGREDIENTS

- about 1.1kg/2lb 7oz pumpkin
- 750ml/1¼ pints/3 cups chicken stock
- 750ml/1¼ pints/3 cups milk
- 10–15ml/2–3 tsp sugar
- 75g/3oz/½ cup cooked white rice
- salt and ground black pepper
- 5ml/1 tsp ground cinnamon, to garnish

COOK'S TIPS

Use butternut squash in place of pumpkin. Use cooked brown rice in place of white rice, if preferred.

1 Remove any seeds or strands of fibre from the pumpkin, cut off the peel and chop the flesh. Put the prepared pumpkin in a pan and add the stock, milk, sugar and seasoning.

2 Bring to the boil, then reduce the heat and simmer for about 20 minutes, until the pumpkin is tender. Drain the pumpkin, reserving the liquid, and purée it in a blender or food processor, then return it to the pan.

3 Bring the soup back to the boil again, throw in the rice and simmer for a few minutes, until the grains are reheated. Check the seasoning, pour into bowls and dust with cinnamon. Serve piping hot, with chunks of fresh, crusty bread.

Energy 148Kcal/627kJ; Protein 8.8g; Carbohydrate 20.7g, of which sugars 13.5g; Fat 4g, of which saturates 2.3g; Cholesterol 11mg; Calcium 308mg; Fibre 2.8g; Sodium 81mg.

Chorba with Ras el Hanout and Noodles

This full-flavoured chorba is the daily soup in many Moroccan households. The ras el hanout gives it a lovely, warming kick. You can purée the soup, if you prefer, but here it is left as it is, finished off with a swirl of yogurt and finely chopped coriander. Garlic lovers may like to add a crushed garlic clove and a little salt to the yogurt.

SERVES FOUR

INGREDIENTS

- 45–60ml/3–4 tbsp olive oil
- 3–4 whole cloves
- 2 onions, chopped
- 1 butternut squash
- 4 celery sticks, chopped
- 2 carrots, chopped
- 8 large, ripe tomatoes
- 5–10ml/1–2 tsp sugar
- 15ml/1 tbsp tomato purée (paste)
- 5–10ml/1–2 tsp ras el hanout
- 2.5ml/½ tsp ground turmeric
- a big bunch of fresh coriander (cilantro), chopped
- 1.75 litres/3 pints/7½ cups vegetable stock
- a handful of dried egg noodles or capellini, broken into pieces
- salt and ground black pepper
- natural (plain) yogurt, to garnish

1 Peel, seed and cut the squash into small chunks. Skin, and roughly chop the tomatoes. In a deep, heavy pan, heat the oil and add the cloves, onions, squash, celery and carrots. Fry until they begin to colour, then stir in the chopped tomatoes and sugar. Cook until the liquid reduces and the tomatoes begin to pulp.

2 Stir in the tomato purée, ras el hanout, turmeric and chopped coriander. Pour in the stock and bring the liquid to the boil. Reduce the heat and simmer, uncovered, for 30–40 minutes until the vegetables are very tender and the liquid has reduced a little.

3 To make a puréed soup, let the liquid cool slightly before processing in a blender or food processor, then pour back into the pan and add the pasta.

4 Alternatively, to make a chunky soup, simply add the pasta to the unblended soup and cook for a further 8–10 minutes, or until the pasta is soft.

5 Season the soup to taste and ladle it into bowls. Spoon a swirl of yogurt into each one, garnish with coriander sprigs and serve with a freshly baked Moroccan loaf.

Energy 265Kcal/1108kJ; Protein 6.9g; Carbohydrate 37.8g, of which sugars 20.2g; Fat 10.2g, of which saturates 1.7g; Cholesterol 0mg; Calcium 158mg; Fibre 8.1g; Sodium 64mg.

LAMB, BEAN AND PUMPKIN SOUP

ASIDE FROM THE GREEN BANANAS, WHICH ARE VERY MUCH AN AFRICAN TOUCH, THIS SOUP COULD HAVE COME FROM ANY OF THE LANDS OF THE MIDDLE EAST. PUMPKIN, CARROT AND TURMERIC GIVE IT A RICH COLOUR AND THE SPICES PROVIDE A WARMTH DESIGNED TO BANISH WINTER CHILLS.

SERVES FOUR

INGREDIENTS

- 115g/4oz black-eyed beans (peas), soaked for 1–2 hours, or overnight
- 675g/1½lb neck of lamb, cut into medium-size chunks
- 5ml/1 tsp chopped fresh thyme, or 2.5ml/½ tsp dried
- 2 bay leaves
- 1.2 litres/2 pints/5 cups stock or water
- 1 onion, sliced
- 225g/8oz pumpkin, diced
- 2 black cardamom pods
- 7.5ml/1½ tsp ground turmeric
- 15ml/1 tbsp chopped fresh coriander (cilantro)
- 2.5ml/½ tsp caraway seeds
- 1 fresh green chilli, seeded and chopped
- 2 green bananas
- 1 carrot
- salt and ground black pepper

1 Drain the beans, place in a pan and cover with cold water. Bring to the boil and boil rapidly for 10 minutes, then reduce the heat and simmer, covered, for 40–50 minutes until tender, adding more water if necessary. Remove from the heat and set aside to cool.

2 Meanwhile, put the lamb in a large pan, add the thyme, bay leaves and stock or water and bring to the boil. Cover and simmer over a medium heat for 1 hour, until tender.

3 Add the onion, pumpkin, cardamoms, turmeric, coriander, caraway seeds, chilli and seasoning and stir. Bring back to a simmer and then cook, uncovered, for 15 minutes, until the pumpkin is tender, stirring occasionally.

4 When the beans are cool, spoon into a blender or food processor with their liquid and process to a smooth purée.

5 Cut the bananas into medium slices and the carrot into thin slices. Stir into the soup with the bean purée. Cook for 10–12 minutes, until the vegetables are tender. Adjust the seasoning and serve.

Energy 442Kcal/1855kJ; Protein 40.8g; Carbohydrate 27.2g, of which sugars 13.1g; Fat 19.7g, of which saturates 9g; Cholesterol 128mg; Calcium 74mg; Fibre 6.4g; Sodium 155mg.

Ghanian Fish and Okra Soup

Okra grows well in many parts of West Africa and the Sudan, and soups like this one were the inspiration for gumbo, which slaves introduced to the Caribbean and North America. Okra thickens the soup and gives it a unique texture and flavour.

SERVES FOUR

INGREDIENTS

- 2 green bananas
- 50g/2oz/¼ cup butter or margarine
- 1 onion, finely chopped
- 2 tomatoes, skinned and finely chopped
- 115g/4oz okra, trimmed
- 225g/8oz smoked haddock or cod fillet, cut into bitesize pieces
- 900ml/1½ pints/3¾ cups fish stock
- 1 fresh red or green chilli, seeded and chopped
- salt and ground black pepper
- chopped fresh parsley, to garnish

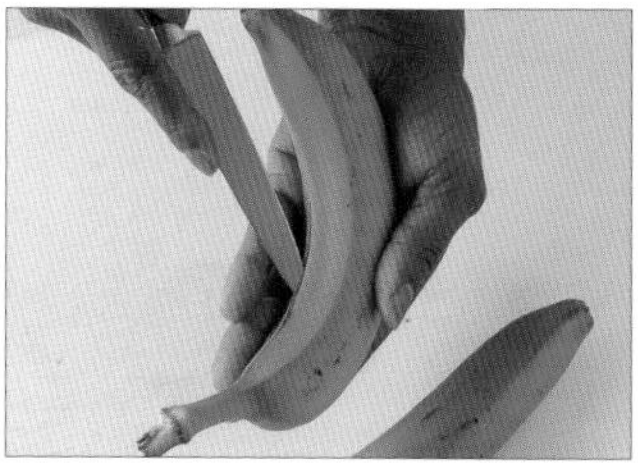

1 Slit the skins of the bananas and place in a large pan. Cover with water, bring to the boil and cook over a medium heat for 25 minutes. Drain.

2 Melt the butter or margarine in a large pan and sauté the onion for about 5 minutes. Stir in the tomatoes and okra and sauté for a further 10 minutes.

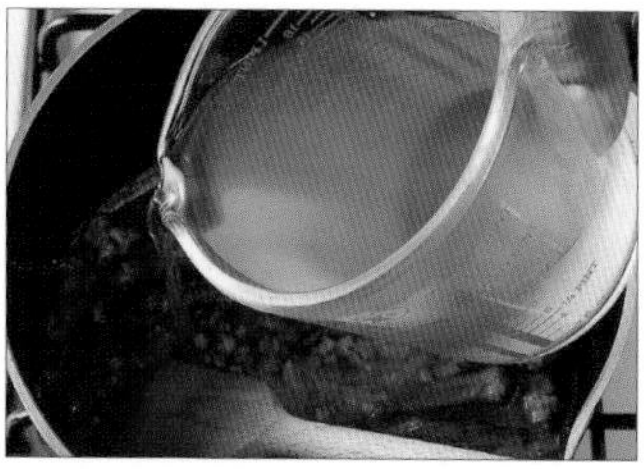

3 Add the fish, fish stock, chilli and seasoning. Bring to the boil, then reduce the heat and simmer for about 20 minutes, until the fish is cooked through and flakes easily.

4 Peel the cooked bananas and cut into slices. Stir into the soup, heat through for a few minutes and then ladle into soup bowls. Sprinkle with chopped parsley and serve.

Energy 295Kcal/1233kJ; Protein 20g; Carbohydrate 24.6g, of which sugars 21.2g; Fat 13.8g, of which saturates 7.5g; Cholesterol 47mg; Calcium 477mg; Fibre 12.7g; Sodium 532mg.

Plantain and Corn Soup

Cameroon is the home of this colourful and unusual soup. It is important to use ripe plantains, which cook down and become beautifully tender. Nutmeg adds the final touch.

SERVES FOUR

INGREDIENTS
- 25g/1oz/2 tbsp butter or margarine
- 1 onion, finely chopped
- 1 garlic clove, crushed
- 275g/10oz yellow plantains, peeled and sliced
- 1 large tomato, peeled and chopped
- 175g/6oz/1 cup corn
- 5ml/1 tsp dried tarragon, crushed
- 900ml/1½ pints/3¾ cups vegetable or chicken stock
- 1 fresh green chilli, seeded and chopped
- pinch of freshly grated nutmeg
- salt and ground black pepper

1 Melt the butter or margarine in a pan over a medium heat, add the onion and garlic and sauté for a few minutes until the onion is soft.

2 Add the plantains, tomato and corn and cook for 5 minutes.

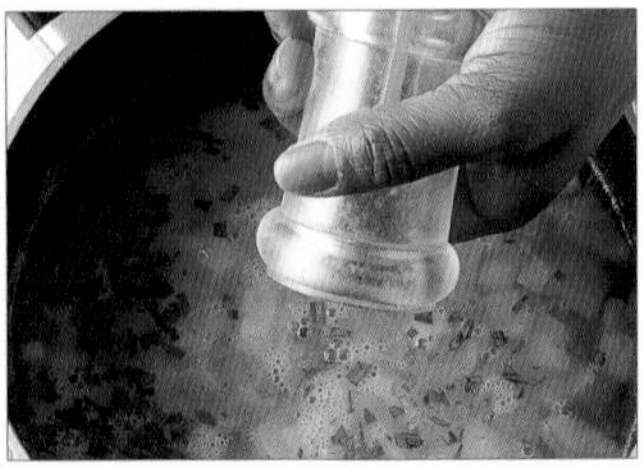

3 Add the tarragon, vegetable or chicken stock, chilli and salt and pepper and simmer for 10 minutes or until the plantain is tender. Stir in the nutmeg and serve immediately.

Groundnut Soup

Groundnuts – or peanuts – are very widely used in sauces in African cooking. Groundnut paste is available from many health food shops and is worth seeking out as it makes a wonderfully rich and creamy soup.

SERVES FOUR

INGREDIENTS
- 45ml/3 tbsp pure groundnut paste or peanut butter
- 1.5 litres/2½ pints/6¼ cups stock
- 30ml/2 tbsp tomato purée (paste)
- 1 onion, chopped
- 2 slices fresh root ginger, peeled and finely chopped
- 1.5ml/¼ tsp dried thyme
- 1 bay leaf
- salt and chilli powder
- 225g/8oz white yam, diced
- 10 small okras, trimmed (optional)

1 Place the groundnut paste or peanut butter in a bowl, add 300ml/½ pint/1¼ cups of the stock and the tomato purée and blend together to make a smooth paste.

2 Spoon the nut mixture into a pan and add the onion, chopped ginger, thyme, bay leaf, salt, chilli powder and the remaining stock. Heat gently until the liquid is simmering.

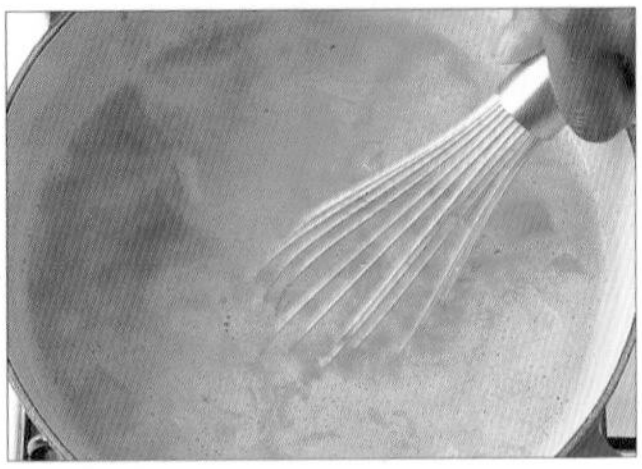

3 Cook for 1 hour, stirring from time to time to prevent the nut mixture sticking.

4 Add the white yam and cook for a further 10 minutes. Add the okra, if using, and simmer until tender. Serve.

COOK'S TIP
Use peanut butter in place of groundnut paste, but only use the smooth variety for this recipe.

TOP Energy 185Kcal/775kJ; Protein 5.8g; Carbohydrate 22.6g, of which sugars 5.2g; Fat 8.3g, of which saturates 1.9g; Cholesterol 0mg; Calcium 66mg; Fibre 3.3g; Sodium 75mg.
BOTTOM Energy 198Kcal/837kJ; Protein 2.7g; Carbohydrate 35.6g, of which sugars 11g; Fat 6g, of which saturates 3.4g; Cholesterol 13mg; Calcium 20mg; Fibre 2.3g; Sodium 162mg.

CHICKEN, TOMATO AND CHRISTOPHENE SOUP

Christophene is a pale green gourd. In southern Africa is is called cho-cho, while elsewhere it is called choko, chayote or vegetable pear. The flesh has a delicate flavour.

SERVES FOUR

INGREDIENTS

- 225g/8oz skinless, boneless chicken breasts
- 1 garlic clove, crushed
- pinch of freshly grated nutmeg
- 25g/1oz/2 tbsp butter or margarine
- ½ onion, finely chopped
- 15ml/1 tbsp tomato purée (paste)
- 400g/14oz can tomatoes, puréed
- 1.2 litres/2 pints/5 cups chicken stock
- 1 fresh red or green chilli, seeded and chopped
- 5ml/1 tsp dried oregano
- 2.5ml/½ tsp dried thyme
- 1 christophene, about 350g/12oz total weight, peeled and diced
- 50g/2oz smoked haddock fillet, skinned and diced
- salt and ground black pepper
- chopped fresh chives, to garnish

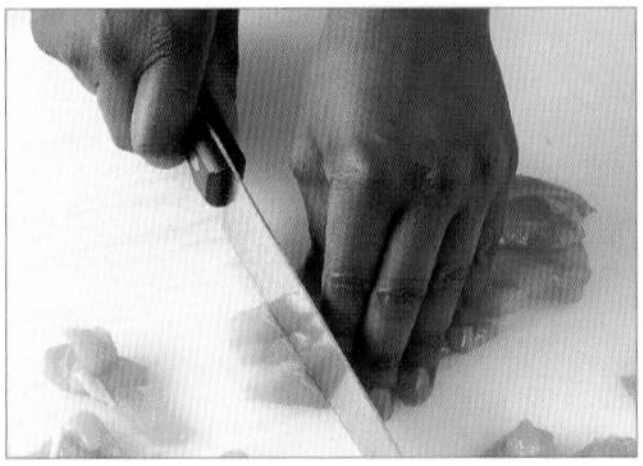

1 Dice the chicken, place in a bowl and season with salt, pepper, garlic and nutmeg. Mix well to flavour the chicken and then set aside for about 30 minutes.

COOK'S TIP

Christophene is a vegetable of the squash family native to central America. The flesh is crisp and light green in colour, and the flavour is delicate and very mild. It may be used in a similar way to courgettes (zucchini) in cooking.

2 Melt the butter or margarine in a large pan, add the chicken and sauté over a medium heat for 5–6 minutes. Stir in the onion and sauté gently for a further 5 minutes, until the onion is slightly softened.

3 Add the tomato purée, puréed tomatoes, stock, chilli, dried herbs and christophene. Bring to the boil, cover and simmer gently for 35 minutes, until the christophene is tender.

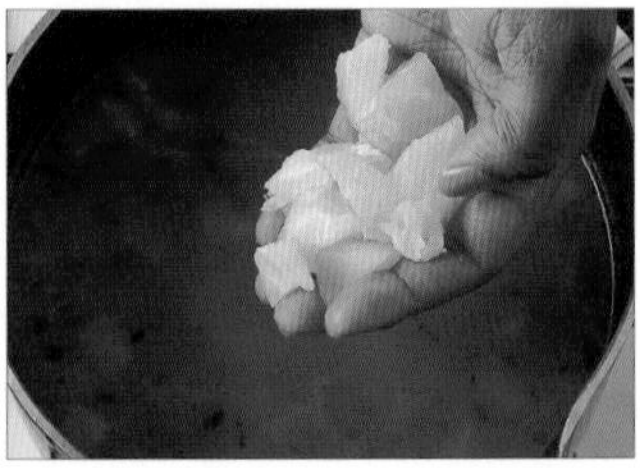

4 Add the smoked fish, simmer for a further 5 minutes, until the fish is cooked through, adjust the seasoning and pour into warmed soup bowls. Garnish with a sprinkling of chopped chives and serve.

Energy 133Kcal/558kJ; Protein 16.7g; Carbohydrate 3.2g, of which sugars 2.4g; Fat 6g, of which saturates 3.5g; Cholesterol 57mg; Calcium 36mg; Fibre 1.1g; Sodium 167mg.

Cameroon Vegetable Soup

Coconut crops up in many popular Cameroonian dishes, including their famous beef and pineapple curry. Here it is teamed with sweet potato and spices to make a tasty soup.

SERVES FOUR

INGREDIENTS

- 30ml/2 tbsp butter or margarine
- ½ red onion, finely chopped
- 175g/6oz each turnip, sweet potato and pumpkin, peeled and roughly chopped
- 5ml/1 tsp dried marjoram
- 2.5ml/½ tsp ground ginger
- 1.5ml/¼ tsp ground cinnamon
- 15ml/1 tbsp chopped spring onion (scallion)
- 1 litre/1¾ pints/4 cups well-flavoured vegetable stock
- 30ml/2 tbsp flaked (sliced) almonds
- 1 fresh red or green chilli, seeded and chopped
- 5ml/1 tsp sugar
- 25g/1oz creamed coconut or 60ml/4 tbsp coconut cream
- salt and ground black pepper
- chopped fresh coriander (cilantro), to garnish

COOK'S TIP

Take care when preparing fresh chillies. Avoid touching your eyes and wash your hands thoroughly afterwards (or wear disposable gloves).

1 Melt the butter or margarine in a large non-stick pan. Fry the onion for 4–5 minutes. Add the chopped vegetables and fry for 3–4 minutes.

2 Add the marjoram, ginger, cinnamon, spring onion, salt and pepper. Sauté over a low heat for about 10 minutes, stirring frequently.

3 Add the vegetable stock, flaked almonds, chilli and sugar and stir well to mix, then cover and simmer gently for 10–15 minutes, until the vegetables are just tender.

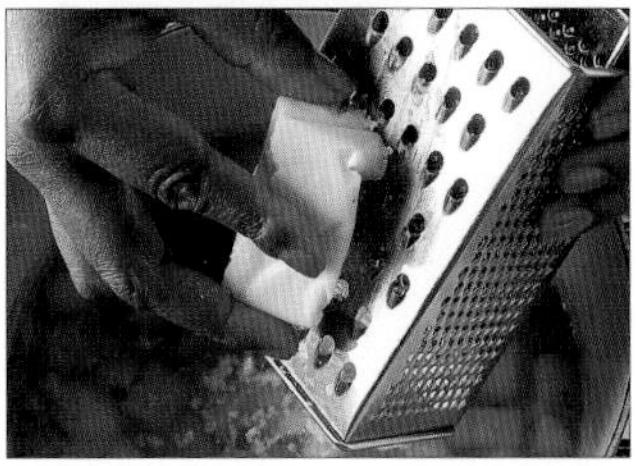

4 Grate the creamed coconut into the soup, or add the coconut cream, and stir to mix. Spoon the soup into warmed bowls and serve, sprinkled with chopped coriander.

Energy 168Kcal/701kJ; Protein 2.3g; Carbohydrate 13.2g, of which sugars 5.5g; Fat 12.2g, of which saturates 7.9g; Cholesterol 16mg; Calcium 50mg; Fibre 2.4g; Sodium 66mg.

Iranian Beef and Herb Soup with Yogurt

This recipe is called aashe maste in Iran. It dates from ancient Persian times, when soup was so important that the word for cook was ash-paz, literally "maker of the soup".

SERVES SIX

INGREDIENTS
- 2 large onions
- 30ml/2 tbsp oil
- 15ml/1 tbsp ground turmeric
- 90g/3½oz/½ cup yellow split peas
- 1.2 litres/2 pints/5 cups water
- 225g/8oz minced (ground) beef
- 200g/7oz/1 cup long-grain rice
- 45ml/3 tbsp each chopped fresh parsley, coriander (cilantro), and chives
- 15g/½oz/1 tbsp butter
- 1 large garlic clove, finely chopped
- 60ml/4 tbsp chopped fresh mint
- 2–3 saffron threads dissolved in 15ml/1 tbsp boiling water (optional)
- salt and ground black pepper
- natural (plain) yogurt and naan bread, to serve

1 Chop one of the onions, then heat the oil in a large pan and fry the onion until golden brown. Add the turmeric, split peas and water, bring to the boil, then reduce the heat and simmer for 20 minutes.

COOK'S TIP

Fresh spinach is also delicious in this soup. Add 50g/2oz finely chopped spinach leaves to the soup with the parsley, coriander and chives.

2 Meanwhile, grate the other onion into a bowl, add the minced beef and seasoning and mix. Using your hands, form the mixture into small balls, about the size of walnuts. Carefully add to the pan and simmer for 10 minutes.

3 Add the rice, then stir in the chopped parsley, coriander and chives and simmer for about 30 minutes, until the rice is tender, stirring frequently.

4 Melt the butter in a small pan and gently fry the garlic. Add the chopped mint, stir briefly, and then sprinkle the mixture over the soup with the saffron liquid, if using. Serve the soup with yogurt and naan bread.

Energy 338Kcal/1409kJ; Protein 14.8g; Carbohydrate 42g, of which sugars 5.3g; Fat 12.5g, of which saturates 4.5g; Cholesterol 28mg; Calcium 64mg; Fibre 2.5g; Sodium 57mg.

SPINACH AND LEMON SOUP WITH MEATBALLS

THIS SOUP – OR A VARIATION OF IT – IS STANDARD FARE THROUGHOUT THE MIDDLE EAST. IN TURKEY, WITHOUT MEATBALLS, IT IS POPULARLY REFERRED TO AS WEDDING SOUP.

SERVES SIX

INGREDIENTS

- 2 large onions
- 45ml/3 tbsp oil
- 15ml/1 tbsp ground turmeric
- 90g/3½oz/½ cup yellow split peas
- 1.2 litres/2 pints/5 cups water
- 225g/8oz minced (ground) lamb
- 450g/1lb spinach, chopped
- 50g/2oz/½ cup rice flour
- juice of 2 lemons
- 1–2 garlic cloves, very finely chopped
- 30ml/2 tbsp chopped fresh mint
- 4 eggs, beaten
- salt and ground black pepper

1 Chop one of the onions, heat 30ml/2 tbsp of the oil in a large frying pan and fry the onion until golden. Add the turmeric, split peas and water, bring to the boil then simmer for 20 minutes.

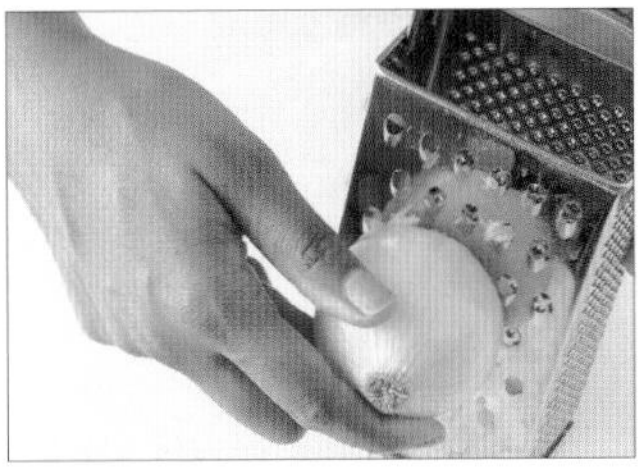

2 Grate the remaining onion into a bowl, add the minced lamb and seasoning and mix. With your hands, form into small balls, about the size of walnuts. Carefully add to the pan and simmer for 10 minutes, then add the spinach, cover and simmer for 20 minutes.

3 Mix the rice flour with about 250ml/8fl oz/1 cup cold water to make a smooth paste, then slowly add to the pan, stirring all the time to prevent lumps. Stir in the lemon juice, season with salt and pepper and cook over a gentle heat for 20 minutes.

4 Meanwhile, heat the remaining oil in a small pan and fry the garlic briefly until golden. Stir in the chopped mint and remove the pan from the heat.

COOK'S TIP

If preferred, use less lemon juice to begin with and then add more to taste once the soup is cooked. Use minced beef or pork in place of minced lamb.

5 Remove the soup from the heat and stir in the beaten eggs. Ladle the soup into warmed soup bowls. Sprinkle the garlic and mint garnish over the soup and serve.

Energy 293Kcal/1222kJ; Protein 18.3g; Carbohydrate 21.6g, of which sugars 5.2g; Fat 15.2g, of which saturates 4.3g; Cholesterol 156mg; Calcium 179mg; Fibre 3.4g; Sodium 185mg.

Olives with Moroccan Marinades

Visit a Moroccan suq and you'll see bowls brimming with fat purple, green and black olives. Marinated, they make a delicious appetizer and keep well in the refrigerator.

SERVES SIX TO EIGHT

INGREDIENTS

- 225g/8oz/1⅓ cups green or tan olives (unpitted) for each marinade

For the Moroccan marinade

- 45ml/3 tbsp chopped fresh coriander (cilantro)
- 45ml/3 tbsp chopped fresh flat leaf parsley
- 1 garlic clove, finely chopped
- good pinch of cayenne pepper
- good pinch of ground cumin
- 30–45ml/2–3 tbsp olive oil
- 30–45ml/2–3 tbsp lemon juice

For the spicy herb marinade

- 60ml/4 tbsp chopped fresh coriander (cilantro)
- 60ml/4 tbsp chopped fresh flat leaf parsley
- 1 garlic clove, finely chopped
- 5ml/1 tsp grated fresh root ginger
- 1 fresh red chilli, seeded and thinly sliced
- ¼ preserved lemon, cut into thin strips

1 Crack the olives, hard enough to break the flesh, but taking care not to crack the pits. Place in a bowl of cold water and leave overnight to remove the excess brine. Drain thoroughly and divide the olives equally between two jars.

COOK'S TIP

Use a sieve (strainer) or fine colander to drain the olives thoroughly.

2 Blend all the ingredients for the Moroccan marinade together, then pour it over the olives in one jar, adding more olive oil and lemon juice to cover, if necessary.

3 To make the spicy herb marinade, mix together the chopped coriander, chopped parsley, garlic, ginger, chilli and preserved lemon. Add to the olives in the second jar. Store the olives in the fridge for at least 1 week, shaking the jars occasionally.

Byesar

The Arab dish byesar is similar to Middle Eastern hummus, but uses broad beans instead of chickpeas. In Morocco, bread is always served with byesar. The bread is torn into pieces, dipped into ground spices and used to scoop up the purée.

SERVES FOUR TO SIX

INGREDIENTS

- 115g/4oz dried broad (fava) beans, soaked overnight
- 2 garlic cloves, peeled
- 5ml/1 tsp cumin seeds
- about 60ml/4 tbsp olive oil
- salt
- fresh mint sprigs, to garnish
- extra cumin seeds, cayenne pepper and bread, to serve

VARIATION

Use dried chickpeas in place of broad beans if you prefer.

1 Put the dried broad beans in a pan with the whole garlic cloves and cumin seeds and add enough water just to cover. Bring to the boil, then reduce the heat, cover and simmer until the beans are tender. Drain, cool and then slip off the outer skin of each bean.

2 Process the beans in a blender or food processor, adding sufficient olive oil and water to give a smooth soft dip. Season to taste with plenty of salt. Garnish with sprigs of mint and serve with extra cumin seeds, cayenne pepper and bread.

TOP Energy 74Kcal/305kJ; Protein 0.6g; Carbohydrate 0.2g, of which sugars 0.2g; Fat 7.9g, of which saturates 1.2g; Cholesterol 0mg; Calcium 38mg; Fibre 1.5g; Sodium 846mg.
BOTTOM Energy 113Kcal/468kJ; Protein 1g; Carbohydrate 2.3g, of which sugars 0.2g; Fat 11.2g, of which saturates 1.6g; Cholesterol 0mg; Calcium 7mg; Fibre 0.5g; Sodium 2mg.

FALAFEL

These tasty deep-fried patties are one of the national dishes of Egypt and are also popular in Israel and other Middle Eastern countries. They make an excellent appetizer.

SERVES SIX

INGREDIENTS
- 450g/1lb/2½ cups dried white beans
- 2 red onions, chopped
- 2 large garlic cloves, crushed
- 45ml/3 tbsp finely chopped fresh parsley
- 5ml/1 tsp ground coriander
- 5ml/1 tsp ground cumin
- 7.5ml/1½ tsp baking powder
- vegetable oil, for deep frying
- salt and ground black pepper
- tomato salad, to serve

1 Soak the white beans overnight in water. Remove the skins and process in a blender or food processor. Add the chopped onions, garlic, chopped parsley, coriander, cumin, baking powder and seasoning and blend again to make a very smooth paste. Allow the mixture to stand at room temperature for at least 30 minutes.

2 Take walnut-size pieces of the mixture and flatten into small patties. Set aside again for about 15 minutes.

3 Heat the oil in a deep, heavy pan until it is very hot and then deep-fry the patties in batches until golden brown. Drain on kitchen paper and then serve hot with a tomato salad.

HUMMUS

This popular Middle Eastern dip is widely available in supermarkets, but nothing compares to the flavour of the home-made variety. It is very easy to prepare.

SERVES FOUR TO SIX

INGREDIENTS
- 175g/6oz/1 cup cooked chickpeas
- 120ml/4fl oz/½ cup tahini paste
- 3 garlic cloves
- juice of 2 lemons
- 45–60ml/3–4 tbsp water
- salt and ground black pepper
- fresh radishes, to serve

For the garnish
- 15ml/1 tbsp olive oil
- 15ml/1 tbsp finely chopped fresh parsley
- 2.5ml/½ tsp paprika
- 4 pitted black olives

1 Place the chickpeas, tahini paste, garlic, lemon juice, seasoning and a little of the water in a blender or food processor. Process until smooth, adding a little more water, if necessary.

2 Alternatively, if you don't have a blender or food processor, mash the ingredients together in a small bowl until smooth in consistency.

3 Spoon the mixture into a shallow dish. Make a dent in the middle and pour the olive oil garnish into it. Garnish with chopped parsley, paprika and olives and serve with the radishes.

COOK'S TIP
Canned chickpeas can be used for hummus. Drain and rinse under cold water before processing.

TOP Energy 409Kcal/1704kJ; Protein 16.9g; Carbohydrate 22.2g, of which sugars 1.5g; Fat 28.7g, of which saturates 4g; Cholesterol 0mg; Calcium 350mg; Fibre 8.1g; Sodium 26mg.
BOTTOM Energy 303Kcal/1282kJ; Protein 18.5g; Carbohydrate 44.7g, of which sugars 5.2g; Fat 6.9g, of which saturates 1.2g; Cholesterol 0mg; Calcium 88mg; Fibre 7.2g; Sodium 16mg.

TABBOULEH

The bulgur wheat that gives this classic Arab salad its delicious nuttiness is not cooked, just soaked in cold water. Tomatoes, fresh herbs and lemon juice add to the flavour.

SERVES FOUR

INGREDIENTS

- 175g/6oz/1 cup fine bulgur wheat
- juice of 1 lemon
- 45ml/3 tbsp olive oil
- 40g/1½oz fresh parsley, finely chopped
- 45ml/3 tbsp fresh mint, chopped
- 4–5 spring onions (scallions), chopped
- 1 green (bell) pepper, seeded and sliced
- salt and ground black pepper
- 2 large tomatoes, diced, and pitted black olives, to garnish

1 Put the bulgur wheat in a bowl. Add enough cold water to cover the wheat and let it stand for at least 30 minutes and up to 2 hours.

2 Drain and squeeze with your hands to remove excess water. The bulgur wheat will swell to double the size. Spread on kitchen paper to dry the bulgur wheat completely.

3 Place the bulgur wheat in a large bowl, add the lemon juice, the oil and a little salt and pepper. Allow to stand for 1–2 hours if possible, in order for the flavours to develop.

4 Add the chopped parsley, chopped mint, spring onions and pepper and mix well. Garnish with diced tomatoes and olives and serve.

ÇAÇIK

Travellers throughout the Middle East know this simple dish. It can be served with flat bread, as an appetizer, or as an accompaniment to a spicy stew or curry.

SERVES FOUR

INGREDIENTS

- ½ cucumber
- 1 small onion
- 2 garlic cloves
- 10g/¼oz fresh parsley
- 475ml/16fl oz/2 cups natural (plain) yogurt
- 1.5ml/¼ tsp paprika
- salt and white pepper
- fresh mint leaves, to garnish

1 Finely chop the cucumber and onion, crush the garlic and finely chop the parsley.

COOK'S TIP

It's not traditional, but other herbs, such as mint or chives used in place of parsley, would be equally good in this dish.

2 Lightly beat the yogurt in a bowl and then add the cucumber, onion, garlic and parsley and season with salt and pepper to taste.

3 Sprinkle with a little paprika and chill for at least 1 hour. Garnish with mint leaves and serve with warm pitta bread or as an accompaniment to meat, poultry and rice dishes.

TOP Energy 199Kcal/828kJ; Protein 3.9g; Carbohydrate 26.5g, of which sugars 3.9g; Fat 9.2g, of which saturates 1.3g; Cholesterol 0mg; Calcium 41mg; Fibre 2.1g; Sodium 13mg.
BOTTOM Energy 77Kcal/321kJ; Protein 6.6g; Carbohydrate 10.7g, of which sugars 10.3g; Fat 1.3g, of which saturates 0.6g; Cholesterol 2mg; Calcium 241mg; Fibre 0.6g; Sodium 101mg.

Roasted Red Peppers with Feta, Capers and Preserved Lemons

Red peppers, particularly the long, slim, horn-shaped variety, feature widely in the cooking of North Africa and the Middle East. Roasting them really brings out their smoky flavour and they taste wonderful with crumbled white cheese. Feta is suggested here, but villagers would just use whatever was available locally, whether from goat's, ewe's or cow's milk. This dish makes a great mezze and also tastes good with kebabs.

SERVES FOUR

INGREDIENTS

- 4 fleshy red (bell) peppers
- 200g/7oz feta cheese, crumbled
- 30–45ml/2–3 tbsp olive oil or argan oil
- 30ml/2 tbsp capers, drained
- peel of 1 preserved lemon, cut into small pieces
- salt

1 Preheat the grill (broiler) on the hottest setting. Roast the red peppers under the grill, turning frequently, until they soften and their skins begin to blacken. (Alternatively, spear the peppers, one at a time, on long metal skewers and turn them over a gas flame, or roast them in a very hot oven.)

2 Place the peppers in a plastic bag, seal and leave them to stand for 15 minutes. Peel the peppers, remove and discard the stalks and seeds and then slice the flesh and arrange on a plate.

3 Add the crumbled feta and pour over the olive or argan oil. Scatter the capers and preserved lemon over the top and sprinkle with a little salt, if required (this depends on whether the feta is salty or not). Serve with chunks of bread to mop up the delicious, oil-rich juices.

Energy 255Kcal/1058kJ; Protein 9.6g; Carbohydrate 12g, of which sugars 11.4g; Fat 19.1g, of which saturates 8.2g; Cholesterol 35mg; Calcium 194mg; Fibre 2.8g; Sodium 727mg.

Artichoke Hearts with Ginger, Honey and Lemons

When globe artichokes are in season, they grace every Moroccan table as a first course or salad. The hearts are often poached in salted water until tender, then chopped and tossed in olive oil with garlic, herbs and preserved lemon. For a more exciting appetizer, the artichokes are cooked in a glorious spiced honey dressing. Preserved lemons, which are available in large jars at every North African market, add a piquant note.

SERVES FOUR

INGREDIENTS

- 30–45ml/2–3 tbsp olive oil
- 2 garlic cloves, crushed
- scant 5ml/1 tsp ground ginger
- pinch of saffron threads
- juice of ½ lemon
- 15–30ml/1–2 tbsp clear honey
- peel of 1 preserved lemon, thinly sliced
- 8 fresh globe artichoke hearts, quartered
- 150ml/¼ pint/⅔ cup water
- salt

1 Heat the olive oil in a small, heavy pan and stir in the garlic. Before the garlic begins to colour, stir in the ginger, saffron, lemon juice, honey and preserved lemon.

2 Add the artichokes to the pan and toss them in the spices and honey. Pour in the water, add a little salt and heat until simmering.

3 Cover the pan and simmer for 10–15 minutes, until the artichokes are tender, turning them occasionally.

4 If the liquid has not reduced, take the lid off the pan and boil for about 2 minutes until reduced to a coating consistency. Serve at room temperature.

COOK'S TIP

To prepare globe artichokes, remove the outer leaves and cut off the stems. Carefully separate the remaining leaves and use a teaspoon to scoop out the choke with all the hairy bits. Trim the hearts and immerse them in water mixed with a squeeze of lemon juice to prevent them from turning black. You can use frozen hearts for this recipe.

Energy 115Kcal/478kJ; Protein 0.8g; Carbohydrate 15.6g, of which sugars 15g; Fat 5.9g, of which saturates 0.9g; Cholesterol 0mg; Calcium 32mg; Fibre 3g; Sodium 32mg.

DOLMEH

THE WORD DOLMEH MEANS "STUFFED" IN PERSIAN, AND GENERALLY REFERS TO ANY VEGETABLE FILLED WITH RICE, HERBS, AND SOMETIMES MEAT.

SERVES FOUR TO SIX

INGREDIENTS
- 250g/9oz vine leaves
- 30ml/2 tbsp olive oil
- 1 large onion, finely chopped
- 250g/9oz minced (ground) lamb
- 50g/2oz/¼ cup yellow split peas
- 75g/3oz/½ cup cooked rice
- 30ml/2 tbsp chopped fresh parsley
- 30ml/2 tbsp chopped fresh mint
- 30ml/2 tbsp chopped fresh chives
- 3–4 spring onions (scallions), finely chopped
- juice of 2 lemons
- 30ml/2 tbsp tomato purée (paste)
- 30ml/2 tbsp sugar
- salt and ground black pepper
- yogurt and pitta bread, to serve

1 Blanch fresh vine leaves if using, in boiling water for 1–2 minutes to soften them, or rinse preserved, bottled or canned vine leaves under cold water.

2 Heat the olive oil in a large frying pan and fry the onion for a few minutes until slightly softened. Add the minced lamb and fry over a medium heat until well browned, stirring frequently. Season with salt and pepper.

3 Place the split peas in a small pan with enough water to cover and bring to the boil. Cover the pan and simmer gently over a low heat for 12–15 minutes, until soft. Drain the split peas if necessary.

4 Stir the split peas, cooked rice, chopped herbs, spring onions, and the juice of one of the lemons into the meat. Add the tomato purée and then knead until thoroughly blended.

5 Place each vine leaf on a chopping board with the vein side up. Place 15ml/1 tbsp of the meat mixture on the leaf and fold the stem end over the meat. Fold the sides in towards the centre and then fold into a neat parcel.

6 Line the base of a large pan with unstuffed leaves and arrange the rolled leaves in layers on top. Stir the remaining lemon juice and sugar into 150ml/¼ pint/⅔ cup water and pour over the leaves. Place a heatproof plate over the dolmeh to keep them in shape.

7 Cover the pan and cook over a very low heat for 2 hours, checking occasionally and adding extra water if necessary. Serve with yogurt and bread.

COOK'S TIP

If using preserved vine leaves, soak them overnight in cold water and then rinse several times before use.

Energy 319Kcal/1336kJ; Protein 18.4g; Carbohydrate 29.8g, of which sugars 16.2g; Fat 14.8g, of which saturates 4.8g; Cholesterol 48mg; Calcium 117mg; Fibre 4.2g; Sodium 98mg.

Baba Ganoush

Legend has it that this famous Middle Eastern appetizer was invented by the ladies of the sultan's harem who vied with one another to win his favour.

SERVES FOUR TO SIX

INGREDIENTS

- 3 aubergines (eggplants)
- 2 garlic cloves, crushed
- 60ml/4 tbsp tahini paste
- juice of 2 lemons
- 15ml/1 tbsp paprika, plus extra for garnishing
- salt and ground black pepper
- chopped fresh parsley, olive oil, plus a few green or black olives, to garnish
- pitta bread or vegetable crudités, to serve

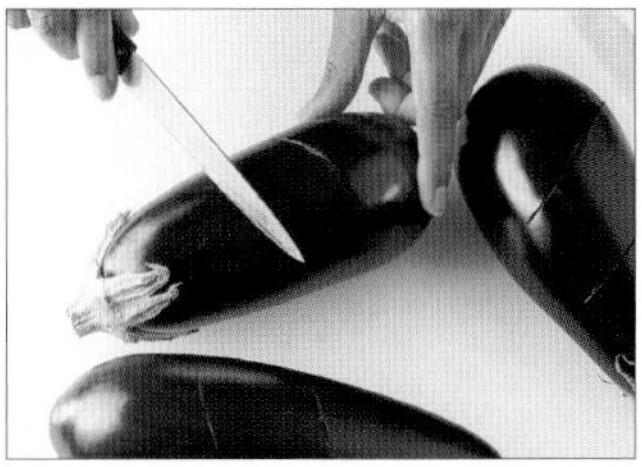

1 Preheat the oven to 190°C/375°F/Gas 5. Slit the skins of the aubergines, place on a baking sheet and bake in the oven for 30–40 minutes, until the skins begin to split.

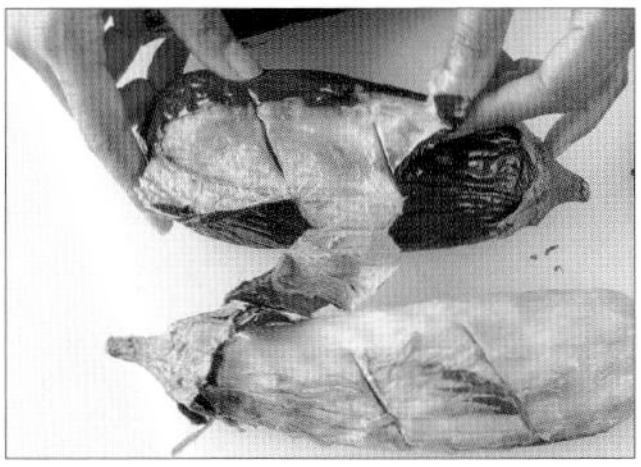

2 Place the aubergines on a chopping board and cool slightly. Carefully peel away the skins from the aubergines.

COOK'S TIP
Tahini paste can be obtained from health food shops, delicatessens and many supermarkets.

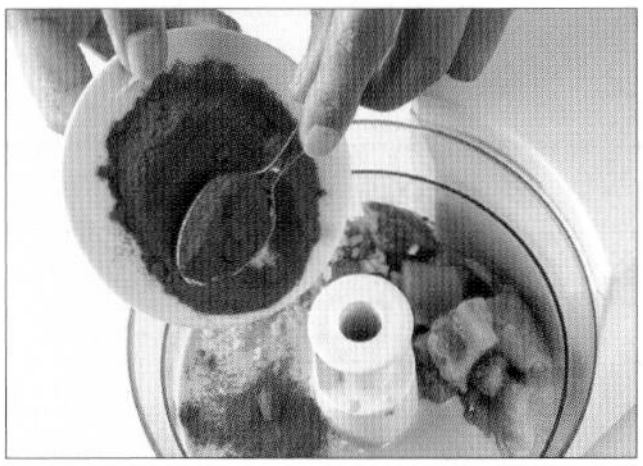

3 Place the aubergine flesh in a blender or food processor. Add the garlic, tahini paste, lemon juice, paprika and salt and pepper. Process to a smooth paste, adding about 15–30ml/1–2 tbsp water if the paste is too thick.

4 Spoon into a dish and make a dip in the centre. Garnish with extra paprika, chopped parsley, a drizzle of olive oil and olives. Serve with hot pitta bread or a selection of vegetable crudités.

Energy 159Kcal/662kJ; Protein 5.5g; Carbohydrate 3.6g, of which sugars 3.2g; Fat 13.9g, of which saturates 2.1g; Cholesterol 0mg; Calcium 168mg; Fibre 4.8g; Sodium 8mg.

STUFFED PEPPERS

Of all the dolmeh, or stuffed vegetables, this is perhaps the most colourful, especially when mixed colours are used. Try to find peppers that are more or less the same size.

SERVES SIX

INGREDIENTS
- 6 mixed (bell) peppers red, yellow and green
- 30ml/2 tbsp olive oil
- 1 large onion, finely chopped
- 3–4 spring onions (scallions), finely chopped
- 250g/9oz minced (ground) lamb
- 2 garlic cloves, crushed (optional)
- 50g/2oz/¼ cup yellow split peas
- 75g/3oz/½ cup cooked rice
- 30ml/2 tbsp finely chopped fresh parsley
- 30ml/2 tbsp finely chopped fresh mint
- 30ml/2 tbsp finely chopped fresh chives
- 5ml/1 tsp ground cinnamon
- juice of 2 lemons
- 30ml/2 tbsp tomato purée (paste)
- 400g/14oz can chopped tomatoes
- knob of butter
- salt and ground black pepper
- natural (plain) yogurt and pitta bread or naan bread, to serve

1 Cut off the mixed pepper tops and set aside. Remove the seeds and cores and trim the bases so they stand squarely. Cook in salted boiling water for 5 minutes, then drain, rinse under cold water and set aside.

2 Heat the oil in a large pan or flameproof casserole and fry the onion and spring onions for about 4–5 minutes until golden brown. Add the minced lamb and fry over a medium heat until well browned, stirring frequently. Stir in the garlic if using.

3 Meanwhile, place the split peas in a small pan with enough water to cover, bring to the boil and then simmer gently for 12–15 minutes until soft. Drain.

4 Stir the split peas, cooked rice, chopped herbs, cinnamon, juice of one of the lemons, and tomato purée into the meat. Season and stir until combined.

5 Spoon the rice and split pea mixture into the peppers and place the reserved lids on top.

6 Pour the chopped tomatoes into a large pan or flameproof casserole and add the remaining lemon juice and butter. Arrange the peppers neatly in the pan with the stems upwards. Bring to the boil and then cover tightly and cook over a low heat for 40–45 minutes, until the peppers are tender.

7 Serve the peppers with the tomato sauce accompanied by yogurt and warm pitta bread or naan bread.

COOK'S TIP

Make sure that the pan or casserole that you choose is just large enough so that the peppers fit quite snugly.

Energy 267Kcal/1115kJ; Protein 13.9g; Carbohydrate 26.1g, of which sugars 15.3g; Fat 12.5g, of which saturates 4.7g; Cholesterol 37mg; Calcium 81mg; Fibre 4.4g; Sodium 84mg.

Imam Bayildi

The name of this much loved Turkish dish translates as "the Imam fainted", and is said to represent his reaction on tasting the superb stuffed aubergines.

SERVES SIX

INGREDIENTS

- 3 aubergines (eggplants)
- 60ml/4 tbsp olive oil
- 1 large onion, chopped
- 1 small red (bell) pepper, seeded and diced
- 1 small green (bell) pepper, seeded and diced
- 3 garlic cloves, crushed
- 5–6 tomatoes, skinned and chopped
- 30ml/2 tbsp chopped fresh parsley
- about 250ml/8fl oz/1 cup boiling water
- 15ml/1 tbsp lemon juice
- salt and ground black pepper
- chopped fresh parsley, to garnish
- bread, salad and yogurt dip, to serve

1 Preheat the oven to 190°C/375°F/ Gas 5. Cut the aubergines in half lengthways and scoop out the flesh, reserving the shells. Set aside.

2 Heat 30ml/2 tbsp of the olive oil and fry the onion and peppers for 5–6 minutes, until both are slightly softened but not too tender.

3 Add the garlic and continue to cook for a further 2 minutes, then stir in the tomatoes, chopped parsley and aubergine flesh. Season and then stir well and fry over a medium heat for 2–3 minutes.

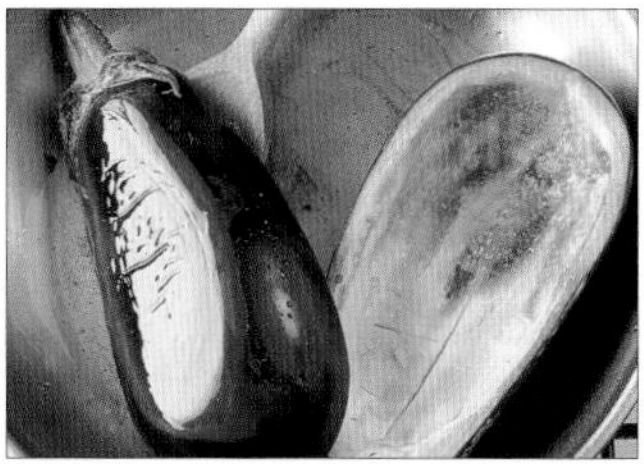

4 Heat the remaining oil in a separate pan and fry the aubergine shells, two at a time, on both sides.

COOK'S TIP

This flavourful dish can be made in advance and is ideal for a buffet table.

5 Stuff the shells with the sautéed vegetables. Arrange the aubergines closely together in an ovenproof dish and pour enough boiling water around the aubergines to come halfway up their sides.

6 Cover with foil and bake in the oven for 45–60 minutes, until the aubergines are tender and most of the liquid has been absorbed.

7 Place a half aubergine on each plate and sprinkle with a little lemon juice. Serve hot or cold, garnished with parsley and accompanied by bread, salad and a yogurt dip.

Energy 128Kcal/532kJ; Protein 2.6g; Carbohydrate 11.4g, of which sugars 10.1g; Fat 8.3g, of which saturates 1.3g; Cholesterol 0mg; Calcium 40mg; Fibre 4.5g; Sodium 14mg.

Spinach and Chickpea Pancakes

Pancakes are popular in those African states that have at some time been occupied by the French. These have a spinach and chickpea filling; high on flavour, low on spice.

SERVES FOUR TO SIX

INGREDIENTS

- 15ml/1 tbsp olive oil
- 1 large onion, chopped
- 250g/9oz fresh spinach
- 400g/14oz can chickpeas, drained
- 2 courgettes (zucchini), grated
- 30ml/2 tbsp chopped fresh coriander (cilantro)
- 2 eggs, beaten
- salt and ground black pepper
- fresh coriander (cilantro) leaves, to garnish

For the pancake batter

- 150g/5oz/1¼ cups plain (all-purpose) flour
- 1 egg
- about 350ml/12fl oz/1½ cups milk
- 15ml/1 tbsp sunflower or olive oil
- butter or oil, for greasing

For the sauce

- 25g/1oz/2 tbsp butter
- 30ml/2 tbsp plain (all-purpose) flour
- about 300ml/½ pint/1¼ cups milk

1 First make the pancakes. Whisk together the flour, a little salt, the egg, milk and 75ml/5 tbsp water to make a fairly thin batter. Stir in the oil.

2 Heat a large griddle, grease lightly and fry the pancakes on one side only, to make eight large pancakes. Set aside while preparing the filling.

3 Heat the oil in a frying pan and fry the onion for 4–5 minutes until soft. Wash the spinach, place in a pan and cook until wilted, shaking the pan occasionally. Chop the spinach roughly.

4 Skin the chickpeas: place them in a bowl of cold water and rub them until the skins float to the surface. Mash the skinned chickpeas roughly with a fork. Add the fried onion, grated courgettes, spinach and chopped coriander. Stir in the beaten eggs, season and mix well.

5 Place the pancakes, cooked side up, on a work surface and place spoonfuls of filling down the centre. Fold one half of the pancake over the filling and roll it up. Place in a large, buttered ovenproof dish and preheat the oven to 180°C/350°F/Gas 4.

6 Melt the butter for the sauce in a small pan, stir in the flour, and then gradually add the milk. Heat gently, stirring continuously, until the sauce is thickened and smooth. Simmer gently for 2–3 minutes, stirring. Season with salt and pepper and pour over the pancakes.

7 Bake in the oven for about 15 minutes, until golden and then serve garnished with coriander leaves.

Energy 560Kcal/2351kJ; Protein 26.2g; Carbohydrate 68.2g, of which sugars 14.8g; Fat 22.1g, of which saturates 7.5g; Cholesterol 166mg; Calcium 473mg; Fibre 8.6g; Sodium 472mg.

SCHLADA

This dish from Morocco is a good example of how recipes migrate. It began as an ancient Arab dish called gazpacho, which means "soaked bread". The Moors took the recipe to Spain. At that stage, the ingredients were simply garlic, bread, olive oil and lemon juice. The Spanish later added tomatoes and peppers, and the dish returned to North Africa, where it became known as schlada, and acquired spices and pickled lemon.

SERVES FOUR

INGREDIENTS

- 3 green (bell) peppers, quartered
- 4 large tomatoes
- 2 garlic cloves, finely chopped
- 30ml/2 tbsp olive oil
- 30ml/2 tbsp lemon juice
- good pinch of paprika
- pinch of ground cumin
- ¼ preserved lemon
- salt and ground black pepper
- fresh coriander (cilantro) and flat leaf parsley, to garnish

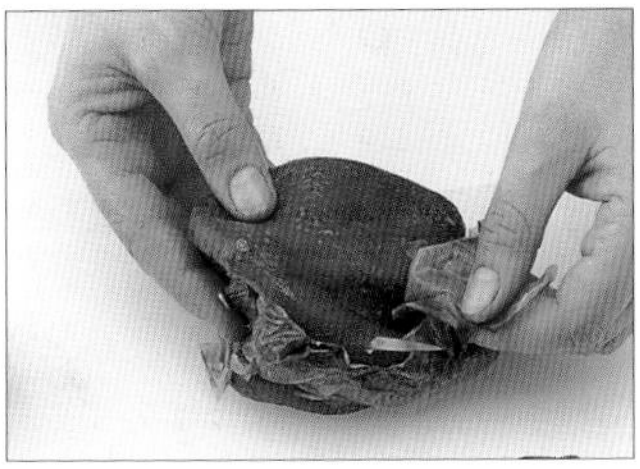

1 Preheat the grill (broiler) to its hottest setting. Grill (broil) the peppers skin side up until the skins are blackened, place in a plastic bag and tie the ends. Leave for about 10 minutes, until the peppers are cool enough to handle and then peel away and discard the skins.

2 Cut the peppers into small pieces, discarding the seeds and core, and place in a serving dish.

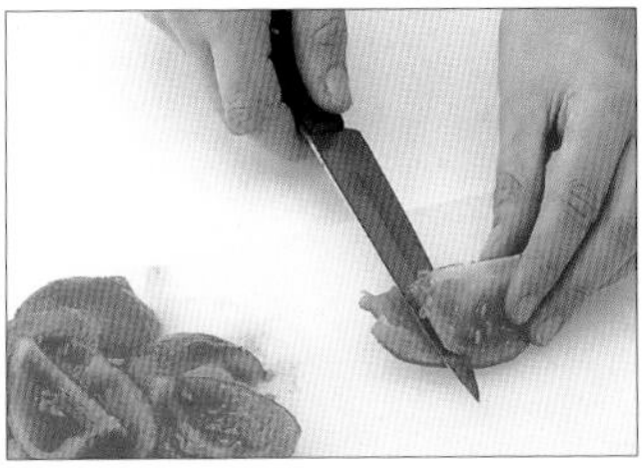

3 Peel the tomatoes by placing in boiling water for 1 minute, then plunging into cold water. Peel off the skins, then quarter them, discarding the core and seeds.

4 Chop the tomatoes roughly and add to the peppers. Scatter the chopped garlic on top and chill for 1 hour.

5 Whisk together the olive oil, lemon juice, paprika and cumin and pour over the salad. Season with salt and pepper.

6 Rinse the preserved lemon in cold water and remove the flesh and pith. Cut the peel into slivers and sprinkle over the salad. Garnish with coriander and flat leaf parsley.

Energy 100Kcal/423kJ; Protein 2.4g; Carbohydrate 9.1g, of which sugars 8.7g; Fat 6.5g, of which saturates 1.1g; Cholesterol 0mg; Calcium 24mg; Fibre 4.2g; Sodium 20mg.

Pan-Fried Baby Squid with Spices

Whether served as an appetizer in Africa or a mezze in the Middle East, baby squid is highly prized. It needs very little cooking and tastes wonderful with this spicy sweet and sour sauce, which teams turmeric and ginger with honey and lemon juice.

SERVES FOUR

INGREDIENTS

- 8 baby squid, prepared, with tentacles
- 5ml/1 tsp ground turmeric
- 15ml/1 tbsp smen or olive oil
- 2 garlic cloves, finely chopped
- 15g/½oz fresh root ginger, peeled and finely chopped
- 5–10ml/1–2 tsp clear honey
- juice of 1 lemon
- 10ml/2 tsp harissa
- salt
- small bunch of fresh coriander (cilantro), chopped, to garnish

1 Pat dry the squid bodies, inside and out, and dry the tentacles. Sprinkle the squid with the ground turmeric.

2 Heat the smen or olive oil in a large, heavy frying pan and stir in the garlic and ginger.

3 Just as the ginger and garlic begin to colour, add the squid and tentacles and fry quickly on both sides over a high heat. (Don't overcook the squid, otherwise it will become rubbery.)

4 Add the honey, lemon juice and harissa and stir to form a thick, spicy, caramelized sauce.

5 Season with salt, sprinkle with the chopped coriander and serve immediately.

COOK'S TIP

Smen is a pungent, aged butter used in Moroccan cooking. It is also savoured with chunks of warm, fresh bread and is used to enhance other dishes including couscous and some tagines.

Energy 154Kcal/647kJ; Protein 19.8g; Carbohydrate 5.8g, of which sugars 4.3g; Fat 5.9g, of which saturates 1g; Cholesterol 281mg; Calcium 54mg; Fibre 1g; Sodium 144mg.

Hot Spicy Prawns with Coriander

Coriander has a long history. Native to the Mediterranean and the Middle East, it was known to the ancient Egyptians, and seeds have been found in the tombs of the pharaohs. Today, coriander is widely grown as a cash crop in North Africa, and it is often used to flavour tagines and similar dishes. The herb's affinity for cumin is well known, so it is not surprising to find the twin flavourings used in this spicy appetizer.

SERVES TWO TO FOUR

INGREDIENTS

- 60ml/4 tbsp olive oil
- 2–3 garlic cloves, chopped
- 25g/1oz fresh root ginger, peeled and grated
- 1 fresh red or green chilli, seeded and chopped
- 5ml/1 tsp cumin seeds
- 5ml/1 tsp paprika
- 450g/1lb uncooked king prawns (jumbo shrimp), shelled
- bunch of fresh coriander (cilantro), chopped
- salt
- 1 lemon, cut into wedges, to serve

1 In a large, frying pan, heat the oil with the garlic. Stir in the ginger, chilli and cumin seeds. Cook briefly, until the ingredients give off a lovely aroma, then add the paprika and toss in the prawns.

2 Fry the prawns over a fairly high heat, turning them frequently, for 3–5 minutes, until just cooked. Season to taste with salt and add the coriander. Serve immediately, with lemon wedges for squeezing over the prawns.

COOK'S TIP

When buying garlic, choose plump garlic with tightly packed cloves and dry skin. Avoid any bulbs with soft, shrivelled cloves or green shoots.

Energy 382Kcal/1591kJ; Protein 40.8g; Carbohydrate 1.1g, of which sugars 0.9g; Fat 23.9g, of which saturates 3.4g; Cholesterol 439mg; Calcium 254mg; Fibre 1.9g; Sodium 440mg.

SNACKS AND STREET FOOD

Stroll around any city in Africa or the Middle East and sooner or later you are bound to encounter a street vendor cooking the regional speciality. What is on the brazier or burner may be roasted corn, kebabs, prawns, plantain snacks or even fried yam balls. Linger and you'll learn about local ingredients and cooking methods; taste and you'll capture the flavour of the place. This chapter introduces some of the dishes you may encounter, and whether you sample them on your travels or recreate them in your own home, you'll discover a world of new and fascinating flavours.

MEAT BRIOUATES

THE MOROCCANS, WHO ENJOY THE TASTE OF SWEET AND SAVOURY TOGETHER, TRADITIONALLY SPRINKLE THESE LITTLE PASTRY SNACKS WITH GROUND CINNAMON AND ICING SUGAR. IT IS AN UNUSUAL BUT DELICIOUS COMBINATION.

MAKES ABOUT TWENTY-FOUR

INGREDIENTS
- 175g/6oz filo pastry sheets
- 40g/1½oz/3 tbsp butter, melted
- sunflower oil, for frying
- fresh flat leaf parsley, to garnish
- ground cinnamon and icing (confectioners') sugar, to serve (optional)

For the meat filling
- 30ml/2 tbsp sunflower oil
- 1 onion, finely chopped
- 1 small bunch of fresh coriander (cilantro), chopped
- 1 small bunch of fresh parsley, chopped
- 375g/13oz lean minced (ground) beef or lamb
- 2.5ml/½ tsp paprika
- 5ml/1 tsp ground coriander
- good pinch of ground ginger
- 2 eggs, beaten

1 First make the filling. Heat the oil in a frying pan and fry the onion and the chopped herbs over a low heat for about 4 minutes, until the onion is softened and translucent.

2 Add the meat to the frying pan and cook for about 5 minutes, stirring frequently, until the meat is evenly browned and most of the moisture has evaporated. Drain away any excess fat and stir in the spices.

3 Cook the spiced meat and onion for 1 minute, and then remove the pan from the heat and stir in the beaten eggs. Stir until they begin to set and resemble lightly scrambled eggs. Set aside.

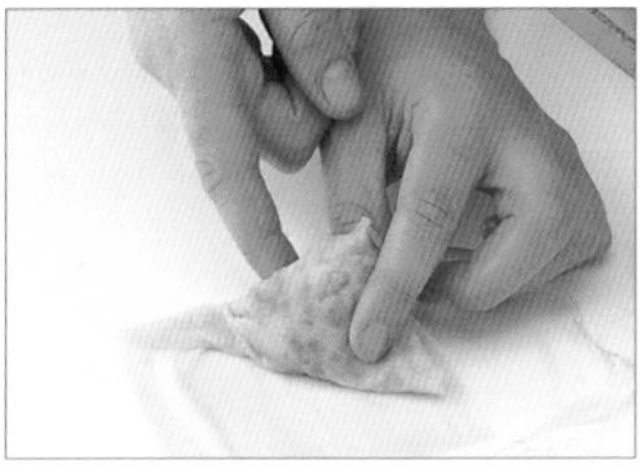

4 Take a sheet of filo pastry and cut into 8.5cm/3½in strips. Cover the remaining pastry with clear film (plastic wrap) to prevent it drying out. Brush the pastry strip with melted butter, then place a heaped teaspoon of the meat filling about 1cm/½in from one end. Fold the corner over to make a triangle shape.

5 Fold the "triangle" over itself and then continue to fold, keeping the triangle shape, until you reach the end of the strip. Continue in this way until all the pastry and filling have been used up. You should make about 24 pastries.

6 Heat about 1cm/½in oil in a heavy pan and fry the briouates in batches for 2–3 minutes until golden, turning once. Drain on kitchen paper and arrange on a serving plate. Serve garnished with fresh parsley and sprinkled with ground cinnamon and icing sugar, if liked.

Energy 95Kcal/396kJ; Protein 4.2g; Carbohydrate 4.8g, of which sugars 0.5g; Fat 6.7g, of which saturates 2.3g; Cholesterol 29mg; Calcium 19mg; Fibre 0.4g; Sodium 30mg.

PRAWN BRIOUATES

In Morocco, briouates are made with a special pastry called ouarka. Like filo, it is very thin and apt to dry out if not kept covered. Making the genuine article is tricky and takes years of practice. Fortunately filo pastry makes a perfect substitute.

MAKES ABOUT TWENTY-FOUR

INGREDIENTS
- 175g/6oz filo pastry sheets
- 40g/1½oz/3 tbsp butter, melted
- sunflower oil, for frying
- 1 spring onion (scallion) and fresh coriander (cilantro) leaves, to garnish
- ground cinnamon and icing (confectioners') sugar, to serve

For the prawn (shrimp) filling
- 15ml/1 tbsp olive oil
- 15g/½oz/1 tbsp butter
- 2–3 spring onions (scallions), finely chopped
- 15g/½oz/2 tbsp plain (all-purpose) flour
- 300ml/½ pint/1¼ cups milk
- 2.5ml/½ tsp paprika
- 350g/12oz cooked peeled prawns (shrimp), chopped
- salt and white pepper

1 First make the filling. Heat the olive oil and butter in a pan and fry the spring onions over a very gentle heat for 2–3 minutes until soft.

2 Stir in the flour, and then gradually add the milk. Heat gently, stirring continuously, until the sauce is thickened and smooth. Simmer gently for 2–3 minutes, stirring.

3 Season the sauce with paprika, salt and pepper and stir in the prawns.

COOK'S TIP

Chilled fresh or frozen filo pastry sheets are widely available from many supermarkets.

4 Take a sheet of filo pastry and cut it in half widthways, to make a rectangle about 18 x 14cm/7 x 5½in. Cover the remaining pastry with clear film (plastic wrap) to prevent it drying out.

5 Brush the pastry with melted butter and then place a heaped teaspoon of filling at one end of the pastry. Roll up like a cigar, tucking in the sides as you go. Continue in this way until you have used all the pastry and filling.

6 Heat about 1cm/½in oil in a heavy pan and fry the briouates, in batches if necessary, for 2–3 minutes until golden, turning occasionally. Drain on kitchen paper, arrange on a serving plate and then serve garnished with a spring onion and coriander leaves, and sprinkled with cinnamon and icing sugar, if liked.

Energy 77Kcal/320kJ; Protein 4.3g; Carbohydrate 5.5g, of which sugars 0.7g; Fat 4.3g, of which saturates 1.6g; Cholesterol 17mg; Calcium 47mg; Fibre 0.2g; Sodium 251mg.

BÖREKS

PROOF POSITIVE THAT COOKING CROSSES CONTINENTS, THESE TURKISH PASTRIES HAVE MUCH IN COMMON WITH THE BRIOUATES OF MOROCCO, BUT LACK THE SWEET CINNAMON COATING. THE TWO CHEESE FILLING IS A FAVOURITE COMBINATION, INEVITABLY ENLIVENED WITH FRESH HERBS AND JUST A PINCH OF NUTMEG. BÖREKS ARE MORE OFTEN BAKED THAN FRIED.

MAKES THIRTY-FIVE TO FORTY

INGREDIENTS

225g/8oz feta cheese, grated
225g/8oz mozzarella, grated
2 eggs, beaten
45ml/3 tbsp chopped fresh parsley
45ml/3 tbsp chopped fresh chives
45ml/3 tbsp chopped fresh mint
pinch of freshly grated nutmeg
225g/8oz filo pastry sheets
45–60ml/3–4 tbsp melted butter
ground black pepper

1 Preheat the oven to 180°C/350°F/ Gas 4. In a bowl, blend the feta and mozzarella cheeses with the beaten eggs. Add the chopped herbs, black pepper and nutmeg, and mix well.

2 Cut the sheets of pastry into four rectangular strips approximately 7.5cm/ 3in wide. Cover all but one or two strips of the pastry with a damp cloth to prevent them from drying out.

3 Brush one strip of pastry at a time with a little melted butter.

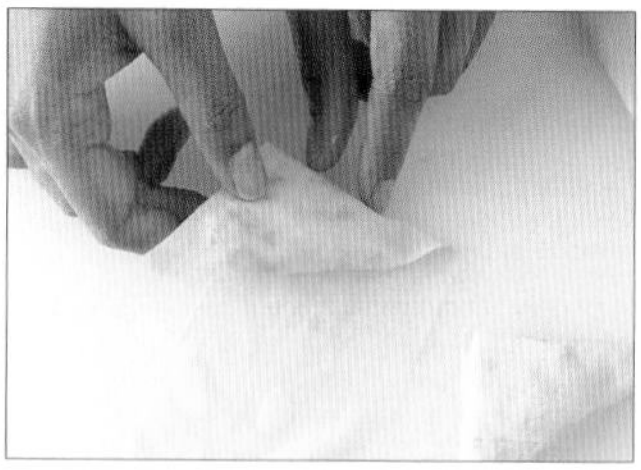

4 Place 5ml/1 tsp of filling at the bottom edge. Fold one corner over the filling to make a triangle shape. Continue folding the pastry over itself until you get to the end of the strip. Keep making triangles until all the filling is used up.

5 Place the böreks on a greased baking sheet and bake in the oven for about 30 minutes, until golden brown and crisp. Serve warm or cold.

COOK'S TIPS

A mixture of almost any cheeses can be used but avoid cream cheeses. Use chopped fresh basil in place of mint.

Energy 64Kcal/269kJ; Protein 3.1g; Carbohydrate 4.1g, of which sugars 0.2g; Fat 4.1g, of which saturates 2.5g; Cholesterol 22mg; Calcium 61mg; Fibre 0.3g; Sodium 131mg.

ASSIETTE OF PLANTAINS

More than half the world's plantains grow between coastal West Africa and the central basin of Zaïre, so it is not surprising that these starchy fruit vegetables have become an important staple. This succulent snack comes from Côte d'Ivoire.

SERVES FOUR

INGREDIENTS
- 2 green plantains
- vegetable oil, for shallow frying
- 1 yellow plantain
- ½ onion
- pinch of garlic powder
- salt and cayenne pepper

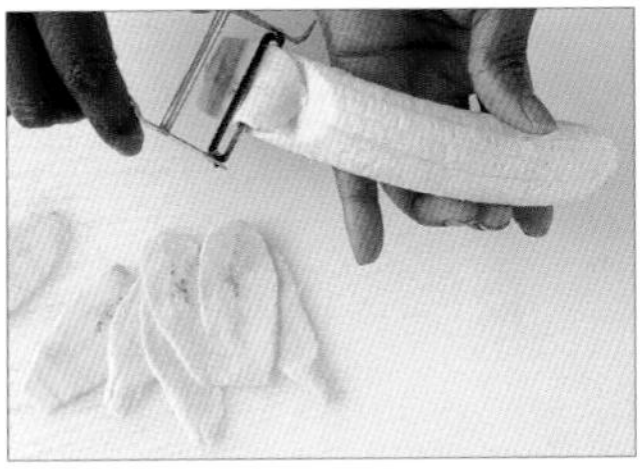

1 Peel one of the green plantains and cut into very thin rounds using a vegetable peeler. Heat the oil in a large frying pan over a moderate heat.

2 Fry the plantain rounds in the oil for about 3 minutes, turning until golden brown. Drain on kitchen paper and keep warm.

3 Coarsely grate the other green plantain and put on a plate. Slice the onion into wafer-thin shreds and mix with the grated plantain.

4 Heat a little more oil in the frying pan and fry handfuls of the mixture, in batches if necessary, for 2–3 minutes, until golden, turning once. Drain on kitchen paper and keep warm with the green plantain rounds.

5 Heat a little more oil in the frying pan and, while it is heating, peel the yellow plantain, cut in half lengthways and dice. Sprinkle with garlic powder and cayenne pepper and then fry until golden brown. Drain on kitchen paper and arrange each variety in shallow dishes. Sprinkle with salt and serve.

Energy 261Kcal/1093kJ; Protein 1.4g; Carbohydrate 34.3g, of which sugars 7.3g; Fat 14.1g, of which saturates 1.7g; Cholesterol 0mg; Calcium 14mg; Fibre 1.7g; Sodium 5mg.

SESAME-COATED MAJOUN

THE NOT-SO-SECRET INGREDIENT THAT TRADITIONALLY GIVES THESE SWEET AND SPICY SNACKS EXTRA FLAVOUR IS HASHISH. IT HAS BEEN OMITTED HERE, FOR OBVIOUS REASONS, BUT IS AS INTEGRAL TO THE GENUINE MOROCCAN RECIPE AS THE SPICES THAT FLAVOUR THE FRUIT, NUT AND HONEY MIX. MAJOUN, OFTEN CALLED HASHISH BALLS, ARE FAMED FOR THEIR NARCOTIC OR APHRODISIAC QUALITIES. THESE MAY NOT HAVE THE SAME EFFECT BUT ARE STILL DELICIOUS.

MAKES ABOUT TWENTY

INGREDIENTS
- 500g/1¼lb/scant 3 cups blanched almonds
- 250g/9oz/1½ cups walnuts
- 500g/1¼lb/3⅓ cups raisins
- 130g/4½oz/generous ½ cup butter
- 250g/9oz/generous 1 cup clear honey
- 7.5ml/1½ tsp ras el hanout
- 7.5ml/1½ tsp ground ginger
- 65–75g/2½–3oz sesame seeds

1 Finely chop the almonds, walnuts and raisins in a food processor or blender until they form a coarse, slightly sticky mixture. Alternatively, pound these ingredients together in batches in a large mortar using a pestle until the correct consistency is reached.

VARIATIONS
Use mixed spice (apple pie spice) or cinnamon in place of ginger. Use dried apricots in place of raisins.

2 Melt the butter in a large, heavy pan and stir in the honey, ras el hanout and ginger. Add the nuts and raisins and stir over a gentle heat for a few seconds until the mixture is thoroughly combined, firm and sticky.

3 Let the mixture cool a little, then shape into about 20 balls. Roll the balls in sesame seeds to coat completely. Serve warm or cold.

Energy 411Kcal/1711kJ; Protein 8.3g; Carbohydrate 29.1g, of which sugars 28.3g; Fat 29.8g, of which saturates 5.5g; Cholesterol 14mg; Calcium 107mg; Fibre 3g; Sodium 61mg.

Tunisian Plantain Snacks

Sweet and crisp, deep-fried slices of plaintain are not only a great street snack, but also make excellent nibbles with drinks. The spice mixture used here – zahtar – is popular throughout North Africa and is also widely used in Turkey and Jordan. Its blend of sesame seeds, sumac and thyme is perfect with plantains, and the chilli adds a warm note.

SERVES TWO TO FOUR AS A SNACK

INGREDIENTS

- 2 large ripe plantains
- sunflower oil, for deep-frying
- 1 dried red chilli, roasted, seeded and chopped
- 15–30ml/1–2 tbsp zhatar
- coarse salt

1 To peel the plantains, cut off their ends with a sharp knife and make two or three incisions in the skin from end to end, then peel off the skin. Cut the plantains into thick slices.

2 Heat the oil for deep-frying in a heavy pan to 180°C/350°F, or until a cube of bread browns in 30–45 seconds. Fry the plantain slices in batches until golden brown. Drain each batch on a double layer of kitchen paper.

3 While still warm, place them in a shallow bowl and sprinkle liberally with the dried chilli, zahtar and salt. Toss them thoroughly and eat immediately.

COOK'S TIP

To roast the chilli, place the chilli in a small, heavy frying pan and cook over a medium heat, stirring constantly, until the chilli darkens and gives off a peppery aroma.

Energy 334Kcal/1408kJ; Protein 1.9g; Carbohydrate 59.4g, of which sugars 14.4g; Fat 11.5g, of which saturates 1.3g; Cholesterol 0mg; Calcium 8mg; Fibre 2.9g; Sodium 4mg.

YAM BALLS

MOST AFRICAN COUNTRIES HAVE A VERSION OF THIS POPULAR SNACK, MADE BY ROLLING A SPICY MIXTURE OF MASHED YAM AND VEGETABLES INTO BALLS, WHICH ARE THEN DEEP FRIED. THE SMOOTH TEXTURE OF THE MASHED YAM CONTRASTS BEAUTIFULLY WITH THE CHOPPED VEGETABLES.

MAKES ABOUT TWENTY-FOUR

INGREDIENTS
- 450g/1lb white yam
- 30ml/2 tbsp finely chopped onion
- 45ml/3 tbsp chopped tomatoes
- 2.5ml/½ tsp chopped fresh thyme
- 1 fresh green chilli, finely chopped
- 15ml/1 tbsp finely chopped spring onion (scallion)
- 1 garlic clove, crushed
- 1 egg, beaten
- salt and ground black pepper
- vegetable oil, for shallow frying
- seasoned flour, for dusting

COOK'S TIP
Add a selection of chopped fresh herbs to the yam mixture; parsley, chives and coriander (cilantro) make a good combination. Mix in 30ml/2 tbsp with the egg and seasoning.

1 Peel the yam, cut into pieces and boil in salted water for about 30 minutes until tender. Drain and mash.

2 Add the onion, tomatoes, thyme, chilli, spring onion, garlic, then stir in the egg and seasoning and mix well.

3 Using a dessertspoon, scoop a little of the mixture at a time and with your hands mould them into balls. Roll the yam balls in the seasoned flour and set aside until you have formed all the mixture into balls.

4 Heat a little oil in a large frying pan, and then fry the balls in batches for a few minutes, until golden brown. Drain the yam balls on kitchen paper and keep them warm while cooking the rest of the mixture. Serve hot.

TATALE

GHANAIANS WOULDN'T DREAM OF THROWING OVER-RIPE PLAINTAINS AWAY. INSTEAD, THEY MASH THEM WITH ONION, CHILLI AND FLOUR AND TRANSFORM THEM INTO THESE TASTY SNACKS.

SERVES FOUR

INGREDIENTS
- 2 over-ripe plantains
- 25–50g/1–2oz/¼–½ cup self-raising (self-rising) flour
- 1 small onion, finely chopped
- 1 egg, beaten
- 5ml/1 tsp palm oil (optional)
- 1 fresh green chilli, seeded and chopped
- salt
- vegetable oil, for shallow frying

1 Peel and mash the plantains. Place in a bowl and add enough flour to bind, stirring thoroughly.

2 Add the onion, egg, palm oil, if using, chilli and salt. Mix well and then leave to stand for 20 minutes.

3 Heat a little oil in a large frying pan. Spoon dessertspoons of mixture into the pan and fry in batches for 3–4 minutes until golden, turning once. Drain the fritters on kitchen paper and serve hot or cold.

TOP Energy 179Kcal/754kJ; Protein 1.7g; Carbohydrate 31.8g, of which sugars 5.9g; Fat 5.9g, of which saturates 0.8g; Cholesterol 0mg; Calcium 21mg; Fibre 1.6g; Sodium 4mg.
BOTTOM Energy 47Kcal/195kJ; Protein 0.6g; Carbohydrate 5.6g, of which sugars 0.4g; Fat 2.6g, of which saturates 0.4g; Cholesterol 8mg; Calcium 5mg; Fibre 0.3g; Sodium 4mg.

BASTELA WITH GINGER AND CASHEW NUTS

Crisp pastry and a melt-in-the-mouth nut and egg filling are what make this delicious pie so special. Versions are made throughout North Africa, and the dish has migrated across the Strait of Gibraltar to southern Spain. In this simplified version, ground cashews are used in place of the more common almonds, and ginger, coriander and cinnamon provide the warm spice notes.

SERVES SIX

INGREDIENTS

- 30ml/2 tbsp olive oil
- 115g/4oz/½ cup butter
- 8 spring onions (scallions), trimmed and chopped
- 2 garlic cloves, chopped
- 25g/1oz fresh root ginger, peeled and chopped
- 225g/8oz/1⅓ cups cashew nuts, roughly chopped
- 5–10ml/1–2 tsp ground cinnamon, plus extra to garnish
- 5ml/1 tsp paprika
- 2.5ml/½ tsp ground coriander
- 6 eggs, beaten
- bunch of fresh flat leaf parsley, finely chopped
- large bunch of fresh coriander (cilantro), finely chopped
- 8 sheets of ouarka or filo pastry
- salt and ground black pepper

1 Preheat the oven to 200°C/400°F/Gas 6. Heat the olive oil with a little of the butter in a heavy pan and stir in the spring onions, garlic and ginger. Add the cashew nuts and cook for a few minutes, then stir in the cinnamon, paprika and ground coriander.

2 Season the mixture well, then add the beaten eggs. Cook, stirring constantly, until the eggs begin to scramble but remain moist. Remove the pan from the heat, add the chopped parsley and fresh coriander, and leave to cool.

VARIATION

Instead of making a single large pie, you can make small, individual pies for a picnic or to serve with drinks at a party. Simply cut the filo into strips or triangles, add a spoonful of the filling and fold them up into tight little parcels, making sure the edges are well sealed.

3 Melt the remaining butter. Separate the sheets of ouarka or filo and keep them under a slightly damp cloth. Brush the base of an ovenproof dish with a little of the melted butter and cover with a sheet of pastry, allowing the sides to flop over the rim.

4 Brush the pastry with a little more of the melted butter and place another sheet of pastry on top of the first. Repeat with another two sheets of pastry to make four layers.

5 Spread the cashew nut mixture on the pastry and fold the pastry edges over the filling. Cover with the remaining sheets of pastry, brushing each one with melted butter and tucking the edges under the pie, as though making a bed.

6 Brush the top of the pie with the remaining melted butter and bake for 25 minutes, until the pastry is crisp and golden. Dust the top of the pie with a little extra ground cinnamon and then serve immediately.

Energy 528Kcal/2190kJ; Protein 15.9g; Carbohydrate 17.6g, of which sugars 3.1g; Fat 44.5g, of which saturates 15.9g; Cholesterol 231mg; Calcium 93mg; Fibre 2.4g; Sodium 300mg.

FISH AND CHERMOULA MINI PIES

These little savoury pies are made with the Moroccan fine pastry ouarka, but filo pastry will work just as well. The filling is highly flavoured with chermoula, which is a mixture of spices and masses of fresh coriander and flat leaf parsley. The chermoula may be made in advance and stored in the refrigerator for a few days. You can vary the filling by adding mussels or scallops, if you like.

MAKES EIGHT

INGREDIENTS
- 500g/1¼lb firm white fish fillets
- 225g/8oz uncooked king prawns (jumbo shrimp)
- 16 sheets of ouarka or filo pastry
- 60–75ml/4–5 tbsp sunflower oil
- 1 egg yolk, mixed with a few drops of water
- salt

For the chermoula
- 75ml/5 tbsp olive oil
- juice of 1 lemon
- 5ml/1 tsp ground cumin
- 5–10ml/1–2 tsp paprika
- 2–3 garlic cloves, crushed
- 1 red chilli, seeded and chopped
- large bunch of fresh flat leaf parsley, chopped
- large bunch of fresh coriander (cilantro), chopped

1 Prepare the chermoula. Combine all the ingredients in a bowl and set aside. Place the fish in a frying pan and add just enough water to cover the fillets.

2 Season the fish with a little salt and heat until just simmering, then cook gently for 3 minutes, until the fish just begins to flake. Use a slotted spoon to remove the fish from the liquid and break it up, taking care to remove all bones as you do so.

3 Poach the prawns in the fish liquor for 10 minutes, until they turn pink, then drain and shell them. Gently toss the prawns and fish in the chermoula, cover and set aside for 1 hour.

4 Preheat the oven to 180°C/350°F/Gas 4 and grease two baking sheets. To make the pies, lay the filo pastry under a damp cloth. Take two sheets of filo: brush one with oil, lay the second one on top, then brush it with oil.

5 Place some of the fish mixture in the middle of the length of the sheet but to one side of its width. Fold the edge of the pastry over the filling, then fold the long side over to cover the filling.

VARIATION
Instead of neat parcels, the filo and filling can be shaped into open boats or slipper shapes, as shown below.

6 Wrap the ends of the pastry around the filling like a collar to make a neat package with the edges tucked in, then brush with egg yolk.

7 Continue as before with the rest of the fish and chermoula mixture. Bake the pies for about 20 minutes, until the pastry is crisp and golden brown. Serve hot or warm.

Energy 236Kcal/984kJ; Protein 18.2g; Carbohydrate 10g, of which sugars 0.4g; Fat 13.9g, of which saturates 2g; Cholesterol 109mg; Calcium 67mg; Fibre 0.9g; Sodium 96mg.

TUNISIAN CHICKEN WINGS WITH ORANGES

THIS IS A GREAT RECIPE FOR THE BARBECUE – IT IS QUICK AND EASY TO PREPARE AND MAKES WONDERFUL FINGER FOOD. THE RUB THAT GIVES THE CHICKEN WINGS THEIR FIERY FLAVOUR IS BASED ON A CLASSIC TUNISIAN SPICE MIX CALLED HARISSA. TO BALANCE THE HEAT, ADD SEGMENTS OF BLOOD ORANGES, EITHER SERVED SEPARATELY OR COOKED ON SKEWERS WITH THE CHICKEN PORTIONS. CHERRY TOMATOES COULD BE USED INSTEAD OF THE ORANGES.

SERVES FOUR

INGREDIENTS

- 60ml/4 tbsp fiery harissa
- 30ml/2 tbsp olive oil
- 16–20 chicken wings
- 4 blood oranges, quartered
- icing (confectioners') sugar
- small bunch of fresh coriander (cilantro), chopped, to garnish
- salt

1 Preheat the grill (broiler) to its hottest setting. Put the harissa in a small bowl with the olive oil and mix to form a loose paste. Add a little salt and stir to combine.

2 Brush harissa mixture over the chicken wings so that they are well coated. Grill (broil) the wings for 5–8 minutes on each side, until cooked and a dark golden brown.

3 Once the wings begin to cook, dip the orange quarters lightly in icing sugar and grill them for a few minutes, until they are slightly burnt but not black and charred. Serve the chicken wings immediately with the oranges, sprinkled with a little chopped fresh coriander.

VARIATION

When blood oranges are out of season, normal oranges can be used instead.

Energy 500Kcal/2077kJ; Protein 44.8g; Carbohydrate 0g, of which sugars 0g; Fat 35.6g, of which saturates 8.9g; Cholesterol 196mg; Calcium 14mg; Fibre 0g; Sodium 132mg.

BUS-STATION KEFTA WITH EGG AND TOMATO

The title says it all. This is the type of snack that is on sale in bus and train stations throughout North Africa and the Middle East. It is cooked on the spot and eaten straight from the pan. Speed is essential when travellers are about to depart, so this is the perfect dish for a quick brunch or supper. Make the tiny meatballs in advance and keep them chilled until they are needed.

SERVES FOUR

INGREDIENTS

- 225g/8oz minced (ground) lamb
- 1 onion, finely chopped
- 50g/2oz/1 cup fresh breadcrumbs
- 5 eggs
- 5ml/1 tsp ground cinnamon
- bunch of flat leaf parsley, chopped
- 30ml/2 tbsp olive oil
- 400g/14oz can chopped tomatoes
- 10ml/2 tsp sugar
- 5ml/1 tsp ras el hanout
- small bunch of fresh coriander (cilantro), roughly chopped
- salt and ground black pepper
- crusty bread, to serve

1 In a bowl, knead the minced lamb with the onion, breadcrumbs, 1 egg, cinnamon, chopped parsley and salt and pepper until well mixed. Lift the mixture in your hand and slap it down into the bowl several times.

2 Take a small amount of mixture and shape it into a small ball about the size of a walnut. Repeat with the remaining mixture to make about 12 balls.

3 Heat the olive oil in a large, heavy frying pan. Fry the meatballs until nicely browned, turning them occasionally so they cook evenly.

4 Stir the tomatoes, sugar, ras el hanout and most of the chopped coriander in to the pan. Bring to the boil, cook for a few minutes to reduce the liquid, and roll the balls round in the sauce. Season to taste with salt and pepper.

5 Make room for the remaining eggs in the pan and crack them into spaces between the meatballs. Cover the pan, reduce the heat and cook for about 3 minutes or until the eggs are just set.

6 Sprinkle with the remaining chopped coriander and serve in the pan, with chunks of bread to use as scoops.

Energy 330Kcal/1381kJ; Protein 21.5g; Carbohydrate 16.7g, of which sugars 6.6g; Fat 20.4g, of which saturates 6.2g; Cholesterol 281mg; Calcium 97mg; Fibre 1.7g; Sodium 264mg

CAMEROONIAN SUYA

SUYA IS SAID TO HAVE ORIGINATED IN GHANA, BUT IS POPULAR THROUGHOUT AFRICA. A SPICY PEANUT RUB GIVES THE SUCCULENT BEEF KEBABS THEIR INIMITABLE FLAVOUR.

SERVES SIX

INGREDIENTS
- 450g/1lb frying (flank) steak
- 2.5ml/½ tsp sugar
- 5ml/1 tsp garlic powder
- 5ml/1 tsp ground ginger
- 5ml/1 tsp paprika
- 5ml/1 tsp ground cinnamon
- pinch of chilli powder
- 10ml/2 tsp onion salt
- 50g/2oz/⅓ cup peanuts, finely crushed
- vegetable oil, for brushing

COOK'S TIP

If cooking the meat on a barbecue, don't cook it too near to the burning coals, or wait until the heat is past its fiercest, to avoid scorching.

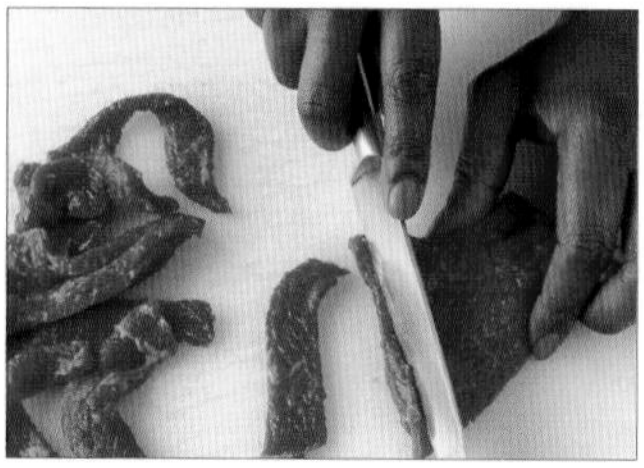

1 Cut the steak into 2.5cm/1in wide strips. Place in a bowl or a shallow dish.

2 Mix the sugar, garlic powder, spices, onion salt and crushed peanuts together in a small bowl, then mix with the steak.

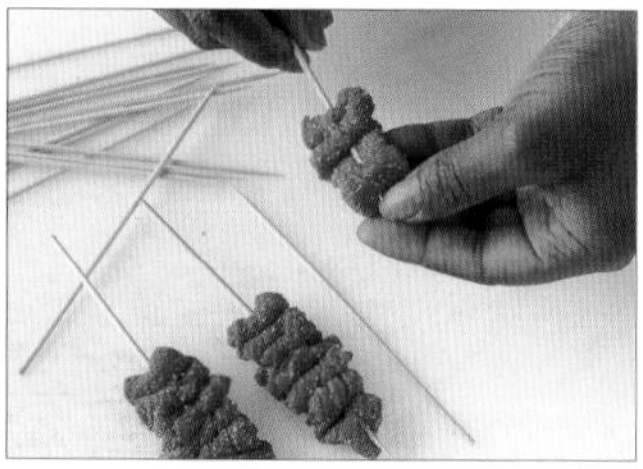

3 Thread the steak on to six satay sticks, pushing the meat close together. Place in a shallow dish, cover loosely with foil and leave to marinate in a cool place for a few hours.

4 Preheat a grill (boiler) or barbecue. Brush the meat with a little oil and then cook on a moderate heat for about 15 minutes, until evenly browned. Serve hot.

AKKRAS

THESE WEST AFRICAN BEAN FRITTERS ARE MADE IN MUCH THE SAME WAY AS MIDDLE EASTERN FALAFEL. SLAVES TOOK THE RECIPE TO THE CARIBBEAN, WHERE IT REMAINS VERY POPULAR TODAY.

SERVES FOUR

INGREDIENTS
- 225g/8oz/1¼ cups dried black-eyed beans (peas)
- 1 onion, chopped
- 1 fresh red chilli, halved, with seeds removed (optional)
- about 150ml/¼ pint/⅔ cup water
- vegetable oil, for deep-frying

1 Soak the black-eyed beans in plenty of cold water for 6–8 hours or overnight. Drain the beans and then briskly rub the beans between the palms of your hands to remove the skins.

2 Return the beans to a bowl, top up with water and the skins will float to the surface. Discard the skins and soak the beans again for 2 hours.

3 Place the beans in a blender or food processor with the onion, chilli, if using, and a little water. Process to make a thick paste. Pour the mixture into a large bowl and whisk for a few minutes.

4 Heat the oil in a large, heavy pan and fry spoonfuls of the mixture for 4 minutes, until golden brown. Serve.

TOP Energy 195Kcal/810kJ; Protein 19.2g; Carbohydrate 1.1g, of which sugars 0.5g; Fat 12.6g, of which saturates 3.8g; Cholesterol 44mg; Calcium 9mg; Fibre 0.5g; Sodium 376mg.
BOTTOM Energy 238Kcal/1004kJ; Protein 13.7g; Carbohydrate 33.4g, of which sugars 3.7g; Fat 6.5g, of which saturates 0.9g; Cholesterol 0mg; Calcium 55mg; Fibre 5.2g; Sodium 10mg.

SIZZLING PRAWNS

IN COASTAL REGIONS OF AFRICA AND THE MIDDLE EAST, STREET FOOD OFTEN MEANS A MAN WITH A PAN COOKING SPICY SEAFOOD OVER A SMALL BRAZIER. PRAWNS COOKED THIS WAY TASTE GREAT.

SERVES FOUR

INGREDIENTS

- 450g/1lb raw king prawns (jumbo shrimp) in their shells
- 30ml/2 tbsp olive oil
- 25–40g/1–1½oz/2–3 tbsp butter
- 2 garlic cloves, crushed
- 5ml/1 tsp ground cumin
- 2.5ml/½ tsp ground ginger
- 10ml/2 tsp paprika
- 1.5ml/¼ tsp cayenne pepper
- lemon wedges and fresh coriander (cilantro) sprigs, to garnish

1 Pull the heads off the prawns and then peel away and discard the shells, legs and tails. Using a sharp knife, cut along the back of each prawn and pull away and discard the dark thread.

2 Heat the olive oil and butter in a frying pan. When the butter begins to sizzle, add the garlic and cook for about 30 seconds.

3 Add the cumin, ginger, paprika and cayenne pepper. Cook briefly, stirring for a few seconds, and then add the prawns. Cook for 2–3 minutes over a high heat, until they turn pink, stirring frequently.

4 Transfer the prawns to four warmed serving dishes and pour the butter and spicy mixture over. Garnish with lemon wedges and coriander and serve.

GRILLED KEFTAS

CLOSELY RELATED TO THE KOFTAS OF INDIA AND THE MIDDLE EAST, THESE SPICY LAMB SAUSAGE SKEWERS WITH A MINT AND YOGURT DRESSING ARE A MOROCCAN SPECIALITY.

MAKES TWELVE TO FOURTEEN

INGREDIENTS

- 675g/1½lb lean lamb
- 1 onion, quartered
- 3–4 fresh parsley sprigs
- 2–3 fresh coriander (cilantro) sprigs
- 1–2 fresh mint sprigs
- 2.5ml/½ tsp ground cumin
- 2.5ml/½ tsp mixed spice (apple pie spice)
- 5ml/1 tsp paprika
- salt and ground black pepper
- Moroccan bread, to serve

For the mint dressing

- 30ml/2 tbsp finely chopped fresh mint
- 90ml/6 tbsp natural (plain) yogurt

1 Roughly chop the lamb, place in a food processor and process until smooth. Transfer to a plate.

2 Add the onion, parsley, coriander and mint to the processor and process until finely chopped. Add the lamb together with the ground spices and seasoning and process again until very smooth. Transfer to a bowl and chill for about 1 hour.

3 Make the dressing. Blend the chopped mint with the yogurt and chill until required.

4 Mould the meat into small sausage shapes and skewer with wooden or metal kebab sticks. Preheat a grill (broiler) or barbecue to a medium heat.

5 Cook the keftas for 5–6 minutes, turning once. Serve immediately with the mint dressing. Moroccan bread makes a good accompaniment.

TOP Energy 182Kcal/756kJ; Protein 19.9g; Carbohydrate 0g, of which sugars 0g; Fat 11.3g, of which saturates 4.2g; Cholesterol 233mg; Calcium 90mg; Fibre 0g; Sodium 252mg.
BOTTOM Energy 111Kcal/463kJ; Protein 11.7g; Carbohydrate 1.7g, of which sugars 1.3g; Fat 6.4g, of which saturates 3g; Cholesterol 43mg; Calcium 29mg; Fibre 0.2g; Sodium 56mg.

MARRAKESH PIZZA

In Morocco, cooks tend to place flavourings inside rather than on top of the dough, so that the flavours permeate right through. The result is surprising – and quite delicious.

MAKES FOUR

INGREDIENTS

- 5ml/1 tsp sugar
- 10ml/2 tsp dried yeast
- 450g/1lb/4 cups strong white bread flour
- 10ml/2 tsp salt
- melted butter, for brushing
- rocket (arugula) salad and olives, to serve

For the filling

- 1 small onion, very finely chopped
- 2 tomatoes, skinned, seeded and chopped
- 25ml/1½ tbsp chopped fresh parsley
- 25ml/1½ tbsp chopped fresh coriander (cilantro)
- 5ml/1 tsp paprika
- 5ml/1 tsp ground cumin
- 50g/2oz/⅓ cup shredded vegetable suet (chilled, grated shortening)
- 40g/1½oz Cheddar cheese, grated

1 First prepare the yeast. Place 150ml/¼ pint/⅔ cup warm water in a small bowl, stir in the sugar and then sprinkle with the yeast. Stir once or twice, then set aside in a warm place for about 10 minutes until frothy.

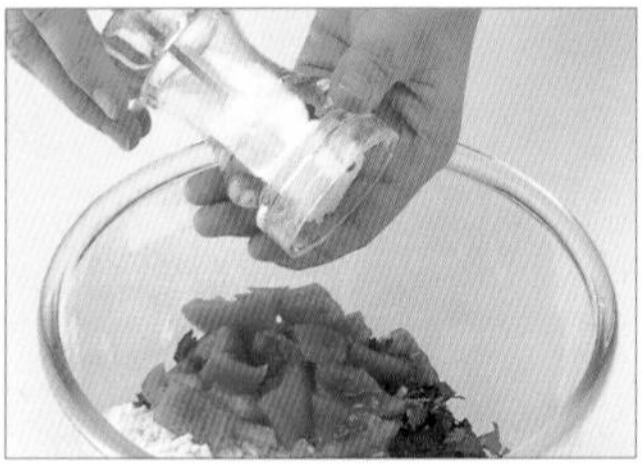

2 Meanwhile, make the filling. Mix together the onion, tomatoes, chopped parsley, chopped coriander, paprika, cumin, suet and cheese, then season with salt and set aside.

3 In a large bowl, mix together the flour and 10ml/2 tsp salt. Add the yeast mixture and enough warm water to make a fairly soft dough (about 250ml/8fl oz/1 cup). Knead the mixture into a ball and then knead on a floured work surface for 10–12 minutes until the dough is firm and elastic.

4 Divide the dough into four pieces and roll each into a rectangle, measuring 20 x 30cm/8 x 12in. Spread the filling down the centre of each rectangle, then fold into three, to make a rectangle 20 x 10cm/8 x 4in.

5 Roll out the dough again, until it is the same size as before and again fold into three to make a smaller rectangle. (The filling will be squeezed out in places, but don't worry – just push it back inside the dough.)

6 Place the pizzas on a buttered baking sheet, cover with oiled clear film (plastic wrap) and leave in a warm place for about 1 hour until slightly risen.

7 Heat a griddle and brush with butter. Prick the pizzas with a fork five or six times on both sides and then fry for about 8 minutes on each side, until crisp and golden.

8 Serve the pizzas immediately, with a little melted butter if liked, and accompanied by rocket salad and black olives.

Energy 548Kcal/2313kJ; Protein 14.2g; Carbohydrate 92.7g, of which sugars 5.3g; Fat 16g, of which saturates 8g; Cholesterol 11mg; Calcium 259mg; Fibre 4.8g; Sodium 1063mg.

Israeli Spiced Seed Breads

Orange flower water scents these delicious breads, which are flavoured with sesame seeds and fennel seeds. They are best served warm, with butter and honey.

MAKES TWELVE

INGREDIENTS

- 5ml/1 tsp sugar
- 10ml/2 tsp dried yeast
- 75g/3oz/6 tbsp butter, melted
- 15ml/1 tbsp orange flower water or almond essence (extract) (optional)
- 400g/14oz/3½ cups strong white bread flour
- 75g/3oz/¾ cup icing (confectioners') sugar
- 5ml/1 tsp salt
- 30ml/2 tbsp sesame seeds
- 15ml/1 tbsp fennel seeds
- beaten egg, to glaze

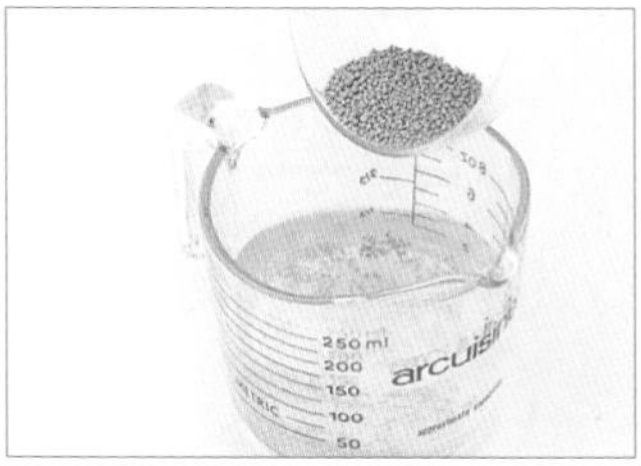

1 First start the yeast. Place 120ml/4fl oz/½ cup warm water in a jug, stir in the sugar and sprinkle the yeast on top. Stir and then set aside for about 10 minutes until frothy.

2 Place the melted butter, orange flower water or almond essence, and 175ml/6fl oz/¾ cup warm water in a separate jug and stir to mix. Stir the flour, icing sugar, salt, sesame seeds and fennel seeds together in the bowl of a food processor fitted with the dough blade.

3 Add the yeast and half of the butter and water mixture to the flour and process so that they slowly combine. Continue processing, adding the remaining butter and water to make a smooth and glossy dough. (You may need to add extra flour/warm water.)

4 Continue processing for 1–2 minutes, then transfer the dough to a floured board and knead by hand for a few minutes until the dough is smooth and elastic.

5 Place in a clean, lightly oiled bowl, cover with clear film (plastic wrap) and leave in a warm place for 1–1½ hours until doubled in size. Knead again for a few minutes and then divide and shape into 12 small balls and flatten slightly with oiled hands. Place on a greased baking sheet, cover with oiled clear film and leave to rise for 1 hour.

6 Preheat the oven to 190°C/375°F/Gas 5. Brush the breads with beaten egg and then bake for 12–15 minutes, until golden brown. Serve warm or cold.

Energy 201Kcal/847kJ; Protein 3.7g; Carbohydrate 32.8g, of which sugars 7.4g; Fat 7g, of which saturates 3.5g; Cholesterol 13mg; Calcium 68mg; Fibre 1.2g; Sodium 204mg.

FISH DISHES

Harvesting the riches of rivers and the sea has always been an important activity for the peoples of Africa and the Middle East, for, as the Angolan proverb says, "The smallest fish is better than an empty dish". The daily catch is sold as soon as the boats return to shore, to be cooked the same day, or preserved by drying, salting or pickling. Africans and Arabs have a vast store of fish recipes, but often prefer the simplest methods of cooking, and grilling, especially over an open fire, is universally popular.

King Prawns in Almond Sauce

A delectable seafood curry from Mauritius, where the prawns are large and succulent and christophene – or cho-cho as it's locally known – is a popular vegetable.

SERVES FOUR

INGREDIENTS

- 450g/1lb raw king prawns (jumbo shrimp)
- 600ml/1 pint/2½ cups water
- 3 thin slices fresh root ginger, peeled
- 10ml/2 tsp curry powder
- 2 garlic cloves, crushed
- 15g/½oz/1 tbsp butter or margarine
- 60ml/4 tbsp ground almonds
- 1 fresh green chilli, seeded and finely chopped
- 45ml/3 tbsp single (light) cream
- salt and ground black pepper

For the vegetables

- 15ml/1 tbsp mustard oil
- 15ml/1 tbsp vegetable oil
- 1 onion, sliced
- ½ red (bell) pepper, seeded and thinly sliced
- ½ green (bell) pepper, seeded and thinly sliced
- 1 christophene, peeled, stoned (pitted) and cut into strips

1 Shell the prawns and place the shells in a pan with the water and ginger. Simmer, uncovered, for 15 minutes until reduced by half. Strain into a jug (pitcher), discard the shells and ginger.

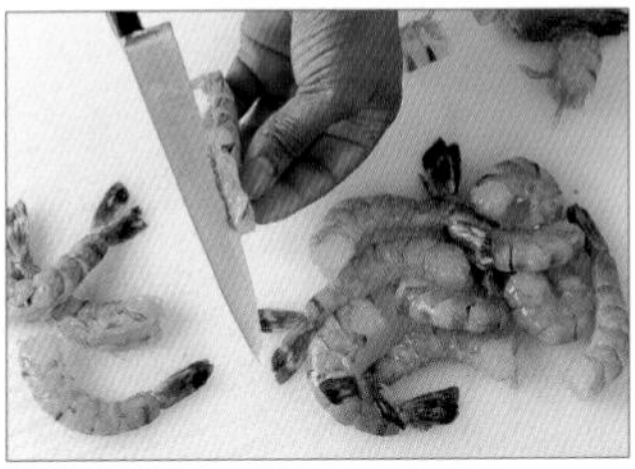

2 De-vein the prawns, place in a bowl and season with the curry powder, garlic and salt and pepper and set aside.

3 Heat the mustard and vegetable oils in a large frying pan, add the vegetables and stir-fry for 5 minutes. Season, spoon into a dish and keep warm.

4 Wipe out the frying pan, then melt the butter or margarine in the pan and sauté the prawns for about 5 minutes, until pink. Spoon over the bed of vegetables, cover and keep warm.

5 Add the ground almonds and chilli to the pan, stir-fry for a few seconds and then add the reserved stock and bring to the boil. Reduce the heat, stir in the cream and cook for a few minutes, without boiling. Pour the sauce over the vegetables and prawns before serving.

Fried Pomfret in Coconut Sauce

Pomfret are found in the Mediterranean, but the best-flavoured fish come from the Indian Ocean. This is how it is cooked in Zanzibar.

SERVES FOUR

INGREDIENTS

- 4 medium pomfret
- juice of 1 lemon
- 5ml/1 tsp garlic powder
- salt and ground black pepper
- vegetable oil, for shallow frying

For the coconut sauce

- 450ml/¾ pint/scant 2 cups water
- 2 thin slices fresh root ginger, peeled
- 25–40g/1–1½oz creamed coconut or 60–90ml/4–6 tbsp coconut cream
- 30ml/2 tbsp vegetable oil
- 1 red onion, sliced
- 2 garlic cloves, crushed
- 1 green chilli, seeded and sliced
- 15ml/1 tbsp chopped fresh coriander (cilantro)

1 Cut the fish in half and sprinkle with the lemon juice. Season with garlic powder, salt and pepper and marinate in a cool place for a few hours.

2 Heat a little oil in a large frying pan. Pat the fish dry, fry in the oil for 10 minutes, turning once. Set aside.

3 To make the sauce, place the water in a pan with the slices of ginger, bring to the boil and simmer until the liquid is reduced to just over 300ml/½ pint/1¼ cups. Remove the ginger and reserve, then add the creamed coconut or coconut cream to the pan and stir until the coconut has melted.

4 Heat the oil in a wok or large pan and fry the onion and garlic for 2–3 minutes. Add the reserved ginger and coconut stock, the chilli and chopped coriander, stir well and then gently add the fish. Simmer for 10 minutes, until the fish is cooked through. Transfer the fish to a warmed serving plate, adjust the seasoning for the sauce and pour over the fish. Serve immediately.

TOP Energy 301Kcal/1251kJ; Protein 24.3g; Carbohydrate 6.1g, of which sugars 5.1g; Fat 20.1g, of which saturates 4.8g; Cholesterol 234mg; Calcium 154mg; Fibre 2.4g; Sodium 244mg.
BOTTOM Energy 210Kcal/875kJ; Protein 23.2g; Carbohydrate 2.3g, of which sugars 2g; Fat 12g, of which saturates 1.5g; Cholesterol 58mg; Calcium 23mg; Fibre 0.2g; Sodium 101mg.

Nigerian Lobster Piri Piri

Dried shrimps intensify the flavour of this seafood dish. The sauce uses easy-to-obtain ingredients like onions, tomatoes and chilli, with chopped ginger for added piquancy.

SERVES TWO TO FOUR

INGREDIENTS

- 60ml/4 tbsp vegetable oil
- 2 onions, chopped
- 5ml/1 tsp chopped fresh root ginger
- 450g/1lb fresh or canned tomatoes, chopped
- 15ml/1 tbsp tomato purée (paste)
- 225g/8oz cooked, peeled prawns (shrimp)
- 10ml/2 tsp ground coriander
- 1 green chilli, seeded and chopped
- 15ml/1 tbsp dried shrimps, ground
- 600ml/1 pint/2½ cups water
- 1 green (bell) pepper, seeded and sliced
- 2 cooked lobsters, halved
- salt and ground black pepper
- fresh coriander (cilantro) sprigs, to garnish

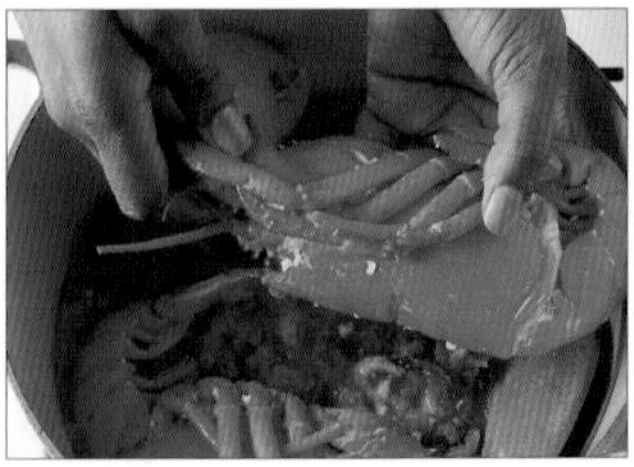

1 Heat the oil in a large, flameproof casserole and fry the onions, ginger, tomatoes and tomato purée for 5 minutes, until the onions are soft. Add the prawns, ground coriander, chilli and ground shrimps and stir well to mix.

2 Stir in the water, green pepper and salt and pepper, bring to the boil and simmer, uncovered, over a medium heat for about 20–30 minutes, until the sauce is reduced.

3 Add the lobsters to the sauce and cook for a few minutes to heat through. Arrange the lobster halves on warmed serving plates and pour the sauce over each one. Garnish with coriander sprigs and serve with fluffy white rice.

VARIATION

Use ground dried crayfish in place of ground dried shrimps, if preferred.

Energy 588Kcal/2464kJ; Protein 64.9g; Carbohydrate 24.5g, of which sugars 20.4g; Fat 26.6g, of which saturates 3.3g; Cholesterol 419mg; Calcium 270mg; Fibre 5.1g; Sodium 918mg.

TILAPIA IN MANGO AND TOMATO SAUCE

THE FLESH OF TILAPIA IS WHITE AND MOIST, WITH A SWEET FLAVOUR THAT IS ACCENTUATED WHEN IT IS COOKED WITH FRUIT, AS HERE. THE FISH IS POPULAR IN AFRICA, AND IN ISRAEL AND LEBANON.

SERVES FOUR

INGREDIENTS

- 4 tilapia
- juice of ½ lemon
- 2 garlic cloves, crushed
- 2.5ml/½ tsp dried thyme
- 30ml/2 tbsp chopped spring onion (scallion)
- vegetable oil, for shallow frying
- plain (all-purpose) flour, for dusting
- 30ml/2 tbsp groundnut (peanut) oil
- 15g/½oz/1 tbsp butter or margarine
- 1 onion, finely chopped
- 3 tomatoes, skinned and finely chopped
- 5ml/1 tsp ground turmeric
- 60ml/4 tbsp white wine
- 1 fresh green chilli, seeded and finely chopped
- 600ml/1 pint/2½ cups well-flavoured fish stock
- 5ml/1 tsp sugar
- 1 under-ripe medium mango, peeled, stoned (pitted) and diced
- 15ml/1 tbsp chopped fresh parsley
- salt and ground black pepper

1 Place the fish in a shallow bowl, drizzle the lemon juice all over the fish and gently rub in the garlic, thyme and some salt and pepper.

2 Place some of the spring onion in the cavity of each fish, cover loosely with clear film (plastic wrap) and leave to marinate for a few hours or overnight in the fridge.

3 Heat a little vegetable oil in a large frying pan, coat the fish with some flour, and then fry the fish on both sides for a few minutes, until golden brown. Remove with a slotted spoon to a plate and set aside.

4 Heat the groundnut oil and butter or margarine in a pan and fry the onion for 4–5 minutes, until soft. Stir in the tomatoes and cook briskly for a few minutes.

5 Add the turmeric, white wine, chilli, fish stock and sugar and stir well. Bring to the boil, then simmer gently, covered, for 10 minutes. Add the fish and cook for about 15–20 minutes.

6 Add the mango, arranging it around the fish, and cook briefly for 1–2 minutes to heat through. Arrange the fish on a warmed serving plate with the mango and tomato sauce poured over. Garnish with chopped parsley and serve immediately.

Energy 238Kcal/998kJ; Protein 23.4g; Carbohydrate 10.1g, of which sugars 9.6g; Fat 10.8g, of which saturates 3.1g; Cholesterol 8mg; Calcium 168mg; Fibre 2g; Sodium 97mg.

TANZANIAN FRIED FISH WITH COCONUT

A SPINACH AND COCONUT MILK SAUCE, STUDDED WITH PRAWNS AND RED CHILLI, LOOKS VERY PRETTY WHEN PUDDLED AROUND GOUJONS OF FRIED FISH THAT HAVE BEEN MARINATED IN SPICES.

SERVES FOUR

INGREDIENTS

- 450g/1lb white fish fillets (cod or haddock)
- 15ml/1 tbsp lemon or lime juice
- 2.5ml/½ tsp garlic powder
- 5ml/1 tsp ground cinnamon
- 2.5ml/½ tsp dried thyme
- 2.5ml/½ tsp paprika
- 2.5ml/½ tsp ground black pepper
- seasoned flour, for dusting
- vegetable oil, for shallow frying
- salt

For the sauce

- 25g/1oz/2 tbsp butter or margarine
- 1 onion, finely chopped
- 1 garlic clove, crushed
- 300ml/½ pint/1¼ cups coconut milk
- 115g/4oz fresh spinach, thinly sliced
- 225–275g/8–10oz cooked, peeled prawns (shrimp)
- 1 fresh red chilli, seeded and finely chopped

2 Blend together the garlic powder, cinnamon, thyme, paprika, black pepper and salt and sprinkle over the fish. Cover loosely with clear film (plastic wrap) and leave to marinate in a cool place or refrigerator for a few hours.

3 Meanwhile, make the sauce. Melt the butter or margarine in a large pan and fry the onion and garlic for 5–6 minutes, until the onion is soft, stirring frequently.

4 Place the coconut milk and spinach in a separate pan and bring to the boil. Cook gently for a few minutes until the spinach has wilted and the coconut milk has reduced a little, then remove from the heat and set aside to cool slightly.

5 Process the spinach mixture in a blender or food processor for 30 seconds then add to the onion with the prawns and red chilli. Stir well and simmer gently for a few minutes then set aside while cooking the fish.

6 Cut the marinated fish into 5cm/2in pieces and dip in the seasoned flour. Heat a little oil in a large frying pan and fry the fish pieces, in batches if necessary, for 2–3 minutes each side, until golden brown. Drain on kitchen paper.

7 Arrange the fish on a warmed serving plate. Gently reheat the sauce and serve separately in a sauce boat or poured over the fish.

VARIATION

Use 1 clove crushed fresh garlic in place of garlic powder.

Energy 259Kcal/1087kJ; Protein 32.5g; Carbohydrate 5.4g, of which sugars 5g; Fat 12.1g, of which saturates 4.3g; Cholesterol 164mg; Calcium 136mg; Fibre 0.8g; Sodium 343mg.

TANZANIAN FISH CURRY

With lakes on its western and northern borders, and the sea to the east, Tanzania has a rich inspiration for its fish dishes. This simple treatment of snapper or bream works well.

SERVES TWO TO THREE

INGREDIENTS
- 1 large snapper or red bream
- 1 lemon
- 45ml/3 tbsp vegetable oil
- 1 onion, finely chopped
- 2 garlic cloves, crushed
- 45ml/3 tbsp curry powder
- 400g/14oz can chopped tomatoes
- 20ml/1 heaped tbsp smooth peanut butter, preferably unsalted
- ½ green (bell) pepper, seeded and chopped
- 2 slices fresh root ginger, chopped
- 1 fresh green chilli, seeded and finely chopped
- about 600ml/1 pint/2½ cups fish stock
- 15ml/1 tbsp finely chopped fresh coriander (cilantro)
- salt and ground black pepper

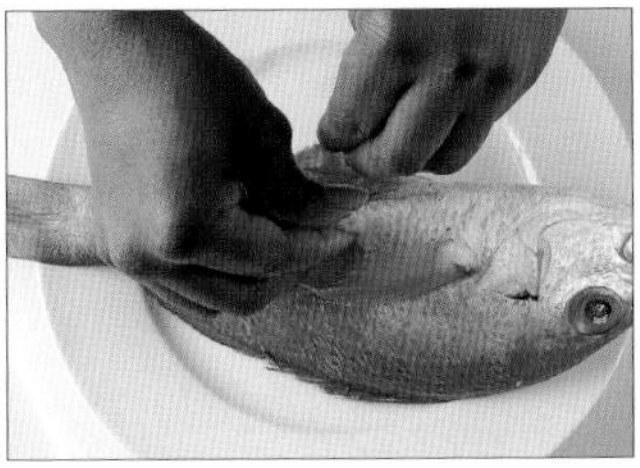

1 Season the fish with salt and pepper and squeeze half a lemon over it. Cover, and leave in a cool place for 2 hours.

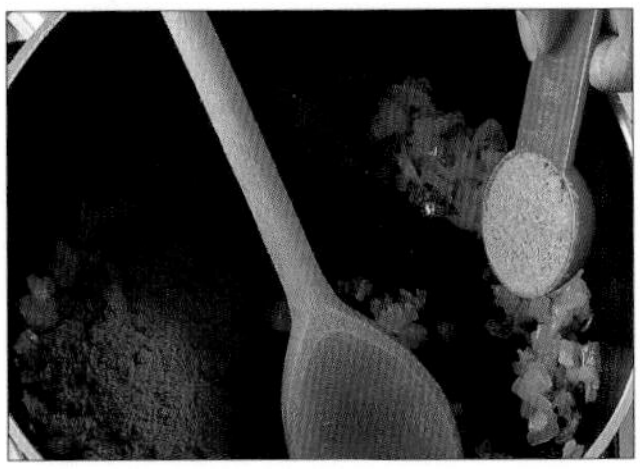

2 Heat the oil in a pan and fry the onion and garlic for 5–6 minutes. Reduce the heat, add the curry powder and stir in.

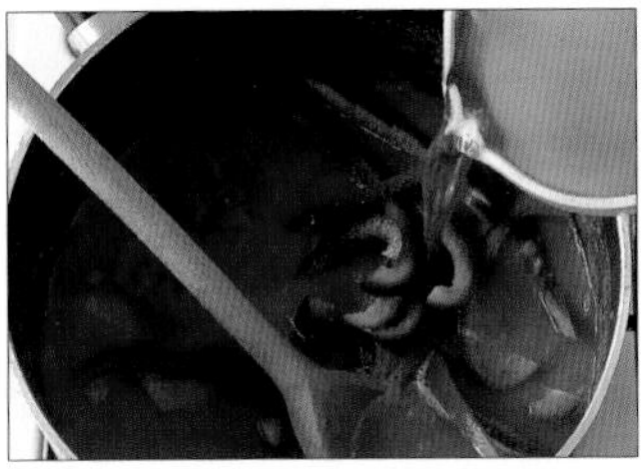

3 Stir in the tomatoes and then the peanut butter, mixing well, then add the green pepper, ginger, chilli and stock. Stir well and simmer gently for 10 minutes.

COOK'S TIP

The fish can be fried before adding to the sauce, if preferred. Dip in seasoned flour and fry in oil in a pan or a wok for a few minutes before adding to the sauce.

4 Cut the fish into pieces and gently lower into the sauce. Simmer for a further 20 minutes or until the fish is cooked, then using a slotted spoon, transfer the fish pieces to a plate.

5 Stir the coriander into the sauce and adjust the seasoning. If the sauce is very thick, add a little stock or water. Return the fish to the sauce, heat through and then serve immediately.

Energy 483Kcal/2020kJ; Protein 44.5g; Carbohydrate 12.8g, of which sugars 10.9g; Fat 28.7g, of which saturates 3.7g; Cholesterol 86mg; Calcium 129mg; Fibre 3.2g; Sodium 364mg.

Fish with Crab Meat and Aubergine

In Mauritius, home of the famous blue swimmer crabs and sand crabs, this shellfish is very popular. Combining it with salmon and aubergine creates a sophisticated dish.

SERVES FOUR

INGREDIENTS

- 450–675g/1–1½lb salmon fillet, skinned and cut into 4 pieces
- 2 garlic cloves, crushed
- juice of ½ lemon
- 15ml/1 tbsp vegetable oil
- 15g/½oz/1 tbsp butter or margarine
- 1 onion, cut into rings
- 175g/6oz fresh or canned crab meat
- salt and ground black pepper

For the aubergine (eggplant) sauce

- 25g/1oz/2 tbsp butter or margarine
- 30ml/2 tbsp chopped spring onion (scallion)
- 2 tomatoes, skinned and chopped
- ½ red (bell) pepper, seeded and finely chopped
- 1 large aubergine (eggplant), peeled and chopped
- 450ml/¾ pint/scant 2 cups fish or vegetable stock
- salt and ground black pepper

1 Place the salmon fillet in a shallow, non-metallic dish, season with the garlic and a little salt and pepper. Sprinkle with the lemon juice, cover loosely with clear film (plastic wrap) and set aside to marinate in a cool place for 1 hour.

2 Meanwhile, make the aubergine sauce. Melt the butter or margarine in a pan and gently fry the spring onion and tomatoes for 5 minutes.

3 Add the red pepper and aubergine, stir together and then add 300ml/½ pint/1¼ cups of the stock. Simmer for 20 minutes, until the aubergines are mushy and the liquid has been absorbed and then mash the mixture together well with a fork.

4 To cook the salmon, heat the oil and butter or margarine in a large frying pan. When the butter has melted, scatter the onion rings over the bottom of the pan and lay the salmon pieces on top. Cover each piece of salmon with crab meat and then spoon the aubergine mixture on top.

5 Pour the remaining stock around the salmon, cover with a lid and cook over a low to moderate heat, until the salmon is cooked through and flakes easily when tested with a knife. The sauce should be thick and fairly dry.

6 Arrange the fish on warmed serving plates, spoon extra sauce over and serve at once.

COOK'S TIP

Use a fish slice or metal spatula to carefully transfer the salmon fillet to serving plates, to prevent breaking up the fish.

Energy 372Kcal/1548kJ; Protein 32.4g; Carbohydrate 6.5g, of which sugars 5.8g; Fat 24.3g, of which saturates 7.9g; Cholesterol 109mg; Calcium 98mg; Fibre 3.1g; Sodium 360mg.

EGYPTIAN BAKED RED SNAPPER

A recipe doesn't have to be elaborate to taste good. This couldn't be simpler, but the fish is delicious when baked whole with its lightly spiced tomato sauce.

SERVES THREE TO FOUR

INGREDIENTS

1 large red snapper, cleaned
juice of 1 lemon
2.5ml/½ tsp paprika
2.5ml/½ tsp garlic powder
2.5ml/½ tsp dried thyme
2.5ml/½ tsp ground black pepper

For the sauce

30ml/2 tbsp palm or vegetable oil
1 onion, peeled and chopped
400g/14oz can chopped tomatoes
2 garlic cloves
1 fresh thyme sprig or 2.5ml/½ tsp dried thyme
1 fresh green chilli, seeded and finely chopped
½ green (bell) pepper, seeded and chopped
300ml/½ pint/1¼ cups fish stock

1 Preheat the oven to 200°C/400°F/Gas 6 and then prepare the sauce. Heat the oil in a pan, fry the onion for 5 minutes, and then add the tomatoes, garlic, thyme and chilli.

2 Add the green pepper and stock. Bring to the boil, stirring, then reduce the heat and simmer, covered, for about 10 minutes, until the vegetables are soft. Remove from the heat and cool slightly and then place in a blender or food processor and process to form a purée.

COOK'S TIP

If you prefer less sauce, remove the foil after 20 minutes and continue baking uncovered, until cooked.

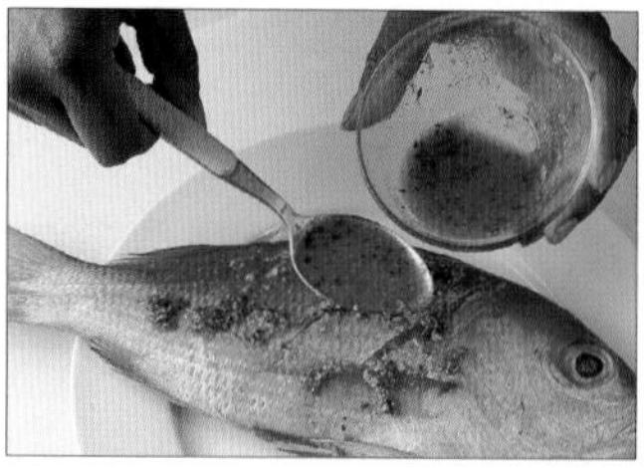

3 Wash the fish well and then score the skin with a sharp knife in a criss-cross pattern. Mix together the lemon juice, paprika, garlic, thyme and black pepper, spoon over the fish and rub in well.

4 Place the fish in a greased baking dish and pour the sauce over the top. Cover with foil and bake for about 30–40 minutes, until the fish is cooked and flakes easily when tested with a knife. Serve with boiled rice.

Energy 198Kcal/837kJ; Protein 33.1g; Carbohydrate 7.4g, of which sugars 6.6g; Fat 4.3g, of which saturates 0.8g; Cholesterol 58mg; Calcium 91mg; Fibre 1.7g; Sodium 201mg.

YELLOWTAIL WITH LEMON AND RED ONION

This delicious game fish is found in South African waters, the flesh can be dry, but simmering it in stock keeps it beautifully moist. Halibut or cod can be substituted.

SERVES FOUR

INGREDIENTS

- 4 yellowtail, halibut or cod steaks or cutlets, about 175g/6oz each
- juice of 1 lemon
- 5ml/1 tsp garlic powder
- 5ml/1 tsp paprika
- 5ml/1 tsp ground cumin
- 4ml/¾ tsp dried tarragon
- about 60ml/4 tbsp olive oil
- plain (all-purpose) flour, for dusting
- 300ml/½ pint/1¼ cups fish stock
- 2 fresh red chillies, seeded and finely chopped
- 30ml/2 tbsp chopped fresh coriander (cilantro)
- 1 red onion, cut into rings
- salt and ground black pepper

1 Place the fish in a shallow, non-metallic bowl. Mix together the lemon juice, garlic powder, paprika, cumin, tarragon, salt and pepper. Spoon over the fish, cover with clear film (plastic wrap) and leave overnight in the fridge.

2 Gently heat the oil in a large frying pan, dust the fish with flour and then fry on each side, until golden brown.

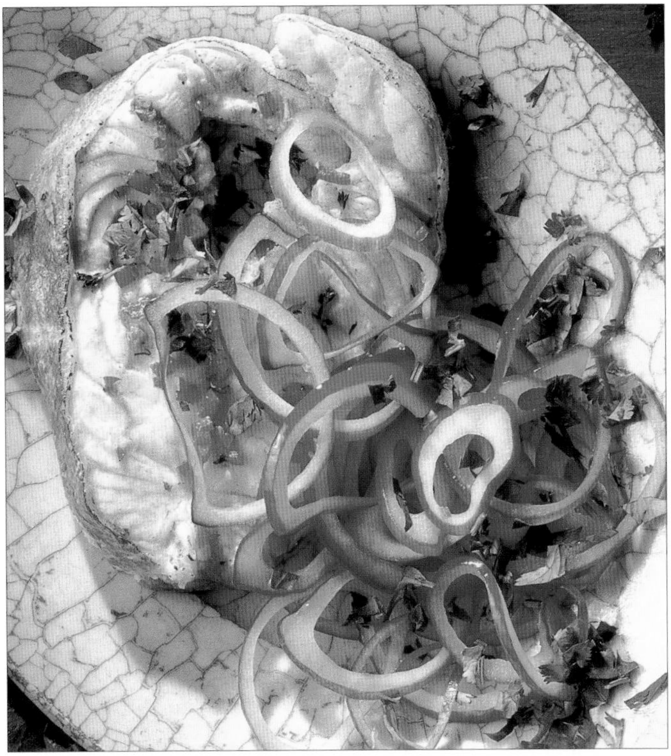

3 Pour the fish stock around the fish, and simmer, covered, for about 5 minutes, until the fish is almost cooked through.

4 Add the red chillies and 15ml/1 tbsp of the chopped coriander to the pan. Simmer for a further 5 minutes.

5 Transfer the fish and sauce to a serving plate and keep warm.

6 Wipe the pan, heat some olive oil in the pan and stir-fry the onion rings until speckled brown. Scatter over the fish with the remaining chopped coriander and serve at once.

Energy 265Kcal/1106kJ; Protein 33g; Carbohydrate 5.4g, of which sugars 1.2g; Fat 12.5g, of which saturates 1.8g; Cholesterol 81mg; Calcium 47mg; Fibre 0.9g; Sodium 109mg.

SPICY SHELLFISH COUSCOUS

THIS IS PRECISELY THE TYPE OF DISH YOU MIGHT ENJOY ON A WARM EVENING AT A BEACH BAR IN CASABLANCA OR TANGIER. THE COUSCOUS IS FLAVOURED WITH HARISSA, A SPICY CHILLI PASTE, BEFORE BEING BAKED IN THE OVEN. IT IS TOPPED WITH MUSSELS AND PRAWNS AND MOISTENED WITH A MARVELLOUSLY CREAMY SAUCE, WHICH JUST BEGS TO BE MOPPED UP WITH BREAD.

SERVES FOUR TO SIX

INGREDIENTS
- 500g/1¼lb/3 cups couscous
- 5ml/1 tsp salt
- 600ml/1 pint/2½ cups warm water
- 45ml/3 tbsp sunflower oil
- 5–10ml/1–2 tsp harissa
- 25g/1oz/2 tbsp butter, diced

For the shellfish broth
- 500g/1¼lb mussels in their shells, scrubbed, with beards removed
- 500g/1¼lb uncooked prawns (shrimp) in their shells
- juice of 1 lemon
- 50g/2oz/¼ cup butter
- 2 shallots, finely chopped
- 5ml/1 tsp coriander seeds, roasted and ground
- 5ml/1 tsp cumin seeds, roasted and ground
- 2.5ml/½ tsp ground turmeric
- 2.5ml/½ tsp cayenne pepper
- 5–10ml/1–2 tsp plain (all-purpose) flour
- 600ml/1 pint/2½ cups fish stock
- 120ml/4fl oz/½ cup double (heavy) cream
- salt and ground black pepper
- small bunch of fresh coriander (cilantro), finely chopped

COOK'S TIP
To roast spices, toss the spices in a heavy pan over a high heat until they begin to change colour and give off a nutty aroma, then tip them into a bowl.

1 Preheat the oven to 180°C/350°F/Gas 4. Place the couscous in a bowl. Stir the salt into the warm water, then pour over the couscous, stirring. Set aside for 10 minutes.

2 Stir the sunflower oil into the harissa to make a paste, then, using your fingers, rub it into the couscous and break up any lumps. Tip into an ovenproof dish, arrange the butter over the top, cover with foil and cook in the oven for about 20 minutes.

3 Meanwhile, put the mussels and prawns in a pan, add the lemon juice and 50ml/2fl oz/¼ cup water, cover and cook for 3–4 minutes, shaking the pan, until the mussels have opened. Drain the shellfish, reserving the liquor, and discard any closed mussels.

4 Heat the butter in a large pan. Cook the shallots for 5 minutes, or until softened. Add the spices and fry for 1 minute. Off the heat, stir in the flour, the fish stock and shellfish cooking liquor. Bring to the boil, stirring. Add the cream and simmer, stirring occasionally, for about 10 minutes. Season with salt and pepper.

5 Shell about two-thirds of the mussels and prawns, then add the shellfish and most of the fresh coriander to the pan. Heat through, then sprinkle with the remaining coriander.

6 Fluff up the couscous with a fork or your fingers, working in the melted butter. To serve, pass round the couscous and ladle the broth over the top.

Energy 734Kcal/3050kJ; Protein 24.5g; Carbohydrate 67.1g, of which sugars 1.5g; Fat 42.3g, of which saturates 21g; Cholesterol 223mg; Calcium 113mg; Fibre 0.2g; Sodium 360mg.

TAGINE OF MONKFISH

THE FISH IS MARINATED IN CHERMOULA, A LEMONY GARLIC AND CORIANDER PASTE, WHICH GIVES IT THAT UNMISTAKABLE MOROCCAN FLAVOUR. MONKFISH IS ROBUST ENOUGH TO HOLD ITS OWN AGAINST THE SPICES AND BLACK OLIVES, AND THE RESULT IS A VERY TASTY DISH. IT DOESN'T REALLY NEED BREAD, AS POTATOES ARE INCLUDED, BUT YOU MAY NOT BE ABLE TO RESIST MOPPING UP THE JUICES.

SERVES FOUR

INGREDIENTS
- 900g/2lb monkfish tail, cut into chunks
- 15–20 small new potatoes, scrubbed, scraped or peeled
- 45–60ml/3–4 tbsp olive oil
- 4–5 garlic cloves, thinly sliced
- 15–20 cherry tomatoes
- 2 green (bell) peppers, grilled (broiled) until black, skinned, seeded and cut into strips
- large handful of kalamata or fleshy black olives
- about 100ml/3½fl oz/scant ½ cup water
- salt and ground black pepper

For the chermoula
- 2 garlic cloves
- 5ml/1 tsp coarse salt
- 10ml/2 tsp ground cumin
- 5ml/1 tsp paprika
- juice of 1 lemon
- small bunch of fresh coriander (cilantro), roughly chopped
- 15ml/1 tbsp olive oil

1 Use a mortar and pestle to make the chermoula: pound the garlic with the salt to a smooth paste. Add the cumin, paprika, lemon juice and chopped coriander, and gradually mix in the oil to emulsify the mixture slightly.

2 Reserve a little chermoula for cooking, then rub the rest of the paste over the monkfish. Cover and leave to marinate in a cool place for 1 hour.

3 Par-boil the potatoes for about 10 minutes. Drain, then cut them in half lengthways. Heat the olive oil in a heavy pan and stir in the garlic. When the garlic begins to colour, add the tomatoes and cook until just softened.

4 Add the peppers to the tomatoes and garlic, together with the remaining chermoula, and season to taste.

5 Spread the potatoes over the base of a tagine, shallow pan or deep, ridged frying pan. Spoon three-quarters of the tomato and pepper mixture over and place the marinated fish chunks on top, with their marinade.

6 Spoon the rest of the tomato and pepper mixture on top of the fish and add the olives. Drizzle a little extra olive oil over the dish and pour in the water.

7 Heat until simmering, cover the tagine or pan with a lid and cook over a medium heat for about 15 minutes, until the fish is cooked through. Serve with fresh, warm crusty bread to mop up the delicious juices.

Energy 406Kcal/1710kJ; Protein 39.6g; Carbohydrate 25.2g, of which sugars 6.5g; Fat 17.1g, of which saturates 2.7g; Cholesterol 32mg; Calcium 98mg; Fibre 5.4g; Sodium 915mg.

SYRIAN BAKED FISH WITH TAHINI

TAHINI IS A SESAME SEED PASTE THAT IS POPULAR THROUGHOUT THE ARAB COUNTRIES IN BOTH SWEET AND SAVOURY DISHES. MOST PEOPLE KNOW IT AS AN INGREDIENT IN AUTHENTIC HUMMUS, BUT IT IS ALSO VERY GOOD WITH FISH. THIS RECIPE COMES FROM TARTOUS, A FISHING TOWN ON SYRIA'S MEDITERRANEAN COASTLINE.

SERVES SIX

INGREDIENTS

- 6 cod or haddock fillets
- juice of 2 lemons
- 60ml/4 tbsp olive oil
- 2 large onions, chopped
- 250ml/8fl oz/1 cup tahini paste
- 1 garlic clove, crushed
- 45–60ml/3–4 tbsp water
- salt and ground black pepper
- boiled rice and a green salad, to serve

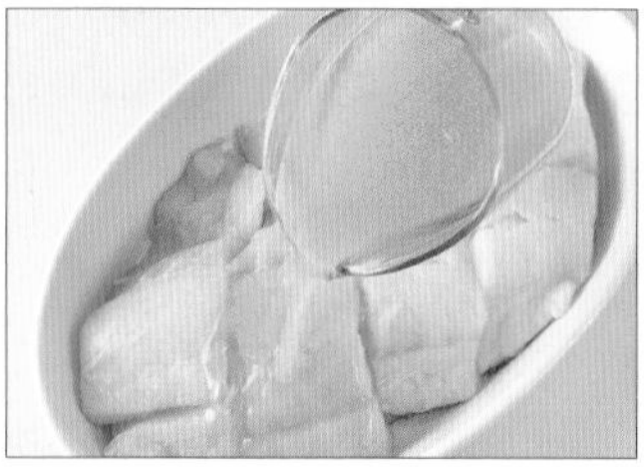

1 Preheat the oven to 180°C/350°F/ Gas 4. Arrange the fish fillets in a shallow ovenproof dish, pour over 15ml/1 tbsp each of the lemon juice and olive oil and bake for 20 minutes.

2 Meanwhile heat the remaining oil in a large frying pan and fry the onions for 6–8 minutes, until well browned and almost crisp.

3 Put the tahini paste, garlic and seasoning in a small bowl and slowly beat in the remaining lemon juice and water, a little at a time, until the sauce is light and creamy.

4 Sprinkle the onions over the fish, pour over the tahini sauce and bake for a further 15 minutes, until the fish is cooked through and the sauce is bubbling. Serve the fish at once with boiled rice and a salad.

Energy 434Kcal/1800kJ; Protein 33.8g; Carbohydrate 0.7g, of which sugars 0.2g; Fat 32.9g, of which saturates 4.7g; Cholesterol 65mg; Calcium 296mg; Fibre 3.4g; Sodium 93mg.

EGYPTIAN BAKED FISH WITH NUTS

The Arabic word for red mullet is Sultan Ibrahim. It is a very popular fish in the Middle East and is often served whole in the fish restaurants of Alexandria and Abu Qir on Egypt's north coast. The sauce for this dish is made with chopped hazelnuts and pine nuts, which not only add flavour, but also thicken the tomato and herb mixture.

SERVES FOUR

INGREDIENTS

- 45ml/3 tbsp sunflower oil
- 4 small red mullet or snapper, gutted and cleaned
- 1 large onion, finely chopped
- 75g/3oz/½ cup hazelnuts, chopped
- 75g/3oz/½ cup pine nuts
- 3–4 tomatoes, sliced
- 45–60ml/3–4 tbsp finely chopped fresh parsley
- 250ml/8fl oz/1 cup fish stock
- salt and ground black pepper
- fresh parsley sprigs, to garnish
- cooked new potatoes or rice, and vegetables or salad, to serve

1 Preheat the oven to 190°C/375°F/ Gas 5. Heat 30ml/2 tbsp of the oil in a frying pan and fry the fish, two at a time, until crisp on both sides.

2 Meanwhile, heat the remaining oil in a large pan or flameproof casserole and fry the onion for 3–4 minutes, until golden. Add the chopped hazelnuts and pine nuts and stir-fry for a few minutes.

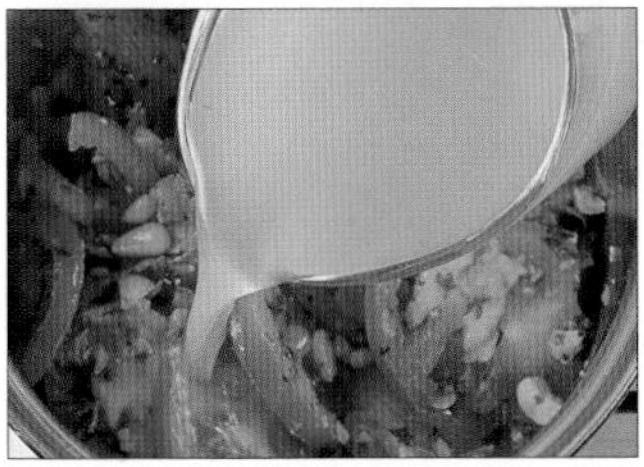

3 Stir in the tomatoes, cook for a few minutes and then add the chopped parsley, seasoning and stock and simmer for 10–15 minutes, stirring occasionally.

4 Place the fish in an ovenproof dish and spoon the sauce over. Bake in the oven for 20 minutes, until the fish is cooked through and flakes easily when tested with a knite.

5 Serve the fish immediately, accompanied by cooked new potatoes or rice, and vegetables or salad.

VARIATION

Other small whole fish, such as snapper or trout, can be used for this recipe if mullet is unavailable.

Energy 470Kcal/1952kJ; Protein 25.8g; Carbohydrate 10.4g, of which sugars 8.3g; Fat 36.4g, of which saturates 2.9g; Cholesterol 0mg; Calcium 166mg; Fibre 4.9g; Sodium 108mg.

Lebanese Fish with Rice

This is a fine example of Saadiyeh, which means a plain fish dish with rice. It is important to use a good quality fish stock, preferably one which you have made yourself from scraps purchased from the fishmonger at the same time as you bought the cod.

SERVES FOUR TO SIX

INGREDIENTS

- juice of 1 lemon
- 45ml/3 tbsp olive oil
- 900g/2lb cod steaks
- 4 large onions, chopped
- 5ml/1 tsp ground cumin
- 2–3 saffron threads
- 1 litre/1¾ pints/4 cups fish stock
- 450g/1lb/2¼ cups basmati or other long grain rice
- 50g/2oz/⅓ cup pine nuts, lightly toasted
- salt and ground black pepper
- fresh flat leaf parsley sprigs, to garnish

1 Whisk together the lemon juice and 15ml/1 tbsp of the oil in a shallow, non-metallic dish. Add the fish, turn to coat well, then cover and leave to marinate for 30 minutes.

2 Heat the remaining oil in a large pan or flameproof casserole and fry the onions for 5–6 minutes, until golden, stirring occasionally.

3 Drain the fish, reserving the marinade, and add to the pan. Fry for 1–2 minutes each side until golden, then add the cumin and saffron.

4 Pour in the fish stock, the reserved marinade and a little salt and pepper. Bring to the boil and then simmer very gently over a low heat for 5–10 minutes, until the fish is nearly done.

5 Transfer the fish to a plate and keep warm, then add the rice to the stock. Bring to the boil and then reduce the heat and simmer very gently for 15 minutes, until nearly all the stock has been absorbed.

6 Arrange the fish over the rice and cover the pan. Cook over a low heat for a further 15–20 minutes.

7 Transfer the fish to a plate, then spoon the rice on to a large, warmed, flat dish and arrange the fish steaks on top. Sprinkle the fish with toasted pine nuts and garnish with parsley sprigs. Serve immediately.

COOK'S TIP

Take care when cooking the rice that the pan does not boil dry. Check it occasionally and add more stock or water if it becomes necessary.

Energy 834Kcal/3483kJ; Protein 54.3g; Carbohydrate 110g, of which sugars 14.5g; Fat 19.5g, of which saturates 2g; Cholesterol 104mg; Calcium 106mg; Fibre 3.7g; Sodium 143mg.

TURKISH COLD FISH

WHOLE FISH, COOKED IN A FLAVOURSOME SAUCE AND SERVED COLD, OFTEN FORM THE CENTREPIECE OF A MIDDLE EASTERN MEAL. THIS VERSION FROM TURKEY CAN ALSO BE MADE USING MACKEREL.

SERVES FOUR

INGREDIENTS

- 60ml/4 tbsp olive oil
- 900g/2lb red mullet or snapper
- 2 onions, sliced
- 1 green (bell) pepper, seeded and sliced
- 1 red (bell) pepper, seeded and sliced
- 3 garlic cloves, crushed
- 15ml/1 tbsp tomato purée (paste)
- 50ml/2fl oz/¼ cup fish stock or water
- 5–6 tomatoes, skinned and sliced or 400g/14oz can chopped tomatoes
- 30ml/2 tbsp chopped fresh parsley
- 30ml/2 tbsp lemon juice
- 5ml/1 tsp paprika
- 15–20 green and black olives
- salt and ground black pepper
- fresh bread and salad, to serve

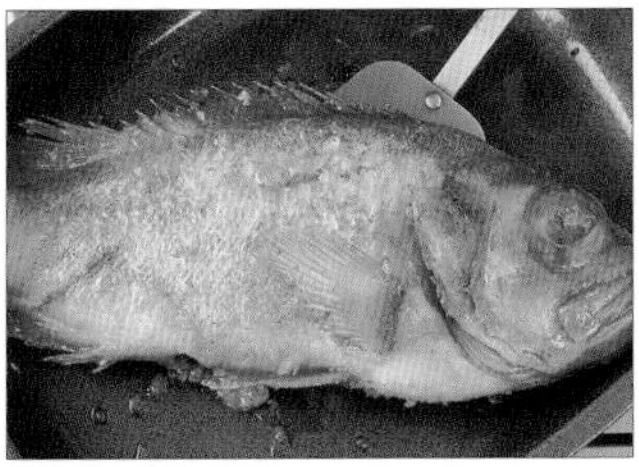

1 Heat 30ml/2 tbsp of the oil in a large, flameproof roasting pan or frying pan and fry the fish on both sides, until golden brown. Remove from the pan, cover and keep warm.

2 Heat the remaining oil in the roasting pan or frying pan and fry the onions for 2–3 minutes, until slightly softened. Add the sliced peppers and continue cooking for 3–4 minutes, then add the garlic and stir-fry for a further minute.

3 Blend the tomato purée with the fish stock or water and stir into the pan with the tomatoes, chopped parsley, lemon juice, paprika and seasoning. Simmer gently without boiling for 15 minutes, stirring occasionally.

4 Return the fish to the roasting pan or frying pan and cover with the sauce. Cook for 10 minutes, then add the olives and cook for a further 5 minutes, until just cooked through.

5 Transfer the fish to a serving dish and pour the sauce over the top. Allow to cool, then cover and chill until completely cold. Serve cold with bread and salad.

VARIATION

One large fish looks spectacular, but it is tricky to both cook and serve. If you prefer, buy four smaller fish and cook for a shorter time, until just tender and cooked through but not overdone.

Energy 352Kcal/1466kJ; Protein 25g; Carbohydrate 15.8g, of which sugars 13.7g; Fat 21.5g, of which saturates 2.5g; Cholesterol 0mg; Calcium 158mg; Fibre 5.3g; Sodium 1124mg.

Red Mullet with Chermoula

The coriander and chilli chermoula marinade gives this dish its distinct flavour. The olives and preserved lemon add a touch of excitement. On their own, these mullet make a delicious appetizer. Served with saffron couscous and a crisp, herb-filled salad, they are delicious as a main course. Choose larger fish if you wish.

SERVES FOUR

INGREDIENTS

- 30–45ml/2–3 tbsp olive oil, plus extra for brushing
- 1 onion, chopped
- 1 carrot, chopped
- ½ preserved lemon, finely chopped
- 4 plum tomatoes, skinned and chopped
- 600ml/1 pint/2½ cups fish stock or water
- 3–4 new potatoes, peeled and diced
- 4 small red mullet or snapper, gutted and filleted
- handful of black olives, pitted and halved
- small bunch of fresh coriander (cilantro), chopped
- small bunch of fresh mint, chopped
- salt and ground black pepper

For the chermoula

- small bunch of fresh coriander (cilantro), finely chopped
- 2–3 garlic cloves, chopped
- 5–10ml/1–2 tsp ground cumin
- pinch of saffron threads
- 60ml/4 tbsp olive oil
- juice of 1 lemon
- 1 hot red chilli, seeded and chopped
- 5ml/1 tsp salt

1 To make the chermoula, pound the ingredients in a mortar with a pestle, or process them together in a food processor, then set aside.

2 Heat the olive oil in a pan. Add the onion and carrot and cook until softened but not browned. Stir in half the preserved lemon, along with 30ml/2 tbsp of the chermoula, the tomatoes and the stock or water.

3 Bring to the boil, then reduce the heat, cover and simmer gently for about 30 minutes. Add the potatoes and simmer for a further 10 minutes, until they are tender.

4 Preheat the grill (broiler) on the hottest setting and brush a baking sheet or grill pan with oil. Brush the fish fillets with olive oil and a little chermoula. Season with salt and pepper, then place skin side up, on the sheet or pan and cook under the grill for 5–6 minutes.

5 Meanwhile, stir the olives, the remaining chermoula and preserved lemon into the sauce and check the seasoning. Serve the fish fillets in wide bowls, spoon the sauce over and sprinkle liberally with chopped coriander and mint.

Energy 374Kcal/1558kJ; Protein 24.7g; Carbohydrate 13.8g, of which sugars 7.2g; Fat 24.9g, of which saturates 2.9g; Cholesterol 0mg; Calcium 193mg; Fibre 4.7g; Sodium 704mg.

Fish in Vine Leaves with Dipping Sauce

Almost any type of firm white fish can be used to make these kebabs. The fish is first marinated in chermoula and then wrapped in vine leaves to seal in the flavours. When cooked, the vine leaf wrapper becomes crisp, contrasting beautifully with its succulent and aromatic contents. The sweet and sour sauce is perfect for dipping.

SERVES FOUR

INGREDIENTS
- about 30 preserved vine leaves
- 4–5 large white fish fillets, skinned, such as haddock, ling or monkfish

For the chermoula
- small bunch of fresh coriander (cilantro), finely chopped
- 2–3 garlic cloves, chopped
- 5–10ml/1–2 tsp ground cumin
- 60ml/4 tbsp olive oil
- juice of 1 lemon
- salt

For the dipping sauce
- 50ml/2fl oz/¼ cup white wine vinegar or lemon juice
- 115g/4oz/generous ½ cup caster (superfine) sugar
- 15–30ml/1–2 tbsp water
- pinch of saffron threads
- 1 onion, finely chopped
- 2 garlic cloves, finely chopped
- 2–3 spring onions (scallions), thinly sliced
- 25g/1oz fresh root ginger, peeled and grated
- 2 hot fresh red or green chillies, seeded and thinly sliced
- small bunch of fresh coriander (cilantro), finely chopped
- small bunch of mint, finely chopped

1 To make the chermoula, pound the ingredients in a mortar with a pestle, or process in a food processor.

2 Rinse the vine leaves in a bowl, then soak them in cold water. Remove any bones from the fish and cut each fillet into about eight bitesize pieces. Coat the pieces of fish in the chermoula, cover and chill for 1 hour.

3 Meanwhile, prepare the dipping sauce. Heat the vinegar or lemon juice with the sugar and water until the sugar has dissolved. Bring to the boil and boil for about 1 minute, then leave to cool. Add the remaining ingredients and mix well to combine. Spoon the sauce into small individual bowls and set aside until ready to serve.

4 Drain the vine leaves and pat dry on kitchen paper. Lay a vine leaf flat on the work surface and place a piece of marinated fish in the centre. Fold the edges of the leaf over the fish, then wrap up the fish and leaf into a small parcel. Repeat with the remaining pieces of fish and vine leaves. Thread the parcels on to kebab skewers and brush with any leftover marinade.

5 Heat the grill (broiler) on the hottest setting and cook the kebabs for 2–3 minutes on each side. Serve immediately, with the sweet and sour chilli sauce for dipping.

Energy 295Kcal/1232kJ; Protein 40.7g; Carbohydrate 3.8g, of which sugars 2.3g; Fat 13g, of which saturates 1.8g; Cholesterol 98mg; Calcium 111mg; Fibre 1.6g; Sodium 139mg.

Chicken Dishes

In the Middle East, chicken is second only to lamb in popularity, and a similar situation exists in Africa. This chapter shows the very different approaches adopted by cooks on either side of the Mediterranean divide. From Morocco come sweet and fruity tagines and a roast with a spicy rub. Senegal contributes a tangy lemon chicken dish, while Sierra Leone's Palaver Chicken is well worth making a fuss about. Crossing to Iran, we discover khoresh, a soup-like stew served over rice, together with a delicious chicken and yogurt dish.

CHICKEN KDRA WITH CHICKPEAS AND ALMONDS

A KDRA IS A TYPE OF TAGINE THAT IS TRADITIONALLY COOKED WITH SMEN, A STRONGLY FLAVOURED CLARIFIED BUTTER, AND PLENTY OF ONIONS. THE ALMONDS IN THIS RECIPE ARE PRE-COOKED UNTIL SOFT, ADDING AN INTERESTING TEXTURE AND FLAVOUR TO THE LIGHTLY SPICED CHICKEN.

SERVES FOUR

INGREDIENTS

- 75g/3oz/½ cup blanched almonds
- 75g/3oz/½ cup chickpeas, soaked overnight and drained
- 4 part-boned chicken breast portions, skinned
- 50g/2oz/¼ cup butter
- 2.5ml/½ tsp saffron threads
- 2 Spanish onions, thinly sliced
- 900ml/1½ pints/3¾ cups chicken stock
- 1 small cinnamon stick
- 60ml/4 tbsp chopped fresh flat leaf parsley, plus extra to garnish
- lemon juice, to taste
- salt and ground black pepper

1 Place the almonds in a pan of water and simmer for 1½–2 hours until fairly soft, then drain and set aside.

2 Cook the chickpeas in a pan of boiling water for 1–1½ hours until they are completely soft. Drain the chickpeas, then place in a bowl of cold water and rub with your fingers to remove the skins. Discard the skins and drain.

3 Place the chicken portions in a pan, together with the butter, half of the saffron, salt and plenty of black pepper. Heat gently, stirring, until the butter has melted.

4 Add the onions and stock, bring to the boil and then add the chickpeas and cinnamon stick. Cover and cook very gently for 45–60 minutes.

5 Transfer the chicken to a serving plate and keep warm. Bring the sauce to the boil and simmer until reduced, stirring frequently. Add the almonds, parsley and remaining saffron and cook for 2–3 minutes. Sharpen the sauce with a little lemon juice, then pour over the chicken and serve, garnished with extra parsley.

CHICKEN WITH TOMATOES AND HONEY

COOKING THE TOMATOES VERY SLOWLY WITH THE AROMATIC SPICES GIVES THE SAUCE FOR THIS CHICKEN DISH A WONDERFULLY INTENSE FLAVOUR, WHICH MELLOWS WHEN THE HONEY IS STIRRED IN.

SERVES FOUR

INGREDIENTS

- 30ml/2 tbsp sunflower oil
- 25g/1oz/2 tbsp butter
- 4 chicken quarters or 1 whole chicken, quartered
- 1 onion, grated or very finely chopped
- 1 garlic clove, crushed
- 5ml/1 tsp ground cinnamon
- good pinch of ground ginger
- 1.3–1.6kg/3–3½lb tomatoes, skinned, cored and roughly chopped
- 30ml/2 tbsp clear honey
- 50g/2oz/⅓ cup blanched almonds
- 15ml/1 tbsp sesame seeds
- salt and ground black pepper
- Moroccan corn bread, to serve

1 Heat the oil and butter in a large, flameproof casserole. Add the chicken quarters and cook over a medium heat for about 3 minutes, until browned.

2 Add the onion, garlic, cinnamon, ginger, tomatoes and seasoning, and heat gently until the tomatoes begin to bubble.

3 Lower the heat, cover and simmer very gently for 1 hour, stirring and turning the chicken occasionally, until it is completely cooked through.

4 Transfer the chicken pieces to a plate and then increase the heat and cook the tomatoes until the sauce is reduced to a thick purée, stirring frequently. Stir in the honey, cook for 1 minute and then return the chicken to the pan and cook for 2–3 minutes to heat through. Dry-fry the almonds and sesame seeds or toast under the grill (broiler).

5 Transfer the chicken and sauce to a warmed serving dish and sprinkle with the almonds and sesame seeds. Serve with Moroccan corn bread.

TOP Energy 477Kcal/1994kJ; Protein 46g; Carbohydrate 21g, of which sugars 8.7g; Fat 23.9g, of which saturates 7.9g; Cholesterol 132mg; Calcium 146mg; Fibre 5.9g; Sodium 185mg.

BOTTOM Energy 610Kcal/2539kJ; Protein 37.7g; Carbohydrate 16.8g, of which sugars 16.4g; Fat 44g, of which saturates 11.4g; Cholesterol 206mg; Calcium 92mg; Fibre 4.5g; Sodium 211mg.

EAST AFRICAN ROAST CHICKEN

Rubbing the skin on the chicken with a spicy herb butter and then marinating it overnight gives it a wonderful flavour. Baste it frequently while it cooks.

SERVES SIX

INGREDIENTS
- 1.8–2kg/4–4½lb chicken
- 30ml/2 tbsp softened butter, plus extra for basting
- 3 garlic cloves, crushed
- 5ml/1 tsp ground black pepper
- 5ml/1 tsp ground turmeric
- 2.5ml/½ tsp ground cumin
- 5ml/1 tsp dried thyme
- 15ml/1 tbsp finely chopped fresh coriander (cilantro)
- 60ml/4 tbsp thick coconut milk
- 60ml/4 tbsp medium-dry sherry
- 5ml/1 tsp tomato purée (paste)
- salt and chilli powder

1 Remove and discard the giblets from the chicken, if necessary, rinse out the cavity and pat the skin dry. Put the butter and all the remaining ingredients in a bowl and mix together well to form a thick paste.

2 Ease the skin of the chicken away from the flesh and push in some of the herb and butter mixture. Rub more of the mixture over the skin, legs and wings of the chicken.

3 Place the chicken in a roasting pan, cover loosely with foil and marinate overnight in the fridge.

VARIATION
Use ground coriander instead of ground cumin or dried thyme.

4 Preheat the oven to 190°C/375°F/Gas 5. Cover the chicken with clean foil and roast for 1 hour, then turn the chicken over and baste with the pan juices. Cover again with foil and roast for a further 30 minutes.

5 Remove the foil and place the chicken breast side up. Rub with a little extra butter and roast for a further 10–15 minutes, until the meat juices run clear and the skin is golden brown. Serve with a rice dish or a salad.

YASSA CHICKEN

Often described as the national dish of Senegal, Yassa can be made with chicken, turkey or fish. The lemon juice marinade gives the sauce its typically tangy taste.

SERVES FOUR

INGREDIENTS
- 150ml/¼ pint/⅔ cup lemon juice
- 60ml/4 tbsp malt vinegar
- 3 onions, sliced
- 60ml/4 tbsp groundnut (peanut) or vegetable oil
- 1kg/2¼lb chicken pieces
- 1 fresh thyme sprig
- 1 fresh green chilli, seeded and finely chopped
- 2 bay leaves
- 450ml/¾ pint/scant 2 cups chicken stock

VARIATION
For a less tangy flavour, you can add less lemon juice, although it does mellow after cooking.

1 Mix the lemon juice, vinegar, onions and 30ml/2 tbsp of the oil together, place the chicken pieces in a dish and pour over the lemon mixture. Cover and leave in a cool place for 3 hours.

2 Heat the remaining oil in a large pan and fry the chicken pieces for 4–5 minutes, until browned.

3 Add the marinated onions to the chicken. Fry for 3 minutes, then add the marinade, thyme, chilli, bay leaves and half the stock.

4 Reduce the heat, cover the pan and simmer for about 35 minutes, until the chicken is cooked, add more stock as the sauce evaporates. Serve hot.

TOP Energy 439Kcal/1824kJ; Protein 43.3g; Carbohydrate 1.2g, of which sugars 1.2g; Fat 27.9g, of which saturates 10.7g; Cholesterol 206mg; Calcium 23mg; Fibre 0g; Sodium 211mg.
BOTTOM Energy 462Kcal/1918kJ; Protein 37.4g; Carbohydrate 8.9g, of which sugars 6.3g; Fat 31g, of which saturates 8g; Cholesterol 163mg; Calcium 43mg; Fibre 1.6g; Sodium 141mg.

Palaver Chicken

It is said that this stew gained its intriguing name because of the arguments that surrounded the right way to cook it. Controversy still rages, with variations existing in Ghana, Liberia and Sierra Leone. Palaver can be made with beef, chicken or fish and always includes a green vegetable such as bitterleaf. Spinach is substituted here.

SERVES FOUR

INGREDIENTS

- 675g/1½lb skinless, boneless chicken breast fillets
- 2 garlic cloves, crushed
- 30ml/2 tbsp butter or margarine
- 30ml/2 tbsp palm or vegetable oil
- 1 onion, finely chopped
- 4 tomatoes, skinned and chopped
- 30ml/2 tbsp peanut butter
- 600ml/1 pint/2½ cups chicken stock or water
- 1 fresh thyme sprig or 5ml/1 tsp dried thyme
- 225g/8oz frozen leaf spinach, defrosted and chopped
- 1 fresh red or green chilli, seeded and chopped
- salt and ground black pepper

1 Cut the chicken breast fillets into thin slices, place in a bowl and stir in the garlic and a little salt and pepper.

2 Melt the butter or margarine in a large frying pan and fry the chicken over a medium heat, turning once or twice to brown evenly. Transfer to a plate using a slotted spoon and set aside.

3 Heat the oil in a large pan and fry the onion and tomatoes over a high heat for 5 minutes, until soft.

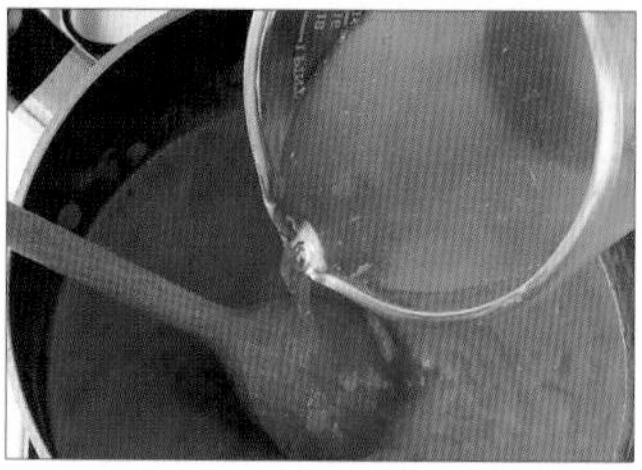

4 Reduce the heat, add the peanut butter and half of the stock or water and blend together well.

5 Cook for 4–5 minutes, stirring all the time to prevent the peanut butter burning, then add the remaining stock or water, thyme, spinach, chilli and seasoning. Stir in the chicken slices and cook over a medium heat for about 10–15 minutes, until the chicken is cooked through.

6 Pour the chicken mixture into a warmed serving dish and serve with boiled yams, rice or ground rice.

COOK'S TIPS

If you're short of time, frozen spinach is more convenient, but chopped fresh spinach, adds a fresher flavour to this recipe. Egusi – ground melon seed – can be used instead of peanut butter.

Energy 387Kcal/1615kJ; Protein 41.1g; Carbohydrate 7.2g, of which sugars 5.8g; Fat 21.7g, of which saturates 7.3g; Cholesterol 89mg; Calcium 131mg; Fibre 2.9g; Sodium 280mg.

KHORESH FESENJAN

A khoresh is a thick stew-like sauce which is served over rice in Iran. This famous version owes its superb flavour to pomegranates and walnuts. Khoresh Fesenjan is often served on festive occasions, when wild duck is used instead of chicken.

SERVES FOUR

INGREDIENTS
- 30ml/2 tbsp vegetable oil
- 4 chicken portions (leg or breast)
- 1 large onion, grated
- 250ml/8fl oz/1 cup water
- 115g/4oz/1 cup finely chopped walnuts
- 75ml/5 tbsp pomegranate purée
- 15ml/1 tbsp tomato purée (paste)
- 30ml/2 tbsp lemon juice
- 15ml/1 tbsp granulated sugar
- 3–4 saffron threads dissolved in 15ml/1 tbsp boiling water
- salt and ground black pepper
- Persian rice and salad leaves, to serve

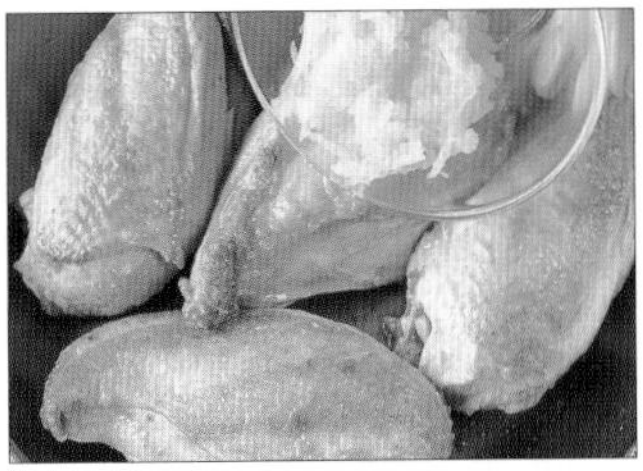

1 Heat 15ml/1 tbsp of the oil in a large pan or flameproof casserole and sauté the chicken portions until golden brown.

2 Add half of the grated onion to the chicken and fry until slightly softened, then add the water and seasoning and bring to the boil. Cover the pan, reduce the heat and simmer for 15 minutes.

3 Meanwhile, heat the remaining oil in a small pan or frying pan and fry the remaining onion for 2–3 minutes, until soft.

4 Add the chopped walnuts to the onion and fry for a further 2–3 minutes over a low heat, stirring frequently and taking great care that the walnuts do not burn.

5 Stir in the pomegranate and tomato purées, lemon juice, sugar and the saffron liquid. Season to taste and then simmer over a low heat for 5 minutes.

6 Pour the walnut sauce over the chicken, ensuring all the pieces are well covered. Cover and simmer for 30–35 minutes, until the meat is cooked and the oil of the walnuts has risen to the surface.

7 Serve immediately with Persian rice and salad leaves.

COOK'S TIP
Pomegranate purée is available from Middle Eastern delicatessens.

Energy 460Kcal/1918kJ; Protein 42.1g; Carbohydrate 12.8g, of which sugars 11.2g; Fat 27g, of which saturates 2.7g; Cholesterol 105mg; Calcium 60mg; Fibre 2.5g; Sodium 148mg.

CHICKEN AND PRESERVED LEMON TAGINE

Moroccan tagines are subtly flavoured stews which are cooked in the conical-lidded dishes from which they get their name. This is the most famous tagine recipe, in which the preserved lemon's mellow flavour contrasts with the earthiness of the olives.

SERVES FOUR

INGREDIENTS

- 30ml/2 tbsp olive oil
- 1 Spanish onion, chopped
- 3 garlic cloves
- 1cm/½in fresh root ginger, peeled and grated, or 2.5ml/½ tsp ground ginger
- 2.5–5ml/½–1 tsp ground cinnamon
- pinch of saffron threads
- 4 chicken quarters, preferably breasts, halved if liked
- 750ml/1¼ pints/3 cups chicken stock
- 30ml/2 tbsp chopped fresh coriander (cilantro)
- 30ml/2 tbsp chopped fresh parsley
- 1 preserved lemon
- 115g/4oz/⅔ cup Moroccan tan olives
- salt and ground black pepper
- lemon wedges and fresh coriander (cilantro) sprigs, to garnish

1 Heat the oil in a large flameproof casserole and fry the onion for 6–8 minutes over a moderate heat until lightly golden, stirring occasionally.

2 Meanwhile, crush the garlic and blend with the ginger, cinnamon, saffron and a little salt and pepper. Stir into the pan and fry for 1 minute.

3 Add the chicken quarters to the pan, in batches if necessary, and fry over a medium heat for 2–3 minutes, until lightly browned.

4 Add the stock, chopped coriander and parsley, bring to the boil and then cover and simmer very gently for 45 minutes, until the chicken is tender.

5 Rinse the preserved lemon, discard the flesh and cut the peel into small pieces. Stir into the pan with the olives and simmer for a further 15 minutes, until the chicken is very tender.

6 Transfer the chicken to a plate and keep warm. Bring the sauce to the boil and bubble for 3–4 minutes, until reduced and fairly thick.

7 Pour the sauce over the chicken and serve, garnished with lemon wedges and coriander sprigs.

Energy 474Kcal/1967kJ; Protein 36.3g; Carbohydrate 5.3g, of which sugars 3.8g; Fat 34.3g, of which saturates 8.1g; Cholesterol 209mg; Calcium 83mg; Fibre 2.6g; Sodium 807mg.

MARRAKESH ROAST CHICKEN

Moroccans invented the spice rub long before it became a trendy deli item. For this traditional dish, a paste made from shallots, garlic, fresh herbs and spices is rubbed into the chicken skin a few hours before roasting, so the flavour permeates the flesh.

SERVES FOUR TO SIX

INGREDIENTS
- 1.8–2kg/4–4½lb chicken
- 2 small shallots
- 1 garlic clove
- 1 fresh parsley sprig
- 1 fresh coriander (cilantro) sprig
- 5ml/1 tsp salt
- 7.5ml/1½ tsp paprika
- pinch of cayenne pepper
- 5–7.5ml/1–1½ tsp ground cumin
- about 40g/1½oz/3 tbsp butter, at room temperature
- ½–1 lemon (optional)
- sprigs of fresh parsley or coriander (cilantro), to garnish

VARIATION
If you are unable to buy shallots, use one small onion instead.

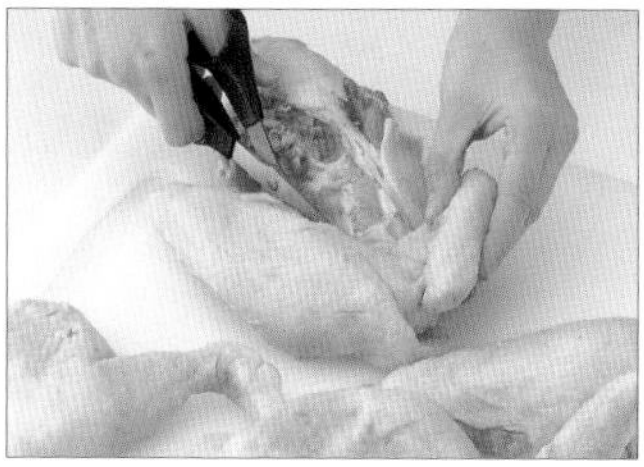

1 Remove and discard the chicken giblets, if necessary, and rinse out the cavity with cold running water. Unless cooking it whole, cut the chicken in half or into quarters using poultry shears or a sharp knife.

2 Place the shallots, garlic, herbs, salt and spices in a blender or food processor and process until the shallots are finely chopped. Add the butter and process to make a smooth paste.

3 Thoroughly rub the paste over the skin of the chicken and then allow it to stand in a cool place for 1–2 hours.

4 Preheat the oven to 200°C/400°F/ Gas 6 and place the chicken in a roasting pan. If using, quarter the lemon and place one or two quarters around the chicken pieces (or in the body cavity if the chicken is whole) and squeeze a little juice over the skin.

5 Roast the chicken in the oven for 1–1¼ hours (2–2¼ hours for a whole bird), until the chicken is cooked through and the meat juices run clear. Baste occasionally during cooking with the juices in the roasting pan. If the skin browns too quickly, cover the chicken loosely with foil or greaseproof (waxed) paper.

6 Allow the chicken to stand for 5–10 minutes, covered in foil, before serving, and then serve garnished with sprigs of fresh parsley or coriander.

Energy 559Kcal/2323kJ; Protein 54.1g; Carbohydrate 0.2g, of which sugars 0.2g; Fat 37.9g, of which saturates 15.3g; Cholesterol 265mg; Calcium 25mg; Fibre 0.1g; Sodium 759mg.

JOLOFF CHICKEN AND RICE

Few visitors to West Africa fail to try this festive chicken and rice dish. It is richly flavoured with tomatoes and can be made with chicken, beef or just with vegetables.

SERVES FOUR

INGREDIENTS

- 1kg/2¼lb chicken, cut into 4–6 pieces
- 2 garlic cloves, crushed
- 5ml/1 tsp dried thyme
- 30ml/2 tbsp palm or vegetable oil
- 400g/14oz can chopped tomatoes
- 15ml/1 tbsp tomato purée (paste)
- 1 onion, chopped
- 450ml/¾ pint/scant 2 cups chicken stock
- 30ml/2 tbsp dried shrimps, ground
- 1 fresh green chilli, seeded and finely chopped
- 350g/12oz/1¾ cups long grain rice, washed

1 Rub the chicken with the garlic and thyme and set aside.

2 Heat the oil in a pan and brown the chicken pieces. Add the tomatoes, tomato purée and onion. Cook over a medium-high heat for about 5 minutes, stirring occasionally at first then more frequently as it thickens.

3 Add the stock and stir well. Bring to the boil, then reduce the heat, cover and simmer for 40 minutes. Add the shrimps and chilli. Cook for 5 minutes.

4 Put the rice in a pan. Scoop 300ml/½ pint/1¼ cups of tomato stock from the chicken into a measuring jug (cup), top up with water to 450ml/¾ pint/scant 2 cups and add to the rice. Cook for 10 minutes to partly absorb the liquid

5 Place a piece of foil on top of the rice, cover and cook over a low heat for 10 minutes, adding a little more water if necessary. Transfer the chicken pieces to a serving plate. Simmer the sauce until reduced by half. Pour over the chicken and serve with the rice.

Energy 719Kcal/2998kJ; Protein 44.1g; Carbohydrate 76.3g, of which sugars 5.4g; Fat 25.9g, of which saturates 7.4g; Cholesterol 163mg; Calcium 54mg; Fibre 1.3g; Sodium 187mg.

KUKU

This delicious tangy chicken stew comes from Kenya. The sauce is thickened with mashed mung beans, and flavoured with chilli and coconut milk.

SERVES FOUR TO SIX

INGREDIENTS

- 6 chicken thighs or pieces
- 2.5–4ml/½–¾ tsp ground ginger
- 50g/2oz dried mung beans
- 60ml/4 tbsp corn oil
- 2 onions, finely chopped
- 2 garlic cloves, crushed
- 5 tomatoes, skinned and chopped
- 1 fresh green chilli, seeded and finely chopped
- 30ml/2 tbsp lemon juice
- 300ml/½ pint/1¼ cups coconut milk
- 300ml/½ pint/1¼ cups water
- 15ml/1 tbsp chopped fresh coriander (cilantro)
- salt and ground black pepper

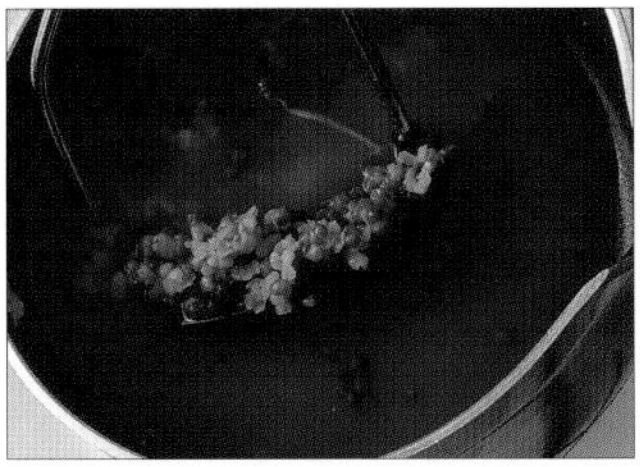

1 Season the chicken pieces with the ginger and a little salt and pepper and set aside in a cool place. Boil the mung beans in plenty of water for 35 minutes until soft. Drain and mash.

2 Heat the oil in a large pan over a medium heat and fry the chicken pieces, in batches if necessary, until evenly browned. Transfer to a plate and set aside. Reserve the juices in the pan.

3 In the same pan, fry the onions and garlic for 5 minutes, then add the chopped tomatoes and green chilli and cook for a further 1–2 minutes, stirring all the time. Add the mashed mung beans and lemon juice.

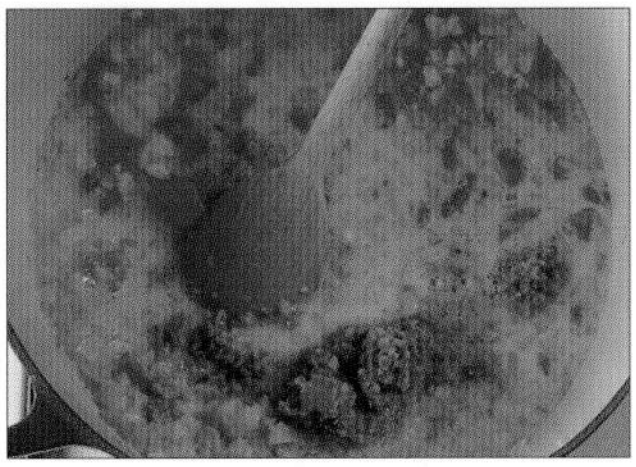

4 Pour the coconut milk in to the pan. Simmer for 5 minutes, then add the chicken pieces and a little water if the sauce is too thick. Stir in the chopped coriander and simmer for about 35 minutes, until the chicken is cooked through. Serve with a green vegetable and rice or chapatis.

Energy 257Kcal/1089kJ; Protein 41.1g; Carbohydrate 18.7g, of which sugars 11.3g; Fat 2.6g, of which saturates 0.8g; Cholesterol 105mg; Calcium 81mg; Fibre 3.7g; Sodium 188mg.

Bistilla

One of the most elaborate dishes in Moroccan cuisine, bistilla often forms the centrepiece at a feast or banquet. It is traditionally made using pigeon, cooked with spices and layered with the wafer-thin pastry known as ouarka. The pie is then cooked over hot coals. This is a simplified version, using filo pastry, which is much easier to handle than ouarka. The dusting of cinnamon and icing sugar on top of the pie is a typical North African refinement, also used on briouates.

SERVES FOUR

INGREDIENTS

- 30ml/2 tbsp sunflower oil, plus extra for brushing
- 25g/1oz/2 tbsp butter
- 3 chicken quarters, preferably breasts
- 1½ Spanish onions, grated or very finely chopped
- good pinch of ground ginger
- good pinch of saffron threads
- 10ml/2 tsp ground cinnamon, plus extra for dusting
- 40g/1½oz/4 tbsp flaked (sliced) almonds
- 1 large bunch of fresh coriander (cilantro), finely chopped
- 1 large bunch of fresh parsley, finely chopped
- 3 eggs, beaten
- about 175g/6oz filo pastry sheets
- 5–10ml/1–2 tsp icing (confectioners') sugar (optional), plus extra for dusting
- salt and ground black pepper

1 Heat the oil and butter in a large flameproof casserole or pan until the butter is melted. Add the chicken pieces and brown for about 4 minutes.

2 Add the onions, ginger, saffron, 2.5ml/½ tsp of the cinnamon and enough water (about 300ml/½ pint/1¼ cups) so that the chicken braises, rather than boils. Season well with salt and pepper.

3 Bring to the boil and then cover and simmer very gently for 45–55 minutes, until the chicken is tender and completely cooked. Meanwhile, dry-fry the almonds in a separate small pan until golden and then set aside.

4 Transfer the chicken to a plate and, when cool enough to handle, remove and discard the skin and bones and cut the flesh into pieces.

5 Stir the chopped coriander and parsley into the pan and simmer the sauce until well reduced and thick. Add the beaten eggs and cook over a very gentle heat until the eggs are lightly scrambled.

6 Preheat the oven to 180°C/350°F/Gas 4. Oil a shallow round ovenproof dish, about 25cm/10in in diameter.

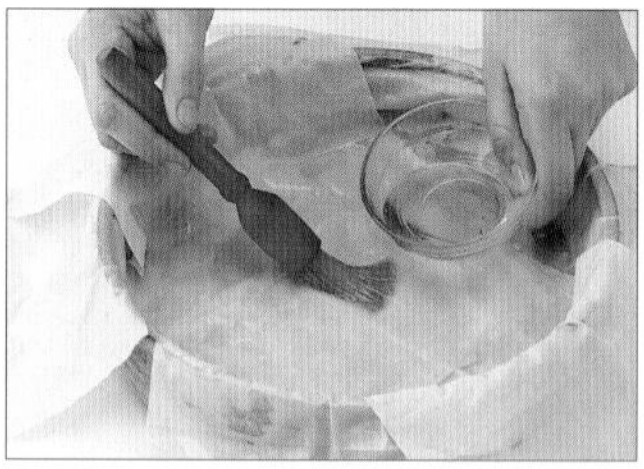

7 Place one or two sheets of filo pastry in a single layer over the bottom of the dish (it will depend on the size of your filo pastry sheets), so that it is completely covered and the edges of the pastry sheets hang over the sides. Brush lightly with oil and make two more layers of filo, brushing with oil between the layers.

8 Place the chicken on the pastry and then spoon the egg and herb mixture on top and spread evenly.

9 Place a single layer of filo pastry on top of the filling (you may need to use more than one sheet of filo pastry).

10 Scatter the almonds over the layer of filo pastry. Sprinkle with some of the remaining cinnamon and the icing sugar, if using.

11 Fold the edges of the filo over the almonds and then make four further layers of filo (using one or two sheets of filo per layer, depending on size), brushing each layer with a little oil. Tuck the filo edges under the pie (as if you were making a bed!) and brush the top layer with oil.

12 Bake in the oven for 40–45 minutes, until golden. Dust the top with icing sugar and use the extra cinnamon to make criss-cross or diagonal lines. Serve immediately.

VARIATIONS

Use standard large onions instead of Spanish onions. Use flaked hazelnuts or whole pine nuts instead of flaked almonds.

Energy 653Kcal/2720kJ; Protein 39.2g; Carbohydrate 33.6g, of which sugars 7.1g; Fat 41.3g, of which saturates 11g; Cholesterol 321mg; Calcium 176mg; Fibre 4.4g; Sodium 224mg.

KHORESH BADEMJAN

THIS CLASSIC PERSIAN DISH, BELIEVED TO HAVE BEEN A FAVOURITE OF KINGS, IS OFTEN SERVED ON FESTIVE OCCASIONS. THE WORD BADEMJAN MEANS AUBERGINES AND THIS IS A WONDERFUL VEHICLE FOR THE DELICIOUS PURPLE VEGETABLE. CUBES OF BEEF CAN BE USED INSTEAD OF CHICKEN.

SERVES FOUR

INGREDIENTS

- 30ml/2 tbsp sunflower oil
- 1 whole chicken or 4 large chicken portions
- 1 large onion, chopped
- 2 garlic cloves, crushed
- 400g/14oz can chopped tomatoes
- 250ml/8fl oz/1 cup water
- 3 aubergines (eggplants), sliced
- 3 (bell) peppers, preferably red, green and yellow, seeded and sliced
- 30ml/2 tbsp lemon juice
- 15ml/1 tbsp ground cinnamon
- salt and ground black pepper
- Persian rice, to serve

1 Heat 15ml/1 tbsp of the oil in a large pan or flameproof casserole and fry the chicken or chicken portions on both sides for about 10 minutes until the skin is a golden brown.

2 Remove the chicken from the pan, and set aside on a warm plate. Add the chopped onion and fry for 4–5 minutes, until golden brown. Return the chicken to the pan.

3 Add the garlic, chopped tomatoes, water and seasoning to the chicken and onion. Bring to the boil, then reduce the heat and simmer slowly, covered, for 10 minutes.

VARIATION
Substitute 1 large red onion or 5–6 shallots instead of standard onion.

4 Meanwhile, heat the remaining oil in a frying pan and fry the aubergines in batches until lightly golden. Transfer to a plate using a slotted spoon. Add the sliced peppers to the pan and fry for a few minutes, until slightly softened.

5 Place the aubergine slices over the chicken or chicken portions and then add the peppers. Sprinkle over the lemon juice and cinnamon, then cover and continue to cook over a low heat for about 45 minutes, until the chicken is cooked.

6 Transfer the chicken to a warmed serving plate and spoon the aubergines and peppers around the edge. Reheat the sauce, if necessary, adjust the seasoning and pour over the chicken. Serve the khoresh with Persian rice.

Energy 467Kcal/1945kJ; Protein 39.9g; Carbohydrate 18.4g, of which sugars 16.2g; Fat 26.4g, of which saturates 7.7g; Cholesterol 163mg; Calcium 63mg; Fibre 5.7g; Sodium 186mg.

TAH CHIN

IRANIANS LOVE THIS RICE DISH AND OFTEN MAKE IT WITH LAMB INSTEAD OF CHICKEN. THE NAME MEANS "ARRANGED AT THE BOTTOM OF THE POT" AND REFERS TO THE WAY THE INGREDIENTS ARE LAYERED. THE YOGURT MARINADE FLAVOURS THE CHICKEN AND MAKES IT BEAUTIFULLY TENDER.

SERVES SIX

INGREDIENTS

- 40g/1½oz/3 tbsp butter
- 1.3–1.6kg/3–3½lb chicken
- 1 large onion, chopped
- 250ml/8fl oz/1 cup chicken stock
- 2 eggs
- 475ml/16fl oz/2 cups natural (plain) yogurt
- 2–3 saffron threads, dissolved in 15ml/1 tbsp boiling water
- 5ml/1 tsp ground cinnamon
- 450g/1lb/scant 2⅓ cups basmati rice, rinsed
- 75g/3oz zereshk (see Cook's Tips)
- salt and ground black pepper
- herb salad, to serve

1 Melt 25g/1oz/2 tbsp of the butter in a large pan and fry the chicken and onion for 4–5 minutes, until the onion is softened and the chicken is browned.

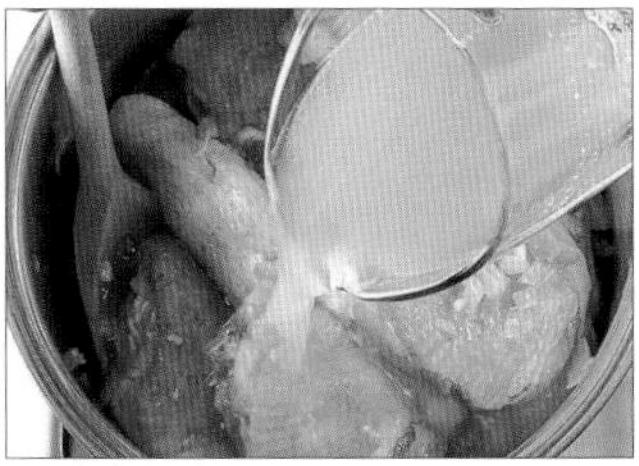

2 Add the chicken stock and salt and pepper, bring to the boil then reduce the heat and simmer for 45 minutes, until the stock is reduced by half.

3 Remove the pan from the heat. Remove the chicken to a plate, and when cool enough to handle, skin and bone the chicken. Cut the flesh into large pieces and place in a large bowl. Discard the bones and reserve the stock.

COOK'S TIPS

Zereshk is a small sour berry that grows on trees by the waterside in the warmer part of Iran.

4 Beat the eggs and blend with the yogurt. Add the saffron liquid and ground cinnamon and season with salt and pepper. Pour over the chicken and leave to marinate for up to 2 hours.

5 Drain the rice and boil it in salted water for 5 minutes. Reduce the heat and simmer for 5 minutes until almost cooked. Drain and rinse in warm water.

6 Transfer the chicken from the yogurt mixture to a dish and mix half the rice into the yogurt.

7 Preheat the oven to 160°C/325°F/Gas 3 and grease a large, 10cm/4in deep, ovenproof dish.

8 Place the rice and yogurt mixture in the bottom of the dish, arrange the chicken pieces in a layer on top and then add the plain rice. Sprinkle with the zereshk.

9 Mix the remaining butter with the reserved stock and pour over the rice. Cover tightly with foil and cook in the oven for 35–45 minutes.

10 Leave the dish to cool for a few minutes. Place on a cold, damp cloth which will help lift the rice from the bottom of the dish, then run a knife around the edges of the dish. Place a large flat plate over the dish and turn out. You should have a rice "cake" which can be cut into wedges. Serve hot with a herb salad.

Energy 682Kcal/2843kJ; Protein 43.4g; Carbohydrate 69g, of which sugars 8.2g; Fat 25.7g, of which saturates 10.2g; Cholesterol 220mg; Calcium 198mg; Fibre 0.6g; Sodium 250mg.

Lebanese Chicken Kebabs

Chicken kebabs are prepared in much the same way all over the Middle East and are a great favourite everywhere. Keep the chicken pieces quite large, so they stay moist.

SERVES SIX TO EIGHT

INGREDIENTS
- 2 small chickens
- 1 large onion, grated
- 2 garlic cloves, crushed
- 120ml/4fl oz/½ cup olive oil
- juice of 1 lemon
- 5ml/1 tsp paprika
- 2–3 saffron threads, dissolved in 15ml/1 tbsp boiling water
- salt and ground black pepper
- naan bread or pitta bread, to serve

1 Cut the chickens into small pieces, removing the bones if preferred, and place the portions in a shallow non-metallic bowl.

2 Mix the onion, garlic, olive oil, lemon juice, paprika and saffron liquid together, and season with salt and pepper.

3 Pour the marinade over the chicken, turning the chicken so that all the pieces are coated evenly.

4 Cover the bowl loosely with clear film (plastic wrap) and leave to marinate in a cool place for at least 2 hours.

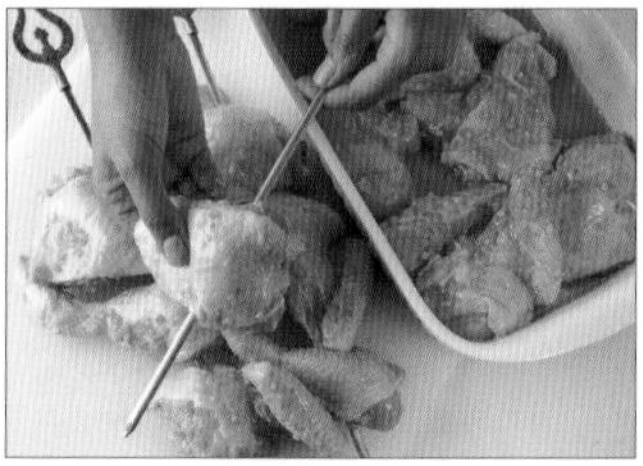

5 Thread the chicken on to long, metal skewers. If barbecuing, once the coals are ready, cook for 10–15 minutes each side. Or, if you prefer, cook under a medium-hot grill (broiler) for about 10–15 minutes each side.

6 Serve with rice and salad. Or remove boneless chicken from the skewers and serve it in pitta as a sandwich, with a garlicky yogurt sauce.

Baked Poussins with Yoghurt and Saffron

In Middle Eastern markets, chickens are often on the small side, and are often split and spatchcocked before being cooked over the coals. Poussins can be treated in the same way, and taste particularly good when marinated in yogurt, saffron and other spices.

SERVES FOUR

INGREDIENTS
- 475ml/16fl oz/2 cups natural (plain) yogurt
- 60ml/4 tbsp olive oil
- 1 large onion, grated
- 2 garlic cloves, crushed
- 2.5ml/½ tsp paprika
- 2–3 saffron threads, dissolved in 15ml/1 tbsp boiling water
- juice of 1 lemon
- 4 poussins, halved
- salt and ground black pepper
- cos or romaine lettuce salad, to serve

1 Blend together the yogurt, olive oil, onion, garlic, paprika, saffron liquid and lemon juice, and season with salt and pepper.

2 Place the poussin halves in a shallow, non-metallic dish, pour over the marinade and then cover and allow to marinate overnight in a cool place or for at least 4 hours in the fridge.

3 Preheat the oven to 180°C/350°F/Gas 4. Arrange the poussins in a greased ovenproof dish and bake in the oven for 30–45 minutes, basting frequently, until cooked. Serve with a lettuce salad.

COOK'S TIP

The poussins can also be cooked on a barbecue, for an authentic and even more delicious taste.

TOP Energy 459Kcal/1904kJ; Protein 36.3g; Carbohydrate 2g, of which sugars 1.4g; Fat 34g, of which saturates 8.8g; Cholesterol 163mg; Calcium 21mg; Fibre 0.4g; Sodium 138mg.
BOTTOM Energy 326Kcal/1358kJ; Protein 24.8g; Carbohydrate 7.6g, of which sugars 6.2g; Fat 22.2g, of which saturates 5.4g; Cholesterol 116mg; Calcium 94mg; Fibre 0.9g; Sodium 113mg.

POUSSINS WITH COURGETTES AND APRICOT STUFFING

COUSCOUS ABSORBS THE LIQUID FROM THE COURGETTES AND MAKES A SUPERB STUFFING. QUAIL AND PARTRIDGE ARE POPULAR IN THE MIDDLE EAST, AND CAN BE USED INSTEAD OF BABY POUSSINS.

SERVES FOUR

INGREDIENTS

- 4 small poussins
- about 40g/1½oz/3 tbsp butter, at room temperature
- 5–10ml/1–2 tsp ground coriander
- 1 large red (bell) pepper
- 1 fresh red chilli
- 15–30ml/1–2 tbsp olive oil
- 120ml/4fl oz/½ cup chicken stock
- 30ml/2 tbsp cornflour (cornstarch)
- salt and ground black pepper
- fresh flat leaf parsley, to garnish

For the stuffing

- 525ml/17fl oz/2¼ cups chicken or vegetable stock
- 275g/10oz/generous 1½ cups couscous
- 2 small courgettes (zucchini)
- 8 ready-to-eat dried apricots
- 15ml/1 tbsp chopped fresh flat leaf parsley
- 15ml/1 tbsp chopped fresh coriander (cilantro)
- juice of ½ lemon

1 First make the stuffing. Bring the stock to the boil and pour it over the couscous in a large bowl. Stir once and then set aside for 10 minutes.

2 Meanwhile, top and tail the courgettes and then grate coarsely. Roughly chop the apricots and add to the courgettes. Preheat the oven to 200°C/400°F/Gas 6.

3 When the couscous has swollen, fluff it up with a fork and then spoon 90ml/6 tbsp into a separate bowl and add the courgettes and chopped apricots to this. Add the chopped herbs, lemon juice and seasoning and stir to make a fairly loose stuffing. Set aside the remaining couscous for serving (see Cook's Tips).

4 Spoon the stuffing loosely into the body cavities of the poussins and secure with string or cocktail sticks. Place the birds in a medium or large flameproof roasting pan so that they fit comfortably but not too closely. Rub the butter into the skins and sprinkle with ground coriander and a little salt and pepper.

COOK'S TIPS

You can reheat the couscous in two ways: either cover the bowl with clear film (plastic wrap) and microwave on High for 2–3 minutes, stirring once or twice, or place in a colander or steamer and set over a pan of simmering water. If liked, finely chopped herbs can be added to the couscous to give colour.

5 Cut the red pepper into medium-sized strips and thinly slice the chilli, discarding the seeds and core. Place in the roasting pan around the poussins and then spoon over the olive oil.

6 Roast in the oven for 20 minutes, then reduce the oven temperature to 180°C/350°F/Gas 4. Pour the stock around the poussins and baste each one with the stock and red pepper/chilli mixture. Return the pan to the oven and roast for a further 30–35 minutes, until the poussins are cooked through and the meat juices run clear, basting occasionally with the stock.

7 When the poussins are cooked, transfer to a warmed serving plate. Blend the cornflour with 45ml/3 tbsp cold water, stir into the stock and peppers in the roasting pan and heat gently, stirring all the time, until the sauce is slightly thickened. Taste, and adjust the seasoning, and then pour into a jug or pour over the poussins. Garnish with flat leaf parsley and serve at once with the reserved couscous.

Energy 593Kcal/2477kJ; Protein 28.1g; Carbohydrate 59.4g, of which sugars 10.2g; Fat 28.5g, of which saturates 10.1g; Cholesterol 137mg; Calcium 64mg; Fibre 2.5g; Sodium 156mg.

MEAT DISHES

In the Middle East, lamb is the dominant meat. A similar situation exists in Morocco and Tunisia, but elsewhere in Africa beef is often the preferred option. Food is often cooked over an open fire, and kebabs are universally enjoyed. Stews range from the lightly spiced tagines of North Africa, which are cooked in distinctive dishes with conical lids, to the rib-sticking ragouts favoured by Nigerian cooks. One of the most unusual dishes featured here is Lebanese Kibbeh, in which two meat mixtures, one with bulgur wheat, are layered in a roasting pan.

Couscous with Lamb Cutlets and Fennel

This style of couscous dish is often served with sour pickles, such as cabbage and hot peppers. Butchers in the Middle East and Africa prepare thin lamb cutlets, sometimes described as rib chops, for grilling or frying. Ask your butcher to do the same for you.

SERVES FOUR

INGREDIENTS

- 45ml/3 tbsp olive oil
- 2 onions, quartered
- 4 garlic cloves, chopped
- 30–45ml/2–3 tbsp tomato purée (paste)
- 10ml/2 tsp harissa
- 4 fennel bulbs, stalks removed and quartered (feathery fronds reserved)
- 50g/2oz/¼ cup butter
- 8 thin lamb cutlets (US rib chops)
- salt and ground black pepper

For the couscous

- 2.5ml/½ tsp salt
- 400ml/14fl oz/1⅔ cups warm water
- 350g/12oz/2 cups medium couscous
- 30ml/2 tbsp sunflower oil
- knob (pat) of butter, diced

1 Heat the olive oil in a heavy pan, add the onions and garlic and cook for 15 minutes, until softened. Mix the tomato purée with the harissa and dilute with a little water. Pour it into the pan with 600ml/1 pint/2½ cups water. Bring to the boil and add the fennel. Reduce the heat, cover and cook for about 10 minutes, until tender.

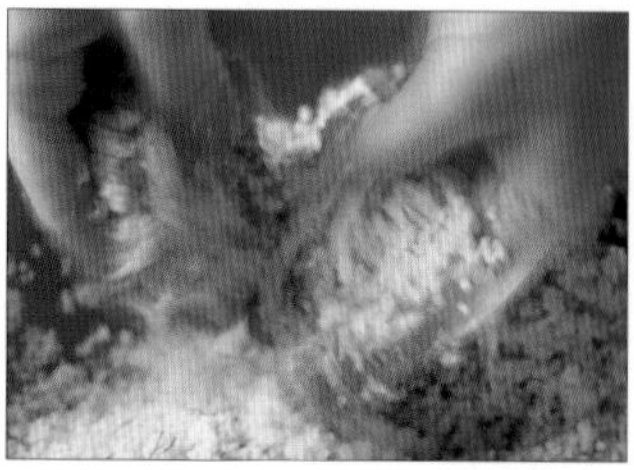

2 Meanwhile, prepare the couscous. Stir the salt into the warm water. Place the couscous in a bowl and cover with the water, stirring. Set aside for 10 minutes. Using your fingers, rub the sunflower oil into the couscous. Set aside.

3 Use a slotted spoon to lift the vegetables from the cooking liquid and transfer to a covered dish; keep warm. Boil the liquid to reduce it. Melt the butter in a heavy frying pan, add the lamb cutlets and brown on both sides. Add the cutlets to the reduced liquid and simmer for 15 minutes, until tender.

4 Preheat the oven to 180°C/350°F/Gas 4. Tip the couscous into an ovenproof dish and arrange the diced butter on top. Chop the fennel fronds and sprinkle over the couscous. Cover with foil and bake in the oven for about 20 minutes.

5 Put the vegetables in the pan with the lamb and heat through. Fluff up the couscous then mound it on to a serving dish. Place the cutlets around the edge and spoon the vegetables over. Moisten with the cooking liquid and serve.

COOK'S TIP

Crunchy pickles make a delicious accompaniment to serve with this dish and are easy to make. Simply combine whole or chopped raw vegetables with white wine vinegar mixed with a little salt and leave to soak for about 3 weeks. The most popular pickled vegetables enjoyed in Morocco are green tomatoes, hot peppers, white cabbage and garlic.

Energy 688Kcal/2862kJ; Protein 35.6g; Carbohydrate 54.5g, of which sugars 7.7g; Fat 37.7g, of which saturates 14.3g; Cholesterol 137mg; Calcium 95mg; Fibre 5.9g; Sodium 421mg.

TAGINE OF SPICED KEFTA WITH LEMON

This North African dish knows no boundaries. It can be found in the tiniest rural villages, in street stalls in the towns and cities, and in the finest restaurants of Casablanca, Fez and Marrakesh. Kefta are lamb meatballs, flavoured with onion, herbs and spices. Poached in a buttery ginger and lemon sauce, with plenty of coriander, they taste wonderful. Bread for mopping up the juices is essential.

SERVES FOUR

INGREDIENTS

- 450g/1lb finely minced (ground) lamb
- 3 large onions, grated
- small bunch of fresh flat leaf parsley, chopped
- 5–10ml/1–2 tsp ground cinnamon
- 5ml/1 tsp ground cumin
- pinch of cayenne pepper
- 40g/1½oz/3 tbsp butter
- 25g/1oz fresh root ginger, peeled and finely chopped
- 1 fresh hot chilli, seeded and finely chopped
- pinch of saffron threads
- small bunch of fresh coriander (cilantro), finely chopped
- juice of 1 lemon
- 300ml/½ pint/1¼ cups water
- 1 lemon, quartered
- salt and ground black pepper

1 To make the kefta, pound the minced lamb in a bowl by using your hand to lift it up and slap it back down into the bowl. Knead in half the grated onions, the parsley, cinnamon, cumin and cayenne pepper. Season with salt and pepper, and continue pounding the mixture by hand for a few minutes. Break off pieces of the mixture and shape them into walnut-size balls.

2 In a lidded heavy frying pan, melt the butter and add the remaining onions with the ginger, chilli and saffron. Cook until the onions just begin to colour, stirring frequently, then stir in the chopped coriander and lemon juice.

3 Pour in the water, season with salt and bring to the boil. Drop in the kefta, reduce the heat and cover the pan. Poach the kefta gently, turning them occasionally, for about 20 minutes.

4 Remove the lid, tuck the lemon quarters around the kefta, raise the heat a little and cook, uncovered, for a further 10 minutes to reduce the liquid slightly.

5 Garnish with parsley and serve the kefka hot, straight from the pan with lots of fresh crusty bread to mop up the delicious juices.

Energy 362Kcal/1503kJ; Protein 24.5g; Carbohydrate 12.9g, of which sugars 9.3g; Fat 24g, of which saturates 12.2g; Cholesterol 108mg; Calcium 134mg; Fibre 4g; Sodium 155mg.

LAMB WITH BLACK-EYED BEANS AND PUMPKIN

Black-eyed beans are popular throughout Africa, and versions of this dish are to be found from Morocco to Malawi. It is in West Africa, however, that the beans are most widely used, which explains why they crop up in the Caribbean, courtesy of slaves who planted them to provide meals with a flavour of home. The pumpkin adds a sweet note.

SERVES FOUR

INGREDIENTS

- 450g/1lb boneless lean lamb or mutton, cubed
- 1 litre/1¾ pints/4 cups chicken or lamb stock or water
- 75g/3oz/scant ½ cup black-eyed beans (peas), soaked for 6 hours, or overnight
- 1 onion, chopped
- 2 garlic cloves, crushed
- 40ml/2½ tbsp tomato purée (paste)
- 7.5ml/1½ tsp dried thyme
- 7.5ml/1½ tsp palm or vegetable oil
- 5ml/1 tsp mixed spice (apple pie spice)
- 2.5ml/½ tsp ground black pepper
- 115g/4oz pumpkin flesh, chopped
- salt and a little hot pepper sauce

1 Put the lamb or mutton in a large pan with the stock or water and bring to the boil. Skim off any foam, then reduce the heat, cover and simmer for 1 hour.

2 Stir in the drained black-eyed beans and continue to cook for about 35 minutes.

VARIATIONS

Mutton is a mature meat with a very good flavour and texture, ideal for stews and casseroles. If mutton is not available, lamb makes a good substitute. Any dried white beans can be used instead of black-eyed beans (peas). If a firmer texture is preferred, cook the pumpkin for about 5 minutes only, until just tender.

3 Add the onion, garlic, tomato purée, thyme, oil, mixed spice, black pepper and salt and hot pepper sauce and cook for a further 15 minutes, until the beans are tender.

4 Add the pumpkin and simmer for 10 minutes, until the pumpkin is very soft or almost mushy. Serve with boiled yam, plantains or sweet potatoes.

Energy 294Kcal/1231kJ; Protein 27.6g; Carbohydrate 15.2g, of which sugars 4.6g; Fat 14.1g, of which saturates 6.1g; Cholesterol 86mg; Calcium 46mg; Fibre 2.6g; Sodium 125mg.

AWAZE TIBS

AN ETHIOPIAN DISH, AWAZE TIBS IS FLAVOURED WITH BERBERE, A POWERFUL BLEND OF CHILLIES WITH LOCAL HERBS AND SPICES. THIS VERSION OFFERS ALTERNATIVE FLAVOURINGS THAT ARE MORE READILY AVAILABLE, BUT FOR A TRULY AUTHENTIC TASTE, LOOK OUT FOR THE PACKAGED SPICE MIX.

SERVES FOUR

INGREDIENTS

- 450g/1lb lamb fillet
- 45ml/3 tbsp olive oil
- 1 red onion, sliced
- 2.5ml/½ tsp peeled, grated fresh root ginger
- 2 garlic cloves, crushed
- ½ fresh green chilli, seeded and finely chopped (optional)
- 15ml/1 tbsp clarified butter or ghee
- salt and ground black pepper

For the berbere

- 2.5ml/½ tsp each chilli powder, paprika, ground ginger, ground cinnamon, ground cardamom seeds and dried basil
- 5ml/1 tsp garlic powder

1 To make the berbere, combine all the ingredients in a small bowl and tip into an airtight container. Berbere will keep for several months if stored in a cool, dry place.

2 Trim the lamb of any fat and then cut the meat into 2cm/¾in cubes.

3 Heat the oil in a large frying pan and fry the meat and onion for 5–6 minutes, until the meat is browned on all sides, stirring occasionally.

4 Add the ginger and garlic to the pan, together with 10ml/2 tsp of the berbere, then stir-fry over a brisk heat for a further 5–10 minutes.

5 Add the chilli, if using, and season well with salt and pepper. Just before serving, add the butter or ghee and stir well.

COOK'S TIPS

Clarified butter is traditionally used for this recipe. It can be made by gently heating butter, preferably unsalted (sweet) butter, up to boiling point and then scooping off and discarding the milk solids that rise to the surface. You are then left with clarified butter, which is a clear yellow liquid. Ghee is an Indian version of clarified butter which is made by simmering butter until all the moisture has evaporated and the butter caramelises. This results in a stronger, sweeter and quite nutty flavour.

Energy 336Kcal/1392kJ; Protein 22g; Carbohydrate 1.2g, of which sugars 0.9g; Fat 27g, of which saturates 10.3g; Cholesterol 92mg; Calcium 9mg; Fibre 0.2g; Sodium 92mg.

Persian Lamb with Split Peas

This dish – Khoresh Ghaimeh – is traditionally served at parties and religious festivals in Iran. The recipe is ancient, and originally used preserved meat.

SERVES FOUR

INGREDIENTS
- 25g/1oz/2 tbsp butter or margarine
- 1 large onion, chopped
- 450g/1lb lean lamb, cut into small cubes
- 5ml/1 tsp ground turmeric
- 5ml/1 tsp ground cinnamon
- 5ml/1 tsp curry powder
- 300ml/½ pint/1¼ cups water
- 2–3 saffron threads
- 90g/3½oz/½ cup yellow split peas
- 3 dried limes
- 3–4 tomatoes, chopped
- 30ml/2 tbsp olive oil
- 2 large potatoes, diced
- salt and ground black pepper
- cooked rice, to serve

1 Melt the butter or margarine in a large pan or flameproof casserole and fry the onion for 3–4 minutes, until golden, stirring occasionally. Add the meat and cook over a high heat for a further 3–4 minutes, until it has browned.

2 Add the turmeric, cinnamon and curry powder and cook for about 2 minutes, stirring frequently.

3 Stir in the water, season well and bring to the boil, then cover and simmer over a low heat for about 30–35 minutes. Stir the saffron into about 15ml/1 tbsp boiling water.

4 Add the saffron liquid to the meat with the split peas, dried limes and tomatoes. Stir well and then simmer, covered, for a further 35 minutes, until the meat is completely tender.

5 Meanwhile, heat the oil in a frying pan and sauté the potatoes for 10–15 minutes, until cooked and golden.

6 Lift out the dried lime and discard. Spoon the meat on to a warmed, large serving dish and scatter the sautéed potatoes on top. Serve the khoresh with cooked rice.

COOK'S TIPS

Dried limes (*Limu amani*) are available in all Middle Eastern shops. However, if you have difficulty obtaining them, use the juice of either 2 limes or 1 lemon instead. If you prefer, you can use beef in place of the lamb in this khoresh.

Energy 463Kcal/1941kJ; Protein 30.3g; Carbohydrate 35.1g, of which sugars 7g; Fat 23.4g, of which saturates 10g; Cholesterol 99mg; Calcium 45mg; Fibre 3.6g; Sodium 162mg.

TURKISH SAUTÉED LAMB WITH YOGURT

IN THE MIDDLE EAST MEAT IS USUALLY STEWED OR COOKED ON THE BARBECUE. THIS DELICIOUS EXCEPTION COMES FROM TURKEY. LAMB IS MARINATED IN YOGURT, PAN-FRIED, AND LAYERED WITH COOKED TOMATOES OVER TOASTED BREAD. IT MUST BE SERVED QUICKLY, WHILE THE TOAST IS CRISP.

SERVES FOUR

INGREDIENTS
- 450g/1lb lean lamb, preferably boned leg, cubed
- 40g/1½oz/3 tbsp butter
- 4 tomatoes, skinned and chopped
- 4 thick slices of white or brown bread, crusts removed
- 250ml/8fl oz/1 cup Greek (US strained plain) yogurt
- 2 garlic cloves, crushed
- salt and ground black pepper
- paprika and fresh mint leaves, to garnish

For the marinade
- 120ml/4fl oz/½ cup Greek (US strained plain) yogurt
- 1 large onion, grated

1 First make the marinade: blend together the yogurt, onion and a little seasoning in a large bowl. Add the cubed lamb, toss to coat all over, and then cover loosely with clear film (plastic wrap) and leave to marinate in a cool place for at least 1 hour.

2 Melt half the butter in a frying pan and fry the meat for 5–10 minutes, until cooked and tender, but still moist. Transfer to a plate using a slotted spoon and keep warm while cooking the tomatoes.

VARIATION
You can also use lean beef or skinless chicken breast fillets, instead of lamb, for this recipe.

3 Melt the remaining butter in the same pan and fry the tomatoes for 4–5 minutes, until soft. Meanwhile, toast the bread and arrange in the bottom of a shallow serving dish.

4 Season the tomatoes and then spread over the toasted bread in an even layer.

5 Blend the yogurt and garlic together and season with salt and pepper. Spoon evenly over the tomatoes.

6 Arrange the pan-fried lamb in a layer on top. Sprinkle with paprika and mint leaves and serve at once.

Energy 463Kcal/1939kJ; Protein 30.3g; Carbohydrate 25.2g, of which sugars 4.8g; Fat 28.3g, of which saturates 14.4g; Cholesterol 107mg; Calcium 158mg; Fibre 1.4g; Sodium 436mg.

KEBAB BAHRG

These kebabs are so popular in their native Iran that many restaurants serve nothing else. The meat is not cubed, as in Africa, but instead is cut into strips before being marinated and threaded onto skewers. Tomatoes are grilled on separate skewers.

SERVES FOUR

INGREDIENTS
- 450g/1lb lean lamb or beef fillet
- 2–3 saffron threads
- 1 large onion, grated
- 4–6 tomatoes, halved
- 15ml/1 tbsp butter, melted
- salt and ground black pepper
- 45ml/3 tbsp sumac (see Cook's Tip), to garnish (optional)
- cooked rice, to serve

1 Using a sharp knife remove and discard any excess fat from the meat and cut the meat into strips, 1cm/½in thick and 4cm/1½in long.

COOK'S TIP
Sumac are red berries that are dried and crushed to a powder.

2 Soak the saffron in 15ml/1 tbsp boiling water, pour into a small bowl and mix with the grated onion. Add to the meat and stir a few times so that the meat is thoroughly coated. Cover loosely with clear film (plastic wrap) and leave to marinate in the fridge overnight.

3 Season the meat with salt and pepper and then thread it on to flat skewers, aligning the strips in neat rows. Thread the tomatoes on to two separate skewers.

4 Grill the kebabs and tomatoes over hot charcoal for 10–12 minutes, basting with butter and turning occasionally. Serve with cooked rice, sprinkled with sumac, if you like.

SHISH KEBAB

One of the first Middle Eastern dishes to achieve global popularity, shish kebab is believed to date from the days of the Ottoman Empire, when soldiers grilled meat on their swords over open fires. The lamb cubes are alternated with colourful vegetables.

SERVES FOUR

INGREDIENTS
- 450g/1lb boned leg of lamb, cubed
- 1 large green (bell) pepper, seeded and cut into squares
- 1 large yellow (bell) pepper, seeded and cut into squares
- 8 baby onions, halved
- 225g/8oz button (white) mushrooms
- 4 tomatoes, halved
- 15ml/1 tbsp melted butter
- bulgur wheat, to serve

For the marinade
- 45ml/3 tbsp olive oil
- juice of 1 lemon
- 2 garlic cloves, crushed
- 1 large onion, grated
- 15ml/1 tbsp chopped fresh oregano
- salt and ground black pepper

1 First make the marinade: blend together the oil, lemon juice, garlic, onion, chopped oregano and seasoning. Place the meat in a shallow, non-metallic dish and pour over the marinade.

2 Cover with clear film (plastic wrap) and leave to marinate in the fridge for 2–3 hours, or overnight.

3 Thread the cubes of lamb on to skewers, alternating with pieces of green and yellow pepper, onions and mushrooms. Thread the tomatoes on to separate skewers.

4 Grill the kebabs and tomatoes over hot charcoal for 10–12 minutes, basting with butter and turning occasionally. Serve with bulgur wheat.

TOP Energy 268Kcal/1119kJ; Protein 23.5g; Carbohydrate 7.9g, of which sugars 6.5g; Fat 16.1g, of which saturates 7.9g; Cholesterol 94mg; Calcium 32mg; Fibre 1.9g; Sodium 130mg.
BOTTOM Energy 340Kcal/1417kJ; Protein 25g; Carbohydrate 11.7g, of which sugars 10.3g; Fat 21.8g, of which saturates 7.3g; Cholesterol 86mg; Calcium 36mg; Fibre 3.4g; Sodium 111mg.

Lebanese Kibbeh

Lamb plays a dual role in this, Lebanon's national dish. The ground meat is mixed with bulgur wheat and then wrapped around a second lamb mixture, this time with spices and nuts. Kibbeh is often made into meatballs, but this tray version is popular, too.

SERVES SIX

INGREDIENTS
- 115g/4oz/⅔ cup bulgur wheat
- 450g/1lb finely minced (ground) lean lamb
- 1 large onion, grated
- 15ml/1 tbsp melted butter
- salt and ground black pepper
- sprigs of fresh mint, to garnish
- cooked rice, to serve

For the filling
- 30ml/2 tbsp oil
- 1 onion, finely chopped
- 225g/8oz minced (ground) lamb or veal
- 50g/2oz/⅓ cup pine nuts
- 2.5ml/½ tsp ground allspice

For the yogurt dip
- 600ml/1 pint/2½ cups Greek (US strained plain) yogurt
- 2–3 garlic cloves, crushed
- 15–30ml/1–2 tbsp chopped fresh mint

1 Preheat the oven to 190°C/375°F/ Gas 5. Rinse the bulgur wheat in a sieve and squeeze out the excess moisture.

2 Mix the lamb, onion and seasoning in a bowl, kneading the mixture to make a thick paste. Add the bulgur wheat and mix well. Set aside.

VARIATION
Use finely minced (ground) lean beef instead of lamb.

3 To make the filling, heat the oil in a frying pan and fry the onion until golden. Add the lamb or veal and cook, stirring, until evenly browned and then add the pine nuts, allspice and salt and pepper.

4 Oil a large baking dish and spread half of the meat and bulgur wheat mixture over the bottom. Spoon over the filling and top with a second layer of the remaining meat and bulgur wheat, pressing down firmly with the back of a spoon.

5 Pour the melted butter over the top and then bake in the oven for 40–45 minutes, until browned on top.

6 Meanwhile make the yogurt dip: blend together the yogurt and garlic, spoon into a serving bowl and sprinkle with the chopped mint.

7 Cut the cooked kibbeh into squares or rectangles and serve garnished with mint sprigs and accompanied by cooked rice and the yogurt dip.

Energy 452Kcal/1883kJ; Protein 29.7g; Carbohydrate 22.8g, of which sugars 11.5g; Fat 27.7g, of which saturates 9.7g; Cholesterol 93mg; Calcium 230mg; Fibre 1.1g; Sodium 178mg.

SHISH BARAK

THIS LEBANESE SPECIALITY IS A FAVOURITE LUNCHTIME DISH IN THE RESTAURANTS OF BEIRUT. DUMPLINGS FILLED WITH LAMB, ONION AND NUTS ARE SIMMERED IN A YOGURT AND EGG SAUCE.

SERVES FOUR

INGREDIENTS
- 30ml/2 tbsp olive oil
- 1 large onion, chopped
- 60ml/4 tbsp pine nuts or chopped walnuts
- 450g/1lb minced (ground) lamb
- 25g/1oz/2 tbsp butter
- 3 garlic cloves, crushed
- 15ml/1 tbsp chopped fresh mint
- salt and ground black pepper
- fresh mint leaves, to garnish
- cooked rice and green salad, to serve

For the dough
- 5ml/1 tsp salt
- 225g/8oz/2 cups plain (all-purpose) flour

For the yogurt sauce
- 2 litres/3½ pints/8 cups natural (plain) yogurt
- 1 egg, beaten
- 15ml/1 tbsp cornflour (cornstarch), blended with 15ml/1 tbsp cold water
- salt and white pepper

1 First make the dough: mix the salt and the flour together and then stir in enough water for the dough to hold together. Cover and leave to rest for 1 hour.

2 Heat the oil in a large frying pan and fry the onion for 3–4 minutes, until soft. Add the pine nuts or walnuts and fry until golden. Stir in the meat and cook until brown. Season, then remove the pan from the heat.

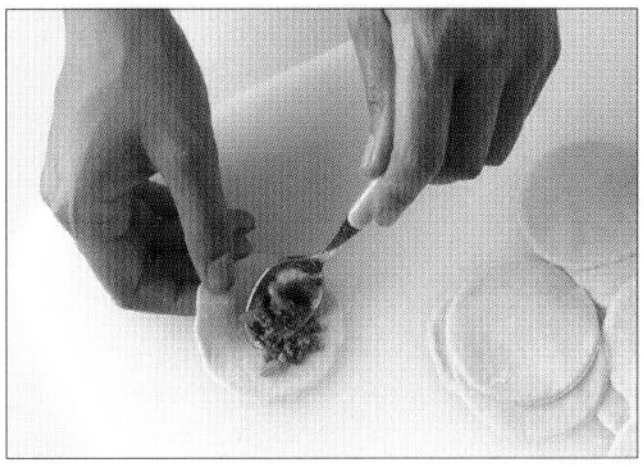

3 Roll out the dough thinly on a floured board. Cut into small rounds 5–6cm/ 2–2½in in diameter. Place 5ml/1 tsp of filling on each one, fold the pastry over and firmly press the edges together to seal. Bring the ends together to form a handle.

4 Meanwhile, make the yogurt sauce: pour the yogurt into a pan and beat in the egg and cornflour mixture. Season with salt and white pepper and slowly bring to the boil, stirring constantly.

5 Cook over a gentle heat until the sauce thickens and then carefully drop in the dumplings and simmer for about 20 minutes.

6 Spoon the dumplings and sauce on to warmed serving plates. Melt the butter in a small frying pan and fry the garlic until golden. Stir in the chopped mint, cook briefly and then pour over the dumplings. Garnish with mint leaves and serve with rice and a green salad.

Energy 820Kcal/3441kJ; Protein 55.4g; Carbohydrate 86.1g, of which sugars 41.8g; Fat 31.5g, of which saturates 13g; Cholesterol 153mg; Calcium 1061mg; Fibre 2.6g; Sodium 1062mg.

LAMB AND VEGETABLE PILAU

ALTHOUGH MANY PEOPLE ASSOCIATE THE PILAU WITH INDIA, THIS METHOD OF COOKING RICE HAS A CLOSE ASSOCIATION WITH THE MIDDLE EAST. ANCIENT PERSIANS CALLED THE DISH PULAW, AND INVENTED EXCITING VARIATIONS, INTRODUCING FRUIT AS WELL AS VEGETABLES AND SPICES.

SERVES FOUR

INGREDIENTS

For the meat curry

- 450g/1lb boned shoulder of lamb, cubed
- 2.5ml/½ tsp dried thyme
- 2.5ml/½ tsp paprika
- 5ml/1 tsp garam masala
- 1 garlic clove, crushed
- 25ml/1½ tbsp vegetable oil
- 900ml/1½ pints/3¾ cups lamb stock or water
- salt and ground black pepper

For the rice

- 30ml/2 tbsp butter or margarine
- 1 onion, chopped
- 175g/6oz potato, diced
- 1 carrot, sliced
- ½ red (bell) pepper, seeded and chopped
- 115g/4oz green cabbage, sliced
- 1 fresh green chilli, seeded and finely chopped
- 60ml/4 tbsp natural (plain) yogurt
- 2.5ml/½ tsp ground cumin
- 5 green cardamom pods
- 2 garlic cloves, crushed
- 350g/12oz/1¾ cups basmati rice
- about 50g/2oz/⅓ cup cashew nuts

1 To make the curry, place the lamb in a large bowl and add the thyme, paprika, garam masala, garlic and salt and pepper. Mix, then cover and set aside to marinate for 2–3 hours.

2 Heat the oil in a large pan and fry the lamb, in batches if necessary, over a medium heat for 5–6 minutes, until browned.

3 Add the stock or water, stir well and then cook, covered, for 35–40 minutes, until the lamb is just tender. Transfer the lamb to a plate or bowl and pour the liquid into a measuring jug (cup), topping up with water if necessary, to make 600ml/1 pint/2½ cups. Set aside.

4 To make the rice, melt the butter or margarine and fry the onion, potato and carrot for 5 minutes.

5 Add the red pepper, cabbage, chilli, yogurt, spices, garlic and the reserved meat stock. Stir well, cover, and then simmer gently for 5–10 minutes, until the cabbage has wilted.

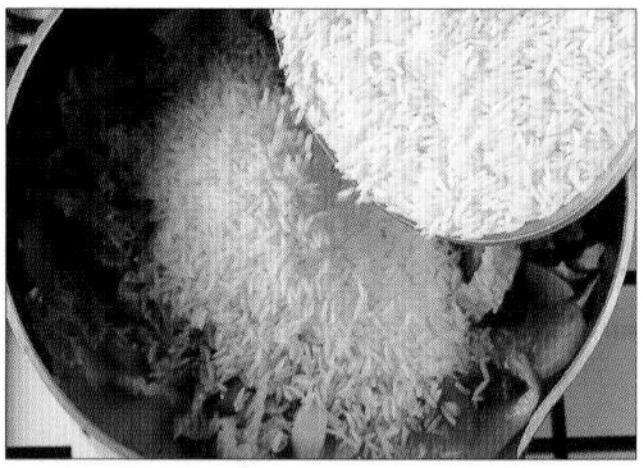

6 Stir in the rice and lamb, cover and simmer over a low heat for 20 minutes, until the rice is cooked. Sprinkle in the cashew nuts and season to taste with salt and pepper. Serve hot.

VARIATIONS

If you prefer, fewer vegetables can be used for this dish and cubed chicken or minced lamb substituted for the cubed lamb. Basmati rice is ideal, but long grain rice may be used instead. The amount of liquid can be varied, depending on whether firm, or well-cooked rice is preferred.

Energy 751Kcal/3135kJ; Protein 33.7g; Carbohydrate 86.3g, of which sugars 7.3g; Fat 30.1g, of which saturates 11.6g; Cholesterol 102mg; Calcium 88mg; Fibre 2.3g; Sodium 200mg.

STUFFED LEG OF LAMB, MOROCCAN STYLE

Throughout North Africa, and in parts of Spain settled by the Moors, this is a favourite way of cooking lamb. The spicy rice stuffing complements the sweetness of the meat.

SERVES SIX

INGREDIENTS

- 1.3–1.6kg/3–3½lb leg of lamb, boned
- 2 garlic cloves, crushed
- 40g/1½oz/3 tbsp butter
- 175ml/6fl oz/¾ cup chicken or lamb stock
- 15ml/1 tbsp cornflour (cornstarch)
- 15ml/1 tbsp apricot jam
- salt and ground black pepper

For the stuffing

- 1 fresh green chilli, seeded
- 2 shallots
- 1 garlic clove
- 1 bunch of fresh coriander (cilantro)
- sprig of fresh parsley
- 25g/1oz/2 tbsp butter
- 10ml/2 tsp ground cumin
- 2.5ml/½ tsp ground cinnamon
- 150g/5oz/¾ cup cooked long grain rice
- 30ml/2 tbsp pine nuts

1 Preheat the oven to 200°C/400°F/Gas 6 and then make the stuffing. Place the chilli, shallots, garlic, coriander and parsley in a blender or food processor and process until very finely chopped.

2 Melt the butter in a small frying pan and fry the shallot and herb mixture for 2–3 minutes over a gentle heat to soften the shallots. Add the cumin and cinnamon and stir well.

3 Place the cooked rice in a bowl, add the pine nuts and then stir in the contents of the pan. Season well with salt and pepper. Set aside.

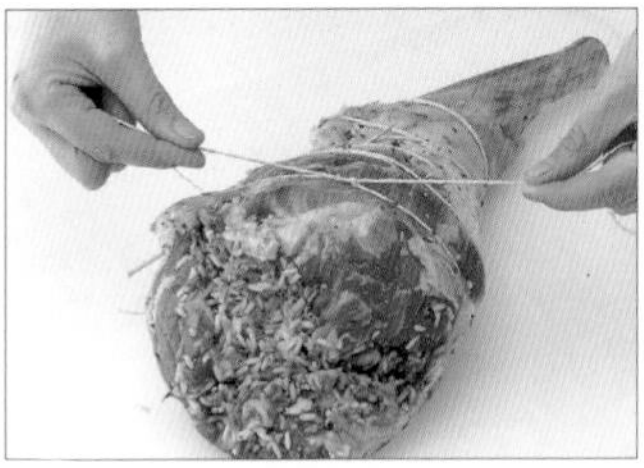

4 Season the meat on both sides with salt and pepper and rub the outside with the crushed garlic and butter. Place the meat, skin side down, on a work surface and spread the stuffing evenly over it. Roll the meat up, secure with a skewer and then tie with cooking string at even intervals.

5 Place in a flameproof roasting pan and roast in the oven for 20 minutes, then reduce the oven temperature to 180°C/350°F/Gas 4 and continue to roast for 1½–2 hours, basting occasionally with the juices from the pan.

6 To make the sauce, pour away the excess fat from the roasting pan and then add the chicken stock. Heat gently, stirring all the time, to deglaze the pan.

7 Blend the cornflour with 30ml/2 tbsp water and add to the roasting pan together with the apricot jam. Gradually bring to the boil, stirring all the time. Strain the sauce into a serving jug and serve with the stuffed lamb.

Energy 414Kcal/1726kJ; Protein 28.1g; Carbohydrate 13.7g, of which sugars 1.1g; Fat 27.8g, of which saturates 12.9g; Cholesterol 124mg; Calcium 46mg; Fibre 0.9g; Sodium 188mg.

BEEF TAGINE WITH SWEET POTATOES

FEZ IS CREDITED WITH MOROCCO'S FINEST TAGINES. THIS IS A PARTICULARLY GOOD ONE, THE SWEET POTATOES AND WARM SPICES PROVIDING A MELLOW COUNTERPOINT TO THE ROBUST FLAVOUR OF THE BEEF. USE A CASSEROLE WITH A TIGHT-FITTING LID TO MIRROR AS CLOSELY AS POSSIBLE THE EFFECT OF COOKING IN THE TRADITIONAL POT THAT GAVE ITS NAME TO THIS TYPE OF STEW.

SERVES FOUR

INGREDIENTS

- 675–900g/1½–2lb braising or stewing beef
- 30ml/2 tbsp sunflower oil
- good pinch of ground turmeric
- 1 large onion, chopped
- 1 fresh red or green chilli, seeded and finely chopped
- 7.5ml/1½ tsp paprika
- good pinch of cayenne pepper
- 2.5ml/½ tsp ground cumin
- 450g/1lb sweet potatoes
- 15ml/1 tbsp chopped fresh parsley
- 15ml/1 tbsp chopped fresh coriander (cilantro)
- 15g/½oz/1 tbsp butter
- salt and ground black pepper

1 Trim the meat and cut into 2cm/¾in cubes. Heat the oil in a flameproof casserole and fry the meat, together with the turmeric and seasoning, over a medium heat for 3–4 minutes, until the meat is evenly browned, stirring frequently.

2 Cover the pan tightly and cook for 15 minutes over a fairly gentle heat, without lifting the lid. Preheat the oven to 180°C/350°F/Gas 4.

VARIATIONS

You can use lean lamb instead of beef. Use swede (rutabaga) in place of the sweet potatoes.

3 Add the onion, chilli, paprika, cayenne pepper and cumin to the pan together with just enough water to cover the meat. Cover tightly and cook in the oven for 1–1½ hours, until the meat is very tender, checking occasionally and adding a little extra water, if necessary, to keep the stew fairly moist.

4 Meanwhile, peel the sweet potatoes and slice them straight into a bowl of salted water to avoid discolouring. Transfer to a pan, bring to the boil, simmer for 2–3 minutes. Drain.

5 Stir the chopped herbs into the meat, adding a little extra water if the stew appears dry. Arrange the potato slices over the meat and dot with the butter. Cover and cook in the oven for a further 10 minutes, until the potatoes feel very tender. Increase the oven temperature to 200°C/400°F/Gas 6 or preheat the grill (broiler) to its hottest setting.

6 Remove the lid of the casserole and cook in the oven or under the grill for a further 5–10 minutes, until the potatoes are golden. Serve at once.

Energy 434Kcal/1819kJ; Protein 39.1g; Carbohydrate 28.9g, of which sugars 10g; Fat 18.8g, of which saturates 6.8g; Cholesterol 114mg; Calcium 66mg; Fibre 3.9g; Sodium 180mg.

Tagine of Beef with Peas and Saffron

Ever since the Persians discovered that the brilliant orange stigmas of a tiny wild flower could be used to colour and flavour food, saffron has been highly prized, not only in the Middle East, but also in Mediterranean countries. The spice is cultivated commercially in Morocco and is a favourite ingredient in dishes like this classic fresh pea and preserved lemon tagine.

SERVES SIX

INGREDIENTS

- 1.2kg/2½lb chuck steak or stewing beef, trimmed and cubed
- 30ml/2 tbsp olive oil
- 1 onion, chopped
- 25g/1oz fresh root ginger, peeled and finely chopped
- 5ml/1 tsp ground ginger
- pinch of cayenne pepper
- pinch of saffron threads
- 1.2kg/2½lb shelled fresh peas
- 2 tomatoes, skinned and chopped
- 1 preserved lemon, chopped
- a handful of brown kalamata olives
- salt and ground black pepper
- bread or couscous, to serve

1 Put the cubed meat in a tagine, flameproof casserole or heavy pan with the olive oil, onion, fresh and ground ginger, cayenne and saffron and season with salt and pepper. Pour in enough water to cover the meat completely and then bring to the boil. Reduce the heat and then cover and simmer for about 1½ hours, until the meat is very tender. Cook for a little longer, if necessary.

2 Add the peas, tomatoes, preserved lemon and olives. Stir well and cook, uncovered, for about 10 minutes, or until the peas are tender and the sauce has reduced. Check the seasoning and serve with bread or plain couscous.

Energy 492Kcal/2049kJ; Protein 57.9g; Carbohydrate 25.6g, of which sugars 7g; Fat 18.2g, of which saturates 6g; Cholesterol 126mg; Calcium 61mg; Fibre 10.1g; Sodium 134mg.

Spicy Beef Koftas with Chickpea Purée

Wherever you go in the Middle East you will encounter these tasty kebabs, as street food, on barbecues, at beach bars and at family meals. The task of pounding the meat – traditionally performed by hand using a mortar and pestle – is much easier in a food processor. It takes just a few minutes to mould the mixture around the skewers, and they don't take long to cook. Chickpea purée is the traditional accompaniment.

SERVES SIX

INGREDIENTS
- 500g/1¼lb finely minced (ground) beef
- 1 onion, grated
- 10ml/2 tsp ground cumin
- 10ml/2 tsp ground coriander
- 10ml/2 tsp paprika
- 4ml/¾ tsp cayenne pepper
- 5ml/1 tsp salt
- small bunch of fresh flat leaf parsley, finely chopped
- small bunch of fresh coriander (cilantro), finely chopped

For the chickpea purée
- 225g/8oz/1¼ cups dried chickpeas, soaked overnight, drained and cooked
- 50ml/2fl oz/¼ cup olive oil
- juice of 1 lemon
- 2 garlic cloves, crushed
- 5ml/1 tsp cumin seeds
- 30ml/2 tbsp light tahini paste
- 60ml/4 tbsp thick Greek (US strained plain) yogurt
- 40g/1½oz/3 tbsp butter, melted
- salt and ground black pepper
- salad and bread, to serve

1 Mix the minced beef with the onion, cumin, ground coriander, paprika, cayenne, salt, chopped parsley and fresh coriander. Knead the mixture well, then pound it until smooth in a mortar with a pestle or in a blender or food processor. Place in a dish, cover and leave to stand in a cool place for 1 hour.

2 Meanwhile, make the chickpea purée. Preheat the oven to 200°C/400°F/Gas 6. In a blender or food processor, process the chickpeas with the olive oil, lemon juice, garlic, cumin seeds, tahini and yogurt until well mixed. Season with salt and pepper, tip the purée into an ovenproof dish, cover with foil and heat through in the oven for 20 minutes.

3 Divide the meat mixture into six portions and mould each on to a metal skewer, so that the meat resembles a fat sausage. Preheat the grill (broiler) on the hottest setting and cook the kebabs for 4–5 minutes on each side.

4 Melt the butter and pour it over the hot chickpea purée. Serve the kebabs with the hot chickpea purée. Serve with salad and bread.

Energy 456Kcal/1898kJ; Protein 26.6g; Carbohydrate 21.8g, of which sugars 3.5g; Fat 29.8g, of which saturates 10.7g; Cholesterol 64mg; Calcium 153mg; Fibre 5.4g; Sodium 463mg.

PERSIAN TANGY BEEF AND HERB KHORESH

In modern-day Iran, as in ancient Persia, rice is eaten at almost every meal. That the diet is never dull is thanks to the khoresh. This is a delicately spiced sauce or stew that serves as a topping, and Persian cooks know dozens of recipes. This is a classic meat khoresh, but there are also vegetarian versions, often with fruit and fresh herbs.

SERVES FOUR

INGREDIENTS

- 45ml/3 tbsp olive oil
- 1 large onion, chopped
- 450g/1lb lean stewing beef, cubed
- 15ml/1 tbsp fenugreek leaf
- 10ml/2 tsp ground turmeric
- 2.5ml/½ tsp ground cinnamon
- 600ml/1 pint/2½ cups water
- 25g/1oz fresh parsley, chopped
- 25g/1oz fresh chives, chopped
- 400g/14oz can red kidney beans
- juice of 1 lemon
- salt and ground black pepper
- cooked rice, to serve

1 Heat 30ml/2 tbsp of the oil in a large pan or flameproof casserole and fry the onion for about 3–4 minutes, until lightly golden. Add the beef and fry for a further 10 minutes until browned on all sides.

2 Add the fenugreek, turmeric and cinnamon and cook for about 1 minute, then add the water and bring to the boil. Cover and simmer over a gentle heat for 45 minutes, stirring occasionally.

3 Heat the remaining oil in a small frying pan and fry the parsley and chives over a medium heat for 2–3 minutes, stirring frequently.

4 Rinse and drain the kidney beans and then stir them into the beef with the fried herbs and lemon juice. Season with salt and pepper. Simmer the stew for a further 30–35 minutes, until the meat is tender. Serve on a bed of cooked rice.

Energy 357Kcal/1491kJ; Protein 32.5g; Carbohydrate 22.9g, of which sugars 7.3g; Fat 15.5g, of which saturates 4g; Cholesterol 71mg; Calcium 117mg; Fibre 7.7g; Sodium 468mg.

Nigerian Meat Stew

Lift the lid on a Nigerian cooking pot and you will generally find a stew inside, which will have been inspired by whatever ingredients were available at market that day – a single type of meat or a mixture, plus vegetables. Occasionally Nigerian women will add dried fish or snails to meat stews.

SERVES FOUR TO SIX

INGREDIENTS
- 675g/1½lb oxtail, chopped
- 450g/1lb stewing beef, cubed
- 450g/1lb skinless, chicken breast fillets, diced
- 2 garlic cloves, crushed
- 1½ onions
- 30ml/2 tbsp palm or vegetable oil
- 30ml/2 tbsp tomato purée (paste)
- 400g/14oz can plum tomatoes
- 2 bay leaves
- 5ml/1 tsp dried thyme
- 5ml/1 tsp mixed spice (apple pie spice)
- salt and ground black pepper

1 Place the oxtail in a large pan, cover with water and bring to the boil. Skim the surface of any froth, then cover and cook for 1½ hours, adding more water as necessary. Add the beef and continue to cook for a further 1 hour.

2 Meanwhile, season the chicken with the crushed garlic and roughly chop one of the onions.

3 Heat the oil in a large pan over a medium heat and fry the chopped onion for about 5 minutes, until soft.

4 Stir the tomato purée in to the onions, cook briskly for a few minutes, then add the chicken. Stir well and cook gently for 5 minutes.

5 Meanwhile, place the plum tomatoes and the remaining half onion in a blender or food processor and process to a purée. Stir into the chicken mixture with the bay leaves, thyme, mixed spice and seasoning.

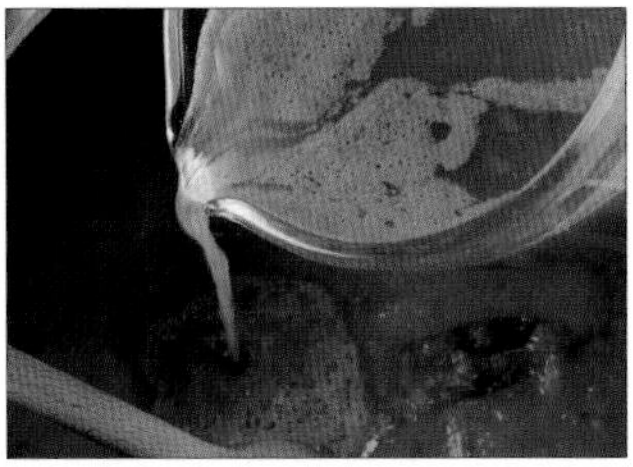

6 Add about 600ml/1 pint/2½ cups of stock from the cooked oxtail and beef and simmer for 35 minutes.

7 Add the oxtail and beef to the chicken. Heat gently, adjust the seasoning and serve hot.

Energy 588Kcal/2472kJ; Protein 88.3g; Carbohydrate 8.8g, of which sugars 7.2g; Fat 22.5g, of which saturates 9g; Cholesterol 281mg; Calcium 56mg; Fibre 1.8g; Sodium 390mg.

Beef Kofta Curry

Koftas come in various shapes and sizes. The basic minced meat mixture can be moulded around a skewer, sausage-style, or shaped into meatballs. In this variation, the more commonly used lamb is replaced by beef, which works well with the hot curry sauce.

SERVES FOUR

INGREDIENTS

For the meatballs
- 450g/1lb minced (ground) beef
- 45ml/3 tbsp finely chopped onion
- 15ml/1 tbsp chopped fresh coriander (cilantro)
- 15ml/1 tbsp natural (plain) yogurt
- about 60ml/4 tbsp plain (all-purpose) flour
- 10ml/2 tsp ground cumin
- 5ml/1 tsp garam masala
- 5ml/1 tsp ground turmeric
- 5ml/1 tsp ground coriander
- 1 fresh green chilli, seeded and finely chopped
- 2 garlic cloves, crushed
- 1.5ml/¼ tsp black mustard seeds
- 1 egg (optional)
- salt and ground black pepper

For the curry sauce
- 30ml/2 tbsp butter
- 1 onion, finely chopped
- 2 garlic cloves, crushed
- 45ml/3 tbsp curry powder
- 4 green cardamom pods
- 600ml/1 pint/2½ cups hot beef stock or water
- 15ml/1 tbsp tomato purée (paste)
- 30ml/2 tbsp natural (plain) yogurt
- 15ml/1 tbsp chopped fresh coriander (cilantro)

1 To make the meatballs, put the beef into a large bowl, add all the remaining meatball ingredients and mix well with your hands. Roll the mixture into small balls or koftas and then put aside on a floured plate until required.

2 To make the curry sauce, heat the butter in a pan over a medium heat and fry the onion and garlic for about 10 minutes, until the onion is soft.

3 Reduce the heat and then add the curry powder and cardamon pods and cook for a few minutes, stirring well.

4 Slowly stir in the stock or water and then add the tomato purée, yogurt and chopped coriander and stir well.

5 Simmer gently for 10 minutes. Add the koftas a few at a time, allow to cook briefly and then add a few more, until all of the koftas are in the pan. Simmer, uncovered, for about 20 minutes, until the koftas are cooked through. Avoid stirring, but gently shake the pan occasionally to move the koftas around. The curry should thicken slightly but if it becomes too dry, add a little more stock or water. Serve hot.

Energy 313Kcal/1301kJ; Protein 25.8g; Carbohydrate 4.9g, of which sugars 3.7g; Fat 21.3g, of which saturates 11.3g; Cholesterol 90mg; Calcium 42mg; Fibre 1g; Sodium 192mg.

GAMBIAN BEEF IN AUBERGINE SAUCE

Beef is popular in The Gambia. It is relatively expensive, though, so is usually reserved for special occasion dishes like this mildly spiced aubergine and beef stew.

SERVES FOUR

INGREDIENTS

- 450g/1lb stewing beef, cubed
- 5ml/1 tsp dried thyme
- 45ml/3 tbsp palm or vegetable oil
- 1 large onion, finely chopped
- 2 garlic cloves, crushed
- 4 canned plum tomatoes, chopped, plus the juice
- 15ml/1 tbsp tomato purée (paste)
- 2.5ml/½ tsp mixed spice (apple pie spice)
- 1 fresh red chilli, seeded and finely chopped
- 900ml/1½ pints/3¾ cups beef stock
- 1 large aubergine (eggplant), about 350g/12oz
- salt and ground black pepper

1 Season the cubed beef with 2.5ml/½ tsp thyme, salt and pepper.

2 Heat 15ml/1 tbsp of the oil in a pan and fry the meat for 8–10 minutes, until browned. Transfer to a bowl and set aside. Add the remaining oil to the pan.

3 Fry the onion and garlic for a few minutes, then add the tomatoes.

4 Simmer for 5–10 minutes, stirring occasionally. Stir in the tomato purée, mixed spice, chilli and remaining thyme, and then add the reserved beef and stock. Bring to the boil, cover and simmer for 30 minutes.

5 Cut the aubergine into 1cm/½in dice. Stir into the beef mixture and cook, covered, for a further 30 minutes, until the beef is completely tender. Adjust the seasoning and serve hot.

Energy 251Kcal/1050kJ; Protein 27.2g; Carbohydrate 7.2g, of which sugars 6.2g; Fat 12.8g, of which saturates 2.9g; Cholesterol 75mg; Calcium 29mg; Fibre 3g; Sodium 87mg.

VEGETARIAN DISHES

When it comes to appetizers and mezzes, vegetarians visiting Africa and the Middle East are spoilt for choice. Main courses are a little more challenging, as there is a tendency in both regions to use meat stock in vegetable dishes. There are, however, some exciting vegetarian dishes to be had. Try a tempting tagine of artichoke hearts, a Turkish spinach and cheese filo pie, summer vegetable kebabs with harissa and yogurt dip, Kenyan mung bean stew, or spinach with ground melon seed.

Classic Casablancan Couscous with Roasted Summer Vegetables

This dish is based on the tradition that a stew served with couscous should include seven vegetables. The number seven is said to bring good luck, and any suitable combination of vegetables can be used, as long as the total adds up to the magic number. To add a flicker of fire to this dish, serve it with a spoonful of harissa. To cool the palate, offer a bowl of thick and creamy yogurt.

SERVES SIX

INGREDIENTS

- 3 red onions, peeled and quartered
- 2–3 courgettes (zucchini), halved lengthways and cut across into 2–3 pieces
- 2–3 red, green or yellow (bell) peppers, seeded and quartered
- 2 aubergines (eggplants), cut into 6–8 long segments
- 2–3 leeks, trimmed and cut into long strips
- 2–3 sweet potatoes, peeled, halved lengthways and cut into long strips
- 4–6 tomatoes, quartered
- 6 garlic cloves, crushed
- 25g/1oz fresh root ginger, sliced
- a few large fresh rosemary sprigs
- about 150ml/¼ pint/⅔ cup olive oil
- 10ml/2 tsp clear honey
- salt and ground black pepper
- natural (plain) yogurt or harissa and bread, to serve

For the couscous

- 500g/1¼lb/3 cups couscous
- 5ml/1 tsp salt
- 600ml/1 pint/2½ cups warm water
- 45ml/3 tbsp sunflower oil
- about 25g/1oz/2 tbsp butter, diced

1 Preheat the oven to 200°C/400°F/Gas 6. Arrange all the vegetables in a roasting pan. Tuck the garlic, ginger and rosemary around the vegetables.

2 Pour lots of olive oil over the vegetables, drizzle with the honey, add salt and pepper, and then roast for about 1½ hours until they are extremely tender and slightly caramelized. The cooking time will depend on the size of the vegetable pieces. Turn them in the oil occasionally.

3 When the vegetables are nearly ready, put the couscous in a bowl. Stir the salt into the water, then pour it over the couscous, stirring to make sure it is absorbed evenly. Leave to stand for 10 minutes to plump up then, using your fingers, rub the sunflower oil into the grains to air them and break up any lumps. Tip the couscous into an ovenproof dish, arrange the butter over the top, cover with foil and heat in the oven for about 20 minutes.

4 To serve, use your fingers to work the melted butter into the grains of couscous and fluff it up, then pile it on a large dish and shape into a mound with a little pit at the top. Spoon some vegetables into the pit and arrange the rest around the dish. Pour the oil from the pan over the couscous or serve separately. Serve immediately with yogurt, or harissa if you prefer, and bread for mopping up the juices.

Energy 561Kcal/2340kJ; Protein 10.4g; Carbohydrate 78.8g, of which sugars 18.7g; Fat 24.6g, of which saturates 3.5g; Cholesterol 0mg; Calcium 101mg; Fibre 7.3g; Sodium 51mg.

TAGINE OF ARTICHOKE HEARTS, POTATOES, PEAS AND SAFFRON

ARTICHOKES ARE A DELICACY IN BOTH THE MIDDLE EAST AND NORTH AFRICA, AND WHEN THE SEASON STARTS, COOKS COMPETE FOR THE PICK OF THE CROP. IN SOME MARKETS IT IS POSSIBLE TO BUY JUST THE ARTICHOKE HEARTS, WHICH SAVES THE SOMEWHAT TEDIOUS TASK OF PREPARATION AT HOME. IF YOU DO NEED TO DO THIS YOURSELF, REMOVE THE OUTER LEAVES, CUT OFF THE STEMS AND SCOOP OUT THE CHOKE AND HAIRY BITS WITH A TEASPOON.

SERVES FOUR TO SIX

INGREDIENTS

- 6 fresh globe artichoke hearts
- juice of 1 lemon
- 30–45ml/2–3 tbsp olive oil
- 1 onion, chopped
- 675g/1½lb potatoes, peeled and quartered
- small bunch of fresh flat leaf parsley, chopped
- small bunch of fresh coriander (cilantro), chopped
- small bunch of fresh mint, chopped
- pinch of saffron threads
- 5ml/1 tsp ground turmeric
- about 350ml/12fl oz/1½ cups vegetable stock
- finely chopped rind of ½ preserved lemon
- 250g/9oz/2¼ cups shelled peas
- salt and ground black pepper
- couscous or bread, to serve

COOK'S TIP

When preparing artichokes, once cut, the flesh of artichokes will blacken. To prevent this from happening, put the artichokes into acidulated water – you can use lemon juice or white wine vinegar.

1 Poach the artichoke hearts very gently in plenty of simmering water with half the lemon juice, for 10–15 minutes, until tender. Drain and refresh under cold water, then drain again.

2 Heat the olive oil in a tagine or heavy pan. Add the onion and cook over a low heat for about 15 minutes, until softened but not browned. Add the potatoes, most of the chopped parsley, the chopped coriander and mint, the remaining lemon juice, and the saffron and turmeric to the pan.

3 Pour in the stock, bring to the boil, then reduce the heat. Cover the pan and cook for about 15 minutes, until the potatoes are almost tender.

4 Stir the preserved lemon, artichoke hearts and peas into the stew, and cook, uncovered, for a further 10 minutes. Season to taste, sprinkle with the remaining parsley, and serve with couscous or chunks of fresh bread.

Energy 260Kcal/1089kJ; Protein 8.6g; Carbohydrate 42g, of which sugars 10.6g; Fat 7.5g, of which saturates 1.2g; Cholesterol 0mg; Calcium 96mg; Fibre 7.9g; Sodium 47mg.

TAGINE OF YAM, CARROTS AND PRUNES

The yams in this Moroccan dish reveal a West African influence. It comes from the Atlas Mountains, where the temperature often drops to below zero in winter, and warming stews are very welcome. This is quite a sweet-tasting dish, thanks to the caramelized vegetables and the prunes. Serve it with couscous and a green salad that includes some bitter leaves, preferably with a sharp lemon and oil dressing.

SERVES FOUR TO SIX

INGREDIENTS

- 45ml/3 tbsp olive oil
- a little butter
- 25–30 button (pearl) onions, blanched and peeled
- 900g/2lb yam or sweet potatoes, peeled and cut into bitesize chunks
- 2–3 carrots, cut into bitesize chunks
- 150g/5oz/generous ½ cup ready-to-eat pitted prunes
- 5ml/1 tsp ground cinnamon
- 2.5ml/½ tsp ground ginger
- 10ml/2 tsp clear honey
- 450ml/¾ pint/scant 2 cups vegetable stock
- small bunch of fresh coriander (cilantro), finely chopped
- small bunch of fresh mint, finely chopped
- salt and ground black pepper

COOK'S TIP

Yams have a brown skin and cream-coloured flesh; sweet potatoes have dark red or orange skin and orange flesh. Buy firm specimens that do not "give".

1 Preheat the oven to 200°C/400°F/Gas 6. Heat the olive oil in a flameproof casserole with the butter and stir in the onions. Cook for about 5 minutes until the onions are tender, then remove half of the onions from the pan and set aside.

2 Add the yam or sweet potatoes and carrots to the pan and cook until lightly browned. Stir in the prunes with the cinnamon, ginger and honey, then pour in the stock. Season well, cover the casserole and transfer to the oven for about 45 minutes.

3 Stir in the reserved onions and bake for a further 10 minutes. Gently stir in the chopped coriander and mint, and serve the tagine immediately.

Energy 454Kcal/1922kJ; Protein 6.2g; Carbohydrate 91.8g, of which sugars 27.1g; Fat 9.5g, of which saturates 1.5g; Cholesterol 0mg; Calcium 111mg; Fibre 7.9g; Sodium 32mg.

Butter Bean, Tomato and Olive Tagine

Vegetarians sometimes struggle to find something hot and substantial to eat when travelling in Africa and the Middle East, as even vegetable stews are often made with meat stock. This tagine takes its moisture from tomatoes and olive oil, however, so fits the bill perfectly. It is hearty enough to be served on its own, with fresh, crusty bread and perhaps a salad. If you are serving it to non-vegetarians, add some sliced chorizo.

SERVES FOUR

INGREDIENTS

- 115g/4oz/⅔ cup butter (lima) beans, soaked overnight
- 30–45ml/2–3 tbsp olive oil
- 1 onion, chopped
- 2–3 garlic cloves, crushed
- 25g/1oz fresh root ginger, peeled and finely chopped
- pinch of saffron threads
- 16 cherry tomatoes
- generous pinch of granulated sugar
- handful of fleshy black olives, pitted
- 5ml/1 tsp ground cinnamon
- 5ml/1 tsp paprika
- small bunch of fresh flat leaf parsley
- salt and ground black pepper

1 Rinse the beans and place them in a large pan with plenty of water. Bring to the boil and boil for about 10 minutes, and then reduce the heat and simmer gently for 1–1½ hours until tender. Drain the beans and refresh under cold running water, then drain again.

COOK'S TIP

If you are in a hurry, you could use two 400g/14oz cans of butter (lima) beans for this tagine. Make sure you rinse the them well before adding, as canned beans tend to be salty.

2 Heat the olive oil in a heavy pan. Add the onion, garlic and ginger, and cook for about 10 minutes, until softened but not browned. Stir in the saffron threads, followed by the cherry tomatoes and a sprinkling of sugar.

3 As the tomatoes begin to soften, stir in the butter beans. When the tomatoes have heated through, stir in the olives, ground cinnamon and paprika. Season to taste and sprinkle over the chopped parsley. Serve immediately.

Energy 146Kcal/615kJ; Protein 7.4g; Carbohydrate 16.2g, of which sugars 3.8g; Fat 6.3g, of which saturates 0.9g; Cholesterol 0mg; Calcium 62mg; Fibre 6g; Sodium 16mg.

Okra and Tomato Tagine

Although this vegetable stew is a North African speciality, similar dishes exist throughout the Middle East. Okra is particularly popular in Egypt, where it is cultivated commercially on a grand scale. The vegetable is also known as "ladies' fingers", a reference to their tapered shape. When cut before being cooked, as in this recipe, the pods ooze a glue-like substance which gives the dish a distinctive texture.

SERVES FOUR

INGREDIENTS

- 350g/12oz okra
- 5–6 tomatoes
- 2 small onions
- 2 garlic cloves, crushed
- 1 fresh green chilli, seeded
- 5ml/1 tsp paprika
- small handful of fresh coriander (cilantro)
- 30ml/2 tbsp sunflower oil
- juice of 1 lemon

1 Trim the okra and then cut it into 1cm/½in lengths. Skin and seed the tomatoes and roughly chop the flesh.

2 Roughly chop one of the onions and place it in a blender or food processor with the garlic, chilli, paprika, coriander and 60ml/4 tbsp water. Process to make a paste.

3 Thinly slice the second onion and fry it in the oil in a pan for 5–6 minutes, until golden brown. Transfer to a plate and set aside. Reduce the heat and pour the onion and coriander paste into the pan. Cook for 1–2 minutes, stirring frequently.

4 Add the okra, tomatoes, lemon juice and about 120ml/4fl oz/½ cup water. Stir well to mix, cover tightly and simmer over a low heat for about 15 minutes, until the okra is tender. Transfer to a serving dish, sprinkle with the fried onion rings and serve.

VARIATION

Use 3–4 shallots instead of onions.

Energy 113Kcal/471kJ; Protein 4.1g; Carbohydrate 9.2g, of which sugars 8g; Fat 7g, of which saturates 1.1g; Cholesterol 0mg; Calcium 181mg; Fibre 5.8g; Sodium 23mg.

Chickpea Tagine

The preserved lemon in this recipe tells you that it comes from North Africa, probably Morocco, where the distinctive yellow globes in glass jars glimmer like miniature suns in the markets. The flavour of preserved – or pickled – lemon is wonderful. Slightly salty, less tart than the fresh fruit, it adds a real zing to the blandness of the chickpeas.

SERVES FOUR

INGREDIENTS

- 150g/5oz/¾ cup chickpeas, soaked overnight, or 2 x 400g/14oz cans chickpeas, rinsed and drained
- 30ml/2 tbsp sunflower oil
- 1 large onion, chopped
- 1 garlic clove, crushed (optional)
- 400g/14oz can chopped tomatoes
- 5ml/1 tsp ground cumin
- 350ml/12fl oz/1½ cups vegetable stock
- ¼ preserved lemon
- 30ml/2 tbsp chopped fresh coriander (cilantro)

1 If using dried chickpeas, cook them in plenty of boiling water for 1–1½ hours until tender. Drain well.

2 Place the chickpeas in a bowl of cold water and rub them between your fingers to remove the skins.

3 Heat the oil in a pan or flameproof casserole and fry the onion and garlic, if using, for 8–10 minutes, until golden.

4 Add the chickpeas, tomatoes, cumin and stock and stir well. Bring to the boil and simmer, uncovered, for 30–40 minutes, until the chickpeas are very soft and most of the liquid has evaporated.

5 Rinse the preserved lemon and cut away the flesh and pith. Cut the peel into slivers and stir it into the chickpeas together with the chopped coriander. Serve immediately with Moroccan bread.

Energy 207Kcal/871kJ; Protein 9.7g; Carbohydrate 26.4g, of which sugars 7.1g; Fat 7.8g, of which saturates 0.9g; Cholesterol 0mg; Calcium 87mg; Fibre 5.6g; Sodium 56mg.

SUMMER VEGETABLE KEBABS WITH HARISSA AND YOGURT DIP

THERE'S NOTHING NEW ABOUT THREADING VEGETABLE CHUNKS ON SKEWERS, BUT THIS METHOD OF TOSSING THEM IN A SPICY OIL AND LEMON JUICE MARINADE MAKES ALL THE DIFFERENCE. SERVE THEM WITH THE HOT AND CREAMY DIP AND YOU'LL HAVE VEGETARIAN GUESTS EATING OUT OF YOUR HANDS – OR THEIRS. THE KEBABS CAN ALSO BE COOKED ON THE BARBECUE, PREFERABLY ON A DEDICATED PORTION OF THE GRILL, WELL AWAY FROM ANY MEAT JUICES.

SERVES FOUR

INGREDIENTS

- 2 aubergines (eggplants), part peeled and cut into chunks
- 2 courgettes (zucchini), cut into chunks
- 2–3 red or green (bell) peppers, seeded and cut into chunks
- 12–16 cherry tomatoes
- 4 small red onions, quartered
- 60ml/4 tbsp olive oil
- juice of ½ lemon
- 1 garlic clove, crushed
- 5ml/1 tsp ground coriander
- 5ml/1 tsp ground cinnamon
- 10ml/2 tsp clear honey
- 5ml/1 tsp salt

For the harissa and yogurt dip

- 450g/1lb/2 cups Greek (US strained plain) yogurt
- 30–60ml/2–4 tbsp harissa
- small bunch of fresh coriander (cilantro), finely chopped
- small bunch of mint, finely chopped
- salt and ground black pepper

1 Preheat the grill (broiler) on the hottest setting. Put all the vegetables in a bowl. Mix together the olive oil, lemon juice, garlic, ground coriander, cinnamon, honey and salt and pour the mixture over the vegetables.

2 Using your hands, turn the vegetables gently in the marinade, then thread them on to metal skewers. Cook the kebabs under the grill, turning them occasionally, until the vegetables are nicely browned all over.

3 To make the dip, put the yogurt in a bowl and beat in the harissa, making it as fiery in taste as you like by adding more harissa. Add most of the chopped coriander and mint, reserving a little to garnish, and season well with salt and pepper. While they are still hot, slide the vegetables off the skewers and dip them into the yogurt dip before eating. Garnish with the reserved herbs.

COOK'S TIP

Make sure you cut the aubergines, courgettes and peppers into fairly even-size chunks, so they will all cook at the same rate.

Energy 274Kcal/1144kJ; Protein 11.1g; Carbohydrate 28.8g, of which sugars 26.2g; Fat 13.7g, of which saturates 2.5g; Cholesterol 1mg; Calcium 303mg; Fibre 5.9g; Sodium 111mg.

Couscous with Dried Fruit Nuts and Cinnamon

In Morocco, this dish of couscous with dates, raisins and nuts frequently forms part of a celebration meal. The dish is often served as a course on its own, just before the dessert. It also tastes good with a spicy tagine, or as a side dish with roasted or grilled meat or poultry. The sugar and cinnamon mixture is traditionally sprinkled in stripes.

SERVES SIX

INGREDIENTS

- 500g/1¼lb/3 cups couscous
- 600ml/1 pint/2½ cups warm water
- 5ml/1 tsp salt
- pinch of saffron threads
- 45ml/3 tbsp sunflower oil
- 30ml/2 tbsp olive oil
- a little butter or smen
- 115g/4oz/½ cup dried apricots, cut into slivers
- 75g/3oz/½ cup dried dates, chopped
- 75g/3oz/generous ½ cup seedless raisins
- 115g/4oz/⅔ cup blanched almonds, cut into slivers
- 75g/3oz/½ cup pistachio nuts
- 10ml/2 tsp ground cinnamon
- 45ml/3 tbsp caster (superfine) sugar

1 Preheat the oven to 180°C/350°F/Gas 4. Put the couscous in a bowl. Mix together the water, salt and saffron and pour it over the couscous, stirring. Leave to stand for 10 minutes. Add the sunflower oil and, using your fingers, rub it through the grains. Set aside.

2 In a heavy pan, heat the olive oil and butter or smen and stir in the apricots, dates, raisins, most of the almonds (reserve some for garnish) and pistachio nuts.

3 Cook until the raisins plump up, then tip the nuts and fruit into the couscous and toss together to mix. Tip the couscous into an ovenproof dish and cover with foil. Place in the oven for about 20 minutes, until heated through.

4 Toast the reserved slivered almonds. Pile the hot couscous in a mound on a large serving dish and sprinkle with the cinnamon and sugar – these are usually sprinkled in stripes down the mound. Scatter the toasted almonds over the top and serve hot.

Energy 567Kcal/2367kJ; Protein 11.9g; Carbohydrate 71.5g, of which sugars 27.9g; Fat 27.7g, of which saturates 3g; Cholesterol 0mg; Calcium 94mg; Fibre 3.3g; Sodium 79mg.

CAMEROONIAN COCONUT RICE

This spicy rice and vegetable medley comes from Buea, which is a small town close to Mount Cameroon in the north west of the country. Use thin coconut milk, which will contribute plenty of flavour without dominating the other ingredients.

SERVES FOUR

INGREDIENTS

- 30ml/2 tbsp vegetable oil
- 1 onion, chopped
- 30ml/2 tbsp tomato purée (paste)
- 600ml/1 pint/2½ cups coconut milk
- 2 carrots, diced
- 1 yellow (bell) pepper, seeded and chopped
- 5ml/1 tsp dried thyme
- 2.5ml/½ tsp mixed spice (apple pie spice)
- 1 fresh green chilli, seeded and chopped
- 350g/12oz/1¾ cups long grain rice
- salt

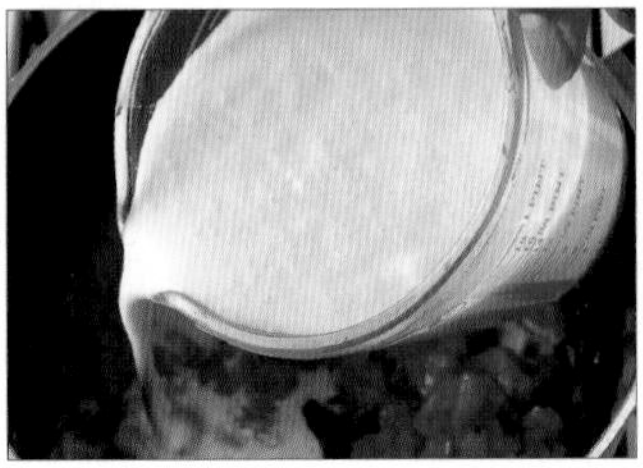

1 Heat the oil in a large pan and fry the onion for 2 minutes. Add the tomato purée and cook over a medium heat for 5–6 minutes, stirring all the time. Add the coconut milk, stir well and bring to the boil.

2 Stir the carrots, pepper, thyme, mixed spice, chilli and rice into the onion mixture, season with salt and bring to the boil. Cover and cook over a low heat, until the rice has absorbed most of the liquid, stirring occasionally. Cover the rice with foil, secure with the lid and steam very gently until the rice is cooked. Serve hot.

CHICKPEA AND OKRA STIR-FRY

This modern treatment of Middle Eastern ingredients typifies what young professionals prepare when time is short. Their mothers would have cooked the chickpeas themselves.

SERVES FOUR

INGREDIENTS

- 450g/1lb okra
- 15ml/1 tbsp vegetable oil
- 15ml/1 tbsp mustard oil
- 15g/½oz/1 tbsp butter
- 1 onion, finely chopped
- 1 garlic clove, crushed
- 2 tomatoes, finely chopped
- 1 fresh green chilli, seeded and finely chopped
- 2 slices of fresh root ginger, peeled
- 5ml/1 tsp ground cumin
- 15ml/1 tbsp chopped fresh coriander (cilantro)
- 400g/14oz can chickpeas, rinsed and drained

VARIATION

Use other canned beans such as black-eyed beans (peas) instead of chickpeas.

1 Wash and dry the okra, trim the ends and roughly chop the flesh.

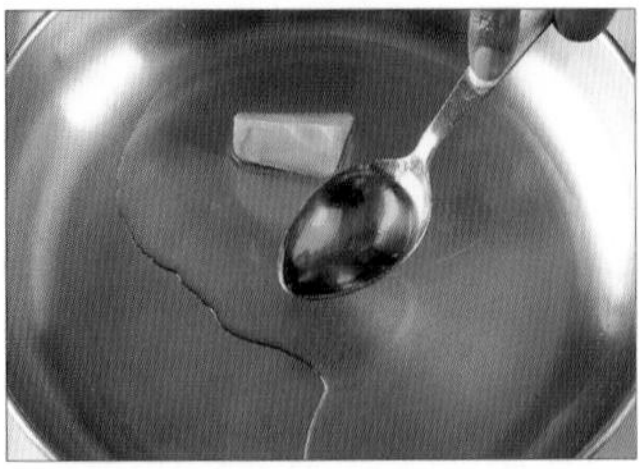

2 Heat the vegetable and mustard oils and the butter in a large frying pan.

3 Fry the onion and garlic for 5 minutes, until the onion is slightly softened. Add the chopped tomatoes, chilli and ginger stir well, then add the okra, cumin and chopped coriander. Simmer for 5 minutes, stirring frequently, and then stir in the chickpeas and seasoning.

4 Cook gently for a few minutes until the chickpeas are heated through, then spoon the mixture into a serving bowl and serve at once.

TOP Energy 448Kcal/1876kJ; Protein 8.6g; Carbohydrate 87.8g, of which sugars 17g; Fat 6.9g, of which saturates 1.1g; Cholesterol 0mg; Calcium 82mg; Fibre 2.6g; Sodium 194mg.

BOTTOM Energy 241Kcal/1010kJ; Protein 10.9g; Carbohydrate 22.2g, of which sugars 5.6g; Fat 12.8g, of which saturates 3.3g; Cholesterol 8mg; Calcium 231mg; Fibre 9.3g; Sodium 257mg.

FATAYER

THIS SPINACH AND CHEESE FILO PIE IS THE TURKISH VERSION OF THAT GREEK FAVOURITE, SPANAKOPITA. SIMILAR RECIPES ARE FOUND THROUGHOUT THE MIDDLE EAST, THE MEDITERRANEAN AND NORTH AFRICA, THE DIFFERENCES BEING IN THE SPICING AND THE TYPE OF PASTRY USED.

SERVES SIX

INGREDIENTS
- 900g/2lb fresh spinach, chopped
- 25g/1oz/2 tbsp butter or margarine
- 2 onions, chopped
- 2 garlic cloves, crushed
- 275g/10oz feta cheese, crumbled
- 115g/4oz/⅔ cup pine nuts
- 5 eggs, beaten
- 2 saffron threads, soaked in 30ml/ 2 tbsp boiling water
- 5ml/1 tsp paprika
- 1.5ml/¼ tsp ground cumin
- 1.5ml/¼ tsp ground cinnamon
- 14 sheets of filo pastry
- about 60ml/4 tbsp olive oil
- salt and ground black pepper
- lettuce leaves, to serve

1 Place the spinach in a large colander, sprinkle with a little salt, rub it into the leaves and leave for 30 minutes to drain the excess liquid.

2 Preheat the oven to 180°C/350°F/ Gas 4. Melt the butter or margarine in a large pan and fry the onions, until golden. Stir in the garlic, feta cheese and pine nuts.

3 Remove the pan from the heat and stir in the eggs, spinach, saffron water and spices. Season with salt and pepper and mix well.

VARIATION
Grated Cheddar, fresh Parmesan or any hard cheese can be added to this dish as well as the feta.

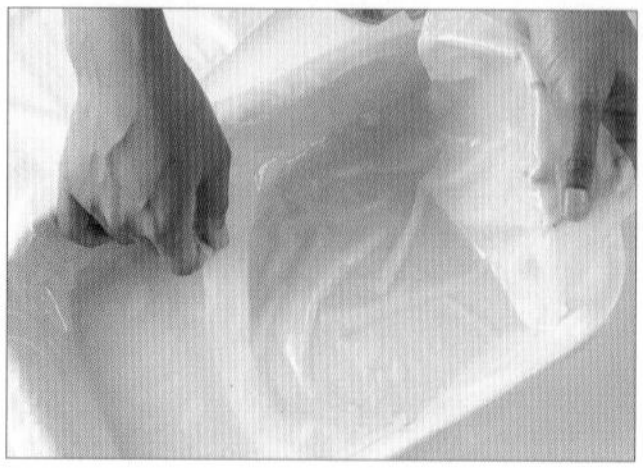

4 Grease a large rectangular baking dish. Take seven of the sheets of filo pastry and brush one side of each with a little olive oil. Place on the bottom of the dish, overlapping the sides.

5 Spoon all of the spinach mixture over the pastry and carefully drizzle 30ml/ 2 tbsp of the remaining olive oil over the top.

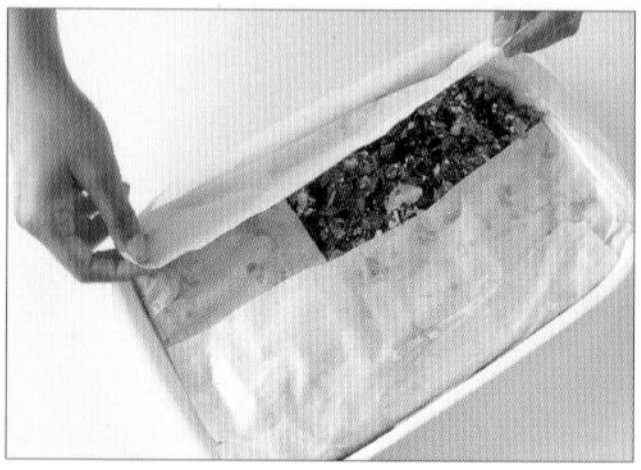

6 Fold the overlapping pastry over the filling. Cut the remaining pastry sheets to the dish size and brush each one with more olive oil. Arrange on top of the filling.

7 Brush with water to prevent curling and then bake in the oven for about 30 minutes, until the pastry is golden brown. Serve with the lettuce leaves.

Energy 565Kcal/2349kJ; Protein 22.7g; Carbohydrate 31.8g, of which sugars 5.6g; Fat 39.5g, of which saturates 11.9g; Cholesterol 200mg; Calcium 500mg; Fibre 4.9g; Sodium 956mg.

KUKU SABZI

THE TRADITIONAL WAY OF CELEBRATING THE NEW YEAR IN IRAN IS TO INVITE SOME FRIENDS OVER TO SHARE IN THIS BAKED EGG AND HERB DISH. IT RESEMBLES A LARGE OVEN-BAKED OMELETTE AND IS FILLED WITH FRESH VEGETABLES. THESE WILL USUALLY BE WHATEVER GREENS ARE IN SEASON AT THE TIME. CHOPPED LETTUCE IS OFTEN INCLUDED, AS IS SPINACH AND FRESH MIXED HERBS.

SERVES FOUR TO SIX

INGREDIENTS

- 2–3 saffron threads
- 8 eggs
- 2 leeks, trimmed and washed
- 115g/4oz fresh spinach
- ½ iceberg lettuce
- 4 spring onions (scallions)
- 45ml/3 tbsp chopped fresh parsley
- 45ml/3 tbsp chopped fresh chives
- 45ml/3 tbsp chopped fresh coriander (cilantro)
- 1 garlic clove, crushed
- 30ml/2 tbsp chopped walnuts (optional)
- 25g/1oz/2 tbsp butter
- salt and ground black pepper
- natural (plain) yogurt and pitta bread, to serve

1 Preheat the oven to 180°C/350°F/ Gas 4. Soak the saffron threads in 15ml/1 tbsp boiling water in a bowl.

2 Beat the eggs in a large bowl. Finely chop the leeks, spinach, lettuce and spring onions.

3 Add the chopped greens to the eggs together with the herbs, garlic, and walnuts, if using. Season with salt and pepper, add the saffron water and stir thoroughly to mix. Melt the butter in a large flameproof, ovenproof dish and pour in the vegetable and egg mixture.

4 Bake in the oven for 35–40 minutes, until the egg mixture is set and the top is golden. Serve warm or cold, cut into wedges, with yogurt and bread.

Energy 230Kcal/955kJ; Protein 15.5g; Carbohydrate 4.2g, of which sugars 3.4g; Fat 17.2g, of which saturates 6.5g; Cholesterol 394mg; Calcium 162mg; Fibre 3.5g; Sodium 225mg.

Egusi Spinach and Egg

This is a superbly balanced dish for those who don't eat meat. Egusi, or ground melon seed, is widely used in West African cooking and adds a creamy texture and a nutty flavour to many recipes. It is especially good with fresh spinach and tomatoes.

SERVES FOUR

INGREDIENTS
- 900g/2lb fresh spinach
- 115g/4oz egusi
- 90ml/6 tbsp groundnut (peanut) or vegetable oil
- 4 tomatoes, skinned and chopped
- 1 onion, chopped
- 2 garlic cloves, crushed
- 1 slice of fresh root ginger, peeled and finely chopped
- 150ml/¼ pint/⅔ cup vegetable stock
- 1 fresh red chilli, seeded and finely chopped
- 6 eggs
- salt

1 Roll the spinach into bundles and cut into strips. Place in a bowl.

2 Cover with boiling water, then drain through a sieve. Press with your fingers to remove excess water. Set aside.

3 Place the egusi in a bowl and gradually add enough water to form a paste, stirring all the time. Set aside.

4 Heat the oil in a pan, add the tomatoes, onion, garlic and ginger and fry over a medium heat for about 10 minutes, stirring frequently.

5 Add the egusi paste, stock, chilli and salt, cook for 10 minutes, then add the spinach and stir it into the sauce. Cook for 15 minutes, uncovered, stirring frequently.

6 Meanwhile hard-boil the eggs, and then stand them in cold water for a few minutes to cool. Shell the eggs and then cut them in half. Arrange the eggs in a shallow serving dish and pour the egusi spinach over the top. Serve hot.

VARIATION

Instead of using boiled eggs, you could make an omelette flavoured with chopped herbs and garlic. Serve it either whole, or sliced, with the egusi sauce. If you can't find egusi, use ground almonds as a substitute.

Energy 436Kcal/1803kJ; Protein 21.5g; Carbohydrate 12.6g, of which sugars 7.5g; Fat 33.3g, of which saturates 5.1g; Cholesterol 285mg; Calcium 464mg; Fibre 7.3g; Sodium 428mg.

GHANIAN BEAN AND GARI LOAF

KIDNEY BEANS AND CAPSICUMS ARE USED TO MAKE THIS TASTY LOAF, WHICH IS THICKENED WITH EGGS AND GROUND CASSAVA. THIS RECIPE IS TYPICAL OF THE CREATIVE DISHES MADE IN GHANA.

SERVES FOUR TO SIX

INGREDIENTS

- 225g/8oz/1¼ cups red kidney beans, soaked overnight
- 15g/½oz/1 tbsp butter or margarine
- 1 onion, finely chopped
- 2 garlic cloves, crushed
- ½ red (bell) pepper, seeded and chopped
- ½ green (bell) pepper, seeded and chopped
- 1 fresh green chilli, seeded and finely chopped
- 5ml/1 tsp chopped fresh mixed herbs
- 2 eggs, beaten
- 15ml/1 tbsp lemon juice
- 75ml/5 tbsp gari (see Cook's Tip)
- salt and ground black pepper

COOK'S TIP

Gari is a course-grained flour, made from a starchy root vegetable, cassava, which is first dried, then ground. Gari is used in a similar way to ground rice.

1 Drain the kidney beans, then place them in a pan, cover with water and boil rapidly for 15 minutes. Reduce the heat and continue boiling for about 1 hour, until the beans are tender, adding more water, if necessary. Drain, reserving the cooking liquid. Preheat the oven to 190°C/375°F/Gas 5 and grease a 900g/2lb loaf tin (pan).

2 Melt the butter or margarine in a large frying pan and fry the onion, garlic and peppers for 5 minutes. Add the chilli, mixed herbs and a little salt and pepper and stir to mix.

3 Place the cooked kidney beans in a large bowl or in a blender or food processor and mash or process to a pulp. Add the onion and pepper mixture and stir well to mix. Cool slightly, then stir in the eggs and lemon juice.

4 Place the gari in a separate bowl and sprinkle generously with warm water. The gari should become soft and fluffy after about 5 minutes.

5 Pour the gari into the bean and onion mixture and stir together thoroughly. If the consistency is too stiff, add a little of the bean cooking liquid. Spoon the mixture evenly into the prepared loaf tin and bake in the oven for 35–45 minutes, until firm to the touch.

6 Cool the loaf in the tin and then turn it out on to a plate. Cut into thick slices and serve.

Energy 303Kcal/1275kJ; Protein 18g; Carbohydrate 42.5g, of which sugars 5g; Fat 7.5g, of which saturates 2.9g; Cholesterol 103mg; Calcium 79mg; Fibre 10.2g; Sodium 70mg.

BLACK-EYED BEAN STEW WITH SPICY PUMPKIN

Gourds of all shapes and sizes are a familiar sight at African markets. Pumpkin makes a tasty and colourful contrasting dish to serve with a simple bean stew.

SERVES THREE TO FOUR

INGREDIENTS

- 225g/8oz/1¼ cups black-eyed beans (peas), soaked for 4 hours or overnight
- 1 onion, chopped
- 1 green or red (bell) pepper, seeded and chopped
- 2 garlic cloves, chopped
- 1 vegetable stock (bouillon) cube
- 1 fresh thyme sprig or 5ml/1 tsp dried thyme
- 5ml/1 tsp paprika
- 2.5ml/½ tsp mixed spice (apple pie spice)
- 2 carrots, sliced
- 15–30ml/1–2 tbsp palm oil
- salt, pepper and hot pepper sauce

For the spicy pumpkin

- 675g/1½lb pumpkin
- 1 onion
- 25g/1oz/2 tbsp butter or margarine
- 2 garlic cloves, crushed
- 3 tomatoes, skinned and chopped
- 2.5ml/½ tsp ground cinnamon
- 10ml/2 tsp curry powder
- pinch of freshly grated nutmeg
- 300ml/½ pint/1¼ cups water
- ground black pepper, to taste

1 Drain the beans, place them in a pan and cover generously with water. Bring the beans to the boil.

2 Add the onion, green or red pepper, garlic, stock cube, thyme and spices. Simmer for 45 minutes, until the beans are just tender. Season to taste with salt and a little hot pepper sauce.

3 Add the carrots and palm oil and continue to cook for about 10–12 minutes, until the carrots are tender, adding a little more water, if necessary. Remove the pan from the heat and set aside.

4 To make the spicy pumpkin, cut the pumpkin into cubes and finely chop the onion.

5 Melt the butter or margarine in a frying pan or heavy pan, and add the pumpkin, onion, garlic, tomatoes, spices and water. Stir well to combine, bring to the boil and simmer until the pumpkin is soft, stirring occasionally.

6 Season with salt, hot pepper sauce and black pepper, to taste. Serve with the black-eyed bean stew.

Energy 420Kcal/1772kJ; Protein 21.5g; Carbohydrate 58.4g, of which sugars 16.9g; Fat 12.9g, of which saturates 6.9g; Cholesterol 18mg; Calcium 165mg; Fibre 12.1g; Sodium 84mg.

KENYAN MUNG BEAN STEW

The local name for this vegetarian stew is dengu. It is a good example of how African cooks add variety and nutrition to a diet that depends largely on seasonal produce.

SERVES FOUR

INGREDIENTS
- 225g/8oz/1 ¼ cups mung beans, soaked overnight
- 25g/1oz/2 tbsp ghee or butter
- 2 garlic cloves, crushed
- 1 red onion, chopped
- 30ml/2 tbsp tomato purée (paste)
- ½ green (bell) pepper, seeded and cut into small cubes
- ½ red (bell) pepper, seeded and cut into small cubes
- 1 fresh green chilli, seeded and finely chopped
- 300ml/½ pint/1 ¼ cups water

1 Put the mung beans in a large pan, cover with water, bring to the boil and boil until the beans are very soft and the water has evaporated. Remove the pan from the heat and mash the beans with a fork or potato masher until smooth. Set aside.

2 Heat the ghee or butter in a separate pan, add the garlic and onion and fry for 4–5 minutes, until golden, then add the tomato purée and cook for a further 2–3 minutes, stirring all the time.

3 Stir in the mashed beans, then add the green and red peppers and chilli.

COOK'S TIP
Mung beans can be found in most Asian shops. If unavailable, use whole green lentils instead.

4 Add the water, stirring well to mix all the ingredients together.

5 Pour the mixture into a clean pan and simmer for about 10 minutes, then spoon into a serving dish and serve immediately.

Energy 224Kcal/944kJ; Protein 14.3g; Carbohydrate 30.2g, of which sugars 4g; Fat 6g, of which saturates 3.5g; Cholesterol 13mg; Calcium 64mg; Fibre 6.9g; Sodium 48mg.

SIDE DISHES AND SALADS

The concept of side dishes is not as clearly defined in the Middle East and Africa as it is in Europe and America. Although a vegetable such fresh green beans might be served solo, with just a simple oil and lemon juice dressing, it is far more common to find composite vegetable dishes. Rice is served at many meals, either plain or with extra ingredients, as in the Persian pilaff or West African Joloff. Breads, especially of the flatbread variety such as chapati, are present at almost every meal, while salads are intriguing, often introducing elements that are relatively unknown outside the country of origin.

CHELO WITH TAHDIG

In Iran, steamed rice – chelo – is served almost every day. The traditional method involves soaking the rice, then steaming it very slowly, so it becomes soft and fluffy, and a crisp golden rice crust or "tahdiq" forms on the bottom of the pan.

SERVES FOUR

INGREDIENTS
- 350g/12oz/1¾ cups long grain rice
- 5ml/1 tsp salt
- 45ml/3 tbsp melted butter
- 2–3 saffron threads, soaked in 15ml/1 tbsp boiling water (optional)

1 Soak the rice in lukewarm water, salted with 15ml/1 tbsp salt for a minimum of 2 hours.

2 When the rice has soaked, and you are ready to cook, fill a non-stick pan with fresh water, add a little salt and bring to the boil.

3 Drain the rice and stir it into the boiling water. Boil for 5 minutes, then reduce the heat and simmer for about 10 minutes, until the rice is almost cooked. Drain the rice and rinse in lukewarm water. Wash and dry the pan.

4 Heat 30ml/2 tbsp of the melted butter in the pan. Make sure it does not burn. Add about 15ml/1 tbsp water and stir in the rice. Cook the rice over a very low heat for 10 minutes, and then pour over the remaining butter.

5 Cover the pan with a clean dishtowel and secure with a tightly fitting lid, lift the corners of the cloth over the lid.

6 Steam the rice for 30–40 minutes. The cloth will absorb the excess steam and the bottom of the rice will turn into a crisp, golden crust called tahdiq. This is regarded by many as the best part of the rice. To serve, if you like, mix 30–45ml/2–3 tbsp of the rice with the saffron water and sprinkle over the top of the rice.

PLAIN PERSIAN RICE

This is a quicker, easier method of cooking chelo. Don't skimp on the soaking time, though, as it softens the grains and improves the flavour of the finished dish.

SERVES FOUR

INGREDIENTS
- 750ml/1¼ pints/3 cups water
- 5ml/1 tsp salt
- 350g/12oz/1¾ cups basmati rice
- 40g/1½oz/3 tbsp butter

1 Place the water and salt in a pan and pour in the rice. Set aside to soak for at least 30 minutes and up to 2 hours.

2 Bring the water and rice to the boil, and then reduce the heat and simmer for 10–15 minutes, until the water is absorbed.

3 Add the butter to the rice, cover the pan with a tight-fitting lid and steam over a very low heat for about 30 minutes. Serve with Khoresh, or any other meat dish.

TOP Energy 398Kcal/1659kJ; Protein 6.6g; Carbohydrate 69.9g, of which sugars 0.1g; Fat 9.7g, of which saturates 5.9g; Cholesterol 24mg; Calcium 19mg; Fibre 0g; Sodium 552mg.
BOTTOM Energy 389Kcal/1620kJ; Protein 6.5g; Carbohydrate 69.9g, of which sugars 0.1g; Fat 8.7g, of which saturates 5.2g; Cholesterol 21mg; Calcium 19mg; Fibre 0g; Sodium 552mg.

Bulgur and Pine Nut Pilaff

A variation on rice pilaff, this is particularly popular in Syria, Jordan and Turkey. The pine nuts accentuate the nutty flavour of the bulgur wheat.

SERVES FOUR

INGREDIENTS
- 30ml/2 tbsp olive oil
- 1 onion, chopped
- 1 garlic clove, crushed
- 5ml/1 tsp ground saffron or turmeric
- 2.5ml/½ tsp ground cinnamon
- 1 fresh green chilli, seeded and finely chopped
- 600ml/1 pint/2½ cups vegetable stock
- 150ml/¼ pint/⅔ cup white wine
- 225g/8oz/1⅓ cups bulgur wheat
- 15g/½oz/1 tbsp butter or margarine
- 30–45ml/2–3 tbsp pine nuts
- 30ml/2 tbsp chopped fresh parsley

1 Heat the oil in a pan and fry the onion, until soft. Add the garlic, saffron or turmeric, ground cinnamon and chopped chilli, and fry for a few seconds more.

2 Add the stock and wine, bring to the boil, then reduce the heat and simmer for 8 minutes.

3 Rinse the bulgur wheat under cold running water, drain and add to the stock mixture. Cover and simmer gently for about 15 minutes until the stock is absorbed.

4 Melt the butter or margarine in a separate small pan, add the pine nuts and fry for a few minutes, until golden. Add to the bulgur wheat with the chopped parsley and fork through.

5 Spoon into a warmed serving dish and serve with a vegetable stew.

VARIATION
You can replace the wine with water or stock, if you prefer.

Joloff Rice

Sometimes referred to as West African paella, this mixed rice dish is made using locally produced palm oil, which gives it a rich flavour and a reddish colour.

SERVES FOUR

INGREDIENTS
- 30ml/2 tbsp vegetable oil
- 1 large onion, chopped
- 2 garlic cloves, crushed
- 30ml/2 tbsp tomato purée (paste)
- 350g/12oz/1¾ cups long grain rice
- 1 fresh green chilli, seeded and chopped
- pinch of salt
- 600ml/1 pint/2½ cups vegetable or chicken stock

1 Heat the oil in a pan and fry the onion and garlic for 4–5 minutes, until soft. Add the tomato purée and fry over a medium heat for about 3 minutes, stirring all the time.

2 Rinse the rice in cold water, drain well and add to the pan with the chilli and a pinch of salt. Cook for 2–3 minutes, stirring all the time to prevent the rice sticking to the base of the pan.

3 Add the stock, bring to the boil, then cover and simmer over a low heat for about 15 minutes.

4 When the liquid is nearly absorbed, cover the rice with a piece of foil, cover the pan and steam, over a low heat, until the rice is cooked. Serve immediately.

TOP Energy 295Kcal/1225kJ; Protein 4.8g; Carbohydrate 32.4g, of which sugars 2.7g; Fat 14.4g, of which saturates 3.1g; Cholesterol 8mg; Calcium 25mg; Fibre 0.7g; Sodium 26mg.
BOTTOM Energy 392Kcal/1637kJ; Protein 7.8g; Carbohydrate 75.7g, of which sugars 4.5g; Fat 6.1g, of which saturates 0.7g; Cholesterol 0mg; Calcium 36mg; Fibre 1.1g; Sodium 20mg.

GARI FOTO

THE NAME SUGGESTS THIS DISH MIGHT INSPIRE GUESTS TO GET OUT THEIR CAMERAS. IT IS A WEST AFRICAN SPECIALITY, THICKENED WITH A COARSE GROUND FLOUR MADE FROM GROUND CASSAVA ROOT.

SERVES FOUR

INGREDIENTS

- 25g/1oz/2 tbsp butter or margarine
- 1 onion, chopped
- 3 tomatoes, skinned and chopped
- 15ml/1 tbsp tomato purée (paste)
- 175g/6oz carrots, chopped
- 115g/4oz/⅔ cup corn
- 175g/6oz red (bell) peppers, seeded and chopped
- 300ml/½ pint/1¼ cups vegetable stock or water
- 1 fresh green chilli, seeded and chopped
- 115g/4oz gari

COOK'S TIP

Gari, used in many African recipes, is a coarse flour made from cassava.

1 Melt the butter or margarine in a non-stick pan and fry the onion and tomatoes until pulpy, stirring frequently.

2 Add the tomato purée and carrots and fry for a few minutes, then stir in the corn, red peppers, stock or water and chilli. Bring to the boil, and then cover and simmer for 5 minutes.

3 Slowly mix the gari into the sauce, stirring constantly, until it is well mixed with the vegetables.

4 Cover the pan and cook over a low heat for 5–8 minutes. Transfer the mixture to a serving dish and serve hot.

FUFU

EVERY AFRICAN COUNTRY HAS A VERSION OF THIS PORRIDGE-LIKE SIDE DISH, DESIGNED TO MOP UP THE LIQUID FROM A STEW. IN SOUTHERN AFRICA IT IS CALLED PUTU AND IS MADE WITH CORN MEAL. WEST AFRICANS PREFER TO USE GROUND RICE, SOMETIMES WITH SEMOLINA.

SERVES FOUR

INGREDIENTS

- 300ml/½ pint/1¼ cups milk
- 300ml/½ pint/1¼ cups water
- 25g/1oz/2 tbsp butter or margarine
- 2.5ml/½ tsp salt
- 15ml/1 tbsp chopped fresh parsley
- 275g/10oz/1½ cups ground rice

COOK'S TIP

Ground rice is creamy white and when cooked it has a slightly grainy texture. Although often used in sweet dishes, it is a tasty grain to serve with savoury dishes too. The addition of milk makes it creamier, but it can be replaced with water, if preferred.

1 Place the milk, water and butter or margarine and salt in a pan, bring to the boil and then turn the heat to low.

2 Add the chopped parsley. Then gradually add the ground rice, stirring vigorously with a wooden spoon to prevent the rice becoming lumpy.

3 Cover the pan and cook over a low heat for about 15 minutes, beating the mixture regularly every 2 minutes to prevent lumps forming.

4 To test if the rice is cooked, rub a pinch of the mixture between your fingers; if it feels smooth and fairly dry, it is ready; if not, continue cooking for a few more minutes and then test again. Serve hot.

TOP Energy 211Kcal/880kJ; Protein 4.6g; Carbohydrate 33.1g, of which sugars 10.9g; Fat 6.7g, of which saturates 3.4g; Cholesterol 13mg; Calcium 32mg; Fibre 3.8g; Sodium 68mg.
BOTTOM Energy 319Kcal/1333kJ; Protein 7.1g; Carbohydrate 56.9g, of which sugars 3.6g; Fat 7.2g, of which saturates 4.1g; Cholesterol 18mg; Calcium 105mg; Fibre 0g; Sodium 316mg.

Tanzanian Vegetable Rice

Kernels of corn and small pieces of carrot and pepper make this a colourful accompaniment. It tastes great with grilled or baked chicken, and can also be used as a filling for baked fish. In Tanzania the rice is often served with a delicious fresh relish called kachumbali.

SERVES FOUR

INGREDIENTS

- 350g/12oz/1¾ cups basmati rice
- 45ml/3 tbsp vegetable oil
- 1 onion, chopped
- 2 garlic cloves, crushed
- 750ml/1¼ pints/3 cups vegetable stock or water
- 115g/4oz/⅔ cup corn
- ½ red or green (bell) pepper, chopped
- 1 large carrot, grated

1 Wash the rice in a sieve under cold running water, then leave to drain for about 15 minutes.

2 Heat the oil in a large pan and fry the onion for a few minutes over a medium heat, until just soft.

3 Add the rice and stir-fry for about 10 minutes, taking care to keep stirring all the time so that the rice doesn't stick to the pan.

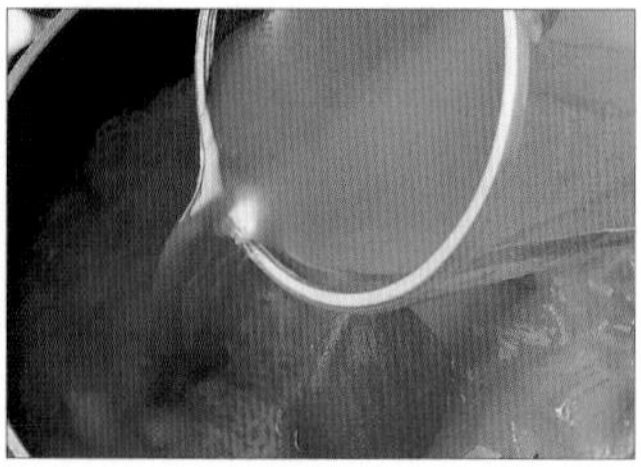

4 Add the garlic and the stock or water and stir well. Bring to the boil and cook over a high heat for 5 minutes, then reduce the heat, cover and cook the rice for 20 minutes.

5 Scatter the corn over the rice, then scatter the pepper on top and lastly sprinkle over the grated carrot.

6 Cover tightly and steam over a low heat until the rice is cooked, then mix the ingredients together with a fork and serve immediately.

Energy 455Kcal/1902kJ; Protein 8.3g; Carbohydrate 84.2g, of which sugars 8.5g; Fat 9.3g, of which saturates 1.1g; Cholesterol 0mg; Calcium 34mg; Fibre 1.9g; Sodium 84mg.

Zereshk Polo

The zereshk, or barberries, that flavour this dish are very small dried berries that are delicious with rice. They are available from most Persian and Middle Eastern food stores.

SERVES FOUR

INGREDIENTS
- 50g/2oz zereshk
- 45ml/3 tbsp melted butter
- 50g/2oz/⅓ cup raisins
- 30ml/2 tbsp granulated sugar
- 5ml/1 tsp ground cinnamon
- 5ml/1 tsp ground cumin
- 350g/12oz/1¾ cups basmati rice, soaked in salted water for 2 hours
- 2–3 saffron threads, soaked in 15ml/1 tbsp boiling water
- salt

1 Thoroughly wash the zereshk in cold water at least 4–5 times to rinse off any bits of grit.

2 Heat 15ml/1 tbsp of the butter in a small frying pan and stir-fry the raisins for 1–2 minutes.

3 Add the zereshk, stir-fry for a few seconds and then add the sugar, and half of the cinnamon and cumin. Cook briefly and then set aside.

4 Drain the rice and then boil it in a pan of salted water for 5 minutes, reduce the heat and simmer for 10 minutes, until almost cooked.

5 Drain and rinse the rice in lukewarm water, and wash and dry the pan. Heat half of the remaining butter in the pan, add 15ml/1 tbsp water and stir in half of the rice.

6 Sprinkle with half of the raisin and zereshk mixture and top with all but 45ml/3 tbsp of the rice. Sprinkle over the remaining raisin mixture.

7 Blend the reserved rice with the remaining cinnamon and cumin and sprinkle over the top of the rice mixture.

8 Dribble the remaining butter over and then cover the pan with a clean dishtowel and secure with a tightly fitting lid, lifting the corners of the cloth back over the lid. Steam the rice over a very low heat for about 30–40 minutes.

9 Just before serving, mix 45ml/3 tbsp of the rice with the saffron water. Spoon the rice on to a large, flat serving dish and sprinkle the saffron rice over the top to garnish.

Energy 465Kcal/1943kJ; Protein 7g; Carbohydrate 87g, of which sugars 17.2g; Fat 9.8g, of which saturates 5.9g; Cholesterol 24mg; Calcium 32mg; Fibre 0.6g; Sodium 77mg.

Shirin Polo

Also known as sweet rice, this colourful dish is traditionally served at Iranian wedding banquets. For a main course, chicken may be added to the rice mixture.

SERVES EIGHT TO TEN

INGREDIENTS
- 3 oranges
- 90ml/6 tbsp granulated sugar
- 45ml/3 tbsp melted butter
- 5–6 carrots, cut into julienne strips
- 50g/2oz/½ cup mixed chopped pistachios, almonds and pine nuts
- 675g/1½lb/3⅓ cups basmati rice, soaked in salted water for 2 hours
- 2–3 saffron threads, soaked in 15ml/1 tbsp boiling water
- salt

COOK'S TIP

Take care to cook this rice over a very low heat as it can burn easily owing to the added sugar and the natural sugar in the carrots.

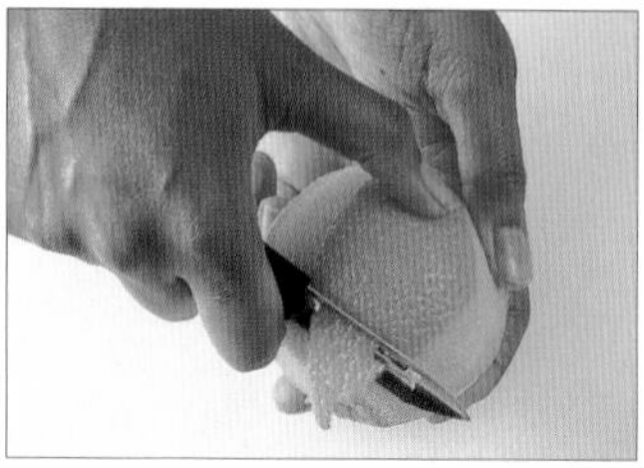

1 Cut the peel from the oranges in wide strips using a potato peeler, and cut the peel into thin shreds.

2 Place the strips of peel in a pan cover with water and bring to the boil. Simmer for a few minutes, and then drain and repeat this process, until you have removed the bitter flavour of the peel.

3 Place the peel back in the pan with 45ml/3 tbsp sugar and 60ml/4 tbsp water. Bring to the boil then simmer, until reduced by half. Set aside.

4 Heat 15ml/1 tbsp of the butter in a pan and fry the carrots for 2–3 minutes. Add the remaining sugar and 60ml/4 tbsp water and simmer for 10 minutes, until the liquid has almost evaporated.

5 Stir the carrots and half of the nuts into the orange peel and set aside. Drain the rice, boil it in a pan of salted water for 5 minutes, then reduce the heat and simmer very gently for 10 minutes, until almost cooked. Drain and rinse.

6 Heat 15ml/1 tbsp of the remaining butter in the pan and add 45ml/3 tbsp water. Fork a little of the rice into the pan and spoon on some of the orange mixture. Make layers until all the mixture has been used.

7 Cook gently for 10 minutes. Pour over the remaining butter and cover with a clean dishtowel. Secure the lid and steam for 30–45 minutes. Garnish with nuts, and drizzle over the saffron water.

Rice with Fresh Herbs

Coriander, chives and dill look pretty scattered among the rice grains in this popular Middle Eastern accompaniment. Serve it with a highly spiced main course.

SERVES FOUR

INGREDIENTS
- 350g/12oz/1¾ cups basmati rice, soaked in salted water for 2 hours
- 30ml/2 tbsp finely chopped fresh parsley
- 30ml/2 tbsp finely chopped fresh coriander (cilantro)
- 30ml/2 tbsp chopped fresh chives
- 15ml/1 tbsp chopped fresh dill
- 3–4 spring onions (scallions), finely chopped
- 60ml/4 tbsp butter
- 5ml/1 tsp ground cinnamon
- 2–3 saffron threads, soaked in 15ml/1 tbsp boiling water
- salt

1 Drain the rice, and then boil it in a pan of salted water for 5 minutes, reduce the heat and simmer for 10 minutes.

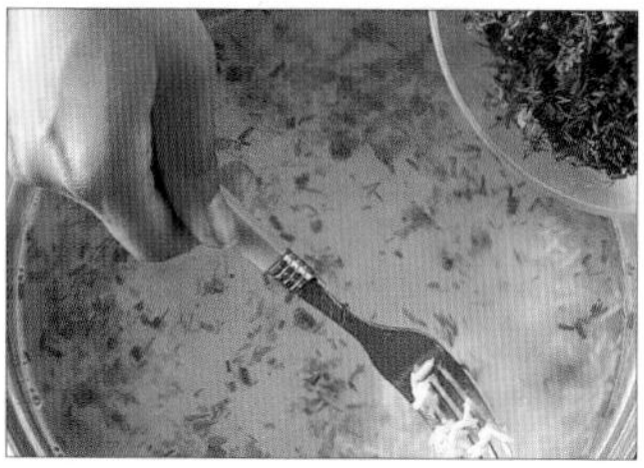

2 Stir in the chopped herbs and spring onions and mix well with a fork. Simmer for a few minutes more, then drain but do not rinse. Wash and dry the pan.

3 Heat half of the butter in the pan, add 15ml/1 tbsp water, then stir in the rice. Cook over a very low heat for 10 minutes, till almost cooked, then add the remaining butter, the cinnamon and saffron water and cover the pan with a clean towel. Secure a tight-fitting lid, and steam for 30–40 minutes. Serve.

TOP Energy 460Kcal/1924kJ; Protein 8.3g; Carbohydrate 87.2g, of which sugars 19.6g; Fat 8.7g, of which saturates 3.4g; Cholesterol 12mg; Calcium 66mg; Fibre 2.2g; Sodium 79mg.
BOTTOM Energy 435Kcal/1809kJ; Protein 7.3g; Carbohydrate 70.7g, of which sugars 0.8g; Fat 13.1g, of which saturates 7.8g; Cholesterol 32mg; Calcium 61mg; Fibre 1.1g; Sodium 98mg.

ETHIOPIAN COLLARD GREENS

ALSO KNOWN AS ABESHA GOMEN, THIS SPICY DISH CAN BE MADE WITH COLLARD GREENS, SPRING GREENS OR KALE. ETHIOPIANS SERVE IT ON A LARGE FLAT PANCAKE-LIKE BREAD CALLED INJERA.

SERVES FOUR

INGREDIENTS
- 450g/1lb collard greens
- 60ml/4 tbsp olive oil
- 2 small red onions, finely chopped
- 1 garlic clove, crushed
- 2.5ml/½ tsp grated fresh root ginger
- 2 fresh green chillies, seeded and sliced
- 150ml/¼ pint/⅔ cup vegetable stock or water
- 1 red (bell) pepper, seeded and sliced
- salt and ground black pepper

1 Wash the collard greens, then strip the leaves from the stalks and steam the leaves over a pan of boiling water for about 5 minutes, until slightly wilted.

2 Set the greens aside on a plate to cool, then place in a sieve or colander and press out the excess water.

3 Using a large sharp knife, slice the collard greens very thinly.

4 Heat the oil in a pan and fry the onions, until browned. Add the garlic and ginger and fry for a few minutes, then add the chillies and a little of the stock or water and cook for 2 minutes.

5 Add the collard greens, red pepper and the remaining stock or water. Season with salt and pepper, mix well, then cover and cook over a low heat for about 15 minutes. Serve immediately.

COOK'S TIPS

Traditionally this dish is cooked with more liquid and for longer. The cooking time has been reduced from 45 minutes to 15 minutes. However, if you fancy a more authentic taste, cook for longer and increase the amount of liquid. Green cabbage or spring greens are a good substitute for collard greens.

GREEN LENTIL SALAD

ANOTHER ETHIOPIAN SPECIALITY, THIS GREEN LENTIL AND TOMATO SALAD IS TRADITIONALLY FLAVOURED WITH SENAFITCH, WHICH IS A PEPPERY HERB FROM WHICH A TYPE OF MUSTARD IS MADE. THIS RECIPE USES ENGLISH MUSTARD INSTEAD.

SERVES FOUR

INGREDIENTS
- 225g/8oz/1 cup green lentils, rinsed
- 2 tomatoes, skinned and chopped
- 1 red onion, finely chopped
- 1 fresh green chilli, seeded and chopped
- 60ml/4 tbsp lemon juice
- 75ml/5 tbsp olive oil
- 2.5ml/½ tsp prepared mustard
- salt and ground black pepepr

1 Place the lentils in a pan, cover with water and bring to the boil. Simmer for 45 minutes until soft, drain, then turn into a bowl and mash lightly.

2 Add the tomatoes, onion, chilli, lemon juice, olive oil, mustard and seasoning. Mix well, adjust the seasoning if necessary, then cool and chill before serving as an accompaniment to meat or fish dishes.

TOP Energy 149Kcal/615kJ; Protein 4.1g; Carbohydrate 6g, of which sugars 4.8g; Fat 12.3g, of which saturates 1.7g; Cholesterol 0mg; Calcium 248mg; Fibre 4.3g; Sodium 24mg.
BOTTOM Energy 192Kcal/816kJ; Protein 14.2g; Carbohydrate 30.2g, of which sugars 3.1g; Fat 2.5g, of which saturates 0.4g; Cholesterol 0mg; Calcium 47mg; Fibre 5.7g; Sodium 12mg.

Sese Plantain and Yam

The word "sese" refers to the wrist action used in tossing the plantain and yam mixture with the oil. There's a definite trick to it, if you wish to avoid splashes. This recipe suggests stirring the ingredients together, which is more decorous and less dangerous.

SERVES FOUR

INGREDIENTS

- 2 green plantains
- 450g/1lb white yam
- 2 tomatoes, skinned and chopped
- 1 fresh red chilli, seeded and chopped
- 1 onion, chopped
- ½ vegetable stock (bouillon) cube
- 15ml/1 tbsp palm oil
- 15ml/1 tbsp tomato purée (paste)
- salt

1 Peel the plantains by cutting them in half, slitting the skin along the natural ridges, and then lifting off the skin in sections. Cut each of the plantain halves into three sections.

2 Prepare the yam, then place the plantains and yam in a large pan with 600ml/1 pint/2½ cups water, bring to the boil and cook for 5 minutes.

3 Add the tomatoes, chilli and onion and simmer for a further 10 minutes, then crumble in the stock cube, stir well, cover and simmer for 5 minutes.

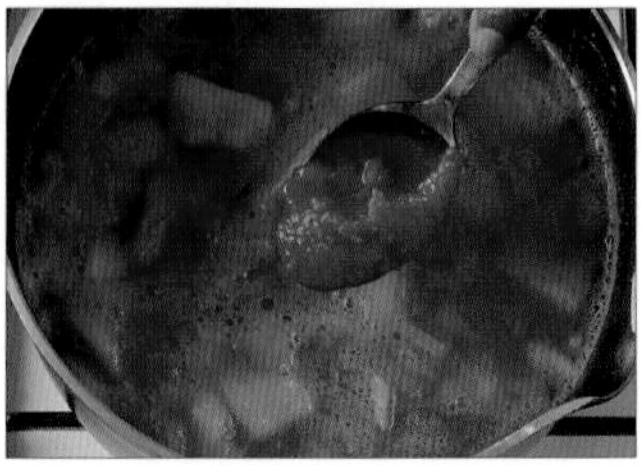

4 Stir in the oil and tomato purée and continue cooking for about 5 minutes, until the plantains are tender. Season with salt and pour into a warmed serving dish. Serve immediately.

Makande

This simple corn and red bean stew is the standard lunch for many Tanzanians, especially those who live in the Kilimanjaro region. When times are good, meat is added.

SERVES THREE TO FOUR

INGREDIENTS

- 225g/8oz/1¼ cups dried red kidney beans, soaked overnight
- 1 onion, chopped
- 2 garlic cloves, crushed
- 75g/3oz creamed coconut or 175ml/6fl oz/¾ cup coconut cream
- 225g/8oz/1⅓ cups frozen corn
- 300ml/½ pint/1¼ cups vegetable stock or water
- salt and ground black pepper

1 Drain the beans and place them in a pan, cover with water and boil rapidly for 15 minutes. Reduce the heat and continue boiling for 1 hour, until the beans are tender, adding more water, if necessary. Drain.

2 Place the beans in a clean pan with the onion, garlic, creamed coconut or coconut cream, corn and salt and pepper.

3 Add the stock or water, bring to the boil and simmer for 20 minutes, stirring occasionally to dissolve or combine the coconut.

4 Adjust the seasoning and spoon into a warmed serving dish. Serve with an onion and tomato salad.

TOP Energy 258Kcal/1097kJ; Protein 3.2g; Carbohydrate 57.1g, of which sugars 8g; Fat 3.5g, of which saturates 1.6g; Cholesterol 0mg; Calcium 32mg; Fibre 3.3g; Sodium 19mg.

BOTTOM Energy 465Kcal/1959kJ; Protein 20.5g; Carbohydrate 56.4g, of which sugars 11.9g; Fat 19.2g, of which saturates 15.1g; Cholesterol 0mg; Calcium 89mg; Fibre 13.1g; Sodium 224mg.

GHANAIAN PRAWN AND PLANTAIN SALAD

USUALLY SERVED AS A SIDE DISH, BUT SUBSTANTIAL ENOUGH FOR LUNCH, THIS FRESH-TASTING SALAD IS A COLOURFUL BLEND OF FRUITS, VEGETABLES, HARD-BOILED EGGS AND FISH.

SERVES FOUR

INGREDIENTS

- 115g/4oz cooked, peeled prawns (shrimp)
- 1 garlic clove, crushed
- 7.5ml/1½ tsp vegetable oil
- 2 eggs
- 1 yellow plantain, halved
- 4 lettuce leaves
- 2 tomatoes
- 1 red (bell) pepper, seeded
- 1 avocado
- juice of 1 lemon
- 1 carrot
- 200g/7oz can tuna or sardines, in brine, drained and flaked
- 1 fresh green chilli, finely chopped
- 30ml/2 tbsp chopped spring onions (scallions)
- salt and ground black pepper

1 Put the prawns in a bowl, add the crushed garlic and a little seasoning. Heat the oil in a small pan, add the prawns and cook over a low heat for a few minutes. Transfer to a plate to cool.

2 Hard-boil the eggs, and then place them in cold water to cool. Shell the eggs and cut them into slices. Set aside.

3 Boil the plantain in a pan of water for 15 minutes, drain, cool, then peel and slice thickly. Set aside.

COOK'S TIP

To make a complete meal, serve this salad with a meat or fish dish. Vary the ingredients, use any canned fish and a mixture of interesting salad leaves.

4 Shred the lettuce and arrange on a large serving plate. Slice the tomatoes and red pepper, and peel, stone and slice the avocado, sprinkling it with a little lemon juice. Arrange the vegetables on the plate over the lettuce. Cut the carrot into matchstick-size pieces and arrange over the other vegetables.

5 Add the plantain, eggs, prawns and tuna or sardines. Sprinkle with the remaining lemon juice, scatter the chilli and spring onions on top and season with salt and pepper to taste. Serve as a lunch-time salad or as a delicious side dish.

Energy 234Kcal/985kJ; Protein 22.1g; Carbohydrate 18g, of which sugars 8.5g; Fat 8.7g, of which saturates 2.1g; Cholesterol 177mg; Calcium 69mg; Fibre 3.3g; Sodium 265mg.

Plantain and Green Banana Salad

The plantains and bananas can be cooked in their skins. If this is done, they will not only retain their soft texture, but will also absorb the dressing more readily.

SERVES FOUR

INGREDIENTS

- 2 firm yellow plantains
- 3 green bananas
- 1 garlic clove, crushed
- 1 red onion
- 15–30ml/1–2 tbsp chopped fresh coriander (cilantro)
- 45ml/3 tbsp sunflower oil
- 25ml/1½ tbsp malt vinegar
- salt and coarse grain black pepper

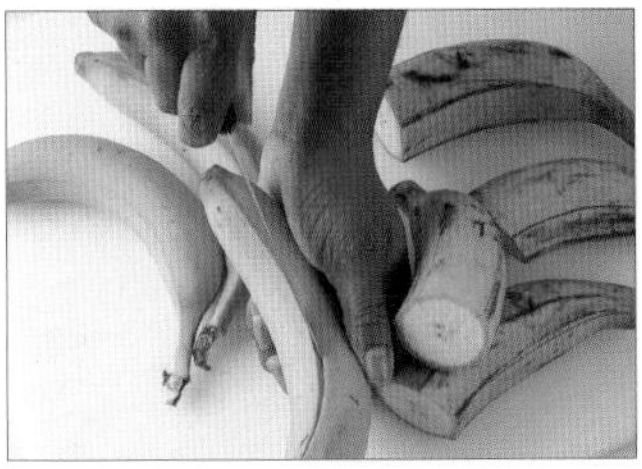

1 Slit the plantains and bananas lengthways along their natural ridges, then cut them in half and place in a large pan.

2 Cover the plantains and bananas with water, add a little salt and bring to the boil. Boil gently for 20 minutes, until tender, then remove the plantains and bananas from the water.

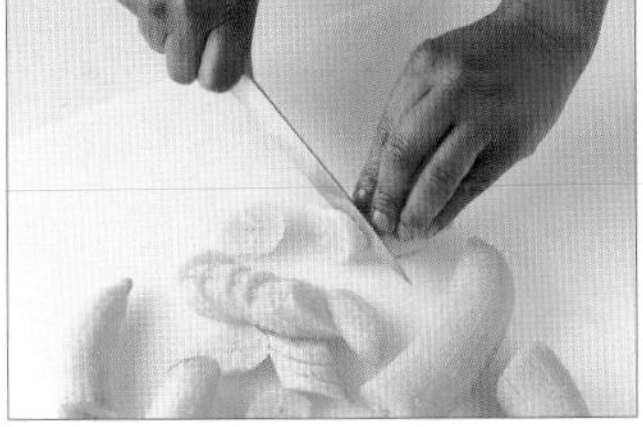

3 When the plantains and bananas are cool enough to handle, peel and cut them into medium-size slices.

4 Put the plantain and banana slices into a bowl and add the garlic, tossing gently to mix.

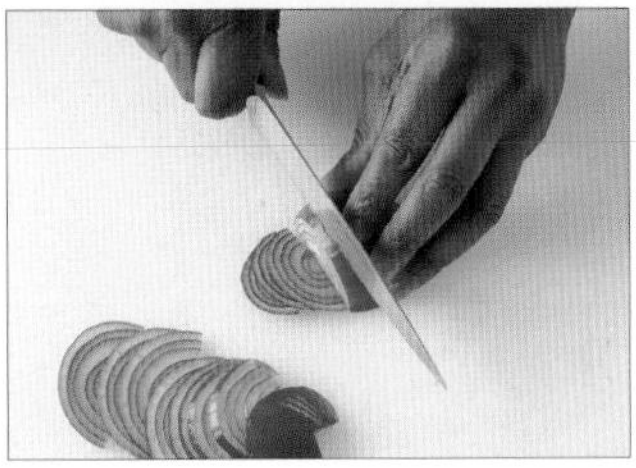

5 Halve the onion and slice it thinly. Add to the bowl with the chopped coriander, oil, vinegar and seasoning. Toss together to mix, then serve as an accompaniment to a main dish.

Energy 256Kcal/1078kJ; Protein 2.3g; Carbohydrate 44.5g, of which sugars 21.7g; Fat 8.9g, of which saturates 1.2g; Cholesterol 0mg; Calcium 31mg; Fibre 2.6g; Sodium 7mg.

BROAD BEAN SALAD AND CARROT SALAD

These two salads are frequently served together. The flavours are complementary, and the intense green of the shelled broad beans provides a perfect contrast to the orange of the carrots. These particular recipes come from Morocco, as is indicated by the preserved lemon in the bean mixture.

SERVES FOUR

INGREDIENTS

For the broad bean salad

- 2kg/4½lb broad (fava) beans
- 60–75ml/4–5 tbsp olive oil
- juice of ½ lemon
- 2 garlic cloves, finely chopped
- 5ml/1 tsp ground cumin
- 10ml/2 tsp paprika
- small bunch of coriander (cilantro),
- 1 preserved lemon, chopped
- salt and ground black pepper
- handful of black olives, to garnish

For the carrot salad

- 450g/1lb carrots, cut into sticks
- 30–45ml/2–3 tbsp olive oil
- juice of 1 lemon
- 2–3 garlic cloves, crushed
- 10ml/2 tsp granulated sugar
- 5–10ml/1–2 tsp cumin seeds, roasted
- 5ml/1 tsp ground cinnamon
- 5ml/1 tsp paprika
- small bunch of coriander (cilantro)
- small bunch of mint

1 To make the broad bean salad, bring a large pan of salted water to the boil. Meanwhile, pod the beans. Put the beans in the pan and boil for about 2 minutes, then drain and refresh the beans under cold running water. Drain. Slip off and discard the thick outer skin.

2 Put the beans in a heavy pan and add the olive oil, lemon juice, garlic, cumin and paprika. Cook the beans gently over a low heat for about 10 minutes, then season to taste with salt and pepper and leave to cool in the pan.

3 Tip the beans into a serving bowl, scraping all the juices from the pan. Chop the coriander and add to the beans with the preserved lemon and garnish with the black olives.

COOK'S TIP

To roast cumin seeds, stir them in a heavy pan over a low heat, until they emit a warm, nutty aroma.

4 To make the carrot salad, steam the carrots over a pan of boiling water for about 15 minutes, until tender. While they are still warm, toss the carrots in a serving bowl with the olive oil, lemon juice, garlic and sugar. Season to taste, then add the cumin seeds, cinnamon and paprika.

5 Finally, chop the coriander and mint, and toss with the carrots. Serve warm or at room temperature.

Energy 299Kcal/1247kJ; Protein 11.1g; Carbohydrate 25.1g, of which sugars 11.4g; Fat 17.8g, of which saturates 2.6g; Cholesterol 0mg; Calcium 136mg; Fibre 11.8g; Sodium 44mg.

ZAHLOUK AND PALE COURGETTE AND CAULIFLOWER SALAD

In Morocco, where these recipes originated, cooks like to use argan oil for special dressings. This rare oil has a reddish tinge and a rich, nutty flavour.

SERVES FOUR

INGREDIENTS

For the zahlouk

- 3 large aubergines (eggplant)
- 3–4 large tomatoes
- 5ml/1 tsp granulated sugar
- 3–4 garlic cloves, crushed
- 60ml/4 tbsp olive oil or argan oil
- juice of 1 lemon
- scant 5ml/1 tsp harissa
- 5ml/1 tsp cumin seeds, roasted and ground
- small bunch of fresh flat leaf parsley
- salt

For the courgette and cauliflower salad

- 60ml/4 tbsp olive oil
- 2–3 small courgettes (zucchini),
- 1 cauliflower, broken into florets
- juice of 1 lemon
- 2–3 garlic cloves, crushed
- small bunch of parsley
- salt and ground black pepper
- 5ml/1 tsp paprika, to garnish

1 To make the zahlouk, peel and cube the aubergines and boil in a pan of plenty of salted water for about 15 minutes, until they are very soft. Drain and squeeze out the excess water, then chop and mash them with a fork.

2 Skin and chop the tomatoes. Put the pulped tomatoes in a pan, stir in the sugar, and cook over a gentle heat, until they are reduced to a thick sauce.

3 Add the mashed aubergines. Stir in the garlic, olive or argan oil, lemon juice, harissa and ground cumin. Chop the parsley and add to the aubergine mix, stir until well mixed. Season with salt to taste.

4 To make the courgette and cauliflower salad, thickly slice the courgettes, then heat about half of the olive oil in a heavy pan and brown the courgettes on both sides. Drain on kitchen paper.

5 Meanwhile, steam the cauliflower over a pan of boiling water for 7–10 minutes, until tender. While the cauliflower is still warm, mash it lightly in a bowl and mix in the remaining olive oil, half the lemon juice and the garlic. Add the courgettes. Finely chop the parsley, and add to the salad together with the remaining lemon juice. Season with salt and pepper.

6 Serve the zahlouk at room temperature with plenty of flat bread. Serve the courgette and cauliflower salad sprinkled with paprika.

Energy 302Kcal/1251kJ; Protein 8.3g; Carbohydrate 12.5g, of which sugars 11.5g; Fat 24.7g, of which saturates 3.7g; Cholesterol 0mg; Calcium 139mg; Fibre 8.6g; Sodium 37mg.

KACHUMBALI

THIS RELISH COMES FROM TANZANIA, WHERE IT IS OFTEN SERVED WITH GRILLED MEAT OR FISH. TANZANIA IS ONE OF THE WORLD'S LEADING CHILLI GROWERS, AND THE VARIETY USED HERE SHOULD BE A HOT ONE FOR AN AUTHENTIC FLAVOUR. JALAPEÑO CHILLIES, WHICH ARE AVAILABLE FROM MOST SUPERMARKETS, WORK WELL IN THIS DISH.

SERVES FOUR TO SIX

INGREDIENTS
- 2 red onions
- 4 tomatoes
- 1 fresh green chilli
- ½ cucumber
- 1 carrot
- juice of 1 lemon
- salt and ground black pepper

VARIATION
This recipe can be made by very finely chopping the onions, tomatoes, cucumber and carrot. This produces a very moist, sauce-like mixture, which is good served inside pitta breads, and eaten as a salad roll.

1 Slice the onions and tomatoes very thinly and place in a bowl.

2 Peel and slice the cucumber and carrot and add to the onions and tomatoes. Slice the chilli lengthways, discard the seeds, and then chop the flesh very finely.

3 Squeeze the lemon juice over the salad. Season with salt and pepper and toss together to mix. Serve as an accompaniment, salad or relish.

COCONUT RELISH

FOR A COOLER, MORE REFRESHING RELISH, TRY THIS MIXTURE OF COCONUT AND LEMON JUICE. THE SMALL AMOUNT OF CHOPPED CHILLI IS JUST ENOUGH TO MAKE THE TASTEBUDS TINGLE.

MAKES ABOUT 50g/2oz

INGREDIENTS
- 50g/2oz fresh or desiccated (dry unsweetened shredded) coconut
- 1 fresh red chilli
- 10ml/2 tsp lemon juice
- 1.5ml/¼ tsp salt
- 10ml/2 tsp water

1 Grate the fresh coconut and place it in a mixing bowl. If using desiccated coconut, add just enough water to moisten it.

2 Cut the chilli in half and remove the seeds. Chop the flesh into fine slices and then chop the slices into tiny pieces. Use about a 1.5ml/¼ tsp, but more if you enjoy the heat.

3 Add the lemon juice, salt, water and chopped chilli to the coconut. Stir thoroughly to mix.

4 Serve the salad as a relish with cold meats or fish, or as an accompaniment to a main dish.

TOP Energy 50Kcal/211kJ; Protein 1.9g; Carbohydrate 10.1g, of which sugars 8.6g; Fat 0.5g, of which saturates 0.1g; Cholesterol 0mg; Calcium 36mg; Fibre 2.6g; Sodium 17mg.
BOTTOM Energy 303Kcal/1250kJ; Protein 2.9g; Carbohydrate 3.2g, of which sugars 3.2g; Fat 31g, of which saturates 26.7g; Cholesterol 0mg; Calcium 13mg; Fibre 6.8g; Sodium 44mg.

COCONUT CHAPATIS

UNUSUALLY, THE DOUGH FOR THESE CHAPATIS IS TWISTED INTO RINGS BEFORE BEING COOKED ON A GRIDDLE OR HEAVY PAN. COCONUT MILK GIVES THEM A LOVELY FLAVOUR.

MAKES NINE TO TEN

INGREDIENTS
- 450g/1lb/4 cups plain (all-purpose) flour
- 2.5ml/½ tsp salt
- 300ml/½ pint/1¼ cups coconut milk
- vegetable oil, for shallow frying

1 Place the flour and salt in a bowl and gradually stir in the coconut milk.

2 Bring the dough together with your hands, then turn it on to a floured surface and knead to form a firm but pliable dough, adding more flour if the dough is on the sticky side.

3 Divide the dough into nine equal-size balls, and roll out each of the balls on a lightly floured surface to form a 21cm/8½in round.

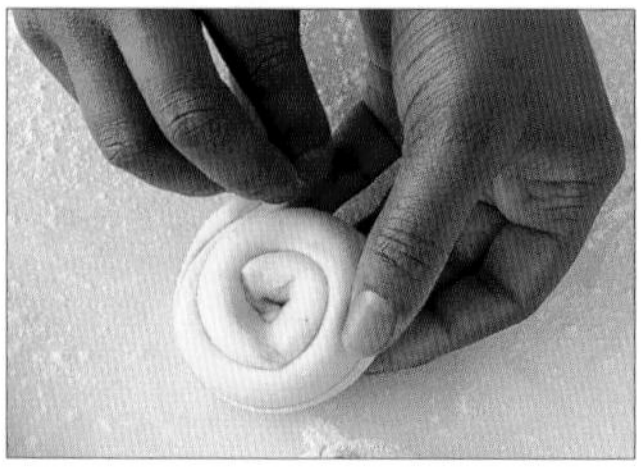

4 Brush the rounds with oil, roll up and twist into a ring, tucking the ends into the middle. Place on a floured board and set aside for 15 minutes.

5 Roll out each of the dough rings to a 5cm/2in round. Brush a heavy frying pan with oil and cook the chapatis for 3–4 minutes on each side, until golden brown. Serve hot as an accompaniment.

MANDAZI

THESE EAST AFRICAN BREADS RESEMBLE DOUGHNUTS. ALTHOUGH THERE ARE SWEETER VERSIONS, THESE SPICY ROUNDS ARE REGARDED AS SAVOURY SNACKS, OR SERVED WITH SOUPS OR STEWS.

MAKES ABOUT FIFTEEN

INGREDIENTS
- 4 or 5 cardamom pods
- 450g/1lb/4 cups self-raising (self-rising) flour
- 45ml/3 tbsp caster (superfine) sugar
- 5ml/1 tsp baking powder
- 1 egg, beaten
- 30ml/2 tbsp vegetable oil, plus oil for deep-frying
- 225ml/7½fl oz/⅞ cup milk or water

1 Slightly crush each of the cardamom pods, shake out the seeds and discard the husks.

2 Grind the cardamom seeds in a small mortar and pestle, then place in a large bowl with the flour, sugar and baking powder. Stir well to mix.

3 Put the egg and oil in a small bowl and beat together, then add to the flour mixture. Mix with your fingers, gradually adding the milk or water to make a dough.

4 Lightly knead the dough until smooth and not sticky when a finger is pushed into it, adding more flour, if necessary. Leave in a warm place for 15 minutes, then roll out to about a 1cm/½in thickness. Cut into 6cm/2½in rounds.

5 Heat the oil in a heavy pan or deep-fryer and deep-fry the mandazis for 4–5 minutes, until golden brown, turning frequently in the oil. Serve.

TOP Energy 179Kcal/762kJ; Protein 4.8g; Carbohydrate 40.8g, of which sugars 2.7g; Fat 0.8g, of which saturates 0.2g; Cholesterol 0mg; Calcium 81mg; Fibre 1.5g; Sodium 44mg.
BOTTOM Energy 149Kcal/631kJ; Protein 3.1g; Carbohydrate 25.9g, of which sugars 3.5g; Fat 4.4g, of which saturates 0.6g; Cholesterol 13mg; Calcium 112mg; Fibre 0.9g; Sodium 152mg.

MOROCCAN BREAD

WARM THIS BREAD IN THE OVEN AND CUT IT INTO THICK SLICES TO SERVE WITH ANY CLASSIC MOROCCAN SAVOURY DISH. IT TASTES GOOD WITH A TAGINE, BUT IS EVEN BETTER WITH A STEW THAT HAS PLENTY OF LIQUID. USE IT TO MOP UP EVERY MORSEL OF SAUCE.

MAKES TWO LOAVES

INGREDIENTS

- 275g/10oz/2½ cups strong white bread flour
- 175g/6oz/1½ cups wholemeal (whole-wheat) flour
- 10ml/2 tsp salt
- about 250ml/8fl oz/1 cup warm milk and water mixed
- 10ml/2 tsp sesame seeds

For the yeast starter

- 150ml/¼ pint/⅔ cup warm milk and water mixed
- 5ml/1 tsp granulated sugar
- 10ml/2 tsp dried yeast

1 First prepare the yeast. Place the warm milk mixture in a small bowl or jug (pitcher), stir in the sugar and then sprinkle with the yeast. Stir, then set aside in a warm place for about 10 minutes, until the yeast is frothy.

2 In a large bowl, mix together the two flours and salt. Add the yeast mixture and enough warm milk and water to make a fairly soft dough. Knead into a ball and then knead on a floured surface for 10 minutes.

3 Divide the dough into two equal pieces and shape into flattened ball shapes. Place on floured baking trays and press down with your hand to make round breads about 13–15cm/5–6in in diameter.

4 Cover the breads with oiled clear film (plastic wrap) or a clean, damp cloth and set aside in a warm place for 1–1½ hours, until risen. The breads are ready to bake when the dough springs back if gently pressed with a finger.

5 Preheat the oven to 200°C/400°F/Gas 6. Sprinkle the loaves with the sesame seeds and bake in the oven for 12 minutes. Reduce the heat to 150°C/300°F/Gas 2 and continue baking for 20–30 minutes, until they are golden brown and sound hollow when tapped underneath. Serve warm.

Energy 770Kcal/3271kJ; Protein 25g; Carbohydrate 162.8g, of which sugars 3.9g; Fat 6.6g, of which saturates 1g; Cholesterol 0mg; Calcium 260mg; Fibre 12.6g; Sodium 1973mg.

Holiday Bread

Three types of seeds – pumpkin, sunflower and sesame – are used to flavour this tasty bread, which is traditionally made on special occasions such as birthdays, weddings or religious festivals. The loaves can be frozen, but should always be served warm.

MAKES TWO LOAVES

INGREDIENTS

- 350g/12oz/3 cups strong white bread flour
- 115g/4oz/1 cup cornmeal
- 10ml/2 tsp salt
- 150ml/¼ pint/⅔ cup warm milk and water mixed
- 25ml/1½ tbsp pumpkin seeds
- 25ml/1½ tbsp sunflower seeds
- 15ml/1 tbsp sesame seeds

For the yeast starter

- 150ml/¼ pint/⅔ cup warm water
- 5ml/1 tsp granulated sugar
- 10ml/2 tsp dried yeast

1 First prepare the yeast. Place the warm water in a small bowl, stir in the sugar and then sprinkle with the yeast. Stir once or twice, then set aside in a warm place for about 10 minutes until the yeast is frothy.

2 In a large bowl, mix together the flour, cornmeal and salt. Add the yeast mixture and enough of the warm milk and water mixture to make a fairly soft dough. Knead the dough into a ball and then knead it on a floured surface for about 5 minutes.

VARIATION

You can use poppy seeds instead of sesame seeds.

3 Add the seeds and knead them into the dough. Continue kneading for about 5–6 minutes, until the dough is firm and elastic.

4 Divide the dough into two equal pieces and shape into balls, flattening each one to make a frisbee shape. Place on floured baking trays and press down with your hand to make round breads about 13–15cm/5–6in in diameter.

5 Cover with oiled clear film (plastic wrap) or a damp cloth and set aside in a warm place for 1–1½ hours, until risen. The bread is ready to bake when it springs back if gently pressed with a finger.

6 Preheat the oven to 200°C/400°F/Gas 6 and bake the breads in the oven for 12 minutes. Reduce the oven temperature to 150°C/300°F/Gas 2 and continue baking for 20–30 minutes until the loaves sound hollow when tapped.

Energy 999Kcal/4211kJ; Protein 28.2g; Carbohydrate 182.7g, of which sugars 3.1g; Fat 20.4g, of which saturates 2.1g; Cholesterol 0mg; Calcium 325mg; Fibre 8.8g; Sodium 1973mg.

Pastries and Desserts

Some of the world's most sumptuous sweet treats are to be found in Middle Eastern pastry shops. Filled with fruit or nuts, then fashioned into elaborate shapes, the pastries emerge from the oven to be coated in syrup or honey. Such delights are not intended to be eaten every day. Family meals usually conclude, as they do in Africa, with fresh fruit. Sherbet is often served, or there may be a fragrant rice pudding. Super-sweet treats like halva and kodafa are saved for special occasions, and are eaten in small portions, with strong coffee or mint tea.

BAKLAVA

The filling for this famous Middle Eastern dessert can be walnuts, almonds or pistachios. This version celebrates the Persian New Year on March 21, the first day of spring.

MAKES ABOUT 38-40

INGREDIENTS
- 350g/12oz/3 cups ground pistachio nuts
- 150g/5oz/1¼ cups icing (confectioners') sugar
- 15ml/1 tbsp ground cardamom
- 150g/5oz/10 tbsp unsalted butter, melted
- 450g/1lb filo pastry

For the syrup
- 450g/1lb/2¼ cups granulated sugar
- 300ml/½ pint/1¼ cups water
- 30ml/2 tbsp rose water

COOK'S TIP
Use ground hazelnuts or almonds instead of pistachio nuts.

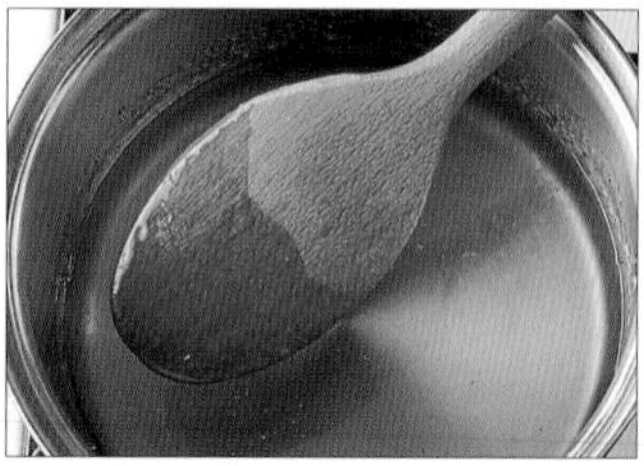

1 First make the syrup. Place the sugar and water in a pan, bring to the boil, then simmer for 10 minutes, until syrupy. Stir in the rose water and then leave to cool.

2 Mix together the nuts, icing sugar and cardamom. Preheat the oven to 160°C/325°F/Gas 3 and brush a large, rectangular baking tin (pan) with a little melted butter.

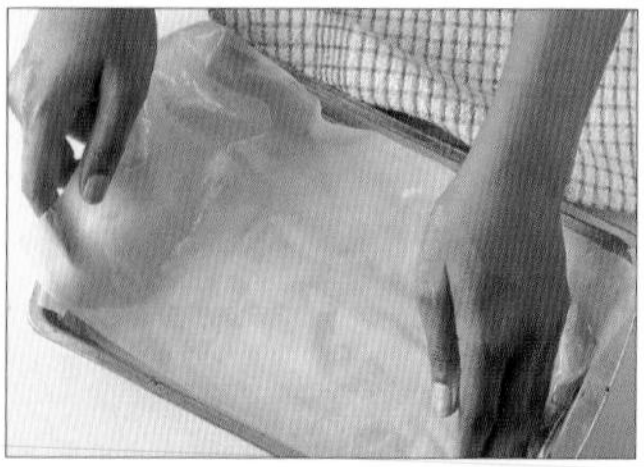

3 Taking one sheet of filo pastry at a time, and keeping the remainder covered with a damp cloth, brush the pastry sheet with melted butter and lay on the bottom of the tin. Continue until you have six buttered layers of pastry in the tin. Spread half of the nut mixture over the pastry, pressing it down with a spoon.

4 Take another six sheets of filo pastry, brush with butter and lay over the nut mixture. Sprinkle over the remaining nuts and top with a final layer of six filo sheets, brushed again with butter. Cut the pastry diagonally into small lozenge shapes using a sharp knife. Pour the remaining melted butter over the top.

5 Bake in the oven for 20 minutes, then increase the oven temperature to 200°C/400°F/Gas 6 and bake for a further 15 minutes, until golden and puffed.

6 Remove from the oven and drizzle about three quarters of the syrup over the pastry, reserving the remainder for serving. Arrange the baklava lozenges on a large glass dish and serve with extra syrup.

Energy 1016Kcal/4258kJ; Protein 13.4g; Carbohydrate 128.9g, of which sugars 108.4g; Fat 53.2g, of which saturates 17.4g; Cholesterol 53mg; Calcium 157mg; Fibre 4.3g; Sodium 468mg.

MA'AMOUL

JEWS EAT THESE DATE AND NUT BISCUITS AT PURIM, CHRISTIANS ENJOY THEM AT EASTER AND MUSLIMS SERVE THEM AT IFTAR, THE AFTER-SUNSET MEAL THAT BREAKS THE RAMADAN FAST. THEY ARE MADE IN SPECIAL WOODEN MOULDS, WHICH SEAL THE ROSE-SCENTED PASTRY AROUND THE FILLING.

MAKES THIRTY-FIVE TO FORTY

INGREDIENTS
- 450g/1lb/4 cups plain (all-purpose) flour
- 225g/8oz/1 cup unsalted butter, diced
- 45ml/3 tbsp rose water
- 60–75ml/4–5 tbsp milk
- icing (confectioners') sugar, for dusting

For the filling
- 225g/8oz/1⅓ cups dried dates, stoned (pitted) and chopped
- 175g/6oz/1 cup walnuts, finely chopped
- 115g/4oz/⅔ cup blanched almonds, chopped
- 50g/2oz/⅓ cup pistachio nuts, chopped
- 120ml/4fl oz/½ cup water
- 115g/4oz/⅔ cup granulated sugar
- 10ml/2 tsp ground cinnamon

1 Preheat the oven to 160°C/325°F/ Gas 3. First make the filling. Place the dates, walnuts, almonds, pistachio nuts, water, sugar and cinnamon in a small pan and cook over a low heat, until the dates are soft and the water has been absorbed. Set aside.

2 Place the flour in a bowl and add the butter, working it into the flour with your fingertips. Add the rose water and milk and knead the dough until soft.

3 Take walnut-size pieces of dough. Roll each one into a ball and hollow with your thumb. Pinch the sides.

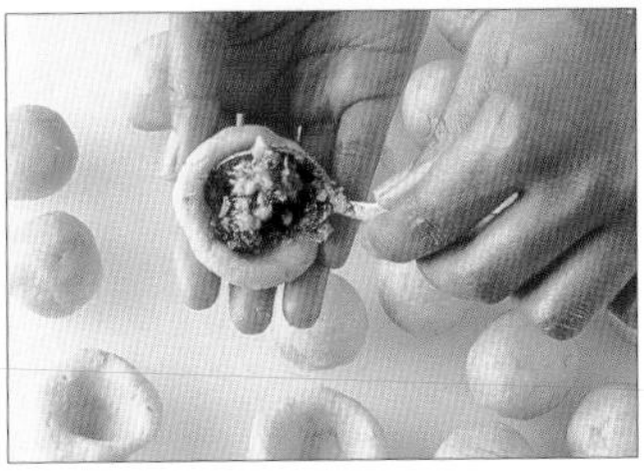

4 Place a spoonful of date mixture in the hollow then press the dough back over the filling to enclose it, press the edges together to seal.

5 Arrange the pastries on a large baking sheet. Press to flatten them slightly. Make little dents with a fork on the top of the pastries.

6 Bake in the oven for 20 minutes. Do not let them change colour or they will become hard. Cool slightly, and sprinkle with sifted icing sugar.

Energy 186Kcal/775kJ; Protein 3.2g; Carbohydrate 18.4g, of which sugars 8.4g; Fat 11.5g, of which saturates 3.9g; Cholesterol 14mg; Calcium 39mg; Fibre 1.2g; Sodium 49mg.

KAAB EL GHZAL

BETTER KNOWN BY THEIR FRENCH NAME OF CORNES DE GAZELLES – GAZELLE HORNS – THESE CURVED PASTRIES FILLED WITH ORANGE-SCENTED ALMOND PASTE ARE ONE OF MOROCCO'S FAVOURITE SWEET TREATS. THEY ARE TRADITIONALLY SERVED AT WEDDINGS.

MAKES ABOUT SIXTEEN

INGREDIENTS
- 200g/7oz/1¾ cups plain (all-purpose) flour
- 25g/1oz/2 tbsp butter, melted
- about 30ml/2 tbsp orange flower water or water
- 1 large egg yolk, beaten
- pinch of salt
- icing (confectioners') sugar, to serve

For the almond paste
- 200g/7oz/1 cups ground almonds
- 115g/4oz/1¾ cups icing (confectioners') sugar or caster (superfine) sugar
- 30ml/2 tbsp orange flower water
- 25g/1oz/2 tbsp butter, melted
- 2 egg yolks, beaten
- 2.5ml/½ tsp ground cinnamon

1 First make the almond paste. Mix together all the ingredients to make a smooth paste.

2 To make the pastry, mix the flour and a pinch of salt and then stir in the melted butter, orange flower water or water, and about three-quarters of the egg yolk. Stir in enough cold water, little by little, to make a fairly soft dough.

3 Knead the dough for about 10 minutes, until smooth and elastic, then place on a floured surface and roll out as thinly as possible. Cut the dough into long strips about 7.5cm/3in wide.

4 Preheat the oven to 180°C/350°F/Gas 4. Take small pieces of the almond paste and roll them between your hands into thin "sausages" about 7.5cm/3in long with tapering ends.

5 Place these in a line along one side of the strips of pastry, about 3cm/1¼in apart. Dampen the pastry edges with water and then fold the other half of the strip over the filling and press the edges together firmly to seal.

6 Using a pastry wheel, cut around each "sausage" (as you would with ravioli) to make a crescent shape. Make sure that the edges are firmly pinched together.

7 Prick the crescents with a fork or a needle and place on a buttered baking tray. Brush with the remaining beaten egg yolk and then bake in the oven for 12–16 minutes, until lightly coloured. Remove to a wire rack, cool and then dust with icing sugar. Serve warm or cold.

Energy 163Kcal/682kJ; Protein 4g; Carbohydrate 18.1g, of which sugars 8.2g; Fat 8.8g, of which saturates 1.5g; Cholesterol 16mg; Calcium 53mg; Fibre 1.3g; Sodium 13mg.

BRIOUATES WITH ALMONDS AND DATES

These Moroccan pastries, made with filo or the local equivalent – ouarka – are a favourite treat. Briouates can be savoury, but these are unashamedly sweet. The filling is a date and almond paste and they are coated in honey and orange flower water.

MAKES ABOUT THIRTY

INGREDIENTS
- 15ml/1 tbsp sunflower oil
- 225g/8oz/1⅓ cups blanched almonds
- 115g/4oz/⅔ cup stoned (pitted) dried dates
- 25g/1oz/2 tbsp butter, softened
- 5ml/1 tsp ground cinnamon
- 1.5ml/¼ tsp almond essence (extract)
- 40g/1½oz/⅓ cup icing (confectioners') sugar
- 30ml/2 tbsp orange flower water or rose water
- 10 sheets of filo pastry
- 50g/2oz/¼ cup butter, melted
- 120ml/4fl oz/½ cup clear honey
- dates, to serve (optional)

1 Heat the oil in a small pan and fry the almonds for a few minutes until golden, stirring all the time. Drain on kitchen paper to cool, then grind the almonds in a coffee or spice mill. Process the dates in a blender or food processor.

2 Spoon the ground almonds into a mixing bowl or into the blender or food processor with the dates, and blend with the softened butter, cinnamon, almond essence, icing sugar and a little flower water to taste. If the mixture feels stiff, work in extra flower water.

3 Preheat the oven to 180°C/350°F/Gas 4. Brush a sheet of filo pastry with melted butter and cut into three equal strips, keeping the remaining sheets covered with clear film (plastic wrap) to prevent them drying out.

4 Place a walnut-size piece of almond paste at the bottom of each strip. Fold one corner over the filling to make a triangle and then fold up, in triangles, to make a neat packet.

5 Brush the filo packet again with a little melted butter and set aside. Repeat steps 3 and 4 to make around 30 pastries.

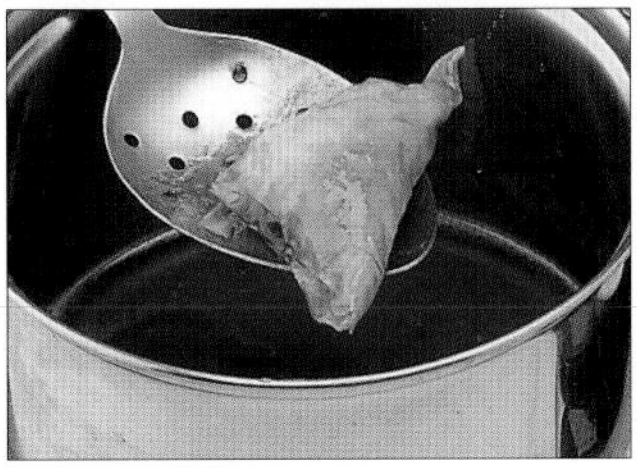

6 While the briouates are cooking, pour the honey and a little orange flower or rose water into a pan and heat very gently. When the pastries are cooked, lower them one by one into the pan and turn them in the honey so that they are thoroughly coated all over.

7 Transfer the briouates to a plate and cool a little before serving, with dates if you wish.

Energy 95Kcal/396kJ; Protein 1.8g; Carbohydrate 7.5g, of which sugars 6g; Fat 6.6g, of which saturates 1.7g; Cholesterol 5mg; Calcium 23mg; Fibre 0.7g; Sodium 17mg.

Ghoriba

Crisp on the outside, but meltingly soft in the middle, these Moroccan almond biscuits are a popular mid-morning snack with coffee or tea.

MAKES ABOUT THIRTY

INGREDIENTS
- 2 egg yolks
- 1 egg white
- 200g/7oz/1¾ cups icing (confectioners') sugar, plus extra for dusting
- 10ml/2 tsp baking powder
- finely grated rind of ½ lemon
- a few drops of vanilla essence (extract)
- about 350g/12oz/3 cups ground almonds
- sunflower oil, for greasing

VARIATION
Use ground hazelnuts instead of ground almonds.

1 Preheat the oven to 180°C/350°F/ Gas 4. In a bowl, beat together the egg yolks and egg white with the icing sugar. Add the baking powder, lemon rind and vanilla essence, with enough of the ground almonds to make a stiff paste. Knead the mixture together with your hands. Oil your hands with sunflower oil.

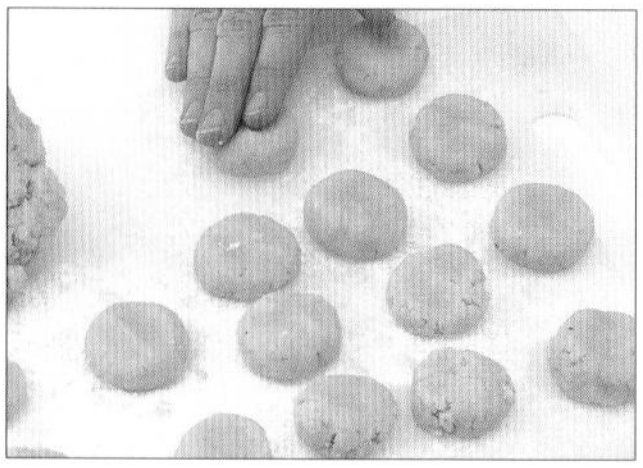

2 Take walnut-size pieces of paste and roll into small balls. Flatten on a board dusted with icing sugar and then place on a greased baking tray about 4cm/1½in apart. Bake for 15 minutes, until golden. Cool on a wire rack.

Honeycomb Pancakes

Like drop scones, these popular pancakes bubble when the batter is spooned into a pan, acquiring a honeycomb texture. Also known as beghrir, they are delicious with butter and honey and are traditionally eaten after sunset during Ramadan.

MAKES ABOUT TWELVE

INGREDIENTS
- 175g/6oz/1½ cups self-raising (self-rising) flour
- 10ml/2 tsp baking powder
- 30ml/2 tbsp caster (superfine) sugar
- 1 egg
- 175ml/6fl oz/¾ cup semi-skimmed (low-fat) milk
- 15ml/1 tbsp rose water or orange flower water
- 15ml/1 tbsp melted butter
- sunflower oil, for greasing

COOK'S TIP
Serve these pancakes warm and topped with a knob (pat) of butter on each one. For a breakfast treat, serve with melted butter and a generous helping of real maple syrup.

1 Mix together the flour, baking powder and sugar in a bowl. Add the egg and milk and blend to make a thick batter. Stir in the rose or orange flower water and then beat in the melted butter.

2 Heat a frying pan and brush the surface with a little oil. Pour in a small ladleful of batter, smoothing with the back of a spoon to make a round about 10cm/4in across. Cook for a few minutes until bubbles appear on the surface, then place on a large plate.

3 Cook the remaining pancakes in the same way and place them on the plate in overlapping circles to make a honeycomb pattern. Serve warm.

TOP Energy 102Kcal/426kJ; Protein 2.8g; Carbohydrate 7.8g, of which sugars 7.5g; Fat 6.9g, of which saturates 0.6g; Cholesterol 13mg; Calcium 33mg; Fibre 0.9g; Sodium 5mg.
BOTTOM Energy 82Kcal/346kJ; Protein 2.4g; Carbohydrate 14.6g, of which sugars 3.5g; Fat 1.9g, of which saturates 1g; Cholesterol 19mg; Calcium 42mg; Fibre 0.5g; Sodium 20mg.

Almond Fingers

This very simple Middle Eastern sweetmeat is also popular in Tunisia. The filo is rolled into cigar shapes, which are filled with a ground nut and rose water paste.

MAKES FORTY TO FIFTY

INGREDIENTS
- 200g/7oz/1¾ cups ground almonds
- 50g/2oz/½ cup ground pistachio nuts
- 50g/2oz/¼ cup granulated sugar
- 15ml/1 tbsp rose water
- 2.5ml/½ tsp ground cinnamon
- 12 sheets of filo pastry
- 115g/4oz/½ cup butter, melted
- icing (confectioners') sugar, to decorate

1 Preheat the oven to 160°C/325°F/Gas 3. Mix together the almonds, pistachio nuts, granulated sugar, rose water and cinnamon for the filling.

2 Cut each sheet of filo pastry into four rectangles. Work with one rectangle at a time, and cover the remaining rectangles with a damp dishtowel to prevent them from drying out.

3 Brush one of the rectangles of filo pastry with a little melted butter and then place a heaped teaspoon of the nut filling in the centre of the pastry.

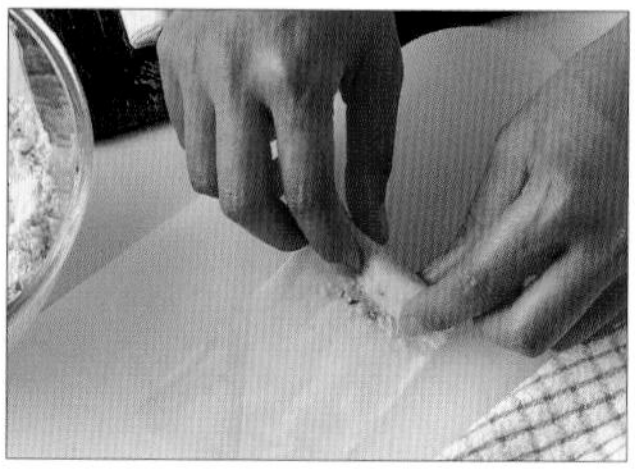

4 Fold in the sides and roll into a finger or cigar shape. Continue making "cigars" until all the filling and pastry have been used up.

5 Place the fingers on a buttered baking sheet and bake in the oven for 30 minutes, until lightly golden.

6 Transfer to a wire rack to cool and then dust with icing sugar.

Coconut Halva

In Egypt, this syrup-soaked sweetmeat is called basbousa. To achieve the most delicious stickiness, pour the cold syrup over the cake as soon as it comes out of the oven.

SERVES FOUR TO SIX

INGREDIENTS
- 115g/4oz/½ cup unsalted butter
- 175g/6oz/generous ¾ cup granulated sugar
- 50g/2oz/½ cup plain (all-purpose) flour
- 150g/5oz/scant 1 cup semolina
- 75g/3oz desiccated (dry unsweetened shredded) coconut
- 175ml/6fl oz/¾ cup milk
- 5ml/1 tsp baking powder
- 5ml/1 tsp vanilla essence (extract)
- whole almonds, to decorate

For the syrup
- 115g/4oz/⅔ cup caster (superfine) sugar
- 150ml/¼ pint/⅔ cup water
- 15ml/1 tbsp lemon juice

1 First make the syrup. Place the sugar, water and lemon juice in a pan, stir to mix and then bring to the boil and simmer for 6–8 minutes, until it thickens. Allow to cool and then chill.

2 Preheat the oven to 180°C/350°F/Gas 4. Melt the butter in a pan. Add the sugar, flour, semolina, coconut, milk, baking powder and vanilla essence and mix thoroughly.

3 Pour the cake mixture into a greased shallow baking tin (pan), level the surface and then bake in the oven for 30–35 minutes, until the top is golden.

4 Remove the halva from the oven and cut into diamond-shaped lozenges. Pour the cold syrup evenly over the top and decorate with a whole almond placed in the centre of each lozenge. Serve hot or cold.

TOP Energy 71Kcal/294kJ; Protein 1.5g; Carbohydrate 3.2g, of which sugars 1.6g; Fat 5.9g, of which saturates 1.8g; Cholesterol 6mg; Calcium 17mg; Fibre 0.5g; Sodium 25mg.
BOTTOM Energy 807Kcal/3391kJ; Protein 8.3g; Carbohydrate 118g, of which sugars 79.4g; Fat 36.9g, of which saturates 25.5g; Cholesterol 64mg; Calcium 125mg; Fibre 3.8g; Sodium 208mg.

Apricot Parcels with Honey Glaze

These parcels can be made with dried apricots that have been poached in syrup before being stuffed with the almond mixture, but fresh fruit is the better option. It has a juicy tartness that cuts through the sweetness of the honey. Roll the filo parcels into any shape, but leave them open so that fruit and pastry benefit from the glaze.

SERVES SIX

INGREDIENTS

- 200g/7oz/1¾ cups blanched almonds, ground
- 115g/4oz/⅔ cup granulated sugar
- 30–45ml/2–3 tbsp orange flower water or rose water
- 12 fresh apricots, slit and stoned (pitted)
- 3–4 sheets of filo pastry, cut into 12 circles or squares
- 30ml/2 tbsp clear honey

1 Preheat the oven to 180°C/350°F/Gas 4. Using your hands or a blender or food processor, bind the almonds, sugar and orange flower or rose water to a soft paste.

2 Take small walnut-size lumps of the paste and roll them into balls. Press a ball of paste into each slit apricot and gently squeeze the fruit closed.

3 Place a stuffed apricot on a piece of filo pastry, fold up the sides to secure the fruit and twist the ends to form an open boat. Repeat with the remaining apricots and filo pastry.

4 Place the filo parcels in a shallow ovenproof dish and drizzle the honey over them. Bake for 20–25 minutes, until the pastry is crisp and the fruit has browned on top.

5 Serve hot or cold with cream, crème fraîche, or a spoonful of yogurt.

Energy 347Kcal/1455kJ; Protein 9g; Carbohydrate 37.8g, of which sugars 27.4g; Fat 18.9g, of which saturates 1.5g; Cholesterol 0mg; Calcium 120mg; Fibre 4.2g; Sodium 8mg.

M'HANNCHA

THE SNAKE, OR M'HANNCHA TO USE THE ARABIC NAME, IS THE MOST FAMOUS SWEET DISH IN MOROCCO. THE COILED PASTRY LOOKS IMPRESSIVE AND TASTES SUPERB. CRISP, BUTTERY FILO IS FILLED WITH ALMOND PASTE THAT HAS BEEN SPICED WITH CINNAMON AND SCENTED WITH ORANGE FLOWER WATER. SERVE M'HANNCHA AS A DESSERT OR AS AN AFTERNOON TREAT WITH MINT TEA.

SERVES EIGHT TO TEN

INGREDIENTS
- 115g/4oz/⅔ cup blanched almonds
- 115g/4oz/½ cup butter, softened, plus 20g/¾oz for cooking nuts
- 300g/11oz/2⅔ cups ground almonds
- 50g/2oz/½ cup icing (confectioners') sugar
- 115g/4oz/⅔ cup caster (superfine) sugar
- 5–10ml/1–2 tsp ground cinnamon
- 15ml/1 tbsp orange flower water
- 3–4 sheets of filo pastry
- melted butter, for brushing
- 1 egg yolk
- icing (confectioner's sugar) and ground cinnamon for the topping

1 Fry the blanched almonds in a little butter until golden brown, then pound them using a pestle and mortar until they resemble coarse breadcrumbs.

2 Place the nuts in a bowl and add the ground almonds, icing sugar, caster sugar, softened butter, cinnamon and orange flower water. Use your hands to form the mixture into a smooth paste. Cover and chill for 30 minutes.

3 Preheat the oven to 180°C/350°F/ Gas 4. Grease a large, round baking tin (pan) or a wide baking sheet.

4 Open out the sheets of filo pastry, keeping them in a pile so they do not dry out, and brush the top one with a little melted butter.

5 Lift one of the filo rolls in both hands and push it together from both ends, like an accordion, to relax the pastry before coiling it in the centre of the tin or baking sheet. Do the same with the other rolls, placing them end to end to form a tight coil like a snake.

6 Take lumps of the almond paste and roll them into fingers. Place them end to end along the long edge of the top sheet of filo, then roll the filo up into a roll the thickness of your thumb, tucking in the ends to stop the filling oozing out.

7 Repeat this with the other sheets of filo, until all the filling is used up.

8 Mix the egg yolk with a little water and brush this over the pastry, then bake in the oven for 30–35 minutes, until crisp and lightly browned.

9 Top the freshly cooked pastry with a liberal sprinkling of icing sugar, and add lines of cinnamon like the spokes of a wheel. Serve at room temperature.

Energy 281Kcal/1168kJ; Protein 4.1g; Carbohydrate 21g, of which sugars 15.8g; Fat 20.6g, of which saturates 8.3g; Cholesterol 56mg; Calcium 56mg; Fibre 1.3g; Sodium 91mg.

EGYPTIAN BREAD AND BUTTER PUDDING

This pudding is rather oddly named, since it contains neither bread nor butter. What it has in common with the classic English dish is the custard, which is poured over layers of fine pastry or crackers. The local name is Omm'Ali, which means "mother of Ali".

SERVES FOUR

INGREDIENTS
- 10–12 sheets of filo pastry
- 600ml/1 pint/2½ cups milk
- 250ml/8fl oz/1 cup double (heavy) cream
- 1 egg, beaten
- 30ml/2 tbsp rose water
- 50g/2oz/½ cup each chopped pistachio nuts, almonds and hazelnuts
- 115g/4oz/¾ cup raisins
- 15ml/1 tbsp ground cinnamon
- single (light) cream, to serve

1 Preheat the oven to 160°C/325°F/Gas 3. Lay the filo pastry sheets on top of each other on a baking sheet and bake in the oven for 15–20 minutes until crisp. Remove from the oven and increase the heat to 200°C/400°F/Gas 6.

2 Scald the milk and cream by pouring them into a pan and heating very gently, until hot but not boiling. Slowly add the beaten egg and the rose water. Cook over a low heat, until it thickens, stirring all the time. Remove from the heat.

3 Crumble the pastry using your hands and then spread it in layers with the nuts and raisins in the base of a greased shallow baking dish.

4 Pour the custard mixture evenly over the nut and pastry base and then bake in the oven for 20 minutes, until golden. Sprinkle with cinnamon and serve with single cream.

Energy 575Kcal/2393kJ; Protein 10.1g; Carbohydrate 38.8g, of which sugars 28.9g; Fat 43.3g, of which saturates 23.4g; Cholesterol 95mg; Calcium 255mg; Fibre 1.7g; Sodium 162mg.

ORANGES IN SYRUP

BOTH BITTER AND SWEET ORANGES ARE EXTENSIVELY CULTIVATED IN THE MIDDLE EAST. OF THE SWEET VARIETIES, JAFFA, WHICH ORIGINATED IN ISRAEL, IS PROBABLY THE BEST KNOWN. THIS METHOD OF SERVING THEM, IN SYRUP SCENTED WITH ORANGE BLOSSOM OR ROSE, IS VERY POPULAR.

SERVES FOUR

INGREDIENTS
- 4 oranges
- 600ml/1 pint/2½ cups water
- 350g/12oz/1¾ cups granulated sugar
- 30ml/2 tbsp lemon juice
- 30ml/2 tbsp orange flower water or rose water
- 50g/2oz/½ cup chopped pistachio nuts, to decorate

1 Peel the oranges with a potato peeler down to the pith.

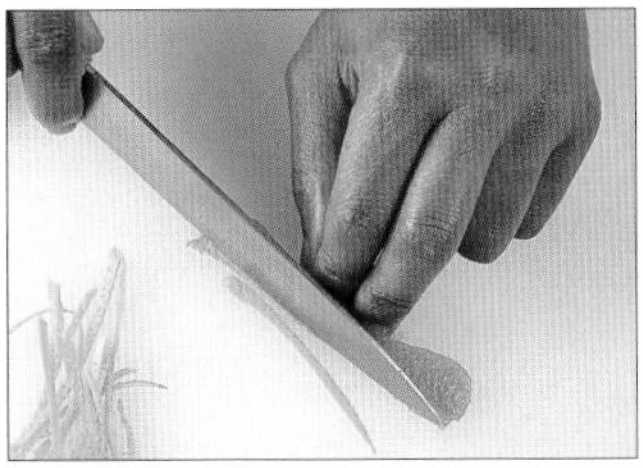

2 Cut the orange peel into fine strips and then boil in water, changing the water several times to remove the bitterness. Drain and set aside until required.

COOK'S TIP
A perfect dessert to serve after a heavy main course dish. Almonds could be substituted for the pistachio nuts, if you like.

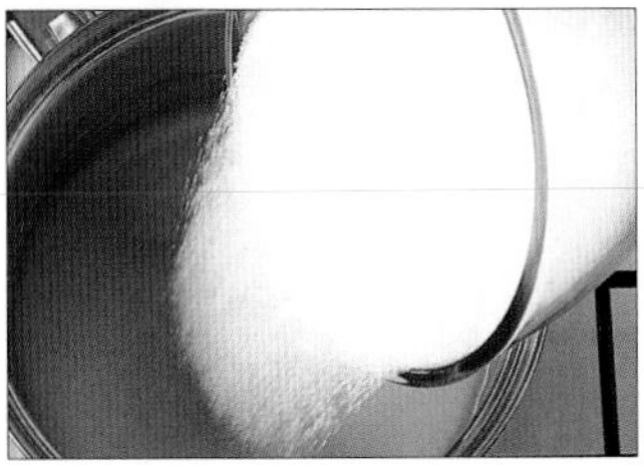

3 Place the water, sugar and lemon juice in a pan. Bring to the boil and add the orange peel. Simmer until the syrup thickens. Stir in the orange flower or rose water, and leave to cool.

4 Completely cut the pith away from the oranges and cut into thick slices. Place in a shallow serving dish and pour over the syrup. Chill for about 1–2 hours. Decorate with pistachio nuts and serve.

Energy 120Kcal/500kJ; Protein 3.6g; Carbohydrate 11.2g, of which sugars 10.9g; Fat 7.1g, of which saturates 0.9g; Cholesterol 0mg; Calcium 70mg; Fibre 2.8g; Sodium 72mg.

FIGS AND PEARS IN HONEY

FRESH FIGS PICKED STRAIGHT FROM THE TREE ARE SO DELICIOUS THAT IT SEEMS ALMOST SACRILEGE TO COOK THEM – UNLESS OF COURSE, YOU TRY THIS SUPERB METHOD.

SERVES FOUR

INGREDIENTS
- 1 lemon
- 90ml/6 tbsp clear honey
- 1 cinnamon stick
- 1 cardamom pod
- 350ml/12fl oz/1½ cups water
- 2 pears
- 8 fresh figs, halved

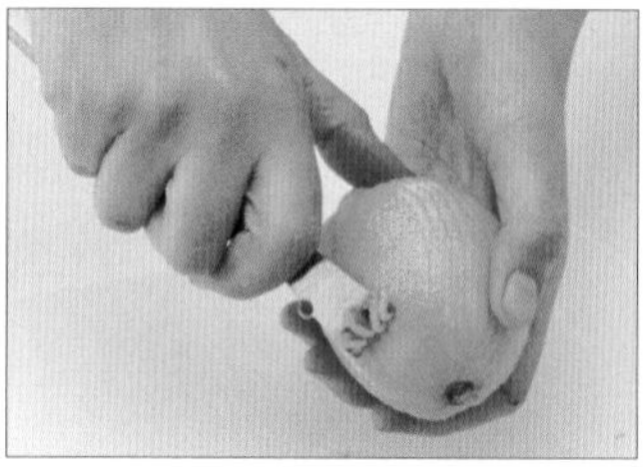

1 Pare the rind from the lemon using a zester or vegetable peeler and cut the rind into very thin strips.

2 Place the lemon rind, honey, cinnamon stick, cardamom pod and the water in a pan and boil, uncovered, for about 10 minutes, until the liquid is reduced by about half.

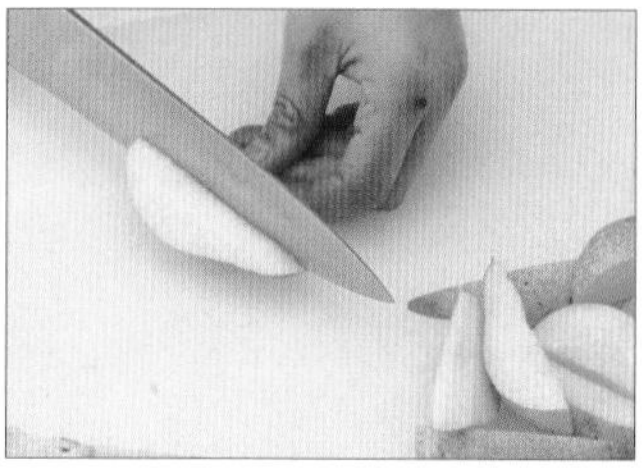

3 Cut the pears into eighths, discarding the core. Leave the peel on or discard, as preferred. Place in the syrup, add the figs and simmer for about 5 minutes, until the fruit is tender.

4 Transfer the fruit to a serving bowl with a slotted spoon. Cook the liquid until syrupy, discard the cinnamon stick and pour over the figs and pears. Serve.

MOROCCAN-STYLE PLUM PUDDING

THERE'S A STRONG FRENCH INFLUENCE IN MOROCCAN COOKING, AS EVIDENCED BY THIS NORTH AFRICAN VERSION OF THE BATTER PUDDING KNOWN AS CLAFOUTI. GROUND RICE AND FLAKED ALMONDS THICKEN THE MILK MIXTURE, WHICH IS FLAVOURED WITH ORANGE FLOWER WATER.

SERVES FOUR

INGREDIENTS
- 450g/1lb fresh plums or other fruit (see Variation)
- 600ml/1 pint/2½ cups skimmed or semi-skimmed (low-fat) milk
- 45ml/3 tbsp ground rice
- 30–45ml/2–3 tbsp caster (superfine) sugar
- 75g/3oz/¾ cup flaked almonds
- 30ml/2 tbsp orange flower water or rose water, to taste
- icing (confectioners') sugar, to decorate

1 Preheat the oven to 190°C/375°F/Gas 5. Stone (pit) and halve the plums. Bring the milk to the boil in a pan.

2 Blend the ground rice with 30–45ml/2–3 tbsp cold water, beating well to remove lumps. Pour the hot milk over the rice then pour back into the pan. Simmer over a low heat for 5 minutes, until it thickens, stirring all the time.

3 Add the caster sugar and flaked almonds and cook gently for a further 5 minutes. Stir in the orange flower or rose water and simmer for 2 minutes.

4 Butter a shallow ovenproof dish and pour in the almond milk mixture. Arrange the prepared fruit on top and then bake in the oven for about 25–30 minutes, until the fruit has softened. Dust with sifted icing sugar and serve.

VARIATION

Apricots, cherries or greengages, can also be used for this pudding.

TOP Energy 186Kcal/790kJ; Protein 1.8g; Carbohydrate 45.9g, of which sugars 45.9g; Fat 0.7g, of which saturates 0g; Cholesterol 0mg; Calcium 110mg; Fibre 4.7g; Sodium 30mg.

BOTTOM Energy 308Kcal/1291kJ; Protein 11g; Carbohydrate 38.1g, of which sugars 28.6g; Fat 13.2g, of which saturates 2.4g; Cholesterol 9mg; Calcium 246mg; Fibre 2.4g; Sodium 69mg.

MINTED POMEGRANATE YOGURT WITH GRAPEFRUIT SALAD

RUBY RED OR SALMON PINK, THE JEWEL-LIKE SEEDS OF THE POMEGRANATE MAKE ANY DESSERT LOOK BEAUTIFUL. HERE THEY ARE STIRRED INTO YOGURT TO MAKE A DELICATE SAUCE FOR A FRESH-TASTING GRAPEFRUIT SALAD. THE FLECKS OF GREEN ARE FINELY CHOPPED FRESH MINT, WHICH COMPLEMENT THE CITRUS FLAVOURS PERFECTLY. SERVE THE COMBINATION FOR BREAKFAST, AS A LIGHT SNACK DURING THE DAY, OR AS A DESSERT AFTER A SPICY MAIN COURSE.

SERVES THREE TO FOUR

INGREDIENTS
- 300ml/½ pint/1¼ cups Greek (US strained plain) yogurt
- 2–3 ripe pomegranates
- small bunch of fresh mint, finely chopped
- clear honey or caster (superfine) sugar, to taste (optional)

For the grapefruit salad
- 2 red grapefruits
- 2 pink grapefruits
- 1 white grapefruit
- 15–30ml/1–2 tbsp orange flower water

To decorate
- handful of pomegranate seeds
- fresh mint leaves

1 Put the yogurt in a bowl and beat well. Cut open the pomegranates and scoop out the seeds, removing and discarding all the bitter pith. Fold the pomegranate seeds and chopped mint into the yogurt. Sweeten with a little honey or sugar, if using, then chill until ready to serve.

2 Peel the red, pink and white grapefruits, cutting off and discarding all the pith. Cut between the membranes to remove the segments, holding the fruit over a bowl to catch the juices.

3 Discard the membranes and mix the fruit segments with the reserved juices. Sprinkle with the orange flower water and add a little honey or sugar, if using. Stir gently then decorate with a few pomegranate seeds.

4 Decorate the chilled yogurt with a sprinkling of pomegranate seeds and mint leaves, and serve with the grapefruit salad.

VARIATION

Alternatively, you can use a mixture of oranges and blood oranges, interspersed with thin segments of lemon. Lime segments work well with the grapefruit and mandarins or tangerines could be used too. As the idea is to create a refreshing, scented salad, juicy melons and kiwi fruit would also be ideal.

Energy 188Kcal/784kJ; Protein 8.8g; Carbohydrate 18g, of which sugars 18g; Fat 10.5g, of which saturates 5.2g; Cholesterol 0mg; Calcium 202mg; Fibre 3.6g; Sodium 82mg.

POACHED PEARS IN SCENTED HONEY SYRUP

Fruit has been poached in honey since ancient times. The Romans did it, as did the Persians, Arabs, Moors and Ottomans. The Moroccans continue the tradition today, adding a little orange rind or aniseed, or even lavender to give a subtle flavouring. Delicate and pretty to look at, these scented pears would provide an exquisite finishing touch to any Middle Eastern or North African meal.

SERVES FOUR

INGREDIENTS
- 45ml/3 tbsp clear honey
- juice of 1 lemon
- 250ml/8fl oz/1 cup water
- pinch of saffron threads
- 1 cinnamon stick
- 2–3 dried lavender heads
- 4 firm pears

VARIATION
Use whole, peeled nectarines or peaches instead of pears.

1 Heat the honey and lemon juice in a heavy pan that will hold the pears snugly. Stir over a gentle heat until the honey has dissolved. Add the water, saffron threads, cinnamon stick and flowers from 1–2 lavender heads. Bring the mixture to the boil, then reduce the heat and simmer for 5 minutes.

2 Peel the pears, leaving the stalks attached. Add the pears to the pan and simmer for 20 minutes, turning and basting at regular intervals, until they are tender. Leave the pears to cool in the syrup and serve at room temperature, decorated with a few lavender flowers.

Energy 66Kcal/278kJ; Protein 0.5g; Carbohydrate 16.5g, of which sugars 16.5g; Fat 0.2g, of which saturates 0g; Cholesterol 0mg; Calcium 17mg; Fibre 3.3g; Sodium 5mg.

BANANA AND MELON IN ORANGE VANILLA SAUCE

The Indian Ocean island of Madagascar is a major producer of vanilla, so it is not surprising to find the spice flavouring this dessert from neighbouring Mozambique.

SERVES FOUR

INGREDIENTS

- 300ml/½ pint/1¼ cups orange juice
- 1 vanilla pod (bean) or a few drops of vanilla essence (extract)
- 5ml/1 tsp finely grated orange rind
- 15ml/1 tbsp granulated sugar
- 4 bananas
- 1 honeydew melon
- 30ml/2 tbsp lemon juice

1 Place the orange juice in a small pan with the vanilla pod or vanilla essence, orange rind and sugar and bring gently to the boil.

2 Reduce the heat and simmer gently for 15 minutes, until the sauce is syrupy. Remove from the heat and leave to cool. Once cool, remove and discard the vanilla pod, if using.

3 Peel and roughly chop the bananas and peel, seed and roughly chop the melon. Place the chopped bananas and melon in a large serving bowl and toss with the lemon juice.

COOK'S TIPS

To check whether a melon is ripe, lightly press the area around the centre of the tip of the melon, the surface should give slightly. A ripe melon will also smell pleasantly sweet.

4 Pour the cooled sauce over the fruit and chill in the refrigerator for at least 1 hour before serving.

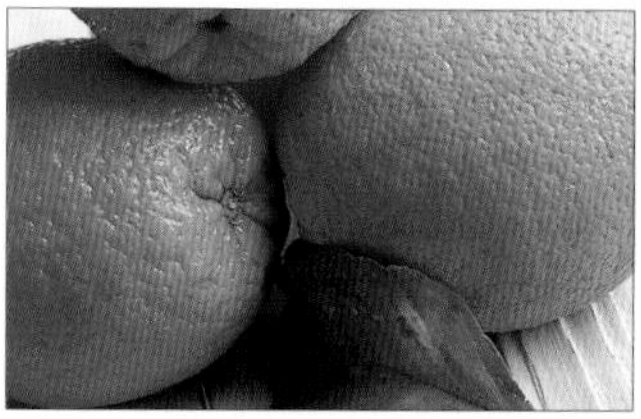

BANANA MANDAZI

Versions of this much-loved dessert – banana fritters – are found throughout Africa, from Kenya to KwaZulu-Natal, in Zaïre and in the west and north of the continent.

SERVES FOUR

INGREDIENTS

- 1 egg
- 2 ripe bananas, roughly chopped
- 150ml/¼ pint/⅔ cup milk
- 2.5ml/½ tsp vanilla essence (extract)
- 225g/8oz/2 cups self-raising (self-rising) flour
- 5ml/1 tsp baking powder
- 45ml/3 tbsp caster (superfine) sugar
- vegetable oil, for deep-frying

1 Place the egg, bananas, milk, vanilla essence, flour, baking powder and sugar in a blender or food processor.

2 Process to make a smooth batter. It should have a creamy dropping consistency. If it is too thick, add a little extra milk. Set aside for 10 minutes.

3 Heat the oil in a heavy pan or deep-fryer. When hot, carefully place spoonfuls of the mixture in the oil and deep-fry for 3–4 minutes, until golden. Remove with a slotted spoon and drain on kitchen paper. Keep warm while cooking the remaining mandazis, then serve at once.

TOP Energy 158Kcal/662kJ; Protein 2.3g; Carbohydrate 37.9g, of which sugars 35.6g; Fat 0.6g, of which saturates 0.1g; Cholesterol 0mg; Calcium 25mg; Fibre 1.9g; Sodium 48mg.

BOTTOM Energy 387Kcal/1637kJ; Protein 8.5g; Carbohydrate 67.7g, of which sugars 24.7g; Fat 11.1g, of which saturates 1.9g; Cholesterol 50mg; Calcium 258mg; Fibre 2.3g; Sodium 237mg.

CAFÉ GLACÉ

ICED COFFEE IS A POPULAR DRINK IN CAPE TOWN; A SWEET INDULGENCE ON THOSE LATE SPRING DAYS BEFORE THE HEAT OF HIGH SUMMER. THIS IS THE LUXURY VERSION.

SERVES FOUR TO SIX

INGREDIENTS
- 30–45ml/2–3 tbsp instant coffee granules or powder
- 15ml/1 tbsp granulated sugar
- 600ml/1 pint/2½ cups milk
- 475ml/16fl oz/2 cups water
- ice cubes and vanilla ice cream
- 4–6 chocolate flakes, to decorate
- 8–12 crisp ice cream biscuits (cookies) or wafers, to serve

COOK'S TIP
You'll need to provide straws and long spoons for eating this dessert. Adjust the amount of coffee and sugar to suit your taste.

1 Dissolve the coffee in 120ml/4fl oz/ ½ cup of boiling water in a small mixing bowl. Add the sugar and stir well until it dissolves. Chill in the refrigerator for at least 2 hours. Mix together the milk and water in a large jug (pitcher). Add the chilled coffee and stir to mix well.

2 Pour the coffee mixture into long glasses until they are three-quarters full. Add ice cubes and the ice cream to the top of each glass. Decorate with the chocolate flakes and serve with the ice cream biscuits.

SWEET PUDDING

WITH ITS DELICATE FLAVOUR AND SILKY SMOOTH TEXTURE, THIS MILK PUDDING WOULD MAKE THE PERFECT FINALE FOR A MIDDLE EASTERN MEAL. STREW THE PLATE WITH ROSE PETALS, IF YOU LIKE.

SERVES FOUR

INGREDIENTS
- 50g/2oz/⅓ cup ground rice
- 45ml/3 tbsp cornflour (cornstarch)
- 1.2 litres/2 pints/5 cups milk
- 75g/3oz/scant ½ cup granulated sugar
- 30ml/2 tbsp rose water
- 50g/2oz/½ cup ground almonds
- 25g/1oz/¼ cup ground pistachio nuts
- ground cinnamon, to decorate
- golden (light corn) syrup or clear honey, warmed, to serve

1 Blend the ground rice and cornflour to a paste with a little cold milk in a small bowl. Set aside.

2 Bring the remaining milk to the boil in a pan, then add the sugar and simmer gently. Gradually add the ground rice paste to the milk, stirring constantly with a wooden spoon to mix.

3 Simmer the mixture over a very gentle heat for 10–15 minutes, until the mixture has thickened, stirring frequently and being very careful not to burn the bottom of the pan, which would damage the very delicate flavour of the rice.

4 Stir in the rose water and half of the ground almonds and simmer for a further 5 minutes.

5 Cool for a few minutes and then pour the rice mixture into a serving bowl or individual dishes. Sprinkle with the remaining ground almonds and ground pistachio nuts and then decorate with a dusting of ground cinnamon. Serve with warmed syrup or honey.

TOP Energy 87Kcal/370kJ; Protein 5.8g; Carbohydrate 11.2g, of which sugars 11g; Fat 2.6g, of which saturates 1.6g; Cholesterol 9mg; Calcium 188mg; Fibre 0g; Sodium 68mg.

BOTTOM Energy 409Kcal/1724kJ; Protein 14.7g; Carbohydrate 55.6g, of which sugars 34.8g; Fat 15.6g, of which saturates 4.6g; Cholesterol 18mg; Calcium 395mg; Fibre 1.2g; Sodium 235mg.

TROPICAL FRUIT PANCAKES

IN THIS SOUTH AFRICAN DESSERT, PANCAKES ARE FILLED WITH A MIXTURE OF MANGOES, BANANAS, KIWI FRUIT AND ORANGES, MOISTENED WITH A HONEYED CITRUS SYRUP FLAVOURED WITH VAN DER HUM, THE LOCAL BRANDY-BASED TANGERINE LIQUEUR.

SERVES FOUR

INGREDIENTS

- 115g/4oz/1 cup self-raising (self-rising) flour
- pinch of freshly grated nutmeg
- 15ml/1 tbsp caster (superfine) sugar
- 1 egg
- 300ml/½ pint/1¼ cups milk
- 15ml/1 tbsp melted butter or margarine, plus extra for frying
- 15ml/1 tbsp fine desiccated (dry unsweetened shredded) coconut (optional)
- whipped fresh cream, to serve

For the filling

- 225g/8oz prepared ripe, firm mango
- 2 bananas
- 2 kiwi fruit
- 1 large orange
- 15ml/1 tbsp lemon juice
- 30ml/2 tbsp orange juice
- 15ml/1 tbsp clear honey
- 30–45ml/2–3 tbsp orange liqueur (optional)

1 Sift the flour, nutmeg and caster sugar into a large bowl, add the egg and most of the milk and beat with a wooden spoon to make a thick, smooth batter.

2 Add the remaining milk, melted butter or margarine, and the coconut, if using, and continue beating until the batter is smooth and of a fairly thin, dropping consistency.

3 Melt a little butter or margarine in a large non-stick frying pan.

4 Swirl the hot fat round the pan then pour in a little batter to cover the base. Fry until golden, then toss or turn with a spatula. Repeat with the remaining mixture to make about eight pancakes.

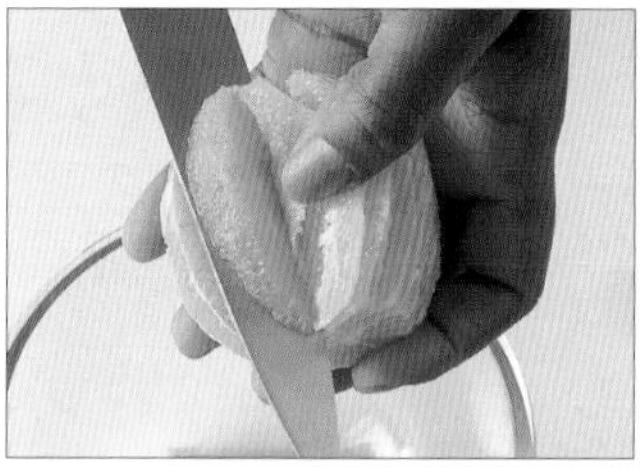

5 Dice the mango, roughly chop the bananas and slice the kiwi fruit. Cut away the peel and pith from the orange and cut into segments.

6 Place the fruit in a bowl. Mix together the lemon and orange juices, honey and orange liqueur, if using, then pour over the fruit. Fold a pancake in half and spoon a little of the fruit in the centre, Fold the corners over. Serve with whipped cream.

Energy 303Kcal/1285kJ; Protein 8.5g; Carbohydrate 56.5g, of which sugars 34g; Fat 6.5g, of which saturates 3.3g; Cholesterol 60mg; Calcium 239mg; Fibre 4.1g; Sodium 182mg.

SPICED NUTTY BANANAS

THIS BAKED BANANA DESSERT FROM CENTRAL AFRICA COULDN'T BE SIMPLER. THE NUTTY CRUST CONTRASTS BEAUTIFULLY WITH THE CREAMY BANANA BENEATH, AND THE RUM SAUCE IS DELICIOUS.

SERVES THREE

INGREDIENTS

- 6 ripe, but firm, bananas
- 30ml/2 tbsp chopped unsalted cashew nuts
- 30ml/2 tbsp chopped unsalted peanuts
- 30ml/2 tbsp desiccated (dry unsweetened shredded) coconut
- 7.5–15ml/½–1 tbsp demerara (raw) sugar
- 5ml/1 tsp ground cinnamon
- 2.5ml/½ tsp freshly grated nutmeg
- 150ml/¼ pint/⅔ cup orange juice
- 60ml/4 tbsp rum
- 15g/½oz/1 tbsp butter or margarine
- double (heavy) cream, to serve

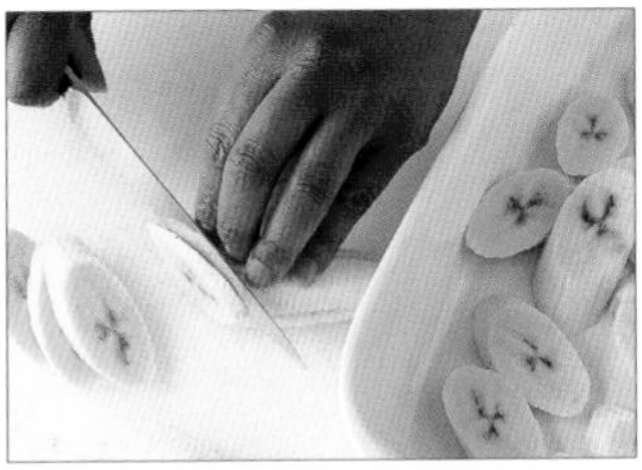

1 Preheat the oven to 200°C/400°F/ Gas 6. Slice the bananas and place them in a greased, shallow ovenproof dish.

2 Mix together the cashew nuts, peanuts, coconut, sugar, cinnamon and nutmeg in a small bowl.

3 Pour the orange juice and rum over the bananas, then sprinkle the nut and sugar mixture over the top.

4 Dot the top with butter or margarine, then bake in the oven for 15–20 minutes, until the bananas are golden and the sauce is bubbly. Serve with double cream.

COOK'S TIPS

Freshly grated nutmeg makes all the difference to this dish. More rum can be added, if preferred. Chopped mixed nuts can be used instead of peanuts.

Energy 455Kcal/1902kJ; Protein 7.7g; Carbohydrate 51.5g, of which sugars 45.3g; Fat 20.6g, of which saturates 10g; Cholesterol 11mg; Calcium 29mg; Fibre 4.4g; Sodium 69mg.

Papaya and Mango with Mango Cream

Make the most of mangoes when they are in season by mixing them with papayas and tossing them in an apricot sauce. A chilled mango cream is the perfect topping.

SERVES FOUR

INGREDIENTS
- 2 large ripe mangoes
- 300ml/½ pint/1¼ cups extra thick double (heavy) cream
- 8 ready-to-eat dried apricots, halved
- 150ml/¼ pint/⅔ cup orange juice or water
- 1 ripe papaya

1 Take one thick slice from one of the mangoes and, while still on the skin, slash the flesh with a sharp knife in a criss-cross pattern to make cubes.

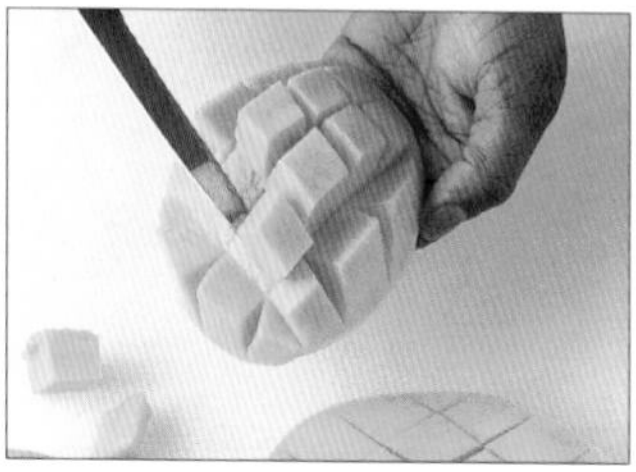

2 Turn the piece of mango inside-out and cut away the cubed flesh from the skin. Place the flesh in a bowl, mash with a fork to a pulp, then add the cream and mix together. Spoon into a freezer-proof container, cover and freeze for about 1–1½ hours, until half frozen.

3 Put the apricots and orange juice or water in a small pan. Bring to the boil, then simmer gently until the apricots are soft, adding a little juice or water, if necessary, to keep moist. Remove the pan from the heat and set aside to cool.

4 Peel, stone (pit) and chop or dice the remaining mango as before and place in a bowl. Cut the papaya in half, remove and discard the seeds and peel. Dice the flesh and add to the mango.

5 Pour the apricot sauce over the fruit and gently toss together so the fruit is well coated.

6 Stir the semi-frozen mango cream a few times until it is spoonable but not soft. Serve the fruit topped with the mango cream.

COOK'S TIP

Mangoes vary tremendously in size. If you can only find small ones, buy three instead of two to use in this dessert.

Energy 462Kcal/1914kJ; Protein 2.6g; Carbohydrate 23g, of which sugars 22.8g; Fat 40.6g, of which saturates 25.1g; Cholesterol 103mg; Calcium 67mg; Fibre 3.6g; Sodium 26mg.

FRESH PINEAPPLE WITH COCONUT

IN THOSE PARTS OF AFRICA WHERE PINEAPPLES ARE GROWN, THE FRUIT AND THE FRESHLY PRESSED JUICE ARE SOLD AT ROADSIDE STALLS. THIS RECIPE CELEBRATES THE FRUIT'S FANTASTIC FLAVOUR.

SERVES FOUR

INGREDIENTS

- 1 fresh pineapple, peeled
- slivers of fresh coconut
- 300ml/½ pint/1¼ cups pineapple juice
- 60ml/4 tbsp coconut liqueur
- 2.5cm/1in piece of preserved stem ginger, plus 45ml/3 tbsp of the syrup

1 Slice the pineapple, arrange in a serving dish and scatter the coconut slivers on top.

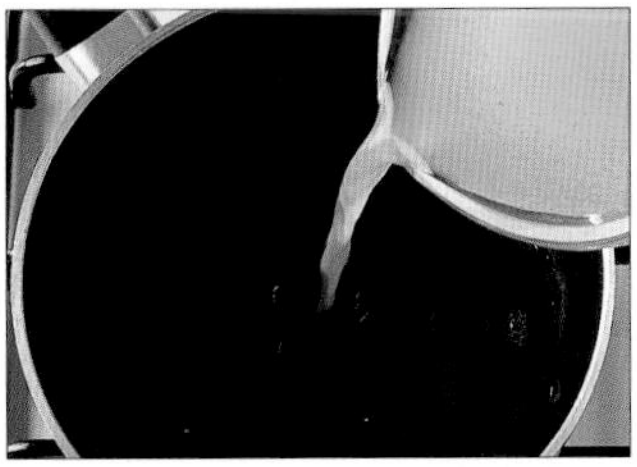

2 Place the pineapple juice and coconut liqueur in a pan and heat gently.

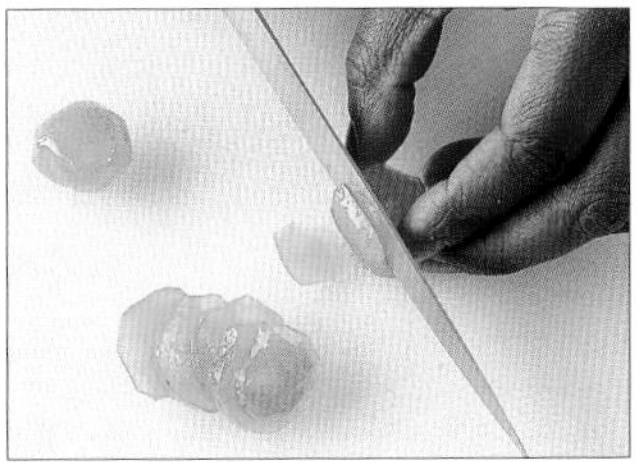

3 Thinly slice the preserved stem ginger and add to the pan together with the ginger syrup. Bring just to the boil and then simmer gently, until the liquid is slightly reduced and the sauce is fairly thick.

4 Pour the sauce over the pineapple and coconut, leave to cool, then chill in the refrigerator before serving.

VARIATION

If fresh coconut is not available, then use desiccated (dry unsweetened shredded) coconut instead.

Energy 175Kcal/744kJ; Protein 1.2g; Carbohydrate 31.9g, of which sugars 31.9g; Fat 2g, of which saturates 1.3g; Cholesterol 0mg; Calcium 43mg; Fibre 2.8g; Sodium 12mg.

FRAGRANT RICE

This rice pudding recipe comes from North Africa, where it is served with a sprinkling of chopped dates and nuts. The fragrant mixture is also used as a filling for pastries.

SERVES FOUR

INGREDIENTS
- 75g/3oz/scant ½ cup short grain rice
- about 900ml/1½ pints/3¾ cups milk
- 30ml/2 tbsp ground rice
- 50g/2oz/¼ cup caster (superfine) sugar
- 40g/1½oz/⅓ cup ground almonds
- 5ml/1 tsp vanilla essence (extract)
- 2.5ml/½ tsp almond essence (extract)
- a little orange flower water (optional)
- 30ml/2 tbsp chopped dried stoned (pitted) dates
- 30ml/2 tbsp pistachio nuts, finely chopped
- 30ml/2 tbsp flaked almonds, toasted

1 Place the rice in a pan with 750ml/1¼ pints/3 cups of the milk and heat gently until simmering. Cook, uncovered, over a very low heat for 30–40 minutes, until the rice is completely tender, stirring frequently and adding more milk, if necessary.

2 Blend the ground rice with the remaining milk and stir into the rice pudding. Slowly bring back to the boil and cook for 1 minute.

COOK'S TIP
Orange flower water is used in surprisingly large quantities in Moroccan sweets and pastries. However, unless you are partial to the strongly perfumed flavour, add it very sparingly, taste, then add more as required.

3 Stir in the sugar, ground almonds, vanilla and almond essences and orange flower water, if using, and cook until the pudding is thick and creamy.

4 Pour into serving bowls and sprinkle with the chopped dates, pistachio nuts and almonds.

ORANGE AND DATE SALAD

Fresh dates are best for this fragrant salad. It is popular throughout the Arab world, and can be served as a dessert or as an accompaniment to roasted meats.

SERVES FOUR TO SIX

INGREDIENTS
- 6 oranges
- 15–30ml/1–2 tbsp orange flower water or rose water (optional)
- lemon juice (optional)
- 115g/4oz/⅔ cup stoned dates (see Cook's Tip)
- 50g/2oz/⅓ cup pistachio nuts
- icing (confectioners') sugar, to taste
- a few whole blanched almonds

COOK'S TIP
Use fresh dates, if you can find them, although dried dates are delicious in this salad, too.

1 Peel the oranges with a sharp knife, removing all the pith, and cut into segments, catching the juices in a bowl. Place the orange segments in a serving dish.

2 Stir in the juice from the bowl together with a little orange flower or rose water, if using, and sharpen with lemon juice, if liked.

3 Chop the dates and pistachio nuts and sprinkle over the salad with a little sifted icing sugar. Chill in the refrigerator for 1 hour.

4 Just before serving, sprinkle over the toasted almonds and a little extra icing sugar and serve.

TOP Energy 343Kcal/1437kJ; Protein 14.3g; Carbohydrate 32.5g, of which sugars 16.8g; Fat 17.9g, of which saturates 3.8g; Cholesterol 13mg; Calcium 327mg; Fibre 2.1g; Sodium 140mg.
BOTTOM Energy 156Kcal/655kJ; Protein 4.4g; Carbohydrate 19.9g, of which sugars 19.6g; Fat 7.1g, of which saturates 0.9g; Cholesterol 0mg; Calcium 101mg; Fibre 4g; Sodium 76mg.

Sweet Couscous with Rose-Scented Fruit Compote

Although couscous is best known for its savoury role, it is also eaten as a dessert or as a nourishing breakfast dish. This sweet, nutritious mixture tastes great with a dried fruit compote. Make the compote a few days ahead, so that the flavours can mingle, and serve it warm, with the freshly cooked sweet couscous. The milk mixture, which is poured over just before the dish is taken to the table, makes it lovely and creamy.

SERVES SIX

INGREDIENTS
- 300ml/½ pint/1¼ cups water
- 225g/8oz/1⅓ cups couscous
- 50g/2oz/scant ⅓ cup raisins
- 50g/2oz/¼ cup butter
- 50g/2oz/¼ cup granulated sugar
- 120ml/4fl oz/½ cup milk
- 120ml/4fl oz/½ cup double (heavy) cream

For the fruit compote
- 225g/8oz/1 cup dried apricots
- 225g/8oz/1 cup stoned (pitted) prunes
- 115g/4oz/¾ cup sultanas (golden raisins)
- 115g/4oz/⅔ cup blanched almonds
- 175g/6oz/generous ¾ cup granulated sugar
- 30ml/2 tbsp rose water
- 1 cinnamon stick

1 Prepare the fruit compote a couple of days in advance. Put the dried fruit and almonds in a bowl and pour in just enough water to cover. Gently stir in the sugar and rose water, and add the cinnamon stick. Cover and leave the fruit and nuts to soak for 48 hours, during which time the water and sugar will form a lovely golden-coloured syrup.

2 To make the couscous, bring the water to the boil in a pan. Stir in the couscous and raisins, and cook gently for 1–2 minutes, until the water has been absorbed. Remove the pan from the heat, cover tightly and leave the couscous to steam for 10–15 minutes. Meanwhile, poach the compote over a gentle heat until warmed through.

COOK'S TIPS

The couscous can be served on its own, drizzled with clear or warmed honey instead of with the dried fruit compote. The compote is also delicious served chilled on its own or with yogurt.

3 Tip the couscous into a bowl and separate the grains with your fingertips. Melt the butter and pour it over the couscous. Sprinkle the sugar over the top then, using your fingertips, rub the butter and sugar into the couscous. Divide the mixture between six bowls.

4 Heat the milk and cream together in a small, heavy pan until they are just about to boil, then pour the mixture over the couscous. Serve immediately, with the dried fruit compote.

Energy 661Kcal/2771kJ; Protein 9.4g; Carbohydrate 95.6g, of which sugars 75.9g; Fat 29.3g, of which saturates 12.1g; Cholesterol 46mg; Calcium 143mg; Fibre 4.8g; Sodium 82mg.

SAFFRON AND CARDAMOM CRÈME CARAMEL WITH BUTTER COOKIES

MANY OF THE CHILLED CREAMY CUSTARDS, MILK PUDDINGS AND RICE PUDDINGS THAT ARE SERVED IN THE MIDDLE EAST ARE FAMILIAR TO VISITORS FROM EUROPE, BUT THERE ARE SUBTLE VARIATIONS. FLAVOURING OFTEN COMES FROM SPICES LIKE SAFFRON OR CARDAMOM, OR FROM FLORAL ESSENCES LIKE ROSE WATER OR ORANGE FLOWER WATER. THIS VERSION OF CRÈME CARAMEL IS A FAVOURITE DESSERT IN NORTH AFRICA. THE RICH, BUTTERY COOKIES ARE AN IRRESISTIBLE ACCOMPANIMENT.

SERVES FOUR TO SIX

INGREDIENTS
- 600ml/1 pint/2½ cups milk
- 115g/4oz/⅔ cup granulated sugar, plus 60ml/4 tbsp for caramel
- pinch of saffron threads
- 2.5ml/½ tsp cardamom seeds
- 15–30ml/1–2 tbsp rose water
- 4 eggs, lightly beaten
- 60ml/4 tbsp boiling water

For the cookies
- 200g/7oz/scant 1 cup butter
- 130g/4½oz/generous 1 cup icing (confectioners') sugar, sifted
- 5–10ml/1–2 tsp orange flower water
- 250g/9oz/2¼ cups plain (all-purpose) flour, sifted
- handful of whole blanched almonds

1 Preheat the oven to 180°C/350°F/Gas 4. Heat the milk, sugar, saffron and cardamom in a pan until the milk is just about to boil. Remove the pan from the heat and set aside to cool. Add the rose water, then gradually pour the mixture onto the eggs in a bowl, beating all the time. Set aside.

2 To make the caramel, heat the 60ml/4 tbsp sugar in a small, heavy pan, until melted and dark brown. Stir in the water, holding the pan at arm's length as the caramel will spit. Let it bubble before tipping it into individual ovenproof dishes. Swirl the dishes to coat the base and sides evenly. Leave to cool.

3 Pour the custard into the dishes and then stand them in a roasting pan. Pour in enough cold water to come two-thirds of the way up the outsides of the dishes. Bake in the oven for about 1 hour, or until the custard has set. Cool, then chill in the refrigerator for several hours or overnight.

4 To make the cookies, melt the butter in a pan and then leave to cool until lukewarm. Stir in the icing sugar and orange flower water, then gradually beat in the flour to form a smooth, stiff dough. Wrap in clear film (plastic wrap) and chill for 15 minutes.

5 Preheat the oven to 180°C/350°F/Gas 4. Grease a baking sheet. Break off walnut-size pieces of dough and roll them into balls. Place on the baking sheet and flatten slightly. Press a whole blanched almond into the centre of each. Bake for 20 minutes, or until golden. Allow to cool slightly on the baking sheet; when firm, transfer to a wire rack.

6 To serve, run a knife around the edges of the crème caramel dishes and invert on to plates. Serve immediately with the butter cookies.

Energy 969Kcal/4064kJ; Protein 17.8g; Carbohydrate 119.9g, of which sugars 72.3g; Fat 50g, of which saturates 29.3g; Cholesterol 306mg; Calcium 338mg; Fibre 2g; Sodium 443mg.

ALMOND AND PISTACHIO ICE CREAMS

Sit at a pavement café in Cairo and you can sample some of the most delicious ice creams in the world. There's keen debate about which tastes the best. Cool green pistachio and snowy almond come high on the list, along with delicate rose water ice cream and vibrant, not-to-be-missed mango. Although pistachio and almond are both nut ices, their flavours are markedly different, and when presented together, they are sensational.

SERVES FOUR

INGREDIENTS

For the almond ice cream
- 150g/5oz/1¼ cups blanched almonds, finely ground
- 300ml/½ pint/1¼ cups milk
- 300ml/½ pint/1¼ cups double (heavy) cream
- 4 egg yolks
- 175g/6oz/generous ¾ cup caster (superfine) sugar
- 30–45ml/2–3 tbsp orange flower water
- 2–3 drops almond essence (extract)

For the pistachio ice cream
- 150g/5oz/1¼ cups pistachio nuts, blanched and finely ground
- 300ml/½ pint/1¼ cups milk
- 300ml/½ pint/1¼ cups double (heavy) cream
- 4 egg yolks
- 175g/6oz/generous ¾ cup caster (superfine) sugar
- 30–45ml/2–3 tbsp rose water
- green food colouring (optional)

1 To make the almond ice cream, put the almonds in a pan with the milk and cream, and bring to the boil. In a large bowl, beat the egg yolks with the sugar, then pour in the hot milk and cream, beating all the time. Pour the mixture back into the pan and stir over a low heat, until it thickens slightly. Do not overheat the custard as, if it approaches simmering point, it will curdle.

2 Stir in the orange flower water and almond essence, and then leave the mixture to cool. Pour the cold mixture into a bowl or freezerproof container and chill, then freeze. Whisk the mixture thoroughly after about 1 hour, when it should be icy around the edges.

3 Continue to freeze the ice cream, whisking it two or three more times, until it is smooth and very thick. Return it to the freezer and leave for several hours or overnight. Alternatively, churn the mixture in an ice cream maker.

4 Make the pistachio ice cream in the same way as the almond ice cream, using the pistachio nuts in place of the almonds and rose water instead of the orange flower water and almond essence. Add a little green food colouring to the pistachio ice cream, if you like.

5 Remove both batches of ice cream from the freezer 10–15 minutes before serving and allow it to soften slightly.

Energy 1735Kcal/7212kJ; Protein 28.4g; Carbohydrate 106.7g, of which sugars 104.8g; Fat 135.8g, of which saturates 59.3g; Cholesterol 618mg; Calcium 478mg; Fibre 5.1g; Sodium 325mg.

Turkish Delight Sorbet

Love Turkish delight, but don't want sticky fingers? Serve this superb sorbet instead. It has all the flavour and aroma of the sweetmeat from which it is made, but is easier to eat. Serve it in small portions with a pot of strong coffee.

SERVES FOUR

INGREDIENTS

- 250g/9oz rose water-flavoured Turkish delight
- 30ml/2 tbsp granulated sugar
- 750ml/1¼ pints/3 cups water
- 30ml/2 tbsp lemon juice
- 50g/2oz white chocolate, broken into squares
- roughly chopped almonds, to decorate

1 Cut the Turkish delight into small pieces with a pair of scissors. Put half the pieces in a heavy pan with the sugar. Pour in half the water. Heat gently until the Turkish delight has dissolved, stirring.

2 Cool, then stir in the lemon juice with the remaining water and Turkish delight. Chill in the refrigerator for several hours.

3 By hand: Pour the mixture into a shallow freezerproof container and freeze for 3–4 hours, beating twice as it thickens. Return to the freezer until ready to serve.
Using an ice cream maker: Churn the mixture until it holds its shape.

4 While the sorbet is freezing, dampen eight very small plastic cups or glasses, then line them with clear film (plastic wrap).

5 Spoon the sorbet into the cups and tap them lightly on the surface to compact the mixture. Cover with the overlapping clear film and freeze for at least 3 hours or overnight.

6 Make a paper piping bag. Put the chocolate in a heatproof bowl and melt it over a pan of gently simmering water. Remove the sorbets from the freezer, let them stand for 5 minutes, then pull them out of the cups.

7 Transfer to serving plates and peel off the clear film. Spoon the melted chocolate into the piping bag, snip off the tip and scribble a design on the sorbet and the plate. Sprinkle the almonds over the top and serve.

Energy 280Kcal/1188kJ; Protein 1.4g; Carbohydrate 63.8g, of which sugars 58g; Fat 3.9g, of which saturates 2.3g; Cholesterol 0mg; Calcium 44mg; Fibre 0g; Sodium 34mg.

Grilled Fruit with Watermelon and Spiced Orange Granitas

For this stunning dessert, sliced fresh pineapple and mango are caramelized alongside halved bananas before being served with a choice of two granitas, one made from puréed watermelon and the other a spicy orange, clove and ginger concoction.

SERVES SIX TO EIGHT

INGREDIENTS
- 1 pineapple
- 1 mango
- 2 bananas
- 45–60ml/3–4 tbsp icing (confectioners') sugar

For the watermelon granita
- 1kg/2¼lb watermelon, seeds removed
- 250g/9oz/1¼ cups caster (superfine) sugar
- 150ml/¼ pint/⅔ cup water
- juice of ½ lemon
- 15ml/1 tbsp orange flower water
- 2.5ml/½ tsp ground cinnamon

For the spiced orange granita
- 900ml/1½ pints/3¾ cups water
- 350g/12oz/1¾ cups caster (superfine) sugar
- 5–6 whole cloves
- 5ml/1 tsp ground ginger
- 2.5ml/½ tsp ground cinnamon
- 600ml/1 pint/2½ cups fresh orange juice
- 15ml/1 tbsp orange flower water

1 To make the watermelon granita, purée the watermelon flesh in a blender. Put the sugar and water in a pan and stir until dissolved. Bring to the boil, simmer for 5 minutes, then cool.

2 Stir in the lemon juice, orange flower water and cinnamon, then beat in the watermelon purée. Pour the mixture into a bowl and place it in the freezer. Stir every 15 minutes for 2 hours and then at intervals for 1 hour, so that the mixture freezes but is slushy.

3 To make the spiced orange granita, heat the water and sugar together in a pan with the cloves, stirring until the sugar has dissolved, then bring to the boil and boil for about 5 minutes. Remove from the heat, leave to cool and then stir in the ginger, cinnamon, orange juice and orange flower water.

4 Remove and discard the cloves, then pour the mixture into a bowl, cover and place in the freezer. Freeze in the same way as the watermelon granita.

5 To serve, peel, core and slice the pineapple. Peel the mango, cut the flesh off the stone (pit) in thick slices. Peel and halve the bananas. Preheat the grill (broiler) on the hottest setting. Arrange the fruit on a baking sheet. Sprinkle with icing sugar and grill (broil) for 3–4 minutes, until slightly softened and lightly browned. Arrange the fruit on a serving platter and scoop the granitas into dishes. Serve immediately.

Energy 606Kcal/2585kJ; Protein 2.9g; Carbohydrate 156.2g, of which sugars 155.5g; Fat 1g, of which saturates 0.2g; Cholesterol 0mg; Calcium 107mg; Fibre 2.8g; Sodium 23mg.

Yogurt Cake with Pistachio Nuts, Crème Fraîche and Passion Fruit

One of the Middle East's favourite ingredients, yogurt, is used to make a beautifully moist cake with a crunchy pistachio topping. It is delicious hot or cold, with a dollop of crème fraîche. Fresh passion fruit pulp adds a tangy note, but this would taste just as good with an apricot compote or a spoonful of Turkish-style sour cherry preserve.

SERVES FOUR TO SIX

INGREDIENTS
- 3 eggs, separated
- 75g/3oz/scant ½ cup caster (superfine) sugar
- seeds from 2 vanilla pods (beans)
- 300ml/½ pint/1¼ cups Greek (US strained plain) yogurt
- grated rind and juice of 1 lemon
- scant 15ml/1 tbsp plain (all-purpose) flour
- handful of pistachio nuts, roughly chopped
- 60–90ml/4–6 tbsp crème fraîche and 4–6 fresh passion fruit or 50g/2oz/½ cup summer berries, to serve

1 Preheat the oven to 180°C/350°F/Gas 4. Line a 25cm/10in square, ovenproof dish with greaseproof (waxed) paper and grease well.

2 Beat the egg yolks with two-thirds of the sugar in a bowl, until pale and fluffy. Beat in the vanilla seeds and then stir in the yogurt, lemon rind and juice, and the flour. In a separate bowl, whisk the egg whites until stiff, then gradually whisk in the rest of the sugar to form soft peaks. Fold the whisked whites into the yogurt mixture. Turn the mixture into the prepared dish.

3 Place the dish in a roasting pan and pour in enough cold water to come about halfway up the outside of the dish. Bake in the oven for about 20 minutes, until the mixture is risen and just set. Sprinkle the pistachio nuts over the cake and then bake for a further 20 minutes, until browned on top.

4 Serve the cake warm or cooled and chilled, with crème fraîche and a spoonful of passion fruit drizzled over the top. Alternatively, sprinkle with a few summer berries such as redcurrants, blackcurrants and blueberries.

Energy 474Kcal/1986kJ; Protein 13.4g; Carbohydrate 49.4g, of which sugars 46g; Fat 26.3g, of which saturates 10g; Cholesterol 170mg; Calcium 195mg; Fibre 2.2g; Sodium 283mg.

Cheese-Filled Jerusalem Kodafa Drenched with Syrup

In Jerusalem, as elsewhere in the Middle East, this super-sweet pastry is a popular street food and you will often see kodafa vendors weaving through the traffic with large trays of the sweetmeat balanced on their heads. Kodafa is usually made with a shredded pastry called kadaif. This version uses couscous, which gives an equally tasty result.

SERVES SIX

INGREDIENTS

- 200–250g/7–9oz/1–1½ cup couscous
- 525ml/17fl oz/2¼ cups boiling water
- 130–200g/4½–7oz/½–1 cup butter, cut into small pieces
- 1 egg, lightly beaten
- pinch of salt
- 400g/14oz/1¾ cups ricotta cheese
- 175–200g/6–7oz cheese, such as mozzarella, Taleggio or Monterey Jack, grated or finely chopped
- 350ml/12fl oz/1½ cups clear honey
- 2–3 pinches of saffron threads or ground cinnamon
- 120ml/4fl oz/½ cup water
- 5ml/1 tsp orange flower water or lemon juice
- 90ml/6 tbsp roughly chopped pistachio nuts

1 Put the couscous in a large bowl and pour over the boiling water. Stir together with a fork, then leave to soak for about 30 minutes, until the water has been completely absorbed.

2 When the couscous is cool enough to handle, break up all the lumps with your fingers.

3 Stir the butter into the couscous, then stir in the beaten egg and salt.

4 Preheat the oven to 200°C/400°F/ Gas 6. Spread half the couscous into a 25–30cm/10–12in round cake tin (pan).

5 In a bowl, combine the cheeses and 30ml/2 tbsp of the honey. Spread the cheese mixture on top of the couscous, then top with the remaining couscous. Press down gently and then bake in the oven for 10–15 minutes.

6 Meanwhile, put the remaining honey, the saffron threads or cinnamon, and the water in a pan. Bring to the boil, then boil for 5–7 minutes, until the liquid forms a syrup. Remove from the heat and stir in the orange flower water or lemon juice.

7 Preheat the grill (broiler) to its hottest setting. When the kodafa is cooked, place it under the grill and cook until it is lightly browned on top and a golden crust is formed.

8 Sprinkle the pistachio nuts on top of the kodafa. Serve warm, cut into wedges, with the syrup.

VARIATIONS

Other versions of this pastry are made with biscuit (cookie) crumbs and broken pistachio nuts. If you like, warm this kodafa through in the microwave before serving it with strong coffee or mint tea.

Energy 702Kcal/2927kJ; Protein 17.6g; Carbohydrate 65.1g, of which sugars 47.6g; Fat 43g, of which saturates 22.7g; Cholesterol 123mg; Calcium 140mg; Fibre 0.9g; Sodium 344mg.

ALMOND MILK

ALMOND MILK HAS BEEN A FAVOURITE BEVERAGE SINCE MEDIEVAL TIMES, WHEN IT WAS VALUED BECAUSE IT COULD BE MADE AS NEEDED, AND DID NOT SOUR LIKE THE DAIRY PRODUCT. IT IS POPULAR THROUGHOUT THE MIDDLE EAST AND NORTH AFRICA, WHICH IS WHERE THIS VERSION COMES FROM. THE ADDITION OF ORANGE FLOWER WATER IS A MOROCCAN REFINEMENT. THE DRINK SHOULD BE SERVED VERY COLD, PREFERABLY IN GLASSES THAT HAVE BEEN FROSTED BY BEING PLACED IN THE FREEZER. IT IS DELICIOUSLY REFRESHING – WONDERFUL ON A HOT DAY.

SERVES EIGHT TO TEN

INGREDIENTS

- 500g/1¼lb/generous 2¾ cups blanched almonds
- 1.2 litres/2 pints/5 cups water
- 200g/7oz/1 cup caster (superfine) sugar
- 15ml/1 tbsp orange flower water

VARIATION

Use blanched hazelnuts instead of almonds if you like.

1 Using a mortar and pestle or a blender, reduce the almonds to a smooth paste. Adding a splash of water will help to make the paste smoother. Put the water and sugar in a large pan and bring to the boil, stirring until the sugar has dissolved. Stir in the almond paste and simmer for 5 minutes.

2 Turn off the heat and stir in the orange flower water. Leave the mixture to cool in the pan so that the flavours mingle, then strain through muslin (cheesecloth) or a fine sieve. Pour the strained milk into glasses and chill thoroughly in the freezer, so that it is almost setting into ice when served.

Energy 48Kcal/198kJ; Protein 4.4g; Carbohydrate 1.2g, of which sugars 1.2g; Fat 2.4g, of which saturates 0.5g; Cholesterol 0mg; Calcium 20mg; Fibre 0g; Sodium 48mg.

MINT TEA

IN MOROCCO, WHERE IT IS THE NATIONAL DRINK, MINT TEA IS KNOWN AS ATAY BI NAHNA. THE MINT LEAVES ARE LEFT TO INFUSE IN THE SWEET BREW SO THAT THE FLAVOUR IS PRONOUNCED. IN OTHER MIDDLE EASTERN LANDS, SUCH AS LEBANON, THE MINT IS ADDED ONLY WHEN SERVING. MINT TEA IS ENJOYED THROUGHOUT THE DAY. IT QUENCHES THE THIRST, EASES A SOCIAL OCCASION, WELCOMES A GUEST AND IS AN ESSENTIAL PART OF THE BARGAINING PROCESS WHEN MAKING A MAJOR PURCHASE.

SERVES TWO

INGREDIENTS

- 10ml/2 tsp Chinese gunpowder green tea
- small bunch of fresh mint leaves
- granulated sugar, to taste

1 Put the tea in a small tea pot and fill with boiling water. Add the mint leaves and leave it to infuse (steep) for 2–3 minutes.

2 Stir in sugar to taste and pour into tea glasses or cups to serve.

COOK'S TIPS

At feasts and on special occasions, the making of mint tea can be an elaborate ceremony: the best green tea is chosen and only fresh spearmint (*Mentha spicata*), of which a well-known cultivar called Moroccan is used. A fine silver-plated, bulbous-shaped teapot is selected for brewing and the heavily sweetened tea is poured rhythmically into fine glasses. For an additional flounce of ceremony, a fresh, fragrant orange blossom or jasmine flower may be floated in each glass. In winter, wormwood is sometimes added for extra warmth, and infusions flavoured with aniseed or verbena are quite common.

Energy 20Kcal/86kJ; Protein 0.2g; Carbohydrate 5.2g, of which sugars 5.2g; Fat 0g, of which saturates 0g; Cholesterol 0mg; Calcium 3mg; Fibre 0g; Sodium 1mg.

INDEX